Modular FORTRAN 77

for Science and Engineering

Gary Bronson

Information Sciences
Fairleigh Dickinson University

Consulting Editors:

Judy Cain, Mathematics & Computer Science, Tompkins-Cortland College
Howard Silver, Electrical Engineering, Fairleigh Dickinson University

Scott/Jones Inc., Publishers
P.O. Box 696
El Granada CA 94018

ISBN 0-9624230-0-9

Printed in the United States of America

Production: Fog Press
Book Manufacturing: Malloy Lithographing

V W X Y   0 1 2

Contents

Preface

Why This Book Was Written

This textbook is designed for a first course in FORTRAN programming. It was written based on two premises. The first premise is that FORTRAN is one of the most powerful and easy to use high-level computer languages available for engineering and scientific applications.

The second premise is that FORTRAN can be taught and written using modular programming techniques in order to stress the specific modular concepts developed over the thirty years since FORTRAN was commercially introduced.

The Need for Flexibility

In writing this text, I soon discovered that most FORTRAN teachers have widely varying opinions on how to teach FORTRAN successfully.

For example, about half of the professors helping in the development of this text felt that formatting should not be introduced until late in the text; while the other half insisted that formatting be introduced early. Similarly, many reviewers indicated that they required the use of the WRITE statement, while just as many insisted that the WRITE statement be avoided in favor of the PRINT statement, to sidestep the need for explicit output unit numbers.

Yet nowhere was this diversity of opinion more apparent than regarding how modularity should be introduced. Many FORTRAN instructors seem to either want, or be willing to tolerate, an introduction of modular concepts as early as possible in the course, but under a host of conditions. There was a general consensus, however, that an early introduction of modularity must be done. Similarly, most reviewers felt that modularity be introduced "in a meaningful way," and not through contrived examples. The teaching of basic programming principles (assignment, selection, repetiton) should not be encumbered with long digressions of argument passing. These conditions seem to echo my own experience, accentuated by the teaching of Pascal and C.

I believe that textbooks don't teach students—professors teach students. A textbook can be a valuable "supporting actor", but the "leading role" belongs to the professor. Thus, regardless of how modularity was introduced in a text, the introduction should be sufficiently flexible so that a variety of professors could mold it to their own way of teaching. As a result, this book was designed to allow any instructor using it to be able to adapt the order of topic presentation to the requirements of each class.

Providing Flexibility

Modularity. Because of all these observations, this book was written to provide a flexible tool to allow each instructor to teach FORTRAN as a modular language to the extent they wish. As one reviewer put it, "The book has successfully managed in Chapter One to introduce the concept of modularity in a painless and effective manner." After Chapter One, the book provides a flexible tool that each professor can use in a variety of ways, depending on *how much* modularity they want to introduce, and *when* they want to introduce it. The Enrichment Section at the end of Chapter Two provides the means for introducing the passing of arguments early in the course.

Print and Write Statements and Formatting. Similarly, the sections on the WRITE statement and formatting provide the means of introducing these topics early. For more advanced classes, any or all of these topics may be introduced early in the course. Equally as effective, any or all of these topics may be skipped until the classroom environment is ready for them. I would not myself teach the PRINT and WRITE statements "back-to-back"—but I have tried to structure the text so that those who prefer to cover the WRITE statement early can omit the PRINT statement, and those who would cover the PRINT statement early can omit the WRITE statement. And in *either* case, explicit formatting can either be initially included or omitted in favor of simpler list-directed output.

Distinctive Features of This Book

Modularity. This book steers a middle course between unstructured programming and modularity. It does it by allowing the instructor to "pick-and-choose" how much, and when, they can introduce modular programming practices.

Flexibility. The key to determining the approach to modularity is the Enrichment Study at the end of Chapter Two. If modular programming is to be a major topic, this section should be covered early. On the other hand, if modular programming is to be covered in the middle of, or late in, the course, then this material should be skipped. Regardless of what the decision is, this book allows professors to customize the coverage of this topic.

Enrichment Studies. Given the many different emphases that can be applied to the teaching of FORTRAN, I have added an Enrichment Study to most of the chapters in this text. These can serve as material for Honors Sections at some schools or can be used to further customize the course to the special interests of students or faculty.

Applications. As the book title implies, this texbookt is primarily designed for students of technology, engineering, and science. The applications reflect this. Many of the applications are of the "tried and true" variety and are not unique to this book. However, some interesting new applications have been added, such as the study of acid rain on pages 147–149. I believe these sorts of applications heighten the interest of students.

Exercises. A wide range of exercises are included in this text. They range from skillbuilders, to programming assignments, to debugging exercises. In addition, there are many program modification assignments.

Class Testing at an Independent Site . I have been especially fortunate to have this material class-tested by one of the Consulting Editors, Judy Cain, Professor of Mathematics & Computer Science at Tompkins-Cortland Community College. Her candid appraisals of her students' reactions have been an enormous aid in the development of material for this book.

Program Testing. Every single FORTRAN 77 program in this text has been successfully run by myself. Many of the programs have also been run independently by reviewers or the Consulting Editors, using different computer systems.

Comparative charts for different compilers. Throughout this text I have tried to allow for differences between the different computing environments in which FORTRAN can be taught. As a result, I have displayed these differences in a table whenever a significant variation seemed to occur.

Readability. The one thing I have found most important in my own teaching is *regardless of what is written about, it must be written so that students can read it.* As a result I have taken every precaution for this material to be clear, unambiguous, and deliberate.

Acknowledgements

This book began as an idea. It became a reality due to the encouragement, skills, and efforts supplied by many people. I would like to acknowledge their contribution.

First, a group of my colleagues at various universities supplied some very detailed responses to some specific, technical questions that my publisher sent out in a survey. I am especially grateful for the attention given this initial survey by Lal Shimpi (Keene State College); Michael Murphy (Norwich University); John Formsma (Los Angeles City College); Allen Hamlin (Palm Beach College); Brian Weinrich (California University of Pennsylvania); Maurice Lind (Jefferson State College); Ralph Frisbie (Ventura College); G.T. Jones (El Camino College); William Dodge (Rensselaer Institute); Ron Goforth (University of Arkansas); Ijaz Awan (Savanah State); James Ball (Indiana State University); Richard Coll (New Jersey Institute of Technology); Don Coleman (Howard University); Gerald Richter (Rutgers University); Don Smith (Texas A&M); Martin Meyers (California State University Sacramento); Ben Mooring (Texas A&M); Jack Kester (University of Dayton); and Don Martin (North Carolina State University).

Also, Jeanne Adams of the X3J3 committee, and Richard Hendrickson, of Spackman & Hendrickson, consultants in St. Paul MN (and also of the X3J3 committee) gave me invaluable insights regarding the new standard of FORTRAN.

Second, this manuscript matured through the reviews, suggestions, criticisms and encouragement of the following colleagues:

Patricia Haseltine
Mathematics & Computer Science
El Camino College

Glenn Williams
Computer Science
Texas A&M University

Carole Conway
Mathematics & Computer Science
Chabot College

John Fleming
Electrical Engineering
Texas A&M University

Daniel Ludwig
Engineering Fundamentals
Virginia Polytechnic University

R. Kenneth Walter
Computer Science
Weber State College

Lewis Miller
Engineering Technology
Canada College

Susan Finch
Computer Information Systems
Pima College

Edward Dionne
Computer & Electrical Engineering
San Jose State University

Richard Lejk
Computer Science
University of North Carolina- Charlotte

Judy Hankins
Mathematics & Computer Science
Middle Tennessee State University

Wesley Scruggs
Computer Science
Brazosport College

James Allert
Computer Science
University of Minnesota, Duluth

S. Srinivasan
Information Science
University of Louisville

David Miller
Computer Science
Oklahoma State University

Richard Martin
Computer Science
Southwest Missouri State University

Bill Clark
Computer Science
Texas A&M University

Barbara Schreur
Computer Engineering
Texas A&I University

No acknowledgement would be complete without mentioning seven very special people. My brother Richard Bronson distilled the issue of modularity in FORTRAN for me, and thus had a profound influence on the final direction this book was to take. My Dean, Dr. Nancy Barret of Farleigh Dickinson University, provided direct encouragement and support. Without her support this text could not have been written.

Additionally, I was fortunate to have two Consulting Editors whose teaching environments and orientations were different from and complimentary to my own. Each of them contributed trenchant and thoughtful criticisms, as well as original work of their own, towards the completion of this text. Judy Cain (who teaches mathematics and computer science at Tompkins-Cortland Community College) and

Howard Silver (who teaches engineering at Fairleigh Dickinson University Teaneck) have both been a delight and a privilege to work with.

My friend and Publisher Richard Jones has been in spirit what every author wishes their publisher was: a partner. It is exciting to author the first book published by a new publishing company, and it is equally rewarding in this age of conglomerate publishing to work with an editor whose word is as good as the deed. It was also rewarding to have Jane Scott Jones working on the project. At many critical junctures and deadlines her humor, warmth, and insights kept us on course.

Jim Beley, the Production Editor at Fog Press, has been an absolute wonder to work with. His attention to detail and high standards have helped in many ways to improve the quality of this book.

Finally, I deeply appreciate the patience, understanding, and love provided by my friend, wife, and partner, Rochelle.

Gary Bronson

Dedicated to Rochelle, Jeremy, David, Matthew.

Getting Started

Chapter One

1.1   Introduction to Programming

A computer is a machine, and like other machines, such as automobiles and lawn mowers, it must be turned on and then driven, or controlled, to do the task it was meant to do. In an automobile, for example, control is provided by the driver, who sits inside of and directs the car. In a computer, the driver is a set of instructions called a program. More formally, a *computer program* is a sequence of instructions used to operate a computer to produce a specific result. *Programming* is the process of writing these instructions in a language to which the computer can respond and that other programmers can understand. The set of instructions that can be used to construct a program is called a *programming language.*

On a fundamental level, all computer programs do the same thing (Figure 1-1); they direct a computer to accept data (input), to manipulate the data (process), and to produce reports (output). This implies that all computer programming languages must provide essentially the same capabilities for performing these operations, and such is indeed the case. The fundamental set of instructions provided by such high-level procedure-oriented computer languages as FORTRAN, BASIC, COBOL, and Pascal is listed in Table 1-1. The term *high-level* means that the statements in these languages resemble English statements. The term *procedure-oriented* means that these languages are primarily used to describe procedures for producing specific results.

If all programming languages provide essentially the same features, why are there so many of them? There are so many languages because there are vast differences in the types of input data, calculations needed, and required output reports. For example, scientific and engineering applications usually require high-precision numerical outputs that are accurate to many decimal places. In addition, these applications typically use many algebraic or trigonometric formulas to produce their results. For example, the determination of a rocket's reentry point, as illustrated in Figure 1-2, requires a trigonometric formula and a high degree of numerical accuracy. For such applications, the FORTRAN programming language, with its algebra-like instructions, is ideal. FORTRAN (an acronym derived from FORmula TRANslation) was introduced commercially in 1957. Originally designed for translating formulas into computer-readable form, FORTRAN was the first high-level language to be developed. The current standard for FORTRAN, commonly referred to as FORTRAN 77, is maintained by the American National Standards Institute (ANSI).

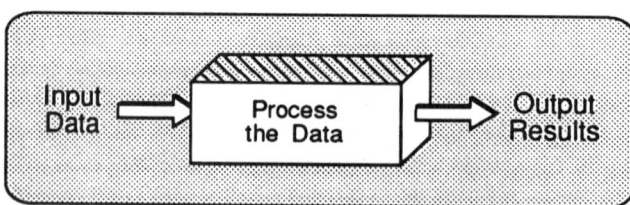

Figure 1-1   All Programs Perform the Same Operations

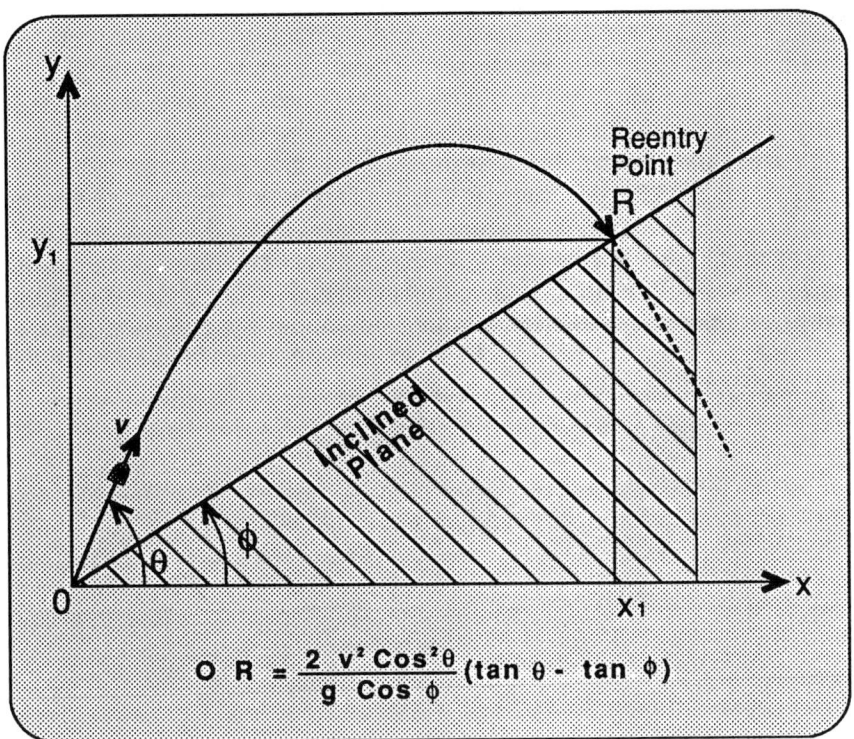

Figure 1-2   FORTRAN Is Ideal for Scientific and Engineering Applications

Table 1-1   **Programming Language Instruction Summary**

Operation	FORTRAN	BASIC	COBOL	Pascal
Input (get the data)	READ	INPUT	READ	READ
		READ/DATA	ACCEPT	READLN
Processing (use the data)	=	LET	COMPUTE	:=
	IF/ELSE	IF/ELSE	IF/ELSE	IF/ELSE
	DO	FOR	PERFORM	FOR
				WHILE
				REPEAT
Output (display the data)	WRITE	PRINT	WRITE	WRITE
	PRINT	PRINT/USING	DISPLAY	WRITELN

Algorithms

Before a program is written, the programmer must have a clear understanding of the desired result and how the proposed program is to produce it. In this regard, it is useful to realize that a computer program describes a procedure for converting a given set of input data into a desired set of outputs.

In computer science, such a procedure is called an algorithm. More specifically, an *algorithm* is defined as a step-by-step sequence of instructions that describes how a computation or task is to be performed. In essence, an algorithm answers the question "What method will be used to solve this problem?" Only after the specific steps required to produce the desired result are known and the algorithm clearly understood can the program be written. Seen in this light, programming is the translation of the selected algorithm into a language that the computer can use.

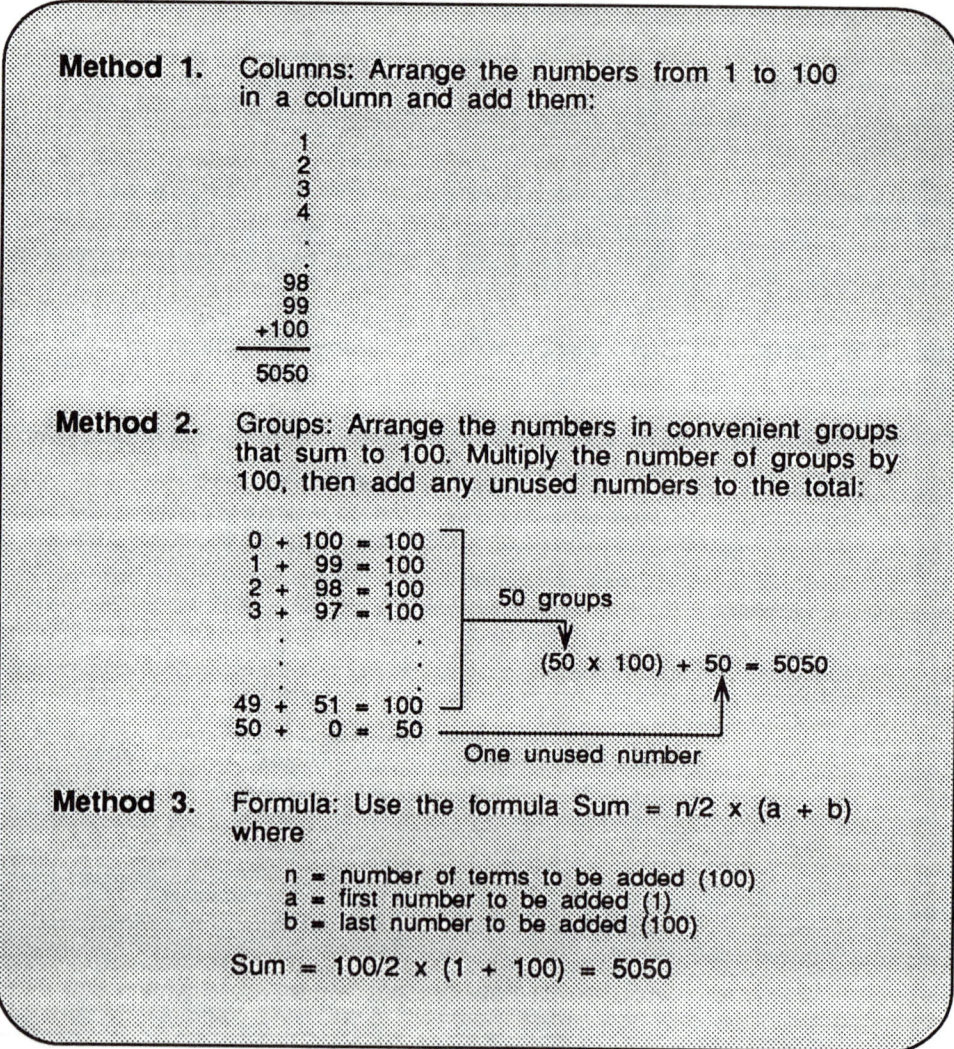

Figure 1-3   **Summing the Numbers 1 Through 100**

To illustrate an algorithm, we shall consider a simple requirement. Assume that a program must calculate the sum of all whole numbers from 1 through 100. Figure 1-3 illustrates three methods we could use to find the required sum. Each method constitutes an algorithm.

Clearly, most people would not bother to list the possible alternatives in a detailed step-by-step manner, as is done in Figure 1-3, and then select one of the algorithms to solve the problem. But then most people do not think algorithmically; they tend to think heuristically. For example, if you had to change a flat tire on your car, you would not think of all the steps required—you would simply change the tire or call someone else to do the job. This is an example of heuristic thinking.

Unfortunately, computers do not respond to heuristic commands. A general statement such as "add the numbers from 1 to 100" means nothing to a computer, because it can only respond to algorithmic commands written in an acceptable language such as FORTRAN. To program a computer successfully, you must clearly understand this difference between algorithmic and heuristic commands. A computer is an "algorithm-responding" machine; it is not a "heuristic-responding" machine. A computer will not understand if you tell it to change a tire or to add the numbers from 1 through 100. Instead, you must give the computer a detailed, step-by-step set of instructions that collectively forms an algorithm. For example, the set of instructions:

```
Set n equal to 100
Set a = 1
Set b equal to 100
Calculate sum = n/2 * (a + b)
Print the sum
```

forms a detailed method, or algorithm, for determining the sum of the numbers from 1 through 100. Notice that these instructions are not a computer program. Unlike a program, which must be written in a language to which the computer can respond, an algorithm can be written or described in various ways. When English-like phrases are used to describe the algorithm (processing steps), as in this example, the description is called *pseudocode*. When mathematical equations are used, the description is called a *formula*. When pictures that employ specifically defined shapes are used, the description is called a *flowchart*. A flowchart provides a pictorial representation of the algorithm using the symbols shown in Figure 1-4. Figure 1-5 illustrates the use of these symbols in depicting an algorithm for determining the average of three numbers.

Because flowcharts are cumbersome to revise, the use of pseudocode to express the logic of an algorithm has gained increasing acceptance among programmers in recent years. Unlike flowcharts, where standard symbols are defined, there are no standard rules for constructing pseudocode. Any short English phrases may be used to describe an algorithm using pseudocode. For example, acceptable pseudocode for describing the steps needed to compute the average of three numbers is:

```
Input the three numbers into the computer
Calculate the average by adding the numbers and
dividing the sum by three
Display the average
```

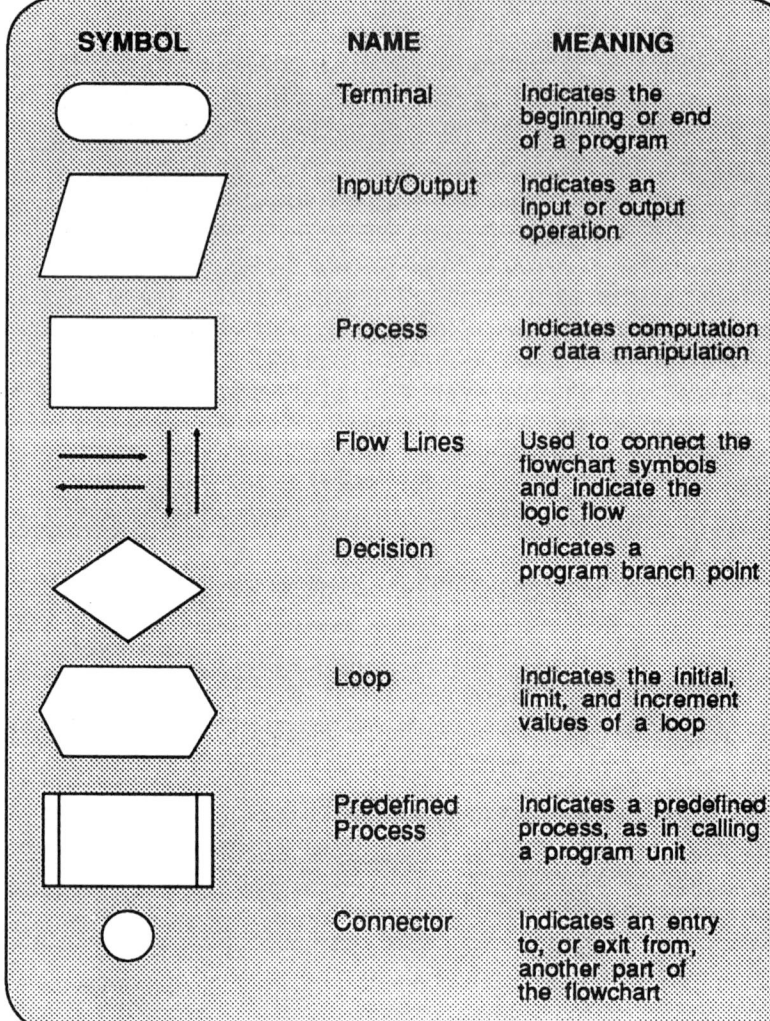

Figure 1-4   Flowchart Symbols

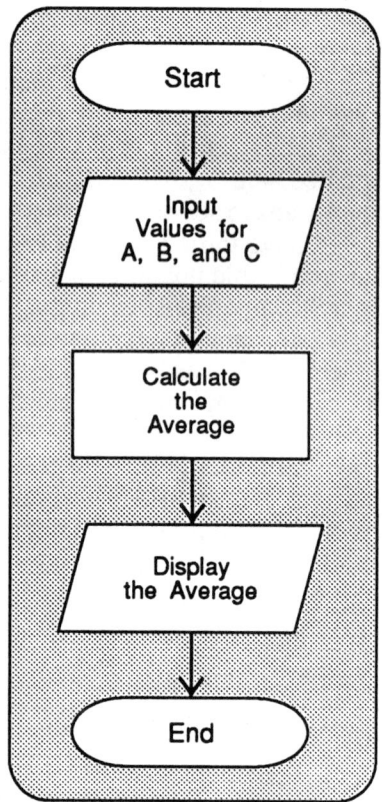

Figure 1-5   Flowchart for Calculating the Average of Three Numbers

Only after the programmer has selected an algorithm and understands the steps required can he or she write the algorithm using computer-language statements. When computer-language statements are used to describe the algorithm, the description is called a *computer program*.

From Algorithms to Programs

After an algorithm has been selected, the programmer must convert it into a form that can be used by a computer. The conversion of an algorithm into a computer program, using a language such as FORTRAN, is called *coding* the algorithm (see Figure 1-6). Much of the remainder of this text is devoted to showing you how to code algorithms into FORTRAN.

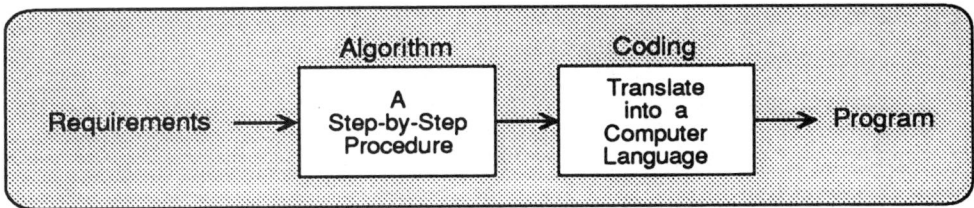

Figure 1-6 Coding an Algorithm

Program Translation

Once a program is written in FORTRAN, it still cannot be executed on a computer without further translation. This is because the internal language of all computers consists of a series of 1s and 0s, called the computer's *machine language*. To generate a machine-language program that can be executed by the computer requires that the FORTRAN program, referred to as a *source program,* be translated into the computer's machine language (see Figure 1-7).

Figure 1-7 Source Programs Must Be Translated

The translation into machine language can be accomplished in two ways. When each statement in a high-level-language source program is translated individually and executed immediately, the programming language used is called an *interpreted language,* and the program doing the translation is called an *interpreter.*

When all the statements in a source program are translated before any one statement is executed, the programming language used is called a *compiled language,* and the program doing the translation is called a *compiler.* FORTRAN is a compiled language. With FORTRAN, the source program is translated as a unit into machine language. The machine-language version of the original source program is a separate entity called the *object program.* (See Appendix A for a complete description of entering, compiling, and running a FORTRAN program.)

Skill Builder Exercises

1. Define the terms:

   a. computer program

   b. programming

   c. program language

   d. FORTRAN

   e. algorithm

   f. pseudocode

   g. flowchart

   h. high-level language

   i. source program

   j. object program

   k. compiler

   l. interpreter

2. Determine a step-by-step procedure and list the steps to do each of the following tasks. (*Note:* There is no single correct answer for any of these tasks. The exercise is designed to give you practice in converting heuristic commands into equivalent algorithms and in making the shift between the thought processes involved in the two types of thinking.)

   a. fix a flat tire

   b. make a telephone call

   c. go to the store and purchase a loaf of bread

   d. roast a turkey

3. Determine and write an algorithm (list the steps) to interchange the contents of two cups of liquid. Assume that a third cup is available to hold the contents of either cup temporarily. Each cup should be rinsed before any new liquid is poured into it.

4. Write a detailed set of instructions, in English, to calculate the dollar amount of money in a piggybank that contains h half-dollars, q quarters, n nickels, d dimes, and p pennies.

5. Write a set of detailed, step-by-step instructions, in English, to find the smallest number in a group of three integer numbers.

6. a. Write a set of detailed, step-by-step instructions, in English, to calculate the change remaining from a dollar after a purchase is made. Assume that the cost of the goods purchased is less than a dollar. The change received should consist of the smallest number of coins possible.

   b. Repeat Exercise 6a, but assume the change is to be given only in pennies.

7. a. Write an algorithm to locate the first occurrence of the name JONES in a list of names arranged in random order.

   b. Discuss how you could improve your algorithm for Exercise 7a if the list of names were arranged in alphabetical order.

8. Write an algorithm to determine the total occurrences of the letter e in any sentence.

9. Determine and write an algorithm to sort four numbers into ascending (from lowest to highest) order.

1.2   Introduction to Modularity

A well-designed program is constructed using a design philosophy similar to that used to construct a well-designed building. It doesn't just happen but depends on careful planning and execution for the final design to accomplish its intended purpose. Just as for a building, an integral part of the design of a program is its structure.

In programming, the term *structure* has two interrelated meanings. The first meaning refers to the program's overall construction, which is the topic of this section. The second meaning refers to the form used to carry out the individual tasks within the program, which is the topic of Chapters 4 and 5. In relation to the first meaning, programs whose structure consists of interrelated segments, arranged in a logical and easily understandable order to form an integrated and complete unit, are referred to as *modular programs* (Figure 1-8). Not surprisingly, modular programs are noticeably easier to develop, correct, and modify than programs constructed otherwise. In general programming terminology, the smaller segments used to construct a modular program are referred to as *modules*.

In a modular program each module is designed and developed

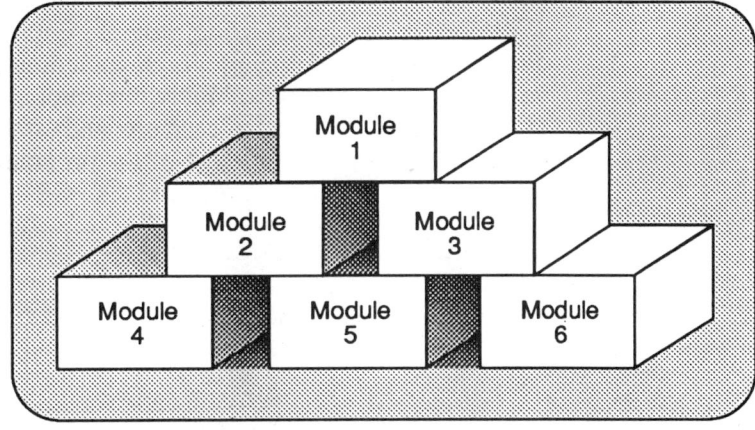

Figure 1-8   A Well-Designed Program Is Built Using Modules

to perform a clearly defined, specific function. This function can be tested and modified without disturbing other modules in the program. The final program is constructed by connecting as many modules as necessary to produce the desired result. Unfortunately, each programming language has its own specific name for modules. In FORTRAN, a module is referred to as a *program unit*.

Program Units

A program unit is essentially a small program in its own right. As such, it must be capable of doing what is required of all programs: receive data, operate on the data, and produce a result (see Figure 1-9). Unlike a larger program, however, a program unit performs only limited operations. Typically, each program unit performs a single task required by the larger program of which it is a part.

A complete program is constructed by combining as many program units as necessary to produce the desired result. The advantage

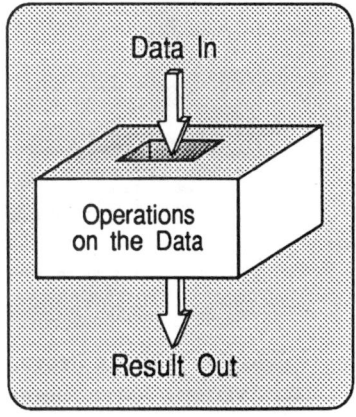

Figure 1-9   A Program Unit Receives Data, Operates on the Data, and Produces a Result

to this modular construction is that the overall design of the program can be developed before any single program unit is written. Once the requirements for a program unit are finalized, it can be programmed and integrated within the overall program as the unit is completed.

FORTRAN provides three common types of program units: the MAIN, SUBROUTINE, and FUNCTION unit types.* Each of these program unit types performs a specific type of task. We shall learn and use all of these unit types as we progress.

It is useful to think of a program unit, regardless of its type, as a small machine that transforms the data it receives into a finished product. For example, Figure 1-10 illustrates a program unit that accepts three numbers and calculates their average to produce an output.

The MAIN Program Unit

A distinct advantage to using program units in FORTRAN is that we can plan the overall structure of the program, including making provisions for testing and verifying the operation of individual units, in advance. We first determine the individual tasks required of each unit and establish how the units will be combined. Only after the overall structure of the program has been designed is each program unit written to perform its required task.

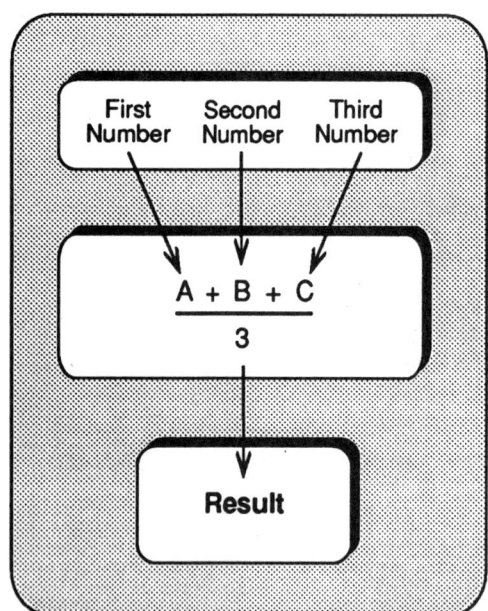

Figure 1-10   A Program Unit That Averages Three Numbers

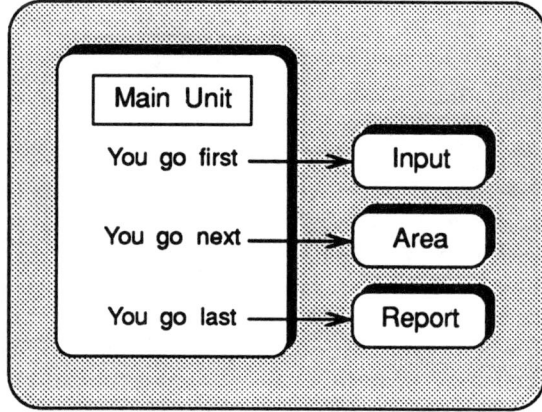

Figure 1-11   The MAIN Program Unit Directs All Other Units

---

* The fourth and last type, BLOCK DATA progam units, described in Section 8.3 is rarely used. All of FORTRAN 77's features, however, are included within the proposal for the new standard (see Chapter 12).

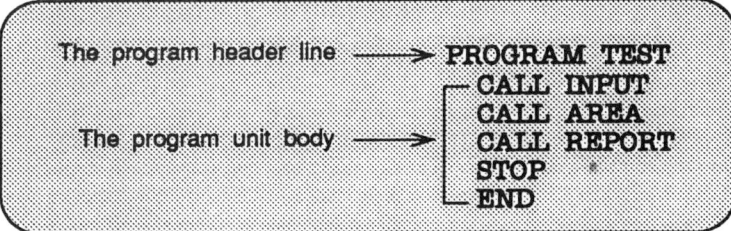

The program header line ⟶ PROGRAM TEST

The program unit body ⟶ CALL INPUT
CALL AREA
CALL REPORT
STOP
END

Figure 1-12 A Sample MAIN **Program Unit**

To provide for the orderly placement and execution of individual program units, every FORTRAN program must have one, and only one, MAIN program unit (Figure 1-11). This MAIN unit is frequently referred to as the *driver unit,* because of its function of telling all other program units the sequence in which they are to be executed.

Figure 1-12 illustrates a complete MAIN program unit. The first line in the program unit, PROGRAM TEST, is called a *header line.* The word PROGRAM in the header line identifies the beginning of a MAIN program unit. The word TEST is a user-selected name for this MAIN unit. The rules for choosing your own program unit names are presented at the end of this section.

The end of a MAIN unit is always designated by the word END written on a line by itself. The words PROGRAM, STOP, and END are examples of FORTRAN keywords. A *keyword* is a word that takes on a special meaning when it is used in a particular way. When the keyword END is placed on a line by itself, it becomes an END statement, which is required as the last statement in the MAIN program unit. Unlike most other programming languages, FORTRAN's keywords are not reserved words (FORTRAN has no reserved words). A *reserved word* is a word that is set aside by the compiler for a special purpose and can be used only in the manner specified by the compiler. Since FORTRAN's keywords are not reserved, it is possible, athough not advisable, to use a keyword such as END for other purposes than an END statement (for example, as the name of a MAIN unit).

Statements following the program header, up to and including the END statement, are collectively referred to as a program unit's body. The *body* of a program unit determines what the unit does. Typically, each statement in the unit's body resides on a line by itself, although a single statement can, as we will see, continue across multiple lines. In no case, however, can multiple FORTRAN 77 statements be written on the same line.[*]

The body of the MAIN program unit illustrated in Figure 1-12 consists of five statements. The keywords CALL in each of the first three statements are commands to execute SUBROUTINE program units. The first statement in the unit's body, CALL INPUT, calls a SUBROUTINE program unit named INPUT into execution. The word CALL informs the compiler that a transfer to a SUBROUTINE program unit is being requested and that the following word, INPUT, is the name of the requested unit.

When the INPUT program unit is finished executing, the AREA program unit is called. After the AREA unit is completed the REPORT program unit is called. The

---

[*] However, multiple statements will be allowed in the proposed new standard (see Chapter 12).

fourth statement is the STOP command. Although the MAIN program unit is complete as written, the SUBROUTINE program units INPUT, AREA, and REPORT must still be written for the whole program to be executed. After these four program units are written, the program, consisting of MAIN, INPUT, AREA, and REPORT, is complete. In the next section we will see how SUBROUTINE program units are constructed.

Symbolic Names

Program unit names such as TEST, INPUT, AREA, and REPORT are all examples of FORTRAN symbolic names. In FORTRAN 77 a *symbolic name* is any combination of letters and digits that:
1. begins with an uppercase letter
2. contains only uppercase letters and digits following the initial letter (no blanks or other symbols allowed)
3. consists of at most six characters

Examples of valid symbolic names are:

NETPAY   AVERAG   TOTL   ADD3   NEWBAL   BESSEL   SUM1

Example of invalid symbolic names are:

2EASY   (begins with a number, which violates Rule 1)
e1223   (begins with a lowercase letter, which violates Rule 1)
ME AN   (contains a blank space, which violates Rule 2)
N_BAL   (contains a special character, which violates Rule 2)
Aokay   (contains lowercase letters, which violates Rule 2)
SALESTAX   (contains too many characters, which violates Rule 3)

A symbolic name should also be a mnemonic when used as a program unit name. A *mnemonic* is a memory aid used to convey information about what the name represents. For example, the program unit name SQUARE is a mnemonic if it is the name of a program unit that calculates the square of a number or the area of a square. The name itself gives some indication of what the program unit does. Examples of valid program unit names that are not mnemonics are:

A123   RHONA   HOWARD   R2D2   C3P0   GOFOR   X4   D

Non-mnemonic symbolic names should not be used as program unit names because they convey no information about what the program unit does.

A non-standard feature you may encounter is the support of symbolic names having more than six characters. Another non-standard extension to FORTRAN is the support of lowercase letters in symbolic names. Although lowercase letters are not part of the FORTRAN 77 standard for symbolic names, many compilers allow their use. Such compilers are then either case sensitive or case insensitive.

A *case-insensitive* compiler does not differentiate between uppercase and lowercase letters. For such compilers symbolic names such as TOTAL, total, and TotAL are equivalent and represent the same name. *Case sensitive* compilers consider these three names as distinct and different entities. In this text we will conform to the FORTRAN 77 standard and use only uppercase letters in symbolic names. We recommend that you do the same. This ensures that your programs will run on any computer supporting the FORTRAN 77 standard.

Skill Builder Exercises

1. State whether the following are valid program unit names. If they are valid, state whether they are mnemonic names. If they are invalid names, state why.

POWER	DENSITY	M123$	NEWBAL	1234	ABCD
TOTAL	TANGENT	ABSVAL	MARRIED	B34A	34AB
TAXES$	A2-B3	NEWBAL	MIN_VAL	SINE	$SINE
COSINE	INVOICES	NETPAY	BALANCE	SOLD	AVERAGE

2. Assume that the following subroutine program units have been written:

    GROPAY, TAXES, NETPAY, and OUTPUT

    a. Write a MAIN program unit that calls these subroutine program units in the order that they are listed.

    b. From their names, what do you think each subroutine program unit in Exercise 2a does?

3. Assume that the following subroutine program units have been written:

    ITEMS, SALETX, BALNCE

    a. Write a MAIN program unit that calls these program units in the order that they are listed.

    b. From their names, what do you think each program unit in Exercise 3a does?

4. Create valid names for subroutine program units that do the following:

    a. find the average of a set of numbers

    b. find the area of a rectangle

    c. find the value of a polynomial

    d. find the density of a steel door

    e. find the maximum value of a set of numbers.

    f. sort a set of numbers from lowest to highest.

5a. Assuming a case-insensitive compiler, determine which of these program unit names are equivalent:

AVERAG	averag	MODE	BESSEL	Mode
Total	besseL	TeMp	Densty	TEMP
denSTY	MEAN	total	mean	moDE

   b. Redo Exercise 5a assuming a case sensitive compiler.

   c. If the compiler adheres strictly to the FORTRAN 77 standard, determine which of the symbolic names in Exercise 5a are invalid.

6. Explain the relationship between an algorithm and a program's modular structure.

Project Structuring Exercises

Most projects, both programming and nonprogramming, can be structured into smaller subtasks or units of activity. These smaller subtasks can often be delegated to different people so that when all the tasks are finished and integrated, the project or program is completed. For Exercises 7 through 12, determine a set of subtasks that, taken together, complete the project. Be aware that there are many possible solutions for each exercise. The only requirement is that the set of subtasks selected completes the required task.

(*Note:* The purpose of these exercises is to have you consider the different ways that complex tasks can be structured. Although there is no one correct solution to these exercises, there are incorrect solutions and solutions that are better than others. An incorrect solution is one that does not fully specify the task. One solution is better than another if it more clearly or easily identifies what must be done.)

7. You are given the task of wiring and installing lights in the attic of your house. Determine a set of subtasks that, taken together, will accomplish this. (**Hint:** The first subtask would be to determine the placement of the light fixtures.)

8. You are given the job of preparing a complete meal for five people next weekend. Determine a set of subtasks, that taken together, accomplish this. (**Hint:** One subtask, not necessarily the first one, would be to buy the food.)

9. You are a sophomore in college and are planning to go to graduate school for a master's degree in electrical engineering. List a set of major objectives that you must fulfill to meet this goal. (**Hint:** One objective is "Take the right courses.")

10. You are given the job of planning a surprise birthday party. Determine a set of subtasks to accomplish this. (**Hint:** One such subtask would be to create a guest list.)

11. You are responsible for planning and arranging the family camping trip this summer. List a set of subtasks that, taken together, accomplish this objective successfully. (**Hint:** One subtask would be to select the campsite.)

12a. A national electrical supply distribution company desires a computer system to prepare its customer invoices. The system must be capable of creating each day's invoices. Additionally, the company wants the capability to retrieve and output a printed report of all invoices that meet certain criteria: for example, all invoices sent in a particular month with a net value of more than a given dollar amount, all invoices sent in a year to a particular client, or all invoices sent to firms in a particular state. Determine three or four major program units into which this system could be separated. (**Hint:** One program unit is "Prepare invoices" to create each day's invoices.)

b. Suppose someone enters incorrect data for a particular invoice, and the error is discovered after the data has been entered and stored by the system. What program unit is needed to take care of correcting this problem? Discuss why such a program unit might or might not be required by most commercial systems.

c. Assume a program unit exists that allows a user to change data that has been incorrectly entered and stored. Discuss the need for including an "audit trail" that would allow for a later reconstruction of the changes made, when they were made, and who made them.

1.3 How Program Units Are Built

A complete FORTRAN program is constructed using one or more program units. Each program unit, regardless of its type, must be constructed using the same form as the MAIN program unit introduced in Section 1.2. Specifically, this includes a program unit header line and a program unit body, as illustrated in Figure 1-13.

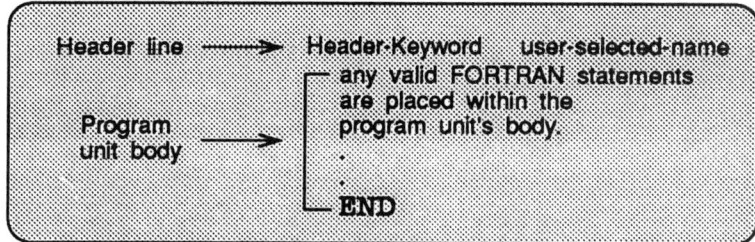

Figure 1-13   A Sample MAIN Program Unit

Program Unit Header Lines

The header line of each program unit is what determines the unit's type. A MAIN program unit is explicitly identified by the header keyword PROGRAM, a SUBROUTINE program unit is identified by the header keyword SUBROUTINE, and a FUNCTION program unit is identified by the header keyword FUNCTION.

Examples of valid MAIN program unit header lines are:

```
PROGRAM TEST
PROGRAM GRAPH
PROGRAM MAIN
PROGRAM SLOPE
```

Each of these header lines identifies the program unit as a MAIN unit. Additionally, a user-selected name must be included on each header line to identify the name of the unit. In the previous examples the first MAIN unit has been named TEST, the second MAIN unit has been named GRAPH, the third MAIN unit has been named MAIN, and the fourth MAIN unit has been named SLOPE. Since each FORTRAN program can have only one MAIN unit, these header lines could not appear together in a single program.

Examples of SUBROUTINE program unit header lines are:

```
SUBROUTINE INPUT
SUBROUTINE AVERGE
SUBROUTINE DISPLY
```

Examples of FUNCTION program unit header lines are:

FUNCTION SHOW( )
FUNCTION HYPER( )

As illustrated, FUNCTION program units require that parentheses be placed after the function's name. In Chapter 2 we will see the purpose of these parentheses. SUBROUTINE and FUNCTION program units are also referred to as *subprogram units*, or subprograms, for short.

Program Unit Bodies

The body of each program unit consists of valid FORTRAN statements and must end with the keyword END, placed on a line by itself. Every program unit statement must conform to certain rules and forms, which collectively are called the language's *syntax*. One of these syntax rules is that every program unit statement (including the header line) must be placed in a certain position on a line. These line positions are referenced by column number, with column number 1 being the first position on the line, column number 2 the second position, and so on.

Figure 1-14 illustrates FORTRAN's coding form, which defines the prescribed form for each line in every program unit. Specifically, as illustrated in Figure 1-14, each line consists of a label field (which includes the comment indicator column), a continuation field, a statement field, and an identification/sequence field. A requirement of FORTRAN is that each statement in a program must have a statement field entry. If a particular statement does not contain any of the other fields, those fields are left blank.

For example, each line in the program previously shown in Figure 1-12 uses only the statement field. Thus, when this program is entered into a computer, each statement must be typed within columns 7 through 72, which constitute the statement field. More typically, the program would be typed using the positioning indicated in Figure 1-15. The additional indentation beyond column 7 of the statements following the program header line is strictly for clarity. This indentation within the statement field is of great help in quickly isolating and locating a specific program unit's header line for programs consisting of many program units.

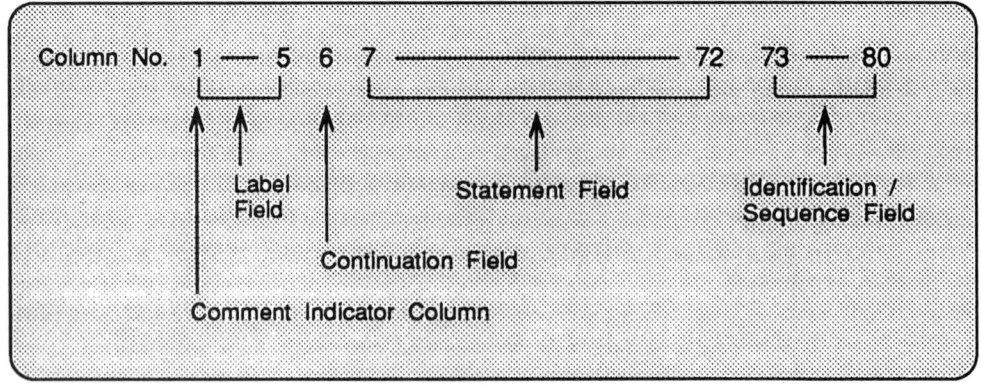

Figure 1-14 The FORTRAN Coding Form

To reinforce the idea that all FORTRAN programs must conform to the FORTRAN coding form, the column heading shown in Figure 1-15 will be retained for all subsequent sample programs listed in this and the next chapter. By Chapter 3 we will assume that you have become familiar with correctly positioning program lines, and the column headings will be dropped. As the identification/sequence field (columns 73–80) is rarely used in any statement, this field will be excluded in all program listings, as it is in Figure 1-15. Each of the fields on the coding form is now explained.

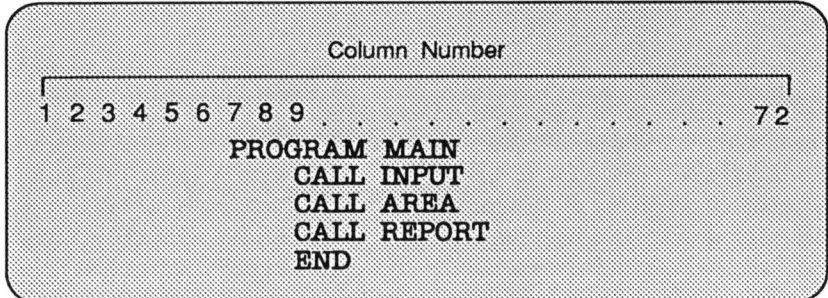

Figure 1-15   Using the FORTRAN Coding Form

Label Field

The label field, consisting of the first five columns in a line, is used for statement numbers. A *statement number* is any integer from 1 to 99999 that is typed into the label field. Although the program statements shown in Figure 1-15 contain no statement numbers, certain statements require a statement number so they may be referenced by other statements in the same program unit (more about this later). If a line does not require a statement number, the label field should be left blank.

Column 1 of the label field is also referred to as the comment indicator column. If either an asterisk (*) or a C is placed in this column, the line becomes a *comment line*. For example,

```
123456789————Column Number ————————————72 73——80
* THIS IS A COMMENT LINE
*       THIS PROGRAM PRINTS OUT A MESSAGE
*            THIS PROGRAM CALCULATES THE SLOPE OF A LINE
```

are all comment lines. Comment lines can be placed anywhere within a program, without restriction, and have no effect on program execution. The compiler ignores all comment lines—they are there strictly for the convenience of anyone reading the program. When used carefully, comment lines can be very helpful in clarifying what a complete program is about, what an individual program unit does, what a specific group of statements is meant to accomplish, or what one line is intended to do.

Continuation Field

An individual FORTRAN statement can consist of up to twenty lines. The first line is always called the *initial line,* and any succeeding lines of the same statement are called *continuation lines.* Initial lines are designated either by leaving column 6, the continuation field, blank or by placing a zero (0) in this field. Continuation lines are specified by placing any nonblank character except zero in column 6. When a statement is continued beyond an initial line, the label field of all continuation lines must be left blank. Comment lines cannot be continued across two lines using the continuation field; every line in a comment must begin with either a * or a C in column 1.

Statement Field

The third field in each line, consisting of columns 7 through 72, is reserved for the actual FORTRAN statement. A statement can be placed anywhere within the statement field. It is customary to write program unit header statements starting in column 7 and to indent each statement in a unit's body by at least two more columns to improve program readability. Every line in a FORTRAN program, except for comment lines, must have an entry in the statement field.

Identification/Sequence Field

The last field of the FORTRAN coding form, consisting of columns 73 through 80, is always ignored by a FORTRAN compiler and is rarely used anymore. This field is a holdover from the early days of FORTRAN, when statements were typed on punched cards consisting of 80 columns. By typing either an identification or a sequence number in this field, a programmer could correctly reorder a deck of cards that was inadvertently dropped or shuffled. The advent of keyboard input has made the need for keeping cards in order, and hence for using the identification/sequence field, obsolete.

Statement Categories

You will have many statements at your disposal in constructing your FORTRAN source programs. All statements, however, belong to one of two broad categories: executable statements and nonexecutable statements. An *executable statement* causes some specific action to be performed by the computer. For example, a statement that tells the computer to add or subtract a number is an executable statement. A *nonexecutable statement* is a statement that describes some feature of either the program or its data but does not cause the computer to perform any action. An example of a nonexecutable statement is a program unit header. A header statement explicitly defines the beginning of a program unit but causes no specific action to be taken by the computer when the program is executed. As the various FORTRAN statements are introduced in the coming sections, we will point out which ones are executable and which are nonexecutable.

Skill Builder Exercises

Note for Exercises 1–3: Assume that the following are valid statements from a FORTRAN program. Using the FORTRAN coding form, show how each statement should be placed on each line entered into the computer.

1.
```
PROGRAM MAIN
CALL GROPAY
CALL TAXES
CALL NETPAY
CALL DISPLAY
STOP
END
```

2.
```
* THIS PROGRAM CALCULATES THE AREA OF A CIRCLE
PROGRAM MAIN
* THE EXECUTABLE STATEMENTS IN THE PROGRAM ARE THE FOLLOWING
CALL RADIUS
CALL AREA
CALL OUTPUT
STOP
END
```

3.
```
* THIS PROGRAM DISPLAYS A FOUR-LINE POEM
PROGRAM MAIN
CALL POEM
STOP
END
SUBROUTINE POEM
* THE NUMBERS 10, 20, 30, AND 40 IN THE NEXT FOUR STATEMENTS
* ARE STATEMENT LABELS THAT BELONGS IN THE LABEL FIELD
10 PRINT *, 'COMPUTERS, COMPUTERS EVERYWHERE'
20 PRINT *, ' AS FAR AS I CAN SEE'
30 PRINT *, 'I REALLY, REALLY LIKE THOSE THINGS'
40 PRINT *, ' OH JOY, OH JOY FOR ME'
RETURN
END
```

4.
```
PROGRAM MAIN
CALL TEST
STOP
END
SUBROUTINE TEST
* THE NUMBER 100 IN THE NEXT STATEMENT IS A
* STATEMENT LABEL THAT BELONGS IN THE LABEL FIELD
100 FORMAT(1X,A,1X,I5)
* THE 100 IN THE NEXT TWO STATEMENTS ARE PART OF THE
* STATEMENTS AND BELONG IN THE STATEMENT FIELD
PRINT 100, '30/5 = ', 30/5
PRINT 100, 'THE SUM OF 2 + 12 IS ', 2 + 12
RETURN
END
```

```
5. PROGRAM MAIN
   CALL TEST
   STOP
   END
   SUBROUTINE TEST
   * THE NUMBERS 100 AND 200 IN THE NEXT TWO STATEMENTS ARE
   * LABELS THAT BELONG IN THE LABEL FIELD
   100 FORMAT(1X,A,2X,A)
   200 FORMAT(1X,I5,2X,F5.3)
   * THE FOLLOWING TWO STATEMENTS ARE CALLED
   * DECLARATION STATEMENTS
   REAL VALUE
   INTEGER COUNT
   PRINT 100, 'VALUE', 'SIN'
   PRINT 100, '-----', '---'
   DO 10 COUNT = 1, 20
   * FOR APPEARANCE ONLY, BEGIN THE NEXT TWO STATEMENTS
   * IN COLUMN 11
   VALUE = 0.1 * I
   PRINT 200, VALUE, SIN(VALUE)
   * THE 10 IN THE NEXT STATEMENT IS A STATEMENT NUMBER
   10 CONTINUE
   RETURN
   END
```

Debugging Exercises

Note for Exercises 6-14: A program "bug" is an error in a program. Some of the most common bugs occur because of the misplacement of statements within the columns of each program line or the misspelling of keywords. Determine the bug in each of the following statements.

6. ```
   123456789————Column Number ————————————72 73——80
   PROGRAM MAIN
   ```

7. ```
   123456789————Column Number ————————————72 73——80
           PROGAM MAIN
   ```

8. ```
   123456789————Column Number ————————————72 73——80
          *THIS IS A COMMENT LINE
   ```

9. ```
   123456789————Column Number ————————————72 73——80
           100 FORMAT(1X,I5)
   ```

10. ```
    123456789————Column Number ————————————72 73——80
                                              CALL REPORT
    ```

11. ```
    123456789————Column Number ————————————72 73——80
    CALL REPORT
    ```

12. ```
    123456789————Column Number ————————————72 73——80
        10   CALL REPORT
    ```
    ```

13. `123456789————Column Number ————————————72 73——80`
```
      C THE NEXT LINE IS AN INITIAL LINE OF A STATEMENT
      PRINT 100, 'THE AVERAGE IS',
      C AND THE NEXT LINE IS A CONTINUATION LINE
    1 AVERAGE
```

14. `123456789————Column Number ————————————72 73——80`
```
      PRGRAM MAIN
      * THIS PROGRAM CALCULATES THE SINE OF AN
        ANGLE
      CALL SINE
      STOP
      END
```

Expanding Your Skills

15. Determine the procedures required to enter a program on your computer system. Also determine how to save the program and reload it from the storage system connected to your computer.

16. Using the procedures determined in Exercise 15, enter and store the following program (make sure to enter the program in accordance with the FORTRAN coding form, as illustrated):

`123456789————Column Number ————————————72`
```
      PROGRAM MAIN
        CALL DISPLY
        STOP
        END
      SUBROUTINE DISPLY
        PRINT *, 'THIS IS A MESSAGE'
        PRINT *, 'THAT WAS DISPLAYED UNDER THE DIRECTION'
        PRINT *, 'OF A FORTRAN PROGRAM'
        RETURN
        END
```

17a. Determine the procedures required to compile and execute a FORTRAN program on your system.

b. Using the procedures determined in Exercises 15 and 17a, enter, compile, and execute the program listed in Exercise 16. Make sure to enter the program in accordance with the FORTRAN coding form.

18. Using the procedures in Exercise 15 and 17a, enter, compile, and execute the following program. Make sure to enter the program in accordance with the FORTRAN coding form:

```
123456789————Column Number ————————————————72
      PROGRAM MAIN
        CALL SHOW
        STOP
        END
      SUBROUTINE SHOW
        REAL ANGLE
        INTEGER I
        PRINT *, 'ANGLE SIN(ANGLE)'
        PRINT *, '————— —————————'
        DO 10 I = 1, 20
          ANGLE = 0.1 * I
          PRINT *, ANGLE, SIN(ANGLE)
   10 CONTINUE
        RETURN
        END
```

1.4   Writing Complete Programs

It is now time to put together the information we have learned in the previous sections and write a complete, working program. A particularly easy program to write is one that displays a message on the standard system display device connected to the computer. Generally, this display device is either a video screen or a printer and is formally referred to as the computer's *standard output device.* Either a PRINT or a WRITE statement can be used to send a message to the standard output device. Both of these statements can be used for either *list-directed output,* in which the placement of the display is under the direction of the FORTRAN compiler, or *user-formatted output,* in which the programmer explicitly controls the positioning of the output display. In this section the list-directed forms of both the PRINT and the WRITE statement are introduced and used within the context of a complete program.

The List-Directed WRITE Statement

The general form of the list-directed WRITE statement is:

```
WRITE(unit number, *) list of items
```

The asterisk before the closing parenthesis in the WRITE statement tells the compiler to use its own default format for displaying the list of items in the statement. The unit number within the WRITE statement's parentheses designates where the message is to be displayed. Table 1-2 lists the unit numbers assigned to the standard output display device by the more commonly used FORTRAN compilers. A space has been left in the table for you to enter the unit numbers used by your compiler to identify your system's standard output device.

One of the simplest items to display on the standard system output device is a single message. A message is any combination of letters, numbers, and special

Table 1-2 Standard Output Device Unit Numbers

Compiler	Unit Number	Example
AT&T PHILON	6 or *	WRITE(6,*) 'HELLO' or WRITE(*,*) 'HELLO'
AUSTEC (R/M)	6 or *	WRITE(6,*) 'OKAY' or WRITE(*,*) 'OKAY'
DEC-VAX	5, 6 or *	WRITE(6,*) 'BYE' or WRITE(*,*) 'BYE'
DTSS	0, 6, or *	WRITE(0,*) 'BYE' or WRITE(6,*) 'BYE' or WRITE(*,*) 'BYE'
IBM	6 or *	WRITE(6,*) 'OKAY' or WRITE(*,*) 'OKAY'
MICROSOFT	6 or *	WRITE(6,*) 'BYE' or WRITE(*,*) 'BYE'
PRIME	1 or *	WRITE(1,*) 'HELLO' or WRITE(*,*) 'HELLO'
Your System:		

characters (such as dollar signs, exclamation points, periods, etc.) enclosed within apostrophes ('), which are also called single quotes, to mark both the beginning and the end of the message. For example, on a DEC-VAX computer, the statement:

```
WRITE(6,*) 'HELLO THERE WORLD!'
```

is a command to display the message HELLO THERE WORLD! on the computer's standard output device. The equivalent statement for a PRIME computer is:

```
WRITE(1,*) 'HELLO THERE WORLD!'
```

The asterisk (*) in both of these statements tells the compiler to use its own default format for creating the display. For messages, the default format is, as you might expect, to display the message exactly as it is written within the apostrophes. (In Chapter 2 we will see how to replace the asterisk with a reference to an explicit user-defined format for controlling the output display.)

More formally, a message in FORTRAN is referred to as a *literal* because it contains literal information consisting of any sequence of numbers, letters, and special characters, such as the exclamation point (!). Literals are also called *character constants,* and the two terms are used interchangeably.

Except for messages within apostrophes and certain specific cases that will be noted as they occur, FORTRAN ignores all *white space* (any combination of blank spaces and tabs). Therefore, blank spaces may be freely inserted within a statement to improve its appearance. For example, all three of the following WRITE statements produce the same result.

```
WRITE(6,*) 'HELLO'
WRITE(6,*)'HELLO'
WRITE (6, *) 'HELLO'
```

Although the spaces separating the parentheses, unit number, comma, asterisk, and message are optional and have no effect on the output, spaces within the apostrophes do affect the display. For example, the statement:

```
WRITE(6,*) 'HELLO'
```

produces a different display than the statement:

```
WRITE(6,*) 'H E L L O'
```

In the first case the message HELLO is displayed, with no spaces between the letters, and in the second case the message H E L L O is displayed, with a space separating each letter from the next.

Now let's put this all together into a working FORTRAN program that can be run on your computer. Consider Program 1-1:*

Program 1-1

```
123456789 ——————— Column Number ————————————————————————72
      PROGRAM MAIN
        CALL DISPLY
        STOP
        END
      SUBROUTINE DISPLY
        WRITE(6,*) 'HELLO THERE WORLD!'
        RETURN
        END
```

Notice that Program 1-1 follows the program structure introduced in the last section: the program has only one main program unit, all header lines and program unit statements are contained within columns 7 through 72, and each statement is placed on a line by itself. It also conforms to a modular program structure where the MAIN program unit is used to call other program units that produce the required results. Since the only result produced by Program 1-1 is a message, only a single subroutine is needed. When Program 1-1 is compiled and executed, the message is correctly displayed on your terminal, as shown in Figure 1-16.

```
HELLO THERE WORLD!
```

Figure 1-16 The Output of Program 1-1

---

* For a Prime computer, the unit number 6 in the WRITE statement must be replaced by 1.

As Program 1-1 is our first complete, working program, we will analyze it in detail to see how this display is produced. The first program unit in Program 1-1 is a MAIN unit, which identifies the start of the FORTRAN program. In this program the MAIN unit is used to call a subroutine named DISPLY. Here, the name of the called subroutine is selected by the programmer according to the rules presented in Section 1.2 for symbolic names. Following the end of the MAIN program unit is a single SUBROUTINE program unit. The subroutine's header line is:

```
SUBROUTINE DISPLY
```

and the body of the subroutine consists of the three statements

```
WRITE(6,*) 'HELLO THERE WORLD!'
RETURN
END
```

The WRITE statement in this subroutine causes the message HELLO THERE WORLD! to be displayed, the RETURN statement returns control to the MAIN unit, and the END statement terminates the subroutine.* Although the display produced by the DISPLY subroutine is extremely simple, it does illustrate the correct structure of a modular program using a single subroutine.

Although Program 1-1 displays only a single message, we can add additional WRITE statements within the subroutine to display more than one message. See if you can read Program 1-2 and determine what it does.**

Program 1-2

```
123456789 ———— Column Number ————————————————72
      PROGRAM MAIN
         CALL DISPLY
         STOP
         END
*
      SUBROUTINE DISPLY
         WRITE(6,*) 'THE SLOPE OF THE LINE'
         WRITE(6,*) ' Y = 5X + 3'
         WRITE(6,*) ' IS 5.'
         RETURN
         END
```

---

* If the RETURN statement is omitted, the subroutine's END statement causes a return to the MAIN unit.

** Again, if this program is to be run on a Prime computer, the unit number in the WRITE statements must be changed to a 1.

When Program 1-2 is compiled and run, the following is displayed:

```
THE SLOPE OF THE LINE
 Y = 5X + 3
 IS 5.
```

As you might have guessed, each WRITE statement in the DISPLY subroutine causes a new line to be displayed. Since the subroutine has three WRITE statements, three individual lines are produced. In each case the message in the WRITE statement is displayed exactly as it appears within the enclosing apostrophes, including spaces. Thus, the single leading space in the second and third messages are retained in the displayed output.

Also notice the sequence in which Program 1-2 is executed. The program begins with the MAIN program unit's nonexecutable program header statement and continues sequentially, statement by statement, until the STOP statement is encountered. The CALL statement transfers control to the DISPLY subroutine, which consists of four executable statements. The statements within the body of this unit are also executed sequentially, with each WRITE statement producing a single line of output. The next-to-last statement in the subroutine is a RETURN statement, which terminates the subroutine's execution and causes control to be passed back to the MAIN unit. The remaining statements in the MAIN program unit are a STOP and an END statement. The STOP statement transfers control back to the computer's operating system. The END statement signals the end of the MAIN program unit for compilation purposes.*

Altering the placement of any of the WRITE statements in the DISPLY subroutine automatically alters the display produced by the complete program. For example, if the statements in Program 1-2 were written in the order shown in Program 1-3, the output shown in Figure 1-17 would be produced.

---

* Although a MAIN program unit may contain both a STOP and END statement at the end of the unit, the STOP statement is not required immediately before an END statement on most FORTRAN 77 compilers, as it was in earlier FORTRAN versions. In these earlier versions, a STOP statement was the last statement actually compiled and translated into machine language. The END statement, in these earlier versions, was a nonexecutable statement that marked the physical end of the program to the compiler and told the compiler to terminate reading any more statements and begin the actual compilation. In FORTRAN 77, the END statement is an executable one that performs both functions; it informs the compiler of the program's physical end and gets translated into machine language. As such, the STOP statement is no longer required immediately before the END statement. For this reason, the convention adopted by this book will be to discontinue using a STOP statement immediately before an END statement in all subsequent MAIN program units. For a similar reason the RETURN statement immediately preceding an END statement in SUBROUTINE units will also be omitted. However, if your computer displays either an error or warning message when the STOP or RETURN statements are omitted, continue to include them in your programs.

Also note that all program units may contain several STOP statements and subroutines may additionally contain several RETURN statements, whereas the END statement must always be the last statement in all program units. For example, a STOP statement might be located within a program unit to halt execution when a detectable error is encountered by the program. The use of a STOP statement in this context requires the selection statements described in Chapter 4.

Program 1-3

```
123456789 ———— Column Number ————————————————72
      PROGRAM MAIN
        CALL DISPLY
      STOP
      END
*
      SUBROUTINE DISPLY
        WRITE(6,*) ' Y = 5X + 3'
        WRITE(6,*) 'THE SLOPE OF THE LINE'
        WRITE(6,*) ' IS 5.'
        RETURN
        END
```

(handwritten annotation: USE CALL TO ADD (W) SUBROUTINE PROG)

```
 Y = 5x + 3
THE SLOPE OF THE LINE
 IS 5.
```

Figure 1-17   The Output from Program 1-3.

Although all of the messages illustrated have used only uppercase letters, this is not required in FORTRAN. Messages can contain any characters, including lower-case letters, percent signs (%), ampersands (&), exclamation points (!), and any other symbol supported by your computer. These characters are allowed within messages because the compiler attributes no significance to them other than to store and display them exactly as they appear in the message. Messages can even include an apostrophe, as long as we indicate that the apostrophe is to be displayed and does not signify the end of the message. This is done by using two consecutive apostrophes. For example, the statement:

```
WRITE(6,*) 'Joe''s grade'
```

produces the display:

```
Joe's grade
```

Finally, it is possible to use the WRITE statements with no output. For example, the statement:

```
WRITE(6,*)
```

causes a blank line to be displayed. Thus, the sequence of statements:

```
WRITE(6,*) 'THE SLOPE OF THE LINE'
WRITE(6,*)
WRITE(6,*) '      Y = 5X + 3'
WRITE(6,*)
WRITE(6,*) '          IS 5.'
```

causes the following double-spaced display:

```
THE SLOPE OF THE LINE

   Y = 5X + 3

      IS 5.
```

The List-Directed PRINT Statement

The unit number in a WRITE statement permits output to be written to units other than the standard output display device. For example, the display can be written directly to a disk or tape unit if the appropriate unit number is used. The routing of results to the standard output device is so common, however, that all FORTRAN 77 compilers, including those listed in Table 1-1, provide an alternative form for the list-directed WRITE statement. This form is the list-directed PRINT statement, which has the general form:

```
PRINT *, list of items
```

For example, the statement:

```
PRINT *, 'HELLO THERE WORLD!'
```

causes the message HELLO THERE WORLD! to be displayed on the standard output device. In this statement the term PRINT *, is equivalent to the term WRITE(1,*) for Prime computers and can be used in place of the term WRITE(6,*) for the other computers listed in Table 1-1. Since, by definition, the PRINT statement can only direct its display to the standard output device, an explicit unit number designating the standard output device is unnecessary. Program 1-4 uses this PRINT statement in place of the WRITE statement used in Program 1-1. Both programs produce the output shown in Figure 1-16.

Program 1-4

```
123456789 ———— Column Number ————————————————————72
PROGRAM MAIN
  CALL DISPLY
  END
SUBROUTINE DISPLY
  PRINT *, 'HELLO THERE WORLD!'
  END
```

As with the WRITE statement, the PRINT statement can be used to produce blank lines. For example, the statement:

```
PRINT *
```

causes a blank line to be displayed (note that there is no comma after the asterisk). Finally, on all computer systems the statement:

```
PRINT *, 'message in here'
```

is equivalent to the statement:

```
WRITE(*,*) 'message in here'
```

As before, the asterisk in the PRINT statement is equivalent to the second asterisk in the WRITE statement and selects the compiler's default formats for the placement of the display. The first asterisk in the WRITE statement is a unit designator (see Table 1-2) that selects the standard output device assigned by the system for output display. For example, on a DEC-VAX computer the following three statements all produce the same display:

```
PRINT *, 'HELLO THERE WORLD!'
WRITE(*,*) 'HELLO THERE WORLD!'
WRITE(6,*) 'HELLO THERE WORLD!'
```

In the remainder of the book we will use the PRINT statement almost exclusively for output to the standard output device to save us the trouble of explicitly including a standard output unit number. For output to any other device, the PRINT statement cannot be used, instead a WRITE statement must be employed to specifically designate the desired output device.

On Using One or More Modules

The number and size of each module in a program depend, respectively, on the number of tasks required by the program and the complexity of each individual task. Even for extremely simple programs it is important to practice writing modular FORTRAN programs to develop the facility of "thinking modular." This ability will benefit the programmer when much larger programs requiring numerous subroutines and more involved tasks must be designed.

By definition, however, modular does not mean that a program must contain a subroutine; it simply means that each program consists of one or more modules appropriate to solving the task at hand. For many programs a single module consisting of only a MAIN program unit, is sufficient. This is especially true when a program is written to illustrate a specific feature of the FORTRAN language.

Using only a single program unit, a FORTRAN program has the form:

```
123456789 ———— Column Number ————————————————72
      PROGRAM name
         valid FORTRAN statements in here
      END
```

For example, Program 1-4, which displays a single message, can be written in this form as:

```
123456789 ———— Column Number ————————————————72
      PROGRAM MAIN
         PRINT *, 'HELLO THERE WORLD!'
      END
```

Notice that this form of the program is obtained by removing the second, third, and fourth lines in Program 1-4. For the remainder of the text, programs that are used to illustrate individual features of the FORTRAN language will adhere to a single program unit format, while more complex programming tasks will be coded using multiple program units.

Additional Exercises for Chapter 1

Skill Builder Exercises

1a. Using either PRINT or WRITE statements, write a FORTRAN program that calls a subroutine to print your name on one line, your street address on a second line, and your city, state, and zip code on the third line.

b. For the program written in Exercise 1a, determine the three statements that can be removed to produce a single-module program.

c. Compile and run the program you have written for either Exercise 1a or Exercise 1b on a computer. (*Note:* To do this, you must understand the procedures for entering, compiling, and running a FORTRAN program on the particular computer you are using.)

2a. Using either PRINT or WRITE statements, write a FORTRAN program that calls a subroutine to print out the following:

```
THE COSECANT OF AN ANGLE
   IS EQUAL TO ONE OVER
      THE SINE OF THE SAME ANGLE.
```

b. For the program written in Exercise 2a, determine the three statements that can be removed to produce a single-module program.

c. Compile and run the program you have written for either Exercise 2a or Exercise 2b.

3a. How many PRINT or WRITE statements should be used to display the following.

```
DEGREES  RADIANS
   0     0.0000
  90     1.5708
 180     3.1416
 270     4.7124
 360     6.2832
```

b. Write a complete FORTRAN program to produce the output illustrated in Exercise 3a.

c. Compile and run the program you have written for Exercise 3b on a computer.

Expanding Your Skills

4. When a PRINT or WRITE statement is used to display a message, the first character in the message is displayed at the beginning of a new line. This character positioning actually represents two distinct operations. What are they?

5a. Most computer operating systems provide the capability for redirecting output intended for the standard output device to some other device. For example, if the standard output device is a video screen, redirection to either a printer or directly to a floppy or hard disk file may be possible. Determine if your computer supports this redirection capability.

b. If your computer supports output redirection, run the program written for Exercise 2a using this feature. Have the display produced by your program redirected to a disk file named DEGREE.

c. If the standard output device for your computer is a video screen, and your system supports output redirection to a printer, run the program written for Exercise 2a using this redirection feature.

1.5   Common Programming Errors

Part of learning any programming language is making the elementary mistakes made by most beginning students. These mistakes can be quite frustrating, since each language seems to have its own set of traps waiting for the unwary. Following are the more common errors made when initially programming in FORTRAN.

1. Starting a statement in either column 1 or column 6 rather than in column 7 or beyond.

2. Continuing a statement beyond column 72. For example, the statement:

```
1234567 ————— Column Number ———————————72 73 —— 80
         PRINT *, 'THIS IS A WONDERFUL DAY BECAUSE THE SUN IS OUT'
```

causes a compiler error message. The message is generated because the statement has no closing apostrophe (recall that characters typed in columns 73 though 80 are ignored by the compiler).

3. Using lowercase rather than uppercase letters. (Some compilers permit lowercase letters. In case insensitive compilers, the lowercase letter can be used in place of its corresponding uppercase equivalent; in case-sensitive compilers, lowercase letters are recognized as distinct from their uppercase equivalents.)

4. Inadvertently misspelling keywords such as PRINT and WRITE: for example, typing PINT instead of PRINT.

5. Omitting the comma after the asterisk in a PRINT statement (except when a blank line is printed using the statement PRINT *).

6. Continuing a comment line over two lines without placing either an asterisk or a C in column 1 of the second line. For example, the comment:

```
123456789 ————— Column Number ———————————80
* THIS COMMENT WILL CAUSE AN ERROR BECAUSE IT INCORRECTLY EXTENDS
OVER TWO LINES
```

results in a FORTRAN error message. This comment is correct when written as:

```
123456789 ————— Column Number ———————————————————————72
* THIS COMMENT IS NOW VALID EVEN
*    THOUGH IT EXTENDS OVER TWO LINES
```

7. Forgetting the keyword SUBROUTINE in a subroutine's header line.

8. Incorrectly typing the letter O for the number zero (0), or vice versa.

9. Incorrectly typing the lowercase letter l or the uppercase letter I for the number 1, or vice versa.

The first seven of these errors are initially the most common but tend to diminish as the programmer gains experience. The last two errors are more persistent and plague even experienced programmers. We suggest that you write a program and specifically introduce each of these errors, one at a time, to see what error messages are produced by your compiler. Later, when these error messages appear due to inadvertent errors in your programming, you will have had experience in understanding the messages and correcting the errors.

1.6   Chapter Summary

1. An *algorithm* is a step-by-step procedure that describes how a computation or task is to be performed.

2. A computer program is a description of an algorithm written in a language that can be used by a computer.

3. FORTRAN provides three commonly used types of program units: the MAIN, SUBROUTINE, and FUNCTION types. Each of these unit types performs a particular type of task.

4. A complete FORTRAN program consists of one or more program units. One of these program units must be a MAIN program unit. The MAIN unit is also called a driver unit when it is primarily used to call other program units.

5. Program units have a header line and a program unit body. The header line includes a header keyword that identifies the type of program unit and contains a user-selected name for the unit. The header keywords for MAIN and SUBROUTINE programs units are PROGRAM and SUBROUTINE, respectively. The last statement in a program unit is the keyword END placed on a line by itself.

6. SUBROUTINE and FUNCTION program units are referred to as *subprogram* units.

7. All program unit statements, including the header line, must comply with the FORTRAN coding form illustrated below:

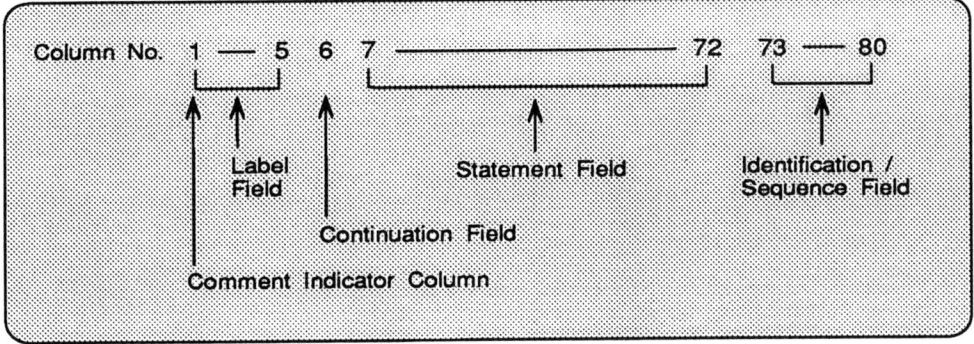

8. If an asterisk (*) or the letter C is placed in column 1, the line becomes a comment line. Comment lines can be placed anywhere in a program unit and are used to clarify either the purpose of the program unit itself or individual sections and lines of code within the program unit.

9. A FORTRAN statement can be continued across multiple lines. When this is done, a nonblank character other than 0 must be placed in column 6 of each continuation line. In no case may multiple statements be placed on the same line.

10. A computer's *standard output device* is the default display device (video terminal or printer) used by your system for the display of text.

11. In *list-directed* output, the placement of the display produced by either a WRITE or a PRINT statement is determined by the compiler's default format specifications.

12. Both PRINT and WRITE statements can be used to display messages on a computer's standard output device. The form of the list-directed PRINT statement for displaying messages is:

```
PRINT *, 'message'
```

The form of the list-directed WRITE statement for displaying messages is:

```
WRITE(unit number, *) 'message'
```

where each compiler has its own unit number for determining where the message is to be displayed. IBM, Prime, and DEC-VAX compilers use unit numbers 6, 1, and either 5 or 6, respectively, as their standard output device numbers. An asterisk may also be used in place of the unit number to designate the standard output device.

The message displayed by PRINT and WRITE statements can include any character supported by your computer. Two consecutive apostrophes ('') are used to designate a single apostrophe within a message.

13. The statement PRINT * causes a blank line to be displayed on the standard output device. The equivalent WRITE statement is WRITE(n,*), where n is the unit number assigned by your system to its standard output device.

14. In a modular program each task performed by the program is accomplished using an individual program unit. The simplest modular FORTRAN program consists of a MAIN program unit only. The program has the form:

```
123456789 ————— Column Number ——————————————72
      PROGRAM name
         valid FORTRAN statements in here
      END
```

An example of such a program is:

```
123456789 ————— Column Number ——————————————72
      PROGRAM SHOW
         PRINT *, 'HELLO THERE WORLD!'
      END
```

An example of a modular program that uses one subroutine in addition to the required MAIN unit is:

```
123456789 ————— Column Number ——————————————72
      PROGRAM MAIN
         CALL DISPLY
      END
      SUBROUTINE DISPLY
         PRINT *, 'HELLO THERE WORLD!'
      END
```

Both programs display the message HELLO THERE WORLD! on the computer's standard output device. The latter program illustrates how a subroutine is called and adheres to the strict usage of a MAIN program unit as a *driver* unit that is only used to call other program units.

15. All statements in a program unit are executed sequentially, one after another, unless a statement causing an alteration of this normal sequence is encountered. There is no "look ahead" capability, where one statement can anticipate the result of another statement later in the program unit.

1.7   Enrichment Study: Computer Hardware and Storage

All computers, from large supercomputers costing millions of dollars to smaller desktop personal computers, must perform a minimum set of functions and provide the capability to:

1. accept input
2. display output
3. store information in a logically consistent format (traditionally binary)
4. perform arithmetic and logic operations on either the input or stored data
5. monitor, control, and direct the overall operation and sequencing of the system

Figure 1-18 illustrates the computer hardware components that support these capabilities. Specifically, this hardware consists of arithmetic and logic, control, memory, and input/output units.

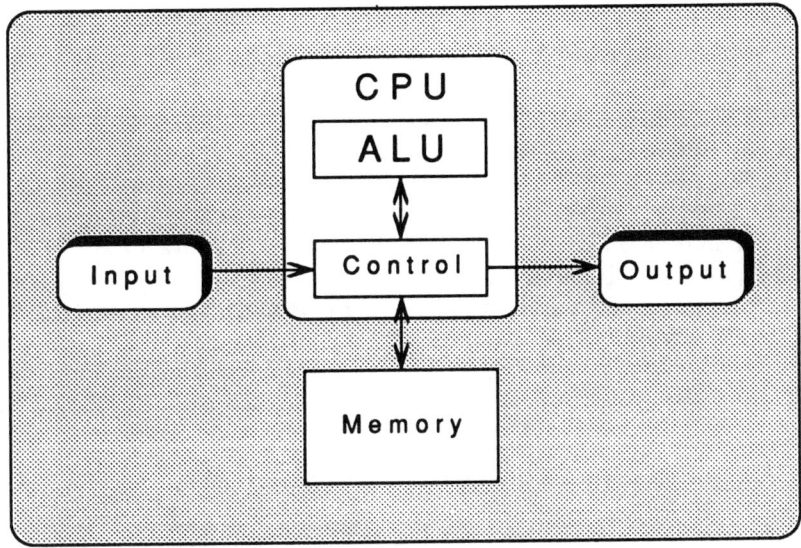

Figure 1-18   Basic Hardware Units of a Computer

The *arithmetic and logic unit* (*ALU*) performs all the arithmetic and logic functions, such as addition, subtraction, and so on., provided by the system.

The *control unit* directs and monitors the overall operation of the computer. It keeps track of where in memory the next instruction resides, issues the signals needed to both read data from and write data to other units in the system, and executes all instructions.

The *memory unit* stores information in a logically consistent format. Typically, both instructions and data are stored in memory, usually in separate and distinct areas.

The *input* and *output* (*I/O*) *units* provide access to and from the computer. These units are the interface to which peripheral devices such as keyboards, cathode ray screens, printers, and card readers are attached.

In the first commercially available computers of the 1950s, all hardware units were built using relays and vacuum tubes. The resulting computers were extremely large pieces of equipment, each capable of making thousands of calculations per second and costing millions of dollars.

With the introduction of transistors in the 1960s, both the size and the cost of computer hardware were reduced. The transistor was approximately one-twentieth the size of its vacuum tube counterpart. The transistors small size allowed manufacturers to combine the arithmetic and logic unit with the control unit into a single new unit. This combined unit is called the *central processing unit* (*CPU*). The combination of the ALU and control units into one CPU made sense because a majority of control signals generated by a program are directed to the ALU in response to arithmetic and logic instructions within the program. Combining the ALU with the control unit simplified the interface between these two units and provided improved processing speed.

The mid-1960s saw the introduction of integrated circuits (ICs), which resulted in still another significant reduction in the space required for a CPU. Initially, integrated circuits were manufactured with up to 100 transistors on a single 1-cm² chip of silicon. Such devices are referred to as small-scale integrated (SSI) circuits. Current versions of these chips contain from hundreds of thousands to over a million transistors and are referred to as very large-scale integrated (VLSI) chips.

VLSI chip technology has provided the means of transforming the giant computers of the 1950s into today's desktop personal computers. Each individual unit required to form a computer (CPU, memory, and I/O) is now manufactured on an individual VLSI chip, and the single-chip CPU is referred to as a *microprocessor.* Figure 1-19 illustrates how the chips are connected internally within current personal computers, such as IBM PCs.

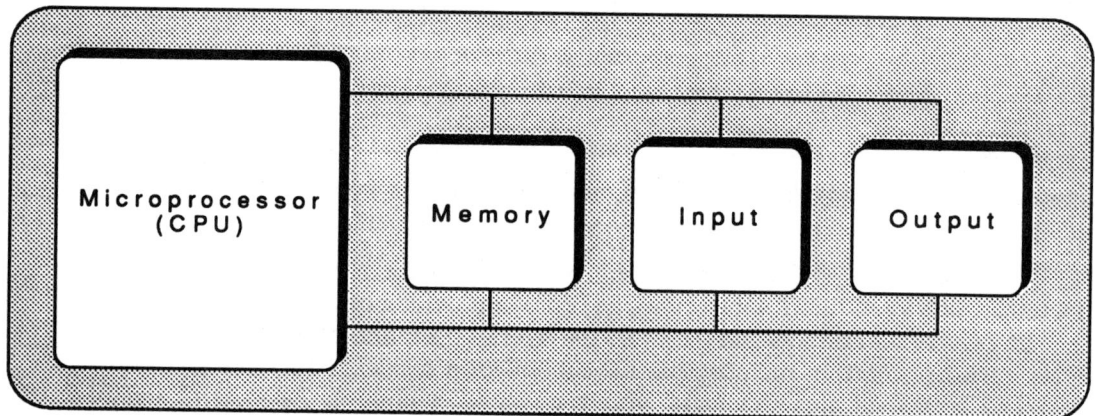

Figure 1-19   VLSI **Chip Connections for a Desktop Computer**

Concurrent with the remarkable reduction in computer hardware size have been an equally dramatic decrease in cost and increase in processing speeds. Equivalent computer hardware that cost over $1million in 1950 can now be purchased for less than $500. If the same reductions had occurred in the automobile industry, for example, a Rolls-Royce could now be purchased for $10! The processing speeds of current computers have also increased by a factor of a thousand over their 1950s predecessors, with the computational speeds of current machines being measured in both millions of instructions per second (MIPS) and billions of instructions per second (BIPS).

Computer Storage

It would be very convenient if a computer stored numbers and letters in its memory and arithmetic and logic units the way that people do. The number 126, for example, would then be stored as 126, and the letter A stored as the letter A. Unfortunately, because of their physical components, computers store information differently than people do.

The smallest and most basic data item in a computer is called a bit. Physically, a bit is really a switch that can be either open or closed. By convention, the open and closed positions of each switch are represented as a 0 and a 1, respectively.

A single bit that can represent the values 0 and 1 by itself has limited usefulness. All computers, therefore, group a set number of bits together for both storage and transmission. The grouping of eight bits to form a larger unit is an almost universal computer standard. Such groups are commonly referred to as bytes. A single byte consisting of eight bits, where each bit is either a 0 or a 1, can represent any one of 256 distinct patterns. These consist of the pattern 00000000 (all eight switches open), the pattern 11111111 (all eight switches closed), and all possible combinations of 0s and 1s in between. Each of these patterns can be used to represent either a letter of the alphabet; other single characters, such as a dollar sign, comma, and so on; a single digit; or numbers containing more than one digit. The patterns of 0s and 1s used to represent letters, single digits, and other single characters are called *character codes* (two such codes, called the ASCII and EBCDIC codes, are presented in Section 2.1). The patterns used to store numbers are called *number codes*, one of which is presented below.

Two's Complement Numbers

The most common number code for storing integer values inside a computer is called the *two's complement* representation. Using this code, the integer equivalent of any bit pattern, such as 10001101, is easy to determine and can be found for either positive or negative integers with no change in the conversion method. For convenience, we will assume byte sized bit patterns consisting of a set of eight bits each, although the procedure carries over directly to larger size bit patterns.

The easiest way to determine the integer represented by each bit pattern is to first construct a simple device called a value box. Figure 1-20 illustrates such a box for a single byte. Mathematically, each value in the box illustrated in Figure 1-20 represents an increasing power of two. Since two's complement numbers must be capable of representing both positive and negative integers, the leftmost position, in addition to having the largest absolute magnitude, also has a negative sign.

Conversion of any binary number, for example, 10001101, simply requires inserting the bit pattern in the value box and adding the values having ones under them. Thus, as illustrated in Figure 1-21, the bit pattern 10001101 represents the integer number −115.

The value box can also be used in reverse, to convert a base 10 integer number into its equivalent binary bit pattern. Some conversions, in fact, can be made by inspection. For example, the base 10 number −125 is obtained by adding 3 to −128. Thus, the binary representation of −125 is 10000011, which equals −128 + 2 + 1. Similarly, the two's complement representation of the number 40 is 00101000, which is 32 plus 8.

Although the value box conversion method is deceptively simple, it is directly related to the underlying mathematical basis of two's complement binary numbers. The original name of the two's complement code was the weighted-sign code, which

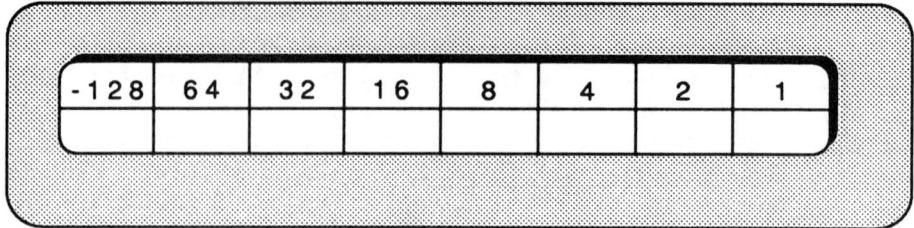

Figure 1-20   An Eight-Bit Value Box

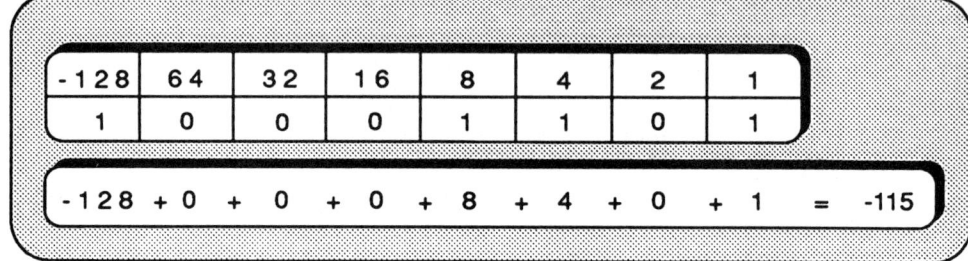

Figure 1-21   Converting 10001101 to a Base 10 Number

correlates directly to the value box. As the name *weighted sign* implies, each bit position has a weight, or value, of two raised to a power and a sign. The signs of all bits except the leftmost bit are positive, and the sign of the leftmost bit is negative.

In reviewing the value box, it is evident that any two's complement binary number with a leading 1 represents a negative number, and any bit pattern with a leading 0 represents a positive number. Using the value box, it is easy to determine the most positive and negative values capable of being stored. The most negative value that can be stored in a single byte is the decimal number –128, which has the bit pattern 10000000. Any other nonzero bit will simply add a positive amount to the number. Additionally, it is clear that a positive number must have a 0 as its leftmost bit. From this you can see that the largest positive eight-bit-two's complement number is 01111111, or 127.

Words and Addresses

One or more bytes may themselves be grouped into larger units, called *words,* which facilitate faster and more extensive data access. For example, retrieving a word consisting of four bytes from a computer's memory results in more information than would be obtained by retrieving a word consisting of a single byte. Such a retrieval is also considerably faster than four individual byte retrievals. This increase in speed and capacity, however, is achieved by an increase in the computer's cost and complexity.

Early personal computers, such as the Apple IIe and Commodore machines, internally stored and transmitted words consisting of single bytes. AT&T 6300 and

IBM PC/XTs use word sizes consisting of two bytes; Digital Equipment, Data General, Prime, and other minicomputers store and process words consisting of four bytes each. Supercomputers, such as the CRAY-1 and Control Data 7000, have six- and eight-byte words, respectively.

The number of bytes in a word determines the maximum and minimum values that can be represented by the word. Table 1-3 lists these values for 1-, 2-, and 4-byte words (each of the values listed can be derived using 8-, 16-, and 32-bit value boxes, respectively).

Table 1-3   Integer Values and Word Size

Word size	Maximum integer value	Minimum integer value
1 byte	127	−128
2 bytes	32,767	−32,768
4 bytes	2,147,483,647	−2,147,483,648

In addition to representing integer values, computers must also store and transmit numbers containing decimal points. Such numbers are mathematically referred to as real numbers. The codes used for real numbers, which are more complex than those used for integers, are presented in Appendix D.

Data and Operations

FORTRAN programs can process different types of data in different ways. For example, calculating the trajectory of a rocket requires that mathematical operations be performed using numerical data, while sorting a list of names requires comparison operations using alphabetic data.

In this chapter we introduce the basic types of data that can be used in FORTRAN programs, with emphasis on numerical data and the mathematical operations (addition, subtraction, multiplication, division, etc.) that can be performed on it. Information is also presented for displaying the results of these calculations using the PRINT and WRITE statements. This information provides us with the ability to write complete FORTRAN programs for elementary engineering and scientific applications.

2.1   Data Constants and Arithmetic Operations

FORTRAN recognizes six basic types of data: integers, real numbers, character strings, logical values, double precision numbers, and complex numbers. The first four of these data types, expressed as constants, are described below. Complex data and double precision data are presented in Chapter 10.

Integer Constants

An *integer constant* in FORTRAN, is any positive or negative number without a decimal point. Examples of valid integer constants are:

    6   −12   +35   1000   186   −6755821   +42

As these examples illustrate, integers may either be signed (have a leading + or − sign) or unsigned (no leading + or − sign). No commas, decimal points, or special symbols, such as the dollar sign, are allowed. Examples of invalid integer constants are:

    $187.62   3,532   4.   8,634,941   2,371.98   +7.0

The largest (most positive) and smallest (most negative) integer values that can be used in a program depend on the amount of storage each computer sets aside for integer values. For IBM 370, DEC-VAX, and Prime computers the most positive integer allowed is 2147483647, and the most negative integer is −2147483648.*

Real Constants

A *real constant* is any number that contains a decimal point. Examples of real constants are:

    +12.125   7.   −8.3   0.0   1351.76   0.66   −6.67   +5.

Notice that the numbers 7., 0.0, and +5. are classified as real constants in FORTRAN, while the same numbers written without a decimal point (7, 0, +5) are classified as integer constants.

The distinction between real and integer constants is made because of the different internal representations that computers use to store these data types. An integer requires storing of the sign and magnitude of the number; a real number requires storing of the sign, integer, and fractional parts of the number. (The interested reader can refer to Appendix D for a more complete explanation of the various internal data representations used for real values.)

Although real numbers can be signed or unsigned, no special symbols, such as the dollar sign and the comma, are permitted. Examples of invalid real constants that contain such special characters are:

    5,326.25   6,459. $10.29

---

* It is interesting to note that in all cases the magnitude of the most negative integer allowed is always one more than the magnitude of the most positive integer. This is because of the method most commonly used to represent integers, called two's complement representation. (For an explanation of two's complement representation see the Enrichment section at the end of Chapter 1.)

Exponential Notation

Real numbers can be written in an exponential notation, which is useful in expressing both very large and very small numbers in compact form. The following examples illustrate how numbers with decimals can be expressed in exponential notation.

Decimal Notation	Exponential Notation
1837.	1.837E
57641.	5.7641E4
234.26	2.3426E2
.00849	8.49E-3
.000265	2.65E-4

In exponential notation, the letter E stands for exponent. The number following the E represents a power of 10 and indicates the number of places the decimal point should be moved to obtain the standard decimal value. The decimal point is moved to the right if the number after the E is positive. It is moved to the left if the number after the E is negative. For example, the E2 in the number 2.3426E2 means move the decimal point two places to the right, so that the number represented is 234.26. The E-3 in the number 8.49E–3 means move the decimal point three places to the left, so that 8.49E–3 is equal to .00849.

Character Constants

The third basic data constant recognized by FORTRAN is the character constant. This data constant is also referred to as either a message, string, or literal and was introduced in Chapter 1. To review, a character constant consists of one or more characters that are enclosed within apostrophes (single quotes). Examples of valid character constants are:

```
'A'
'**&!##!!'
'$3,256.22'
'VELOCITY'
'HELLO THERE WORLD!'
'THE SINE OF THE ANGLE IS:'
```

The number of characters within a character constant is the *length* of the constant. For example, the length of the character constant '$3,256.22' is nine, and the length of the character constant 'A' is one. If an apostrophe is required within a character constant, two apostrophes are used. For example, the string 'DR. JOHNSON''S DOG' is a character constant of length 17 consisting of the characters:

```
DR. (space) JOHNSON'S (space) DOG
```

Character constants are typically represented in a computer using either the ASCII or the EBCDIC code. ASCII, pronounced "As-Key," is an acronym for American Standard Code for Information Interchange. EBCDIC, pronounced "Ebb-sih-dick," is an acronym for Extended Binary Coded Decimal Interchange Code. Each of these codes assigns individual characters to a specific pattern of 0s and 1s. Table 2-1 lists the correspondence between bit patterns and the uppercase letters of the alphabet used by the ASCII and EBCDIC codes.

Table 2-1   The ASCII and EBCDIC Uppercase Letter Codes

Letter	ASCII code	EBCDIC code	Letter	ASCII code	EBCDIC code
A	01000001	11000001	N	01001110	11010101
B	01000010	11000010	O	01001111	11010110
C	01000011	11000011	P	01010000	11010111
D	01000100	11000100	Q	01010001	11011000
E	01000101	11000101	R	01010010	11011001
F	01000110	11000110	S	01010011	11100010
G	01000111	11000111	T	01010100	11100011
H	01001000	11001000	U	01010101	11100100
I	01001001	11001001	V	01010110	11100101
J	01001010	11010001	W	01010111	11100110
K	01001011	11010010	X	01011000	11100111
L	01001100	11010011	Y	01011001	11101000
M	01001101	11010100	Z	01011010	11101001

Using Table 2-1, we can determine how the character constant 'SMITH', for example, is stored inside a computer that uses the ASCII character code. Using the ASCII code, this sequence of characters requires five bytes of storage (one byte for each letter) and would be stored as illustrated in Figure 2-1.

Logical Constants

There are only two logical data values in FORTRAN. These are the logical constants:

.TRUE.   and   .FALSE.

The periods surrounding the words TRUE and FALSE are part of the constants. Without the periods the words become symbolic names rather than logical values.

Logical data is useful in programming because all computers have the ability to select a course of action based on the state of a programmer-specified condition.

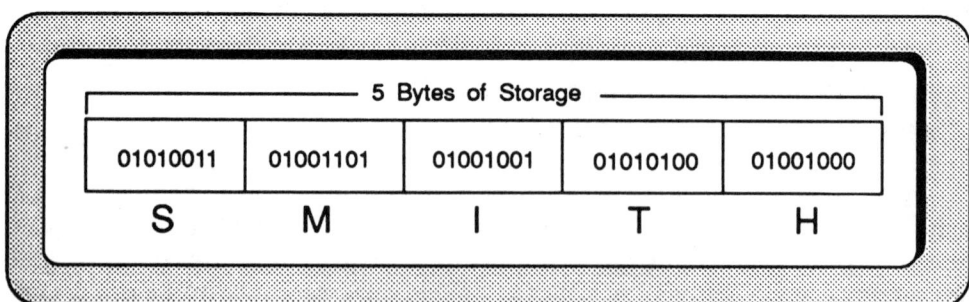

Figure 2-1   The Letters SMITH Stored Inside a Computer using the ASCII Code

Any condition has one of two possible outcomes: either the condition is satisfied, or it is not. In computer and mathematical terms, a condition that is satisfied is considered to be true; a condition that is not satisfied is considered to be false. The two logical constants in FORTRAN correspond to these outcomes and are used extensively in programs that incorporate decision-making statements.

Arithmetic Operations

Integers and real numbers may be added, subtracted, multiplied, divided, and raised to a power. The symbols for performing arithmetic operations in FORTRAN are shown in Table 2-2.

Table 2-2   FORTRAN's Arithmetic Operators

Operator	Operation
+	Addition
–	Subtraction
*	Multiplication
/	Division
**	Exponentiation (raising to a power)

A *simple arithmetic expression* consists of an arithmetic operator connecting two arithmetic operands in the form:

```
operand operator operand
```

Examples of simple arithmetic expressions are:

```
6 + 2
17 - 5
12.75 + 9.3
.06 * 14.8*
26.7 / 3.0
3.1416 ** 2
```

The spaces around the arithmetic operators in these examples are inserted strictly for clarity. They may be omitted without affecting the value of the expression.

The value of any arithmetic expression can be displayed using either a PRINT or a WRITE statement. For example, the value of the expression .06 * 14.8 can be displayed using the statement:

```
PRINT *, .06 * 14.8
```

Here, the expression, with no surrounding apostrophes, is included directly in the PRINT statement. When this statement is executed, the indicated multiplication

---

* Some compilers require a leading digit before a decimal point. For such compilers .06 must be written as 0.06.

is performed, and the output, .888000, is displayed on the standard output device. As this output shows, six digits to the right of the decimal point are displayed. For real number output using list-directed PRINT or WRITE statements, the exact number of decimal digits is compiler dependent. If the value to be displayed does not have the requisite number of decimal digits, zeros are added to the number to fill the fractional part. If the number has more than the default number of decimal digits (six, in this example), the fractional part is rounded to the default number of decimal places.

In addition to calculating and displaying the value of an expression, the list of items in both PRINT and WRITE statements can also include a message. For example, the PRINT statement:

```
PRINT *, 'THE VALUE OF THE EXPRESSION .06 * 14.8 IS ', .06*14.8
```

contains two items in its output list. The first item is a message, which is enclosed in apostrophes, and the second item is an arithmetic expression. When this statement is executed within a complete FORTRAN program, the display:

```
THE VALUE OF THE EXPRESSION .06 * 14.8 is      .888000
```

is produced. See if you can determine the output that is produced by the following sequence of statements:

```
PRINT *, '.06 * 14.8'
PRINT *, .06 * 14.8
PRINT *, '06 * 14.8 IS', .06 * 14.8
```

The first PRINT statement contains a message, which is enclosed in apostrophes. As the message consists of the characters .06 * 14.8, these characters will be displayed by the PRINT statement when it is executed. The second PRINT statement does not contain a message because no apostrophes are used. Thus, the value of the expression .06 * 14.8, which is .888000, is calculated and displayed when this statement is executed. Finally, the third PRINT statement contains both a message and an expression. When this statement is executed, the message will be displayed first, and the value of the arithmetic expression will be calculated and displayed next. This produces the output:

```
.06 * 14.8 IS    .888000
```

Program 2-1 illustrates using a PRINT statement to display the results of simple arithmetic expressions within the context of a complete program.

The output of Program 2-1 is:

```
OPERATION          VALUE
15.2 + 2.0       17.200000
15.2 - 2.0       13.200000
15.2 * 2.0       30.400000
15.2 / 2.0        7.600000
15.2 ** 2.0     231.040000
```

Program 2-1

```
PROGRAM SHOWOP
  PRINT *, 'OPERATION            VALUE'
  PRINT *, '15.2 + 2.0', 15.2 + 2.0
  PRINT *, '15.2 - 2.0', 15.2 - 2.0
  PRINT *, '15.2 * 2.0', 15.2 * 2.0
  PRINT *, '15.2 / 2.0', 15.2 / 2.0
  PRINT *, '15.2 ** 2.0', 15.2 ** 2.0
  END
```

Notice that when a PRINT (or WRITE) statement is used to display more than one item, as in the statement:

```
PRINT *,'15.0 + 2.0', 15.0 + 2.0
```

the individual items must be separated by commas. In this case the first item is a message enclosed within apostrophes. The second item is an arithmetic expression, the result of which is also displayed by the PRINT statement.

Expression Types

An expression that contains only integer operands is called an *integer expression,* and the result of the expression is an integer value. Similarly, an expression containing only real operands is called a *real expression,* and the result of a real expression is a real value. An expression containing both integer and real operands is called a *mixed-mode expression.* Although it is better not to mix integer and real operands when performing an arithmetic operation (the one exception being raising a real value to an integer power), predictable results are obtained when integer and real values are used in the same simple arithmetic expression. A simple arithmetic expression containing both an integer and real data value is evaluated by converting the integer value to a real number, with the result of the operation being real. For example,

```
5 + 3. =  5. + 3. = 8.  (a real value)
16 * 1.  = 16. * 1. = 16. (a real value)
42. / 2  = 42. / 2. = 21. (a real value)
```

Integer Division

A trap for the unwary in FORTRAN can occur when an integer value is divided by another integer value. In such a case the result of the integer expression, as has already been mentioned, will be an integer. For example, dividing the integer 7 by the integer 2 yields an integer result. Since integers cannot contain a fractional part, the anticipated result, 3.5, is not obtained. In FORTRAN, the fractional part of the result obtained when dividing two integers is dropped (truncated). For example,

```
7/2 is 3
9/4 is 2
7/5 is 3
```

Operator Precedence and Associativity

Besides such simple expressions as 5 + 12 and .08 * 26.2, we frequently need to create more complex arithmetic expressions. FORTRAN, like most other programming languages, requires that certain rules be followed in the writing of expressions containing more than one arithmetic operator. These rules are:

1. Two arithmetic operators must never be placed adjacent to one another. For example, 5 / * 6 is invalid because the two operators / and * are placed next to each other. The expression 5 ** 6, however, is valid and does not violate this rule because the double asterisk is the exponentiation operator.
2. Any expression, real or integer, may be raised to an integer power, but only positive real expressions may be raised to a real power. For example, –2.5 ** 3 is valid and –2.25 ** 3.5 is invalid.
3. Parentheses may be used to form groupings, and all expressions enclosed within parentheses are evaluated first. For example, in the expression (6 + 4) / (2 + 3), the 6 + 4 and 2 + 3 are evaluated first to yield 10 / 5. The 10 / 5 is then evaluated to yield 2.

    Sets of parentheses may also be enclosed by other parentheses. For example, the expression (2 * (3 + 7)) / 5 is valid. When parentheses are used within parentheses, the expressions in the innermost parentheses are always evaluated first.

    The evaluation continues from innermost to outermost parentheses until the expressions of all parentheses have been evaluated. The number of right-facing parentheses, (, must always equal the number of left-facing parentheses,), so that there are no unpaired sets.
4. Parentheses cannot be used to indicate multiplication. The multiplication operator, *, must be used. For example, the expression (3 + 4) (5 + 1) is invalid. The correct expression is (3 + 4) * (5 + 1).

As a general rule, parentheses should be used to specify logical groupings of operands and to indicate clearly, to both the computer and any programmer reading the expression, the intended order of arithmetic operations. In the absence of parentheses, expressions containing multiple operators are evaluated by the priority,

Table 2-3   Operator Precedence and Associativity

Operator	Associativity
**	right to left
* /	left to right
+ –	left to right

or precedence, of each operator. Table 2-3 shows the precedence and lists the associativity of the operators considered in this section.

The precedence of an operator establishes its priority relative to all other operators. Operators at the top of Table 2-3 have a higher priority than operators at the bottom of the table. In expressions with multiple operators, an operator with higher precedence is used before an operator with lower precedence. For example, in the expression 6 + 4 / 2 + 3, the division is done before the addition, yielding an intermediate result of 6 + 2 + 3. The additions are then performed, left to right, to yield a final result of 11.

When the minus sign precedes an operand, as in the expression –*A* ** *B*, the minus sign negates (reverses the sign of) the number with the same priority level as subtraction. For example, the expression -6 ** 2 is calculated as –(6**2), which equals –36.

Expressions containing operators with the same precedence are evaluated according to their associativity. This means that evaluation for addition and subtraction, as well as multiplication and division, is from left to right, and successive exponents are evaluated from right to left as each operator is encountered. For example, in the expression 8 + 40 / 8 * 2 + 4, the multiplication and division operators are of higher precedence than the addition operator and are evaluated first. Both the multiplication and division operators, however, are of equal priority. Therefore, these operators are evaluated according to their left-to-right associativity, yielding:

```
8 +   40 / 8 * 2 + 4  =
8 +        5 * 2 + 4  =
8 +           10 + 4
```

The addition operations are now performed, again from left to right, yielding:

```
18 + 4 = 22
```

When two exponentiation operations occur sequentially, the resulting expression is evaluated from right to left. Thus, the expression 2**2**4 is evaluated as 2**16, which equals 65,536.

Note that in evaluating an expression with more than one operator, the result of each intermediate calculation is determined by the data types of the values used in the calculation. For example, 5/2. * 3 evaluates to the real number 7.5, while 5/2 * 3.0 evaluates to the real number 6.0.

In both expressions the division is done before the multiplication (left-to right-associativity). In the first expression, however, the division of an integer and a real value is involved. The result of this mixed-mode operation is the real number 2.5. Multiplying the real number 2.5 by the integer number 3 results in a second mixed-mode operation whose result is the real number 7.5. In the second expression the division involves two integers. The intermediate result produced by this integer expression is the integer value 2; multiplying this integer by the real number 3.0 results in a final real value of 6.0.

Skill Builder Exercises

1. Determine data types appropriate for the following data:
   a. the average of four grades
   b. the number of days in a month
   c. the length of the Golden Gate Bridge
   d. the numbers in a state lottery
   e. the distance from Brooklyn, New York, to Newark, New Jersey
   f. the names in a mailing list

2. Convert the following numbers into standard decimal form:

   6.34E5   1.95162E2   8.395E1   2.95E-3   4.623E-4

3. Write the following decimal numbers using exponential notation:

   126.   656.23   3426.95   4893.2   .321   .0123   .006789

4. Using the system reference manuals for your computer, determine the character code used by your computer.

5a. Show how the name MARTHA would be stored inside a computer that uses the ASCII code. That is, draw a figure similar to Figure 2-1 for the letters KINGSLEY.

   b. Show how the name MARTHA would be stored inside a computer that uses the EBCDIC code.

6a. Repeat Exercise 5a using the letters of your own last name.

   b. Repeat Exercise 5b using the letters of your own last name.

7. Listed below are correct algebraic expressions and incorrect FORTRAN expressions corresponding to them. Find the errors and write corrected FORTRAN expressions.

Algebra	FORTRAN expression
a. $(2)(3) + (4)(5)$	(2) (3) + (4) (5)
b. $\dfrac{6+18}{2}$	6 + 18 / 2
c. $\dfrac{4.5}{12.2 - 3.1}$	4.5 / 12.2 - 3.1
d. $4.6(3.0 + 14.9)$	4.6 (3.0 + 14.9)
e. $(12.1 + 18.9)(15.3 - 3.8)$	(12.1 + 18.9) (15.3 - 3.8)

8. Determine the value of the following integer expressions:
   a. $3 + 4 * 6$
   b. $3 * 4 / 6 + 6$
   c. $2 * 3 / 12 * 8 / 4$
   d. $10 * (1 + 7 * 3)$
   e. $20 - 2 / 6 + 3$
   f. $20 - 2 / (6 + 3)$
   g. $(20 - 2) / 6 + 3$
   h. $(20 - 2) / (6 + 3)$

9. Determine the value of the following real expressions:

a. 3.0 + 4.0 * 6.0

b. 3.0 * 4.0 / 6.0 + 6.0

c. 2.0 * 3.0 / 12.0 * 8.0 / 4.0

d. 10.0 * (1.0 + 7.0 * 3.0)

e. 20.0 – 3.0 / 6.0 + 3.0

f. 20.0 – 3.0 / (6.0 + 3.0)

g. (20.0 – 2.0) / 6.0 + 3.0

h. (20.0 – 2.0) / (6.0 + 3.0)

10. Evaluate the following mixed-mode expressions and list the data types of the results. In evaluating the expressions, be aware of the data types of all intermediate calculations.

a. 10.0 + 15 / 2 + 4.3

b. 10.0 + 15.0 / 2 + 4.3

c. 3.0 * 4 / 6 + 6

d. 3 * 4.0 / 6 + 6

e. 20.0 – 2 / 6 + 3

f. 10 + 17 * 3 + 4

g. 10 + 17 / 3. + 4

11. Assuming that AMOUNT has the integer value 1, M has the integer value 50, N has the integer value 10, and P has the integer value 5, evaluate the following expressions:

a. N / P + 3

b. M / P + N – 10 * AMOUNT

c. M – 3 * N + 4 * AMOUNT

d. AMOUNT / 5

e. 18 / P

f. –P * N

g. –M / 20

h. (M + N) / (P + AMOUNT)

i. M + N / P + AMOUNT

12. Repeat Exercise 11 assuming that AMOUNT has the real value 1.0, M has the real value 50.0, N has the real value 10.0, and P has the real value 5.0.

Expanding Your Skills

13. Enter, compile, and run Program 2-1 on your computer system.

14. Rewrite Program 2-1 so that it contains one subroutine (*Hint:* Review Program 1-2 in Chapter 1.)

15. Since computers use different representations for storing integer, real, and character values, discuss how a program might alert the computer to the data types of the various values it will be using.

Note: For the following exercise you should have an understanding of basic computer storage concepts. Specifically, if you are unfamiliar with the concept of a byte, refer to the Enrichment section at the end of Chapter 1 before doing the next exercise.

16. Although the total number of bytes varies from computer to computer, memory sizes of 65,536 to more than 1 million bytes are common. In computer language, the letter K is used to represent the number 1024, which is 2 raised to the 10th power. Thus, a memory size of 64K is really 64 times 1024, or 65,536 bytes, and a memory size of 512K consists of 512 times 1024, or 524,288 bytes. Using this information, calculate the actual number of bytes in:

   a. a memory containing 64K bytes

   b. a memory containing 128K bytes

   c. a memory containing 192k bytes

   d. a memory containing 256k bytes

   e. a memory consisting of 64K words, where each word consists of 2 bytes

   f. a memory consisting of 64K words, where each word consists of 4 bytes

   g. a floppy diskette that can store 360K bytes

2.2 Variables and Declaration Statements

All integer, real, character, and logical values used in a computer program are stored and retrieved from the computer's memory unit. Conceptually, individual memory locations in the memory unit are arranged like the rooms in a large hotel. Like hotel rooms, each memory location has a unique address ("room number"). Before high-level languages such as FORTRAN existed, memory locations were referenced by their addresses. For example, storing the integer values 45 and 12 in the memory locations 1652 and 2548 (see Figure 2-2), respectively, required instructions equivalent to:

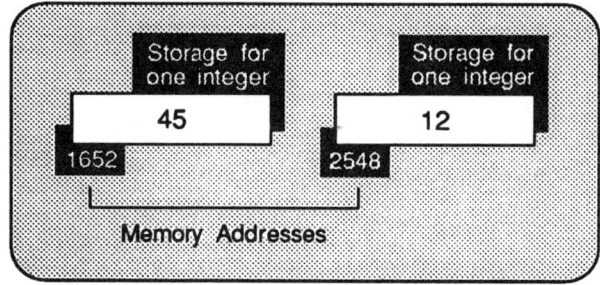

put a 45 in location 1652
put a 12 in location 2548

To add the two numbers just stored and save the result in another memory location, for example, at location 3000, required a statement comparable to:

add the contents of location 1652
to the contents of location 2548
and store the result in location 3000

Figure 2-2   Enough Storage for Two Integers

Clearly, this method of storage and retrieval is cumbersome. In high-level languages such as FORTRAN, symbolic names are used in place of actual memory addresses. Symbolic names used in this manner are called *variables*. A variable is simply a name given by the programmer to a memory storage location. The term *variable* is used because the value stored in the variable can change, or vary. For each name that the programmer uses, the computer keeps track of the actual memory address corresponding to that name. In our hotel room analogy, this is equivalent to putting a name on the door of a room, for example, BLUE room, and referring to the room by this name rather than using the actual room number.

In FORTRAN the selection of variable names is left to the programmer as long as the variable name is chosen according to the rules used for selecting symbolic names given in Chapter 1. A variable name can thus consist of from one to six uppercase letters or digits, the first of which must be a letter, with no embedded special characters.

As with program unit names, variable names should be mnemonics that give some indication of the variable's use. For example, a good name for a variable used to store a value that is the total of some other values would be SUM or TOTAL. Similarly the variable name WIDTH is a good choice if the value stored in the variable represents a width. Variable names that give no indication of the value stored, such as R2D2, LINDA, BILL, and GETUM, should not be selected.

Now assume the first memory location illustrated in Figure 2-2, that has address 1652, is given the name FIRST. Also assume that memory location 2548 is given the variable name SECOND, and memory location 3000 is given the variable name TOTAL, as illustrated in Figure 2-3.

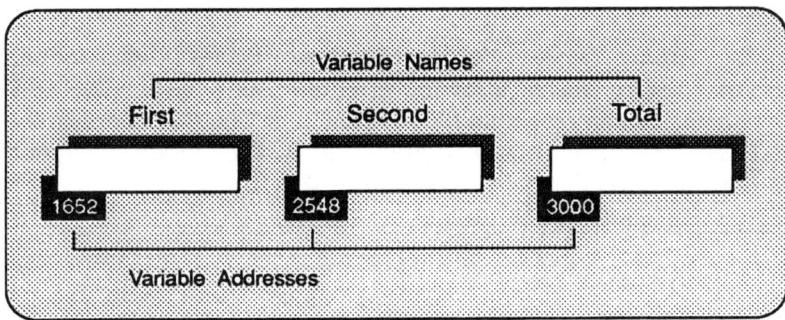

Figure 2-3   Naming Storage Locations

Using these variable names, storing 45 in location 1652 and 12 in location 2548 and adding the contents of these two locations is accomplished by the FORTRAN statements:

```
FIRST = 45
SECOND = 12
TOTAL = FIRST + SECOND
```

Each of these three statements is called an assignment statement because it tells the computer to assign (store) a value into a variable. Assignment statements always have an equal (=) sign and one variable name immediately to the left of the equal sign. The value on the right of the equal sign is determined first; this value is assigned to the variable on the left of the equal sign. The blank spaces in the assignment statements are inserted for readability. We will have more to say about assignment statements in the next section, but for now we can use them to store values in variables.

A variable name is useful because it frees the programmer from concern over where data is physically stored inside the computer. We simply use the variable name and let the computer deal with where in memory the data are actually stored. Before storing a value into a variable, however, we must clearly define the type of data to be stored in it. This requires telling the computer in advance the names of the variables that will be used for integers, the names that will be used for real numbers, and the names that will be used to store the other FORTRAN data types.

Declaration Statements

Naming a variable and specifying the data type that can be stored in it are accomplished using declaration statements. Declaration statements, which are also called specification statements, are nonexecutable statements that have the general form:

```
data type   variable name
```

where data type designates a valid FORTRAN data type (INTEGER, REAL, CHARACTER, etc.), and variable name is a user-selected variable name. For example, variables used to hold integer values are declared using the declaration statement:

```
INTEGER variable name
```

Thus, the declaration statement:

```
INTEGER TOTAL
```

declares TOTAL as the name of a variable capable of storing an integer value. Declaration statements must be placed after the program unit's header line and before any other statements contained within the program unit's body. For example, if the variable TOTAL is to be used in a MAIN program unit, its declaration statement would be placed in the unit as:

```
123456789 ———— Column Number ————————————————72
      PROGRAM MAIN
         INTEGER TOTAL
```

Notice that the declaration statement is written on a line by itself within columns 7 through 72 (the statement field).

Variables used to hold real values are declared using the keyword REAL, variables used to hold character data are declared using the keyword CHARACTER, and variables used for logical data are declared using the key word LOGICAL. For example, the statement:

```
REAL AVERGE
```

declares that AVERGE is a variable name that will be used to store a real value.

Program 2-2 illustrates the declaration and use of four real variables. The list-directed PRINT statement is then used to display the contents of one of these variables.

The placement of the declaration statements in Program 2-2 is straightforward, although we will shortly see that the four individual declarations can be combined into a single declaration. Note that the statements within the box of asterisks, including the box itself, are comment lines because of the asterisks in column 1. When Program 2-2 is run, the following output is displayed:

```
THE AVERAGE OF THE GRADES IS      91.250000
```

Two comments about the PRINT statement made in Program 2-2 should be made. First, as was also noted with respect to Program 2-1, if more than one item is to be displayed using the PRINT statement, the individual items in the list must be separated by commas. Second, if a variable name is one of the items in the display list, as in Program 2-2, the value stored in the variable is displayed rather than the variable name. When the PRINT statement sees a variable name in its output list, it first goes to the variable and retrieves the value stored. It is this value that is displayed. The same is true for the equivalent WRITE statement. For example, the statement:

```
WRITE(6,*) 'THE AVERAGE OF THE GRADES IS ', AVERGE
```

displays the same two items as Program 2-2. The first item printed is the message and the second item is the value stored in the variable AVERGE. As with the PRINT statement, the two items in the WRITE statement are separated by a comma. Since the compiler's default format, as specified by the asterisk in both the PRINT and the WRITE statements, is used, the spacing of the output display and the number of digits displayed to the right of the decimal point depend on the default format of the compiler (in Section 2.4 we will see how to explicitly designate our own output formats).

Program 2-2

```
123456789 ———— Column Number ————————————————————72
      PROGRAM DECLAR
***********************************************************
*      THIS PROGRAM DECLARES FOUR REAL VARIABLES. THE      *
*      TOTAL AND AVERAGE OF THE FIRST TWO VARIABLES ARE     *
*      COMPUTED.                                            *
***********************************************************
      REAL GRADE1
      REAL GRADE2
      REAL TOTAL
      REAL AVERGE
*
      GRADE1 = 85.5
      GRADE2 = 97.0
      TOTAL = GRADE1 + GRADE2
      AVERGE = TOTAL/2.0
      PRINT *,'THE AVERAGE OF THE GRADES IS ', AVERGE
      END
```

(Handwritten annotations:)
Real Grade1, Grade2, Average
Grade1 = 85.8
Grade2 = 97.0
Average = [Grade1 + Grade2] / 2.0
Print
End

Just as integer and real variables must be declared before they can be used, variables used to store logical values and character constants must also be suitably declared. Logical variables are declared using the keyword LOGICAL. For example, the declaration statement:

```
LOGICAL BINARY
```

declares that the variable name BINARY will be used to hold a logical value. This means that either the value .TRUE. or the value .FALSE. can be stored in this variable.

Character variables are declared using the keyword CHARACTER. Since character constants can be of varying length, the declaration of a character constant should include the maximum number of characters that the variable will store. If the string length is omitted, a default length of one is assumed. For example, the declaration:

```
CHARACTER CH
```

declares CH to be a character variable capable of holding a single character. By adding a length specifier, as in either the declaration statement:

```
CHARACTER*14 TITLE
```

or the declaration statement

```
CHARACTER TITLE*14
```

the variable TITLE is declared to be a character variable capable of holding 14 characters.

Multiple Declarations

Variables having the same data type always can be grouped together and declared using a single declaration statement. The general form of such a declaration statement is:

```
data type variable list
```

where data type must be a valid FORTRAN data type (INTEGER, REAL, CHARACTER, etc.), and the list is replaced by a list of variable names. For example, the four separate declarations:

```
REAL GRADE1
REAL GRADE2
REAL TOTAL
REAL AVERGE
```

can be replaced by the single declaration statement:

```
REAL GRADE1, GRADE2, TOTAL, AVERGE
```

In the case of a CHARACTER declaration, the optional length specifier applies to each variable in the list. For example, the declaration:

```
CHARACTER*20  CODE, TITLE
```

declares both CODE and TITLE to be variables of length 20. A separate length specifier can also be designated for any individual character variable in the declaration list, regardless of the general length specifier given for the complete list. For example, the declaration:

```
CHARACTER*15 NAME, STREET, CITY, STATE*2, ZIP*5, CODE
```

specifies the variables NAME, STREET, CITY, and CODE as character variables of length 15, STATE to be a character variable of length 2, and ZIP to be a character variable of length 5.

Notice that declaring multiple variables in a single declaration statement requires that the data type of the variables be given only once and that all the variables in the list be separated by commas. The space after each comma is inserted for readability and is not required.

Implicit Declarations

Specifying the data type of a variable using a declaration statement is referred to as *explicit data typing*. Programming languages that require all variables be declared before they can be used are called *strongly typed languages*. In this regard FORTRAN is considered a *weakly typed language* because it does not require a declaration for every variable. In the absence of a declaration, FORTRAN assumes the following data typing: any variable beginning with an I, J, K, L, M, or N is an integer variable, and any variable not beginning in one of these letters is a real variable. For example, if the variables ALPHA, BETA, INTVAL, and ICOUNT were used in a program without being explicitly declared, INTVAL and ICOUNT would be created as integer variables and ALPHA and BETA as real variables.

Despite the fact that FORTRAN allows default data declarations for real and integer variables, it is good programming practice to explicitly declare all variables used in a program. An explicit declaration provides the programmer with the opportunity to carefully decide on the names of the variables that will be used and the data types that will be stored within them. It also provides a summary of all variables that have been used, which is extremely helpful if additional variables need to be named. All of the programs in this text will adhere to the programming practice of explicitly declaring all variable names.

Specifying Storage Allocation

Declaration statements perform both a software and a hardware function. From a software perspective, declaration statements always provide a convenient, up-front list of all variables and their data types. In addition to this software role, declaration statements also serve a distinct hardware task. Since each data type has its own storage requirements (an integer uses less room than a real number, for example), the computer can allocate sufficient storage for a variable only after it knows the variable's data type. Because variable declarations provide this information, they also inform the computer of the physical memory storage that must be reserved for each variable. (In the hotel analogy introduced at the beginning of this section, this is equivalent to connecting adjoining rooms to form larger suites.)

Figure 2-4 illustrates the series of operations set in motion by declaration statements in performing their memory allocation function. As illustrated, declaration statements both cause sufficient memory to be allocated for each data type and "tag" the reserved memory locations with a name. This name is, of course, the variable's name.

Within a program, the declared variable name is used by a programmer to reference the contents of the variable (that is, the variable's value). Where in memory this value is stored is generally of little concern to the programmer. The computer, however, must be concerned with where each value is stored. In this task the computer uses the variable's name to locate the desired value. Knowing the variable's data type allows the computer to access the correct number of locations for each type of data.

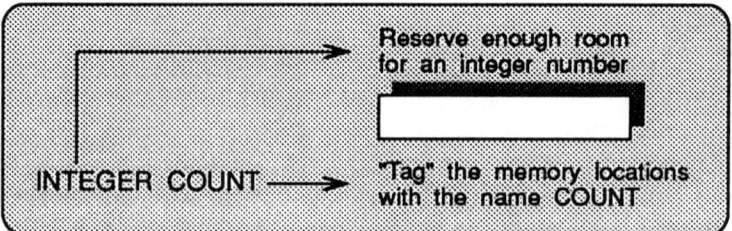

Figure 2-4(a)   Defining the INTEGER Variable Named COUNT

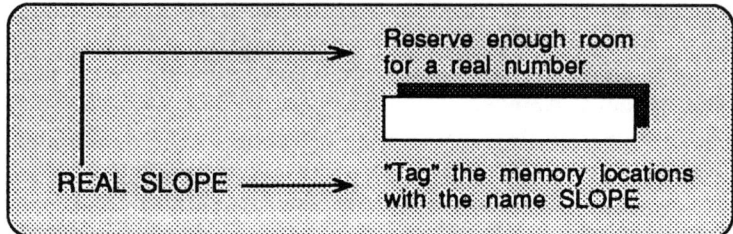

Figure 2-4(b)   Defining the REAL Variable Named SLOPE

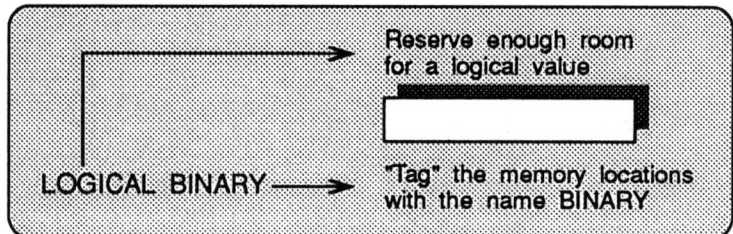

Figure 2-4(c)   Defining the LOGICAL Variable Named BINARY

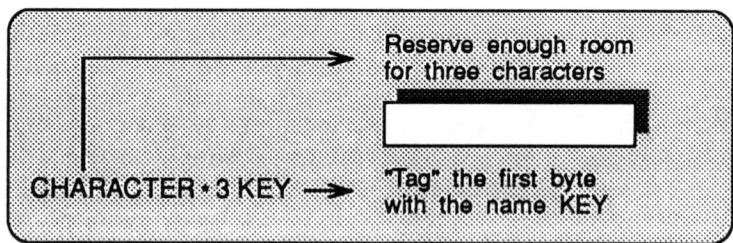

Figure 2-4(d)   Defining the CHARACTER Variable Named KEY

Skill Builder Exercises

1. State whether the following variable names are valid or not. If they are invalid, state the reason why.

```
PROD-A      C1234      ABCD       -C3        12345
NEWBAL      WATTS      $TOTAL     NEW$AL     A1B2C3D4
9AB6        SUM.OF     AVERAGE    GRADE1     FINGRAD
```

2a. State whether the following variable names are valid or not. If they are invalid, state the reason why.

```
SLSTAX      A243       R2D2       FIRST_NUM  CC-A1
HARRY       SUE        C3P0       TOTAL      SUM
MAXNUM      OKAY       A          AWSOME     GOFOR
3SUM        FOR        TOT.A1     C$FIVE     NETPAY
```

b. List which of the valid variable names found in Exercise 2a normally should not be used because they convey no information about the variable.

3a. Write a declaration statement to declare that the variable COUNT will be used to store an integer.

b. Write a declaration statement to declare that the variable GRADE will be used to store a real number.

c. Write a declaration statement to declare that the variable KEYCH will be used to store a single character.

4. For each of the following, write a single declaration statement:

   a. NUM1, NUM2, and NUM3 used to store integer numbers   *Read NUM1.*

   b. GRADE1, GRADE2, GRADE3, and GRADE4 used to store real numbers

   c. CH, LET1, LET2, LET3, and LET4 used to store character types of sizes 1, 3, 3, 7, and 9 respecively.

5. For each of the following, write a single declaration statement:

   a. FIRNUM and SECNUM used to store integers

   b. PRICE, YIELD, and COUPON used to store real numbers

   c. MATRTY to store a character constant consisting of nine letters

6. Rewrite each of these declaration statements as three individual declarations:

   a. INTEGER MONTH, DAY, YEAR   d. CHARACTER INKEY, CH, CHOICE

   b. REAL HOURS, RATE, OTIME   e. CHARACTER*5, CODE, CITY*10, ZIP

   c. REAL PRICE, AMOUNT, TAXES

7. Every variable has at least two items associated with it. What are these two items?

Expanding Your Skills

8a. Rewrite Program 2-2 so that it uses only a single declaration statement; then enter, compile, and run the program on your computer system.

If you're working with subroutines...
   b. Rewrite the program you wrote for Exercise 8a so that it contains one subroutine. (*Hint:* Review Program 1-2 in Chapter 1.)

Note for Exercises 9 through 11: These exercises assume you are familiar with the Enrichment material presented in Section 1.7. For these exercises assume that a character requires one byte of storage, an integer two bytes, and a real number four bytes and that variables are assigned consecutive storage locations in the order they are declared. Memory bytes are shown in Figure 2-5.

9a. Using Figure 2-5 and assuming that the variable name RATE is assigned to the byte having memory address 159, determine the addresses corresponding to each variable declared in the following statements:

```
REAL RATE
CHARACTER CH1, CH2, CH3, CH4
INTEGER NUM, COUNT
```

   b. Repeat Exercise 9a, but substitute the actual bit patterns that a computer using the ASCII code would use to store the characters in the variables CH1, CH2, CH3, and CH4 assuming the following assignment statements. (*Hint:* Use Table 2-1.)

```
CH1 = 'O'
CH2 = 'K'
CH3 = 'A'
CH4 = 'Y'
```

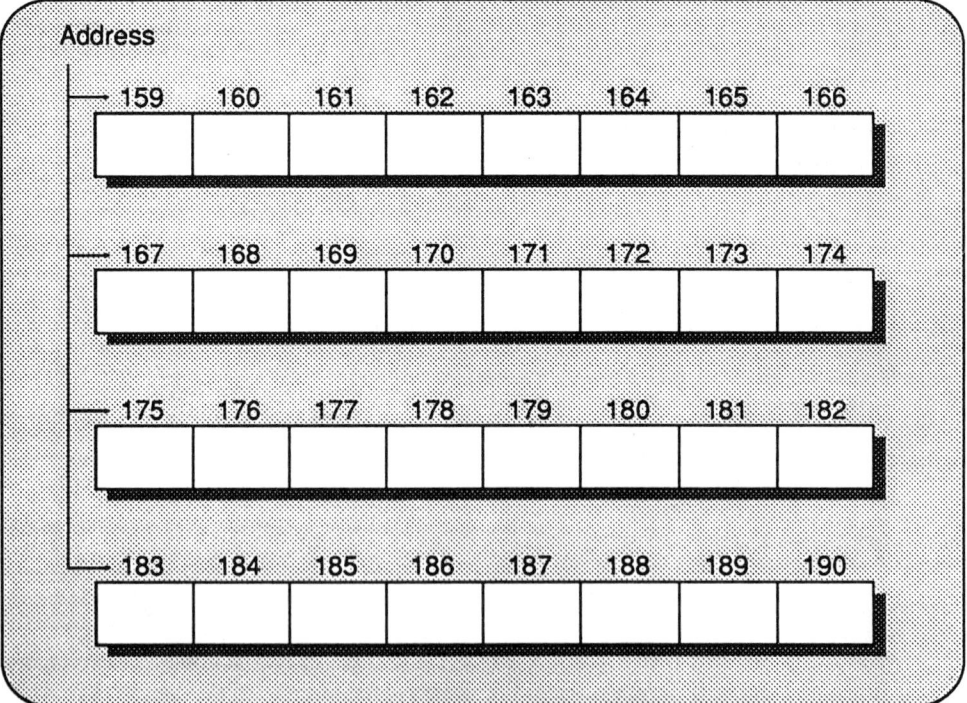

Figure 2-5 Memory Bytes for Exercises 9, 10, and 11

10. Using Figure 2-5 and assuming that the variable named CN1 is assigned to the byte at memory address 159, determine the addresses corresponding to each variable declared in the following statements:

```
CHARACTER CN1, CN2, CN3, CN4, CN5
CHARACTER*2 CN6, CN7, KEY*1, SCH*4
CHARACTER*4 INC1
```

11. Using Figure 2-5 and assuming that the variable name MILES is assigned to the byte at memory address 159, determine the addresses corresponding to each variable declared in the following statements:

```
REAL MILES
INTEGER COUNT, NUM
CHARACTER KEY1, KEY2*3, KEY3
```

2.3   Assignment Statements

The most basic FORTRAN statement for both assigning values to variables and performing computations is the assignment statement. This statement has the general form:

$$VARIABLE \; = \; expression$$

The simplest arithmetic expression in FORTRAN is a single constant, and in each of the following assignment statements, the expression to the right of the equal sign is a constant:

```
LENGTH = 25
WIDTH = 17.5
```

In these assignment statements, the value of the constant to the right of the equal sign is assigned to the variable on the left side of the equal sign. It is extremely important to note that the equal sign in FORTRAN does not have the same meaning as an equal sign in algebra. The equal sign in an assignment statement tells the computer to first determine the value of the expression to the right of the equal sign and then to store (or assign) that value in the variable to the left of the equal sign. In this regard, the FORTRAN statement LENGTH = 25 is read "LENGTH is assigned the value 25." The blank spaces in the assignment statement are inserted for readability only.

When a value is assigned to a variable for the first time, the variable is said to be *initialized*. Subsequent assignment statements can, of course, be used to change the value assigned to a variable. For example, assume the following statements are executed one after another:

```
SLOPE = 3.7
SLOPE = 6.28
```

The first assignment statement assigns the value of 3.7 to the variable named SLOPE. Since this is the first time a value is assigned to this variable, it is also correct to say that SLOPE is initialized to 3.7. The next assignment statement causes the computer to assign a value of 6.28 to SLOPE. The 3.7 that was in SLOPE is erased and replaced with the new value of 6.2, because a variable can store only one value at a time. In this regard it is sometimes useful to think of the variable to the left of the equal sign as a temporary parking spot in a huge parking lot. Just as an individual parking spot can only be used by one car at a time, each variable can store only one value at a time. The "parking" of a new value in a variable automatically causes the computer to remove any value previously parked there.

In its most general form, a FORTRAN expression is any combination of constants and variables that can be evaluated to yield a result. Thus, the expression in an assignment statement can be used to perform calculations using the arithmetic operators introduced in Section 2.1 (see Table 2-2). Examples of assignment statements using expressions containing these operators are:

```
SUM = 3 + 7
DIFF = 15 - 6
PRODUC = .05 * 14.6
TALLY = COUNT + 1
NEWTOT = 18.3 + TOTAL
TAXES = .06 * AMOUNT
TOTWET = WEIGHT * FACTOR
AVERGE = SUM / ITEMS
NEWVAL = NUMBER ** POWER
```

As always in an assignment statement, the equal sign directs the computer first to calculate the value of the expression to the right of the equal sign and then to store this value in the variable to the left of the equal sign. For example, in the assignment statement TOTWET = WEIGHT * FACTOR, the expression WEIGHT * FACTOR is first evaluated to yield a result. This result, which is a number, is then stored in the variable TOTWET.

In writing assignment statements, you must be aware of two important considerations. Since the expression to the right of the equal sign is evaluated first, all variables used in the expression must be initialized if the result is to make sense. For example, the assignment statement TOTWET = WEIGHT * FACTOR will only cause a valid number to be stored in TOTWET if the programmer first takes care to put valid numbers in WEIGHT and FACTOR. Thus, the sequence of statements:

```
WEIGHT = 155.0
FACTOR = 1.06
TOTWET = WEIGHT * FACTOR
```

ensures that we know the values being used to obtain the result that will be stored in the variable to the left of the equal sign. Figure 2-6 illustrates the values stored in the variables WEIGHT, FACTOR, and TOTWET.

The second consideration to keep in mind is that since the value of an expression is stored in the variable to the left of the equal sign, there must only be one variable listed in this position. For example, the assignment statement:

```
AMOUNT + EXTRA = 1462 + 10 - 24
```

is invalid. The right-side expression evaluates to the integer 1448, which can only be stored in a variable. Since AMOUNT + EXTRA is not the valid name of a memory

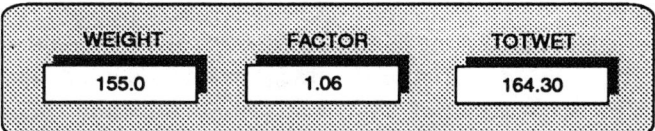

Figure 2-6 Values Stored in the Variables

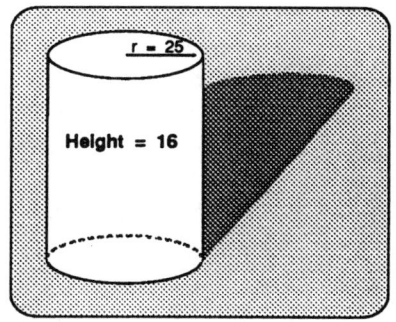

location (it is not a valid variable name), the computer does not know where to store the value 1448. Program 2-3 illustrates the use of assignment statements to calculate the volume of a cylinder. As illustrated in Figure 2-7, the volume of a cylinder is determined by the formula *Volume = pi r²h,* where *r* is the radius of the cylinder, *h* is the height, and *pi* is the constant 3.1416 (accurate to four decimal places).

Figure 2-7 Determining the Volume of a Cylinder

Program 2-3

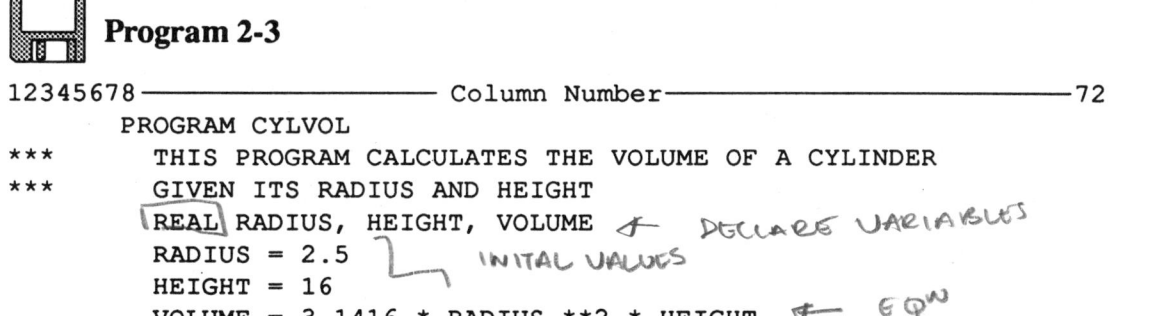

```
12345678 ——————————— Column Number ————————————————72
        PROGRAM CYLVOL
***     THIS PROGRAM CALCULATES THE VOLUME OF A CYLINDER
***     GIVEN ITS RADIUS AND HEIGHT
        REAL RADIUS, HEIGHT, VOLUME
        RADIUS = 2.5
        HEIGHT = 16
        VOLUME = 3.1416 * RADIUS **2 * HEIGHT
        PRINT *, 'THE VOLUME OF THE CYLINDER IS ', VOLUME
        END
```

When Program 2-3 is compiled and executed, the output is:

```
THE VOLUME OF THE CYLINDER IS 314.160000
```

Notice the order in which statements are executed in Program 2-3. The program begins with the program header line and continues sequentially, statement by statement, until the END statement is encountered. All computer programs execute in this manner. The computer works on one statement at a time, executing that statement with no knowledge of what the next statement will be. This explains why all variables used in an expression must have values assigned to them before the expression is evaluated.

When the computer executes the statement VOLUME = 3.1416 * RADIUS **2 * HEIGHT in Program 2-3, it uses whatever value is stored in the variables RADIUS and HEIGHT at the time the assignment statement is executed. If no values have been specifically assigned to these variables before they are used in the assignment statement, the computer uses whatever values happen to occupy these variables when they are referenced (on some systems all variables are automatically initialized to zero). The computer does not look ahead to see if you assign values to these variables later in the program.

Assignment Variations

Although only one variable is allowed immediately to the left of the equal sign in an assignment expression, the variable on the left of the equal sign can also be used on the right of the equal sign. For example, the assignment statement TOTAL = TOTAL + 20 is valid. Clearly, in algebra, TOTAL could never be equal to itself plus 20. But in FORTRAN, the statement TOTAL = TOTAL + 20 is not an equation—it is a statement that is evaluated in two distinct steps. The first step is to calculate the value of TOTAL + 20. The second step is to store the computed value in TOTAL. See if you can determine the output of Program 2-4.

The assignment statement TOTAL = 15 initializes the value in TOTAL to the number 15, as shown in Figure 2-8.

The first PRINT statement causes both a message and the value stored in TOTAL to be displayed. The output produced by this statement is:

```
THE NUMBER STORED IN TOTAL IS       15
```

The second assignment statement in Program 2-4, TOTAL = TOTAL + 25, causes the computer to retrieve the 15 stored in TOTAL and add 25 to this number, yielding the number 40. The number 40 is then stored in the variable on the left side of the equal sign, which is the variable TOTAL. The 15 that was in TOTAL is overwritten and replaced with the new value of 40, as shown in Figure 2-9.

 Program 2-4

```
123456789——————————— Column Number——————————————72
      PROGRAM MAIN
        INTEGER TOTAL
        TOTAL = 15
        PRINT *, 'THE NUMBER STORED IN TOTAL IS ', TOTAL
        TOTAL = TOTAL + 25
        PRINT *, 'THE NUMBER NOW STORED IN TOTAL IS ', TOTAL
        END
```

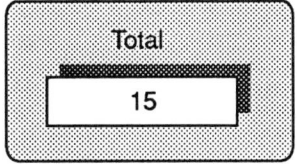

**Figure 2-8   The Integer
15 is Stored in** TOTAL

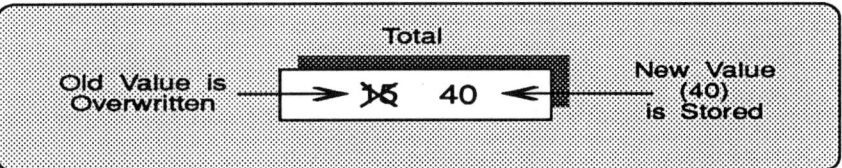

Figure 2-9 TOTAL = TOTAL + 25 **Causes
a New Value to Be Stored in** TOTAL

Accumulating

Assignment expressions like TOTAL = TOTAL + 25 are very common in programming
and are required in accumulating subtotals when data are entered one number at a
time. For example, if we want to add the numbers 62, 40, 55, and 90 in calculator
fashion, the following statements could be used:

Statement	Value in TOTAL
TOTAL = 0	0
TOTAL = TOTAL + 62	62
TOTAL = TOTAL + 40	102
TOTAL = TOTAL + 55	157
TOTAL = TOTAL + 90	247

The first statement initializes TOTAL to 0. This removes any number ("garbage"
value) stored in the memory locations corresponding to TOTAL and ensures we start
with 0. (This is equivalent to clearing a calculator before doing any computations.)
As each number is added, the value stored in TOTAL is increased accordingly. After
completion of the last statement, TOTAL contains the total of all the added numbers.

Program 2-5 illustrates the effect of these statements by displaying TOTAL's
contents after each addition is made.

Program 2-5

```
123456789————————————— Column Number—————————————72
    PROGRAM MAIN
      INTEGER TOTAL
      TOTAL = 0
      PRINT *, 'THE VALUE OF TOTAL IS INITIALLY SET TO ', TOTAL
      TOTAL = TOTAL + 62
      PRINT *, '   TOTAL IS NOW ', TOTAL
      TOTAL = TOTAL + 40
      PRINT *, '   TOTAL IS NOW ', TOTAL
      TOTAL = TOTAL + 55
      PRINT *, '   TOTAL IS NOW ', TOTAL
      TOTAL = TOTAL + 90
      PRINT *, '   THE FINAL VALUE IN TOTAL IS ', TOTAL
      END
```

The output produced by Program 2-5 is:

```
THE VALUE OF TOTAL IS INITIALLY SET TO                0
    TOTAL IS NOW            62
    TOTAL IS NOW           102
    TOTAL IS NOW           157
    THE FINAL VALUE IN TOTAL IS          247
```

Although it is clearly easier to add the numbers by hand than to use the sequence of assignment statements listed, these statements do illustrate the subtotaling effect of repeated assignment statements having the form:

> VARIABLE = VARIABLE + *added value*

We will find many uses for this type of statement when we become more familiar with the repetition statements introduced in Chapter 5.

Counting

A variation of the accumulating assignment statement is the counting statement. Counting statements have the form:

> VARIABLE = VARIABLE + *fixed number*

Examples of counting statements are:

```
I = I + 1
N = N + 1
ICOUNT = ICOUNT + 1
J = J + 2
M = M + 2
KK = KK + 3
```

In each of these examples the same variable is used on both sides of the equal sign. After the statement is executed, the value of the respective variable is increased by a fixed amount. In the first three examples, the variables I, N, and ICOUNT have all been increased by one. In the next two examples, the respective variables have been increased by two, and in the final example the variable KK has been increased by three. Variable names beginning in I, J, K, L, M, or N are conventionally used for counter variables to stress their integer nature (recall that variable names beginning in these letters are implicitly specified as integer variables). The following sequence of statements illustrate the use of a counter.

Statement	Value in ICOUNT
ICOUNT = 0	0
ICOUNT = ICOUNT + 1	1
ICOUNT = ICOUNT + 1	2
ICOUNT = ICOUNT + 1	3
ICOUNT = ICOUNT + 1	4

Skill Builder Exercises

1. Write an assignment statement to calculate the circumference of a circle. The equation for determining the circumference, c, of a circle is $c = 2\ pi\ r$, where r is the radius, and pi equals 3.1416.

2. Write an assignment statement to calculate the area of a circle. The equation for determining the area, a, of a circle is $a = pi\ r^2$, where r is the radius and $pi = 3.1416$.

3. Write an assignment statement to convert temperature in degrees Fahrenheit to degrees Celsius. The equation for this conversion is $Celsius = 5/9\ (Fahrenheit - 32)$.

4. Write an assignment statement to calculate the round trip distance, d, in feet, of a trip that is s miles long, one way.

5. Write an assignment statement to calculate the elapsed time, in minutes, that it takes to make a trip. The equation for computing elapsed time is $elapsed\ time = total\ distance\ /\ average\ speed$. Assume that the distance is in miles and the average speed is in miles/hour.

ELAPSED TIME =

6. Write an assignment statement to calculate the nth term in an arithmetic sequence. The formula for calculating the value, v, of the nth term is $v = a + (n-1)d$, where a is the first number in the sequence and d is the difference between any two numbers in the sequence.

7. Write an assignment statement to calculate the maximum height, h, of a projectile. The formula for determining the maximum height is $h = (v^2 \sin^2 \theta)/2g$, where v is the initial velocity of the projectile, θ is the angle at which the projectile is fired, and g is the gravitational constant equal to 32.2 ft/sec^2.

8. Write an assignment statement to calculate the linear expansion in a steel beam as a function of temperature increase. The formula for linear expansion, l, is $l = l_o[1+a(T_f-T_o)]$, where l_o is the length of the beam at temperature T_o, a is the coefficient of linear expansion, and T_f is the final temperature of the beam.

9. Coulomb's law states that the force F, acting between two electrically charged spheres, is given by the formula $F = k\ q_1\ q_2/\ r^2$, where q_1 is the charge on the first sphere, q_2 is the charge on the second sphere, r is the distance between the centers of the two spheres, and k is a proportionality constant. Write an assignment statement to calculate the force F.

10. Write an assignment statement to determine the maximum bending moment, M, of a beam. The formula for maximum bending moment is $M = X\ W\ (L - X)\ /\ L$, where X is the distance from the end of the beam that a weight, W, is placed, and L is the length of the beam.

11. Determine the output of the following program:

```
      PROGRAM MAIN
*** A PROGRAM ILLUSTRATING INTEGER TRUNCATION ***
      INTEGER NUM1, NUM2
      NUM1 = 9/2
      NUM2 = 17/4
      PRINT *, 'THE FIRST INTEGER DISPLAYED IS', NUM1
      PRINT *, 'THE SECOND INTEGER DISPLAYED IS', NUM2
      END
```

12. Determine the output produced by the following program:

```
PROGRAM MAIN
  REAL AVERGE
  AVERGE = 26.27
  PRINT *, 'THE AVERAGE IS', AVERGE
  AVERGE = 682.3
  PRINT *, 'THE AVERAGE IS', AVERGE
  AVERGE = 1.968
  PRINT *, 'THE AVERAGE IS', AVERGE
  END
```

13. Determine the output produced by the following program:

```
PROGRAM MAIN
  REAL SUM
  SUM = 0.0
  PRINT *, 'THE SUM IS', SUM
  SUM = SUM + 26.27
  PRINT *, 'THE SUM IS', SUM
  SUM = SUM + 1.968
  PRINT *, 'THE FINAL TOTAL IS', SUM
  END
```

14a. Determine what each statement causes to happen in the following program:

```
PROGRAM MAIN
  INTEGER NUM1
  INTEGER NUM2
  INTEGER TOTAL
  NUM1 = 25
  NUM2 = 30
  TOTAL = NUM1 + NUM2
  PRINT *, NUM1, '+', NUM2, '=', TOTAL
  END
```

 b. What is the output that will be produced when the program listed in Exercise 14a is compiled and executed?

Debugging Exercises

Note for Exercises 15 through 18: Identify the errors in the sections of code listed in each exercise:

15.
```
PROGRAM MAIN
  INTEGER LENGTH, WIDTH, AREA
  WIDTH = 20
  AREA = LENGTH * WIDTH
```

16.
```
PROGRAM MAIN
  AREA = LENGTH * WIDTH
  LENGTH = 15
  WIDTH = 20
```

17.
```
PROGRAM MAIN
  INTEGER LENGTH, WIDTH, AREA
  LENGTH = 16
  WIDTH = 24
  LENGTH * WIDTH = AREA
```

18.
```
PROGRAM MAIN
   INTEGER LENGTH = 20, WIDTH = 10, AREA
   AREA = LENGTH * WIDTH
```

19. By mistake a student reordered the statements in Program 2-5 as follows:

```
PROGRAM MAIN
   INTEGER TOTAL
   TOTAL = 0
   TOTAL = TOTAL + 62
   TOTAL = TOTAL + 40
   TOTAL = TOTAL + 55
   TOTAL = TOTAL + 90
   PRINT *, 'THE VALUE OF TOTAL IS INITIALLY SET TO ', TOTAL
   PRINT *, '   TOTAL IS NOW ', TOTAL
   PRINT *, '   TOTAL IS NOW ', TOTAL
   PRINT *, '   TOTAL IS NOW ', TOTAL
   PRINT *, '   THE FINAL VALUE IN TOTAL IS ', TOTAL
   END
```

Determine the output that this program produces.

Programming Exercises

20a. Enter, compile, and execute Program 2-3 on your computer system.

If you're working with subroutines...

  b. Rewrite Program 2-3 so that it contains one subroutine.

  c. Execute the program written for Exercise 20b on a computer.

21a. Enter, compile, and execute Program 2-4 on your computer system.

If you're working with subroutines...

  b. Rewrite Program 2-4 so that it contains one subroutine.

  c. Execute the program written for Exercise 21b on a computer.

22. Enter, compile, and execute Program 2-5 on your computer system.

23. Using Program 2-3, determine the volume of cylinders having the following radii and heights:

Radius (in.)	Height (in.)
1.62	6.23
2.86	7.52
4.26	8.95
8.52	10.86
12.29	15.35

24. Modify Program 2-3 to calculate the weight, in pounds, of the steel cylinder whose volume was found by the program. The formula for determining the weight is *weight* = .28 *(pi)*$(r^2)(h)$, where r is the radius (in inches) and h is the height (in inches) of the cylinder.

25. The circumference of an ellipse (see Figure 2-10) is given by the formula:

$$Circumference = pi * \sqrt{2(a^2 + b^2)}$$

Using this formula, write a FORTRAN program to calculate the circumference of an ellipse having a minor radius of 2.5 inches and a major radius of 6.4 inches. (*Hint:* The square root can be taken by raising the real quantity $2(a^2 + b^2)$ to the 0.5 power.)

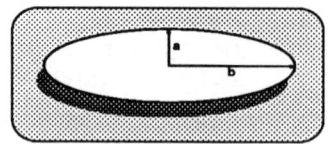

Figure 2-10   The Minor Radius *a* and the Major Radius *b* of an Ellipse

26a. The combined resistance of three resistors connected in parallel, as shown in Figure 2-11, is given by the equation:

$$Combined\ resistance = \cfrac{1}{\cfrac{1}{R_1} + \cfrac{1}{R_2} + \cfrac{1}{R_3}}$$

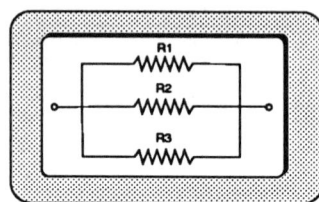

Figure 2-11   Three Resistors Connected in Parallel

Write a FORTRAN program to calculate and display the combined resistance when the three resistors $R_1 = 1000$, $R_2 = 1000$, and $R_3 = 1000$ are connected in parallel. Your program should produce the display THE COMBINED RESISTANCE, IN OHMS, IS xxxxx, where the xs are replaced by the value of the combined resistance computed by your program.

b. How do you know that the value calculated by your program is correct?

c. Once you have verified the output produced by your program, modify it to determine the combined resistance when the resistors $R_1 = 1500$, $R_2 = 1200$, and $R_3 = 2000$ are connected in parallel.

27a. Write a FORTRAN program to calculate and display the value of the slope of the line connecting the two points whose coordinates are (3,7) and (8,12). Use the fact that the slope between two points having coordinates (x_1,y_1) and (x_2,y_2) is *slope* = $(y_2 - y_1)$ / $(x_2 - x_1)$. Your program should produce the display THE SLOPE IS xxxx, where the xs are replaced by the value calculated by your program.

b. How do you know that the result produced by your program is correct?

c. Once you have verified the output produced by your program, modify it to determine the slope of the line connecting the points (2,10) and (12,6).

28a. Write a FORTRAN program to calculate and display the coordinates of the midpoint of the line connecting the two points given in Exercise 27a. Use the fact that the coordinates of the midpoint between two points having coordinates (x_1,y_1) and (x_2,y_2) are $((x_1+x_2)/2, (y_1+y_2)/2)$. Your program should produce the following display:

```
THE X MIDPOINT COORDINATE IS xxx
THE Y MIDPOINT COORDINATE IS xxx
```

where the xs are replaced with the values calculated by your program.

b. How do you know that the midpoint values calculated by your program are correct?

c. Once you have verified the output produced by your program, modify it to determine the midpoint coordinates of the line connecting the points (2,10) and (12,6).

29a. For the electrical circuit shown in Figure 2-12, the branch currents I_1, I_2, and I_3 can be determined using the formulas

$$I_1 = \frac{E_2 R_3 + E_1 (R_1 + R_3)}{(R_1 + R_3)(R_2 + R_3) - (R_3)^2}$$

$$I_2 = \frac{E_1 R_3 + E_2 (R_1 + R_3)}{(R_1 + R_3)(R_2 + R_3) - (R_3)^2}$$

$$I_3 = I_1 - I_2$$

Using these formulas, write a FORTRAN program to compute the branch currents when $R_1 = 10$ ohms, $R_2 = 4$ ohms, $R_3 = 6$ ohms, $E_1 = 12$ volts, and $E_2 = 9$ volts. The display produced by your program should be:

```
BRANCH CURRENT 1 IS xxxx
BRANCH CURRENT 2 IS xxxx
BRANCH CURRENT 3 IS xxxx
```

where the *x*s are replaced by the values determined in your program.

b. How do you know that the branch currents calculated by your program are correct?

c. Once you have verified the output produced by your program, modify it to determine the loop currents for the values $R_1 = 1500$, $R_2 = 1200$, $R_3 = 2000$, $E_1 = 15$, and $E_2 = 12$.

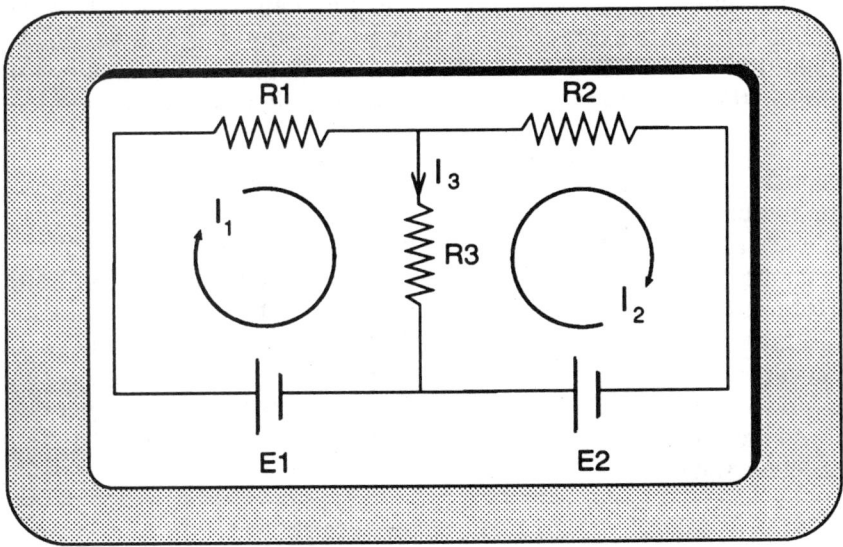

Figure 2-12 An Electrical Circuit

2.4 Formatted Output

Besides calculating correct results, it is extremely important for a program to present its results clearly and attractively. Typically, in fact, most users of a program judge it based on the perceived ease of data entry and the style and presentation of the output. For many applications, especially when a program is being developed, the list-directed PRINT and WRITE statements introduced in Chapter 1 are sufficient. Occasions do arise, however, that require more explicit programmer control of the output format. This explicit control is provided using *user-formatted* output, where the spacing and appearance of the display are directly specified by the programmer.

User-Formatted PRINT and WRITE Statements

The output display produced by both PRINT and WRITE statements can be explicitly defined using the user-formatted version of these statements rather than their list-directed versions. In fact, both list-directed and user-formatted versions are variations of more general forms for these statements. For the PRINT statement, this more general form is:

```
PRINT format identifier, item list
```

The item list is a list of any valid FORTRAN expressions, which include constants, variables, and arithmetic expressions including both constants and variables. The format identifier in the PRINT statement allows us to control the precise form in which items in the expression list are displayed. Specifically, the format identifier can be:

1. an asterisk
2. a format specification
3. a reference to a FORMAT statement that contains a format specification

An asterisk, as we have already seen, selects the compiler's list-directed (default) format. In place of the asterisk, an explicit format specification can be used. A more useful approach is to place this explicit format specification in a separate FORMAT statement that is referenced by the PRINT statement. This approach allows the same format control to be referenced by any number of PRINT statements and is the approach we will adopt. Using this approach, the required form of the user-formatted PRINT statement is:

```
PRINT n, item list
```

where *n* is a number from 1 to 99999 that refers to a FORMAT statement, and the item list is a list of FORTRAN expressions, as in the list-directed version. The FORMAT statement referenced by the PRINT statement must use the same number, *n,* in its label field. For example, a sample user-formatted PRINT statement and its associated FORMAT statement are:

```
123456789 ————— Column Number ————————————————72
     PRINT 10, AVERGE
  10 FORMAT(' ','THE AVERAGE IS',F5.2)
```

The statement label 10 was chosen arbitrarily, and any other valid integer between 1 and 99999 could have been selected.

The same options available to the PRINT statement are also provided by the WRITE statement. Specifically, the general form of the WRITE statement that references a FORMAT statement is:

> WRITE *(unit number,n) expression list*

where the unit number, as before, designates where the display is to be sent, and *n* is the label number of a FORMAT statement. For example, assuming that unit number 6 designates the standard output device, the statement pair:

```
     WRITE (6, 10) AVERGE
  10 FORMAT(' ','THE AVERAGE IS',F5.2)
```

produces the same output as the statements

```
     PRINT 10, AVERGE
  10 FORMAT(' ','THE AVERAGE IS',F5.2)
```

FORMAT Statements

FORMAT statements referenced by the user-formatted versions of both the PRINT and WRITE statements consist of a statement label, the keyword FORMAT, and a format specification list having the general form:

> *n*   FORMAT *(specification list)*

where *n* is a statement label, which is a number from 1 to 99999, that is placed in columns 1 through 5 (the label field). As we have already seen, the statement label in the FORMAT statement is used to connect the format specification to a corresponding PRINT or WRITE statement. The specification list in the statement designates both the vertical and horizontal positioning of the display. The vertical positioning specifies whether the displayed line is placed at the top of the next printed page (for displays printed on paper), on the next line, double spaced, or with no vertical spacing (called overprinting). Horizontal positioning determines the number of items displayed on a single line, the spacing between items on the same line, and the number of digits that are displayed for each value. An example of a FORMAT statement is:

```
  10 FORMAT(' ','THE AVERAGE IS',F5.2)
```

The specification list in this FORMAT statement consists of three items, each of which must be separated from the others by a comma.

The first item in a specification list is called the *carriage control character* and specifies the vertical positioning of the line to be printed. Table 2-4 lists the most commonly used carriage control characters and the effect each produces.

Table 2-4 Carriage Control Characters

Character	Effect
+	No vertical spacing: return to column 1 of the current line and overprint the current display.
a blank space	Single spacing: advance to the next space line before displaying any data.
0	Double spacing: advance two lines before displaying any data.
1	Top-of-page (paper output only): advance to the top of the next page before displaying any data.

For example, the carriage control character specified by the FORMAT statement:

```
10 FORMAT(' ','THE AVERAGE IS',F5.2)
```

is the character constant ' '. The space within apostrophes, as listed in Table 2-4, specifies that single spacing has been selected.

Carriage control characters, as their name implies, were originally designed for controlling the carriage of a standard printer. When used with a printer, the top-of-page carriage control character causes the current page to be ejected and the top of the next page to be placed under the print mechanism. The overprint control causes no motion of the carriage; this causes the new line to print on top of the existing one, which is called overprinting. With video screens these two specifiers do not have the same effect. Generally, the top-of-page has no effect on a video screen, and the overprint erases the existing line before the next line is displayed.

Before actually displaying a line of text on an output device, the computer first constructs the line internally within its memory unit. The memory area reserved for constructing the line is called a *buffer* (see Figure 2-13). The buffer is automatically cleared (filled with blanks) before being used to construct a new line. Once the line is constructed, the contents of the buffer are sent out for display as a complete entity. The first location of the buffer is used to store the carriage control character. When the complete contents of the buffer are sent to the display unit, the carriage control character tells the display device where to vertically position the next line. Thus, the second character in the buffer becomes the first character actually displayed.

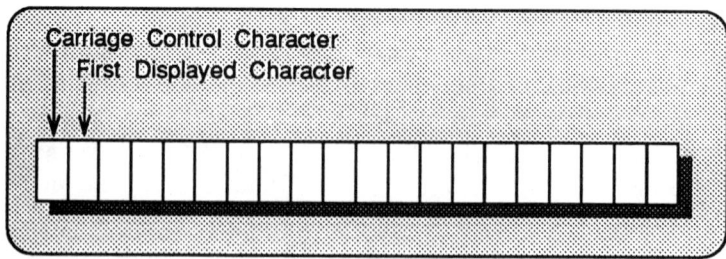

Figure 2-13   An Output Buffer

The same buffer mechanism is employed for list-directed output, except that the compiler places a blank space in the first buffer position (single spacing) and fills the rest of the buffer with the indicated data in accordance with its own format specifications. Following are the more common FORMAT specifications for explicit user control of how data is entered into the buffer and ultimately displayed. A complete listing of all format specifications is presented in Appendix B.

Literal Specification

A literal specification consists of one or more characters enclosed within apostrophes and permits the direct placement of the enclosed characters in the memory buffer. Thus, carriage control characters can be placed in the buffer by enclosing the selected carriage control character within apostrophes and placing the resulting character constant as the first item in the specification list. Similarly, any other character constant can be entered in the buffer using a literal specification. For example, the FORMAT statement:

```
10 FORMAT (' ','INVENTORY REPORT:')
```

sets the carriage control for single spacing and places the 17 characters INVENTORY REPORT: in positions 2 through 18 of the buffer. When referenced by a PRINT statement, as in the combination of statements

```
    PRINT 10
10  FORMAT (' ','INVENTORY REPORT:')
```

the following display is produced:

```
INVENTORY REPORT:
12345678911111111
        01234567
```

The italicized numbers under the display correspond to the column positions that the characters above would occupy on the output line. Thus, the I is displayed in column 1, and the colon, :, is placed in column 17.

When no carriage control character is included in a format specifier, the first character intended for display by default fills the first position of the output buffer and becomes the carriage control character. For example, what do you think the display produced by the sequence of statements:

```
    PRINT 10
10  FORMAT ('1999 PROFIT PROJECTIONS')
```

would be?

Here the carriage control specification was omitted. Since the computer always uses the first character in the specification list as a carriage control, the 1 in the number 1999 is used for this purpose. The actual message, displayed at the top of a new page, becomes:

```
999 PROFIT PROJECTIONS
12345678911111111111222
        0123456789012
```

As before, the numbers under the display indicate the column position of each displayed character. It should be noted that since FORMAT statements are non-executable, the actual placement of a FORMAT statement can come before or after the PRINT or WRITE statement that references it. Some programmers prefer to place all FORMAT statements together, at either the beginning or end of a program (before the END statement), while other programmers prefer to place an individual FORMAT statement close to the PRINT or WRITE statement that references it. All of these approaches are appropriate.

Although literal specifications are extremely useful for specifying carriage control characters and messages that can be used for report or column headings, this specification does not permit us to display numeric values stored in variables. For this we need two format specifiers, one for integers (I) and another for real numbers (F).

The I Specification

The I specification is required for displaying the contents of an integer variable under user-formatting control. The general form of this specification is:

$$\boxed{\text{I}\,w}$$

where the I specifies that an integer number will be displayed, and the w designates the maximum field width size to be filled. For example, assuming the variables ICOUNT, MINVAL, and MAXVAL contain the values shown in Figure 2-14, the combination of statements:

```
      PRINT  20, ICOUNT, MINVAL, MAXVAL
  20  FORMAT(' ',I3,I4,I5)
```

produces the display:

```
    8   12    16
123456789111
          012
```

The numbers 3, 4, and 5 in the I specifications are all field width specifiers. The 3 causes the first integer to be displayed in a total field width of three spaces, in this case, two blank spaces followed by the number 8. The field width specifier in the second integer specification, I4, causes two blank spaces and the number 12 to be

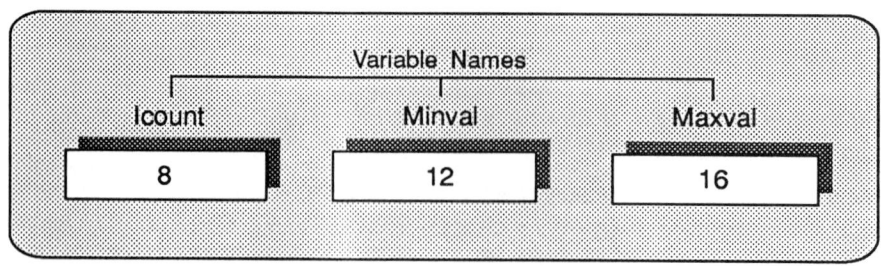

Figure 2-14 The Variables ICOUNT, MINVAL, and MAXVAL in Memory

printed for a total field width of four spaces. The last field width specifier causes the 16 to be printed in a field of five spaces, which includes three blanks and the number 16. As illustrated, for field widths that are large enough to contain the desired integer, the number is right justified within the designated field. If the field width specifier is too small for the integer to be displayed, the field is filled with asterisks. For example, assuming the number 28194 is stored in the variable ITOTAL, the statements:

```
        PRINT 30, ITOTAL
30      FORMAT(' ',I4)
```

produce the display:

```
****
```

Here the field width of four is not large enough to contain the integer, so the field is filled with asterisks. If the integer to be displayed is a negative number, the field width must be large enough to contain both the minus sign and the magnitude of the number, or asterisks will be printed.

An extremely useful display is produced by combining a literal message specification with a numerical specification. For example, the sequence of statements:

```
        INTEGER IPOWER
        IPOWER = 2**10
        PRINT 30, IPOWER
30      FORMAT(' ','2 RAISED TO THE 10TH = ',I4)
```

produces the display:

```
2 RAISED TO THE 10TH = 1024
123456789111111111122222222
          0123456789012345
```

Here the display not only presents the results of a calculation but also gives an indication of what the numerical value represents.

The F Specification

The F specification (the F stands for floating point) defines the format of the output for displaying values of real variables and expressions in decimal (as opposed to exponential) form. The general form of this specification is:

$$\boxed{\texttt{Fw.d}}$$

The F in the specification must be present and designates that a decimal number will be displayed. In addition, the two field width specifiers, denoted as w and d, separated by a period, must also be present. The first specifier (w) determines the total width of the display, including space for a sign and the number's decimal point. The second specifier (d) determines how many digits are printed to the right of the decimal point. For example, the statements:

```
        SLOPE = 25.67
        PRINT 16, SLOPE
16      FORMAT(' ',F9.3)
```

produce the display:

```
   25.670
123456789
```

As before, field position numbers have been placed under the output to clearly mark the display field. The specification F9.3 tells the computer to display a real number in a total field width of 9 spaces, with three digits displayed to the right of the decimal point. Since the number contains only two digits to the right of the decimal point, the decimal part of the number is padded with a trailing zero. Numbers are always right-justified in the field.

If the portion of the total field width allocated to the integer portion of a decimal number is too small to fit the integer part of the number, the display is filled with asterisks. For field widths that can accommodate the integer portion of a decimal number, the fractional part of the number is always displayed with the number of specified digits. If the fractional part contains fewer digits than specified, the number is padded with trailing zeros; if the fractional part contains more digits than called for in the specifier, the number is rounded to the indicated number of decimal places. Program 2-6 illustrates these effects using PRINT statements to display the values of two floating point arithmetic expressions.

 Program 2-6

```
123456789──────────── Column Number ────────────72
      PROGRAM MAIN
      PRINT 10, 16.3 + 2.1
      PRINT 10, 18.621 + 2.116
  10  FORMAT(' ','THE VALUE OF THE EXPRESSION IS ',F5.2)
      END
```

The output of Program 2-6 is:

```
THE VALUE OF THE EXPRESSION IS 18.40
THE VALUE OF THE EXPRESSION IS 20.74
123456789111111111122222222223333333
         012345678901234567890123456
```

Notice that the values displayed on both lines of the output are contained within individual fields five spaces wide with two positions beyond the decimal point. The first value displayed has been padded with a trailing zero to fill the fractional part of the field, and the second value has been rounded to two decimal places. Also notice that both PRINT statements in the program reference the same FORMAT statement.

One caution should be mentioned here. The FORMAT statement does check the values it is given. Thus, if an integer specification is used (I3, for example), and the value given the statement is a real number, the program will display an error message on output. Similarly, if a real specification is used (F5.2, for example), and the corresponding number is an integer, an error message on output will also be produced.

The X Specification

The X specification is used to create blank fields by causing the computer to skip over a specified number of spaces. To illustrate the usefulness of creating a blank field first, consider the FORMAT statement:

```
100 FORMAT (' ',I3,I4)
```

This statement defines two integer fields with no intervening space between them. The first field occupies columns 1, 2, and 3 and is immediately followed by the second field. Using the X edit descriptor, we can insert any desired number of blank spaces in the output before a field is used. The general form of the X edit specification is:

$$\boxed{nX}$$

where n is an integer number defining how many spaces should be skipped over (left blank). For example, the FORMAT statement:

```
100 FORMAT (' ',1X,I3,2X,I3)
```

causes a single space to be skipped over before the first integer field is used. After the first integer is displayed, two additional spaces are skipped over, and then the second integer field is used. For example, the following sequence of statements:

```
        INTEGER NUM1, NUM2
        NUM1 = 726
        NUM2 = 345
        PRINT 100, NUM1, NUM2
100     FORMAT (' ',1X,I3,2X,I3)
```

produces the display:

```
726   345
123456789
```

The X specification may also be used as a substitute for the single space carriage control specification, ' '. For example, the 1X in the FORMAT statement:

```
10 FORMAT(1X,I4)
```

causes one blank space to fill the first position in the memory buffer in the same manner as the ' ' literal specification. Thus, the literal specification ' ' and the 1X specification can be used interchangeably for carriage control purposes. Additionally, since FORTRAN defaults to single spacing when an unrecognized control character is used, any noncontrol code placed in the first buffer position also causes single spacing to occur. For example, both of the following FORMAT statements produce single-spaced output lines:

```
45 FORMAT('7',I5)
66 FORMAT(30X,'HELLO WORLD!')
```

The first FORMAT statement specifies that an integer is to be displayed in a field with a width of 5, starting at column 1. Because a separate carriage control specification has not been included in the second FORMAT statement, this statement specifies that the message HELLO WORLD! is to be displayed after 29 blank spaces (not 30) have been skipped over. The first blank space designated by the specification 30X is used as the carriage control.

The A Specification

The A specification (the A stands for alphanumeric) defines the output format for displaying character data. The most common form of this specification is:

```
Aw
```

where the A designates that alphanumeric data will be displayed and the *w* is an optional field width specifier designating the maximum character size of the display. For example, the statements:

```
      PRINT 10, 'HAVE A HAPPY DAY'
10    FORMAT (A25)
```

includes both the A edit specification and a field width specifier of 25. This specification causes the character constant HAVE A HAPPY DAY to be displayed in a field width of 25, as follows:

```
          HAVE A HAPPY DAY
12345678911111111112222222
          0123456789012345
```

As illustrated, if the specified field width is larger than the character constant to be displayed, the constant is right-justified in the field and padded with leading blanks. If the field width specifier is too small for the string to be displayed, only the first *w* characters of the constant will be output. For example, the statements:

```
      PRINT 10, 'HELLO THERE WORLD!'
10    FORMAT (A5)
```

produce the display:

```
HELLO
12345
```

When the A edit specification is used without a field width specifier, the output is displayed in a field sufficiently large to hold the required number of characters. Thus, the statements:

```
      PRINT 10, 'HAVE A HAPPY DAY'
10    FORMAT (A)
```

produce the display:

```
HAVE A HAPPY DAY
1234567891111111
          0123456
```

In using the A specification it is the programmer's responsibility to ensure that character data are actually being used. Attempting to display a number, either real or integer, using the A specification will produce an error message or an unpredictable display.

Additional Format Control Characters

Many other format specifications exist in addition to the literal, I, F, A, and X specifications. The more useful of these additional specifications include repeat specifications, multiple line control, and tab control. The specifications providing these features are now described (a complete list of format specifications is presented in Appendix B).

Repeat Counts

A repeat count allows both single and groups of format specifications to be repeated. For example, the specification:

```
10 FORMAT (' ',F5.2,F5.2,F5.2)
```

uses the same specifier, F5.2, three times in succession. Using a repeat count of 3, this statement can be rewritten as:

```
10 FORMAT (' ',3F5.2)
```

Notice that the repeat count simply allows us to shorten the format specifier by eliminating the need to retype the same specifier explicitly. In addition to repeating a single format specifier, a repeat count also can be used with larger groupings of specifications. For example, the statement:

```
20 FORMAT (' ',1X,I3,2X,I3,2X,I3,2X,F4.2,1X,F5.2,1X,F5.2)
```

repeats the sequence I3,2X three times and the sequence 1X,F5.2 twice. Enclosing these sequences in parentheses and using repeat counts of 3 and 2, respectively, results in the following equivalent FORMAT statement.

```
20 FORMAT (' ',1X,3(I3,2X),F4.2,2(1X,F5.2))
```

All of the format specifiers presented so far (I, F, A, and X) may use repeat counts. The following format specifiers are nonrepeatable.

The Slash (/) Specification

The slash (/) specification, which can be placed anywhere within a specification list, forces the output buffer to display its contents immediately and then to clear itself. For example, the statements:

```
     PRINT 65
65   FORMAT(' ','HELLO',/,' ','THERE',//,' ','WORLD!')
```

produce the following display:

```
HELLO
THERE

WORLD!
```

This display is produced as follows: The carriage control ' ' and the word HELLO in the format specifier initially fill the first six locations of the output buffer with a blank and the characters H, E, L, L, and O. The first slash then forces the contents of the buffer to be displayed, producing the first output line. The buffer is then cleared and is filled with a blank followed by the characters T, H, E, R, and E. The next slash causes the contents of the buffer to be displayed again, producing the second line of output, and the buffer is again cleared. The second slash in the sequence // once again causes the contents of the buffer to be displayed. Since there is nothing in the buffer, a blank line is displayed. Finally, the buffer is filled with a blank space and the characters W, O, R, L, D, and !. The closing parenthesis of the format specifier then forces the contents of the buffer to be displayed, producing the last output line.

Two facts with respect to the slash edit descriptor should be kept in mind. First, since the slash causes the contents of the buffer to be displayed and the buffer cleared, the first character following a sequence of one or more slashes should be a carriage control character. Second, the commas enclosing the slash edit descriptor are always optional. For example, omitting the commas surrounding the slashes in the previous format statement produces the equivalent statement:

```
65 FORMAT(' ','HELLO'/' ','THERE'//' ','WORLD!')
```

Tab Specifications

The tab specifications provide tab capabilities and permit display fields to begin at any specified position. The first form of this specification is:

$$\boxed{\text{T}c}$$

where c is an integer representing an absolute column number at which the next field is to begin. For example, the FORMAT statement:

```
30 FORMAT (' ',T15,I3,T45,F5.2)
```

causes the first field, I3, to start at column 15 and the second field, F5.2, to begin at column 45 on the output line. Tabbing "backward" usually is permitted. For example, the FORMAT statement:

```
35 FORMAT(' ',T24,I5,T10,I2,T30,I6)
```

will cause the first integer field, I5, to begin at column 24 and the second field to begin at column 10. Finally, the last integer field, I6, begins at column 30.

In addition to absolute tabbing provided by the T edit descriptor, the TL and TR edit descriptors provide left (backward) and right (forward) relative positioning. The general form of the tab left (backward) specification is:

$$\boxed{\text{TL}n}$$

where n is an integer denoting how many spaces to the left, relative to the current position, should be backspaced. The general form of the tab right (forward) specification is:

$$\boxed{\text{TR}n}$$

where n is an integer denoting how many spaces to the right, relative to the current position, should be skipped over. For example, the statements:

```
    PRINT 22, 123,'HELLO',4567
 22 FORMAT(' ',T7,I3,TL9,A5,TR4,I4)
```

produce the output:

```
HELLO 1234567
1234567891111
        0123
```

The first tab in the format, T7, causes the display to tab over to column 7, which is the first space used by the I3 field. The number 123 is entered into this field position, at which point the current column position is 10. Tabbing back from column 10 with the TL9 descriptor places the starting column of the second field, A5, at column 1. After the word HELLO is displayed in columns 1 through 5, the current column position becomes 6. Tabbing forward from this position four spaces places the starting position of the last field at column 10.

Since relative tabbing to the right is the same as skipping over spaces, the conversion sequences TRn and nX can be used interchangeably. For example, the statement:

```
10 FORMAT(' ',I3,TR5,F6.2)
```

produces the same display as does the statement:

```
20 FORMAT(' ',I3,5X,F6.2)
```

Skill Builder Exercises

1. Determine and write out the display produced by the following statements:

```
a.        NUM1 = 7
          PRINT 10, NUM1
    10    FORMAT (' ',1X,I1)
b.        NUM1 = 7
          PRINT 20, NUM1
    20    FORMAT (' ',1X,I4)
c.        NUM1 = 29876
          PRINT 30, NUM1
    30    FORMAT (' ',1X,I4)
d.        SECNUM = 7.92
          PRINT 40, SECNUM
    40    FORMAT (1X,F5.2)
e.        SECNUM = 5.762
          PRINT 50, SECNUM
    50    FORMAT (1X,F5.2)
f.        SECNUM = 82.625
          PRINT 60, SECNUM
    60    FORMAT (1X,F5.2)
g.        SECNUM = 523.462
          PRINT 70, SECNUM
    70    FORMAT (1X,F5.2)
h.        SECNUM = 924.
          PRINT 80, SECNUM
    80    FORMAT (1X,F6.2)
```

```
i.      PRINT 10, 'THE NUMBER IS ', 26.27
        PRINT 10, 'THE NUMBER IS ', 682.3
        PRINT 10, 'THE NUMBER IS ', 1.968
    10 FORMAT (1X,A,1X,F6.2)
j.      PRINT 20, 26.27
        PRINT 20, 682.3
        PRINT 20, 1.968
        PRINT 30
        PRINT 20, 26.27 + 682.3 + 1.968
    20 FORMAT(1X,F6.2)
    30 FORMAT(1X,'——')
k.      PRINT 30, 26.27
        PRINT 30, 682.3
        PRINT 30, 1.968
        PRINT 40
        PRINT 30, 26.27 + 682.3 + 1.968
    30 FORMAT(' ',3X,F6.2)
    40 FORMAT(' ',T4,'——')
l.      PRINT 50, 34.164
        PRINT 50, 10.003
        PRINT 60, '——'
        PRINT 50, 34.164 + 10.003
    50 FORMAT (' ',8X,F5.2)
    60 FORMAT (' ',T9,A)
```

2. Determine the output produced by the following program:

```
        PROGRAM MAIN
        REAL AVERAGE
        AVERGE = 26.27
        PRINT 10, AVERGE
        AVERGE = 682.3
        PRINT 10, AVERGE
        AVERGE = 1.968
        PRINT 10, AVERGE
    10  FORMAT (1X,'THE AVERAGE IS',1X,F6.2)
        END
```

3. Write out the display produced by the following statements (assume that unit number 6 designates the standard output device):

```
a.      MUM1 = 7
        WRITE(6,10) NUM1
    10  FORMAT (' ',1X,I1)
b.      NUM1 = 7
        WRITE(6,20) NUM1
    20  FORMAT (' ',1X,I4)
c.      NUM1 = 29876
        WRITE(6,30) NUM1
    30  FORMAT (' ',1X,I4)
d.      SECNUM = 7.92
        WRITE(6,40) SECNUM
    40  FORMAT (1X,F5.2)
e.      SECNUM = 5.762
        WRITE(6,50) SECNUM
    50  FORMAT (1X,F5.2)
```

```
f.      SECNUM = 82.625
        WRITE(6,60) SECNUM
     60 FORMAT (1X,F5.2)
g.      SECNUM = 523.462
        WRITE(6,70) SECNUM
     70 FORMAT (1X,F5.2)
h.      SECNUM = 924.
        WRITE(6,80) SECNUM
     80 FORMAT (1X,F5.2)
i.      WRITE(6,10) 'The number is ', 26.27
        WRITE(6,10) 'The number is ', 682.3
        WRITE(6,10) 'The number is ', 1.968
     10 FORMAT (1X,A,1X,F6.2)
j.      WRITE (6,20) 26.27
        WRITE (6,20) 682.3
        WRITE (6,20) 1.968
        WRITE (6,30)
        WRITE (6,20) 26.27 + 682.3 + 1.968
     20 FORMAT(1X,F6.2)
     30 FORMAT(1X,'——')
k.      WRITE (6,30) 26.27
        WRITE (6,30) 682.3
        WRITE (6,30) 1.968
        WRITE (6,40)
        WRITE (6,30) 26.27 + 682.3 + 1.968
     30 FORMAT (' ',3X,F6.2)
     40 FORMAT (' ',T4,'——-')
l.      WRITE (6,50) 34.164
        WRITE (6,50) 10.003
        WRITE (6,60)
        WRITE (6,50) 34.164 + 10.003
     50 FORMAT (' ',8X,F5.2)
     60 FORMAT (' ',T9,'——-')
```

4a. Determine the output displayed by the following program:

```
        PROGRAM MAIN
        REAL PRICE, SALSTX, TOTAL
        PRICE = 36.0
        SALSTX = .05 * PRICE
        TOTAL = PRICE + SALSTX
        PRINT 55, SALSTX
        PRINT 60, TOTAL
     55 FORMAT (1X,'THE SALES TAX IS $',F7.3)
     60 FORMAT (1X,'THE TOTAL BILL IS $',F7.3)
        END
```

b. Rewrite the FORMAT statements in the program listed in Exercise 4a to produce the display:

```
THE SALES TAX IS $ 1.80
THE TOTAL BILL IS $37.80
```

c. Compile and execute the program written for Exercise 4b to verify the output.

5. Determine and write out the display produced by the following statements. (*Note:* Assume unit number 6 is the standard output device.)

a.
```
    INUM = 4
    WRITE (6,10) INUM
10  FORMAT (1X,I1)
```
b.
```
    INUM = 4
    WRITE (6,20) INUM
20  FORMAT (1X,I4)
```
c.
```
    INUM = 32736
    WRITE (6,30) INUM
30  FORMAT (1X,I4)
```
d.
```
    TNUM = 8.64
    WRITE (6,40) TNUM
40  FORMAT (1X,F5.2)
```
e.
```
    TNUM = 7.562
    WRITE (6,50) TNUM
50  FORMAT (1X,F5.2)
```
f.
```
    TNUM = 87.735
    WRITE (6,60) TNUM
60  FORMAT (1X,F5.2)
```
g.
```
    TNUM = 523.462
    WRITE (6,70) TNUM
70  FORMAT (1X,F5.2)
```
h.
```
    TNUM = 863.
    WRITE (6,80) TNUM
80  FORMAT (1X,F5.2)
```

Programming Exercises

6. Using either PRINT or WRITE statements, write a FORTRAN program that displays the results of the expressions (3.0 * 5.0), (7.1 * 8.3 – 2.2), and (3.2 / (6.1 * 5)) on three separate lines. Each value displayed should be limited to two decimal positions to the right of the decimal point. Calculate the value of these expressions manually to verify that the displayed values are correct.

7. The combined resistance of three resistors connected in parallel, as shown in Figure 2-15, is given
by the equation

$$Combined\ resistance = \cfrac{1}{\cfrac{1}{R_1}+\cfrac{1}{R_2}+\cfrac{1}{R_3}}$$

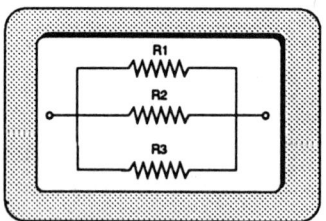

Using this formula, write a FORTRAN program to
calculate and display the combined resistance when
the three resistors $R_1 = 1000$, $R_2 = 1000$, and $R_3 =$
1000 are connected in parallel. The output should
produce the display: THE COMBINED RESISTANCE IS

Figure 2-15   Three Resistors Connected in Parallel

xxxx.xx OHMS, where xxxx.xx denotes that the calculated value should be placed in a field width of 7 columns, with two positions to the right of the decimal point.

8a. Write a FORTRAN program to calculate and display the value of the slope of the line connecting the two points whose coordinates are (3,7) and (8,12). Use the fact that the slope between two points having coordinates (x_1, y_1) and (x_2, y_2) is slope $= (y_2 - y_1) / (x_2 - x_1)$. The display produced by your program should be: THE VALUE OF THE SLOPE IS xxx.xx, where xxx.xx denotes that the calculated value should be placed in a field wide enough for three places to the left of the decimal point and two places to the right of it.

b. Write a FORTRAN program to calculate and display the coordinates of the midpoint of the line connecting the two points given in Exercise 8a. Use the fact that the coordinates of the midpoint between two points having coordinates (x_1, y_1) and (x_2, y_2) are $((X_1+X_2)/2, (Y_1+Y_2)/2)$. The display produced by your program should be:

```
THE X COORDINATE OF THE MIDPOINT IS xxx.xx
THE Y COORDINATE OF THE MIDPOINT IS xxx.xx
```

where xxx.xx denotes that the calculated value should be placed in a field wide enough for three places to the left of the decimal point and two places to the right of it.

9. Write a FORTRAN program to calculate and display the maximum bending moment, M, of a beam, which is supported on both ends (see Figure 2-16). The formula for maximum bending moment is $M = X W (L - X) / L$, where X is the distance from the end of the beam that a weight, W, is placed, and L is the length of the beam. Let $W = 500$ lbs., $X = 10$ ft., and $L = 25$ ft. The display produced by your program should be:

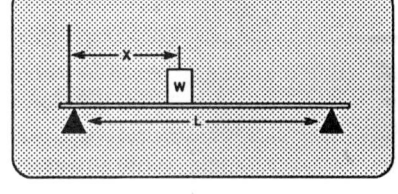

Figure 2-16   **Calculating the Maximum Bending Moment**

```
THE MAXIMUM BENDING MOMENT IS xxxx.xxxx
```

where xxxx.xxxx denotes that the calculated value should be placed in a field wide enough for four places each to the right and to the left of the decimal point.

10. For the electrical circuit shown in Figure 2-17, the branch currents I_1, I_2, and, I_3 can be determined using the formulas:

$$I_1 = \frac{E_2 R_3 + E_1 (R_1 + R_3)}{(R_1 + R_3)(R_2 + R_3) - (R_3)^2}$$

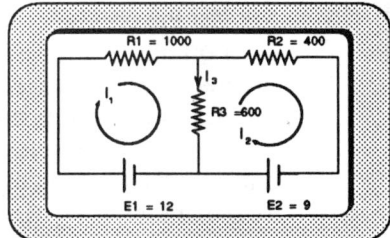

$$I_2 = \frac{E_1 R_3 + E_2 (R_1 + R_3)}{(R_1 + R_3)(R_2 + R_3) - (R_3)^2}$$

Figure 2-17   **Calculating Loop Currents in an Electrical Circuit**

$$I_3 = I_1 - I_2$$

Using these formulas, write a FORTRAN program to compute the branch currents when $R_1 = 1000$ ohms, $R_2 = 400$ ohms, $R_3 = 600$ ohms, $E_1 = 12$ volts, and $E_2 = 9$ volts. The display produced by your program should be:

```
BRANCH CURRENT 1 IS xx.xxxxx
BRANCH CURRENT 2 IS xx.xxxxx
BRANCH CURRENT 3 IS xx.xxxxx
```

where xx.xxxx denotes that the calculated value should be placed in a field wide enough for two places to the left of the decimal point and four places to the right of it.

2.5   Top-Down Program Development

Recall from Section 1.1 that writing a FORTRAN program is essentially the last step in the programming process. The first step in the process is determining what is required and selecting the algorithm to be coded into FORTRAN. In this section we present a five-step program development procedure, called top-down development, for converting programming problems into working FORTRAN programs. To make this development procedure more meaningful, we first apply it to a simple programming problem. The key part of the development procedure, called top-down design, is then applied to a more complicated program requirement. As we will see, designing a program using a top-down approach results in a modular program design.

The five steps in the top-down development procedure are to:

1. determine the desired output items that the program must produce
2. determine the input items
3. design the program as follows:
   a. either select an algorithm for transforming the input items into the desired outputs or design one using a top-down design technique
   b. check the chosen algorithm, by hand, using specific input values
   c. determine variable names for the selected algorithm
4. code the algorithm into FORTRAN
5. test the program using selected test data

Formally, steps 1 and 2 in the development procedure are referred to as the program *analysis phase;* step 3 is called the *design phase,* step 4 the *coding phase,* and step 5 the *testing phase.*

In the analysis phase of program development (steps 1 and 2), we are concerned with extracting the complete input and output information supplied by the problem. Together these two items are referred to as the problem's input/output, or I/O. Only after a problem's I/O has been determined is it possible to select an algorithm for transforming the inputs into the desired outputs. For example, consider the following simple programming problem:

The electrical resistance of a metal wire, in ohms, is given by the formula $R = (mL)/A$, where m is the resistivity of the metal; L is the length of the wire, in feet; and A is the cross-sectional area of the wire, in circular mils. Using this information, write a FORTRAN program to calculate the resistance of a wire that is 125 feet long, has a cross-sectional area of 500 circular mils, and is copper. The resistivity of copper is 10.4.

Step 1: Determine the Desired Output

The first step in developing a program for this problem statement is determining the required outputs (step 1 of the development procedure). Frequently, the statement of the problem will use such words as *calculate, print, determine, find,* or *compare,* which can be used to determine the desired outputs.

For our sample problem statement, the key phrase is "to calculate the resistance of a wire." This clearly identifies an output item. Since there are no other such phrases in the problem, only one output item is required.

Step 2: Determine the Input Items

After the desired output has been clearly identified, step 2 of the development process requires that all the input items be identified. It is essential at this stage to distinguish between input items and input values. An input item is the name of an input quantity, while an input value is a specific number or quantity that the input item can be. For example, in our sample problem statement the input items are the resistivity, m, the length of the wire, L, and the cross-sectional area of the wire, A. Although these input items have specific numerical values, these input item values are generally not of importance in step 2.

The reason that input values are not needed at this point is that the initial selection of an algorithm typically is independent of specific input values; the algorithm depends on knowing what the output and input items are and if there are any special limits. Let us see why this is so, as we determine a suitable algorithm for our sample problem statement.

Step 3a: Determine an Algorithm

From the problem statement it is clear that the algorithm for transforming the input items to the desired output is given by the formula $R = (mL)/A$. Notice that this formula can be used regardless of the specific values assigned to m, L, and A. Although we cannot produce an actual numerical value for the output item, resistance, unless we have actual numerical values for the input items, the correct relationship between inputs and outputs is expressed by the formula. Recall that this is precisely what an algorithm provides: a description of how the inputs are to be transformed into outputs that work for all inputs. Thus, the complete algorithm, in pseudocode, for solving this problems is:

> *Assign values to m, L, and A*
> *Calculate the resistance using the formula R = (mL)/A*
> *Display the result*

Step 3b: Do a Hand Calculation

After an algorithm is selected, the next step in the design procedure, step 3b, is to check the algorithm manually using specific data. Performing a manual calculation, either by hand or using a calculator, helps to ensure that you really do understand the problem. An added feature of doing a manual calculation is that the results can be used later to verify the operation of your program in the testing phase. Then, when the final program is used with other data, you will have established a degree of confidence that a correct result is being calculated.

Doing a manual calculation requires that we have specific input values that can be applied to the algorithm to produce the desired output. For this problem three input values are given: a resistivity of 10.4, a cross-sectional area of 500 circular mils, and a length of 125 feet. Substituting these values into the formula, we obtains a resistance of 2.6 ohms for the copper wire.

Step 3c: Select Variable Names

The last step in the design phase (step 3c) is to choose the names of variables to hold the input, output, and any intermediate calculated items determined in the analysis phase (steps 1 and 2). Let us use the variables named RESTVY, AREA, and LENGTH for the input items resistivity, area, and length, respectively; and a variable named RESIST for the calculated output, the resistance of the wire. All of these names are arbitrary, and any valid symbolic names can be used in their place.

Step 4: Write the Program

After variable names for the chosen algorithm have been selected, all that is required of our program is to declare these variables, initialize the input variables appropriately, compute the resistance variable, and print the calculated resistance value. Program 2-7 performs these steps.

 Program 2-7

```
123456789<——————————— Column Number
      PROGRAM OHMS
***      THIS PROGRAM CALCULATES THE RESISTANCE, IN OHMS, OF A WIRE
         REAL RESTVY, AREA, LENGTH, RESIST
         RESTVY = 10.4
         AREA = 500
         LENGTH = 125
***      DETERMINE THE WIRE'S RESISTANCE
         RESIST = (RESTVY * LENGTH) / AREA
         PRINT *, 'THE RESISTANCE OF THE WIRE (IN OHMS) IS', RESIST
         END
```

When program 2-7 is executed, the following output is produced:

```
THE RESISTANCE OF THE WIRE (IN OHMS) IS   2.600000
```

Once a working program that produces a result has been written, the final step in the development process, testing the program, can begin.

Step 5: Test the Program

The purpose of testing is to verify that a program works correctly and actually fulfills its requirements. Once testing has been completed, the program can be used to calculate outputs for differing input data without the need for retesting. This is, of course, the real value in writing a program; the same program can be used over and over with new input data.

In theory, testing would reveal all existing program errors (in computer terminology, a program error is called a *bug*). In practice, this would require checking all possible combinations of statement execution. Because of the time and effort required, this is usually an impossible goal except for extremely simple programs such as Program 2-7. (We illustrate why this is generally an impossible goal in Chapter 4, which describes FORTRAN's IF statements.)

The inability to completely test most programs has led to various testing methodologies. The simplest of these methods is to verify the program's operation for carefully selected sets of input data. One set of input data that always should be used is the data that was selected for the hand calculation made previously in step 3b of the development procedure. If testing reveals an error (bug), the process of debugging, which includes locating, correcting, and verifying the correction, can be initiated. It is important to realize that although this type of verification testing may reveal the presence of an error, it does not necessarily indicate the absence of one. Thus, the fact that a test does not reveal an error does not indicate that another bug is not lurking somewhere else in the program.

Modularity and Top-Down Design

The design of Program 2-7 was relatively simple. The design of a more complex program's structure can be considerably more involved. Designing a program in its more elaborate form, is similar to receiving the pieces of a puzzle (the inputs) and deciding how to arrange them to form a completed structure (the desired output). Unlike a jigsaw puzzle, however, the pieces of a program design puzzle can be arranged in many different ways, depending on the algorithm chosen for transforming the inputs into the desired outputs. In this regard, the program designer is very similar to an architect who must draw up the plans for a house.

The general procedure for designing programs (step 3 in our development procedure) is called *top-down design*. The purpose of top-down design is to design an algorithm in such a way that the program structure corresponding to the algorithm is modular. To achieve this goal, the design starts from the highest-level requirement and proceeds to the parts that must be constructed. As an example, consider an inventory reporting program that is required to keep track of the number of parts in inventory. The required output for this program is a description of all parts carried in inventory and the number of units of each item in stock; the given inputs are the initial inventory quantity of each part, the number of items sold, the number of items returned, and the number of items purchased.

For these I/O specifications, a designer initially could organize the requirements for the program into the three sections illustrated in Figure 2-18. This is called a *first-level structure diagram* because it represents the first overall structure of the program selected by the designer.

In top-down design, the lower boxes in the structure diagram are refined until the tasks indicated in the boxes are small enough to be programmed as individual program units. For example, both the data entry and report sections shown in Figure 2-18 would be further refined into suitable

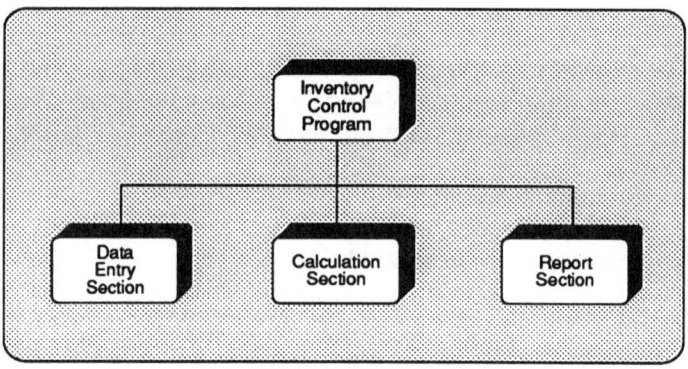

Figure 2-18   First-Level Structure Diagram

segments. The data entry section certainly must include provisions for entering the data. Since it is the system designer's responsibility to plan for contingencies and human error, provisions also must be made for changing incorrect data after an entry has been made and for deleting a previously entered value altogether. Similar subdivisions for the report section also can be made. Figure 2-19 illustrates a second-level structure diagram for an inventory tracking system that includes these further refinements.

The process of refinement continues until the last level of tasks can be coded using individual program units. Notice that the design produces a tree-like structure whose levels branch out as we move from the top of the structure to the bottom. When the design is complete, it specifies both how many program units are needed and the calling sequence of each unit (that is, lower-level units are called from higher-level ones). The individual algorithms specified for each box on the final structure diagram, which are coded using separate subprograms, are frequently described using either flowcharts or pseudocode.

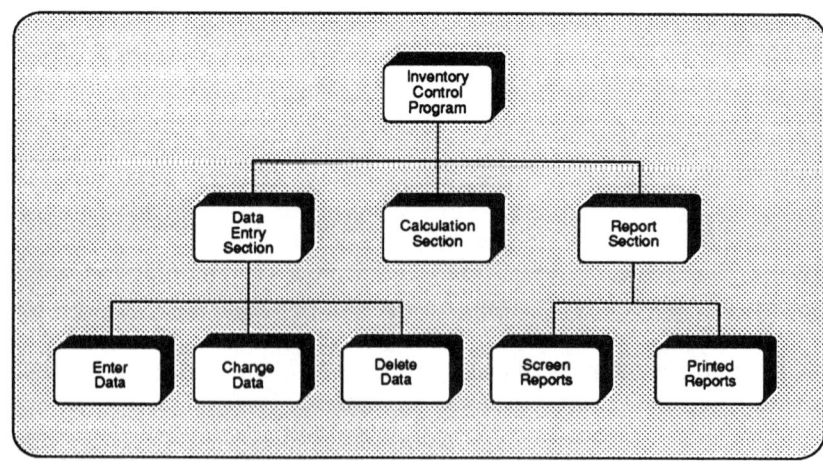

Figure 2-19   Second-Level Refinement Structure Diagram

Exercises

Note: In each of these exercises a programming problem is given. Read the problem statement first and then answer the questions pertaining to the problem.

1. Write a FORTRAN program that calculates the amount, in dollars, contained in a piggybank. The bank contains half-dollars, quarters, dimes, nickels, and pennies.

   a. For this programming problem, how many outputs are required?

   b. How many inputs does this problem have?

   c. Determine an algorithm for converting the input items into output items.

   d. Test the algorithm written for part c using the following sample data: half-dollars = 0, quarters = 17, dimes = 24, nickels = 16, and pennies = 12.

2. Write a program to calculate the value of *Distance,* in miles, given the relationship:

   *Distance = Rate * Elapsed time*

   a. For this programming problem, how many outputs are required?

   b. How many inputs does this problem have?

   c. Determine an algorithm for converting the input items into output items.

   d. Test the algorithm written for part c using the following sample data: *Rate* is 55 miles per hour and *Elapsed time* is 2.5 hours.

   e. How must the algorithm you determined in part c be modified if the elapsed time was given in minutes instead of hours?

3a. Write a program to determine the value of *Ergies,* given the relationships:
   *Ergies = Fergies * $\sqrt{Lergies}$*
   *Lergies = 2 * pi * e^{mu}*

   a. For this programming problem, how many outputs are required?

   b. How many inputs does this problem have?

   c. Determine an algorithm for converting the input items into output items.

   d. Test the algorithm written for part c using the following sample data: *Fergies* = 14.65, *pi* = 3.1416, *mu* = 1.672, and *e* = 2.7818.

4. Write a program to display the following name and address:
   Mr. J. Knipper
   63 Seminole Way
   Dumont, NJ 07030

   a. For this program problem, how many lines of output are required?

   b. How many inputs does this problem have?

   c. Determine an algorithm for converting the input items into output items.

5. Write a FORTRAN program to determine how far a car has traveled after 10 seconds assuming the car is initially traveling at 60 miles per hour and the driver applies the brakes to uniformly decelerate at a rate of 12 miles/sec^2. Use the fact that *distance = st − (1/2)dt^2*, where *s* is the initial speed of the car, *d* is the deceleration, and *t* is the elapsed time.

a. For this programming problem, how many outputs are required?

b. How many inputs does this problem have?

c. Determine an algorithm for converting the input items into output items.

d. Test the algorithm written for part c using the data given in the problem.

6. Consider the folowing programming problem: in 1627, Manhattan Island was sold to the Dutch settlers for approximately $24. If the proceeds of that sale had been deposited in a Dutch bank paying 5 percent interest, compounded annually, what would the principal balance be at the end of 1990? A display is required as follows: Balance as of December 31, 1990, is xxxxxx, where xxxxxx is the amount calculated by your program.

a. For this programming problem, how many outputs are required?

b. How many inputs does this problem have?

c. Determine an algorithm for converting the input items into output items.

d. Test the algorithm written for part c using the data given in the problem statement.

7. Write a program that calculates and displays the weekly gross pay and net pay of two individuals. The first individual is paid an hourly rate of $8.43, and the second individual is paid an hourly rate of $5.67. Both individuals have 20 percent of their pay withheld for income tax purposes, and both pay 2 percent of their net pay, before taxes, for medical benefits.

a. For this programming problem, how many outputs are required?

b. How many inputs does this problem have?

c. Determine an algorithm for converting the input items into output items.

d. Test the algorithm written for part c using the following sample data: the first person works 40 hours during the week, and the second person works 35 hours per week.

8. The formula for the standard normal deviation z, used in statistical applications is:

$$z = \frac{x - \mu}{r}$$

where μ refers to a mean value and r to a standard deviation. Using this formula, write a program that calculates and displays the value of the standard normal deviation when $x = 85.3$, $\mu = 80$, and $r = 4$.

a. For this programming problem, how many outputs are required?

b. How many inputs does this problem have?

c. Determine an algorithm for converting the input items into output items.

d. Test the algorithm written for part c using the data given in the problem.

9. The equation of the normal (bell-shaped) curve used in statistical applications is:

$$y = \frac{1}{r\sqrt{2\,pi}}\ e^{-\frac{1}{2}[(x - \mu)/r]^2}$$

Using this equation, write a FORTRAN program to calculate the value of *y*.

a. For this programming problem, how many outputs are required?

b. How many inputs does this problem have?

c. Determine an algorithm for converting the input items into output items.

d. Test the algorithm written for part c using the intrinsic exponential function, assuming $\mu = 90$, $r = 4$, $x = 80$, and $pi = 3.1416$.

2.6   Applications

In this section we apply the top-down development procedure presented in the previous section to two specific applications. Although each application is different, the top-down development procedure can be applied to any programming problem to produce a completed program.

Application 1: Pendulum Clocks

Pendulums used in clocks keep relatively accurate time because when the length of a pendulum is relatively large compared to the maximum arc of its swing, the time to complete one swing is independent of both the pendulum's weight and the maximum displacement of the swing. When this condition is satisfied, the relationship between the time to complete one swing and the length of the pendulum is given by the formula:

length = *g* [*time*/(2 *pi*)]²

where *pi*, accurate to four decimal places, is equal to 3.1416 and *g* is the gravitational constant equal to 32.2 ft/sec². When the time of a complete swing is given in seconds, the length of the pendulum is in feet. Using the given formula, write a FORTRAN program to calculate and display the length of a pendulum needed to produce a swing that will be completed in one second. The length should be displayed in inches.

Program Development

Using our five-step development procedure, we have:

Step 1: Determine the Desired Outputs
For this problem, a single output is required by the program: the length of the pendulum. The problem also specifies that the actual value be displayed in units of inches.

Step 2: Determine the Input Items
The input items required for this problem are the time to complete one swing, the gravitational constant, *g*, and *pi*.

Step 3: Design the Program
a. The algorithm for transforming the three input items into the desired output item is given by the formula *length* = *g* [*time*/(2 *pi*)]². Since this formula

calculates the length in feet, we will have to multiply the result by 12 to convert the answer into inches.

b. A hand calculation, using the data that $g = 32.2$, *time* $= 1$, and *pi* $= 3.1416$, yields a length of 9.78 inches for the pendulum.

c. We select the variable name TIME for the time and XLENTH for the length. (Since the length can be a real number, we select a variable name for this item that does not begin in either I, J, K, L, M, or N; this ensures consistency with earlier versions of FORTRAN, where these letters are required as initial letters for integer variable names.) As *g* and *pi* are constants that do not change, we will not assign them to variables; instead, their values will be directly incorporated in the assignment statement used to determine the pendulum's length.

Step 4: Write the Program
Program 2-8 provides the necessary code.

 Program 2-8

```
PROGRAM MAIN
  REAL TIME, XLENTH
  TIME = 1.0
  XLENTH = 12 * 32.2 * (TIME/(2*3.1416))**2
  PRINT *, 'THE LENGTH OF THE PENDULUM (IN INCHES) MUST BE ', XLENTH
  END
```

Program 2-8 begins with a program header line and ends with an *END* statement. Additionally, Program 2-8 contains a variable declaration statement, two assignment statements, and one output statement. The assignment statement TIME = 1.0 is used to initialize the TIME variable. The assignment statement:

```
XLENTH = 12 * 32.2 * (TIME/(2*3.1416))**2
```

calculates a value for the variable XLENTH. Notice that the 12 is used to convert the calculated value from feet into inches. Also notice the placement of parentheses in the expression (TIME/(2*3.1416)). Both sets of parentheses are needed. The inner set of parentheses ensures that the value of *pi* is multiplied by 2 before the division is performed. If these parentheses were not included, the value of TIME would first be divided by 2, and then the quantity TIME/2 would be multiplied by 3.1416. Finally, the outer parentheses ensure that the total quantity (TIME/(2*3.1416)) is squared. When Program 2-8 is compiled and executed, the following output is produced:

```
THE LENGTH (IN INCHES) OF THE PENDULUM MUST BE  9.787582
```

Step 5: Test the Program
The last step in the development procedure is testing the output of the program. Since the displayed value agrees with our previous hand calculation, we have

established a degree of confidence in the program. This permits us to use the program for different values of time. It should be noted that if the parentheses were not correctly placed in the assignment statement that calculated a value for XLENTH, the displayed value would not agree with our previous hand calculation. This would have alerted us to the fact there was an error in the program.

Application 2: Telephone Switching Networks

A directly connected telephone network is one in which all telephones in the network are directly connected and do not require a central switching station to establish calls between two telephones. For example, financial institutions on Wall Street use such a network to maintain direct and continuously open phone lines between institutions.

The number of direct lines, L, needed to maintain a directly connected network for N telephones is given by the formula:

$$L = N(N-1)/2$$

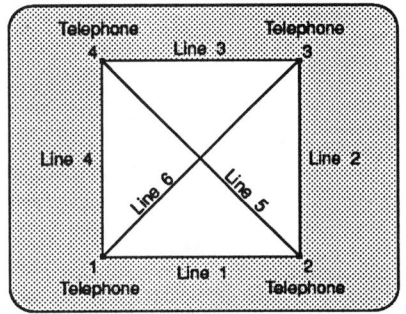

Figure 2-20 Directly Connecting Four Telephones

For example, directly connecting four telephones, without the use of a central switching station, requires six individual lines (see Figure 2-20). Adding a fifth telephone to the network illustrated in Figure 2-20 would require an additional four lines, for a total of 10 lines.

Using the given formula, write a program that determines the number of direct lines required for 100 subscribers and the additional lines required if 10 new subscribers are added to the network.

Program Development

Using our five-step development procedure, we have:

Step 1: Determine the Desired Outputs

For this program, two outputs are required: the number of direct lines for 100 telephones and the additional number of lines needed when 10 new telephones are added into the existing network.

Step 2: Determine the Input Items

The input items required for this problem are the number of subscribers, denoted as N in the formula.

Step 3: Design the Program

a. The first output is easily obtained using the formula $L = (N-1)/2$. Although there is no formula given for additional lines, we can use the given formula to determine the total number of lines needed for 110 subscribers. Subtracting the number of lines for 100 subscribers from the number of lines needed for 110 subscribers will then yield the number of additional lines required. Thus, the complete algorithm for our program, in pseudocode, is:

Calculate the number of direct lines for 100 subscribers
Calculate the number of direct lines for 110 subscribers
Calculate the additional lines needed, which is the difference between the second and
    first calculation
Display the number of lines for 100 subscribers
Display the additional lines needed

b. A hand calculation, using the data given yields that:

$L = 100(100 - 1)/2 = 100(99)/2 = 4950$ lines

for 100 subscribers and that $L = 5995$ direct lines needed for 110 subscribers. Thus, an additional 1045 lines would be needed to directly connect the 10 additional telephones into the existing network.

c. We select the variable name NUMIN for the initial number of 100 subscribers, NUMFIN for the final number of 110 subscribers, LINES1 for the initial number of lines, and LINES2 for the final number of lines. As all of these numbers are integer quantities, it is appropriate that these variable names begin with one of the letters J, K, L, M, or N; this ensures consistency with earlier versions of FORTRAN, where these letters are required as initial letters for integer variables.

Step 4: Write the Program

Program 2-9 provides the necessary code.

 Program 2-9

```
123456789 ──────────────── Column Number ──────────────────
      PROGRAM MAIN
        INTEGER NUMIN, NUMFIN,LINES1,LINES2
          NUMIN=100
          NUMFIN=110
          LINES1 = NUMIN*(NUMIN - 1)/2
          LINES2 = NUMFIN*(NUMFIN -1)/2
          PRINT *,'THE NUMBER OF LINES ORIGINALLY NEEDED IS ' LINES1
          PRINT *,' THERE ARE ', LINES2 - LINES1, ' NEW LINE NEEDED'
          END
```

As before, the FORTRAN program begins with a program header line and ends with an END statement. Since the number of lines between subscribers must be an integer (a fractional line is not possible) the variables LINES1 and LINES2 are specified as integer variables. The first two assignment statements initialize the variables NUMIN and NUMFIN. The next assignment statement calculates the number of lines needed for 100 subscribers, and the last assignment statement calculates the number of lines for 110 subscribers. The first PRINT statement is used to display a message and the result of the first calculation. The second PRINT statement is used to display the difference between the two calculations. The following output is produced when Program 2-9 is compiled and executed:

```
THE NUMBER OF LINES FOR 100 SUBSCRIBERS IS  4950
   THERE ARE  1045 NEW LINES NEEDED
```

Additional Exercises for Chapter Two

1a. Modify Program 2-8 to calculate the length of a pendulum that produces an arc that takes two seconds to complete.

   b. Compile and execute the program written for Exercise 1a on a computer.

If you're working with subroutines...

   c. Rewrite Program 2-8 so that it contains one subroutine.

2a. Modify Program 2-8 to determine the time it takes a three-foot pendulum to complete one swing. Your program should produce the following display:

```
THE TIME TO COMPLETE ONE SWING (IN SECONDS) IS  xxxx
```

where xxxx is replaced by the actual value calculated by your program.

   b. Compile and execute the program written for Exercise 2a on a computer. Make sure to do a hand calculation so that you can verify the results produced by your program.

   c. After you have verified the results of the program written in Exercise 2a, modify the program to calculate the time it takes a four-foot pendulum to complete one swing.

If you're working with subroutines...

   d. Rewrite the program written for Exercise 2a so that it contains one subroutine.

3a. Modify Program 2-9 to calculate and display the total number of lines needed to directly connect 1000 individual phones to each other.

   b. Compile and execute the program written for Exercise 3a on a computer.

4a. Modify Program 2-9 so that the variable NUMFIN is initialized to 10, which is the additional number of subscribers to be connected to the existing network. Make any other changes in the program so that the program produces the same display as does Program 2-9.

   b. Compile and execute the program written for Exercise 4a on a computer. Check that the display produced by your program matches the display shown in the text.

If you're working with subroutines...

   c. Rewrite the program written for Exercise 4a so that it contains one subroutine.

5a. Write, compile, and execute a FORTRAN program to convert temperature in degrees Fahrenheit to degrees Celsius. The equation for this conversion is *Celsius* = 5.0/9.0 (*Fahrenheit* – 32.0). Have your program convert and display the Celsius temperature corresponding to 98.6 degrees Fahrenheit. Your program should produce the display:

```
FOR A FAHRENHEIT TEMPERATURE OF xxxx  DEGREES
THE CELSIUS TEMPERATURE IS xxxx DEGREES
```

where appropriate values are inserted by your program in place of the xs.

b. Check the values computed by your program. After you have verified that your program is working correctly, modify it to convert 86.5 degrees Fahrenheit into its equivalent Celsius value.

6a. Write, compile, and execute a FORTRAN program to calculate the dollar amount contained in a piggybank. The bank currently contains 12 half-dollars, 20 quarters, 32 dimes, 45 nickels, and 27 pennies. Your program should produce the following display:

```
THE VALUE OF MONEY, IN DOLLARS, IS xxxx
```

where xxxx is replaced by the actual value calculated by your program.

b. Check the values computed by your program. After you have verified that your program is working correctly, modify it to determine the dollar value of a bank containing no half-dollars, 17 quarters, 19 dimes, 10 nickels, and 42 pennies.

7a. Write, compile, and execute a FORTRAN program to calculate the elapsed time it took to make a 183.67-mile trip. The equation for computing elapsed time is *elapsed time = total distance / average speed*. Assume that the average speed during the trip was 58 miles / hour. Your program should produce the display:

```
THE TIME FOR THE TRIP WAS xxxx HOURS
```

where the xs are replaced with the value calculated by your program.

b. Check the values computed by your program. After you have verified that your program is working correctly, modify it to determine the elapsed time it takes to make a 372-mile trip at an average speed of 67 miles/hour.

8a. Write, compile, and execute a FORTRAN program to calculate the sum of the numbers from 1 to 100. The formula for calculating this sum is $sum = (n/2)(2*a + (n-1)d$, where n is the number of terms to be added, a is the first number, and d is the difference between each number. Your program should produce the display:

```
THE SUM OF THE NUMBERS IS xxxx
```

where the xs are replaced by the sum computed by your program.

b. Check the values computed by your program. After you have verified that your program is working correctly, modify it to determine the sum of the integers from 100 to 1000.

9a. Newton's law of cooling states that when an object with an initial temperature T is placed in a surrounding substance of temperature A, it will reach a temperature $TFIN$ in t minutes according to the formula:

$$TFIN = (T - A) e^{-kt} + A$$

In this formula e is the irrational number 2.71828 rounded to five decimal places (commonly known as Euler's number), and k is a thermal coefficient, which depends on the material being cooled. Using this formula, write, compile, and execute a FORTRAN program that determines the temperature reached by an object after 20 minutes when it is placed in a glass of water whose temperature is 60 degrees. Assume that the object initially has a temperature of 150 degrees and has a thermal coefficient of 0.0367. Your program should produce the display:

```
THE FINAL TEMPERATURE IS xxxx
```

where the xs are replaced by the value calculated by your program.

b. Check the value computed by your program. After you have verified that your program is working correctly, modify it to determine the temperature reached by an object after 10 minutes when it is placed in a glass of water whose temperature is 50 degrees.

10a. Given an initial deposit of money, A, in a bank that pays interest annually, the amount of money at a time N years later is given by the formula:

$$AMOUNT = A * (1 + I)^N$$

where I is the interest rate as a decimal number (e.g., 9.5 percent is .095). Using this formula, write, compile, and execute a FORTRAN program that determines the amount of money that will be available in four years if $10,000 is deposited in a bank that pays 10 percent interest annually. Your program should produce the display:

```
THE VALUE AFTER xx YEARS IS yyyyy
```

where the xs are replaced by the number of years and the ys by the value of money calculated by your program.

b. Check the value computed by your program by hand. After you have verified that your program is working correctly, modify it to determine the amount of money available if $24 is invested at 4 percent for 300 years.

11a. If an initial deposit of A dollars is made in a bank, and the interest, I, is compounded M times a year, the amount of money available after N years is given by the expression:

$$A * (1 + I/M)^{M*N}$$

Using this expression, write, compile, and run a FORTRAN program to determine the amount of money available after 10 years if $5000 is invested in a bank paying 6 percent interest compounded quarterly ($M = 4$).

b. Check the value computed by your program. After you have verified that your program is working correctly, modify it to determine the amount of money available if $1000 is invested at 8 percent, compounded quarterly, for 10 years.

12a. Effective annual interest is the rate that must be compounded annually to generate the same interest as a stated rate compounded over a stipulated conversion period. For example, a stated rate of 8 percent compounded quarterly is equivalent to an effective annual rate of 8.24 percent. The relationship between the effective annual rate, E, and the stated rate, I, compounded M times a year is $E = (1 + I/M)^M - 1$. Using this formula, write, compile, and execute a FORTRAN program to determine the effective annual rate for a stated rate of 6 percent compounded four times a year (quarterly). Your program should produce the display:

```
THE EFFECTIVE INTEREST IS xxxx
```

where the xs are replaced by the value calculated by your program.

   b. Check the value computed by your program. After you have verified that your program is working correctly, modify it to determine the effective annual rate for a stated rate of 8 percent compounded monthly.

13a. The present value of a dollar amount is the amount of money that must be deposited in a bank account today to yield a specified dollar amount in the future. For example, if a bank is currently paying 8 percent interest annually, you would have to deposit $6,947.90 in the bank today to have $15,000 in 10 years. Thus, the present value of the $15,000 is $6,947.90. Using this information, write, compile, and execute a FORTRAN program that calculates how much must be deposited in a bank today to provide exactly $8,000 in 9 years at an annual interest rate of 8 percent. Use the formula:

Present value = Future amount / (1.0 + annual interest rate)^{Years}

   b. Check the value computed by your program. After you have verified that your program is working correctly, modify it to determine the amount of money that must be invested in a bank today to yield $15,000 in eighteen years at an annual rate of 6 percent.

14a. The set of linear equations:

$$a_{11}X_1 + a_{12}X_2 = c_1$$
$$a_{21}X_1 + a_{22}X_2 = c_2$$

can be solved using Cramer's rule as:

$$X_1 = \frac{c_1 a_{22} - a_{12} c_2}{a_{11} a_{22} - a_{12} a_{21}}$$

$$X_2 = \frac{c_2 a_{11} - a_{21} c_1}{a_{11} a_{22} - a_{12} a_{21}}$$

Using these equations, write, compile, and execute a FORTRAN program to solve for the X_1 and X_2 values that satisfy the following equations:

$$3X_1 + 4X_2 = 40$$
$$5X_1 + 2X_2 = 34$$

   b. Check the values computed by your program. After you have verified that your program is working correctly, modify it to solve the following set of equations:

$$3X_1 + 12.5X_2 = 22.5$$
$$4.2X_1 - 6.3X_2 = 30$$

2.7 Common Programming Errors

The common programming errors associated with the material presented in this chapter are:

1. Forgetting to separate variable names with commas in all declaration, PRINT, and WRITE statements.

2. Using a variable in an expression before the variable has been initialized. In such a case, whatever value happens to be in the variable will be used when the expression is evaluated, and the result will be meaningless.

3. Misspelling a variable's name within a program. For example, assume that the following declaration is made:

```
REAL VOLTS, CURRNT, RESIST
```

Now assume that the variable CURRNT is misspelled in the assignment statement:

```
VOLTS = CURNT * RESIST
```

The program would treat CURNT as a new REAL variable and use whatever value happened to be in the variable's storage locations (see previous error), effectively assigning a "garbage" value to VOLTS. Finding this error or even knowing that one occurred could be extremely troublesome.

4. Storing an incorrect data type in a variable. This error is not detected by the compiler. Here, the assigned value is converted to the data type of the variable to which it is assigned. For example, if LENGTH has been declared an integer variable, the assignment LENGTH = 26.95894 assigns the value 26 to LENGTH.

5. Dividing integer values incorrectly. This error usually is disguised within a larger expression and can be very troublesome to detect. For example, the expression 7.26 + 4/5 + 8.95 yields the same result as the expression 7.26 + 8.95 because the integer division of 4/5 is 0.

6. Mixing data types in the same expression without clearly understanding the effect produced. Since FORTRAN allows expressions with "mixed" data types, it is important to be clear about the order of evaluation and the data type of all intermediate calculations. As a general rule, data types should never be mixed in an expression unless a specific effect is desired.

7. Not using parentheses to clarify the intended order of computation in an expression.

8. Attempting multiple assignments within one statement. For example, the statement $A = B = C = 10$ is an invalid assignment statement.

9. Specifying a field width in a FORMAT statement that does not include sufficient space for both the decimal point and sign of a real number.

2.8 Chapter Summary

1. The six basic types of data recognized by FORTRAN are integer, real, double precision, character, logical, and complex data. Each of these types of data is typically stored in a computer using different amounts of memory.

2. Every variable in a FORTRAN program should be declared with the type of value it can store. Declarations within a program unit must be placed as the first statements within the unit. Variables of the same type should be declared using a single declaration statement.

3. An *expression* is any combination of constants and/or variables that can be evaluated to yield a result.
4. Assignment statements are used to store values into variables. The general form of an assignment statement is:

> VARIABLE = *expression*

5. PRINT and WRITE statements are used to display the values of expressions. In *list-directed* output, the format of the display is determined by the compiler. In *user-formatted* output, the format of the display is explicitly specified by the programmer.
6. The general form of the list-directed PRINT statement is:

> PRINT *, *item list*

where the item list can contain any number of valid FORTRAN expressions. The equivalent WRITE statement is:

> WRITE(*unit number,**) *item list*

where the unit number is an integer number that designates where the output is to be displayed.
7. The general form of the user-formatted version of the PRINT statement is:

> PRINT *n*, *item list*

where *n* is the statement number of a FORMAT statement and the item list can consist of any number of valid FORTRAN expressions. The equivalent WRITE statement is:

> WRITE(*unit number, n*) *item list*

8. A FORMAT statement consists of a statement label, the keyword FORMAT, and a format specification list. The general form of this statement is:

> *n* FORMAT (*specification list*)

where *n* is a statement label that is referenced by cither a PRINT or a WRITE statement. When used with a PRINT or a WRITE statement, the first character in the specification list is a carriage control character that determines the vertical spacing of the output. The remaining specification determines the horizontal spacing and form of the output.
9. A simple FORTRAN program using only a MAIN program unit has the form:

```
123456789 ───── Column Number─────────────────────72
        PROGRAM HEADER LINE
            declaration statements
            all other statements
            END
```

This general form is also valid for subroutine program units. For example, the program:

```
123456789——————————— Column Number——————————————72
        PROGRAM SHOW
         CALL TEST
         END
  *

        SUBROUTINE TEST
          declaration statements
          all other statements
          END
```

consists of two program units, both of which follow the general form required of all program units.

10. Although assignment and output statements can be placed in any order within a program unit after the declaration statements, it only makes sense to use PRINT or WRITE statements for displaying the contents of a variable after a proper value has been assigned to it. Similarly, a variable should only be used in an expression after the variable has been properly initialized. Comment statements may be placed anywhere in the program and have no effect on program execution.

2.9   Enrichment Study: Exchanging Data with Subroutines

As we saw in Chapter 1, a subroutine is called into action using the CALL statement. For example, the statement:

```
    CALL CIRCUM
```

initiates the execution of a subroutine named CIRCUM. This statement is used in Program 2-10 to illustrate its use in calling a subroutine to determine the circumference of a circle.

 **Program 2-10**

```
123456789——————————— Column Number——————————————72
      PROGRAM MAIN
        CALL CIRCUM
        END
  *

      SUBROUTINE CIRCUM
        REAL RADIUS, CCUM
        RADIUS = 2.24
        CCUM = 2.0 * 3.1416 * RADIUS
        PRINT *, 'THE CIRCUMFERENCE IS ',CCUM
        END
```

When Program 2-10 is compiled and executed, the following output is obtained:

```
THE CIRCUMFERENCE IS      14.074370
```

As written, Program 2-10 makes no provision for passing data from the main program unit into the CIRCUM subroutine or for passing data back from the subroutine to the main unit. Let us see how to rectify this situation so that data can be exchanged between the two program units used in Program 2-10.

In exchanging data between two program units, we must be concerned with both the sending and the receiving sides of the data exchange. Let us first look at the sending of data into a subroutine.

In its most general form, a subroutine is called into action using a CALL statement having the form:

```
CALL subroutine name (argument list)
```

Except for the addition of the parentheses and the argument list, this is identical to the CALL statement introduced in Chapter 1. The purpose of the parentheses following the subroutine name is to provide a pipeline through which data can be exchanged with the subroutine. The items that are passed to the subroutine through the parentheses are called *arguments* of the subroutine. For example, the statement:

```
CALL AREA(3.5)
```

both calls a subroutine named AREA and makes the number 3.5 available to it. Here the argument list consists of the single number 3.5, which is referred to as an *actual* argument of the called function. Similarly, the statement:

```
CALL DISPLY(2.67, 8)
```

calls a subroutine named DISPLY and makes two actual arguments, the real constant 2.67 and the integer constant 8, available to the called subroutine. In addition to constants, variables may also be used as actual arguments in a subroutine statement call. For example, the statement:

```
CALL CIRCUM(3.1416, RADIUS)
```

calls a subroutine named CIRCUM and makes both the constant 3.1416 and the variable RADIUS available to it. To illustrate the use of this CALL statement within a main program unit to both call and exchange data to the CIRCUM subroutine, consider Program 2-11. Included within the program is an appropriate CIRCUM subroutine to receive the transmitted data. The complete program, consisting of both main and subroutine program units, produces the same output as Program 2-10.

The CALL statement, as previously described, both calls the CIRCUM subroutine into action and makes two actual arguments available to it. Let's now see how the subroutine is constructed to correctly receive these two arguments.

The header line of the subroutine:

```
SUBROUTINE CIRCUM(PI,RAD)
```

prepares the subroutine to deal with two data items. The names PI and RAD, contained within parentheses, are called *dummy* arguments of the subroutine and are selected by the programmer according to the rules used to select variable names. The names selected for dummy arguments may, but do not have to, be the same as the actual argument names used in the CALL statement.

Program 2-11

```
123456789——————————— Column Number —————————————72
        PROGRAM MAIN
          REAL RADIUS
          RADIUS = 2.24
          CALL CIRCUM(3.1416,RADIUS)
          END
*
        SUBROUTINE CIRCUM(PI,RAD)
          REAL PI, RAD, CCUM
          CCUM = 2.0 * PI * RAD
          PRINT *, 'THE CIRCUMFERENCE IS ', CCUM
          END
```

The purpose of the dummy arguments in a subroutine header is to provide names by which the subroutine can access values transmitted through the CALL statement. Thus, the name PI is used within the subroutine to refer to the first value transmitted by the CALL statement, and the name RAD references the second value passed at the time of the subroutine call. As illustrated in Figure 2-21, the formal arguments PI and RAD effectively open one side of the two pipelines into the main program unit. On the CALL side of the pipeline the arguments are known as the constant 3.1416 and the variable RADIUS; on the subroutine side of the pipeline, the two arguments are known by their dummy argument names, PI and RAD.

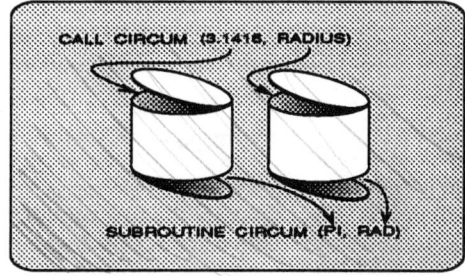

Figure 2-21   Exchanging Data with a Subroutine

The subroutine itself does not know where the data items made available to it come from. As far as the subroutine is concerned, the dummy arguments PI and RAD are treated as variables that have been initialized externally. As such, however, dummy arguments must still be declared, either explicitly using a declaration statement or implicitly using FORTRAN's implicit data typing rules.

When an explicit argument declaration statement is used, as it is in Program 2-11, it is placed immediately after the subroutine's header line. Once declared, an argument can be used anywhere within the subroutine in the same manner as a variable. Also, as illustrated in Program 2-11, variables used by the subroutine (in this case, the variable CCUM) should also be declared. The variable declarations can be made on a line by themselves or included within the declarations of the dummy arguments. Although the arguments and variables within a declaration statement can be listed in any order, it makes for clearer reading if all dummy arguments are declared before any variables.

Caution

Since an actual argument and its corresponding dummy argument both reference the same memory locations (see Figure 2-21), it is essential that corresponding arguments have the same declared data type. If the data types of the arguments do not match, the subroutine will interpret the internal computer code for the transmitted data differently than anticipated by the CALL statement. In such a case, the received value will bear no obvious relationship to the transmitted value. To avoid this error, which is not reported by the compiler, it is a good idea to display the values received by the subroutine. Once it has been verified that correct values have been received, the display can be removed.

Exercises for Enrichment Study

1. Write subroutine headers, argument declarations, and CALL statements for the following:

   a. A subroutine named TEST() having a real dummy argument named EXPER. The corresponding actual argument used in calling TEST() is named VALUE.

   b. A subroutine named MINUTE() having an integer dummy argument named ITIME. The corresponding actual argument used in calling MINUTE() is named LSECND.

   c. A subroutine named KEY() having a character dummy argument named CODE. The corresponding actual argument used in calling KEY() is also named CODE.

   d. A subroutine named YIELD() having a real dummy argument named RATE and an integer dummy argument named N. The actual arguments used in calling YIELD() are named COUPON and IYEARS.

   e. A subroutine named RAND() having two real dummy arguments named SEED and RANDNO, respectively. The actual arguments used in calling RAND() are named SEED and RVAL.

2a. Write a subroutine named AREA() that accepts two dummy real arguments named WIDTH and XLENTH. The subroutine should calculate the area of a rectangle by multiplying the passed data and should then display the calculated area.

   b. Include the AREA() subroutine written for Exercise 2a in a working program. The main program unit should correctly call and pass the values 4.4 and 2.0 to AREA(). Make sure to do a hand calculation to verify the result displayed by your program.

3a. Write a subroutine named TOTAMT() that accepts four actual integer arguments named IQUART, IDIMES, NICKEL, and IPENNY, which represent the number of quarters, dimes, nickels, and pennies in a piggybank. The subroutine should determine the dollar value of the number of quarters, dimes, nickels, and pennies passed to it and display the calculated value.

   b. Include the TOTAMT() subroutine written for Exercise 3a in a working program. The main program unit should correctly call and pass the values of 26 quarters, 80 dimes,

100 nickels, and 216 pennies to TOTAMT(). Make sure to do a hand calculation to verify the result displayed by your program.

4a. The time in hours, minutes, and seconds is to be passed to a subroutine named TOTSEC(). Write TOTSEC() to accept these values, determine the total number of seconds in the passed data, and display the calculated value.

b. Include the TOTSEC() subroutine written for Exercise 4a in a working program. The main program unit should correctly call TOTSEC() and display the value returned by the subroutine. Use the following test data to verify your program's operation: hours = 10, minutes = 36, and seconds = 54. Make sure to do a hand calculation to verify the result displayed by your program.

Completing the Basics

In the first two chapters we explored how results are displayed using FORTRAN's output statements and how numerical data is stored and processed using variables and assignment statements. In this chapter we complete our introduction to FORTRAN by presenting additional processing and input capabilities.

3.1 Intrinsic Functions

As we have seen, assignment statements can be used to perform arithmetic computations. For example, the assignment statement:

```
PWATTS = RESIST * CURRNT ** 2
```

squares the value in CURRNT, multiplies by the value in RESIST, and then assigns the resulting value to PWATTS. Although raising a number to a power is easily done using the exponentiation operator (**), finding a trigonometric value using FORTRAN's arithmetic operators is not as simple. To facilitate the calculation of trigonometric, logarithmic, and other mathematical calculations frequently required in scientific and engineering programs, FORTRAN provides standard preprogrammed routines, called *intrinsic functions*, that can be included in a program.

Before using a FORTRAN intrinsic function, the programmer must know:
- the name of the desired intrinsic function
- what the intrinsic function does
- the type of data required by the intrinsic function
- the data type of the result returned by the intrinsic function

To illustrate the use of FORTRAN's intrinsic functions, consider the intrinsic function named SQRT, which calculates the square root of a number. The square root of a number is computed using the expression:

```
SQRT(number)
```

where the intrinsic function name, in this case SQRT, is followed by parentheses containing the number for which the square root is desired. The purpose of the parentheses following the function name is to provide a funnel through which data can be passed to the function (see Figure 3-1). The items that are passed to the function through the parentheses are called *arguments* of the function and constitute its input data. For example, the following expressions are used to compute the square root of the arguments 4.0, 17.0, 25.0, 1043.29, and 6.4516:

```
SQRT(4.0)
SQRT(17.0)
SQRT(25.0)
SQRT(1043.29)
SQRT(6.4516)
```

The argument to the function named SQRT must be a positive real value. The SQRT function computes the square root of its argument, and the returned result is itself a real value. The values returned by the previous expressions are:

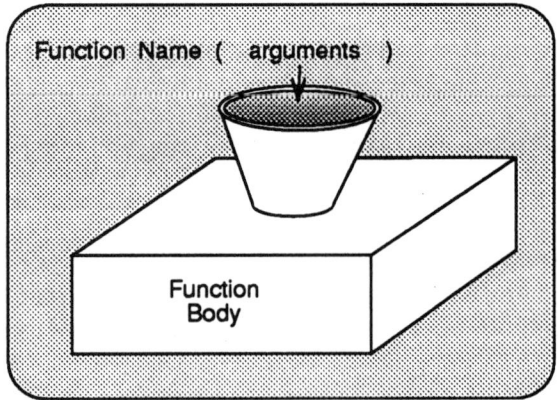

Figure 3-1 Passing Data to a Function

Expression	Value returned
SQRT(4.0)	2.000000
SQRT(17.0)	4.123106
SQRT(25.0)	5.000000
SQRT(1043.29)	32.300000
SQRT(6.4516)	2.540000

Table 3-1 lists the more commonly used intrinsic functions provided in FORTRAN in addition to the SQRT function. Although some of the intrinsic functions listed require more than one argument, all functions, by definition, return a single value. Table 3-2 lists the value returned by selected functions using example arguments. Note that the argument types for the examples agree with those given in Table 3-1 for the specified function.

Whenever an intrinsic function is used, it is called into action by giving the name of the function and passing any data to it within the parentheses following the function's name (see Figure 3-2).

The arguments that are passed to a function need not be single constants. Expressions can also be arguments, provided that the expression can be computed to yield a value of the required data type. For example, the following arguments are valid for the given functions:

```
SQRT(4.0 + 5.3 * 4.0)         ABS(2.3 * 4.6)
SQRT(16.0 * 2.0 - 6.7)        SIN(THETA - PHI)
SQRT(X * Y - Z/3.2)           COS(2.0 * OMEGA)
```

The expressions in parentheses are first evaluated to yield a specific value. Thus, values would have to be assigned to the variables X, Y, Z, THETA, PHI, and OMEGA before their use in the above expressions. After the value of the argument is calculated, it is passed to the function.

Table 3-1 Common FORTRAN Functions

Function name and argument(s)	Argument type(s)	Returned value	Description
ABS(R)	REAL	REAL	Absolute value of R
IABS(I)	INTEGER	INTEGR	Absolute value of I
INT(R)	REAL	INTEGER	Integer part of R
REAL(I)	INTEGE	REAL	Convert an integer to a real
FLOAT(I)	INTEGER	EEAL	Same as REAL(I)
MOD(I1,I2)	INTEGER	INTEGER	Integer remainder of I1 / I2
SQRT(R)	REAL	REAL	Square root of R
SIN(R)	REAL	REAL	Sine of R (R in radians)
COS(R)	REAL	REAL	Cosine of R (R in radians)
TAN(R)	REAL	REAL	Tangent of R (R in radians)
EXP(R)	REAL	REAL	e raised to the R power
ALOG(R)	REAL	REAL	Natural log of R
ALOG10(R)	REAL	REAL	Common log (base 10) of R
MAX0(I1,I2,..,IN)	INTEGER	INTEGER	Returns largest argument
AMAX1(R1,R2,..,RN)	REAL	REAL	Returns largest argument
MIN0(I1,I2,..,IN)	INTEGER	INTEGER	Returns smallest argument
AMIN1(R1,R2,..,RN)	REAL	REAL	Returns smallest argument

Table 3-2   Selected Function Examples

Examples	Returned value
ABS(-7.362)	7.3620000
IABS(-3)	3
INT(-16.892)	-16
REAL(29)	29.000000
MOD(17,3)	2
MOD(9,5)	4
MAX0(5, 1, 6, 9, 2)	9
AMAX1(3.67, 9.8, 2.456)	9.800000
MIN0(5, 1, 6, 9, 2)	1
AMIN1(3.67, 9.8, 2.456)	2.4560000

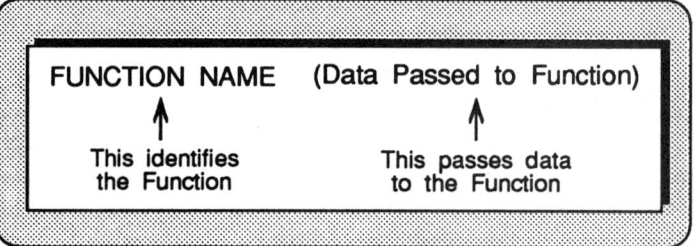

Figure 3-2   Using and Passing Data to a Function

Functions may be included as part of larger expressions. The value returned by the function is computed before any other operation is performed, for example:

```
4 * SQRT(4.5 * 10.0 - 9.0) - 2.0 =
    4 * SQRT(36.000000) - 2.0 =
        4 * 6.000000 - 2.0 =
            24.000000 - 2.0 = 22.000000
```

and:

```
3.0 * ALOG(30 * .514) =
    3.0 * ALOG(15.42) =
        3.0 * 2.735665 = 8.206995
```

The step-by-step evaluation of:

```
3.0 * SQRT(5 * 33 - 13.71) / 5
```

is:

Step	Result
1. Perform multiplication in argument	3.0 * SQRT(165 – 13.71) / 5
2. Complete argument calculation	3.0 * SQRT(151.290000) / 5
3. Return a function value	3.0 * 12.300000 / 5
4. Perform the multiplication	36.900000 / 5
5. Perform the division	7.380000

Program 3-1 illustrates the use of the SQRT function to determine the time it takes a ball to hit the ground after it has been dropped from an 800-foot tower. The mathematical formula used to calculate the time, in seconds, that it takes to fall a given distance, in feet, is:

*time = sqrt (2 * distance / g)*

where *g* is the gravitational constant equal to 32.2 ft/sec².

 Program 3-1

```
PROGRAM MAIN
  REAL TIME, HEIGHT
  HEIGHT = 800
  TIME = SQRT(2.0 * HEIGHT / 32.2)
  PRINT *, 'IT WILL TAKE ', TIME, ' SECONDS'
  PRINT *, ' TO FALL ', HEIGHT, ' FEET.'
  END
```

Following is the output of Program 3-1.

```
IT WILL TAKE 7.049074 SECONDS
TO FALL 800.000000 FEET.
```

As used in Program 3-1, the value returned by the SQRT function is assigned to the variable TIME. The value returned by any function may always be used as any other value of the same type. This means that the returned value may be assigned to a variable (as in Program 3-1), included within larger expressions, or even used as an argument to another function. For example, the expression:

```
SQRT (SIN (ABS (THETA) ) )
```

is valid. Since parentheses are present, the computation proceeds from the inner to the outer pairs of parentheses. Thus, the absolute value of *THETA* is computed first and used as an argument to the SIN function. The value returned by the SIN function is then used as an argument to the SQRT function.

It must be noted that the arguments of all intrinsic trigonometric functions (SIN, COS, etc.) must be in radians. Thus, to obtain the sine of an angle that is given in degrees, you must first convert the angle to radian measure. This is accomplished easily by multiplying the angle by the term (3.1416/180.). For example, to obtain the sine of 30 degrees, the expression SIN(30 * 3.1416/180.) should be used.

Skill Builder Exercises

1. Write function calls to determine:

   a. the square root of 6.37

   b. the square root of $X - Y$

   c. the sine of 30 degrees

   d. the sine of 60 degrees

   e. the integer part of the number 19.37

   f. the absolute value of $A^2 - B^2$

   g. the remainder of 7 divided by 2

   h. the value of e raised to the third power

2. For $A = 10.6, B = 13.9, C = -3.42$, determine the value of:

   a. `INT(A)`
   b. `INT(C)`
   c. `ABS(A) + ABS(B)`
   d. `SQRT(ABS(A - B))`
   e. `AMIN1(A, B)`
   f. `AMIN1(A, B, C)`
   g. `AMAX1(A, B, C)`
   h. `AMAX1(2*SQRT(A), B-C)`
   i. `MINO(INT(A), INT(B), INT(ABS(C)))`
   j. `MOD(9,4)`
   k. `MOD(17,3)` l. `MOD(3,17)`

3. Write FORTRAN statements for the following:

   a. $b = \sin x - \cos x$

   b. $b = \sin^2 x - \cos^2 x$

   c. $area = (c * b * \sin a)/2$

   d. $c = \sqrt{a^2 + b^2}$

   e. $p = \sqrt{|m - n|}$

   f. $sum = \dfrac{a(r^n - 1)}{r - 1}$

   g. x is the largest value of the real variables P, Q, R, S, and T

   h. y is the smallest value of the real variables P, Q, R, S, and T

Programming Exercises

4. Write, compile, and execute a program that calculates and returns the fourth root of the number 81.0, which is 3. When you have verified that your program works correctly, use it to determine the fourth root of 1,728.8964. Your program should make use of the SQRT function.

5. Write, compile, and execute a FORTRAN program that calculates the distance between two points whose coordinates are (7,12) and (3,9). Use the fact that the distance between

two points having coordinates (x_1, y_1) and (x_2, y_2) is *distance = sqrt($[x_1 - x_2]^2 + [y_1 - y_2]^2$)*. When you have verified that your program works correctly by calculating the distance between the two points manually, use your program to determine the distance between the points (–12,–15) and (22,5).

6. If a 20 foot ladder is placed on the side of a building at a 75-degree angle, as illustrated in Figure 3-3, the height at which the ladder touches the building can be calculated as *height* = 20 * *sin* 75°. Calculate this height by hand and then write, compile, and execute a FORTRAN program that determines and displays the value of the height. When you have verified that your program works correctly, use it to determine the height of a 25-foot ladder placed at an angle of 85 degrees.

Figure 3-3 Calculating the Height of a Ladder Against a Building

7. The maximum height reached by a ball thrown with an initial velocity v, in meters/sec, at an angle of q is given by the formula *height* = $(.5 * v^2 * \sin^2 q) / 9.80$. Using this formula, write, compile, and execute a FORTRAN program that determines and displays the maximum height reached when the ball is thrown at 15 meters/sec at an angle of 60 degrees. Calculate the maximum height manually and verify the result produced by your program. After you have verified that your program works correctly, use it to determine the height reached by a ball thrown at 7 miles/hour at an angle of 45 degrees.

8. For small values of x, the value of $\sin(x)$ can be approximated by the power series:

$$x - \frac{x^3}{6} + \frac{x^5}{120}$$

As with the SIN function, the value of x must be in radians. Using this power series, write, compile, and execute a FORTRAN program that approximates the sine of 180/3.1416 degrees, which equals 1 radian. Additionally, have your program use the SIN function to calculate the sine and display both calculated values and the absolute difference of the two results. Verify the approximation produced by your program. After you have verified that your program is working correctly, use it to approximate the value of the sine of 62.2 degrees.

9. The polar coordinates of a point consist of the distance, r, from a specified origin and an angle, θ, with respect to the x axis. The x and y coordinates of the point are related to its polar coordinates by the formulas:

$x = r \cos \theta$

$y = r \sin \theta$

Using these formulas, write a FORTRAN program that calculates the x and y coordinates of the point whose polar coordinates are $r = 10$ and $\theta = 30$ degrees. Verify the results produced by your program by calculating the results manually. After you have verified that your program is working correctly, use it to convert the polar coordinates $r = 12.5$ and $\theta = 67.8$ degrees into rectangular coordinates.

10. A model of worldwide population growth, in billions of people, since 1985, is given by the equation:

    $$population = 4.88e^{.02 \, [Year - 1985]}$$

    Using this formula, write, compile, and execute a FORTRAN program to estimate the worldwide population in the year 1995. Verify the result displayed by your program by calculating the answer manually. After you have verified that your program is working correctly, use it to estimate the world's population in the year 2012.

11. A model to estimate the number of grams of a certain radioactive isotope left after N years is given by the formula:

    $$Remaining \; material = (Original \; material) \; e^{-.00012 \, N}$$

    Using this formula, write, compile, and execute a FORTRAN program to determine the amount of radioactive material remaining after 1000 years, assuming an initial amount of 100 grams. Using a hand calculation, verify the display produced by your program. After you have verified that your program is working correctly, use it to determine the amount of radioactive material remaining after 275 years, assuming an initial amount of 250 grams.

12. The number of years that it takes for a certain isotope of uranium to decay to one-half of an original amount is given by the formula:

    $$Half\text{-}life = \ln(2)/k$$

    where k equals .00012. Using this formula, write, compile, and execute a FORTRAN program that calculates and displays the half-life of this uranium isotope. Using a hand calculation, verify the result produced by your program. After you have verified that your program is working correctly, use it to determine the half-life of a uranium isotope having a $k = .00026$.

13. The amplification of electronic circuits is measured in units of decibels, which is calculated as:

    $$10 \; \text{LOG} \; (P_O/P_I)$$

    where P_O is the power of the output signal and P_I is the power of the input signal. Using this formula, write, compile, and execute a FORTRAN program that calculates and displays the decibel amplification in which the output power is 50 watts and the input power is 1 watt. Using a hand calculation, verify the result displayed by your program. After you have verified that your program is working correctly, use it to determine the amplification of a circuit whose output power is 4.639 watts and input power is 1 watt.

14. The loudness of a sound is measured in units of decibels, calculated as:

    $$10 \; \text{LOG} \; (SL/RL)$$

    where SL is intensity of the sound being measured and RL is a reference sound intensity level. Using this formula, write a FORTRAN program that calculates and displays the decibel loudness of a busy street having a sound intensity of 10,000,000 RL. Using a hand calculation, verify the result produced by your program. After you have verified that your program is working correctly, use it to determine the sound level, in decibels, of the following sounds::

    a. a whisper of sound intensity 200 RL

    b. a rock band playing at a sound intensity of 1,000,000,000,000 RL

    c. an airplane taking off at a sound intensity of 100,000,000,000,000 RL

15. The dollar change remaining after an amount PAID is used to pay a restaurant check of amount CHECK can be calculated using the following FORTRAN statements:

```
* DETERMINE THE AMOUNT OF PENNIES IN THE CHANGE
      CHANGE = (PAID - CHECK)*100
* DETERMINE THE NUMBER OF DOLLARS IN THE CHANGE
      DOLLAR = INT(CHANGE/100)
```

a. Using the previous statements as a starting point, write a FORTRAN program that calculates the number of dollar bills, quarters, dimes, nickels, and pennies in the change when $10 is used to pay a bill of $6.07.

b. Without compiling or executing your program, check the effect, by hand, of each statement in the program and determine what is stored in each variable as each statement is encountered.

c. When you have verified that your algorithm works correctly, compile and execute your program. Verify that the result produced by your program is correct. After you have verified that your program is working correctly, use it to determine the change when a check of $12.36 is paid using a $20 bill.

16a. For display purposes, the F FORMAT specification allows the programmer to round all outputs to the desired number of decimal places. However, this can, yield seemingly incorrect results when used in financial programs that require all monetary values to be displayed to the nearest penny. For example, the display produced by the statements:

```
      REAL A, B
      A = 1.674
      B = 1.322
      PRINT 100, A
      PRINT 100, B
      PRINT 110
      C = A + B
      PRINT 100, C
100 FORMAT(1X,F4.2)
110 FORMAT(1X,'———')
```

is:

```
1.67
1.32
———
3.00
```

Clearly, the sum of the displayed numbers should be 2.99 and not 3.00. The problem is that although the values in A and B have been displayed with two decimal digits, they were added internal to the program as three-digit numbers. The solution is to round the values in A and B before they are added by the statement C = A + B. Using the INT function, devise a method to round the values in the variables A and B to the nearest hundredth (penny value) before they are added.

b. Include the method you have devised for exercise 16a into a working program that produces the following display:

```
1.67
1.32
———
2.99
```

3.2 The List-Directed READ Statement

Data for programs that are going to be executed only once may be included directly in the program. For example, if we wanted to multiply the numbers 300.0 and .05, we could use Program 3-2.

 Program 3-2

```
PROGRAM MAIN
  REAL FIRNUM, SECNUM, PRODCT
  FIRNUM = 300.0
  SECNUM = .05
  PRODCT = FIRNUM * SECNUM
  PRINT *, FIRNUM,' TIMES ', SECNUM,' IS ', PRODCT
  END
```

The output displayed by Program 3-2 is:

```
300.000000 TIMES .050000 IS 15.000000
```

Program 3-2 can be shortened, as illustrated in Program 3-3. Both programs, however, suffer from the same basic problem in that they must be rewritten in order to multiply different numbers.

 Program 3-3

```
PROGRAM MAIN
  PRINT *, '300.00 TIMES .05 IS ', 300.00 * .05
  END
```

Except for the practice provided to the programmer in writing, entering, and running the program, programs that do the same calculation only once, on the same set of numbers, are clearly not very useful. After all, it is simpler to use a calculator to multiply two numbers than to enter and run either Program 3-2 or 3-3.

To overcome the necessity of rewriting and compiling a program for each new set of data, a READ statement can be used. The READ statement permits data to be entered into a program while it is executing. Just as the PRINT and WRITE statements display a copy of the value stored inside a variable, the READ statement allows the user to enter a value at the terminal while the program is executing (see Figure 3-4).

Figure 3-4 READ Is Used to Enter Data;
PRINT and WRITE Are Used to Display Data

The entered value is then stored directly in a variable. Additionally, like its output statement counterparts, the READ statement has both list-directed and user-formatted versions. In this section the list-directed version is presented. The user-formatted version of the READ statement is described in Section 3.3.

The list-directed READ statement is used to accept data from a terminal, card reader, or auxiliary storage device such as a disk without the need of an explicit format specifier. FORTRAN 77 provides two distinct forms for its list-directed READ statement. The most general of these forms is:

```
READ (unit number, *) list of variables
```

The asterisk (*) in the READ statement specifies that the compiler's list-directed format is to be used. The *unit number* within the statement's parentheses designates where the input is coming from. Initially, we will only be reading data from either the keyboard or card reader connected to the computer, referred to as the computer's *standard input device*. Table 3-3 lists the unit numbers assigned to the standard input device by the more commonly used FORTRAN compilers. A space has been left in the table for you to enter your system's standard input unit number.

For example, assuming that unit number 5 denotes the standard input device, the statement READ (5,*) FIRNUM tells the computer to read its standard input device for a single value that is to be stored in the variable FIRNUM.

When a statement such as READ (5,*) FIRNUM is encountered, the computer stops program execution and waits for a number to be entered at the computer's standard input device (for the remainder of the text we assume this is a keyboard). When a number is typed and the ENTER key is pressed, the READ statement stores the entered value in the variable FIRNUM. The program then continues execution with the next statement following the READ. To see this, consider Program 3-4, where we have assumed that unit number 5 designates the keyboard.

The first PRINT statement in Program 3-4 displays a message that tells the person at the terminal what should be typed. When a message is used in this manner it is called a *prompt*. In this case the prompt tells the user to type a number. The computer then executes the next statement, which is a READ statement. The READ statement puts the computer into a temporary pause (or wait) state for as long as it takes the

Table 3-3   Standard Input Device Unit Numbers

Compiler	Unit number	Example
AT&T Philon	5 or *	READ (5,*) FIRNUM
		or
		READ (*,*) FIRNUM
AUTEC (R/M)	5 or *	READ (5,*) SECNUM
		or
		READ (*,*) SECNUM
DEC-VAX	5, 6 or *	READ (5,*) SLOPE
		or
		READ (6,*) SLOPE
		or
		READ (*,*) SLOPE
DTSS	0, 5, or *	READ (0,*) FIRNUM
		or
		READ (5,*) FIRNUM
		or
		READ (*,*) FIRNUM
IBM	5 or *	READ (5,*) SECNUM
		or
		READ (*,*) SECNUM
Microsoft	5 or *	READ (5,*) SLOPE
		or
		READ (*,*) SLOPE
Prime	1 or *	READ (1,*) FIRNUM
		or
		READ (*,*) FIRNUM
Your System		

 Program 3-4

```
PROGRAM MAIN
  REAL FIRNUM, SECNUM, PRODCT
  PRINT *,'PLEASE TYPE IN A NUMBER: '
  READ (5,*) FIRNUM
  PRINT *, 'PLEASE TYPE IN ANOTHER NUMBER: '
  READ (5,*) SECNUM
  PRODCT = FIRNUM * SECNUM
  PRINT *, FIRNUM,' TIMES ', SECNUM,' IS ', PRODCT
  END
```

user to type a value. The user signals the READ statement that input is ready for reading by pressing the RETURN key after the value has been typed. The entered value is stored in the variable whose name is in the READ statement, and the computer is taken out of its paused state. Program execution then proceeds with the next statement, which in Program 3-4 is a PRINT statement. This statement causes the next message to be displayed. The next READ statement again puts the computer into a temporary wait state while the user types a second value. This second number is stored in the variable SECNUM.

The following sample run was made using Program 3-4:

```
PLEASE TYPE IN A NUMBER:
300.
PLEASE TYPE IN ANOTHER NUMBER:
0.05
300.00000 TIMES 0.050000 IS 15.000000
```

In Program 3-4, each READ statement is used to store one value into a variable. The READ statement, however, can be used to enter and store as many values as there are variables in the variable list. For example, again assuming that unit number 5 designates the standard input device, the statement:

```
READ (5,*) FIRNUM, SECNUM
```

results in two values being read from the terminal and assigned to the variables FIRNUM and SECNUM. If the data entered at the terminal were:

```
0.052 245.79
```

the variables FIRNUM and SECNUM would contain the values 0.052 and 245.79, respectively. When actually entering numbers such as 0.052 and 245.79, you must leave at least one space between the numbers or separate them with a comma. The space or comma between the entered numbers clearly indicates where one number ends and the next begins. Inserting more than one space between numbers has no effect on the READ statement. In this sense, list-directed input provides a kind of free-form input.

Any number of READ statements may be included in a program, and any number of values may be input using a single READ statement. *When entering a character value in response to a list-directed* READ *statement, however, the entered data must be enclosed in apostrophes.* Program 3-5 illustrates using the READ statement to input three numbers from the standard input device. The program then calculates and displays the average of the numbers entered.

The following sample run was made using Program 3-5:

```
ENTER THREE INTEGER NUMBERS:
22, 56, 73
THE AVERAGE OF THE NUMBERS IS: 50.333333
```

Note that the data entered at the standard input device for this sample run consist of the input:

```
22, 56, 73
```

Program 3-5

```
PROGRAM MAIN
  INTEGER NUM1, NUM2, NUM3
  REAL AVERGE
  PRINT *, 'ENTER THREE INTEGER NUMBERS: '
  READ (5,*) NUM1, NUM2, NUM3
  AVERGE = (NUM1 + NUM2 + NUM3) / 3.0
  PRINT *, 'THE AVERAGE OF THE NUMBERS IS: ',AVERGE
  END
```

In response to this line of input, Program 3-5 stores the value 22 in the variable NUM1, the value 56 in the variable NUM2, and the value 73 in the variable NUM3 (see Figure 3-5). Since the average of three integer numbers can be a real number, the variable AVERGE, which is used to store the average, is declared as a real variable. Note also that the parentheses are needed in the assignment statement AVERGE = (NUM1 + NUM2 + NUM3) / 3.0. Without these parentheses, the only value that would be divided by 3.0 would be the integer in NUM3 (since division has a higher precedence than addition). As previously noted, the commas in the input are not required as long as one or more spaces separate the individual data items.

Had the user inadvertently entered real values instead of integers in response to the prompt in Program 3-5, the real values would have been truncated to integers. This happens because the READ statement is "clever" enough to make a few data type conversions. Thus, if a real number is entered when an integer is expected, the READ statement only uses the integer part of the number. Similarly, if an integer is entered in response to a READ statement that expects a real number, the READ

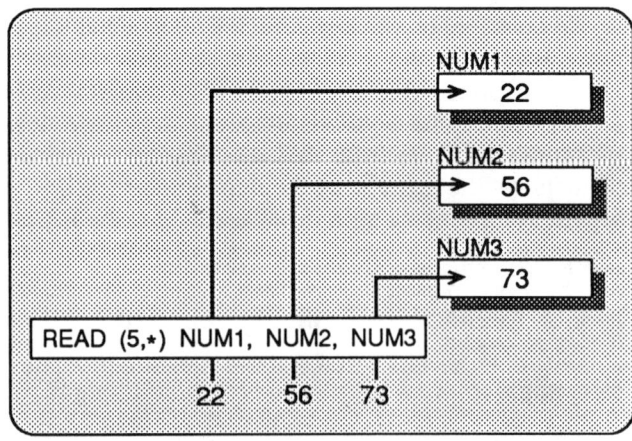

Figure 3-5 Reading Data into the Variables NUM1, NUM2, **and** NUM3

statement automatically adds a decimal point at the end of the integer before storing the number. For example, assume that REANUM has been declared as a real variable, INTNUM as an integer variable, and the statement:

```
READ (5,*) REANUM, INTNUM
```

is being executed. For purposes of illustration, assume that the following line of data is entered at the standard input device:

```
22 26.75 45.62
```

The READ statement converts the 22 to the real number 22.0 and stores this value in the variable REANUM. The statement continues reading the input, expecting an integer value. As far as READ is concerned, the fractional part of the number 26.75 is extraneous input and is ignored. Thus, the integer number 26 is stored in INTNUM.* The remaining data entered on the same line, 45.62, is extra input and is ignored. However, if less data is entered than the number of variables in the READ statement, the READ statement will continue to make the computer pause until sufficient data has been entered.

Default to Standard Input

The input of data from the standard input device is so common that FORTRAN 77 provides a second form of the READ statement that automatically defaults to this device for its data entry. This second form of the list-directed READ statement is:

```
READ *, list of variables
```

Here the term READ *, is equivalent to the term READ $(n,*)$, where n is the standard input device's unit number. Since, by definition, this second form of the READ statement can accept its input only from the standard input device, the unit number is omitted from the statement. In both forms of the READ statement the asterisk tells the compiler that list-directed (free-form) input is to be used. Program 3-6 illustrates this second form of the READ statement. In this program the user is prompted to enter the temperature in degrees Fahrenheit. The entered value is converted to degrees Celsius using the algorithm *Celsius* = (5.0 / 9.0) * (*Fahrenheit* − 32.0), and the equivalent Celsius temperature is displayed.

Following is a sample run using Program 3-6. In response to the prompt, a Fahrenheit temperature of 212 degrees, which corresponds to the boiling point of water, was entered. In Celsius this corresponds to 100 degrees, which agrees with the output produced by the program.

```
ENTER THE TEMPERATURE IN DEGREES FAHRENHEIT
212
THE EQUIVALENT CELSIUS TEMPERATURE IS 100.000000
```

Table 3-4 summarizes the various forms provided for list-directed input from the standard input device. Also included are corresponding forms for list-directed output to the standard output device. All of the READ statements in the table perform an identical input function, and all of the WRITE and PRINT statements accomplish

---

* On some systems a "type mismatch" error is displayed.

Program 3-6

```
PROGRAM TEMPCN
*** THIS PROGRAM CONVERTS AN ENTERED FAHRENHEIT
*** TEMPERATURE INTO AN EQUIVALENT CELSIUS VALUE
      REAL FAHREN, CELSUS
      PRINT *, 'ENTER THE TEMPERATURE IN DEGREES FAHRENHEIT: '
      READ *, FAHREN
      CELSUS = (5.0/9.0)* (FAHREN - 32.0)
      PRINT *, ' THE EQUIVALENT CELSIUS TEMPERATURE IS ',CELSUS
      END
```

Table 3-4   Summary of Standard Input and Output List-Directed Statements

Input	Output
READ (*n*,*) variable list	WRITE (*k*,*) expression list
READ (*,*) variable list	WRITE (*,*) expression list
READ *, variable list	PRINT *, expression list

Note: *n* is the standard input device number and *k* is the standard output device number

an identical output function. Additionally, any of the statements listed in the table can be freely intermixed within a single program.

Notice from the table that all of the READ statements in the first column are equivalent, just as all of the WRITE statements in the second column are equivalent. For example, on an IBM computer the statement:

```
READ (5,*) NUM1
```

can be replaced by the statement:

```
READ *, NUM1
```

and both of these statements can be replaced by:

```
READ (*,*) NUM1
```

The first asterisk in this last statement is a unit designator (see Table 3-3) that selects the computer's standard input device. The second asterisk selects the compiler's default formats for the entry of the data. As with user-formatted output, this asterisk can be replaced with an explicit format specification, the topic of the next section.

Skill Builder Exercises

1. For each of the following declaration statements, write a single list-directed READ statement, using either form of the READ statement, that will cause the computer to pause while data for the declared variables is entered by a user.

   a. `INTEGER NUMBER`

   b. `REAL GRADE`

   c. `CHARACTER KEYVAL*8`

   d. `INTEGER MONTH, YEAR`
      `REAL SCORE`

   e. `CHARACTER CH*4`
      `INTEGER NUM1, NUM2`

   f. `REAL CAPTAL, RATE, AMOUNT`

   g. `CHARACTER*4 LETTR1, LETTR2, KEY*8`
      `INTEGER NUM1, NUM2, NUM3`

   h. `REAL OHMS1, OHMS2, OHMS3, VOLTS1, VOLTS2, VOLTS3`

2. Given the following declaration statements:

```
INTEGER NUM1,NUM2
REAL TEMP, AMBINT
CHARACTER*5 VAL1, VAL2
```

   determine and correct the errors in the following READ statements, assuming that the first form of the READ statement presented in the text is to be used.

   a. `READ * (NUM1, NUM2, VAL2)`

   b. `READ (NUM1, NUM2), *`

   c. `READ (NUM1,I4)`

   d. `READ INTO TEMP AND AMBINT`

   e. `READ VAL1, VAL2`

   f. `READ * NUM1, TEMP`

3. Redo Exercise 2 assuming that the second form of the READ statement presented in the text is to be used.

Programming Exercises

4a. Modify Program 3-6 to convert Celsius degrees into equivalent Fahrenheit values. Make sure that an appropriate prompt and output line are displayed and that the conversion algorithm is suitably altered.

   b. Compile and execute the program written for Exercise 4a. Verify your program by calculating by hand, and then using your program, the Fahrenheit equivalent of the following test data:

      Test data set 1: 0 degrees Celsius
      Test data set 2: 50 degrees Celsius
      Test data set 3: 100 degrees Celsius

When you are sure your program is working correctly, use it to complete the following table:

Celsius	Fahrenheit
45	
50	
55	
60	
65	
70	

5. Write, compile, and execute a FORTRAN program that displays the following prompt:

```
ENTER THE RADIUS OF A CIRCLE:
```

After accepting a value for the radius, your program should calculate and display the area of the circle. (*Note:* area = 3.1416 * radius^2.) For testing purposes, verify your program using a test input radius of 3 inches. After manually checking that the result produced by your program is correct, use your program to complete the following table:

Radius (inches)	Area (square inches)
1.0	
1.5	
2.0	
2.5	
3.0	
3.5	

6a. Write, compile, and execute a FORTRAN program that displays the following prompts:

```
ENTER THE MILES DRIVEN:
ENTER THE GALLONS OF GAS USED:
```

After each prompt is displayed, your program should use a READ statement to accept data from the keyboard for the displayed prompt. After the gallons of gas used has been entered, your program should calculate and display miles per gallon obtained. This value should be included in an appropriate message and calculated using the equation *miles per gallon = miles / gallons used.* Verify your program using the following test data:

Test data set 1: miles = 276, gas = 10 gallons
Test data set 2: miles = 200, gas = 15.5 gallons

When you have completed your verification, use your program to complete the following table:

Miles driven	Gallons used	MPG
250	16	
275	18	
312	19.54	
296	17.39	

b. For the program written for Exercise 6a, determine how many verification runs are required to ensure the program is working correctly and give a reason supporting your answer.

7a. Write, compile, and execute a FORTRAN program that displays the following prompts:

```
ENTER A NUMBER:
ENTER A SECOND NUMBER:
ENTER A THIRD NUMBER:
ENTER A FOURTH NUMBER:
```

After each prompt is displayed, your program should use a READ statement to accept a number from the keyboard for the displayed prompt. After the fourth number has been entered, your program should calculate and display the average of the numbers. The average should be included in an appropriate message. Check the average displayed by your program using the following test data:

Test data set 1: 100, 100, 100, 100
Test data set 2: 100, 0, 100, 0

When you have completed your verification, use your program to complete the following table:

Numbers	Average
92, 98, 79, 85	
86, 84, 75, 86	
63, 85, 74, 82	

b. Repeat Exercise 7a, making sure that you use the same variable name, NUMBER, for each number input. Also use the variable SUM for the sum of the numbers. (*Hint:* To do this, you must use the statement SUM = SUM + NUMBER after each number is accepted. Review the material on accumulating presented in Section 2.3.)

8a. Write, compile, and execute a FORTRAN program that computes and displays the value of the second order polynomial $ax^2 + bx + c$ for any user-input values of the coefficients $a, b, c,$ and the variable x. Have your program first display a message informing the user as to what the program will do and then display suitable prompts to alert the user to enter the desired data. (*Hint:* Use a prompt such as ENTER THE COEFFICIENT OF THE X SQUARED TERM:)

b. Check the result produced by your program using the following test data:

Test data set 1: $a = 0, b = 0, c = 22, x = 56$
Test data set 2: $a = 0, b = 22, c = 0, x = 2$
Test data set 3: $a = 22, b = 0, c = 0, x = 2$
Test data set 4: $a = 2, b = 4, c = 5, x = 2$
Test data set 5: $a = 5, b = -3, c = 2, x = 1$

When you have completed your verification, use your program to complete the following table:

a	b	c	x	polynomial value
2	17	-12	1.3	
3.2	2	15	2.5	
3.2	2	15	-2.5	
-2	10	0	2	
-2	10	0	4	
-2	10	0	5	
-2	10	0	6	
5	22	18	8.3	
4.2	-16	-20	-5.2	

9. The number of bacteria, B, in a certain culture that is subject to refrigeration can be approximated by the equation $B = 300,000\ e^{-.032t}$, where t is the time, in hours, that the culture has been refrigerated. Using this equation, write, compile, and execute a single FORTRAN program that prompts the user for a value of time, calculates the number of bacteria in the culture, and displays the result. For testing purposes, check your program using a test input of 10 hours. When you have verified the operation of your program, use it to determine the number of bacteria in the culture after 12, 18, 24, 36, 48, and 72 hours.

10. Write, compile, and execute a program that calculates and displays the square root value of a user-entered real number. Recall that the square root of a number can be found by either using the SQRT function or by raising the number to the 1/2 power. (*Hint:* Do not use integer division—can you see why?) Verify your program by calculating the square roots of the following data: 25, 16, 0, and 2. When you have completed your verification, use your program to determine the square root of 32.25, 42, 48, 55, 63, and 79.

11. Write, compile, and execute a program that calculates and displays the fourth root of a user-entered number. Recall from elementary algebra that the fourth root of a number can be found either by using the SQRT function twice or by by raising the number to the 1/4 power. (*Hint:* Do not use integer division—can you see why?) Verify your program by calculating the fourth root of the following data: 81, 16, 1, and 0. When you have completed your verification, use your program to determine the fourth root of 42, 121, 256, 587, 1240, and 16,256.

12. For the series circuit shown in Figure 3-6, the voltage drop, V_2, across resistor R_2 and the power, P_2, delivered to this resistor are given by the equations $V_2 = I\,R_2$ and $P_2 = I\,V_2$, where $I = E / (R_1 + R_2)$. Using these equations, write, compile, and execute a FORTRAN program that prompts the user for values of E, R_1, and R_2, calculates the voltage drop and power delivered to R_2, and displays the results. Check your program using the test data $E = 10$ volts, $R_1 = 100$ ohms, and $R_2 = 200$ ohms. When you have completed your verification, use your program to complete the following table:

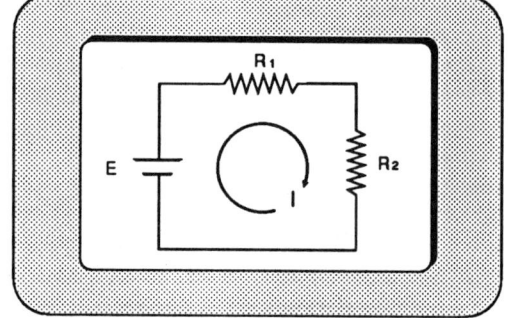

Figure 3-6   Calculating the Voltage Drop

E	R_1	R_2	Voltage drop	Power delivered
(volts)	(ohms)	(ohms)	(volts)	(watts)
10	100	100		
10	100	200		
10	200	200		
20	100	100		
20	100	200		
20	200	200		

13. Write, compile, and execute a FORTRAN program that computes the combined resistance of three parallel resistors. The values of each resistor should be accepted using a READ statement (use the formula for combined resistance given in Exercise 26 of Section 2.3). Verify the operation of your program by using the following test data:

Test data set 1: $R_1 = 1000$, $R_2 = 1000$, and $R_3 = 1000$
Test data set 2: $R_1 = 1000$, $R_2 = 1500$, and $R_3 = 500$

When you have completed your verification, use your program to complete the following table:

R_1 (volts)	R_2 (ohms)	R_3 (ohms)	Combined resistance (ohms)
3000	3000	3000	
6000	6000	6000	
2000	3000	1000	
2000	4000	5000	
4000	2000	1000	
10000	100	100	

14. Using READ statements, write, compile, and execute a FORTRAN program that accepts the x and y coordinates of two points. Have your program determine and display the midpoints of the two points (use the formula given in Exercise 28 of Section 2.3 on page 70). Verify your program using the following test data:

Test data set 1: point 1 = (0,0), point 2 = (16,0)
Test data set 2: point 1 = (0,0), point 2 = (0,16)
Test data set 3: point 1 = (0,0), point 2 = (–16,0)
Test data set 4: point 1 = (0,0), point 2 = (0,–16)
Test data set 5: point 1 = (–5,–5), point 2 = (5,5)

When you have completed your verification, use your program to complete the following table.

Point 1	Point 2	Midpoint
(4,6)	(16,18)	
(22,3)	(8,12)	
(–10,8)	(14,4)	
(–12,2)	(14,–4)	
(–4,–6)	(20,16)	
(–4,–6)	(–16,–18)	

15. Write, compile, and execute a FORTRAN program that calculates and displays the amount of money, A, available in N years when an initial deposit of X dollars is deposited in a bank account paying an annual interest rate of R percent. Use the relationship that $A = X(1.0 + R/100)^N$. The program should prompt the user to enter appropriate values and use READ statements to accept the data. In constructing your prompts, use statements such as ENTER THE AMOUNT OF THE INITIAL DEPOSIT. Verify the operation of your program by calculating by hand the amount of money available for the following test data:

Test data set 1: $1000 invested for 10 years at 0 percent interest
Test data set 2: $1000 invested for 10 years at 6 percent interest

When you have completed your verification, use your program to determine the amount of money available for the following cases:

a. $1000 invested for 10 years at 8 percent interest
b. $1000 invested for 10 years at 10 percent interest
c. $1000 invested for 10 years at 12 percent interest
d. $5000 invested for 15 years at 8 percent interest
e. $5000 invested for 15 years at 10 percent interest
f. $5000 invested for 15 years at 12 percent interest
g. $24 invested for 300 years at 4 percent interest

16. Program 3-4 prompts the user to input two numbers, where the first value entered is stored in FIRNUM and the second value is stored in SECNUM. Using this program as a starting point, write a program that swaps the values stored in the two variables.

17. Write a FORTRAN program that prompts the user to type in an integer number. Have your program accept the number as an integer and immediately display the integer using a PRINT statement. Run your program three times. The first time you run the program, enter a valid integer number, the second time enter a real number, and the third time enter a character constant (recall that a character constant must be surrounded by apostrophes). Using the output display, see what number your program actually accepted from the data you entered. What happened, if anything, and why?

18. Repeat Exercise 17 but have your program declare the variable used to store the number as a real variable. Run the program four times. The first time enter an integer, the second time enter a decimal number with less than six decimal places, the third time enter a number having more than six decimal places, and the fourth time enter a character constant (recall that a character constant must be surrounded by apostrophes). Using the output display, keep track of what number your program actually accepted from the data you typed in. What happened, if anything, and why?

19. Repeat Exercise 17 but have your program declare the variable used to store the number as a character variable having a length of four characters. Run the program four times. The first time enter character data having four or fewer characters (recall that input character data must be surrounded by apostrophes), the second time enter a character constant having more than four characters, the third time enter an integer, and the fourth time enter a decimal number. Using the output display, keep track of what value your program actually accepted from the data you typed in. What happened, if anything, and why?

20a. Why do you think that most successful applications programs contain extensive data input validity checks? (*Hint:* Review Exercises 17, 18, and 19.)

 b. What do you think is the difference between a data type check and a data reasonableness check?

 c. Assume that a program requests that the velocity and acceleration of a car be entered by the user. What are some checks that could be made on the data entered?

3.3   The Formatted READ Statement *

Just as the list-directed output statements PRINT and WRITE have their user-formatted counterparts, the list-directed READ statements do also. As with the list-directed READ statements, the user-formatted counterparts come in two forms. The most general of these forms is:

```
READ (unit number, format specifier) variable list
```

where unit number designates where the input will be entered and the format specifier designates the specific spacing of the input data on the input unit. Acceptable format specifiers include:

1. an asterisk, which specifies a list-directed format
2. the statement number of a FORMAT statement
3. a literal format control character constant, enclosed in parentheses surrounded by apostrophes

For user-selected input formatting, the last two options are used. For example, assuming that the variables NUM1 and NUM2 have been declared as integers, the statement:

```
READ (1,10) NUM1, NUM2
```

specifies that the two integers are to be read from unit number 1 using the format defined in FORMAT statement 10. For purposes of illustration, assume the following FORMAT statement:

```
10 FORMAT(I2,3X,I4)
```

This FORMAT statement specifies that the input line consists of two integer fields separated by three spaces. The first integer must occupy columns 1 and 2 of the line and the second 6 through 9.

Using this format demands that the entered data conform exactly to the fields specified. For example, assuming that unit number 1 corresponds to the standard input device, consider the sequence of statements:

```
      INTEGER NUM1, NUM2
      READ (1,10) NUM1, NUM2
10 FORMAT(I2,3X,I4)
```

If the data entered is:

```
45   6732        ←——— data entered
123456789        ←——— column number
```

the value 45 is assigned to the variable NUM1 and the value 6732 is assigned to NUM2. If instead the data entered is placed as follows:

```
4   673 2        ←——— data entered
123456789        ←——— column number
```

---

* This topic may be omitted on first reading without loss of subject continuity.

the number 4 is assigned to NUM1 and the number 732 is assigned to NUM2. Note that the blanks embedded in each field are effectively ignored. *

As illustrated by this example, a FORMAT statement by itself is neither an input or a output format. The format refers to an input line only because it is referenced by a READ statement. Additionally, when a format specification is used for input, the first character is not interpreted as a carriage control code. Carriage control only has meaning in a format specification used for output. The format specifications for reading integer, real, and character data and for skipping over designated input fields, as expected, are essentially the same as those used for writing these items and are presented at the end of this section.

Default to Standard Input

In addition to the more general form of the user-formatted READ statement that can receive input from any device, an alternate form is provided in FORTRAN 77 for standard input data entry. This alternate form is:

```
READ k, list of variables
```

Here, the term READ k, is equivalent to the term READ (n,k), where n is the unit number of the standard input device, and k is a reference to a FORMAT statement. As an example of this alternate form, consider the sequence of statements:

```
    INTEGER NUM1, NUM2
    READ 10, NUM1, NUM2
10 FORMAT(I4,I3)
```

This form of the READ statement designates that the data will be entered at the standard input device. The referenced FORMAT statement specifies that the input line entered at the standard input device consists of two integer fields, the first of which occupies columns 1 through 4 of the line and the second of which occupies columns 5, 6, and 7.

Assuming that the keyboard is the standard input unit, if the data entered at the keyboard in response to these statements is:

```
4567329        ←—— data entered
1234567        ←—— column number
```

the value 4567 is assigned to the variable NUM1 and the value 329 is assigned to NUM2. If instead the following data is entered:

```
4567 123       ←—— data entered
123456789      ←—— column number
```

the number 456, which is the contents of columns 1 through 4, is assigned to NUM1, and the contents of columns 5, 6, and 7, which is interpreted as the number 71, is assigned to NUM2.** Note that the blank in column 6 is effectively ignored.

In the early days of FORTRAN, during the 1960s and 1970s, the standard input device was almost always a card reader. For these devices, which read a standard

---

* Some FORTRAN compilers consider embedded blanks to be zeros.

** For compilers that consider embedded blanks to be zeros, NUM2 would be assigned the number 710.

card having 80 columns, explicit user-designated formatting was the preferred method of data entry. Such formatting allowed cards to be prepared by data entry clerks using a standard format. The cards were then read by the program using an appropriate FORMAT statement. Although user-formatted input is still defined for keyboard input, it is rarely used for this purpose because of the additional level of complexity that is not present in its free-form list-directed counterpart. Nevertheless, user-formatted input does have its place. Typically, it is used with the first form of the READ statement presented for reading data stored on a medium such as a magnetic disk or tape. The use of user formatting for these storage mediums can result in savings of storage space due to the fixed-form field widths employed. The saving of storage space will become clearer when we encounter user-formatted input of data files in Chapter 9.

Input Edit Descriptors

The commonly used edit descriptors for user-formatted input are essentially the same as those used for user-formatted output. They are presented below as they relate to data input.

Integer Input

The I edit descriptor is used for reading user-formatted integer data. The form of this descriptor, which is the same as for user-formatted integer data output, is:

$$\boxed{r\text{I}w}$$

where r is the repeat factor, I denotes an integer, and w is the width of the integer field. For example, the statements:

```
   INTEGER I, J, K
   READ (2,10) I, J, K
10 FORMAT(I3,I4,I5)
```

specify an input line of three integer fields having lengths of 3, 4, and 5 columns, respectively. For the following input line:

```
678 -3 4   29
123456789111
         012
```
↑
Column number 1

the number 678 is assigned to I, -3 to J, and 429 to K. Note that blanks are ignored in an input field, and a number can be placed in any position within a field.*

---

* Again, some compilers interpret embedded blanks as zeros.

Real Number Input

The F edit descriptor can be used for reading real numbers. The form of this descriptor, which is the same as for user-formatted real data output, is:

$$rFw.d$$

where r is the repeat factor, F denotes a real number, w denotes total field width, and d denotes the number of digits to the right of the decimal point. If a decimal point is included in the input number, the number can be placed anywhere within the defined field. For example, the statements:

```
     REAL A, B, C
     READ (2,10) A, B, C
 10  FORMAT(F6.2,2F4.1)
```

define three input fields: the first has a field width of 6, and the next two, because of the repeat count, both have field widths of 4. For the following input line:

```
 54.23 6.1 9.6
 12345678911111
         01234
```

↑
Column number 1

the value 54.23 within the first field is assigned to *A*, the value 6.1 in the second field is assigned to *B*, and the value 9.6 in the third field is assigned to *C*. Within the three fields, each number can be placed in any position without affecting the values assigned to the variables *A, B,* and *C*.

The decimal point actually can be omitted from a user-formatted real number. When the decimal point is omitted in the input data, the *d* format specification automatically assigns the last *d* positions in the field as the fractional part of the number. For example, if the previous input line was:

```
 5423   61   96
 12345678911111
         01234
```

↑
Column number 1

the same values as before are assigned to the variables *A, B,* and *C*.

Real values may also be entered in scientific notation using the F edit descriptor. For example, the numbers 1.79E2, .925E+2, and 26.7E–3 may all be placed in fields described by the F descriptor. When the exponent is preceded by a sign, as in the numbers .925E+2 and 26.7E–3, the E can be omitted. Thus, these two numbers can also be stored in their defined fields as .925+2 and 26.7–3.

Character Input

The A edit descriptor is used for reading formatted character data. As with output, the input version of the A edit descriptor has the two forms:

$$\boxed{r\text{A and }r\text{A}w}$$

where *r* is a repeat factor, A denotes character data, and *w* is an optional field width specifier. In the first form, the character field is determined by the length declared for the variable in its CHARACTER declaration. For example, the statements:

```
    CHARACTER STRNG1*3, STRNG2*4, STRNG3*5
    READ (2,10) STRNG1, STRNG2, STRNG3
10  FORMAT (3A)
```

define three character variables of length 3, 4, and 5, respectively, and three corresponding field lengths. For the following input line:

```
NOW IS THE TIME
123456789111111
        012345
```

↑
Column number 1

the character constant NOW is assigned to STRNG1, the constant bISb (where b denotes a blank space) is assigned to STRNG2, and the constant THEbT is assigned to STRNG3. As with all data input, any extra data on a line are ignored. Note that character data entered in response to a user-formatted input statement do not require apostrophes surrounding the input data. (As noted previously, apostrophes are required when entering data in response to a list-directed READ statement.)

When a field width is used with the A edit descriptor, it defines the width of the input character field. If this field width is larger than the length declared for the character variable, the rightmost characters in the input field up to the number of characters declared for the variable are used. If the field width is smaller than the length declared for the character variable, the input characters are stored, left justified in the character variable, and the remaining positions in the variable are padded with trailing blanks. For example, the statements:

```
    CHARACTER*4 STRNG1, STRNG2, STRNG3
    READ (2,10) STRNG1, STRNG2, STRNG3
10  FORMAT (A4,A6,A2)
```

define three character variables of length 4, and three input fields of widths 4, 6, and 2, respectively. For the following input line:

```
RAREEARTHMETALS
123456789111111
        012345
```

↑
Column number 1

the characters RARE in the first field of four are assigned to STRNG1. In the second field of six, the rightmost four characters, RTHM, are assigned to STRNG2, and the first two characters in the field are ignored. Finally, the two characters ET in the third field are padded with two trailing blank spaces and assigned to STRNG3. The rest of the characters on the line are considered extra input and are ignored.

Positional Editing

The X, T, and TR positional edit descriptors can be used to skip over designated columns of input data. For example, the statement:

```
10 FORMAT(1X,I4,3X,F5.2)
```

specifies four input fields. The first field consists of one column, the second is an integer field four spaces wide, the third is a field of three columns, and the fourth is a real field five spaces wide. Fields specified by the X edit descriptor are skipped over on input. This means that any data in these fields is ignored.

The TR (tab right) edit descriptor works in the same manner as the X edit descriptor. For example, the statement:

```
20 FORMAT(TR4,F5.2,TR7,F7.3)
```

is exactly equivalent to the statement:

```
20 FORMAT(4X,F5.2,7X,F7.3)
```

Finally, the T edit descriptor specifies an absolute column position in the input line. For example, the statement:

```
20 FORMAT(T20,I4)
```

specifies that the designated integer field begins at column 20 in the line.

Exercises

1. For the following READ statements, write appropriate variable declaration statements.

```
a.    READ (1,10) WATTS
   10 FORMAT(F8.2)
b.    READ (5,20) TEMP
   20 FORMAT(F5.2)
c.    READ (*,30) COUNT
   30 FORMAT(I4)
d.    READ (1,40) NUM1, NUM2, VALUE, CH1
   40 FORMAT(I4,I5,F3.2,A6)
e.    READ (5,50) COUNT, VOLTS, OHMS
   50 FORMAT(I2,2F6.2)
f.    READ (*,60) AVERGE, IFLAG, KEY, CODE
   60 FORMAT(F7.3,I1,2A6)
```

2. Given the following declaration statements:

```
INTEGER NUM1,NUM2
REAL TEMP, AMBINT
CHARACTER*5 VAL1, VAL2
```

determine and correct the errors in the following statements. Assume that the maximum integer value that will be read into NUM1 and NUM2 is 9999 and that the real variables TEMP and AMBINT have a maximum integer part of 999 with at most three digits to the right of the decimal point.

```
a.    READ (1,10,NUM1)
b.    READ (5,20) (NUM1,NUM2,NUM3)
c.    READ (*,30),TEMP,AMBINT
```

```
d.      READ (1,10) NUM1
    10 FORMAT(F5.2)
e.      READ (5,20) NUM1, TEMP, VAL1
    20 FORMAT(3I4)
f.      READ (*,30) NUM1, AMBINT, VAL1
    30 FORMAT(A,I2,F7.4)
```

3. List the starting and ending column numbers for all input fields defined by the following statements:

a. 10 FORMAT(I4,F5.2,I5)

b. 20 FORMAT(F5.3,I6,A8)

c. 30 FORMAT(1X,F5.2,2X,A20)

d. 40 FORMAT(2(1X,I5))

e. 60 FORMAT(1X,2(I3,2X),F5.2,2(1X,I3))

4. The following is a valid FORTRAN program.

```
PROGRAM MAIN
    INTEGER NUM1, NUM2
    READ (*,10)NUM1, NUM2
10  FORMAT(I4,I3)
    PRINT *, NUM1, NUM2
    END
```

When this program is run, the user enters the data 1 234 5. For this data input, determine the output produced by the program.

5. Determine if the following program will work. Discuss what should be changed in the program, if anything.

```
PROGRAM MAIN
    CHARACTER*8, MESSGE
    INTEGER NUM1, NUM2
    READ (5,10) MESSGE, NUM1, NUM2
    WRITE(6,10) MESSGE, NUM1, NUM2
10  FORMAT(1X,A,2(1X,I3))
    END
```

6a. Write, compile, and run a FORTRAN program that accepts two integer numbers from the standard input device using the FORMAT statement:

10 FORMAT(I2,I4)

The program should display the numbers entered to verify correct data input.

b. Determine what your program will display for the following data input line:

```
45678           ←—— data entered
123456          ←—— column number
```

c. Verify your answer to Exercise 6b by running your program and entering the designated input line.

7a. Write, compile, and run a FORTRAN program that accepts two real numbers from the standard input device using the FORMAT statement:

10 FORMAT(1X,F7.2,2X,F5.2)

The program should display the numbers entered to verify correct data input.

b. Determine what your program will display for the following data input line:

```
    6.78     23.4  ←— data entered
12345678911111
         01234
↑
Column number 1
```

c. Determine what your program will display for the following data input line:

```
6.78      23.4   ←— data entered
123456789111
         012
↑
Column number 1
```

d. Determine what your program will display for the following data input line:

```
      678 234    ←— data entered
123456789111111
         012345
↑
Column number 1
```

e. Verify your answers to Exercises 7b, 7c, and 7d by running your program and entering the designated input line.

f. Run the program written for Exercise 7a using the following data input line:

```
 678          234  ←— data entered
12345678911111
         01234
↑
Column number 1
```

Using the display produced by your program determine how your compiler interprets trailing blank spaces in an input field.

8. Write, compile, and execute a FORTRAN program that accepts four real numbers from the standard input device using the FORMAT statement:

```
10 FORMAT(4(1X,F5.2))
```

Your program should read the input, determine the average of the four numbers read, and display the average. Verify the output produced by your program using the following test data:

Test data set 1: 100, 100, 100, 100
Test data set 2: 100, 0, 100, 0

When you have completed your verification, use your program to complete the following table:

Numbers	Average
92, 98, 79, 85	
86, 84, 75, 86	
63, 85, 74, 82	

9. Using the FORMAT statement:

```
10 FORMAT(4(1X,F6.2))
```

write, compile, and execute a FORTRAN program that reads an input line and interprets the first and second numbers on the input line as the coordinates of one point and the third and fourth numbers as the coordinates of a second point. Using the formula given in Exercise 28 of Section 2.3, have your program compute and display the midpoint of the two points entered. Verify your program using the following test data:

Test data set 1: point 1 = (0,0), point 2 = (16,0)
Test data set 2: point 1 = (0,0), point 2 = (0,16)
Test data set 3: point 1 = (0,0), point 2 = (–16,0)
Test data set 4: point 1 = (0,0), point 2 = (0,–16)
Test data set 5: point 1 = (–5,–5), point 2 = (5,5)

When you have completed your verification, use your program to complete the following table:

Point 1	Point 2	Midpoint
(4, 6)	(16, 18)	
(22, 3)	(8, 12)	
(6.3, 8.2)	(18.25, 24.32)	
(4.0, 4.0)	(10.0, –5.0)	
(–2.0, 5.0)	(4.0, 5.0)	

3.4   Named Constants: The PARAMETER Statement

Certain constants used within a program may have a more general meaning that is recognized outside the context of the program. Examples of these types of constants include the number 3.1416, which is the value of *pi* accurate to four decimal places; 32.2 ft/sec^2, which is the gravitational constant (see, for example, Program 3-1); and the number 2.71828, which is Euler's number accurate to five decimal places.

The meaning of certain other constants appearing in a program is defined strictly within the context of the application being programmed. For example, in a program to determine bank interest charges, the value of the interest rate takes on a special meaning. Similarly, in determining the weight of various-sized objects, the density of the material being used takes on a special significance. Numbers such as these are referred to by programmers as *magic numbers*. By themselves the numbers are quite ordinary, but in the context of a particular application they have a special ("magical") meaning. Frequently, the same magic number appears repeatedly within the same program. This recurrence of the same constant throughout a program is a potential source of error should the constant have to be changed. For example, if the interest rate changes, or a new material is employed with a different density, the programmer will have the cumbersome task of changing the value of the magic number everywhere it appears in the program. Multiple changes, however, are subject to error: if just one value is overlooked and not changed, the result obtained when the program is run will be incorrect.

To avoid the problems of having a magic number spread throughout a program and to clearly permit identification of more universal constants, such as *pi,* FORTRAN allows the programmer to give these constants their own symbolic names. Then, instead of using the constant throughout the program, the symbolic name is used instead. In the case of magic numbers, should the number ever need to be changed, the change can be made once at the point where the symbolic name is equated to the actual constant value.

Equating constants to symbolic names is accomplished using the PARAMETER statement. The general form of this statement is:

```
PARAMETER (name1 = expression, name2 = expression, etc.)
```

For example, the number 3.1416 can be equated to the symbolic name PI using the PARAMETER statement:

```
PARAMETER (PI = 3.1416)
```

Constants named in this fashion are called both *named constants* and *symbolic constants,* and we shall use both terms interchangeably.

Once a constant has been named, the name can be used in any FORTRAN statement in place of the number itself. For example, the assignment statement:

```
CIRCUM = 2 * PI * RADIUS
```

makes use of the named constant PI. This statement must, of course, appear after PI has been named in a PARAMETER statement. As with variables, the names of the symbolic constants must be declared prior to being used in a PARAMETER statement. For example, the naming of PI would be used with a declaration statement as follows:

```
REAL PI
PARAMETER (PI = 3.1416)
```

Other than the requirement that a PARAMETER statement must appear after the declarations for its named constants, PARAMETER and declaration statements can be freely intermixed. Both types of statements must, however, be placed at the top of a program unit immediately following the program unit's header line. Program 3-7 illustrates the use of a PARAMETER statement to calculate the weight of a steel cylinder. The density of the steel is 0.284 lb/in^3.

Notice in Program 3-7 that a single PARAMETER statement defines two named constants: PI and DENSTY. The following run was made using Program 3-7 to determine the weight of a cylinder with a radius of 3 inches and a height of 12 inches.

```
ENTER THE RADIUS OF THE CYLINDER
3
ENTER THE HEIGHT OF THE CYLINDER
12
 THE CYLINDER WEIGHS        96.359150 POUNDS.
```

Program 3-7

```
      PROGRAM MAIN
*** THIS PROGRAM DETERMINES THE WEIGHT OF A STEEL CYLINDER
*** BY MULTIPLYING THE VOLUME OF THE CYLINDER TIMES ITS DENSITY
*** THE VOLUME OF A CYLINDER IS (PI * RADIUS**2 * HEIGHT)
      REAL PI, DENSTY, RADIUS, HEIGHT, WEIGHT
      PARAMETER (PI = 3.1416, DENSTY = 0.284)
      PRINT *, 'ENTER THE RADIUS OF THE CYLINDER'
      READ *, RADIUS
      PRINT *, 'ENTER THE HEIGHT OF THE CYLINDER'
      READ *, HEIGHT
      WEIGHT = DENSTY * PI * RADIUS**2 * HEIGHT
      PRINT *, ' THE CYLINDER WEIGHS ', WEIGHT, ' POUNDS.'
      END
```

The advantage of using the named constant PI in Program 3-7 is that it clearly identifies the value 3.1416 in terms recognizable to most people. The advantage of using the named constant DENSTY is that it permits a programmer to change the value of the density for another material without having to search through the program to see where the density is used. Of course, if many different materials are to be considered, the density should be changed from a named constant to a variable. A natural question arises, then, as to the difference between named constants and variables.

The value of a variable can be altered anywhere within a program. By its nature a named constant is a constant value that must not be altered after it is defined. Naming a constant rather than assigning the value to a variable ensures that the value in the constant cannot be subsequently altered. Whenever a named constant appears in an instruction, it has the same effect as the constant it represents. Thus, DENSTY in Program 3-7 is simply another way of representing the number 0.284. Since DENSTY and the number 0.284 are equivalent, the value of DENSTY may not be changed subsequently within the program. Once DENSTY has been defined as a constant, an assignment statement such as:

```
DENSTY = 0.156
```

is meaningless and will result in an error message, because DENSTY is not a variable. Since DENSTY is only a substitute for the value 0.284, this statement is equivalent to writing the invalid statement 0.284 = 0.156.

In addition to using the PARAMETER statement to name constants, as in Program 3-7, this statement can also be used to equate the value of a constant expression to a symbolic name. A *constant expression* is an expression consisting of operators and constants only. For example, the statement:

```
PARAMETER (CONVRT = 3.1416/180.0)
```

equates the value of the constant expression 3.1416/180.0 to the symbolic name CONVRT. The symbolic name, as always, can be used in any statement following its definition. For example, since the expression 3.1416/180.0 is required for converting degrees to radians, the symbolic name selected for this conversion factor can be conveniently used whenever such a conversion is required. Thus, in the assignment statement:

```
HEIGHT = DISTNC * SIN(ANGLE*CONVRT)
```

the symbolic constant CONVRT is used to convert the value in ANGLE to radian measure.

A previously defined named constant can also be used in a subsequent PARAM-ETER statement. For example, the following sequence of statements is valid:

```
REAL PI, CONVRT
PARAMETER (PI = 3.1416, CONVRT = PI/180.)
```

Since the constant 3.1416 has been equated to the symbolic name PI, it can be used legitimately in any subsequent definition, even within the same PARAMETER statement. Program 3-8 uses the named constant CONVRT to convert a user-entered angle, in degrees, into its equivalent radian measure for use by the SIN function.

 Program 3-8

```
PROGRAM MAIN
  REAl PI, CONVRT, ANGLE
  PARAMETER (PI = 3.1416, CONVRT = PI/180.0)
  PRINT *, 'ENTER THE ANGLE (IN DEGREES)'
  READ *, ANGLE
  PRINT *, ' THE SINE OF THE ANGLE IS ', SIN(ANGLE*CONVRT)
  END
```

Following is a sample run using Program 3-8:

```
ENTER THE ANGLE (IN DEGREES)
30
 THE SINE OF THE ANGLE IS 5.000000 E-01
```

The use of PARAMETER statements is not restricted to integer and real constants. A constant of any data type can be named, with the only requirement being that the data type of the named constant be declared and a constant of the correct type be equated to the declared name. For example, the pair of statements:

```
CHARACTER*7 UNITS
PARAMETER (UNITS = 'NANOSEC')
```

declares UNITS to be a symbolic name of type CHARACTER. Its use in the PARAMETER changes its status to a symbolic constant (it no longer can be used as a variable) and equates a constant of the correct data type to it.

A useful feature in defining a symbolic character constant is that the length of the constant need not be specified in the declaration statement. If the "dummy" length specifier, (*), is used in the declaration statement, the actual length of the character constant is determined by the compiler when the PARAMETER statement is encountered. Thus, the previous declaration for UNITS can be replaced by the declaration:

```
CHARACTER*(*) UNITS
```

The use of the "dummy" length specifier makes subsequent modifications to the named constant much easier because it eliminates the need to count the length of each character string. For example, if it is required to change UNITS to 'NANOSECONDS', all that needs to be modified is the PARAMETER statement. The new PARAMETER statement becomes:

```
PARAMETER (UNITS = 'NANOSECONDS')
```

and no change to the declaration for UNITS is necessary.

Statement Ordering

We have introduced a variety of statements. In using the various statement types, certain placement rules must be followed. For the statements we have presented these rules are:

1. The END statement must be the last statement of every program unit. This statement consists of the keyword END with no spaces allowed between any of the letters (on some compilers spaces are permitted).
2. Comment lines may appear anywhere in a program unit, except as the last line of a program unit.
3. FORMAT statements may appear anywhere between the program header line and the END statement.
4. PARAMETER and declaration statements, which collectively (along with additional statements to be introduced) are referred to as *specification* statements, may be intermixed and must appear before all executable statements. Executable statements, which may be freely intermixed, include all assignment, WRITE, PRINT, and READ statements.

A review of Programs 3-7 and 3-8 will verify that they adhere to these statement placement rules. Any violations of these rules will result in a compiler error message.

Figure 3-7 summarizes the relationships described by these statement placement rules. Horizontal lines in the figure indicate statement types that cannot be intermixed. For example, the line between PARAMETER and assignment statements indicates that these two types of statements must not be intermixed. Since PARAMETER statements appear above the line, all PARAMETER statements in a program unit must appear before any assignment statement is used. Similarly, all of the other statements below this same line, such as the PRINT statement, cannot be intermixed with any statement above the line. Thus, PRINT statements cannot be intermixed with either program header lines or PARAMETER statements, and all PRINT statements must appear after the last PARAMETER statement in a program unit.

Statements separated by dashed vertical lines in Figure 3-7 can be freely intermixed. Thus, comment lines can be intermixed with any statement in a program unit except for an END statement. Similarly, FORMAT statements may appear anywhere between the program header line and END statement and may be intermixed with any other statement within these two bounds.

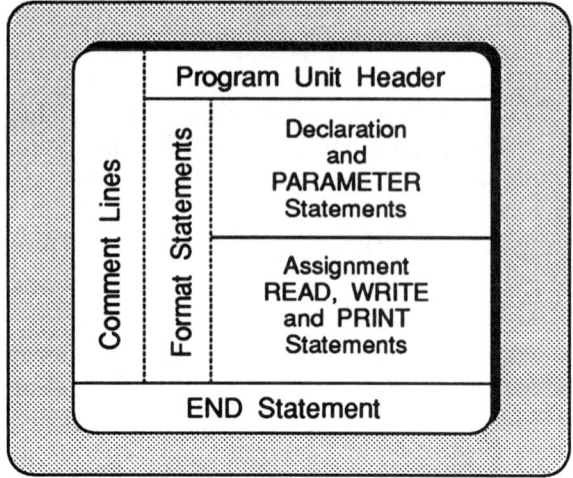

Figure 3-7   Required Statement Placement

Exercises

1. Modify Program 3-1 to use the named constant GRAV in place of the value 32.2 used in the program. Compile and execute your program to verify that it produces the same result as shown in the text.

2. Modify Program 3-6 to use the named constant FACTOR in place of the expression (5.0/9.0) used in the program. Compile and execute your program to verify that it produces the same result as shown in the text.

3. Rewrite the following program using a PARAMETER statement for the constant 3.1416.

```
PROGRAM MAIN
   REAL RADIUS, CIRCUM, AREA
   PRINT *, 'ENTER A RADIUS'
   READ *, RADIUS
   CIRCUM = 2.0 * 3.1416 * RADIUS
   AREA = 3.1416 * RADIUS**2
   PRINT *, 'THE CIRCUMFERENCE IS ', CIRCUM
   PRINT *, 'THE AREA IS ', AREA
   END
```

4. Rewrite the following program so that the variable PRIME is changed to a named constant.

```
PROGRAM MAIN
   REAL PRIME, AMOUNT, INTRST
   PRIME = 0.08
   PRINT *, 'ENTER THE AMOUNT' READ *, AMOUNT
   INTRST = PRIME * AMOUNT
   PRINT *, 'THE INTEREST EARNED IS ', INTRST
   END
```

3.5   Applications

In this section we present two applications to further illustrate both the use of READ statements to accept user input data and the use of intrinsic functions for performing calculations.

Application 1: Acid Rain

The use of coal as the major source of steam power began with the Industrial Revolution. Currently, coal is one of the principal sources of generating electrical power in many industrialized countries.

Since the middle of the nineteenth century it has been known that the oxygen used in the burning process combines with the carbon and sulfur in the coal to produce both carbon dioxide and sulfur dioxide. When these gases are released into the atmosphere, the sulfur dioxide combines with the water and oxygen in the air to form sulfuric acid, which itself is transformed into separate hydronium ions and sulfates (see Figure 3-8). It is the hydronium ions in the atmosphere that fall to earth, either as components of rain or as a dry deposit, which changes the acidity level of lakes and forests.

The acid level of rain and lakes is measured on a pH scale using the formula:

$$pH = -Log_{10} \text{ (concentration of hydronium ions)}$$

where the concentration of hydronium ions is measured in units of moles/liter. A pH value of 7 indicates a neutral value (neither acid nor alkaline), while levels below 7 indicate the presence of an acid, and levels above 7 indicate the presence of an

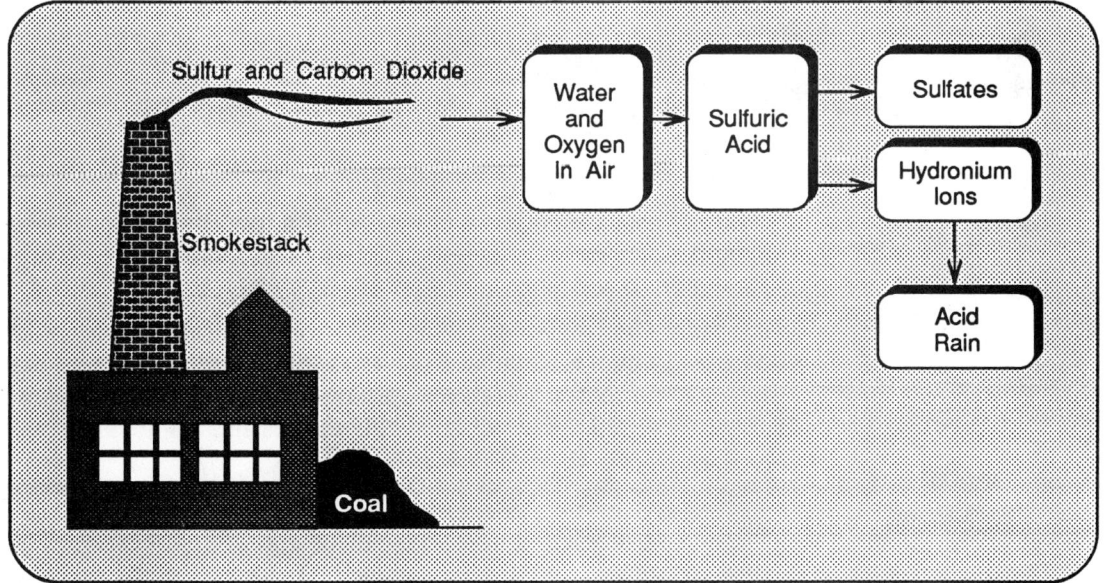

Figure 3-8   The Formation of Acid Rain

alkaline substance. For example, sulfuric acid has a pH value of approximately 1, lye has a pH value of approximately 13, and water typically has a pH value of 7. Marine life usually cannot survive in water with a pH level below 4.

Using the formula for pH, we will write a FORTRAN program that calculates the pH level of a substance based on a user-input value for the concentration of hydronium ions.

Program Development

Using the top-down development procedure described in Chapter 2, we have:

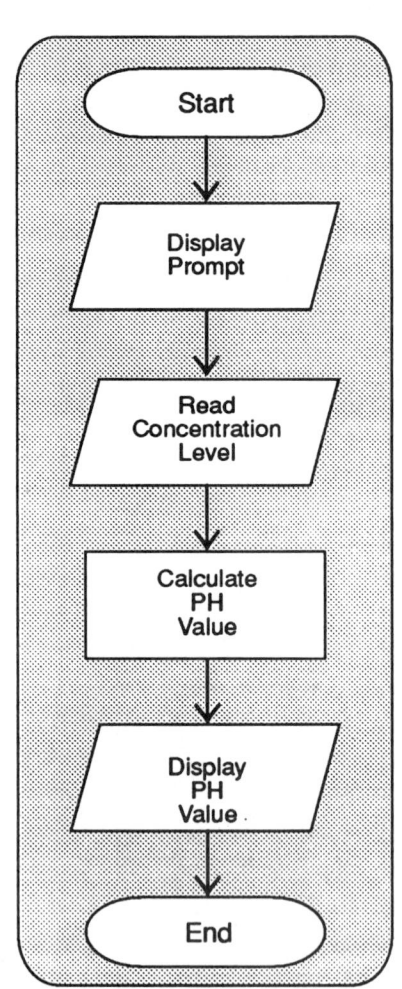

Figure 3-9 The Selected Algorithm as a Flowchart

Step 1: Determine the Desired Outputs

Although the statement of the problem provides technical information on the composition of acid rain, from a programming viewpoint this is a rather simple problem. Here there is only one required output: a pH level.

Step 2: Determine the Input Items

For this problem there is only one input item, the concentration level of hydronium ions.

Step 3a: Determine an Algorithm

The processing required to transform the input to the required output is a rather straightforward use of the pH formula provided. The flowchart representation of the complete algorithm for entering the input data, processing the data to produce the desired output, and displaying the output is illustrated in Figure 3-9.

The pseudocode representation of the algorithm depicted in Figure 3-9 is:

Display a prompt to enter an ion concentration level
Read a value for the concentration level
Calculate a PH level using the given formula
Display the calculated value

Step 3b: Do a Hand Calculation

To ensure that we understand the formula used in the algorithm, we will do a hand calculation. We can use the result of this calculation to verify the result produced by the program.

Assuming a hydronimum concentration of .0001 (any value would do), the pH level is calculated as $- \text{LOG}_{10} \, 10^{-4}$. Either by knowing that the logarithm of 10 raised to a power is the power itself, or by using a log table, the value of this expressions is found to be $-(-4) = 4$.

Step 3c: Select Variable Names

The last step required before the selected algorithm is described in FORTRAN is to select variable names for the input, output, and any intermediate variables required by the algorithm. For this problem we will select the variable names HYDRON for the input variable and PHLEVL for the calculated pH level (any valid variable name could have been selected).

Step 4: Write the Program

Program 3-9 describes the selected algorithm in FORTRAN using the variable names chosen in Step 3c.

 Program 3-9

```
PROGRAM MAIN
    REAL HYDRON, PHLEVL
    PRINT *, 'ENTER THE HYDRONIUM ION CONCENTRATION LEVEL:
    READ *, HYDRON
    PHLEVL = - ALOG10 (HYDRON)
    PRINT *, 'THE PH LEVEL IS: ',PHLEVL
    END
```

Program 3-9 begins with a program header line and a declaration statement that declares two real variables, HYDRON and PHLEVL. The program then displays a prompt requesting input data from the user. After the prompt is displayed, a READ statement is used to store the entered data in the variable HYDRON. Finally, a value for PHLEVL is calculated, using the intrinsic logarithmic function, and displayed. As always, the program is terminated with an END statement.

Step 5: Test the Program

A test run using Program 3-9 produced the following:

```
ENTER THE HYDRONIUM ION CONCENTRATION LEVEL:
0.0001
THE PH LEVEL IS: 4.000000
```

As the program performs a single calculation, and the result of this test run agrees with our previous hand calculation, the program has been completely tested. It now can be used to calculate the pH level of other hydronium concentrations with confidence that the results being produced are accurate.

Application 2: Sine Approximation

The sine of an angle x, in radians, can be approximated using the polynomial:

$$x - \frac{x^3}{6} + \frac{x^5}{120}$$

Using this polynomial, write a program that approximates the sine of a user-entered angle using the first, second, and third terms, respectively, of the approximating polynomial. For each approximation, display the value calculated by FORTRAN's intrinsic sine function, the approximate value, and the absolute difference between the two. Make sure to verify your program using a hand calculation. Once the verification is complete, use the program to approximate the sine of 62.5 degrees.

Program Development

Using the top-down development procedure described in Chapter 2, we have:

Step 1: Determine the Desired Outputs

This program requires a total of nine outputs, arrived at as follows: the statement of the problem specifies that three approximations are to be made, using one, two, and three terms of the approximating polynomial, respectively. For each approximation to the sine, three output values are required: the value of the sine produced by the intrinsic SIN function, the approximation value, and the absolute difference between the two values. Figure 3-10 illustrates, in symbolic form, the structure of the required output display.

Sine	Approximation	Difference
Intrinsic Function Value	1st Approximate Value	1st Difference
Intrinsic Function Value	2nd Approximate Value	2nd Difference
Intrinsic Function Value	3rd Approximate Value	3rd Difference

Figure 3-10   Required Output Display

The output indicated in Figure 3-10 can be used to get a feel for what the program must look like. Realizing that each line in the display can be produced only by executing either a PRINT or a WRITE statement, it should be clear that three such statements must be executed. Additionally, since each output line contains three computed values, each PRINT or WRITE statement executed will have three items in its expression list.

Step 2: Determine the Input Items

The only input to the program consists of the angle whose sine is to be approximated. This will require a single prompt and a READ statement to input the necessary value.

Step 3a: Determine an Algorithm

Before any output item can be calculated, it will be necessary to have the program prompt the user for an input angle and then have the program accept a user-entered value. Since this angle will be in degrees, and both the SIN function and the approximating polynomial require radian measure, the input angle will have to be converted into radians.

The actual output display consists of two header lines followed by three lines of calculated data. The heading lines can be produced using two PRINT or WRITE statements. Now let us see how the actual data being displayed is produced.

The first item on the first data output line illustrated in Figure 3-10, the sine of the angle, can be obtained using the SIN( ) function. The second item on this line, the approximation to the sine, can be obtained by using the first term in the polynomial that was given in the program specification. Finally, the third item on the line can be calculated using the ABS( ) function on the difference between the first two items. When all of these items are calculated, a single PRINT or WRITE statement can be used to display the three results on the same line.

The second output line illustrated in Figure 3-10 displays the same type of items as the first line, except that the approximation to the sine requires using two terms of the approximating polynomial. Notice also that the first item on the second line, the sine of the angle, is the same as the first item on the first line. This means that this item does not have to be recalculated, and the value calculated for the first line can simply be displayed a second time. Once the data for the second line has been calculated, a single PRINT or WRITE statement can be used to display the required values.

Finally, only the second and third items on the last output line shown in Figure 3-10 need to be recalculated, since the first item on this line is the same as previously calculated for the first line. The second item on the third line is calculated using all three terms of the polynomial, and the last item on this line is obtained as the absolute difference between the first two items. Once the data for this last line has been calculated, a single PRINT or WRITE statement can be used to display the complete line.

Thus, for this problem, the complete algorithm described in pseudocode is:

> *Display a prompt for the input angle*
> *Read an angle in degrees*
> *Convert the angle to radian measure*
> *Display the heading lines*
> *Calculate the sine of the angle*
> *Calculate the first approximation*
> *Calculate the first difference*
> *Print the first output line*
> *Calculate the second approximation*
> *Calculate the second difference*
> *Print the second output line*
> *Calculate the third approximation*
> *Calculate the third difference*
> *Print the third output line*

Step 3b: Do a Hand Calculation

To ensure that we understand the processing used in the algorithm, we will do a hand calculation. We can use the result of this calculation to verify the result produced by the program that we write. For test purposes, any angle will do, and we will select a value of 30 degrees. Converting this angle to radian measure requires multiplying it by the factor 3.1416/180.0, which corresponds to 0.523600 radians.

For this test value the following approximations to the sine are obtained:

Using the first term of the polynomial the approximation is:

$$0.523600$$

Using the first two terms of the polynomial, the approximation is:

$$0.523600 - (0.523600)^3 / 6 = .499675$$

Using all three terms of the polynomial, the approximation is:

$$0.499675 + (0.523600)^5 / 120 = .500003$$

Notice that in using all three terms of the polynomial, that it was not necessary to recalculate the value of the first two terms. Instead, we used the value previously calculated in our second approximation. All of the approximations are extremely close to 0.5, which is the actual sine of 30 degrees.

Step 3c: Select Variable Names

The last step required before the selected algorithm is described in FORTRAN is to select variable names for the input, output, and any intermediate variables required by the algorithm. For this problem we select the variable names ANGLE for the input angle entered by the user and RADIAN for its equivalent radian measure. The conversion factor 3.1416/180.0 to convert the input angle from degrees into radians will be given the name CONVRT and constructed as a named constant using the PARAMETER statement. Finally, the variable names SINE, APPROX, and DIF will be declared for the sine of the angle, the approximation to the sine, and the difference between these two quantities, respectively. As always, any valid variable names could have been selected.

Step 4: Write the Program

Program 3-10 represents a description of the selected algorithm in FORTRAN.

Program 3-10

```
      PROGRAM MAIN
*** THIS PROGRAM APPROXIMATES THE SINE OF AN ANGLE, IN DEGREES
*** USING ONE, TWO, AND THREE TERMS OF AN APPROXIMATING POLYNOMIAL
      REAL RADIAN, CONVRT, SINE, APPROX, DIF
      PARAMETER (CONVRT = 3.1416/180.0)
      PRINT *, 'ENTER AN ANGLE (IN DEGREES)'
      READ *, ANGLE
*** CONVERT THE ANGLE TO RADIAN MEASURE
      RADIAN = CONVRT * ANGLE
*** PRINT TWO HEADER LINES
      PRINT *,'  SINE          APPROXIMATION DIFFERENCE'
      PRINT *,'  ------------ -------------- ----------'
*** CALCULATE THE SINE USING THE INTRINSIC FUNCTION
      SINE = SIN(RADIAN)
*** CALCULATE THE FIRST APPROXIMATION AND DISPLAY A LINE
      APPROX = RADIAN
      DIF = ABS(SINE - APPROX)
      PRINT *, SINE, APPROX, DIF
*** CALCULATE THE SECOND APPROXIMATION AND DISPLAY A LINE
      APPROX = APPROX - (RADIAN ** 3 / 6.0)
      DIF = ABS(SINE - APPROX)
      PRINT *, SINE, APPROX, DIF
*** CALCULATE THE THIRD APPROXIMATION AND DISPLAY A LINE
      APPROX = APPROX + (RADIAN ** 5 / 120.0)
      DIF = ABS(SINE - APPROX)
      PRINT *, SINE, APPROX, DIF
      END
```

Notice that the input angle is immediately converted to radians after it is read. The two header lines are then printed prior to any approximations being made. The value of the sine is then computed using the intrinsic sine function and is assigned to the variable SINE. This assignment permits this value to be used in the three difference calculations and be displayed three times without the need for recalculation.

Since the approximation to the sine is "built up" using more and more terms of the approximating polynomial, only the new term for each approximation is calculated and added to the previous approximation. Finally, to permit the same variables to be reused, the values in them are immediately printed before the next approximation is made. Following is a sample run produced by Program 3-10.

```
ENTER AN ANGLE (IN DEGREES)
30
SINE                APPROXIMATION       DIFFERENCE
------------        -------------       -----------

5.000011E-01        5.236000E-01        2.359891E-02
5.000011E-01        4.996752E-01        3.258522E-04
5.000011E-01        5.000032E-01        2.098380E-06
```

Step 5: Test the Program

The first two columns of output data produced by the sample run agree with our hand calculation. (If you are unfamiliar with exponential notation, review Section 2.1.) A hand check of the last column verifies that it contains the correct value differences between the first two columns.

As the program only performs seven calculations, and the result of the test run agrees with our hand calculations, the program has been completely tested. It can now be used with other input angles with confidence that the results it produces are correct.

Additional Exercises for Chapter Three

1a. Enter, compile, and run Program 3-9 on your computer system.

b. Rewrite Program 3-9 using formatted READ and PRINT statements.

c. If you're working with subroutines, modify Program 3-9 so that the hydronium ion concentration is entered in the main program unit and passed to a subroutine named PHCALC. The PHCALC subroutine should be used to calculate the pH level and display the resultant value. Enter, compile, and run the modified program. (*Note:* Review Section 2.8 for exchanging data with a subroutine.)

2a. Enter, compile, and run Program 3-10 on your computer system.

b. If you're working with subroutines, modify Program 3-10 so that the input angle is entered in the main program unit and passed to a subroutine named APCALC. The APCALC subroutine should be used to convert the passed angle to radian measure, perform the remaining calculations, and produce the required display. (*Note:* Review Section 2.8 for exchanging data with a subroutine.)

3. By mistake a student wrote Program 3-10 as follows:

```
      PROGRAM MAIN
***   THIS PROGRAM APPROXIMATES THE SINE OF AN ANGLE, IN DEGREES
***   USING ONE, TWO, AND THREE TERMS OF AN APPROXIMATING POLYNOMIAL
      REAL RADIAN, CONVRT, SINE, APPROX, DIF
      PARAMETER (CONVRT = 3.1416/180.0)
***   PRINT TWO HEADER LINES
      PRINT *,' SINE           APPROXIMATION DIFFERENCE'
      PRINT *,' ─────────────  ─────────────  ─────────────'
      PRINT *, 'ENTER AN ANGLE (IN DEGREES)'
      READ *, ANGLE
```

```
*** CONVERT THE ANGLE TO RADIAN MEASURE
        RADIAN = CONVRT * ANGLE
*** CALCULATE THE SINE USING THE INTRINSIC FUNCTION
        SINE = SIN(RADIAN)
*** CALCULATE THE FIRST APPROXIMATION AND DISPLAY A LINE
        APPROX = RADIAN
        DIF = ABS(SINE - APPROX)
        PRINT *, SINE, APPROX, DIF
*** CALCULATE THE SECOND APPROXIMATION AND DISPLAY A LINE
        APPROX = APPROX - (RADIAN ** 3 / 6.0)
        DIF = ABS(SINE - APPROX)
        PRINT *, SINE, APPROX, DIF
** CALCULATE THE THIRD APPROXIMATION AND DISPLAY A LINE
        APPROX = APPROX + (RADIAN ** 5 / 120.0)
        DIF = ABS(SINE - APPROX)
        PRINT*, SINE, APPROX, DIF
        END
```
Determine the output that will be produced by this program.

4a. The formula for the standard normal deviation, z, used in statistical applications is:

$$z = \frac{X - \mu}{r}$$

where μ refers to a mean value and r to a standard deviation.

Using this formula, write a program that calculates and displays the value of the standard normal deviation when $X = 85.3$, $\mu = 80$, and $r = 4$.

b. Rewrite the program written in Exercise 4a to accept the values of x, μ, and r as user inputs while the program is executing.

5a. The equation of the normal (bell-shaped) curve used in statistical applications is:

$$y = \frac{1}{r \sqrt{2\,pi}}\, e^{-(1/2)[(x-u)/r]^2}$$

Using this equation, and assuming $\mu = 90$ and $r = 4$, write a program that determines and displays the value of y when $x = 80$.

b. Rewrite the program written in Exercise 5a to accept the values of x, μ, and r as user inputs while the program is executing.

6a. Write, compile, and execute a program that calculates and displays the gross pay and net pay of two individuals. The first individual works 40 hours and is paid an hourly rate of $8.43. The second individual works 35 hours and is paid an hourly rate of $5.67. Both individuals have 20 percent of their pay withheld for income tax purposes, and both pay 2 percent of their net pay, before taxes, for medical benefits.

b. Redo Exercise 6a assuming that the individuals' hours and rate will be entered when the program is run.

7. The volume of oil stored in a underground 200-foot deep cylindrical tank is determined by measuring the distance from the top of the tank to the surface of the oil. Knowing this distance and the radius of the tank, the volume of oil in the tank can be determined using the formula *Volume* = *pi radius*^{2} (200 – distance). Using this information, write, compile, and execute a FORTRAN program that accepts the radius and distance measurements, calculates the volume of oil in the tank, and displays the two input values and the calculated volume. Verify the results of your program by doing a hand calculation using the following test data: radius is 10 feet, distance is 12 feet.

8. The perimeter, underground surface area, and volume of an in-ground pool are given by the following formulas:

> *Perimeter* = 2(*length* + *width*)
> *Volume* = *length* * *width* * *average depth*
> *Underground surface area* = 2(*length* + *width*)*average depth* + *length* * *width*

Using these formulas as a basis, write a FORTRAN program that accepts the length, width, and average depth measurements, calculates the perimeter, volume, and underground surface area of the pool, and produces the following display:

LENGTH	WIDTH	DEPTH	PERIMETER	VOLUME	UNDERGROUND SURFACE AREA
xxxxx	xxxxx	xxxxx	yyyyy	yyyyy	yyyyy

where xxxxx and yyyyy represent input and calculated quantities, respectively. In writing your program, make the following two calculations immediately after the input data has been entered: *length* * *width* and *length* + *width*. The results of these two calculations should then be used, as appropriate, in the assignment statements for determining the perimeter, volume, and underground surface area. Verify the results of your program by doing a hand calculation using the following test data: length is 25 feet, width is 15 feet, and average depth is 5.5 feet. When you have verified that your program is working, use it to complete the following table.

LENGTH	WIDTH	DEPTH	PERIMETER	VOLUME	UNDERGROUND SURFACE AREA
25	10	5			
25	10	5.5			
25	10	6			
25	10	6.5			
30	12	5			
30	12	5.5			
30	12	6			
30	12	6.5			

3.6 Common Programming Errors

The errors commonly associated with the material presented in this chapter are:

1. Forgetting to separate with commas all variable names within a READ statement.
2. Using an intrinsic function without providing the correct number of arguments having the proper data type.
3. Incorrectly defining a FORMAT specification that does not correctly correspond to the data items being displayed. For example, specifying a field width too small to accommodate the displayed item. In its most common occurrence, this usually takes the form of not specifying sufficient room for a real number's decimal point and a possible leading negative sign.
4. A major programming error is the rush to code and run a program before the programmer fully understands what is required and the algorithms and procedures that will be used to produce the desired result. A symptom of this haste to get a program entered into the computer is the lack of either an outline of the proposed program or a written program itself (see the Enrichment section at the end of this chapter). Many problems can be caught just by checking a copy of the program, either handwritten or listed from the computer, before it is compiled.
5. Another error is the unwillingness to test a program in depth. After all, since you wrote the program, you assume it is correct, or you would have changed it before it was compiled. It is extremely difficult to back away and test your own software honestly. As a programmer, you must constantly remind yourself that just because you think your program is correct does not make it so. Finding errors in your own program is a sobering experience, but one that will help you become a master programmer.

3.7 Chapter Summary

1. FORTRAN provides intrinsic functions for calculating trigonometric, logarithmic, and other mathematical computations typically required in scientific and engineering programs.
2. Data passed to an intrinsic function are called *arguments* of the function. Arguments are passed to an intrinsic function by including each argument, separated by commas, within the parentheses following the function's name. Each intrinsic function has its own requirements for the number and data types of the arguments that must be provided.
3. Each intrinsic function operates on its arguments to calculate a single value.
4. Functions may be included within larger expressions.
5. The READ statement is used for data input. The general form of this statement is:

```
READ(n, fmt) list of variables
```

where *n* is a unit number designating from where the input will be read and *fmt* specifies the format of the input. When an asterisk (*) is used for the unit number, the computer's standard input unit is specified. If an asterisk is used for the format specification, the compiler's list-directed format is selected.

6. For standard unit input, an alternative form of the READ statement can be used. This alternative form is:

> READ *fmt, list of variables*

The *fmt* in this statement can either be an asterisk, which designates list-directed input, an explicit format control specification, or the statement label of a FORMAT statement. In the latter two instances, user-designated formatting is selected.

7. When the computer encouters a READ statement, it temporarily suspends further statement execution until sufficient data has been entered for the number of variables contained in the READ statement.

8. It is a good programming practice to display a message, prior to a READ statement, that alerts the user as to the type and number of data items to be entered. Such a message is called a *prompt*.

9. A PARAMETER statement is used to equate a constant to a symbolic name. The general form of the PARAMETER statement is:

> PARAMETER (*name1 = expression, name2 = expression, etc.*)

For example, the number 3.1416 can be equated to the symbolic name PI using the PARAMETER statement:

```
PARAMETER (PI = 3.1416)
```

Once a symbolic name has been equated to a value, another value may not be assigned to the symbolic name.

10. When using FORTRAN's various statement types, certain placement rules must be followed. These rules are:

   i. The END statement must be the last statement of every program unit. This statement consists of the keyword END with no spaces between any of the letters.

   ii. Comment lines may appear anywhere in a program unit, except as the last line of a program unit.

   iii. FORMAT statements may appear anywhere between the program header line and the END statement.

   iv. PARAMETER and declaration statements, which collectively (along with additional statements to be introduced) are referred to as *specification* statements, may be intermixed and must appear before all executable statements. Executable statements, such as assignment, WRITE, PRINT, and READ statements, may be freely intermixed with each other.

3.8   Enrichment Study: Program Life Cycle

Just as people and products have a life cycle, so do programs. A program's life cycle is divided into three main stages, as illustrated in Figure 3-11. These stages consist of program development, program documentation, and program maintenance.

The development stage is where a program is initially developed. It is at this stage that requirements must be understood and the structure of the program planned using the top-down development procedure presented in Section 2.5. The documentation stage, as its name implies, consists of creating, both within the program and in separate documents, sufficient user and programmer support references and explanations. At the maintenance stage, the program is modified or enhanced as new demands and requirements are obtained or program errors are detected. Complete courses and textbooks are devoted to each of these three program stages. Our purpose in listing them is to put the actual writing of a program in perspective with the total effort needed to produce professional engineering and scientific software.

The writing of a program in a computer language is formally called *coding* (informally, of course, it is called programming). And that, after all, is what we have been doing—writing programs in a language, or code, that can be decoded and used by the computer. As we saw in Section 2.5, the coding of a program is but one component in the program's development stage. The total development effort is composed of four distinct phases, as illustrated in Figure 3-12.

Listed below are both the steps in the top-down development procedure corresponding to each development phase and the relative amount of effort that typically is expended on each phase in large engineering and scientific programming projects. As can be seen from this listing, the coding phase is not the major effort in overall program development.

Phase	Top-down development step	Effort
Analysis	Steps 1 and 2	10%
Design	Step 3	20%
Coding	Step 4	20%
Testing	Step 5	50%

Many new programmers have trouble because they spend the majority of their time coding the program without first spending sufficient time understanding and designing it. In this regard, it is worthwhile to remember the programming saying "It is impossible to write a successful program for a problem or application that is not fully understood."

It is for this reason that the analysis phase is one of the most important, because if the requirements are not fully and completely understood before programming begins, the results are almost always disastrous. Once a program structure is created and the program is written, new or reinterpreted requirements often cause havoc. An analogy with house construction is useful to illustrate this point.

Imagine designing and building a house without fully understanding the architect's specifications. After the house is completed, the architect tells you that a bathroom is required on the first floor, where you have built a wall between the kitchen and the dining room. In addition, that particular wall is one of the main

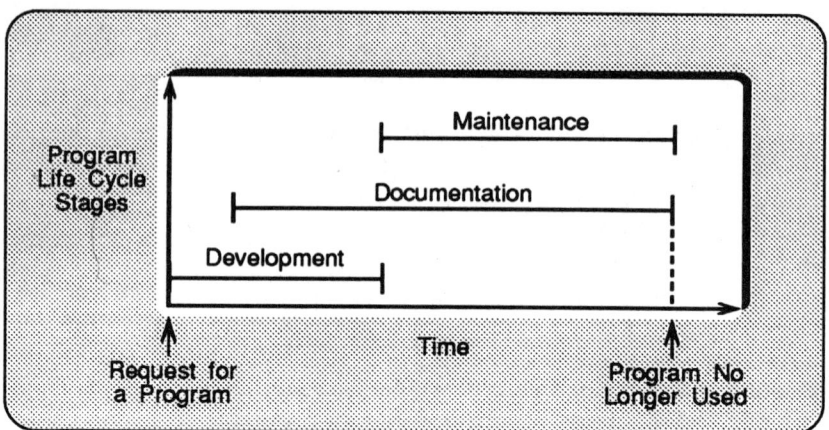

Figure 3-11   A Program's Life Cycle

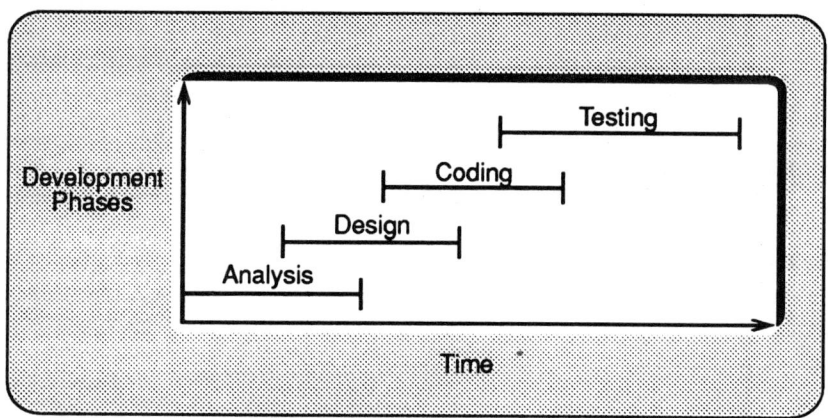

Figure 3-12   The Phases of Program Development

support walls for the house and contains numerous pipes and electrical cables. In this case, adding one bathroom requires a major modification to the basic structure of the house.

Experienced programmers know the importance of analyzing and understanding a program's requirements before coding, if for no other reason than that they too have constructed programs that later had to be entirely dismantled and redone. The following exercise should give you a sense of this experience.

Figure 3-13 illustrates the outlines of six individual shapes from a classic children's puzzle. Assume that as one or more shapes are given, starting with shapes A and B, an easy-to-describe figure must be constructed.

Typically, shapes A and B are initially arranged to obtain a square, as illustrated in Figure 3-14. Next, when shape C is considered, it is usually combined with the

Figure 3-13   Six Individual Shapes

existing square to form a rectangle, as illustrated in Figure 3-15. Then, when pieces D and E are added, they are usually arranged to form another rectangle, which is placed alongside the existing rectangle to form a square, as shown in Figure 3-16.

The process of adding new pieces onto the existing structure is identical to constructing a program and then adding to it as each subsequent requirement is understood. The problem arises when the program is almost finished and a requirement is added that does not fit easily into the established pattern. For example, assume that the last shape (shape F) is now to be added (see Figure 3-17). This last piece does not fit into the existing pattern that has been constructed. In order to include this piece with the others, the pattern must be completely dismantled and restructured.

Unfortunately, many programmers structure their programs in the same manner used to construct Figure 3-16. Rather than taking the time to understand the complete set of requirements, new programmers frequently start coding based on the understanding of only a small subset of the total requirements. Then, when a subsequent requirement does not fit the existing program structure, the programmer is forced to dismantle and restructure either parts or all of the program.

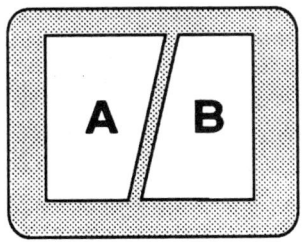

Figure 3-14   Typical First Figure

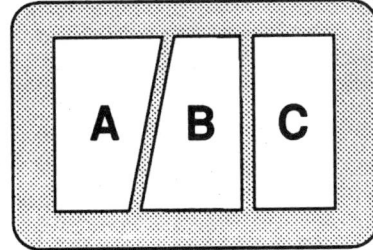

Figure 3-15   Typical Second Figure

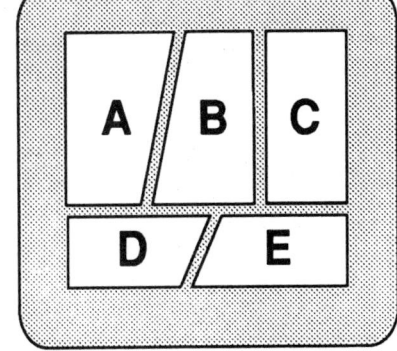

Figure 3-16   Typical Third Figure

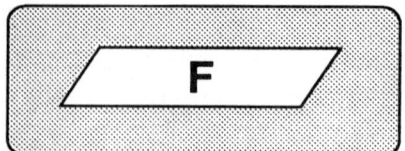

Figure 3-17   The Last Piece

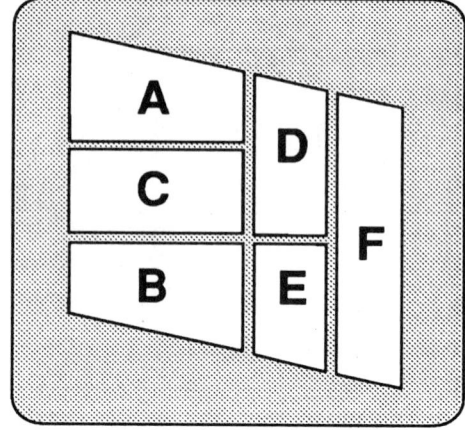

Figure 3-18   Including All the Pieces

Now, let's approach the problem of creating a figure from another view. If we started by arranging the first set of pieces as a parallelogram, all the pieces could be included in the final figure, as illustrated in Figure 3-18.

It is worthwhile observing that the piece that caused us to dismantle the first figure (Figure 3-16) actually sets the pattern for the final figure illustrated in Figure 3-18. This is often the case with programming requirements. The requirement that seems to be the least clear is frequently the one that determines the main interrelationships of the program. Thus, it is essential to include and understand all the known requirements before coding is begun. In practical terms, this means doing the analysis and design before attempting any coding.

Selection

Chapter Four

The field of programming, as a distinct discipline, is still a relatively new activity. It should not be surprising, then, that many advances have occurred in the theoretical foundations of this field. One of the most important of these advances was the recognition in the late 1960s that any algorithm, no matter how complex, could be constructed using combinations of standardized sequence, selection, and repetition *flow of control* structures.

The term *flow of control* refers to the order in which a program's statements are executed. Unless directed otherwise, the normal flow of control for all programs is *sequential*. This means that statements are executed in sequence, one after another, in the order in which they are placed within the program.

Selection and repetition structures permit the sequential flow of control to be altered in precisely defined ways. As you might have guessed, the selection structure is used to select which statements are to be performed next, and the repetition structure is used to repeat a set of statements. In this chapter we present FORTRAN's selection statements. As selection requires choosing between alternatives, we begin this chapter with a description of FORTRAN's selection criteria.

4.1   Relational Expressions

Besides providing computational capabilities (addition, subtraction, multiplication, division, etc.), all computers have the ability to compare quantities. Because many seemingly "intelligent" decision-making situations can be reduced to the level of choosing between two quantities, this comparison capability can be used to create a remarkable intelligencelike facility.

The expressions used to compare quantities are called *relational expressions*. A simple relational expression consists of a relational operator connecting two variable and/or constant operands, as shown in Figure 4-1.

FORTRAN's relational operators are listed in Table 4-1. These relational operators may be used with all of FORTRAN's data types but must be typed exactly as shown. Thus, while the following examples:

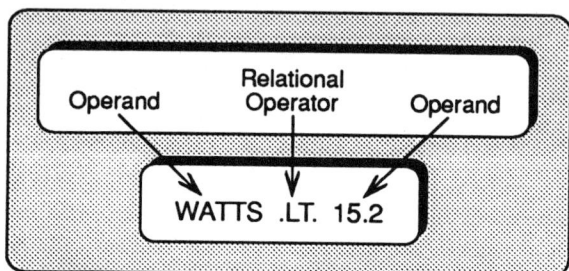

Figure 4-1   Anatomy of a Simple Relational Expression

```
AGE .GT. 40
3 .LT. 4
DAY .NE. 5
LENGTH .LE. 50
FLAG .EQ. DONE
```

```
2.0 .GT. 3.3
TEMP .GT. 98.6
IDNUM .EQ. 682
HOURS .GT. 40
```

are all valid, the following:

```
LENGTH LT 50       (periods are missing)
2.0 > 3.3          (invalid operator)
FLAG .EQUAL. DONE  (invalid operator)
```

are invalid.

Table 4-1   FORTRAN's Relational Operators

Relational operator	Meaning	Example
.LT.	Less than	AGE .LT. 30
.GT.	Greater than	HEIGHT .GT. 6.2
.LE.	Less than or equal to	TAXBLE .LE. 20000
.GE.	Greater than or equal to	TEMP .GE. 98.6
.EQ.	Equal to	GRADE .EQ. 100
.NE.	Not equal to	NUMBER .NE. 250

Relational expressions are also called *conditions,* and we will use both terms interchangeably. Like all FORTRAN expressions, relational expressions are evaluated to yield a result. For relational expressions this result is either the logical constant .TRUE. or .FALSE. For example, the value of the expression 3 .LT. 4 is always .TRUE., and the value of the expression 2.0 .GT. 3.3 is always .FALSE.

FORTRAN displays the value of a relational expression as either a T or an F, where T denotes a true value and F a false value.

Thus, the statements:

```
PRINT *, 'THE VALUE OF 3 .LT. 4 IS', 3 .LT .4
PRINT *, 'THE VALUE OF 2.0 .GT. 3.0 IS', 2.0 .GT. 3.3
```

can be used to display the value of the expressions 3 .LT. 4 and 2.0 .GT. 3.3, respectively, and produce the display:

```
THE VALUE OF 3 .LT. 4 IS T
THE VALUE OF 2.0 .GT. 3.0 IS F
```

The value of a condition such as HOURS .GT. 40 depends on the value stored in the variable HOURS. In a FORTRAN program, a condition such as this is typically used as part of a selection statement. In these statements, which are presented in the next section, the selection of which statement is to be executed next is based on the value of the condition (true or false).

Character data can also be compared using relational operators. For example, in both the ASCII and the EBCDIC codes the letter A is stored using a code having a lesser numerical value than the letter B, the code for a B is lesser in value than the code for a C, and so on. For character sets coded in this manner, the following conditions are evaluated as listed below.

Expression	Value
'A' .GT. 'D'	.FALSE.
'E' .LE. 'M'	.TRUE.
'G' .EQ. 'K'	.FALSE.
'J' .GE. 'M'	.FALSE.
'F' .NE. 'P'	.TRUE.

Comparing letters is essential in alphabetizing names or using characters to select a particular choice in decision-making situations.

Logical Operators

In addition to simple relational expressions as conditions, more complex conditions can be created using the logical operations AND, OR, and NOT. These operations are represented by the respective symbols:

```
.AND.
.OR.
.NOT.
```

When the AND operator, .AND., is used between two relational expressions, the resulting condition is called a *logical expression* and is true only if both single relations are true by themselves. Thus, the logical condition:

```
(VOLTGE .GT. 48) .AND. (MILAMP .LT. 10)
```

is true only if VOLTGE is greater than 48 and MILAMP is less than 10. The parentheses surrounding the individual relational expressions are used for clarity only, because the logical .AND. operator has a lower precedence than the relational operators (.GT., .LT., .EQ., etc.).

The logical OR operator, .OR., must also be applied between two relational expressions, and the resulting expression referred to as a logical expression. With the .OR. operator, the resulting condition is true if either one or both of the two individual conditions is true. Thus, the condition:

```
(VOLTGE .GT. 48) .OR. (MILAMP .LT. 10)
```

is true if either VOLTGE is greater than 48, or MILAMP is less than 10 or if both conditions are true. Again, the parentheses around the relational expressions are used only for clarity, since the .OR. operator has a lower precedence than all relational operators.

For the declarations:

```
INTEGER I,J
REAL A,B,COMPLET
```

the following represent valid logical expressions:

```
A .GT. B
I .EQ. J .OR. A .LT. B .OR. COMPLET .GT. B
A/B .GT. 5.0 .AND. I .LE. 20
```

Before these complex conditions can be evaluated, the values of A, B, I, J, and COMPLET must be known. Assuming A = 12.0, B = 2.0, I = 15, J = 30, and COMPLET = 0.0, the previous expressions yield the following results:

Expression	Value
`A .GT. B`	`.TRUE.`
`I .EQ. J .OR. A .LT. B .OR. COMPLET .GT. B`	`.FALSE.`
`A/B .GT. 5.0 .AND. I .LE. 20`	`.TRUE.`

Although it is better not to construct relational or logical expressions using different data types, FORTRAN will automatically convert integer operands to real values when they are compared to real values. Numerical operands, however, should not be compared to either character or logical operands. Similarly, character operands should be compared to only character operands and logical operands compared to only logical operands.

The NOT operator is used to change a relational or logical expression to its opposite state. That is, if an expression is true, then .NOT.*expression* is false. Similarly, if an expression is false to begin with, then .NOT.*expression* is true. For example, assuming the number 26 is stored in the variable VOLTGE, the expression VOLTGE .GT. 48 is false, and the expression .NOT.(VOLTGE .GT. 48) is true.

Both relational and logical operators have a hierarchy of execution similar to that for the arithmetic operators. Table 4-2 lists the precedence of these operators in relation to the other operators we have used.

Table 4-2   Operator Precedence and Associativity
(from Highest to Lowest Precedence)

Type	Symbol	Associativity
Exponentiation	**	Right to left
Multiplication, division	* /	Left to right
Addition, subtraction, negation	+ −	Left to right
Relational (all have the same precedence)	.LT. .LE. .GT. .GE. .EQ. .NE.	Left to right
Logical	.NOT.	Left to Right
Logical	.AND.	Left to right
Logical	.OR.	Left to right

The following examples illustrate the evaluation of various relational expressions. These examples assume the following declarations and assignments:

```
CHARACTER KEY
INTEGER I, J, K
REAL X

KEY = 'M'
I = 5
J = 7
K = 12
X = 22.5
```

Expression	Equivalent expression	Value
I + 2 .EQ. K − 1	(I + 2) .EQ. (K − 1)	.FALSE.
3 * I − J .LT. 22	((3 * I) − J) .LT. 22	.TRUE.
I + 2 * J .GT. K	(I + (2 * J)) .GT. K	.TRUE.
K + 3 .LE. − J + 3 * I	(K + 3) .LE. ((−J) + (3*I))	.FALSE.
'A' .NE. 'B'	'A' .NE. 'B'	.TRUE.
KEY .GT. 'P'	KEY .GT. 'P'	.FALSE.
20.5 .GE. X + 10.2	20.5 .GE. (X + 10.2)	.FALSE.

As with arithmetic expressions, parentheses can be used both to alter the assigned operator priority and to improve the readability of relational and logical expressions. Since expressions within parentheses are evaluated first, the following complex condition is evaluated as:

```
(6 * 3 .EQ. 36 / 2) .OR. (13 .LT. 3 * 3 + 4) .AND. .NOT.(6 − 2 .LT. 5)
    (18 .EQ. 18) .OR. (13 .LT. 9 + 4) .AND. .NOT.(4 .LT. 5)
        (True) .OR. (13 .LT. 13) .AND. .NOT.(True)
        (True) .OR. (False) .AND. (False)
        (True) .OR. (False)
            (True)
```

Exercises

1. Determine the value of the following expressions. Assume that all variables are integers and A = 5, B = 2, C = 4, D = 6, and E = 3.

   a. `A .GT. B`
   b. `A .NE. B`
   c. `A * C .NE. D * B`
   d. `D * B .EQ. C * E`
   e. `A * B`
   f. `MOD(D,B) .NE. MOD(C,B)`
   g. `MOD(A,B) * C .EQ. D`
   h. `MOD(C,B) * A .EQ. 0`
   i. `MOD(B,C) * A .EQ. 0`

2. Write relational expressions to express the following conditions (use variable names of your own choosing):

   a. A person's age is equal to 30.

   b. A person's temperature is greater than 98.6.

   c. A person's height is less than six feet.

   d. The current month is 12 (December).

   e. The letter input is K.

   f. A person's age is equal to 30 and the person is taller than six feet.

   g. The current day is the 15th day of the 1st month.

   h. A person is older than 50 or has been employed at the company for at least 5 years.

   i. A person's identification number is less than 500, and the person is older than 55.

   j. A length is greater than two feet and less than three feet.

3. Determine the value of the following expressions, assuming that all variables are integers and that A = 5, B = 2, C = 4, and D = 5.

   a. `A .EQ. 5`
   b. `B * D .EQ. C * C`
   c. `MOD(D,B) * C .GT. 5 .OR. MOD(C,B) * D .GT. 7`

4. Using parentheses, rewrite the following expressions to correctly indicate their order of evaluation. Then evaluate each expression assuming all variables are integers and that A = 5, B = 2, and C = 4.

   a. `A / B .NE. C .AND. C / B .NE. A`
   b. `A / B .NE. C .OR. C / B .NE. A`
   c. `MOD(B,C) .EQ. 1 .AND. MOD(A,C) .EQ. 1`
   d. `MOD(B,C) .EQ. 1 .AND. MOD(A,C) .EQ. 1`

4.2   The IF-ELSE Structure

The IF-ELSE structure directs the computer to perform a series of one or more instructions based on the result of a comparison. For example, the state of New Jersey has a two-level state income tax structure. If a person's taxable income is less than $20,000, the New Jersey State income tax rate is 2 percent. For incomes exceeding $20,000, a different rate is applied. The IF-ELSE structure can be used in this situation to determine the correct tax based on whether the taxable income is less than or equal to $20,000. The general form of the IF-ELSE structure is:

```
IF (condition) THEN
   statement 1
   statement 2
          .
          .
          .
   statement n
ELSE
   statement n+1
          .
          .
          .
   statement m
ENDIF
```

This structure is formally constructed using three separate FORTRAN statements each of which must reside on a line by itself: a block IF statement having the form IF (*condition*) THEN, an ELSE statement consisting of the keyword ELSE, and an ENDIF statement consisting of the keyword ENDIF.

The condition in the block IF statement is evaluated first. If the condition is True, statements 1 through *n* are executed. If the condition is False, the statements after the keyword ELSE are executed. Thus, one of the two sets of statements (either statement 1 through statement *n* or statement *n*+1 through statement *m*) is always executed, depending on the value of the condition. The flowchart for the IF-ELSE structure is shown in Figure 4-2.

For a specific example of an IF-ELSE structure, we will construct a FORTRAN program for determining New Jersey State income taxes. As previously described, these taxes are assessed at 2 percent of taxable income for incomes less than or equal to $20,000. For taxable income greater than $20,000, state taxes are 2.5 percent of the income that exceeds $20,000 plus a fixed amount of $400. Thus, the condition to be tested is whether taxable income is less than or equal to $20,000. An appropriate IF-ELSE structure for this situation is:

```
IF (INCOME .LE. 20000.0) THEN
   TAXES = .02 * INCOME
ELSE
   TAXES = .025 * (INCOME - 20000.0) + 400.0
ENDIF
```

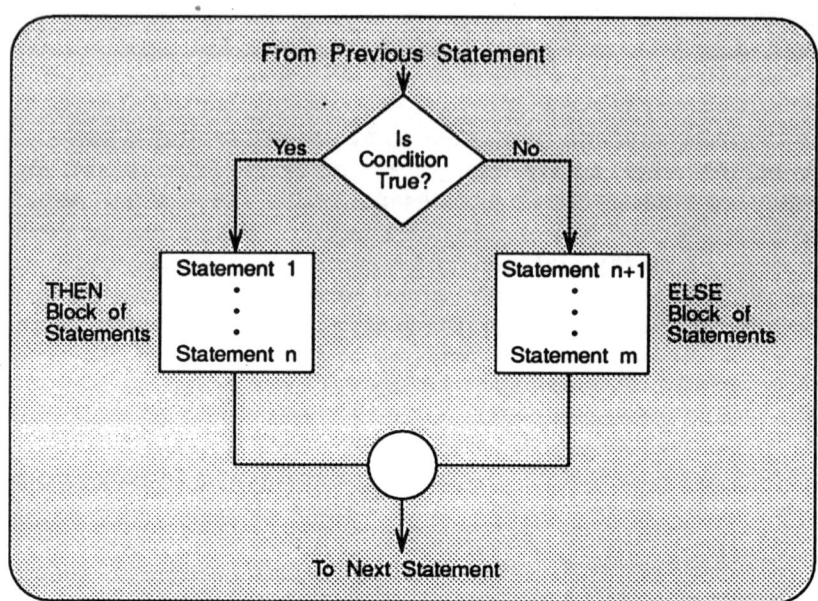

Figure 4-2   The IF-ELSE Flowchart

Recall that the relational operator .LE. represents the relation "less than or equal to." If the value of INCOME is less than or equal to 20000.0, the condition is true, and the statement TAXES = .02 * INCOME is executed. If the value of INCOME is not less than or equal to 20000.0, the condition is false, and the statement after the reserved word ELSE is executed. Program 4-1 illustrates the use of this statement in a complete program.

A blank line was inserted before and after the IF-ELSE structure to highlight it in the complete program. We will continue to do this throughout the text to emphasize the structure being presented.

 Program 4-1

```
PROGRAM MAIN
  REAL INCOME, TAXES
  PRINT *,'PLEASE TYPE IN THE TAXABLE INCOME: '
  READ *,INCOME
*
  IF (INCOME .LE. 20000.0) THEN
    TAXES = .02 * INCOME
  ELSE
    TAXES = .025 * (INCOME - 20000.0) + 400.0
  ENDIF
*
  PRINT *,'TAXES ARE $ ', TAXES
  END
```

To illustrate the selection provided by the IF-ELSE structure in Program 4-1, the program was run twice with different input data. The results are:

```
PLEASE TYPE IN THE TAXABLE INCOME:
10000.
TAXES ARE $ 200.000000
```

and:

```
PLEASE TYPE IN THE TAXABLE INCOME:
30000.
TAXES ARE $ 650.000000
```

Although the use of FORMAT statements would improve the appearance of the output (see Exercise 3 at the end of this section), observe that the taxable income input in the first run of the program was less than $20,000, and the tax was correctly calculated as 2 percent of the number entered. In the second run, the taxable income was more than $20,000, and the ELSE part of the IF-ELSE structure was used to yield a correct tax computation of:

```
.025 * (30000. - 20000.) + 400. = 650.
```

Although only a single statement was needed in both the IF and ELSE parts of the structure used in Program 4-1, any number of statements could have been included. Program 4-2 illustrates the use of multiple statements within a IF-ELSE structure.

Program 4-2 checks whether the entered letter is an F (notice that the F must be entered within apostrophes). If it is, the two statements within the IF part of the

---

 Program 4-2

```
PROGRAM MAIN
  CHARACTER TYPE
  REAL TEMP, FAHREN, CELSUS
  PRINT *,'ENTER THE TEMPERATURE TO BE CONVERTED: '
  READ *,TEMP
  PRINT *,'ENTER ''F'' IF THIS TEMPERATURE IS FAHRENHEIT'
  PRINT *,' OR ''C'' IF THE TEMPERATURE IS CELSIUS: '
  READ *, TYPE
*
  IF (TYPE .EQ. 'F') THEN
    CELSUS = (5.0 / 9.0) * (TEMP - 32.0)
    PRINT *,'THE EQUIVALENT CELSIUS TEMPERATURE IS ', CELSUS
  ELSE
    FAHREN = (9.0 / 5.0) * TEMP + 32.0
    PRINT *,'THE EQUIVALENT FAHRENHEIT TEMPERATURE IS', FAHREN
  ENDIF
*
  END
```

IF-ELSE structure are executed. Any other letter results in execution of the two statements within the ELSE part. Following is a sample run of Program 4-2.

```
ENTER THE TEMPERATURE TO BE CONVERTED:
212
ENTER 'F' IF THIS TEMPERATURE IS FAHRENHEIT
OR 'C' IF THE TEMPERATURE IS CELSIUS:
'F'
THE EQUIVALENT CELSIUS TEMPERATURE IS    100.000000
```

One-Way Selection: The Block IF and Logical IF Statements

As we have seen, the IF-ELSE structures that we have been using consist of three separate FORTRAN statements: a block IF statement, an ELSE statement, and an ENDIF statement. The block IF statement, IF (*condition*) THEN, can be followed by any number of valid FORTRAN statements. It must, however, always be used with an ENDIF statement. Use of the ELSE statement with a block IF statement is optional. When the ELSE statement is not used, the block IF statement combined with the ENDIF takes the shortened and frequently useful form:

```
IF (condition)    THEN
   statement 1
   statement 2
          .
          .
          .
   statement n
ENDIF
```

The statement or statements following the IF (*condition*) are only executed if the condition is true. The flowchart for this combination of statements is illustrated in Figure 4-3.

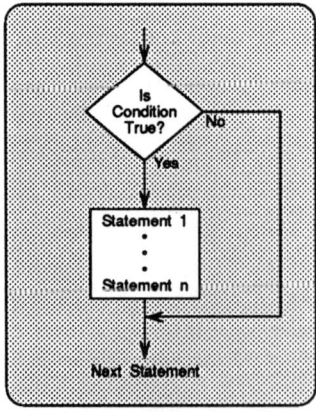

Figure 4-3   Flowchart for the Block IF structure

Program 4-3

```
PROGRAM MAIN
  INTEGER IDNUM
  REAL LIMIT, MILES, OMILES
  LIMIT = 2000.0
  PRINT *,'PLEASE TYPE IN CAR NUMBER AND MILEAGE: '
  READ *, IDNUM, MILES
  PRINT *
*
  IF(MILES .GT. LIMIT) THEN
    PRINT *,'CAR ', IDNUM, ' IS OVER THE LIMIT'
    OMILES = MILES - LIMIT
    PRINT *, 'BY', OMILES, ' MILES'
  ENDIF
*
  PRINT *,'END OF PROGRAM OUTPUT.'
  END
```

Program 4-3 uses a block IF statement to selectively display messages for cars that have been driven more than 2000 miles.

As an illustration of its one-way selection criteria in action, Program 4-3 was run twice, each time with different input data. Only the input data for the first run causes the statements within the block IF to be executed.

```
PLEASE TYPE IN CAR NUMBER AND MILEAGE:
56 3742.4

CAR     56 IS OVER THE LIMIT
BY    1742.400000 MILES
END OF PROGRAM OUTPUT.
```

and:

```
PLEASE TYPE IN CAR NUMBER AND MILEAGE:
16 354
END OF PROGRAM OUTPUT.
```

A useful alternative to this form of the block IF statement is possible when only a single statement needs to be executed when the tested condition is true. For this case the logical IF statement, having the simplified form:

```
IF (condition) statement
```

can be used. For example, the statements:

```
IF (SPEED .GT. 22896.0) PRINT *, 'THE SPEED IS', SPEED
IF (NUMBER .LT. 0) NEGSUM = NEGSUM + NUMBER
IF (BALNCE .LT. REORD .AND. TIME .GT. 5) READ *, NEWVAL
```

are all examples of logical IF statements. In each case, the single statement following the condition is executed only if the tested condition is true.

In addition to the restriction that only one executable statement may follow the logical IF's condition, this executable statement is further limited in that it may not be another logical IF statement or the DO statement that is described in the next chapter.

Nested IF Statements

Although a second IF statement may never be included within a logical IF statement, no such restriction is placed on the statements that may be included within a block IF or ELSE statement. The inclusion of one or more IF statements within a block IF or ELSE statement results in a *nested* IF statement. For example, the following nested IF statement includes a logical IF statement nested within the block IF part of an IF-ELSE structure:

```
IF (TIME .LT. 9) THEN
  PRINT *, 'SNAP'
  IF (DIST .GT. 6) PRINT *, 'CRACKLE'
ELSE
  PRINT *, 'POP'
ENDIF
```

In this construction, when TIME has a value less than nine, the word SNAP is printed, and the condition in the "inner" logical IF statement is evaluated. If the condition DIST .GT. 6 is also true, the word CRACKLE is displayed after the word SNAP. The word POP is only displayed if TIME is greater than or equal to nine.

The process of nesting IF statements can be extended indefinitely. For example, both the PRINT *, 'SNAP' and the PRINT *, 'POP' statements may be replaced by any other IF statement. (Since logical IF statements cannot contain other IF statements, the statement PRINT *, 'CRACKLE' can not be replaced with another IF statement.) As always, the indentation we have used is entirely for program readability and is irrelevant as far as the compiler is concerned.

Generally, when one or more IF statements are nested within a single block IF statement or the block IF part of an IF-ELSE structure, the resulting statement tends to be confusing and is best avoided. However, an extremely useful construction occurs when an ELSE statement contains an IF-ELSE structure. This takes the form shown at the left.

The indentation we have used is not required but distinguishes the "inner" IF-ELSE structure from the "outer" IF-ELSE structure. This form of a nested IF statement is so common in programming that FORTRAN provides a special statement, called the ELSEIF statement, to simplify its creation. The ELSEIF statement is the topic of the next section.

```
IF  (condition 1)
THEN
  statement 1
      .
      .
      .
  statement n
ELSE
  IF  (condition 2) THEN
    statement n + 1
        .
        .
        .
    statement p
  ELSE
    statement p + 1
        .
        .
        .
    statement q
  ENDIF
ENDIF
```

Exercises

1. Write appropriate IF statements for each of the following conditions:

   a. If ANGLE is equal to 90 degrees, print the message "THE ANGLE IS A RIGHT ANGLE"; otherwise print the message "THE ANGLE IS NOT A RIGHT ANGLE."

   b. If the temperature is above 100 degrees, display the message "ABOVE THE BOILING POINT OF WATER"; otherwise display the message "BELOW THE BOILING POINT OF WATER."

   c. If the number is positive, add the number to POSSUM; otherwise add the number to NEGSUM.

   d. If the voltage is less than .5 volts, set the variable FLAG to zero; otherwise set FLAG to one.

   e. If the difference between VOLTS1 and VOLTS2 is less than .001, set the variable APPROX to zero; otherwise calculate APPROX as the quantity (VOLTS1 – VOLTS2) / 2.0.

   f. If the frequency is above 60, display the message "FREQUENCY IS TOO HIGH."

   g. If the difference between TEMP1 and TEMP2 exceeds 2.3 degrees, calculate ERROR as (TEMP1 – TEMP2) * FACTOR.

   h. If X is greater than Y, and Z is less than 20, read in a value for P.

   i. If DIST is greater than 20 and less than 35, read in a value for TIME.

2. Write IF statements corresponding to the conditions illustrated by each of the following flowcharts.

a.
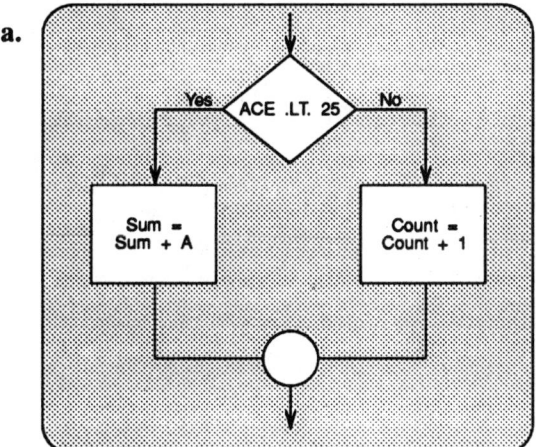

b.
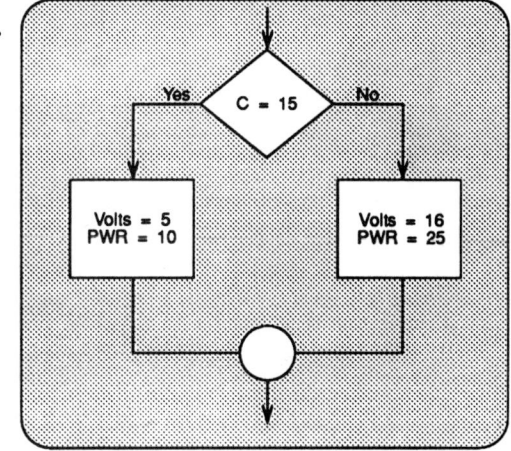

c.

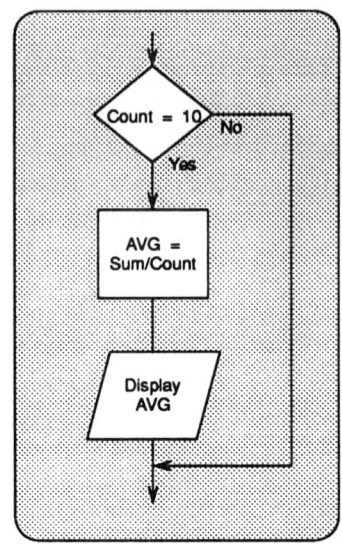

d.

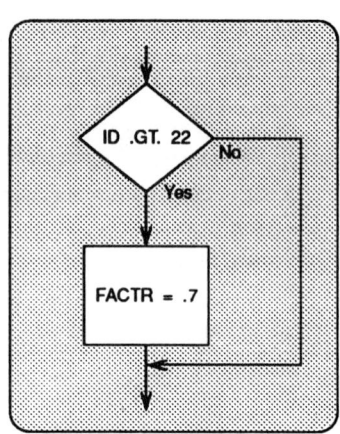

e.

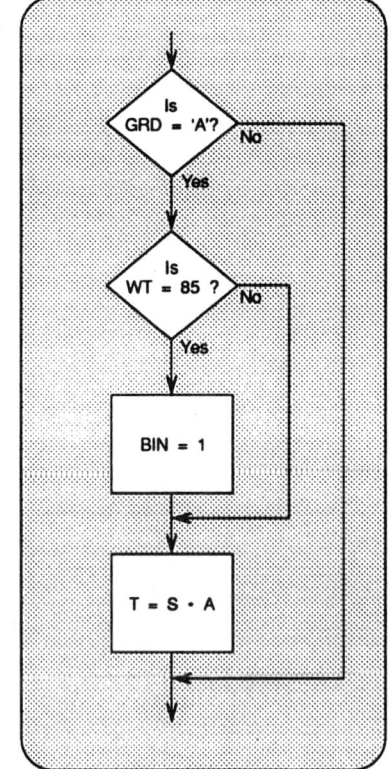

f.

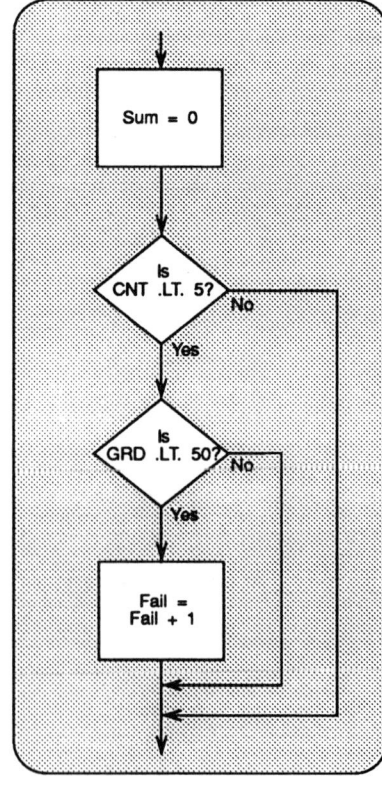

3. Using format statements, rewrite Program 4-1 to have all displayed currency values rounded and displayed to the nearest cent.

4. Write a FORTRAN program that asks the user to input two numbers. If the first number entered is greater than the second number, the program should print the message "THE FIRST NUMBER IS GREATER"; otherwise it should print the message "THE FIRST NUMBER IS SMALLER." Test your program by entering the numbers 5 and 8 and then the numbers 11 and 2. What do you think your program will display if the two numbers entered are equal? Test this case.

   If you are using subroutines, write this program so that the two numbers are input to the MAIN program unit and the determination and display of the appropriate message are performed by a subroutine.

5a. If money is left in a particular bank for more than two years, the interest rate given by the bank is 8.5 percent; otherwise the interest rate is 7 percent. Write a FORTRAN program that uses the READ statement to accept the number of years into the variable NYRS and display the appropriate interest rate depending on the input value.

   If you are using subroutines, write this program so that the number of years is input to the MAIN program unit and the determination and display of the interest rate are performed by a subroutine.

  b. How many runs should you make for the program written in Exercise 5a to verify that it is operating correctly? What data should you input in each of the program runs?

6a. In a pass/fail course, a student passes if the grade is greater than or equal to 70 and fails if the grade is lower. Write a FORTRAN program that accepts a grade and prints either the message "A PASSING GRADE" or the message "A FAILING GRADE," as appropriate.

   If you are using subroutines, write this program so that the numerical grade is input to the MAIN program unit and the determination and display of the appropriate message are performed by a subroutine.

  b. How many runs should you make for the program written in Exercise 6a to verify that it is operating correctly? What data should you input in each of the program runs?

7a. Write a FORTRAN program to compute and display a person's weekly salary as determined by the following conditions:

   If the hours worked are less than or equal to 40, the person receives $8.00 per hour; otherwise the person receives $320.00 plus $12.00 for each hour worked over 40 hours.

   The program should request the hours worked as input and should display the salary as output.

   If you are using subroutines, write this program so that the hours worked are input to the MAIN program unit and the determination and display of the weekly salary are performed by a subroutine.

  b. How many runs should you make for the program written in Exercise 7a to verify that it is operating correctly? What data should you input in each of the program runs?

8a. Write a program that displays either "I FEEL GREAT TODAY!" or "I FEEL DOWN TODAY #$*!" depending on the input. If the character U is entered in the variable CODE, the first message should be displayed; otherwise the second message should be displayed.

(Recall that a character constant must be entered within apostrophes if a list-directed READ statement is used and without apostrophes if a user-directed READ statement is used.)

If you are using subroutines, write this program so that the letter code is input to the MAIN program unit and the determination and display of the appropriate message are performed by a subroutine.

b. How many runs should you make for the program written in Exercise 8a to verify that it is operating correctly? What data should you input in each of the program runs?

9a. A senior salesperson is paid $400 a week, and a junior salesperson $275 a week. Write a FORTRAN program that accepts as input a salesperson's status in the character variable status. (Recall that a character constant must be entered within apostrophes if a list-directed READ statement is used and without apostrophes if a user-directed READ statement is used.) If status equals S, the senior person's salary should be displayed; otherwise the junior person's salary should be output.

If you are using subroutines, write this program so that the letter code is input to the MAIN program unit and the determination and display of the appropriate salary are performed by a subroutine.

b. How many runs should you make for the program written in Exercise 9a to verify that it is operating correctly? What data should you input in each of the program runs?

10. Write a FORTRAN program that accepts a character using the READ statement and determines if the character is an uppercase letter. An uppercase letter is any character that is greater than or equal to A and less than or equal to Z. If the entered character is an uppercase letter, display the message "THE CHARACTER ENTERED IS AN UPPERCASE LETTER." If the entered letter is not uppercase, display the message "THE CHARACTER ENTERED IS NOT AN UPPERCASE LETTER."

If you are using subroutines, write this program so that the character is input to the MAIN program unit and the determination and display of the appropriate message are performed by a subroutine.

11. Repeat Exercise 10 to determine if the character entered is a lowercase letter. A lowercase letter is any character greater than or equal to a and less than or equal to z.

If you are using subroutines, write this program so that the character is input to the MAIN program unit and the determination and display of the appropriate message are performed by a subroutine.

4.3 The IF-ELSEIF Structure

The last selection structure provided in FORTRAN 77 uses an ELSEIF statement. An ELSEIF statement can only be used with a block IF statement. When it is included with a block IF and ELSE statement, the complete IF-ELSEIF structure has the form:

```
IF (condition 1) THEN
   statement 1
      .
      .
      .
   statement n
ELSEIF (condition 2) THEN
   statement n+1
      .
      .
      .
   statement p
ELSEIF (condition 3) THEN
   statement p+1
      .
      .
      .
   statement q
ELSE
   statement q+1
      .
      .
      .
   statement r
ENDIF
```

Each condition is evaluated in the order it appears in this structure. For the first condition that is true, the corresponding statements are executed, and the remainder of the structure is not executed. Thus, if condition 1 is true, only statements 1 through n are executed; otherwise condition 2 is tested. If condition 2 is then true, only statements $n+1$ through p are executed; otherwise condition 3 is tested. The final ELSE statement, which is optional, is only executed if none of the previous conditions are satisfied. This serves as a default or "catchall" case that is frequently useful for detecting an error condition. Although only two ELSEIF statements are illustrated here, any number of ELSEIF statements may be used in the structure, which must be terminated with an ENDIF statement.

To illustrate using an ELSEIF statement, Program 4-4 displays a person's marital status corresponding to a letter input. The following letter codes are used:

Marital status	Input code
Married	M
Single	S
Divorced	D
Widowed	W

 Program 4-4

```
PROGRAM MAIN
  CHARACTER MRCODE
  PRINT *,'ENTER A MARITAL CODE (IN APOSTROPHES): '
  READ *, MRCODE
*
  IF (MRCODE .EQ. 'M') THEN
    PRINT *,'INDIVIDUAL IS MARRIED.'
  ELSEIF (MRCODE .EQ. 'S') THEN
    PRINT *,'INDIVIDUAL IS SINGLE.'
  ELSEIF (MRCODE .EQ. 'D') THEN
    PRINT *,'INDIVIDUAL IS DIVORCED.'
  ELSEIF (MRCODE .EQ. 'W') THEN
    PRINT *,'INDIVIDUAL IS WIDOWED.'
  ELSE
    PRINT *,'AN INVALID CODE WAS ENTERED.'
  ENDIF
*
  END
```

As a further example of an IF-ELSEIF structure, we determine the monthly income of a salesperson using the following commission schedule:

Monthly Sales	Income
Greater than or equal to $50,000	$375 plus 16% of sales
Less than $50,000 but greater than or equal to $40,000	$350 plus 14% of sales
Less than $40,000 but greater than or equal to $30,000	$325 plus 12% of sales
Less than $30,000 but greater than or equal to $20,000	$300 plus 9% of sales
Less than $20,000 but greater than or equal to $10,000	$250 plus 5% of sales
Less than $10,000	$200 plus 3% of sales

The following statements can be used to determine the correct monthly income, where the variable MSALES is used to store the salesperson's current monthly sales:

```
IF (MSALES .GE. 50000.00) THEN
   INCOME = 375.00 + 0.16 * MSALES
ELSEIF (MSALES .GE. 40000.00) THEN
   INCOME = 350.00 + 0.14 * MSALES
ELSEIF (MSALES .GE. 30000.00) THEN
   INCOME = 325.00 + 0.12 * MSALES
ELSEIF (MSALES .GE. 20000.00) THEN
   INCOME = 300.00 + 0.09 * MSALES
ELSEIF (MSALES .GE. 10000.00) THEN
   INCOME = 250.00 + 0.05 * MSALES
ELSE
   INCOME = 200.00 + 0.03 * MSALES
ENDIF
```

Notice that this example makes use of the fact that ELSEIF statements are executed in sequence only until a true condition is found. Thus, the first condition checks for the highest monthly sales. If the salesperson's monthly sales are less than $50,000, the next ELSEIF statement checks for the next highest sales amount, and so on, until the correct sales category is obtained.

 Program 4-5

```
PROGRAM MAIN
  REAL MSALES, INCOME
  PRINT *,'ENTER THE VALUE OF MONTHLY SALES: '
  READ *, MSALES
*
  IF (MSALES .GE. 50000.00) THEN
     INCOME = 375.00 + 0.16 * MSALES
  ELSEIF (MSALES .GE. 40000.00) THEN
     INCOME = 350.00 + 0.14 * MSALES
  ELSEIF (MSALES .GE. 30000.00) THEN
     INCOME = 325.00 + 0.12 * MSALES
  ELSEIF (MSALES .GE. 20000.00) THEN
     INCOME = 300.00 + 0.09 * MSALES
  ELSEIF (MSALES .GE. 10000.00) THEN
     INCOME = 250.00 + 0.05 * MSALES
  ELSE
     INCOME = 200.00 + 0.03 * MSALES
  ENDIF
*
  PRINT *,'THE INCOME IS $', INCOME
  END
```

Program 4-5 uses ELSEIF statements to calculate and display the income corresponding to the value of monthly sales input in the READ statement.

A sample run using Program 4-5 is illustrated below.

```
ENTER THE VALUE OF MONTHLY SALES:
44255.80
THE INCOME IS $ 6545.812000
```

Exercises

1. Modify Program 4-4 to accept both lowercase and uppercase letters as marriage codes. For example, if a user enters either an m or an M, the program should display the message "INDIVIDUAL IS MARRIED."

2. **If you are using subroutines,** modify Program 4-4 so that the marital code is passed to a subroutine named STATUS. The subroutine should accept the passed value and display the same message as determined in Program 4-4.

3. An angle is considered to be an acute angle if it is less than 90 degrees, an obtuse angle if it is greater than 90 degrees, and a right angle if it is equal to 90 degrees. Using this information, write a FORTRAN program that accepts an angle, in degrees, and displays the type of angle corresponding to the degrees entered.

   If you are using subroutines, write this program so that the angle is input within the MAIN program unit and the determination and display of angle type are performed by a subroutine.

4. The grade level of undergraduate college students is typically determined according to the following schedule:

Number of credits completed	Grade level
Less than 32	Freshman
32 to 63	Sophomore
64 to 95	Junior
96 or more	Senior

   Using this information, write a FORTRAN program that accepts the number of credits a student has completed, determines the student's grade level, and displays the grade level.

   If you are using subroutines, write this program so that the number of credits is input within the MAIN program unit and the determination and display of the grade level are performed by a subroutine.

5. A student's letter grade is calculated according to the following schedule:

Numerical grade	Letter grade
Greater than or equal to 90	A
Less than 90 but greater than or equal to 80	B
Less than 80 but greater than or equal to 70	C
Less than 70 but greater than or equal to 60	D
Less than 60	F

   Using this information, write a FORTRAN program that accepts a student's numerical grade, converts the numerical grade to an equivalent letter grade, and displays the letter grade.

If you are using subroutines, write this program so that the numerical grade is input within the MAIN program unit and the determination and display of the letter grade are performed by a subroutine.

6. The interest rate used on funds deposited in a bank is determined by the amount of time the money is left on deposit. For a particular bank, the following schedule is used:

Time on deposit	Interest rate
Greater than or equal to 5 years	.095
Less than 5 years but greater than or equal to 4 years	.090
Less than 4 years but greater than or equal to 3 years	.085
Less than 3 years but greater than or equal to 2 years	.075
Less than 2 years but greater than or equal to 1 year	.065
Less than 1 year	.058

Using this information, write a FORTRAN program that accepts the time that funds are left on deposit and displays the interest rate corresponding to the time entered.

If you are using subroutines, write this program so that the amount of money on deposit is input within the MAIN program unit and the determination and display of the interest rate are performed by a subroutine.

7. Write a FORTRAN program that accepts a number followed by one space and then a letter. If the letter following the number is an F, the program is to consider the entered number as a Fahrenheit temperature, convert it to an equivalent Celsius value, and print a suitable display message. If the letter following the number is a C, the program is to consider the number as a Celsius temperature, convert it to an equivalent Fahrenheit value, and print a suitable display message. If the letter is neither an F nor a C the program is to print a message that the data entered is incorrect and then terminate. Use ELSEIF statements in your program and make use of the conversion formulas:

Celsius = (5.0 / 9.0) * (Fahrenheit − 32.0)
Fahrenheit = (9.0 / 5.0) * Celsius + 32.0

If you are using subroutines, write this program so that the temperature and temperature-type designation are input within the MAIN program unit and the determination and display of the corresponding temperature are performed by a subroutine.

8. Using the commission schedule from Program 4-5, the following program calculates monthly income (note that four of the logical IF statements have been continued across two lines):

```
      PROGRAM MAIN
        REAL MSALES, INCOME
        PRINT *,'ENTER THE VALUE OF MONTHLY SALES: '
        READ *, MSALES
***
        IF (MSALES .GE. 50000.00) INCOME = 375.00 + 0.16 * MSALES
        IF (MSALES .GE. 40000.00 .AND. MSALES .LT. 50000.00)
     +    INCOME = 350.00 + 0.14 * MSALES
        IF (MSALES .GE. 30000.00 .AND. MSALES .LT. 40000.00)
     +    INCOME = 325.00 + 0.12 * MSALES
        IF (MSALES .GE. 20000.00 .AND. MSALES .LT. 30000.00)
     +    INCOME = 300.00 + 0.09 * MSALES
        IF (MSALES .GE. 10000.00 .AND. MSALES .LT. 20000.00)
     +    INCOME = 250.00 + 0.05 * MSALES
```

```
IF (MSALES .LT. 10000.00) INCOME = 200.00 + 0.03 * MSALES
PRINT *,'THE INCOME IS $', INCOME
END
```

a. Will this program produce the same output as Program 4-5?

b. Do you think that one program is better than the other? Why or why not?

9. The following program was written to produce the same result as Program 4-5:

```
PROGRAM MAIN
   REAL MSALES, INCOME
   PRINT *,'ENTER THE VALUE OF MONTHLY SALES: '
   READ *, MSALES
*
   IF (MSALES .LT. 10000.00) THEN
      INCOME = 200.00 + 0.03 * MSALES
   ELSEIF (MSALES .GE. 10000.00) THEN
      INCOME = 250.00 + 0.05 * MSALES
   ELSEIF (MSALES .GE. 20000.00) THEN
      INCOME = 300.00 + 0.09 * MSALES
   ELSEIF (MSALES .GE. 30000.00) THEN
      INCOME = 325.00 + 0.12 * MSALES
   ELSEIF (MSALES .GE. 40000.00) THEN
      INCOME = 350.00 + 0.14 * MSALES
   ELSE
      INCOME = 375.00 + 0.16 * MSALES
   ENDIF
*
   PRINT *,'THE INCOME IS',INCOME
END
```

a. Will this program run?

b. What does this program do?

c. For what values of monthly sales does this program calculate the correct income?

10. Using a FORMAT statement, rewrite Program 4-5 so that it displays all currency values to the nearest penny value in conventional dollar-and-cents format.

4.4 Applications

Three major uses of FORTRAN's IF statements are (1) to select appropriate processing paths, (2) to filter undesirable data from being processed at all, and (3) to create repeating sections of code. In this section we present examples of the first two uses. The use of IF statements in creating repeating sections of code is presented in Chapter 5.

Application 1: Solving Quadratic Equations

A *quadratic equation* is an equation that has the form $ax^2 + bx + c = 0$ or that can be algebraically manipulated into this form. In this equation, x is the unknown variable, and a, b, and c are known constants. Although the constants b and c can be any numbers, including zero, the value of the constant a cannot be zero (if a is zero, the equation would become a *linear equation* in x). Examples of quadratic equations are:

$5x^2 + 6x + 2 = 0$
$x^2 - 7x + 20 = 0$
$34x^2 + 16 = 0$

In the first equation, $a = 5$, $b = 6$, and $c = 2$; in the second equation, $a = 1$, $b = -7$, and $c = 20$; and in the third equation, $a = 34$, $b = 0$, and $c = 16$.

The real roots of a quadratic equation can be calculated using the quadratic formula as:

$$\text{root 1} = \frac{-b + \sqrt{b^2 - 4ac}}{2a}$$

and:

$$\text{root 2} = \frac{-b - \sqrt{b^2 - 4ac}}{2a}$$

A FORTRAN program that solves for the two roots of a quadratic equation, without any data validation statements, would use the user-entered values of a, b and c to directly calculate a value for each of the roots. However, if the user entered a value of 0 for a, the division by $2a$ would result in an error. Another error occurs when the value of the term $b^2 - 4ac$, which is called the *discriminant,* is negative, because the square root of a negative number cannot be taken. The complete logic for correctly determining the roots of a quadratic equation, including the steps necessary to determine that a valid quadratic equation is being processed, is illustrated in Figure 4-4.

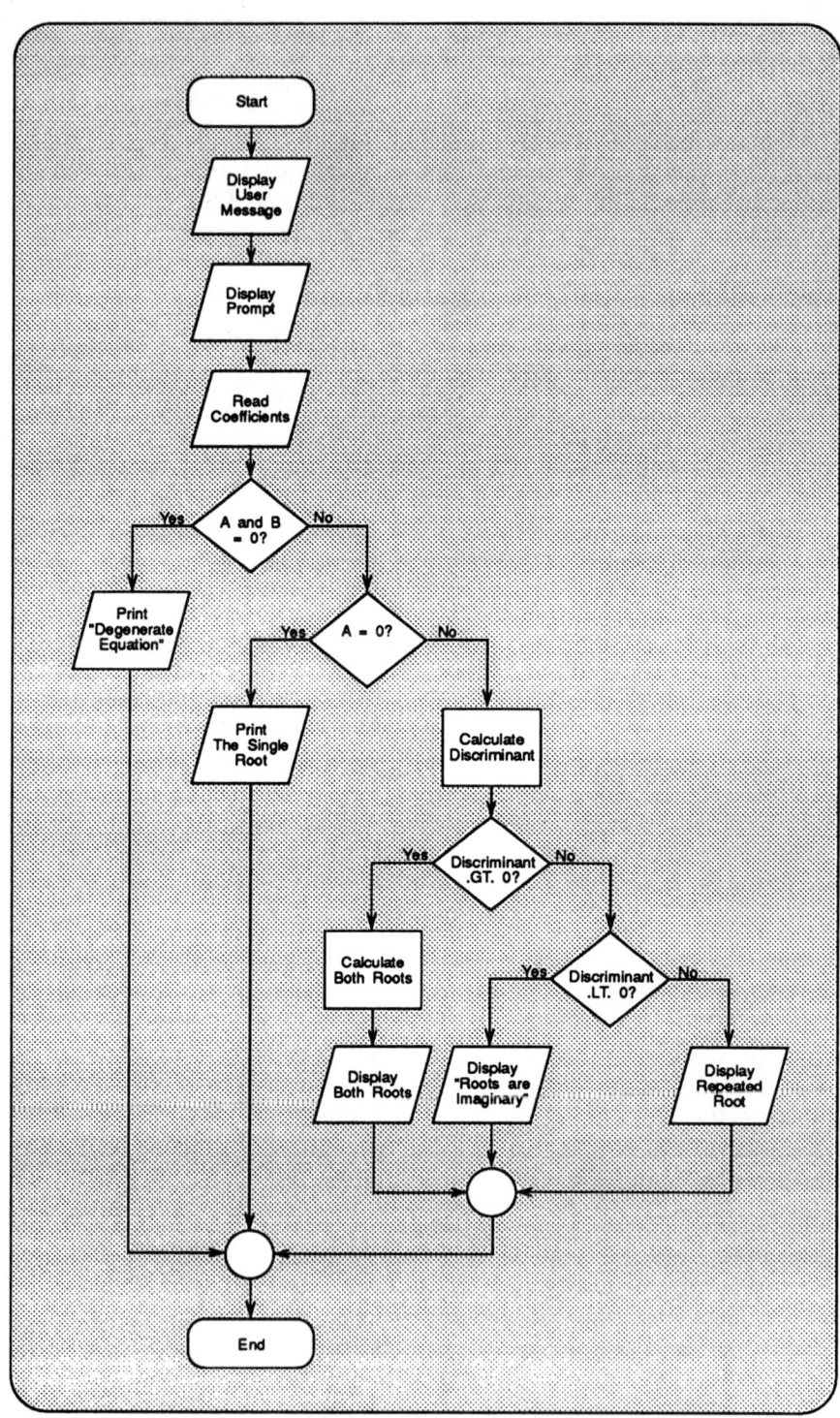

Figure 4-4   Program Logic Flowchart

The pseudocode corresponding to this figure is:

display a program purpose message
accept user-input values for a, b, and c
if a = 0 and b = 0, then
    display a message saying that the equation
    is degenerate (has no solution)
else if a = zero then
    calculate the single root equal to −c/b
    display the single root
else
    calculate the discriminant
    if the discriminant > 0 then
        solve for both roots using the quadratic formula
        display the two roots
    else if the discriminant < 0 then
        display a message that there are no real roots
    else
        calculate the repeated root equal to −b/(2a)
        display the repeated root
    endif
endif

Notice in both the flowchart and the equivalent pseudocode that we have used nested IF-ELSEIF structures. The outer IF-ELSEIF structure is used to validate the entered coefficients and determine that we have a valid quadratic equation. The inner IF-ELSEIF is then used to determine if the equation has two real roots (discriminant > 0), two imaginary roots (discriminant < 0), or repeated roots (discriminant = 0). The equivalent FORTRAN code for this problem is listed in Program 4-6.

Following are two sample runs of Program 4-6.

```
THIS PROGRAM CALCULATES THE ROOTS OF A
    QUADRATIC EQUATION OF THE FORM
          AX² + BX + C = 0

PLEASE ENTER VALUES FOR A, B, AND C:
1 2 -35
THE TWO REAL ROOTS ARE     5.000000 AND     -7.000000
```

and:

```
THIS PROGRAM CALCULATES THE ROOTS OF A
    QUADRATIC EQUATION OF THE FORM
          AX² + BX + C = 0

PLEASE ENTER VALUES FOR A, B, AND C:
0 0 16
THE EQUATION IS DEGENERATE AND HAS NO ROOTS
```

The first run solves the quadratic equation $x^2 + 2x − 35 = 0$, which has the real roots $x = 5$ and $x = −7$. The input data for the second run results in the equation $0x^2 + 0x + 16 = 0$. As this degenerates into the mathematical impossibility $16 = 0$, the program correctly identifies this as a degenerate equation.

Program 4-6

```
      PROGRAM MAIN
* THIS PROGRAM SOLVES FOR THE ROOTS OF A QUADRATIC EQUATION
      REAL A, B, C, DISC, ROOT1, ROOT2
      PRINT *, 'THIS PROGRAM CALCULATES THE ROOTS OF A'
      PRINT *, ' QUADRATIC EQUATION OF THE FORM'
      PRINT *, '            2'
      PRINT *, '        AX + BX + C = 0'
      PRINT *
      PRINT *, 'PLEASE ENTER VALUES FOR A, B, AND C: '
      READ *, A,B,C
* OUTER IF-ELSEIF STATEMENT
      IF (A .EQ. 0.0 .AND. B .EQ. 0.0) THEN
         PRINT *, 'THE EQUATION IS DEGENERATE AND HAS NO ROOTS'
      ELSE IF (A .EQ. 0.0) THEN
         PRINT *, 'THE EQUATION HAS THE SINGLE ROOT X = ', -C / B
      ELSE
         DISC = B**2 - 4*A*C
* INNER IF-ELSEIF STATEMENT
          IF (DISC .GT. 0.0) THEN
            DISC = SQRT(DISC)
            ROOT1 = (-B + DISC) / (2.0*A)
            ROOT2 = (-B - DISC) / (2.0*A)
            PRINT *, 'THE TWO REAL ROOTS ARE ', ROOT1, ' AND', ROOT2
          ELSEIF (DISC . LT. 0.0) THEN
            PRINT *, 'BOTH ROOTS ARE IMAGINARY'
          ELSE
            PRINT *, 'BOTH ROOTS ARE EQUAL TO ', -B / (2.0*A)
          ENDIF
      ENDIF
      END
```

Application 2: Data Validation

An important use of FORTRAN's IF statements is to validate data by checking for clearly invalid cases. For example, a date such as 5/33/86 contains an obviously invalid day. Similarly, the division of any number by zero, for example, 14/0, within a program, should not be allowed. Both of these examples illustrate the need for a technique called *defensive programming*, where the program includes code to check for improper data before an attempt is made to process it further. The defensive programming technique of checking user input data for erroneous or unreasonable data is referred to as *input data validation*.

Consider the case where we are to write a FORTRAN program to calculate the square root and the reciprocal of a user-entered number. Since the square root of a negative number does not exist as a real number, and the reciprocal of zero cannot be taken, our program will contain input data validation statements to screen the user-input data and avoid these two cases.

The flowchart describing the processing required for our program is shown in Figure 4-5. The pseudocode corresponding to this flowchart logic is:

display a program purpose message
accept a user input number
if the number is negative then
    print a message that the square root
    cannot be taken
else
    calculate and display the square root
endif
if the number is zero then
    print a message that the reciprocal
    cannot be taken
else
    calculate and display the reciprocal
endif

The FORTRAN code corresponding to Figure 4-5 is listed in Program 4-7.

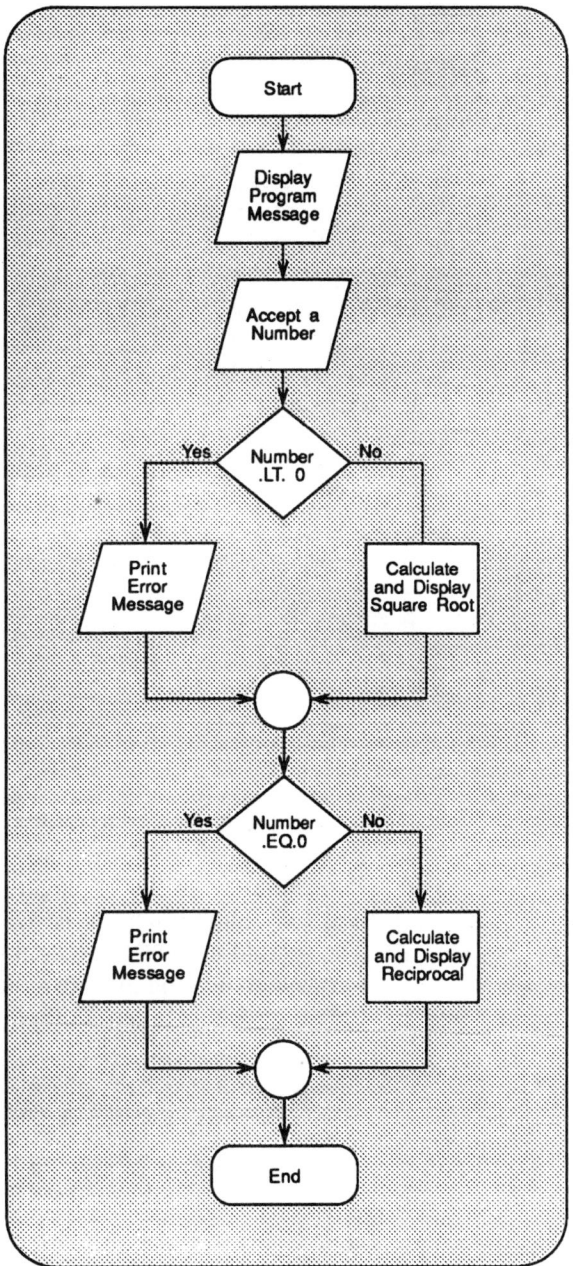

Figure 4-5   Program Logic Flowchart

Program 4-7

```
PROGRAM MAIN
  REAL USENUM
  PRINT *, 'THIS PROGRAM CALCULATES THE SQUARE ROOT AND'
  PRINT *, 'RECIPROCAL (1/NUMBER) OF A NUMBER'
  PRINT *
  PRINT *, ' PLEASE ENTER A NUMBER: '
  READ *, USENUM
  IF (USENUM .LT. 0.0) THEN
    PRINT *, 'THE SQUARE ROOT OF A NEGATIVE NUMBER'
    PRINT *, ' DOES NOT EXIST.'
  ELSE
    PRINT *, 'THE SQUARE ROOT OF ', USENUM, ' IS ', SQRT(USENUM)
  ENDIF
  IF (USENUM .EQ. 0.0) THEN
    PRINT *, 'THE RECIPROCAL OF ZERO DOES NOT EXIST'
  ELSE
    PRINT *,'THE RECIPROCAL OF ', USENUM, ' IS ', 1.0 / USENUM
  ENDIF
  END
```

Program 4-7 is a rather straightforward program containing two separate (nonnested) IF-ELSE structures. The first IF-ELSE checks for a negative input number. If the input number is negative, a message indicating that the square root of a negative number cannot be taken is displayed; otherwise the square root is taken. The second IF-ELSE statement checks if the entered number is zero. If it is zero, a message indicating that the reciprocal of zero cannot be taken is displayed; otherwise the reciprocal is taken. Following are two sample runs of Program 4-7.

```
THIS PROGRAM CALCULATES THE SQUARE ROOT AND
RECIPROCAL (1/NUMBER) OF A NUMBER
   PLEASE ENTER A NUMBER:
5
THE SQUARE ROOT OF 5.000000 IS 2.236068
THE RECIPROCAL OF 5.000000 IS 2.000000 E-01
```

and:

```
THIS PROGRAM CALCULATES THE SQUARE ROOT AND
RECIPROCAL (1/NUMBER) OF A NUMBER
   PLEASE ENTER A NUMBER:
-6
THE SQUARE ROOT OF A NEGATIVE NUMBER
   DOES NOT EXIST.
THE RECIPROCAL OF -6.000000 IS -1.666667 E-01
```

Additional Exercises for Chapter 4

1a. Write a program that accepts two real numbers and a select code from a user. If the entered select code is 1, have the program add the two previously entered numbers and display the result; if the select code is 2, the numbers should be multiplied; and if the select code is 3, the first number should be divided by the second number.

If you are using subroutines, write this program so that the two real numbers are input within the MAIN program unit and the determination and display of the appropriate result are performed by a subroutine.

b. Determine what the program written in Exercise 1a does when the entered numbers are 3 and 0 and the select code is 3.

c. Modify the program written in Exercise 1a so that division by 0 is not allowed and an appropriate message is displayed when such a division is attempted.

2a. Write a program to display the following two prompts:

```
ENTER A MONTH (USE A 1 FOR JAN, ETC.):
ENTER A DAY OF THE MONTH:
```

Have your program accept and store a number in the variable MONTH in response to the first prompt and accept and store a number in the variable DAY in response to the second prompt. If the month entered is not between 1 and 12 inclusive, print a message informing the user that an invalid month has been entered. If the day entered is not between 1 and 31, inclusive, print a message informing the user that an invalid day has been entered.

If you are using subroutines, write this program so that the two values are input within the MAIN program unit and the determination and display of the appropriate error message are performed by a subroutine.

b. What will your program do if the user types a number with a decimal point for the month? How can you ensure that your IF statements check for an integer number?

c. In a non–leap year February has 28 days; the months January, March, May, July, August, October, and December have 31 days; and all other months have 30 days. Using this information, modify the program written in Exercise 2a to display a message when an invalid day is entered for a user-entered month. For this program, ignore leap years.

3a. The quadrant that a line drawn from the origin resides in is determined by the angle that the line makes with the positive *X* axis as follows:

Angle from the positive X axis	Quadrant
Between 0 and 90 degrees	I
Between 90 and 180 degrees	II
Between 180 and 270 degrees	III
Between 270 and 360 degrees	IV

Using this information, write a FORTRAN program that accepts the angle of the line as user input and determines and displays the quadrant appropriate to the input data. (*Note:* If the angle is exactly 0, 90, 180, or 270 degrees, the corresponding line does not reside in any quadrant but lies on an axis.)

If you are using subroutines, write this program so that the angle is input within the MAIN program unit and the determination and display of the appropriate quadrant are performed by a subroutine.

b. Modify the program written for Exercise 3a so that a message is displayed that identifies an angle of zero degrees as the positive X axis, an angle of 90 degrees as the positive Y axis, an angle of 180 degrees as the negative X axis, and an angle of 270 degrees as the negative Y axis.

4a. All years that are evenly divisible by 400 or are evenly divisible by 4 and not evenly divisible by 100 are leap years. For example, since 1600 is evenly divisible by 400, the year 1600 was a leap year. Similarly, since 1988 is evenly divisible by 4 but not by 100, 1988 was also a leap year. Using this information, write a FORTRAN program that accepts the year as a user input, determines if the year is a leap year, and displays an appropriate message that tells the user if the entered year is or is not a leap year.

If you are using subroutines, write this program so that the year is input within the MAIN program unit and the determination and display of the appropriate message are performed by a subroutine.

b. Using the code written in Exercise 4a, redo Exercise 2c such that leap years are taken into account.

5. Based on an automobile's model year and weight, the state of New Jersey determines the car's weight class and registration fee using the following schedule:

Model year	Weight	Weight class	Registration fee
1970 or earlier	Less than 2700 lbs	1	$16.50
	2700 to 3800 lbs	2	25.50
	More than 3800 lbs	3	46.50
1971 to 1979	Less than 2700 lbs	4	27.00
	2700 to 3800 lbs	5	30.50
	More than 3800 lbs	6	52.50
1980 or later	Less than 3500 lbs	7	19.50
	3500 or more lbs	8	52.50

Using this information, write a FORTRAN program that accepts the year and weight of an automobile and determines and displays the weight class and registration fee for the car.

If you are using subroutines, write this program so that the year and weight are input within the MAIN program unit and the determination and display of the appropriate weight class and registration fee are performed by a subroutine.

6. Modify Program 4-6 so that the imaginary roots are calculated and displayed when the discriminant is negative. For this case, the two roots of the equation are:

$$x_1 = \frac{-b}{2a} + \frac{\sqrt{-(b^2 - 4ac)}}{2a} \; i$$

and:

$$x_2 = \frac{-b}{2a} - \frac{\sqrt{-(b^2 - 4ac)}}{2a} \; i$$

where i is the imaginary number symbol for the square root of -1. (*Hint:* Calculate the real and imaginary parts of each root separately.)

7. In the game of Blackjack the cards 2 through 10 are counted at their face values, regardless of suit; all face cards (jack, queen, and king) are counted as 10; and an ace is counted as either a 1 or an 11, depending on the total count of all the cards in a player's hand. The ace is counted as 11 only if the resulting total value of all cards in a player's hand does not exceed 21; otherwise it is counted as a 1. Using this information, write a FORTRAN program that accepts three card values as inputs (a 1 corresponding to an ace, a 2 corresponding to a two, and so on), calculates the total value of the hand appropriately, and displays the value of the three cards with a printed message.

4.5   Common Programming Errors

The common programming errors related to FORTRAN's selection statements include the following:

1. Forgetting the periods that must surround all relational and logical operators.
2. Trying to use arithmetic operators, such as =, <, and > instead of the correct FORTRAN relational operators (.EQ., .LE., .GT., etc.).
3. Trying to use a logical operator without a relational expression or logical variable. For example, the expression I .NE. 5 .OR. 10 is invalid. The expression A .NE. 5 .OR. A .NE. 10 in which the .OR. operator connects two relational expressions is valid.
4. Omitting the keyword THEN from a block IF statement or putting it in a logical IF statement.
5. Omitting the final ENDIF from a block IF statement, whether or not the block IF includes either the ELSEIF or the ELSE statement. This can create especially tricky logic problems when two IF statements are placed in sequence. For example, the section of code:

```
IF (AGE .GT. 25) THEN
         .
         .
         .
IF (EMPLYD .LT. 10) THEN
         .
         .
         .
ELSE
         .
         .
         .
ENDIF
```

is missing one ENDIF statement, which will be caught by the compiler when the statement is compiled. Now, however, you must be careful to place the missing ENDIF correctly. Placing an ENDIF immediately before or after the existing ENDIF creates a nested IF-ELSE statement, while placing the ENDIF before the second block IF creates a sequence of two nonnested block IF statements. The correct placement depends on the logic required.

6. This error presents a typical debugging problem. Here an IF statement appears to select an incorrect choice, and the programmer mistakenly concentrates on the tested condition as the source of the problem. For example, assume that the following IF-ELSE statement is part of your program:

```
IF (KEY .EQ. 'F') THEN
   XTEMP = (5.0/9.0)*(TEMP - 32.0)
   PRINT *, 'CONVERSION TO CELSIUS DONE'
ELSE
   XTEMP = (9.0/5.0) * TEMP + 32.0
   PRINT *, 'CONVERSION TO FAHRENHEIT DONE'
ENDIF
PRINT *, 'THE CONVERTED TEMPERATURE IS ', XTEMP
```

This statement will always display "CONVERSION TO CELSIUS DONE" when the variable KEY contains an F. Therefore, if this message is displayed when you believe KEY does not contain an F, investigation of KEY's value is called for. As a general rule, whenever a selection statement does not act as you think it should, make sure to test your assumptions about the values assigned to the tested variables using either PRINT or WRITE statements. If an unanticipated value is displayed, you have at least isolated the source of the problem to the variables themselves rather than the structure of the IF statement. From there you will have to determine where and how the incorrect value was obtained.

7. The last error common to selection statements is a subtle one and is really a numerical accuracy problem relating to REAL numbers. Because of the way computers store these values, tests for equality of REAL values or variables using the relational operator .EQ. should be avoided. The reason for this is that many decimal numbers, for example, .1, cannot be represented exactly in binary using a finite number of bits. Thus, testing for exact equality for such numbers can fail. When equality of REAL values is desired, it is better to require that the absolute value of the difference between operands be less than some extremely small value. Thus, for REAL operands the general condition:

```
operand 1 .EQ. operand 2
```

should be replaced by the condition:

```
ABS(operand 1 - operand 2) .LT. 0.000001
```

where the value 0.000001 can be altered to any other acceptably small value. Thus, if the difference between the two operands is less than 0.000001 (or any other user-selected amount), the two operands are considered essentially equal. For example, if X and Y are real variables, a condition such as:

```
(X/Y .EQ. 0.35)
```

should be programmed as:

```
(ABS(X/Y - 0.35) .LT. 0.000001)
```

This latter condition ensures that slight inaccuracies in representing real numbers in binary do not affect evaluation of the tested condition. Since all computers have an exact binary representation of zero, comparisons for exact equality to zero don't encounter this numerical accuracy problem (see, for example, Programs 4-6 and 4-7).

4.6 Chapter Summary

1. Relational expressions, which are also called *simple conditions,* are used to compare operands. The value of a relational expression is either .T. (true) or .F. (false). Relational expressions are created using the following relational operators:

Relational operator	Meaning	Example
.LT.	Less than	AGE .LT. 30
.GT.	Greater than	HEIGHT .GT. 6.2
.LE.	Less than or equal to	TAXABLE .LE. 20000
.GE.	Greater than or equal to	TEMP .GE. 98.6
.EQ.	Equal to	GRADE .EQ. 100
.NE.	Not equal to	NUMBER .NE. 250

2. More complex conditions can be constructed from relational expressions using FORTRAN's .AND., .OR., and .NOT. logical operators.

3. A block IF statement is used to select one or more statements for execution based on the value of a condition. The block IF statement has the form:

```
IF (condition) THEN
```

and must always be used with an ENDIF statement. Additionally, one ELSE statement and any number of ELSEIF statements may be used with a block IF statement to provide multiple selection criteria. The common selection structures that can be created using a block IF statement include the following forms:

a. Form 1: Simple IF-THEN:

```
IF (condition) THEN
   statement 1
   statement 2
      .
      .
      .
   statement n
ENDIF
```

Here, the statements between the block IF and ENDIF statements are only executed if the condition being tested is true. The block IF and ENDIF statements must be written on separate lines.

b. Form 2: Simple IF-ELSE:

```
IF (condition) THEN
   statement 1
   statement 2
        .
        .
        .
   statement n
ELSE
   statement n+1
        .
        .
        .
   statement m
ENDIF
```

This is a two-way selection structure. Here the ELSE statement is used with the block IF to select between two alternative sets of statements based on the value of a condition. If the condition is true, statements 1 through n are executed; otherwise, statements $n+1$ through m are executed. The block IF, ELSE, and ENDIF statements must be written on separate lines.

c. Form 3: Simple ELSEIF:

```
IF (condition 1) THEN
   one or more statements in here
ELSEIF (condition 2) THEN
   one or more statements in here
ELSE
   one or more statements in here
ENDIF
```

This is a three-way selection structure. Once a condition is satisfied, only the statements between that condition and the next ELSEIF or ELSE are executed, and no further conditions are tested. The ELSE statement is optional, and the statements corresponding to the ELSE statement are only executed if neither condition 1 nor condition 2 is true. The block IF, ELSEIF, ELSE and ENDIF statements must be written on separate lines.

d. Form 4: Multiple ELSEIFs:

```
IF (condition) THEN
   one of more statements in here
ELSEIF (condition 2) THEN
   one or more statements in here
               .
               .
               .
ELSEIF (condition n) THEN
   one or more statements in here
ELSE
   one or more statements in here
ENDIF
```

This is a multiway selection structure. Once a condition is satisfied, only the statements between that condition and the next ELSEIF or ELSE are executed, and no further conditions are tested. The ELSE statement is optional, and the statements corresponding to the ELSE statement are only executed if none of the conditions tested are true. The block IF, ELSEIF, ELSE and ENDIF statements must be written on individual lines.

4. A logical IF statement is a one-way selection statement that has the general form:

```
IF (condition) statement
```

where the single statement following the condition can be any executable FORTRAN statement except a block IF, logical IF, END, or a repetition statement, described in Chapter 5.

5. Block IF, ELSE, and ELSEIF statements may themselves contain logical IF, block IF, ELSE, and ELSEIF statements. Such constructions are called nested IF statements.

4.7   Enrichment Study: A Closer Look at Errors, Testing, and Debugging

The ideal in programming is to efficiently produce readable, error-free programs that work correctly and can be modified or changed with a minimum of testing required for reverification. In this regard, it is useful to know the different types of errors that can occur, when they are detected, and how they can be corrected.

Compile-Time and Runtime Errors

An error in a program can be detected either before it is compiled, while it is being compiled, while it is being run, after it has been executed and the output is being examined, or not at all. Errors that are detected by the compiler are formally referred to as *compile-time* errors, and errors that occur while the program is being run are formally referred to as *runtime* errors.

Although there is no formal name for errors that are detected either before a program is compiled or after a program is executed, there are methods for locating errors at these times. The method for detecting errors after a program has been executed is formally referred to as *program verification and testing*. The method for detecting errors before a program is compiled is called *desk checking*. Desk checking refers to the procedure of checking a program, by hand, at a desk or table for syntax and logic errors, which are described next.

Syntax and Logic Errors

Computer literature distinguishes between two primary types of errors, called syntax and logic errors, respectively. A *syntax error* is an error in the structure or spelling of a statement. For example, the statement:

```
IF (A .LT B)
  PINT * 'THERE ARE FIVE ERRORS HERE
  PRINT *, 'CAN YOU FIND TEM?'
ENDIF
```

contains five syntax errors. These errors are:

1. The relational operator LT is not followed by a period.
2. The keyword THEN is missing from the first line.
3. The keyword PRINT is misspelled in the second line.
4. There is a comma missing after the asterisk in the second line.
5. The closing apostrophe is missing in the second line.

All of these errors will be detected by the compiler when the program is compiled. This is true of all syntax errors—since they violate the basic rules of FORTRAN, if they are not discovered by desk checking, the compiler will detect them and display an error message indicating that a syntax error exists.* In some cases the error message is extremely clear and the error is obvious, and in other cases it takes a little detective work to understand the error message displayed by the compiler. Since all syntax errors are detected at compile time, the terms *compile-time error* and *syntax errors* are frequently used interchangeably. Strictly speaking, however, compile time refers to when the error was detected, and syntax refers to the type of error detected.

Note that the misspelling of the word THEM in the second PRINT statement is not a syntax error. As far as the compiler is concerned, the second PRINT statement satisfies all of the syntactical requirements for a valid PRINT statement. This spelling error is a rather simple example of a logic error.

Logic errors are characterized by erroneous, unexpected, or unintentional errors that are a direct result of some flaw in the program's logic. These errors, which are never caught by the compiler, may be detected either by desk checking, by program testing, by accident when a user obtains an obviously erroneous output, or while the

---

*   They may not, however, all be detected at the same time. Frequently, one syntax error "masks" another error and the second error is only detected after the first error is corrected.

program is executing. In this latter case a runtime error occurs that results in an error message being generated and/or abnormal and premature program termination.

Since logic errors may not be detected by the computer, they are always more difficult to detect than syntax errors. If not detected by desk checking, a logic error will usually reveal itself in one or both of two ways. In one instance the program executes to completion but produces incorrect results. A simple example of this is the misspelling of the word THEM in the code illustrated previously. More generally, logic errors of this type include:

- No output: caused by either an omission of a PRINT statement or a sequence of statements that inadvertently bypasses a PRINT statement.
- Unappealing or misaligned output: always caused by an error in either a PRINT or WRITE statement.
- Incorrect numerical results: always caused by either incorrect values assigned to the variables used in an expression, the use of an incorrect arithmetic expression, an omission of a statement, round-off error, or the use of an improper sequence of statements.

See if you can detect the logic error in Program 4-8.

 Program 4-8

```
      PROGRAM MAIN
* COMPOUND INTEREST PROGRAM
      INTEGER NYEARS
      REAL CAPTAL, AMOUNT, RATE
      PRINT *, 'THIS PROGRAM CALCULATES THE AMOUNT OF MONEY'
      PRINT *, 'IN A BANK ACCOUNT FOR AN INITIAL DEPOSIT'
      PRINT *, 'INVESTED FOR N YEARS AT AN INTEREST RATE R.'
      PRINT *
      PRINT *, ' ENTER THE INITIAL AMOUNT IN THE ACCOUNT: '
      READ *, AMOUNT
      PRINT *, ' ENTER THE INTEREST RATE (EX. 5 FOR 5%): '
      READ *, RATE
      CAPTAL = AMOUNT * (1 + RATE/100.) ** NYEARS
      PRINT *, ' THE FINAL AMOUNT OF MONEY IS ', CAPTAL
      END
```

Following is a sample run of Program 4-8.

```
THIS PROGRAM CALCULATES THE AMOUNT OF MONEY
IN A BANK ACCOUNT FOR AN INITIAL DEPOSIT
INVESTED FOR N YEARS AT AN INTEREST RATE R.

 ENTER THE INITIAL AMOUNT IN THE ACCOUNT:
1000.
 ENTER THE INTEREST RATE (EX. 5 FOR 5%):
5
 THE FINAL AMOUNT OF MONEY IS 1000.000000
```

As indicated in the output, the final amount of money is identical to the initial amount input. Did you spot the error in Program 4-8 that produced this apparently erroneous output?

Unlike a misspelled output message, the error in Program 4-8 causes a mistake in a computation. Here the error is that the program does not initialize the variable NYEARS before this variable is used in the calculation of CAPTAL. When the assignment statement that calculates CAPTAL is executed, the computer uses whatever value is stored in NYEARS. On those systems that initialize all variables to zero, the value zero will be used for NYEARS. However, on those systems that do not initialize all variables to zero, whatever "garbage" value that happens to occupy the storage locations corresponding to the variable NYEARS will be used (the manuals supplied with your compiler will indicate which of these two actions your compiler takes). In either case, an error is produced.

The second major type of logic error is one in that may cause the program to prematurely terminate execution and almost always results in a system error message being displayed. Examples of this type of error are attempts to divide by zero or to take the square root of a negative number. When this type of logic error occurs, it is a runtime error.

Testing and Debugging

In theory, a comprehensive set of test runs would reveal all logic errors and ensure that a program will work correctly for any and all combinations of input and computed data. In practice this requires checking all possible combinations of statement execution. Because of the time and effort required, this is an impossible goal except for extremely simple programs. Let us see why this is so. Consider Program 4-9.

Program 4-9 has two paths that can be executed when it is run. The first path, which is executed when the input number is 7, is the sequence:

```
PRINT *, 'ENTER A NUMBER: '
READ *, NUMBER
PRINT *, 'WHAM!'
```

The second path, which is executed whenever any number except 7 is input, includes the sequence of instructions:

```
PRINT *, 'ENTER A NUMBER: '
READ *, NUMBER
PRINT *, 'SLAM!'
```

Program 4-9

```
PROGRAM MAIN
   INTEGER NUMBER
   PRINT *, 'ENTER A NUMBER: '
   READ *, NUMBER
   IF (NUMBER .EQ. 7) THEN
      PRINT, * 'WHAM!'
   ELSE
      PRINT * ,'SLAM!'
   ENDIF
   END
```

To test each possible path through Program 4-9 requires two runs of the program, with a judicious selection of test input data to ensure that both paths of the IF-ELSE structure are exercised. The addition of one more IF-ELSE structure in the program increases the number of possible execution paths by a factor of two and requires four (2^2) runs of the program for complete testing. Similarly, two additional IF-ELSE structures increase the number of paths by a factor of four and require eight (2^3) runs for complete testing; three additional IF-ELSE structures would produce a program that required sixteen (2^4) test runs.

Now consider a modestly sized program consisting of four program units (one MAIN unit and three subroutine units), with each unit containing five IF-ELSE structures. The complete program thus contains 20 IF-ELSE structures. There are 32 (2^5) possible paths through each program unit; there are 1,048,576 (2^{20}) possible paths through the complete program, assuming each program unit is executed. The time needed to create individual test data to exercise each path and the actual computer runtime required for all the test data clearly become prohibitive. For this and larger programs, the complete testing of all program paths, referred to as *exhaustive testing,* is a practical impossibility.

The inability to fully test all combinations of statement execution sequences has led to the programming saying "there is no error-free program." It has also led to the realization that any testing that is done should be well thought out to maximize the possibility of locating errors. An important corollary to this is the realization that although a single test can reveal the presence of an error, it does not verify the absence of one. The fact that one error is revealed by testing does not indicate that another error is not lurking somewhere else in the program; the fact that one test revealed no errors does not indicate that there are no errors.

Once an error is discovered, however, the programmer must locate where it occurs and then fix it. In computer jargon, a program error is referred to as a "bug," and the process of isolating, correcting, and verifying the correction is called "debugging."

Although there are no hard-and-fast rules for isolating the cause of an error, some useful techniques can be applied. The first of these is a preventive technique. Frequently, many errors are simply introduced by the programmer in the rush to code and run a program before fully understanding what is required and how the result is to be achieved. A symptom of this haste to get a program entered into the computer is the lack of an outline of the proposed program (pseudocode or flowcharts) or of a handwritten program itself. Many errors can be eliminated simply by desk checking a copy of the program before it is ever entered or compiled.

A second useful technique is to mimic the computer and execute each statement, by hand, as the computer would. This means writing down each variable as it is encountered in the program and listing the value that should be stored in the variable as each input and assignment statement is encountered. Doing this also sharpens your programming skills, because it requires that you fully understand what each statement in your program causes to happen. Such a check is called *program tracing*.

A third, very powerful debugging technique is to use one or more diagnostic PRINT statements to display the values of selected variables. For example, consider again Program 4-8. Since this program produced an incorrect value for CAPTAL, it is worthwhile to place PRINT statement immediately before the assignment statement for CAPTAL to display the value of all variables used in the computation. If the displayed values are correct, the problem is in the assignment statement that computes CAPTAL; if the values are incorrect, we must determine where the incorrect values were obtained.

In this same manner, another use of PRINT statements in debugging is to immediately display the values of all input data. This technique is referred to as *echo printing*. It is useful in establishing that the computer is correctly receiving and interpreting the input data.

Finally, no discussion of debugging is complete without mentioning the primary ingredient needed for successful isolation and correction of errors. This is the attitude and spirit you bring to the task. Since you wrote the program, your natural assumption is that it is correct, or you would have changed it before it was compiled. It is extremely difficult to back away and honestly test and find errors in your own software. As a programmer, you must constantly remind yourself that just because you think your program is correct does not make it so. Finding errors in your own programs is a sobering experience, but one that will help you become a master programmer. It can also be exciting and fun if approached as a detection problem with you as the master detective.

Repetition

The programs examined so far have been useful in illustrating the correct structure of FORTRAN programs and in introducing fundamental input, output, assignment, and selection capabilities. By this time you should have gained enough experience to be comfortable with the concepts and mechanics of the FORTRAN programming process. It is now time to move up a level in our knowledge and abilities.

The real power of most computer programs resides in their ability to repeat the same calculation or sequence of instructions many times over, each time using different data, without the necessity of rerunning the program for each new set of data values. In this chapter we explore the FORTRAN statements that permit this.

5.1   The DO-WHILE Structure

The DO-WHILE structure is a general repetition construction that can be used in a variety of programming situations. In pseudocode a DO-WHILE structure has the general form:

```
do-while (condition) is true
    statement 1
    statement 2
          .
          .
          .
    statement n
enddo
```

The condition contained within the parentheses is evaluated in exactly the same manner as a condition in an IF statement; the difference is how the condition is used. As we have seen, when the condition is true in an IF statement, the statements following the condition are executed once. In a DO-WHILE structure, the statements following the condition are executed repeatedly as long as the condition remains true. This means that somewhere in the DO-WHILE structure there must be a statement that alters the value of the tested condition. As we will see, this is indeed the case. For now, however, considering just the condition and the statements following the condition, the process used by the computer in evaluating a DO-WHILE structure is:

Step 1. Test the condition
Step 2. If the condition is true
       a. execute the statements following the parentheses
       b. go back to step 1
    else
       exit the DO-WHILE structure

Notice that step 2b forces program control to be transferred back to step 1. The transfer of control back to the start of a DO-WHILE structure in order to reevaluate the condition is called a program loop. The DO-WHILE structure literally loops back on itself to recheck the condition until it becomes false. The flowchart for a DO-WHILE loop is illustrated in Figure 5-1.

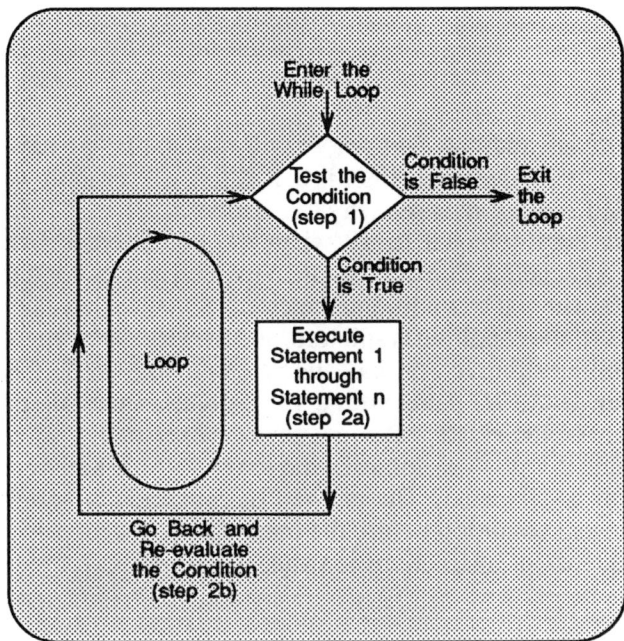

Figure 5-1 The DO-WHILE Loop Flowchart

Construction of a DO-WHILE loop in FORTRAN 77 requires the use of a block IF statement. The general FORTRAN 77 version of a DO-WHILE structure is:[*]

```
k IF (condition) THEN
      statement 1
      statement 2
            .
            .
            .
      statement n
      GO TO k
   ENDIF
```

Notice that this construction is a standard block IF statement with the addition of the new statement GO TO k, where k is the value of the statement number corresponding to the IF statement. The GO TO statement, which always has the form GO TO k, is called an *unconditional transfer of control statement*. Whenever this statement is encountered, execution is automatically transferred to the statement having the label specified in the GO TO statement.

To make this a little more tangible, consider the relational condition COUNT .LE. 10 and the statement PRINT *, COUNT. Using these, we can write the following DO-WHILE structure:

---

[*] See page 495 for an example of a directly implemented DO-WHILE statement.

```
5 IF (COUNT .LE. 10) THEN
    PRINT *, COUNT
    GO TO 5
  ENDIF
```

Although the above structure is valid, the alert reader will realize that we have created a situation in which the PRINT statement either is called forever (or until we stop the program) or is not called at all. Let us see why this happens.

If COUNT has a value less than or equal to 10 when the condition is first evaluated, the PRINT statement is executed. The GO TO statement then causes control to be transferred back to line 10, where the condition is retested. Since we have not changed the value stored in COUNT, the condition is still true, and the PRINT statement is reexecuted. This process continues forever, or until the program containing this statement is stopped by the user. If COUNT starts with a value greater than 10, the condition is false to begin with, and the PRINT statement never is executed.

How do we set an initial value in COUNT to control what the DO-WHILE structure does the first time the condition is evaluated? The answer, of course, is to assign values to each variable in the tested condition before the condition is encountered. For example, the following sequence of instructions is valid:

```
    COUNT = 1
10  IF (COUNT .LE. 10) THEN
      PRINT *, COUNT
      GO TO 10
    ENDIF
```

Using this sequence of instructions, we have ensured that COUNT starts with a value of one. We could assign any value to COUNT in the assignment statement—the important thing is to assign some value. In practice, the assigned value depends on the application.

We must still change the value of COUNT so that we can finally exit the loop. This requires a condition such as COUNT = COUNT + 1 to increment the value of COUNT each time the loop is executed. For example:

```
    COUNT = 1
10  IF (COUNT .LE. 10) THEN
      PRINT *, COUNT
      COUNT = COUNT + 1
      GO TO 10
    ENDIF
```

Let us now analyze this sequence of instructions. The first assignment statement sets COUNT equal to one. The IF statement is then entered, and the condition is evaluated for the first time. Since the value of COUNT is less than or equal to 10, the condition is true, and the statements within the IF statement are executed. The first statement within the IF statement causes the PRINT statement to display the value of COUNT. The next statement adds one to the value currently stored in COUNT, making this value equal to two. The GO TO statement now causes the program to loop back to retest the condition. Since COUNT is still less than or equal to 10, the statements within the loop are again executed. This process continues until the value of COUNT reaches 11. Program 5-1 illustrates these statements in an actual program.

Program 5-1

```
PROGRAM MAIN
      INTEGER COUNT
      COUNT = 1
5     IF (COUNT .LE. 10) THEN
        PRINT *, COUNT
        COUNT = COUNT + 1
        GO TO 5
      ENDIF
      END
```

The output for Program 5-1 is:

```
1
2
3
4
5
6
7
8
9
10
```

There is nothing special about the name COUNT used in Program 5-1 or the statement label assigned to the IF line. Any valid integer variable name could have been used, and any integer number between one and 99999 could have been used for the statement label.

Before we consider other examples of the DO-WHILE structure, two comments concerning Program 5-1 are in order. First, the statement COUNT = COUNT + 1 can be replaced with any statement that changes the value of COUNT. A statement such as COUNT = COUNT + 2, for example, would cause every second integer to be displayed. Second, it is the programmer's responsibility to ensure that COUNT is changed in a way that ultimately leads to a normal exit from the loop. For example, if we replace the statement COUNT = COUNT + 1 with the statement COUNT = COUNT −1, the value of COUNT will never reach 11, and an infinite loop is created (an infinite loop is a loop that never terminates). The computer will not reach out, touch you, and say, "Excuse me, you have created an infinite loop." It just keeps executing over and over (in this case, displaying numbers) until you realize that the program is not working as you expected or until it reaches the maximum time allocated for each run, if your system has one.

Now that you have some familiarity with the DO-WHILE structure, see if you can read and determine the output of Program 5-2.

Program 5-2

```
PROGRAM MAIN
   INTEGER I
*
   I = 10
22 IF (I .GE. 1) THEN
      PRINT *, I
      I = I - 1
      GO TO 22
   ENDIF
   END
```

The assignment statement in Program 5-2 initially sets the INTEGER variable I to 10. The IF statement then checks to see if the value of I is greater than or equal to one. While the condition is true, the value of I is displayed by the PRINT statement, and the value of I is decremented by one. When I finally reaches zero, the condition is false, and the program exits the DO-WHILE structure. Thus, the following display is obtained when Program 5-2 is run:

```
10
 9
 8
 7
 6
 5
 4
 3
 2
 1
```

To illustrate the power of the DO-WHILE structure, consider the task of printing a table of numbers from 1 to 10 with their squares and cubes. This can be done with the simple DO-WHILE structure illustrated in Program 5-3.

Program 5-3

```
PROGRAM MAIN
    INTEGER NUM
    PRINT *, ' NUMBER SQUARE CUBE'
    PRINT *, ' ------ ------ ----'
*
    NUM = 1
25  IF (NUM .LT. 11) THEN
        PRINT *, NUM, NUM**2, NUM**3
        NUM = NUM + 1
        GO TO 25
    ENDIF
    END
```

When Program 5-3 is run, the following display is produced:*

NUMBER	SQUARE	CUBE
1	1	1
2	4	8
3	9	27
4	16	64
5	25	125
6	36	216
7	49	343
8	64	512
9	81	729
10	100	1000

Note that the condition used in Program 5-3 is NUM .LT. 11. For the integer variable NUM, this condition can be replaced by the equivalent condition NUM .LE. 10. The choice of which to use is entirely up to you.

If we want to use Program 5-3 to produce a table of 1000 numbers, all we do is change the condition in the IF statement from I .LT. 11 to I .LT. 1001. Changing the 11 to 1001 produces a table of 1000 lines—not bad for a simple five-line DO-WHILE structure.

As a final example, consider the task of producing a Celsius-to-Fahrenheit temperature-conversion table. Assume that Fahrenheit temperatures corresponding to Celsius temperatures ranging from 5 to 50 degrees are to be displayed in increments of five degrees. The desired display can be obtained with the series of statements:

---

* The spacing required to produce alignment of the headings with the column of numbers was determined by trial and error. This, of course, is a disadvantage of list-directed output.

```
            CELSUS = 5
   122   IF (CELSUS .LE. 50) THEN
            FAHREN = (9.0/5.0) * CELSUS + 32.0
            PRINT *, CELSUS, FAHREN
            CELSUS = CELSUS + 5
            GO TO 122
         ENDIF
```

As before, the DO-WHILE structure begins with a block IF statement and ends with the keyword ENDIF. Prior to entering the DO-WHILE loop, we have made sure to assign a value to the operand being evaluated, and there is a statement to alter the value of CELSUS to ensure an exit from the DO-WHILE loop. Program 5-4 illustrates the use of this code in a complete program.

 Program 5-4

```
      PROGRAM MAIN
* A PROGRAM TO CONVERT CELSIUS TO FAHRENHEIT
      INTEGER CELSUS
      REAL FAHREN
      PRINT *, ' DEGREES DEGREES'
      PRINT *, ' CELSIUS FAHRENHEIT'
      PRINT *, ' ------- ----------'
      CELSUS = 5
  122 IF (CELSUS .LE. 50) THEN
         FAHREN = (9.0/5.0) * CELSUS + 32.0
         PRINT *, CELSUS, FAHREN
         CELSUS = CELSUS + 5
         GO TO 122
      ENDIF
      END
```

The display obtained when Program 5-4 is executed is:[*]

```
DEGREES   DEGREES
CELSIUS   FAHRENHEIT
-------   ----------
      5    41.000000
     10    50.000000
     15    59.000000
     20    68.000000
     25    77.000000
     30    86.000000
     35    95.000000
     40   104.000000
     45   113.000000
     50   122.000000
```

[*] As in Program 5-3, the alignment of the headings is determined by trial and error.

Programming Exercises

1. Rewrite Program 5-1 to print the numbers 2 to 10 in increments of two. The output of your program should be:

```
2
4
6
8
10
```

2. Rewrite Program 5-4 to produce a table that starts at a Celsius value of -10 and ends with a Celsius value of 60, in increments of 10 degrees.

3a. For the following program, determine the total number of items displayed. Also determine the first and last numbers printed.

```
    PROGRAM MAIN
      INTEGER NUM
      NUM = 0
20    IF (NUM .LE. 20) THEN
         NUM = NUM + 1
         PRINT *, NUM
         GO TO 20
      ENDIF
      END
```

b. Enter and run the program from Exercise 3a on a computer to verify your answers to the exercise.

c. How would the output be affected if the two statements within the DO-WHILE loop structure were reversed (that is, if the PRINT statement was made before the NUM = NUM + 1 statement)?

Note for Exercises 4 through 9: **If you have been programming with subroutines, write** each of the following programs with a single subroutine that is called from the MAIN program unit.

4. Write a FORTRAN program that converts gallons to liters. The program should display gallons from 10 to 20 in one-gallon increments and the corresponding liter equivalents. Use the relationship liters = 3.785 * gallons.

5. Write a FORTRAN program that converts feet to meters. The program should display feet from 3 to 30 in three-foot increments and the corresponding meter equivalents. Use the relationship meters = feet / 3.28.

6. A machine purchased for $28,000 is depreciated at a rate of $4000 a year for seven years. Write and run a FORTRAN program that computes and displays a depreciation table for seven years. The table should have the form:

Year	Depreciation	End-of-year value	Accumulated depreciation
1	4000	24000	4000
2	4000	20000	8000
3	4000	16000	12000
4	4000	12000	16000
5	4000	8000	20000
6	4000	4000	24000
7	4000	0	28000

7. An automobile travels at an average speed of 55 miles per hour for four hours. Write a FORTRAN program that displays the distance, in miles, that the car has traveled after .5, 1, 1.5, etc., hours until the end of the trip.

8a. An approximate conversion formula for converting Fahrenheit to Celsius temperatures is:

```
Celsius = (Fahrenheit - 30) / 2
```

Using this formula, and starting with a Fahrenheit temperature of zero degrees, write a FORTRAN program that determines when the approximate equivalent Celsius temperature differs from the exact equivalent value by more than four degrees. (*Hint:* Use a DO-WHILE loop that terminates when the difference between approximate and exact Celsius equivalents exceeds four degrees.)

b. Using the approximate Celsius conversion formula given in Exercise 8a, write a FORTRAN program that produces a table of Fahrenheit temperatures, exact Celsius equivalent temperatures, approximate Celsius equivalent temperatures, and the difference between the correct and approximate equivalent Celsius values. The table should begin at zero degrees Fahrenheit, use two-degree Fahrenheit increments, and terminate when the difference between exact and approximate values differs by more than four degrees.

9. The value of Euler's number, e, can be approximated using the formula:

```
e = 1 + 1/1! + 1/2! + 1/3! + 1/4! + 1/5! + . . .
```

Using this formula, write a FORTRAN program that approximates the value of e using a DO-WHILE loop that terminates when the difference between two successive approximations is less than 10 E-7.

10. The value of sin x can be approximated using the formula:

$$\sin x = \frac{x^3}{3!} + \frac{x^5}{5!} + \frac{x^7}{7!} + \frac{x^9}{9!} \quad . \quad . \quad .$$

Using this formula, determine how many terms are needed to approximate the value returned by the intrinsic SIN function with an error less than 1 E-6, when $x = 30$ degrees. (*Hints:* Use a DO-WHILE loop that terminates when the difference between the value returned by the intrinsic SIN function and the approximation is less than 1 E-6. Also note that x must first be converted to radian measure and that the alternating sign in the approximating series can be determined as $(-1)^{**}(n+1)$, where n is the number of terms used in the approximation.)

5.2   READing Within a Loop

Including a READ statement within a DO-WHILE loop produces very adaptable and powerful programs. To understand the concept involved, consider Program 5-5, where a DO-WHILE loop is used to accept and then display four user-entered numbers, one at a time. Although the program uses a very simple idea, it highlights the flow of control concepts needed to produce more useful programs.

 Program 5-5

```
PROGRAM MAIN
    INTEGER COUNT
    REAL NUM
    PRINT *, 'THIS PROGRAM WILL ASK YOU TO ENTER SOME NUMBERS.'
    COUNT = 1
10  IF (COUNT .LE. 4) THEN
       PRINT *, 'ENTER A NUMBER: '
       READ *, NUM
       PRINT *, ' THE NUMBER JUST ENTERED IS ', NUM
       COUNT = COUNT + 1
       GO TO 10
    ENDIF
    END
```

Following is a sample run of Program 5-5. The numbers 10, 18.3, 291, and 83 were input in response to the appropriate prompts.

```
THIS PROGRAM WILL ASK YOU TO ENTER SOME NUMBERS.
ENTER A NUMBER:
10
    THE NUMBER JUST ENTERED IS 10.000000
ENTER A NUMBER:
18.3
    THE NUMBER JUST ENTERED IS 18.299999
ENTER A NUMBER:
291
    THE NUMBER JUST ENTERED IS 291.000000
ENTER A NUMBER:
83
    THE NUMBER JUST ENTERED IS 83.000000
```

Let us review the program to clearly understand how the output was produced. The first message displayed is caused by the execution of the first PRINT statement.

This statement is outside and before the loop, so it is executed once before any statement within the loop.

Once the DO-WHILE loop is entered, the statements within it are executed as long as the tested condition is true. The first time through the loop the message "ENTER A NUMBER:" is displayed. The program then executes the READ statement, which forces the computer to wait for a number to be entered at the keyboard. Once a number is typed and the Return key is pressed, the second PRINT in the loop displays the number that was entered. The variable COUNT is then incremented by one. This process continues until four passes through the loop have been made and the final value of COUNT is five. Each pass causes the message "ENTER A NUMBER:" to be displayed, the READ statement to be executed, and the message "THE NUMBER JUST ENTERED IS " to be displayed. (Notice that an exact representation of the fractional part of the number 18.3 is not displayed. This reinforces the point made in Section 4.5 that exact representation of fractional numbers should not be assumed.) Figure 5-2 illustrates the flow of control for Program 5-5.

Program 5-5 can be modified in order to use the entered data rather than simply to display it. For example, let us add the numbers entered and display the total. To do this, we must be very careful in how we add the numbers, since the same variable, NUM, is used for each number entered. Because of this, the entry of a new number in Program 5-5 automatically causes the previous number stored in NUM to be lost. Thus, each number entered must be added to the total before another number is entered. The required sequence is:

enter a number
add the number to the total

How do we add a single number to a total? A statement such as TOTAL = TOTAL + NUM does the job perfectly. This is the accumulating statement introduced in Section 2.3. After each number is entered, the accumulating statement adds the number into the TOTAL, as illustrated in Figure 5-3. The flow of control required for adding the numbers is illustrated in Figure 5-4.

Observe that in Figure 5-4 we have made a provision for initially setting TOTAL to zero before the DO-WHILE loop is entered. If we were to clear TOTAL inside the DO-WHILE loop, it would be set to zero each time the loop was executed, and any previously stored value would be erased.

Program 5-6 incorporates the necessary modifications to Program 5-5 to total the entered numbers. As indicated in the flow diagram shown in Figure 5-4, the statement TOTAL = TOTAL + NUM is placed immediately after the READ statement. Putting the accumulating statement at this point in the program ensures that the entered number is immediately added into the total.

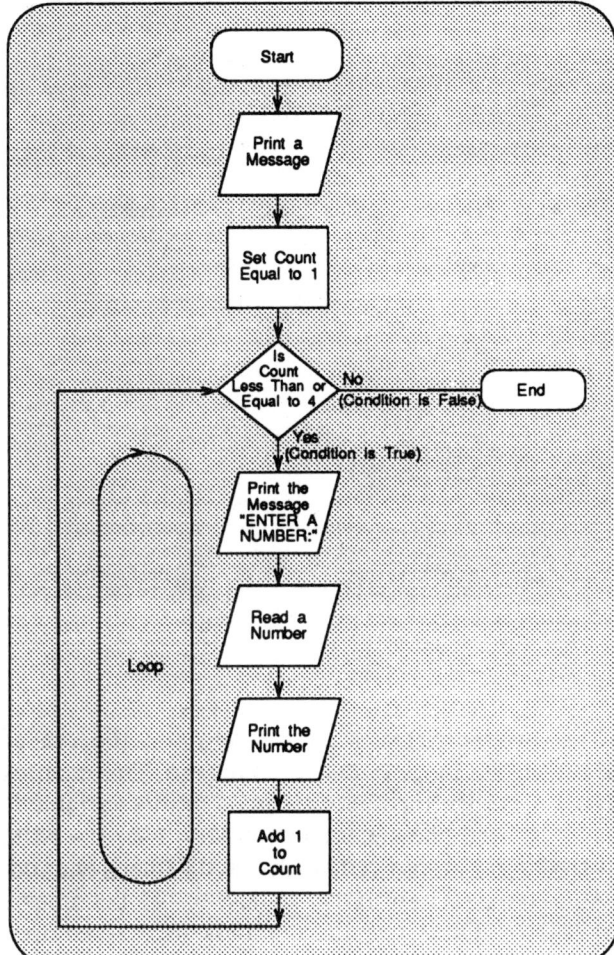

Figure 5-2   Flowchart for Program 5-5

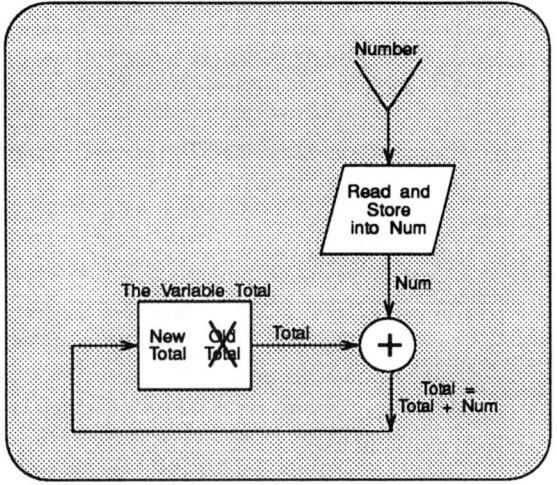

Figure 5-3   Accepting and Adding a Number to a Total

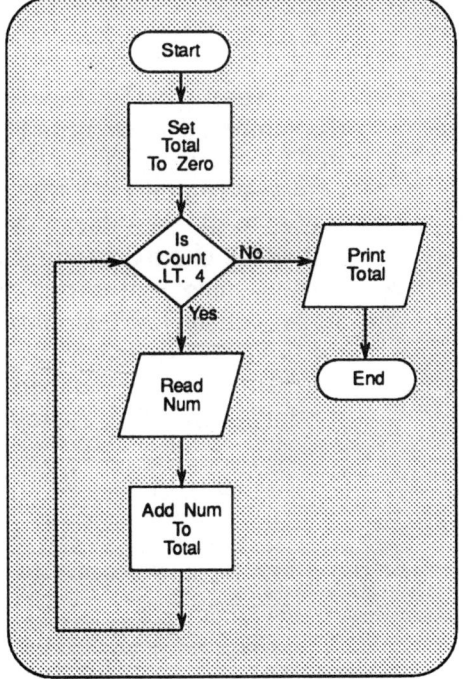

Figure 5-4   Accumulation Flowchart

Program 5-6

```
PROGRAM MAIN
   INTEGER COUNT
   REAL NUM, TOTAL
   PRINT *, 'THIS PROGRAM WILL ASK YOU TO ENTER SOME NUMBERS.'
   COUNT = 1
   TOTAL = 0
10    IF (COUNT .LE. 4) THEN
      PRINT *, 'ENTER A NUMBER: '
      READ *, NUM
      TOTAL = TOTAL + NUM
      PRINT *, ' THE TOTAL IS NOW ', TOTAL
      COUNT = COUNT + 1
      GO TO 10
   ENDIF
   PRINT *, 'THE FINAL TOTAL IS ', TOTAL
   END
```

Let us review Program 5-6. The variable TOTAL was created to store the total of the numbers entered. Prior to the DO-WHILE loop, TOTAL is set to zero. This ensures that any previous value present in the storage locations assigned to this variable is erased. When the DO-WHILE loop is entered, the statement TOTAL = TOTAL + NUM is used to add the value of the entered number into TOTAL. As each value is entered, it is added into the existing TOTAL to create a new TOTAL. Thus, TOTAL becomes a running subtotal of all the values entered. Only when all numbers are entered does TOTAL contain the final sum of all the numbers. After the DO-WHILE loop is finished, the last PRINT statement displays the final sum.

Using the same numbers (10, 18.3, 291, and 83) that were entered in the sample run for Program 5-5, the following sample run of Program 5-6 was made:

```
THIS PROGRAM WILL ASK YOU TO ENTER SOME NUMBERS.
ENTER A NUMBER:
10
   THE TOTAL IS NOW 10.000000
ENTER A NUMBER:
18.3
   THE TOTAL IS NOW 28.299999
ENTER A NUMBER:
291
   THE TOTAL IS NOW 319.299999
ENTER A NUMBER:
83
   THE TOTAL IS NOW 402.299999
THE FINAL TOTAL IS 402.299999
```

Having used an accumulating assignment statement to add the numbers entered, we can now go further and calculate the average of the numbers. First, however, we must decide where to calculate the average—within the DO-WHILE loop or outside it?

Calculating an average requires that both a final sum and the number of items in that sum be available. The average is then computed by dividing the final sum by the number of items. Thus, we must ask, "At what point in the program are both the correct sum and the number of items available?"

We see that the final sum in Program 5-6 is available after the DO-WHILE loop is finished. In fact, the whole purpose of the DO-WHILE loop is to ensure that the numbers are entered and correctly added to produce a correct sum. After the loop is finished, we also have a count of the number of items used in the sum. However, because of the way the DO-WHILE loop was constructed, the number in COUNT when the loop is finished is five, which is one more than the number of items (four) used to obtain the total. Knowing this, we simply subtract one from COUNT before using it to determine the average. With this as background, see if you can read and understand Program 5-7.

 Program 5-7

```
PROGRAM MAIN
    INTEGER COUNT
    REAL NUM, TOTAL, AVERGE
*
    PRINT *, 'THIS PROGRAM WILL ASK YOU TO ENTER SOME NUMBERS.'
    COUNT = 1
    TOTAL = 0
10  IF (COUNT .LE. 4) THEN
        PRINT *, 'ENTER A NUMBER: '
        READ *, NUM
        TOTAL = TOTAL + NUM
        COUNT = COUNT + 1
        GO TO 10
    ENDIF
    COUNT = COUNT - 1
    AVERGE = TOTAL / COUNT
    PRINT *, 'THE AVERAGE OF THE NUMBERS IS ', AVERGE
    END
```

Program 5-7 is almost identical to Program 5-6 except for the calculation of the average. We have also removed the repeating display of the total within the loop and the final display of it after the loop. The loop in Program 5-7 is simply used to enter and add four numbers. Immediately after the loop is exited, the average is computed and displayed.

Following is a sample run using Program 5-7:

```
THIS PROGRAM WILL ASK YOU TO ENTER SOME NUMBERS.
ENTER A NUMBER:
10
ENTER A NUMBER:
18.3
ENTER A NUMBER:
291
ENTER A NUMBER:
83
THE AVERAGE OF THE NUMBERS IS 100.574999
```

Sentinels

In many situations, the exact number of items to be entered is not known in advance, or the items are too numerous to count beforehand. For example, when entering a large amount of research data, we might not want to take the time to count the number of actual data items that are to be entered. In cases like this, it is desirable to enter data continuously and at the end to type in a special data value to signal the end of data input.

In computer programming, a data value used to signal either the start or the end of a series of data items is called a *sentinel*. The sentinel value must, of course, be selected so as not to conflict with legitimate data values. For example, if we were constructing a program that accepts a student's grades, and assuming that no extra credit is given that could produce a grade higher than 100, we could use any number higher than 100 as a sentinel value. Program 5-8 illustrates this concept. In this program data is continuously requested and accepted until a number larger than 100

 Program 5-8

```
PROGRAM MAIN
   REAL GRADE, TOTAL
   TOTAL = 0.0
   PRINT *, 'TO STOP ENTERING GRADES, TYPE IN ANY NUMBER'
   PRINT *, ' GREATER THAN 100.'
10 IF (GRADE .LE. 100) THEN
      PRINT *, 'ENTER A GRADE: '
      READ *, GRADE
      TOTAL = TOTAL + GRADE
      GO TO 10
   ENDIF
   PRINT *, 'THE TOTAL OF THE GRADES IS ', TOTAL - GRADE
   END
```

is entered. Entry of a number higher than 100 alerts the program to exit the DO-WHILE loop and display the sum of the numbers entered.

Following is a sample run using Program 5-8. As long as grades less than or equal to 100 are entered, the program continues to request and accept additional data. When a number greater than 100 is entered, the program adds this number to TOTAL and exits the DO-WHILE loop. Outside of the loop and within the PRINT statement, the value of the sentinel that was added to TOTAL is subtracted, and the sum of the legitimate grades that were entered is displayed.

```
TO STOP ENTERING GRADES, TYPE IN ANY NUMBER
  GREATER THAN 100.
ENTER A GRADE:
84
ENTER A GRADE:
75
ENTER A GRADE:
93
ENTER A GRADE:
88
ENTER A GRADE:
101
THE TOTAL OF THE GRADES IS 340.000000
```

Notice that Program 5-8 differs from previous examples in that termination of the loop is controlled by an externally supplied value rather than a fixed count condition. The loop in Program 5-8 will continue indefinitely until the sentinel value is encountered. DO-WHILE loops are well suited to handle sentinel values because of the loop's IF statement.

Breaking Out of a Loop

It is sometimes necessary to prematurely break out of a loop when an unusual error condition is detected. The means of doing this is provided by the GO TO statement that we have been using to force repetition of the DO-WHILE loop. For example, execution of the following DO-WHILE loop is immediately terminated if a number greater than 76 is encountered.

```
10      IF (COUNT .LE. 10) THEN
           PRINT *, 'ENTER A NUMBER: '
           READ *, NUM
           IF (NUM .GT. 76) GO TO 15
           GO TO 10
        ENDIF
15      next statement
```

The use of a GO TO statement in this manner violates pure structured programming principles because it provides a second, nonstandard exit from a loop. Nevertheless, this technique is extremely useful for breaking out of loops when an unusual condition is detected.

The statement that the "breakout" GO TO statement refers to can be any executable statement within the program, except that it should not be a statement internal to another loop. Can you see why? Entering a loop in the middle causes the initializing statements for the variables controlling the loop to be skipped, so that there is no control over how the entered loop will terminate.

Exercises

1. Rewrite Program 5-6 to compute the total of eight numbers.

2. Rewrite Program 5-6 to display the prompt:

   PLEASE TYPE IN THE TOTAL NUMBER OF DATA VALUES TO BE ADDED:

   In response to this prompt, the program should accept a user-entered number and then use this number to control the number of times the DO-WHILE loop is executed. Thus, if the user enters 5 in response to the prompt, the program should request the input of five numbers and display the total after five numbers have been entered.

3. By mistake, a programmer put the statement AVERGE = TOTAL / COUNT within the DO-WHILE loop immediately after the statement TOTAL = TOTAL + NUM in Program 5-7. Thus, the DO-WHILE loop becomes:

   ```
   10      IF (COUNT .LE.4) THEN
              PRINT *, 'ENTER A NUMBER: '
              READ *, NUM
              TOTAL = TOTAL + NUM
              AVERGE = TOTAL / COUNT
              COUNT = COUNT + 1
              GO TO 10
           ENDIF
   ```

   Will the program yield the correct result with this DO-WHILE loop?

   From a programming perspective, which DO-WHILE loop is better to use, and why?

4. Rewrite Program 5-7 to compute the average of ten numbers.

5. Rewrite Program 5-7 to display the prompt:

   PLEASE TYPE IN THE TOTAL NUMBER OF DATA VALUES TO BE AVERAGED:

   In response to this prompt, the program should accept a user-entered number and then use this number to control the number of times the DO-WHILE loop is executed. Thus, if the user enters 6 in response to the prompt, the program should request the input of six numbers and display the average of the next six numbers entered.

6a. Modify Program 5-8 to compute the average of the grades entered.

 b. Run the program written in Exercise 6a on a computer and verify the results.

7a. Write, compile, and execute a FORTRAN program that accepts a set of 10 numbers, finds the largest number of the entered values, and displays this value after all numbers have been entered.

 b. Modify the program written for Exercise 7a to also display the position of the largest entered number (that is, was it the first, second, third, etc., number entered?).

8. In addition to the arithmetic average of a set of numbers, both a geometric and a harmonic mean can be calculated. The geometric mean of a set of n numbers $x_1, x_2, \ldots x_n$ is defined as:

   $$\sqrt[n]{x_1 * x_2 * \ldots * x_n}$$

and the harmonic mean as:

$$\frac{n}{\dfrac{1}{x_1} + \dfrac{1}{x_2} + \ldots + \dfrac{1}{x_n}}$$

Using these formulas, write a FORTRAN program that continues to accept numbers until the number 999 is entered and then calculates and displays both the geometric and harmonic means of the entered numbers. (*Hint:* It will be necessary for your program to correctly count the number of values entered.)

9a. The following data was collected on a recent automobile trip.

	Mileage	Gallons
Start of trip:	22495	Full tank
	22841	12.2
	23185	11.3
	23400	10.5
	23772	11.0
	24055	12.2
	24434	14.7
	24804	14.3
	25276	15.2

Write a FORTRAN program that accepts mileage and gallons values and calculates miles per gallon (mpg) achieved for that segment of the trip. Miles per gallon is obtained as the difference in mileage between fill-ups divided by the number of gallons of gasoline used in the fill-up.

b. Modify the program written for Exercise 9a to additionally compute and display the cumulative mpg achieved after each fill-up. The cumulative mpg is calculated as the difference between each fill-up mileage and the mileage at the start of the trip divided by the sum of the gallons used to that point in the trip.

10a. Write a FORTRAN program to convert Celsius degrees to Fahrenheit. The program should request the starting Celsius value, the number of conversions to be made, and the increment between Celsius values. The display should have appropriate headings and list the Celsius value and the corresponding Fahrenheit value. Use the relationship Fahrenheit = (9.0 / 5.0) * Celsius + 32.0.

b. Run the program written in Exercise 10a on a computer. Verify that your program starts at the correct Celsius value and contains the exact number of conversions specified in your input data.

11a. Modify the program written in Exercise 10a to request the starting Celsius value, the ending Celsius value, and the increment. Thus, instead of the condition checking for a fixed count, the condition will check for the ending Celsius value.

b. Run the program written in Exercise 11a on a computer. Verify that your output starts and ends at the correct values.

12a. A bookstore summarizes its monthly transactions by keeping the following information for each book in stock:

> book identification number
> inventory balance at the beginning of the month
> number of copies received during the month
> number of copies sold during the month

Write a FORTRAN program that accepts this data for each book and then displays the book identification number and an updated book inventory balance using the relationship new balance = inventory balance at the beginning of the month + number of copies received during the month – number of copies sold during the month. Your program should use a DO-WHILE loop with a fixed count condition so that information on only three books is requested.

b. Run the program written in Exercise 12a on a computer. Review the display it produces and verify that the output is correct.

13. Modify the program you wrote for Exercise 12a to keep requesting and displaying results until a sentinel identification value of 999 is entered. Run the program on a computer.

14a. The outstanding balance on Rhona Karp's car loan is $8000. Each month Rhona is required to make a payment of $300, which includes both interest and principal repayment of the car loan. The monthly interest is calculated as 0.10/12.0 of the outstanding balance of the loan. After the interest is deducted, the remaining part of the payment is used to pay off the loan. Using this information, write a FORTRAN program that produces a table indicating the beginning monthly balance, the interest payment, the principal payment, and the remaining loan balance after each payment is made. Your output should resemble and complete the entries in the following table until the outstanding loan balance is zero.

Beginning balance	Interest payment	Principal payment	Ending loan balance
8000.00000000	66.66666667	233.33333333	7766.66666667
7766.66666667	64.72222223	235.27777777	7531.38888890
7531.38888890	.	.	.
.	.	.	.
.	.	.	.
.	.	.	0.00000000

b. Modify the program written in Exercise 14a to display the total of the interest and principal paid at the end of the table produced by your program.

5.3 The DO Statement

As we have seen, the condition used to control a DO-WHILE loop can be used either to test the value of a counter or to test for a sentinel value. Loops controlled by a counter are referred to as fixed-count loops, because the loop is executed a fixed number of times. The creation of fixed-count loops always requires initializing a counter variable, testing the counter variable, and modifying the counter variable. The general form we have used for these steps has been:

```
        initialize counter
    k   IF (counter .LT. final value) THEN
        statement 1
                .
                .
                .
        statement n
        counter = counter + increment
        GO TO
        ENDIF
```

The need to initialize, test, and alter a counter to create a fixed-count loop is so common that FORTRAN provides a special statement, called the DO statement, that groups all of these operations together on a single line. The general form of the DO statement is:

```
DO  k  variable = initial, final, increment
```

Although the DO statement looks a little complicated, it is really quite simple if we consider each of its parts separately. The *k* in the DO statement is the label of the last executable statement to be performed in the loop. Following the statement label are five items: a variable name, an equal sign, an initial value, a final value, and an increment value. Except for the increment, each of these items must be present in a DO statement, including the comma used to separate the initial and final values. If an increment is included, a comma must also be used to separate the increment value from the final value.

The variable name can be any valid FORTRAN name and is referred to as the loop counter (typically the counter is chosen as an integer variable); *initial* is the starting (initializing) value assigned to the counter; *final* is the maximum or minimum value the counter can have and determines when the loop is finished; and *increment* is the value that is added to or subtracted from the counter each time the loop is executed. If the increment is omitted, it is assumed to be one. Examples of valid DO statements are:

```
DO 5 COUNT = 1, 7, 1
DO 25 I = 5, 15, 2
DO 16 KK = 1, 20
```

In the first DO statement, the counter variable is named COUNT, the initial value assigned to COUNT is 1, the loop will be terminated when the value in COUNT exceeds 7, and the increment value is 1. In the next DO statement, the counter variable is named I, the initial value of I is 5, the loop will be terminated when the value in I exceeds 15, and the increment is 2. In the last DO statement, the counter variable is named KK, the initial value of KK is 1, the loop will be terminated when the value of KK exceeds 20, and a default value of 1 is used for the increment.

By convention, a CONTINUE statement is used to terminate DO loops. The CONTINUE statement is a "placeholder" statement that is used where a statement is syntactically required but no action is called for. As such, the CONTINUE statement is primarily used as a transfer point for other statements. The general form of this statement is:

```
k CONTINUE
```

where *k* is a statement number. When placed at the end of a DO loop, the value of *k* must be the same as the value referenced in the DO statement. Thus, the general form of a complete DO loop is:

```
DO k counter = initial, final, increment
   statement 1
   statement 2
         .
         .
         .
   statement n
k    CONTINUE
```

Here the DO statement is the first statement of the loop and determines how many times the statements 1 through *n* are executed. The CONTINUE statement performs no action but determines the end of the loop. It causes a transfer back to the beginning of the loop if the loop is to be executed again or serves as the exit point when the loop is completed.

Consider the loop contained within Program 5-9 as a specific example of a DO loop.

 Program 5-9

```
PROGRAM MAIN
   INTEGER COUNT
   PRINT *, ' NUMBER SQUARE ROOT'
   PRINT *, ' ------ -----------'
   DO 10 COUNT = 1, 5
     PRINT *, COUNT, SQRT(COUNT)
10   CONTINUE
   END
```

When Program 5-9 is executed, the following display is produced:

```
NUMBER        SQUARE ROOT
------        -----------
  1           1.000000
  2           1.414214
  3           1.732051
  4           2.000000
  5           2.236068
```

The first two lines displayed by the program are produced by the two PRINT statements placed before the DO statement. The remaining output is produced by the DO loop. This loop begins with the DO statement and ends with the CONTINUE statement (note that the CONTINUE's statement label number matches that given in the DO statement). This loop is executed as follows:

The initial value assigned to the counter variable COUNT is 1. Since the value in COUNT does not exceed the final value of 5, the statements in the loop, including the CONTINUE statement, are executed. The execution of the PRINT statement within the loop produces the display:

```
1   1.000000
```

The CONTINUE statement is then encountered and control is transferred back to the DO statement. The DO statement then increments the value in COUNT to 2, tests if COUNT is greater than 5, and repeats the loop, producing the display:

```
2   1.414214
```

This process continues until the value in COUNT exceeds the final value of 5, producing the complete output table. For comparison purposes, an equivalent DO-WHILE loop to the DO loop contained in Program 5-9 is:

```
       COUNT = 1
10     IF (COUNT .LE. 5) THEN
          PRINT *, COUNT, SQRT(COUNT)
          COUNT = COUNT + 1
          GO TO 10
       ENDIF
```

As seen in this example, the difference between the DO and DO-WHILE loops is the placement of the initialization, condition test, and incrementing items. The grouping together of these items in the DO statement is very convenient when fixed-count loops must be constructed. See if you can determine the output produced by Program 5-10.

Program 5-10

```
PROGRAM MAIN
   INTEGER COUNT
   DO 15 COUNT = 12, 20, 2
      PRINT *, COUNT
15    CONTINUE
   END
```

Did you figure it out? The loop starts with COUNT initialized to 12, stops when COUNT exceeds 20, and increments COUNT in steps of 2. The actual statements executed include all statements following the DO statement up to and including the CONTINUE statement. The output of Program 5-10 is:

```
12
14
16
18
20
```

DO Loop Structure

Now that we have seen a few simple examples of DO loop structures, it is useful to summarize the rules that all DO loops must adhere to:

1. The last statement in a DO loop can be any executable statement except a GO TO, IF, ELSEIF, ELSE, ENDIF, END, STOP, RETURN, or another DO statement. (Always placing a CONTINUE statement as the last statement of a DO loop ensures that you will never violate this rule.)
2. The DO loop counter variable may be either a real or an integer variable.
3. The initial, final, and increment values may all be replaced by variables or expressions, as long as each variable has a value previously assigned to it, and the expressions can be evaluated to yield a number. For example, the DO statement:
    ```
    DO 10 ICOUNT = BEGIN, BEGIN + 10.0, AUGMNT
    ```
    is valid and can be used as long as values have been assigned to the variables BEGIN and AUGMNT before this statement is encountered in a program.
4. The initial, final, and increment values may be positive or negative, but the loop will not be not executed at all if any one of the following is true:
    a. The initial value is greater than the final value and the increment is positive.
    b. The initial value is less than the final value and the increment is negative.
    c. The increment is zero.

5. A GO TO statement may be embedded within the DO loop to cause a transfer out of the loop.

Once a DO loop is correctly structured, it is executed as follows:*

Step 1. The initial value is assigned to the counter variable.

Step 2. The value in the counter is compared to the final value. For positive increments if the value is less than or equal to the final value, then:

all loop statements are executed

the counter is incremented, and step 2 is repeated

For negative increments if the value is greater than or equal to the fixed value, then:

all loop statements are executed

the counter is decremented asnd step 2 is repeated

else

the loop is terminated

It is extremely important to realize that no statement within the loop should ever alter the value in the counter because the increment or decrement of the loop counter is automatically done by the DO statement. The value in the counter may itself be displayed, as in Program 5-10, or may be used in an expression to calculate some other variable. It must never, however, be used either on the left-hand side of an assignment statement or in a READ statement within the loop. Also notice that when a DO loop is completed, the counter contains the last value that exceeds the final tested value.

Figure 5-5 illustrates the internal workings of the DO loop for positive increments. To avoid the necessity of always illustrating these steps, a simplified set of flowchart symbols is available for describing DO loops. Using the fact that a DO statement can be represented by the flowchart symbol:

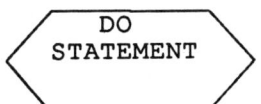

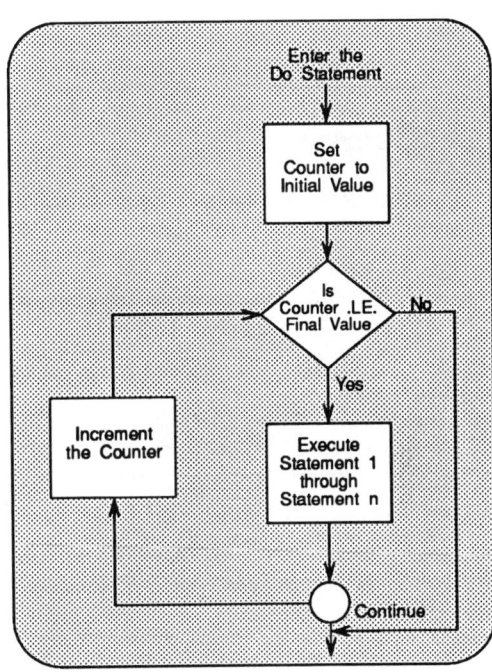

Figure 5-5   DO Loop Flowchart for Positive Increments

---

*   The number of times that a DO loop is executed is determined by the expression:

INT ((*final value* – *initial value* + *increment*) / *increment*)

If this expression results in a negative value, the loop is not executed.

Complete DO loops can alternatively be illustrated as shown in Figure 5-6.

To understand the enormous power of DO loops, consider the task of printing a table of numbers from 1 to 10, including their squares and cubes, using a DO statement. Such a table was previously produced using a DO-WHILE loop in Program 5-3. You may wish to review Program 5-3 and compare it to Program 5-11 to get a further sense of the equivalence between DO and DO-WHILE loops.

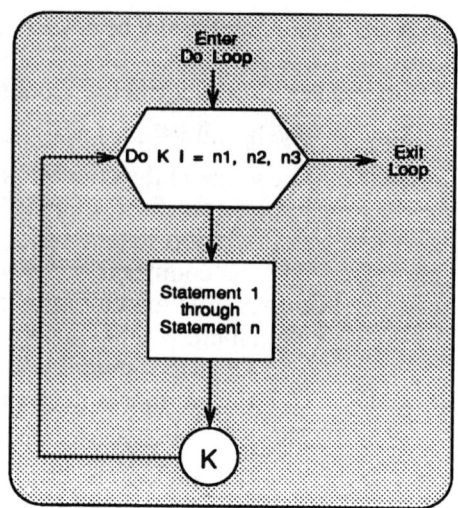

Figure 5-6   Simplified DO Loop

 Program 5-11

```
PROGRAM MAIN
  INTEGER NUM
  PRINT *, ' NUMBER SQUARE CUBE'
  PRINT *, ' ------ ------ ----'
  DO 30, NUM = 1,10
     PRINT *, NUM, NUM**2, NUM**3
30   CONTINUE
  END
```

When Program 5-11 is run, the display produced is:

NUMBER	SQUARE	CUBE
1	1	1
2	4	8
3	9	27
4	16	64
5	25	125
6	36	216
7	49	343
8	64	512
9	81	729
10	100	1000

Simply changing the number 10 in the DO statement of Program 5-11 to 1000 creates a loop that is executed 1000 times and produces a table of numbers from 1 to 1000. As with the DO-WHILE loop, this small change produces an immense increase in the processing and output provided by the program.

Skill Builder Exercises

1. Write individual DO statements for the following cases:

   a. Use a counter named I that has an initial value of 1, a final value of 20, and an increment of 1.

   b. Use a counter named ICOUNT that has an initial value of 1, a final value of 20, and an increment of 2.

   c. Use a counter named J that has an initial value of 1, a final value of 100, and an increment of 5.

   d. Use a counter named ICOUNT that has an initial value of 20, a final value of 1, and an increment of –1.

   e. Use a counter named ICOUNT that has an initial value of 20, a final value of 1, and an increment of –2.

   f. Use a counter named COUNT that has an initial value of 1.0, a final value of 16.2, and an increment of 0.2.

   g. Use a counter named XCNT that has an initial value of 20.0, a final value of 10.0, and an increment of –0.5.

2. Determine the number of times that each DO loop is executed for the DO statements written for Exercise 1.

3. Determine the value in TOTAL after each of the following loops is executed.

   a.
   ```
           TOTAL = 0
           DO 10 I = 1, 10
             TOTAL = TOTAL + I
        10  CONTINUE
   ```
   b.
   ```
           TOTAL = 1
           DO 10 COUNT = 1, 10
             TOTAL = TOTAL * 2
        10  CONTINUE
   ```
   c.
   ```
           TOTAL = 0
           DO 10 I = 10, 15
             TOTAL = TOTAL + I
        10  CONTINUE
   ```
   d.
   ```
           TOTAL = 50
           DO 15 I = 1, 10
             TOTAL = TOTAL - I
        15  CONTINUE
   ```
   e.
   ```
           TOTAL = 1
           DO 20 ICNT = 1, 8
             TOTAL = TOTAL * ICNT
        20  CONTINUE
   ```
   f.
   ```
           TOTAL = 1.0
           DO 25 J = 1, 5
             TOTAL = TOTAL / 2.0
        25  CONTINUE
   ```

4. Determine the errors in the following DO statements:

   a. DO I = 1,10
   b. DO 10 COUNT 5,10
   c. DO 5 JJ = 1 10 2
   d. DO 15 KK = 1, 10, -1
   e. DO 20 KK = -1, -20

5. Determine the output of the following program:

```
      PROGRAM MAIN
        INTEGER I
        DO 10 I = 20, 0, -4
          PRINT *, I
10      CONTINUE
        END
```

6. Modify Program 5-11 to produce a table of the numbers 0 through 20 in increments of 2, with their squares and cubes.

7. Modify Program 5-11 to produce a table of numbers from 10 to 1, instead of 1 to 10 as it currently does.

Programming Exercises

Note for Exercises 8 through 13: **If you have been programming with subroutines,** write each of the following programs with a single subroutine that is called from the MAIN program unit.

8. Write and run a FORTRAN program that displays a table of 20 temperature conversions from Fahrenheit to Celsius. The table should start with a Fahrenheit value of 20 degrees and be incremented in values of 4 degrees. Recall that Celsius = (5.0/9.0) * (Fahrenheit – 32).

9. The expansion of a steel bridge as it is heated to a final Celsius temperature, T_F, from an initial Celsius temperature, T_0, can be approximated using the formula:

   Increase in length = $a * L * (T_F - T_0)$

where a is the coefficient of expansion, which for steel is 11.7 E–6, and L is the length of the bridge at temperature T_0. Using this formula, write a FORTRAN program that displays a table of expansion lengths for a steel bridge that is 7365 meters long at 0 degrees Celsius, as the temperature increases to 40 degrees in 5-degree increments.

10. The probability that an individual telephone call will last less than t minutes can be approximated by the exponential probability function:

   Probability that a call lasts less than t minutes = $1 - e^{-t/a}$

where a is the average call length and e is Euler's number (2.71828). For example, assuming that the average call length is 2.5 minutes, the probability that a call will last less than one minute is calculated as $1 - e^{-1/2.5} = 0.3297$.

Using this probability function, write a FORTRAN program that calculates and displays a list of probabilities of a calls lasting less than 1 to less than 10 minutes, in 1-minute increments.

11a. The arrival rate of customers in a busy New York bank can be estimated using the Poisson probability function:

$$P(x) \ = \ \frac{a^x \ e^{-a}}{x!}$$

where x is the number of customer arrivals per minute, a is the average number of arrivals per minute, and e is Euler's number (2.71828). For example, if the average number of customers entering the bank is three customers per minute, then a is equal to three. Thus, the probability of zero customers arriving in any one minute is:

$$P(x+0) \ = \ \frac{3^0 e^{-3}}{0!} = .0498$$

and the probability of one customer arriving in any one minute is:

$$P(x+1) \ = \ \frac{3^1 e^{-3}}{1!} = .1494$$

Using the Poisson probability function, write a FORTRAN program that calculates and displays the probability of 0 to 20 customer arrivals when the average arrival rate is 3 customers per minute.

b. The formula given in Exercise 11a is also applicable for estimating the arrival rate of planes at a busy airport (here, an arriving "customer" is an incoming airplane). Using this formula, modify the program written in Exercise 11a to accept the average arrival rate as an input data item. Then run the modified program to determine the probability of 0 to 10 planes attempting to land in any 1-minute period at an airport during peak arrival times. Assume that the average arrival rate for peak arrival times is 2 planes per minute.

12. Write and run a program that calculates and displays the amount of money available in a bank account that initially has $1000 deposited in it and that earns 8 percent interest a year. Your program should display the amount available at the end of each year for a period of 10 years. Use the relationship that the money available at the end of each year equals the amount of money in the account at the start of the year plus .08 times the amount available at the start of the year.

13. A machine purchased for $28,000 is depreciated at a rate of $4000 a year for seven years. Write and run a FORTRAN program that computes and displays a depreciation table for seven years. The table should have the form:

```
              Depreciation schedule
              ----------------------
                             End-of-year    Accumulated
   Year       Depreciation      value       depreciation
   ----       ------------   -----------    ------------
    1             4000          24000           4000
    2             4000          20000           8000
    3             4000          16000          12000
    4             4000          12000          16000
    5             4000           8000          20000
    6             4000           4000          24000
    7             4000              0          28000
```

14. A well-regarded manufacturer of widgets has been losing 4 percent of its sales each year. The annual profit for the firm is 10 percent of sales. This year the firm has had $10 million in sales and a profit of $1 million. Determine the expected sales and profit for the next 10 years. Your program should complete and produce a display as follows:

```
            Sales and profit projection
            ---------------------------
   Year          Expected sales          Projected profit
   ----          --------------          ----------------
   1             $10000000.00            $1000000.00
   2             $ 9600000.00            $ 960000.00
   3                   .                       .
   .                   .                       .
   .                   .                       .
   .                   .                       .
   10                  .                       .
   Totals:       $     .                 $     .
```

5.4 DO Loop Programming Techniques

In this section we present four common programming techniques associated with DO loops. All of these techniques are common knowledge to experienced FORTRAN programmers.

Technique 1: Variable Parameters

The initial, final, and increment values in a DO statement are formally called the parameters of the DO statement. Although each parameter must be known and set before the DO statement is executed, these values may be set using variables rather than constant values. For example, the four statements:

```
I = 5
J = 10
K = 1
DO 20 COUNT = I, J, K
```

produce the same effect as the single statement:

```
DO 20 COUNT = 5,10,1
```

The advantage of the first DO statement, where variables are used for the initial, final, and increment parameters, is that it allows us to assign values to these variables external to the DO statement. This is especially useful when READ statements are used to set the actual values. To make this more tangible, consider Program 5-12.

In Program 5-12, we have used a variable name for the final parameter only. Since this parameter must be set before the DO statement is executed, a READ statement has been placed before the DO statement to allow the user to decide what the final value should be. Notice that this arrangement permits the user to set the size of the table at run time rather than having the programmer set the table size at compile time. This also makes the program more general, since it now can be used to create a variety of tables without the need for reprogramming and recompiling.

Program 5-12

```
      PROGRAM MAIN
* THIS PROGRAM DISPLAYS A TABLE OF NUMBERS, THEIR SQUARES AND CUBES
* STARTING FROM THE NUMBER 1. THE FINAL NUMBER IN THE TABLE
* IS DECIDED BY THE USER
      INTEGER NUM, IFINAL
      PRINT *, 'ENTER THE FINAL NUMBER: '
      READ *, IFINAL
      PRINT *, ' NUMBER SQUARE CUBE'
      PRINT *, ' ------ -----------'
      DO 30, NUM = 1, IFINAL
         PRINT *, NUM, NUM**2, NUM**3
  30     CONTINUE
      END
```

Technique 2: READing Within a DO Loop

Using a READ statement inside a DO loop produces the same effect as when this statement is used inside a DO-WHILE loop. For example, in Program 5-13 a READ statement is used to input a set of numbers. As each number is input, it is added to a total. When the DO loop is exited, the average is calculated and displayed.

 Program 5-13

```
      PROGRAM MAIN
* THIS PROGRAM CALCULATES THE AVERAGE OF FIVE USER-ENTERED NUMBERS
      INTEGER COUNT
      REAL NUM, TOTAL, AVERGE
*
      TOTAL = 0.0
*
      DO 10 COUNT = 1,5
         PRINT *, 'ENTER A NUMBER: '
         READ *, NUM
         TOTAL = TOTAL + NUM
  10     CONTINUE
      AVERGE = TOTAL / (COUNT-1)
      PRINT *, 'THE AVERAGE OF THE DATA ENTERED IS ', AVERGE
      END
```

The DO statement in Program 5-13 creates a loop that is executed five times. The user is prompted to enter a number each time through the loop. After each number is entered, it is immediately added to the total. Notice that TOTAL is initialized to zero before the DO statement is executed. Also notice that the value in COUNT is reduced by one in the calculation of the average. The reason for this is that upon completion of the DO statement, the counter always contains the first value that exceeds the final tested value. The loop in Program 5-13 is executed as long as the value in COUNT is less than or equal to five and is terminated when COUNT becomes six (the increment to six, in fact, is what causes the loop to end). Thus, to obtain the proper average, the five entered numbers must be divided by five and not by the value of six stored in COUNT.

Technique 3: Selection Within a DO Loop

Another common programming technique is to use a DO loop to cycle through a set of numbers and select those numbers that meet one or more criteria. For example, assume that we want to find both the positive and the negative sums of a set of numbers. The criterion here is whether the number is positive or negative, and the logic for implementing this program is given by the pseudocode:

> *Do for each number*
> *Enter a number*
> *If the number is greater than zero*
> *add the number to the positive sum*
> *else*
> *add the number to the negative sum*
> *Enddo*

Program 5-14 describes this algorithm in FORTRAN for the case where five numbers are to be entered.

Following is a sample run using Program 5-14.

```
ENTER A NUMBER (POSITIVE OR NEGATIVE):
10
ENTER A NUMBER (POSITIVE OR NEGATIVE):
-10
ENTER A NUMBER (POSITIVE OR NEGATIVE):
5
ENTER A NUMBER (POSITIVE OR NEGATIVE):
-7
ENTER A NUMBER (POSITIVE OR NEGATIVE):
11
  THE POSITIVE TOTAL IS 26.00000000
  THE NEGATIVE TOTAL IS -17.0000000
```

Technique 4: Evaluating Functions of One Variable

DO loops can be conveniently constructed to determine and display the values of single variable functions for a set of values over any specified interval. For example, assume that we want to know the values of the function:

$$Y = 10X^2 + 3X - 2$$

Program 5-14

```
      PROGRAM MAIN
* THIS PROGRAM COMPUTES THE POSITIVE AND NEGATIVE SUMS OF A SET
* OF 5 USER ENTERED NUMBERS
      INTEGER I
      REAL USENUM, POSTOT, NEGTOT
      POSTOT = 0.0
      NEGTOT = 0.0
      DO 10 I = 1,5
         PRINT *, 'ENTER A NUMBER (POSITIVE OR NEGATIVE): '
         READ *, USENUM
         IF (USENUM .GT. 0) THEN
            POSTOT = POSTOT + USENUM
         ELSE
            NEGTOT = NEGTOT + USENUM
         ENDIF
  10     CONTINUE
         PRINT *,' THE POSITIVE TOTAL IS ', POSTOT
         PRINT *,' THE NEGATIVE TOTAL IS ', NEGTOT
         END
```

for X between two and five. Assuming that X has been declared as an integer variable, the following DO loop can be used to calculate the required values.

```
      DO 10 X = 2, 5
         Y = 10* X ** 2 + 3 * X - 2
         PRINT *, X, Y
  10 CONTINUE
```

For this loop we have used the variable X as both the counter variable and the unknown (independent variable) in the function. For each value of X from two to five, a new value of Y is calculated and displayed. This DO loop is contained within Program 5-15, which also displays appropriate headings for the values printed.

The following is displayed when Program 5-15 is executed:

```
      X VALUE        Y VALUE
      -------        -------
         2              44
         3              97
         4             170
         5             263
```

Two items are of importance here. The first is that any function of a single variable can be tabulated using a single DO loop. The method requires substituting

Program 5-15

```
PROGRAM MAIN
    INTEGER X,Y
    PRINT *,' X VALUE Y VALUE'
    PRINT *,' ------- -------'
    DO 10 X = 2,5
        Y = 10 * X ** 2 + 3 * X - 2
        PRINT *, X, Y
10      CONTINUE
    END
```

the desired equation into the DO loop in place of the equation used in Program 5-15 and adjusting the counter values to match the desired solution range.

The second item of note is that we are not constrained to using integer values for the counter variable. For example, by specifying a noninteger increment, we can obtain solutions for fractional values. This is shown in Program 5-16, where the equation $Y = 10X^2 + 3X - 2$ is evaluated in the range $X = 2$ to $X = 6$ in increments of 0.5.

 Program 5-16

```
PROGRAM MAIN
    REAL X, Y
    PRINT *,' X VALUE    Y VALUE'
    PRINT *,' --------   ---------'
    DO 10 X = 2.0, 6.0, 0.5
        Y = 10.0 * X ** 2 + 3.0 * X - 2.0
        PRINT *, X, Y
10      CONTINUE
    END
```

Notice that X and Y have been declared as REALs in Program 5-16, to allow these variables to take on fractional values. The following is the output produced by this program.

```
X VALUE         Y VALUE
--------        ----------
2.000000         44.000000
2.500000         68.000000
3.000000         97.000000
3.500000        131.000000
4.000000        170.000000
4.500000        214.000000
5.000000        263.000000
5.500000        317.000000
6.000000        376.000000
```

Exercises

1. (Setting Loop Parameters) Modify Program 5-12 to accept the starting and increment values of the table produced by the program.

2. (Setting Loop Parameters) Write a FORTRAN program that converts Fahrenheit temperatures to Celsius in increments of five degrees. The initial value of the Fahrenheit temperature and the total conversions to be made are to be requested as user input during program execution. Recall that Celsius = (5.0/9.0) * (Fahrenheit − 32.0)

3a. (Setting Loop Parameters) Modify the program written for Exercise 12 of the previous section (Section 5-3) to initially prompt the user for the amount of money deposited in the account.

b. Modify the program written for Exercise 3a to additionally prompt the user for the number of years that should be used.

c. Modify the program written for Exercise 3a to additionally prompt the user for both the interest rate and the number of years to be used.

4. (Reading Within a Loop) Write and run a FORTRAN program that accepts six Fahrenheit temperatures, one at a time, and converts each value entered to its Celsius equivalent before the next value is requested. Use a DO loop in your program. The conversion required is Celsius = (5.0/9.0) * (Fahrenheit − 32).

5. (Reading Within a Loop) Write and run a FORTRAN program that accepts 10 individual values of gallons, one at a time, and converts each value entered to its liter equivalent before requesting the next value. Use a DO loop in your program. The conversion required is liters = 3.785 * gallons.

6. (Setting Loop Parameters and Reading Within a Loop) Modify the program written for Exercise 4 to initially request the number of data items that will be entered and converted.

7. (Selection) Modify Program 5-14 so that the number of entries to be READ in is specified by the user when the program is executed.

8. (Selection) Modify Program 5-14 so that it displays the average of the non-zero positive and negative numbers. (*Hint:* Be careful not to include the number zero as a negative number.) Test your program by entering the numbers 17, −10, 19, 0, and −4. The positive average displayed by your program should be 18; and the negative average, −7.

9a. (Selection) Write a FORTRAN program that selects and displays the maximum value of five numbers that are to be entered when the program is executed. (*Hint:* Use a DO loop with both a READ and an IF statement internal to the loop.)

  b. Modify the program written for Exercise 9a so that it displays both the maximum value and the position in the input set of numbers where the maximum occurs.

10. (Evaluating Functions) Modify Program 5-16 to produce a table of Y values for the following:

  a. $Y = 3X^5 - 2X^3 + X$
  for X between 5 and 10 in increments of .2

  b. $Y = 1 + x + \dfrac{x^2}{2} + \dfrac{x^3}{6} + \dfrac{x^4}{24}$
  for X between 1 and 3 in increments of .1

  c. $Y = 2e^{.8t}$ for t between 4 and 10 in increments of .2

11. (Evaluating Functions) A model of worldwide population, in billions of people, is given by the equation:

```
Population = 4.88(1 + e.02*t)
```

where t is the time in years ($t = 0$ represents January 1985, and $t = 1$ represents January 1986). Using this formula, write a FORTRAN program that displays a monthly population table for the months January 1990 though December 1991.

12. (Evaluating Functions) The x and y coordinates, as a function of time, t, of a projectile fired with an initial velocity v at an angle of θ with respect to the ground is given by:

```
x = v t cos(θ)
y = v t sin(θ)
```

Using these formulas, write a FORTRAN program that displays a table of x and y values for a projectile fired with an initial velocity of 500 ft/sec at an angle of 22.8 degrees. (*Hint:* Remember to convert to radian measure.) The table should contain values corresponding to the time interval 0 to 10 seconds in increments of half seconds.

5.5 Nested Loops

There are many situations in which it is very convenient to have a loop contained within another loop. Such loops are called nested loops. A simple example of a nested loop is:

```
      DO 10 I = 1, 4          ──────  Start of outer loop
         PRINT *, 'I IS NOW ', I
         DO 5 J = 1, 3         ──────  Start of inner loop
            PRINT *, ' J = ', J
   5     CONTINUE              ──────  End of inner loop
  10     CONTINUE              ──────  End of outer loop
```

The first loop, controlled by the value of I, is called the outer loop. The second loop, controlled by the value of J, is called the inner loop. Notice that all statements

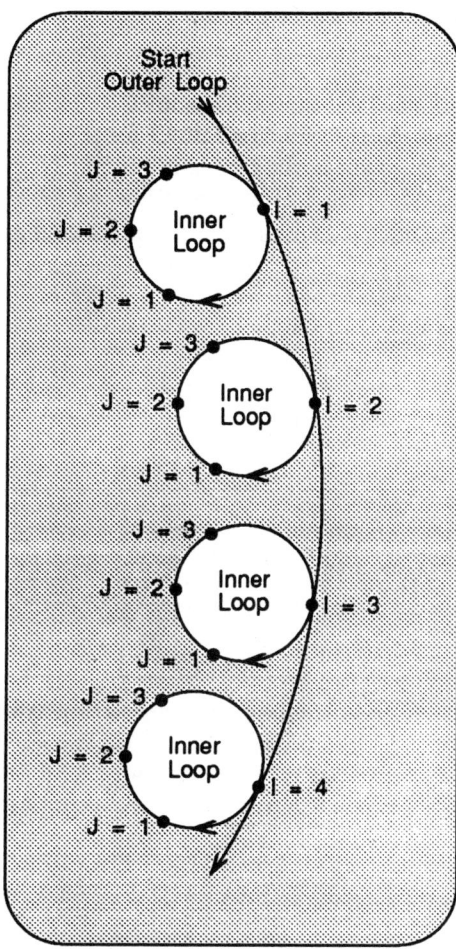

in the inner loop are contained within the boundaries of the outer loop and that we have used a different variable to control each loop. For each single trip through the outer loop, the inner loop runs through its entire sequence. Thus, each time the I counter increases by one, the inner DO loop executes completely. This situation is illustrated in Figure 5-7.

Program 5-17 includes the above code in a working program.

Following is the output of a sample run of Program 5-17:

```
I IS NOW 1
   J = 1
   J = 2
   J = 3
I IS NOW 2
   J = 1
   J = 2
   J = 3
I IS NOW 3
   J = 1
   J = 2
   J = 3
I IS NOW 4
   J = 1
   J = 2
   J = 3
```

Figure 5-7   For Each I, J Makes a Complete Loop

Program 5-17

```
      PROGRAM MAIN
         INTEGER I,J
***      START OF OUTER LOOP
         DO 10 I = 1,4
           PRINT *, 'I IS NOW ',I
***        START OF INNER LOOP
           DO 5 J = 1,3
             PRINT *, ' J = ',J
    5      CONTINUE
   10    CONTINUE
         END
```

The only requirements that must be adhered to in creating nested loops are:

1. An inner loop must be fully contained within an outer loop.
2. The inner loop and outer loop counter variables cannot be the same.
3. An outer loop counter variable must not be altered within an inner loop.

Let us use a nested loop to compute the average grade for each student in a class of 20 students. Each student has taken four exams during the course of the semester. The final grade for each student is calculated as the average of the four examination grades.

Program Analysis

The pseudocode for this example is:

```
Do 20 times
   Set student grade total to zero
   Do 4 times
     read in a grade
     add the grade to the student grade total
   End inner do
   Calculate student's average grade
   Print student's average grade
End outer do
```

As described in the pseudocode, an outer loop consisting of 20 passes will be used to calculate the average for each student. The inner loop will consist of four passes, with one examination grade entered in each inner loop pass. As each grade is entered, it is added to the total for the student, and at the end of the loop the average is calculated and displayed. Program 5-18 uses a nested loop to make the required calculations.

 Program 5-18

```
      PROGRAM MAIN
* THIS PROGRAM CALCULATES THE AVERAGE GRADE FOR 20 STUDENTS
      INTEGER I, J
      REAL GRADE, TOTAL, AVERGE
* THIS IS THE START OF THE OUTER LOOP
      DO 30 I = 1, 20
        TOTAL = 0.0
        DO 15 J = 1,4
          PRINT *, 'ENTER AN EXAM GRADE FOR THIS STUDENT: '
          READ *, GRADE
          TOTAL = TOTAL + GRADE
   15     CONTINUE
        AVERGE = TOTAL / 4.0
        PRINT *, 'THE AVERAGE FOR THIS STUDENT IS ', AVERGE
   30   CONTINUE
      END
```

In reviewing Program 5-18, pay particular attention to the initialization of TOTAL within the outer loop before the inner loop is entered. TOTAL is initialized 20 times, once for each student. Also notice that the average is calculated and displayed immediately after the inner loop is finished. Since the statements that compute and print the average are also contained within the outer loop, 20 averages are calculated and displayed. The entry and addition of each grade within the inner loop use summation techniques we have seen before, and they should now be familiar to you.

Programming Exercises

Note for Exercises 1 through 6: **If you have been programming with subroutines,** write each of the following programs with a single subroutine that is called from the MAIN program unit.

1. Four experiments are performed, each experiment consisting of six test results. The results for each experiment are given below. Write a program using a nested loop to compute and display the average of the test results for each experiment.

   ```
   1st experiment results: 23.2  31.5  16.9  27.5  25.4  28.6
   2nd experiment results: 34.8  45.2  27.9  36.8  33.4  39.4
   3rd experiment results: 19.4  16.8  10.2  20.8  18.9  13.4
   4th experiment results: 36.9  39.5  49.2  45.1  42.7  50.6
   ```

2. Modify the program written for Exercise 1 so that the number of test results for each experiment is entered by the user. Write your program so that a different number of test results can be entered for each experiment.

3a. A bowling team consists of five players. Each player bowls three games. Write a FORTRAN program that uses a nested loop to enter each player's individual scores and then computes and displays the average score for each bowler. Assume that each bowler has the following scores:

   ```
   1st bowler: 286  252  265
   2nd bowler: 212  186  215
   3rd bowler: 252  232  216
   4th bowler: 192  201  235
   5th bowler: 186  236  272
   ```

 b. Modify the program written for Exercise 3a to calculate and display the average team score. (*Hint:* Use a second variable to store the total of all the players' scores.)

4. Rewrite the program written for Exercise 3a to eliminate the inner loop. To do this, you will have to input three scores for each bowler rather than one at a time. Each score must be stored in its own variable name before the average is calculated.

5. Write a program that calculates and displays values for Y when:

   $Y = XZ/(X-Z)$

   Your program should calculate Y for values of X ranging between 1 and 5 and values of Z ranging between 2 and 10. X should control the outer loop and be incremented in steps of 1, and Z should be incremented in steps of 2. Your program should also display the message "FUNCTION UNDEFINED" when the X and Z values are equal.

6. Write a program that calculates and displays the yearly amount available if $1000 is invested in a bank account for 10 years. Your program should display the amounts available for interest rates from 6 percent to 12 percent, inclusive, at 1 percent increments. Use a nested loop, with the outer loop having a fixed count of 7 and the inner loop a fixed count of 10. The first iteration of the outer loop should use an interest rate of 6 percent and should display the amount of money available at the end of the first 10 years. In each subsequent pass through the outer loop, the interest rate should be increased by 1 percent. Use the relationship that the money available at the end of each year equals the amount of money in the account at the start of the year plus the interest rate times the amount available at the start of the year.

5.6 REPEAT-UNTIL Loops

Both DO-WHILE and DO loops evaluate a condition at the start of the repetition loop. There are cases, however, where it is more convenient to test the condition at the end of the loop. For example, suppose we have constructed the following DO-WHILE loop to convert Fahrenheit temperatures to Celsius:

```
      PRINT *,'ENTER A TEMPERATURE: '
      READ *, TEMP
10    IF (TEMP .NE. SENTNL) THEN
         CELSUS = 5.0/9.0 * (TEMP -32.0)
         PRINT *, 'THE EQUIVALENT CELSIUS TEMPERATURE IS ', CELSUS
         PRINT *,'ENTER A TEMPERATURE: '
         READ *, TEMP
         GO TO 10
      ENDIF
```

Here the variable SENTNL represents an agreed-upon sentinel value. When the user enters this value, the loop is terminated. Notice that using this DO-WHILE loop has required us to place a prompt and a READ statement before the loop to force initial execution of the statements within the DO-WHILE loop. These same two statements are then repeated within the loop.

The REPEAT-UNTIL loop structure allows us to execute a set of statements before a condition is evaluated. In many situations this can be used to eliminate the duplication illustrated in the previous example. A general form of a REPEAT-UNTIL loop is:

```
k       statement 1
        statement 2
                .
                .
                .
        statement n
        IF (condition) GO TO k
```

The important concept with REPEAT-UNTIL loops is that all statements within the loop are executed at least once before a condition is tested. Although we have used a logical IF statement as the last statement in the loop, both IF-ELSE statements and block IF statements can also be used. A flow-control diagram illustrating the operation of the REPEAT-UNTIL loop is shown in Figure 5-8.

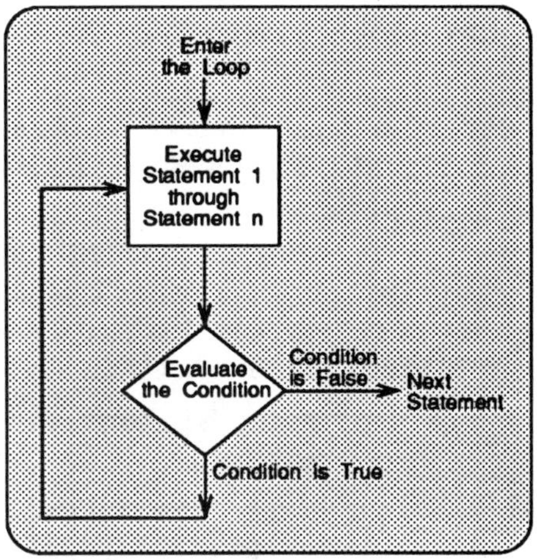

As illustrated in Figure 5-8, all statements within the REPEAT-UNTIL loop are executed once before the condition is evaluated. Then, if the condition is true, the statements within the loop are executed again. This process continues until the condition evaluates to false. For example, consider the following REPEAT-UNTIL loop:

Figure 5-8   Flowchart for the REPEAT-UNTIL Loop

```
10      PRINT *,'ENTER A TEMPERATURE: '
        READ *, TEMP
        CELSUS = 5.0/9.0 * (TEMP -32.0)
        PRINT *, 'THE EQUIVALENT CELSIUS TEMPERATURE IS ', CELSUS
     IF (TEMP .NE. SENTNL) GO TO 10
```

Observe that only one PRINT statement and one READ statement are required because the tested condition is evaluated at the end of the loop.

Validity Checks

REPEAT-UNTIL loops are particularly useful in filtering user-entered input and providing data validity checks. For example, assume that an operator is required to enter a valid customer identification number between the numbers 1000 and 1999. A number outside this range is to be rejected and a new request for a valid number made. The following section of code provides the necessary data filter to verify the entry of a valid identification number:

```
5       PRINT *, 'ENTER AN IDENTIFICATION NUMBER: '
        READ *, IDNUM
     IF (IDNUM .LT.1000 .OR. IDNUM .GT. 1999) GO TO 5
```

Here, a request for an identification number is repeated until a valid number is entered. This section of code is "bare bones" in that it neither alerts the operator to the cause of the new request for data nor allows premature exit from the loop if a valid identification number cannot be found. An alternative that removes the first drawback is:

```
5       PRINT *, 'ENTER AN IDENTIFICATION NUMBER: '
        READ *, IDNUM
     IF (IDNUM .LT.1000 .OR. IDNUM .GT. 1999) THEN
           PRINT *, 'AN INVALID NUMBER WAS JUST ENTERED'
           PRINT * 'PLEASE CHECK THE ID NUMBER AND RE-ENTER'
           GO TO 5
     ENDIF
```

Here we have used a block IF statement instead of a logical IF statement to terminate the loop.

Additional Exercises for Chapter 5

Note for Exercises 1 through 3: **If you have been programming with subroutines,** write each of the following programs with a single subroutine that is called from the MAIN program unit.

1a. Using a REPEAT-UNTIL loop, write a program to accept a grade. The program should request a grade continuously as long as an invalid grade is entered. An invalid grade is any grade less than 0 or greater than 100. After a valid grade has been entered, your program should display the value of the grade entered.

b. Modify the program written for Exercise 1a so that the user is alerted when an invalid grade has been entered.

c. Modify the program written for Exercise 1b so that it allows the user to exit the program by entering the number 999.

d. Modify the program written for Exercise 1b so that it automatically terminates after five invalid grades are entered.

2a. Write a program that continuously requests a grade to be entered. If the grade is less than 0 or greater than 100, your program should print an appropriate message informing the user that an invalid grade has been entered; otherwise the grade should be added to a total. When a grade of 999 is entered, the program should exit the repetition loop and compute and display the average of the valid grades entered.

b. Run the program written in Exercise 2a on a computer and verify the program using appropriate test data.

3a. Write a program to reverse the digits of a positive integer number. For example, if the number 8735 is entered, the number displayed should be 5378. (*Hint:* Use a REPEAT-UNTIL loop to continuously strip off digits of the number. For example, if the variable NUM initially contains the number entered, the units digit is obtained as MOD(NUM,10). After a units digit is obtained, integer division by 10 sets up the number for the next iteration. Thus, MOD(8735,10) is 5, and (8735/10) is 873. The REPEAT-UNTIL loop should continue as long as the remaining number is not zero.)

b. Run the program written in Exercise 3a on a computer and verify the program using appropriate test data.

5.7   Common Programming Errors

Eight errors are commonly made by beginning FORTRAN programmers when creating loops. The first three of these pertain to the tested condition and have already been encountered with the FORTRAN's IF statements.

1. Failure to enclose the condition in a DO-WHILE structure within parentheses. (This is the same error encountered using IF statements.)
2. Failure to follow the IF statement used to create a DO-WHILE loop with the keyword THEN. (Again, this is a common error associated with IF statements.)

3. Testing for equality in DO-WHILE and REPEAT-UNTIL loops when comparing real operands. For example, the condition (FNUM .EQ. 0.01) should be replaced by an equivalent test requiring that the absolute value of FNUM − .01 be less than an acceptable amount. The reason for this is that all numbers are stored in binary form. Using a finite number of bits, decimal numbers such as .01 have no exact binary equivalent, so that tests requiring equality with such numbers can fail.
4. Failure to put the statement label on the DO-WHILE loop's IF statement within columns one through five.
5. Failure to have a statement within a DO-WHILE loop that alters the tested condition in a manner that terminates the loop.
6. Modifying a DO statement's counter variable within the DO loop.
7. Transferring control into the middle of a DO loop.
8. Failure to have a statement within a REPEAT-UNTIL loop that alters the tested condition in a manner that terminates the loop.

5.8 Chapter Summary

1. The general form of a FORTRAN DO-WHILE loop is:

```
k     IF (condition) THEN
         statement 1
         statement 2

              .
              .
              .

         statement n
         GO TO k
         ENDIF
```

Since a DO-WHILE loop checks its condition at the top of the loop, any variables in the tested condition must have values assigned before the loop is encountered. Additionally, one of the statements within the loop must alter the condition in such a way that the loop ultimately terminates.
2. Sentinels are prearranged values used to signal either the start or the end of a series of data items. Typically, sentinels are used to create DO-WHILE loop conditions that terminate the loop when the sentinel value is encountered.
3. The DO statement is extremely useful in creating loops that must be executed a fixed number of times. The initializing value, final value, and increment used by the loop counter are all included within the DO statement. The general form of a DO loop is:

```
        DO k counter = initial, final, increment
            statement 1
            statement 2
                .
                .
                .
            statement n
k       CONTINUE
```

4. Both DO-WHILE and DO loops evaluate a condition at the start of the loop. The REPEAT-UNTIL loop checks its expression at the end of the loop. This ensures that the body of a DO loop is executed at least once. A general form of a REPEAT-UNTIL loop is:

```
k           statement 1
            statement 2
                .
                .
                .
            statement n
    IF (condition) GO TO k
```

As with the DO-WHILE loop, the REPEAT-UNTIL loop must contain a statement that alters its tested condition in such a way that the loop ultimately terminates.

Arrays

Chapter Six

The variables used so far have all had a common characteristic: each variable could only be used to store a single value at a time. For example, although the variables KEY, COUNT, and GRADE specified in the statements:

```
CHARACTER KEY
INTEGER COUNT
REAL GRADE
```

are of different data types, each variable can only store one value of the specified data type. These types of variables are called scalar variables. A *scalar variable* is a single variable that cannot be further subdivided or separated into a legitimate data type.

Frequently, we may have a set of values, all of the same data type, that form a logical group. For example, Table 6-1 illustrates three groups of items. The first group is a list of five real temperatures, the second group is a list of four character codes, and the last group is a list of six integer voltages.

A simple list containing individual items of the same scalar data type is called a single dimension array. In this chapter we describe how single dimension arrays are specified, initialized, stored inside a computer, and used. Additionally, we explore the use of single dimension arrays with example programs and present the procedures for declaring and using multidimensional arrays.

Table 6-1   Three Lists of Items

Temperatures	Codes	Voltages
95.75	Z	12
83.0	C	5
97.625	K	3
72.5	L	55
86.25		16
		6

6.1 Single Dimension Arrays

A single dimension array, which is also called a one dimension array, is a list of values of the same data type. For example, consider the list of temperatures in Table 6-2.

All the temperatures in the list are real numbers and must be declared as such. However, the individual items in the list do not have to be declared separately. The items in the list can be declared as a single unit and stored under a common variable name called the array name. For convenience, we will choose TEMP as the name for the list in Table 6-2. To

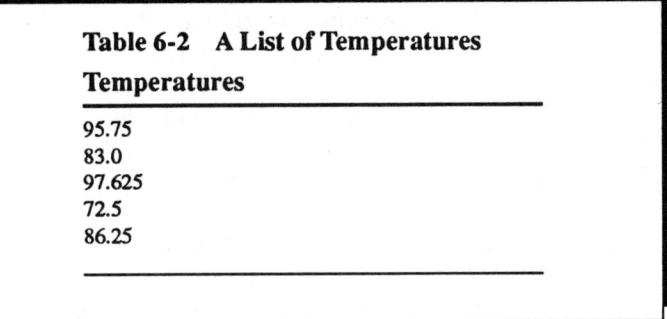

Table 6-2   A List of Temperatures

Temperatures

95.75
83.0
97.625
72.5
86.25

specify that TEMP is to store five individual real values requires the declaration statement REAL TEMP(5). Notice that this declaration statement gives the array (or list) name, the data type of the items in the array, and the number of items in the array. Further examples of array declarations are:

```
INTEGER VOLTS(6)
CHARACTER CODE(4)
REAL AMOUNT(100)
```

Each array has sufficient memory reserved for it to hold the number of data items given in the declaration statement. Thus, the array named VOLTS has storage reserved for 6 integers, the AMOUNT array has storage reserved for 100 real numbers, and the CODE array has storage reserved for 4 individual characters. Figure 6-1 illustrates the storage reserved for the VOLTS and CODE arrays.

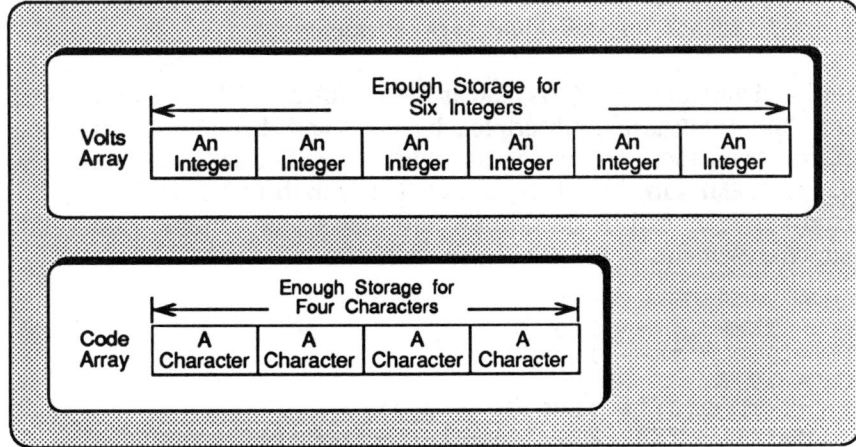

Figure 6-1   The VOLTS and CODE Arrays in Memory

Each item in an array is called an *element* or component of the array. The individual elements stored in the arrays illustrated in Figure 6-1 are stored sequentially, with the first array element stored in the first reserved location, the second element stored in the second reserved location, and so on, until the last element is stored in the last reserved location.

Some unique means of identifying each element is required to provide access to individual elements in a one dimension array. Since elements in the array are stored sequentially, any individual element can be accessed by giving the name of the array and the element's position. This position is called the element's *index* or *subscript* value (the two terms are synonymous). The first element has an index of 1, the second element has an index of 2, and so on. In FORTRAN, the array name and index of the desired element are combined by listing the index in parentheses after the array name. For example, given the specification REAL TEMP(5), TEMP(1) refers to the first temperature stored in the TEMP array, TEMP(2) refers to the second temperature stored in the TEMP array, TEMP(3) refers to the third temperature stored in the TEMP array, TEMP(4) refers to the fourth temperature stored in the TEMP array, and TEMP(5) refers to the fifth temperature stored in the TEMP array.

Figure 6-2 illustrates the TEMP array in memory with the correct designation for each array element. Each individual element is called an indexed variable or a subscripted variable, since both a variable name and an index or subscript value must be used to reference the element. Remember that the index or subscript value gives the position of the element in the array, not the element's value.

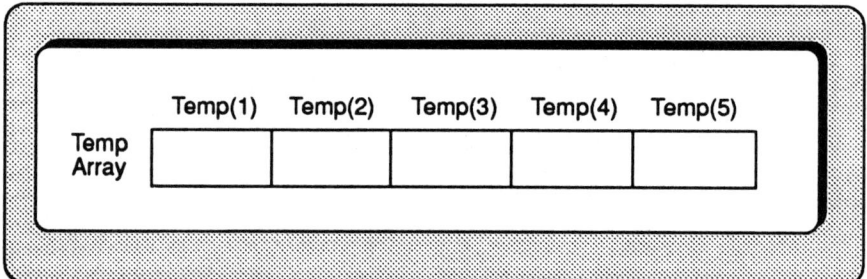

Figure 6-2   Identifying Individual Array Elements

The subscripted variable TEMP(1) is read as "TEMP sub one." This is a shortened way of saying "the TEMP array subscripted by one" and distinguishes the first element in an array from a scalar variable that could be specified as TEMP1. Similarly, TEMP(2) is read as "TEMP sub two," TEMP(3) as "TEMP sub three," and so on.

Subscripted variables can be used anywhere that scalar variables are valid. Examples using the elements of the TEMP array are:

```
TEMP(1) = 95.75
TEMP(2) = TEMP(1) - 11.0
TEMP(3) = 5.0 * TEMP(1)
TEMP(4) = 79.0
TEMP(5) = (TEMP(2) + TEMP(3) - 3.1) / 2.2
SUM = TEMP(1) + TEMP(2) + TEMP(3) + TEMP(4) + TEMP(5)
```

The subscript contained within parentheses need not be an integer constant, and any expression that evaluates to an integer may be used as a subscript. In each case, of course, the value of the expression must be within the valid subscript range defined when the array is specified. For example, assuming that I and J are integer variables, the following subscripted variables are valid:

```
TEMP(I)
TEMP(2*I)
TEMP(J-I)
```

One extremely important advantage of using integer expressions as subscripts is that it allows sequencing through an array by using a loop. This makes statements such as:

```
SUM = TEMP(1) + TEMP(2) + TEMP(3) + TEMP(4) + TEMP(5)
```

unnecessary. The subscript values in this statement can be replaced by a DO loop counter to access each element in the array sequentially. For example, the code:

```
        SUM = 0
        DO 10 I = 1,5
          SUM = SUM + TEMP(I)
10      CONTINUE
```

sequentially retrieves each array element and adds the element to SUM. Here the variable I is used both as the counter in the DO loop and as a subscript. As I increases by one each time through the loop, the next element in the array is referenced. The procedure for adding the array elements within the DO loop is similar to the accumulation procedure we have used before.

The advantage of using a DO loop to sequence through an array becomes apparent when working with larger arrays. For example, if the TEMP array contained 100 values rather than just 5, simply changing the number 5 to 100 in the DO statement is sufficient to sequence through the 100 elements and add each temperature to the sum.

As another example of using a DO loop to sequence through an array, assume that we want to locate the maximum value in an array of 1000 elements named VOLTS. The procedure we will use to locate the maximum value is to initially assume that the first element in the array is the largest number. Then, as we sequence through the array, the maximum is compared to each element. When an element with a higher value is located, that element becomes the new maximum. The following code does the job.

```
        XMAX = VOLTS(1)
        DO 10 I = 2, 100
          IF (VOLTS(I) .GT. XMAX) XMAX = VOLTS(I)
10      CONTINUE
```

The search for a new maximum value starts with the second element of the array and continues through the last element. Each element is compared to the current maximum, and when a higher value is encountered it becomes the new maximum.

The DIMENSION Statement[*]

In addition to creating arrays using explicit declaration statements, as we have done, arrays may also be implicitly declared and sized using a DIMENSION statement. This statement has the form:

```
DIMENSION array name(number of array elements)
```

For example, the statement:

```
DIMENSION LOTTO(6)
```

creates an array named LOTTO having six elements, and the statement:

```
DIMENSION AREA(10)
```

creates an array named AREA having 10 elements. Since the name LOTTO begins with an L, LOTTO is an integer array unless explicitly declared otherwise (recall FORTRAN's implicit type rule that any variable beginning in I, J, K, L, M, or N is an integer). Similarly, since the name AREA does not begin in either I, J, K, L, M, or N, this is an array of real numbers unless explicitly declared otherwise.

The advantage of DIMENSION statements is that a single DIMENSION statement can be used to specify arrays of different types. For example, the single specification:

```
DIMENSION LOTTO(6), AREA(10)
```

creates both an integer and a real array.

DIMENSION statements can also be combined with explicit typing statements, and this must be done, for example, if a DIMENSION statement is used to create arrays of characters. For example, the statements:

```
CHARACTER CODE
DIMENSION CODE(20)
```

create an array of characters having 20 elements, where each element is a single character. Similarly, the declaration statements:

```
CHARACTER*4 CODE
DIMENSION CODE(20)
```

make each element in the CODE array four characters in length. In these cases, however, it is easier to use one of the following single explicit declarations:

```
CHARACTER CODE(20)
```

or:

```
CHARACTER*4 CODE(20)
```

We will continue to use explicit data typing throughout the text for both scalar and array variables.

Input and Output of Array Values

Individual array elements can be assigned values interactively using the READ statement. Examples of individual data entry statements are:

---

[*] This topic may be omitted on initial reading without loss of subject continuity.

```
READ *, TEMP(1)
READ *, TEMP(1), TEMP(2), TEMP(3)
READ *, TEMP(4), VOLTS(6)
```

In the first statement a single value will be read and stored in the variable named TEMP(1). The second statement will cause three values to be read and stored in the variables TEMP(1), TEMP(2), and TEMP(3), respectively. Finally, the last READ statement can be used to read values into the variables TEMP(4) and VOLTS(6).

Alternatively, a DO loop can be used to cycle through the array for interactive data input. For example, the code:

```
DO 15 I = 1,5
   PRINT *, 'ENTER A TEMPERATURE: '
   READ *, TEMP(I)
15 CONTINUE
```

prompts the user for five temperatures. The first temperature entered is stored in TEMP(1), the second temperature entered in TEMP(2), and so on, until five temperatures have been input. Program 6-1 illustrates the use of this code in a complete program.

 Program 6-1

```
PROGRAM MAIN
  REAL TEMP(5)
  DO 15 I = 1,5
    PRINT *, 'ENTER A TEMPERATURE: '
    READ *, TEMP(I)
15  CONTINUE
  PRINT *, 'THE ELEMENTS OF THE TEMP ARRAY ARE:'
  PRINT *, TEMP (1), TEMP(2), TEMP(3), TEMP(4), TEMP(5)
  END
```

Following is a sample run using Program 6-1.

```
ENTER A TEMPERATURE:
96.75
ENTER A TEMPERATURE:
83.0
ENTER A TEMPERATURE:
97.625
ENTER A TEMPERATURE:
72.5
ENTER A TEMPERATURE:
86.25
THE ELEMENTS OF THE TEMP ARRAY ARE:
   96.750000    83.000000    97.625000    72.500000    86.250000
```

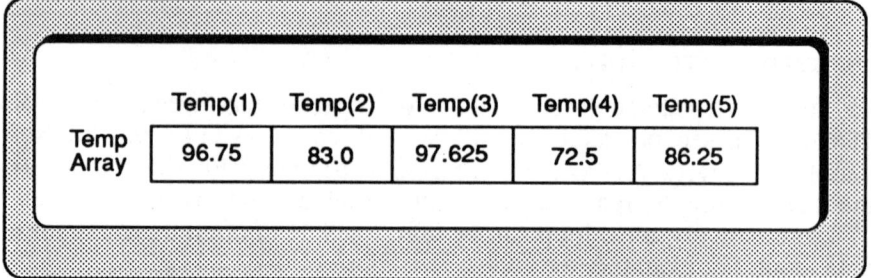

	Temp(1)	Temp(2)	Temp(3)	Temp(4)	Temp(5)
Temp Array	96.75	83.0	97.625	72.5	86.25

Figure 6-3   The Elements of the TEMP Array

Figure 6-3 illustrates the storage of these values in the TEMP array.

Just as a READ statement is used to input values into array elements, both PRINT and WRITE statements can be used to display array elements. Notice in Program 6-1 that a single PRINT statement was used to display the values in the subscripted values TEMP(1) through TEMP(5). Further examples of PRINT statements using subscripted variables are:

```
      PRINT *, VOLTS(6)
      PRINT *, 'THE VALUE OF ELEMENT ', I, ' IS, TEMP(I)
      DO 25 N = 5, 20
        PRINT *, N, AMOUNT(N)
25    CONTINUE
```

The first PRINT statement displays the value of the subscripted variable VOLTS(6). The second PRINT statement displays the value of the subscript I and the value of TEMP(I). Before this statement can be executed, I would have to have an assigned value. Finally, the last example includes a PRINT statement within a DO loop. Both the value of the index and the value of the elements from 5 to 20 are displayed.

Program 6-2 illustrates the use of two DO loops: the first to input values into a 10-element array named AREA, and the second to display the values.

Program 6-2

```
      PROGRAM MAIN
      REAL AREA(10)
      DO 15 I = 1,10
        PRINT *, 'ENTER AN AREA: '
        READ *, AREA(I)
15    CONTINUE
      PRINT *, 'THE ELEMENTS OF THE ARRAY ARE:'
      DO 20 I = 1,10
        PRINT *, AREA(I)
20    CONTINUE
      END
```

Alternative Array Input/Output

Programs 6-1 and 6-2 use similar techniques for the input and display of subscripted variables as used for scalar variables. Two other techniques, called *array name I/O* and *implied DO loops,* are available specifically for the input and output of array elements.

In array name I/O, the name of the array is used to read or display array values without the necessity of using individual subscripts. The general form of the list-directed array name input statement is:

```
READ *, array name
```

For example, if A is the name of an array, the statement:

```
READ *, A
```

causes the computer to temporarily pause and wait for values of each element in the array to be entered. The first entered value is assigned to A(1), the second to A(2), and so on, until the array has been completely filled with values. Similarly, the list-directed output statement:

```
PRINT *, A
```

causes all of the values in the A array to be displayed, starting with A(1) and ending with the last element in the array. Program 6-3 illustrates the use of these two statements:

 Program 6-3

```
PROGRAM MAIN
   INTEGER A(5)
   PRINT *, 'ENTER FIVE NUMBERS: '
   READ *, A
   PRINT *, 'THE VALUES FOR A(1) THROUGH A(5) ARE:'
   PRINT *, A
   END
```

Following is a sample run using program 6-3:

```
ENTER FIVE NUMBERS:
36 42 1 18 63
THE VALUES FOR A(1) THROUGH A(5) ARE:
          36              42              1           18          63
```

Notice that in Program 6-3 the statement READ *, A is equivalent to the longer statement:

```
READ *, A(1), A(2), A(3), A(4), A(5)
```

and the statement PRINT *, A is equivalent to the longer statement:

```
PRINT *, A(1), A(2), A(3), A(4), A(5)
```

The final technique for inputting and displaying array elements uses implied DO loops. An implied DO loop is simply an alternate form of a standard DO loop in which all returned elements are placed on the same line. For example, PRINT *, (A(I), I=1,5) is equivalent to both PRINT *, A and PRINT *, A(1), A(2), A(3), A(4), A(5).

Similarly, an implied DO loop may also be used on input. Program 6-4 uses an implied DO loop to enter the first, third, and fifth elements of a 10-element array and also to display the array's first 5 elements.

Following is a sample run of Program 6-4.

```
ENTER THREE NUMBERS:
33 26 45
THE VALUES FOR A(1) THROUGH A(5) ARE:
33              17              26              2              45
```

 Program 6-4

```
PROGRAM MAIN
    INTEGER A(10)
    PRINT *, 'ENTER THREE NUMBERS: '
    READ *, (A(I), I=1,5,2)
    A(2) = 17
    A(4) = 2
    PRINT *, 'THE VALUES FOR A(1) THROUGH A(5) ARE:'
    PRINT *, (A(I), I = 1,5)
    END
```

Skill Builder Exercises

1. Write array declarations for the following:

   a. a list of 100 real voltages named VOLTS

   b. a list of 50 real temperatures named TEMPS

   c. a list of 30 characters, each representing a single character code, named CODE

   d. a list of 100 integer years named YEARS

   e. a list of 32 real velocities named VELOCY

   f. a list of 1000 real distances named DISTNC

   g. a list of 6 integer code numbers named CODE

2. Write appropriate notation for the first, third, and seventh elements of the following arrays:

a. INTEGER GRADES(20)
b. REAL VOLTS(10)
c. REAL AMPS(16)
d. INTEGER DIST(15)
e. REAL VELOC(25)
f. REAL TIME(100)

3a. Write individual READ statements that can be used to enter values into the first, third, and seventh elements of each of the arrays specified in Exercises 2a through 2f.

b. Write a DO loop that can be used to enter values for the complete array specified in Exercise 2a.

4a. Write individual PRINT statements that can be used to print the values from the first, third, and seventh elements of each of the arrays specified in Exercises 2a through 2f.

b. Write a DO loop that can be used to display values for the complete array specified in Exercise 2a.

5. List the elements that will be displayed by the following sections of code:

```
a.        DO 10 K = 1,5,2
              PRINT A(K)
      10  CONTINUE
b.        DO 15 J = 3,10
              PRINT B(J)
      15  CONTINUE
```
c. PRINT *, (A(J), J = 1,5)
d. PRINT *, (B(K), K = 3,12,3)
e. PRINT *, (C(I), I = 2,10,2)

Expanding Your Skills

6. All of the array specifications we have used specify only the upper index value of the array. This type of specification, which is the most commonly encountered one in FORTRAN, has the effect of forcing the first array element to have an index value of 1.

It is possible in FORTRAN 77 to specify a lower as well as an upper index value. For example, the specification REAL VOLTS(-10:7) specifies an array of eighteen elements: the first element is accessed as VOLTS(-10), the second element as VOLTS(-9), the eleventh element as VOLTS(0), and the eighteenth element as VOLTS(7). Although specifying a lower index value is not commonly used, situations may arise that make such a designation useful. For example, in storing population data for the years 1950 through 1990, a specification such as POP(1950:1990) could be used. This specification creates an array named POP consisting of 41 elements, where the first element is accessed as POP(1950), and the last element as POP(1990). For the following array specifications, determine the total amount of elements in each array and the correct notation for the first, third, and seventh elements in the array.

a. INTEGER GRADES(-10:10)
b. REAL VOLTS(-10:5)
c. REAL AMPS(-16:0)
d. INTEGER DIST(0:15)
e. REAL VELOC(-2:25)
f. REAL TIME(-5:95)

Programming Exercises

Note for Exercises 4 through 9: **If you have been programming with subroutines,** write each of the following programs with a single subroutine that is called from the MAIN program unit.

7a. Write a program to input the following values into an array named VOLTS: 10.95, 16.32, 12.15, 8.22, 15.98, 26.22, 13.54, 6.45, 17.59. After the data has been entered, have your program output the values.

b. Repeat Exercise 7a, but after the data has been entered, have your program display it in the following form:

```
10.95  16.32  12.15
 8.22  15.98  26.22
13.54   6.45  17.59
```

8. Write a program to input eight integer numbers into an array named TEMP. As each number is input, add the numbers into a total. After all numbers are input, display the numbers and their average.

9a. Write a program to input 10 positive integer numbers into an array named FMAX and determine the maximum value entered. Your program should contain only one loop, and the maximum should be determined as array element values are being input. (*Hint:* Set the maximum equal to −10000 before the loop used to input the numbers.)

b. Repeat Exercise 9a, keeping track of both the maximum element in the array and the index number for the maximum. After displaying the numbers, print the two messages:

```
THE MAXIMUM VALUE IS: ____
THIS IS ELEMENT NUMBER ____    IN THE LIST OF NUMBERS
```

Have your program display the correct values in place of the underlines in the messages.

c. Repeat Exercise 9b, but have your program locate the minimum data value entered.

10a. Write a program to input the following integer numbers into an array named GRADE: 89, 95, 72, 83, 99, 54, 86, 75, 92, 73, 79, 75, 82, 73. As each number is input, add the numbers to a total. After all numbers are input and the total is obtained, calculate the average of the numbers and use the average to determine the deviation of each value from the average. Store each deviation in an array named DEVIAT. Each deviation is obtained as the element value less the average of all the data. Have your program display each deviation alongside its corresponding element from the GRADE array.

b. Calculate the variance of the data used in Exercise 10a. The variance is obtained by squaring each individual deviation and dividing the sum of the squared deviations by the number of deviations.

Write a program that specifies three single dimension arrays named VOLTS, CURRNT, and RESIST. Each array should be capable of holding 10 elements. Using a DO loop, input values for the CURRNT and RESIST arrays. The entries in the VOLTS array should be the product of the corresponding values in the CURRNT and RESIST arrays (thus, VOLTS(I) = CURRNT(I) * RESIST(I)). After all of the data have been entered, display the following output:

```
VOLTAGE CURRENT RESISTANCE
------- ------- ----------
```

Display the appropriate values under each column heading.

12a. Write a program that allows user inputs of 10 real numbers into an array named RAW. After the numbers are entered into the array, your program should cycle through RAW 10 times. During each pass through the array, your program should select the lowest value in RAW and place the selected value in the next available slot in an array named SORTED. Thus, when your program is complete, the SORTED array should contain the numbers in RAW in sorted order from lowest to highest. (*Hint:* Make sure to reset the lowest value selected during each pass to a very high number so that it is not selected again. You will need a second DO loop within the first DO loop to locate the minimum value for each pass.)

b. The method used in Exercise 12a to sort the values in the array is very inefficient. Can you determine why? What might be a better method of sorting the numbers in an array?

6.2 The DATA Statement and Array Initialization

Array elements can be initialized within a program unit at compile time, using DATA statements. Since DATA statements can also be used to initialize scalar variables, we will consider the scalar case first.

A DATA statement is a specification statement having the general form:

```
DATA    variable list/value list/, variable list/value list/ ...
```

Examples of DATA statements are:

```
DATA LENGTH, WIDTH, RADIUS /22,33.4,86.8/
DATA W,X,Y,Z /6.,8.,10.,12./
DATA I,J,K /1,5,6/,ICOUNT,SUM /23,42.5/
```

The first DATA statement assigns the value 22 to the variable LENGTH, the value 33.4 to the variable WIDTH, and the value 86.8 to the variable RADIUS. The second DATA statement assigns the values 6., 8., 10., and 12., respectively, to the variables W, X, Y, and Z. Finally, the third DATA statement assigns the values 1, 5, and 6, respectively, to the variables I, J, and K, and the values 23 and 42.5 to the respective variables ICOUNT and SUM.

The primary requirement in constructing DATA statements is that there be the same number of values in each value list as there are variables in the corresponding variable list. For example, if the variable list A,B,C,D,E,F,G is used, its associated value list must contain seven values.

Although each value list must contain sufficient values for its associated variable list, the value list can use repeat counts. For example, the value list 3*4.6 is equivalent to the value list 4.6,4.6,4.6. Further examples of repeat counts are listed in Table 6-3.

DATA statements are useful because they permit many variables to be initialized in a single statement rather than in multiple assignment statements. For example, if

Table 6-3   Repeat Count Examples

Using a repeat count	Equivalent value list
/ 5 * 3.2 /	/ 3.2, 3.2, 3.2, 3.2, 3.2/
/ 4 * 2 /	/ 2, 2, 2, 2 /
/ 2 * (1.3, 2), 3 * 1 /	/ 1.3, 2, 1.3, 2,1, 1,1 /

the variables A, B, C, and D are to be initialized at the beginning of a program unit, a single DATA statement can be used instead of four individual assignment statements. It is important to note that DATA statements must only appear at the top of a program unit after all declaration statements and before any executable statements. Thus, for example, a DATA statement cannot be used within a DO loop or later in a program unit to subsequently modify the value of a variable. If the variables initialized by a DATA statement must be modified, either assignment or READ statements must be used.

The ability to initialize many variables with a single statement makes the DATA statement particularly useful in initializing arrays. This initialization of array elements can be done by individual element name, by array name, or by using implied DO loops.

Initialization by Array Element Name

Individual array elements can be initialized using a DATA statement by including the names of the array elements within the list of variables. Examples of this type of array element initialization are:

```
DATA A(1), A(3), A(5)  /4.5,6.2,8.3/
```
and:

```
DATA B(1), B(2), B(3)  /3*22.6/
```

The first DATA statement initializes the variables A(1), A(3), and A(5) to the respective values 4.5, 6.2, and 8.3, while the second DATA statement uses a repeat count to store the value 22.6 into each of the variables B(1), B(2), and B(3).

Initialization by Array Name

Array elements can also be initialized with a DATA statement by listing the name of the array and sufficient values to fill the complete array. For example, assuming an array named GRADES is specified by:

```
INTEGER GRADES(10)
```

the statement:

```
DATA GRADES/14,24,26,33,35,42,46,19,4,20/
```

initializes GRADES(1) with the value 14, GRADES(2) with the value 24, and so on, until GRADES(10) is initialized to the value 20.

Similarly, the statement:

```
DATA GRADES/10*92/
```

uses a repeat count to initialize all elements to 92, and the statement:

```
DATA GRADES/2*(50,60,70,80,90)/
```

initializes the GRADES array with the repeating sequence of values 50, 60, 70, 80, and 90.

Implied DO Loops

The third method of using DATA statements to initialize array elements is to use an implied DO loop. For example, assuming an array named SLOPES is specified by:

```
REAL SLOPES(15)
```

the statement:

```
DATA (SLOPES(I), I = 1,4)/14,16,18,5/
```

makes the following assignments:

```
SLOPES(1) = 14
SLOPES(2) = 16
SLOPES(3) = 18
SLOPES(4) = 5
```

Repeat counts can also be used with implied DO loops. For example, the statement:

```
DATA (SLOPES(I), I = 1, 15, 2)/8*12/
```

assigns the value 12 to all array elements having an odd subscript value. Notice that the implied DO loop starts with the element SLOPES(1), ends with the element SLOPES(15), and includes eight elements. Thus, the list of values must also contain eight values.

Exercises

1. Write array declarations and initializing DATA statements for the following:

   a. A list of ten integer grades: 89, 75, 82, 93, 78, 95, 81, 88, 77, 82.

   b. A list of five real amounts: 10.62, 13.98, 18.45, 12.68, 14.76.

   c. A list of 100 real interest rates; the first 6 rates are 6.29, 6.95, 7.25, 7.35, 7.40, 7.42.

   d. A list of 64 real temperatures; the first 4 temperatures are 78.2, 69.6, 68.5, 83.9.

   e. A list of 15 character codes; the first 7 codes are G, K, M, Q, R, W, X.

2. Write array and DATA specification statements to store the following values in an array named VOLTS: 16.24, 18.98, 23.75, 16.29, 19.54, 14.22, 11.13, 15.39. Include these statements in a program that displays the values in the array.

3. Write a program that uses a DATA statement to store the following numbers in an array named SLOPES: 17.24, 25.63, 5.94, 33.92, 3.71, 32.84, 35.93, 18.24, 6.92. Your program should locate and display both the maximum and the minimum values in the array.

4. Write a program that uses a DATA statement to store the following values in an array named PRICES: 9.92, 6.32, 12.63, 5.95, 10.29. Your program should also create two arrays named UNITS and AMOUNT, each capable of storing five real numbers. Using a loop and a READ statement, have your program accept five user-input numbers into the UNITS array when the program is run. Your program should store the product of the corresponding values in the PRICES and UNITS arrays in the AMOUNT array (for example, AMOUNT(1) = PRICES(1) * UNITS(1)) and display the following output (fill in the table appropriately):

```
PRICE    UNITS  AMOUNT
-----    -----  ------
 9.92      .       .
 6.32      .       .
12.63      .       .
 5.95      .       .
10.29      .       .
                 ------
TOTAL              .
```

5a. Write an array declaration and DATA initialization statements to store the four strings of characters:

```
'  INPUT THE FOLLOWING DATA '
'--------------------------'
'ENTER THE DATE: '
'ENTER THE ACCOUNT NUMBER: '
```

   in elements 1 through 4 of an array name MESSGE. (*Hint:* Use the array specification statement CHARACTER*26 MESSGE(4).)

   b. Include the array declaration and DATA statements written in Exercise 5a in a program that uses the PRINT statement to display the individual messages. For example, the statement PRINT *, MESSGE(1) should cause the first message to be displayed.

6a. Write an array and DATA specification statement to store the individual characters T, E, S, T, I, N, and G into a character array named STRTST, specified as CHARACTER STRTST(7). Include these specification statements in a program to display the characters using the following loop:

```
      DO 10 I = 1,7
         PRINT *, STRTST(I)
  10  CONTINUE
```

b. Modify the DO loop in Exercise 6a to display only the array characters I, N, and G.

6.3 Two Dimension Arrays

A two dimension array consists of both rows and columns of elements. For example, the array of numbers:

```
 8   16    9   52
 3   15   27    6
14   25    2   10
```

is called a two dimension array of integers. This array consists of three rows and four columns. To reserve storage for this array, both the number of rows and the number of columns must be included in the array's declaration. Calling the array VALS, the correct declaration for this two dimension array is:

```
INTEGER VALS(3,4)
```

Similarly, the declarations:

```
REAL VOLTS(10,5)
CHARACTER*4 CODE(6,26)
```

specify that the array VOLTS consists of 10 rows and 5 columns of real numbers and that the array CODE consists of 6 rows and 26 columns, with each element capable of holding 4 characters.

To make it possible to locate an element in a two dimension array, each element is identified by its position in the array. As illustrated in Figure 6-4, the term VALS(2,4) uniquely identifies the element in row 2, column 4. As with single dimension array variables, double dimension array variables can be used anywhere that scalar variables are valid. Examples using elements of the VALS array are:

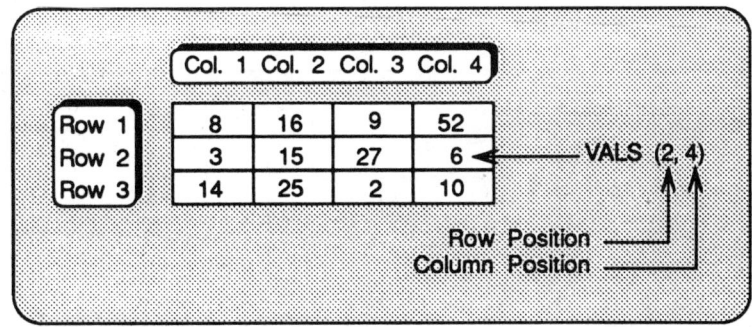

Figure 6-4   Each Array Element Is Identified by Its Row and Column Position

```
WATTS = VALS(2,3)
VALS(1,1) = 62
NEWNUM = 4 * (VALS(2,1) - 5)
SUMR1 = VALS(1,1) + VALS(1,2) + VALS(1,3) + VALS(1,4)
```

The last statement causes the values of the four elements in row 1 to be added and the sum to be stored in the scalar variable SUMR1.

As with single dimension arrays, two dimension arrays can be specified explicitly within a declaration statement or with a declaration statement followed by a dimension statement. For example, both:

```
REAL AREA(3,4)
```

and:

```
REAL AREA
DIMENSION AREA(3,4)
```

produce a real array named AREA having three rows and four columns. This same array is produced using the single specification statement:

```
DIMENSION AREA(3,4)
```

which uses FORTRAN's implied data typing to declare the array (recall that any variable name not beginning in I, J, K, L, M, or N is considered a real variable). As with all FORTRAN type declarations, a single declaration statement can always be used to specify variables of the same type. Thus, for example, the declaration:

```
INTEGER SLOPE, VOLTS(75), TEMPS(52,7)
```

specifies SLOPE to be a scalar integer variable, VOLTS to be a single dimension integer array consisting of 75 elements, and TEMPS to be a two dimension integer array having 52 rows and 7 columns.

As with single dimension arrays, two dimension arrays can be initialized using DATA statements following the array declaration. For example, the statements:

```
INTEGER VALS(3,4)
DATA VALS/ 8,3,14,16,15,25,9,27,2,52,6,10/
```

create and initialize each element of the VALS array. Figure 6-5 lists the initializations performed by the DATA statement.

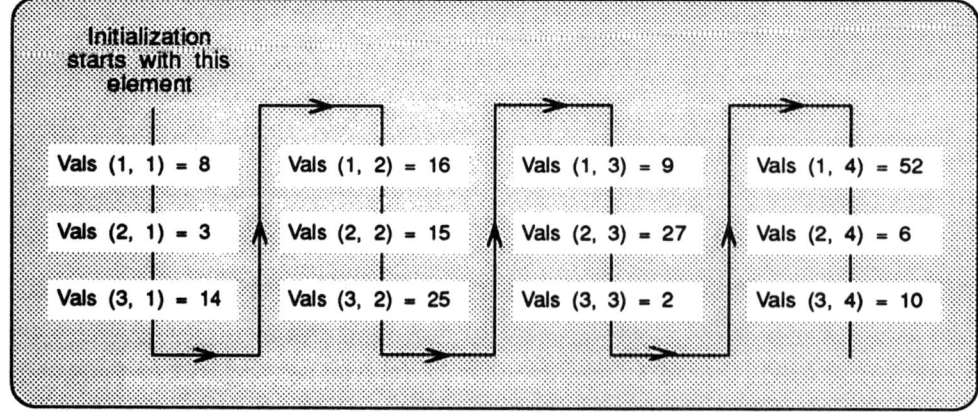

Figure 6-5   Storage and Initialization of the VALS() **Array**

As illustrated in Figure 6-5, the initialization of a two dimension array is done in column order. First, the elements of the first column are initialized, then the elements of the second column are initialized, and so on, until the initializations are completed. This column ordering is also the same ordering used to store two dimension arrays. That is, array element (1,1) is stored first, followed by element (2,1), followed by element (3,1), and so on. Following the first column's elements are the second column's elements, and so on for all the columns of the array.

As with single dimension arrays, two dimension arrays may be displayed by individual element notation, by array name, or by using DO loops (either explicit or implied). This is illustrated by Program 6-5, which displays all of the elements of a three-by-four two dimension array using three different techniques.

 Program 6-5

```
      PROGRAM MAIN
        INTEGER I, J, VALS(3,4)
        DATA VALS/ 8,3,14,16,15,25,9,27,2,52,6,10/
*** DISPLAY BY EXPLICIT ELEMENT
        PRINT *, 'DISPLAY OF VALS() BY EXPLICIT ELEMENT'
        PRINT *, VALS(1,1), VALS(1,2), VALS(1,3), VALS(1,4)
        PRINT *, VALS(2,1), VALS(2,2), VALS(2,3), VALS(2,4)
        PRINT *, VALS(3,1), VALS(3,2), VALS(3,3), VALS(3,4)
*** DISPLAY BY NESTED DO LOOPS WITH THE INNER LOOP IMPLIED
        PRINT *
        PRINT *, 'DISPLAY OF VALS() USING NESTED DO LOOPS'
        DO 15 I = 1,3
           PRINT *, (VALS(I,J), J = 1,4)
   15   CONTINUE
*** DISPLAY USING AN ARRAY OUTPUT STATEMENT
        PRINT *
        PRINT *, 'DISPLAY OF VALS() USING ARRAY NAME OUTPUT'
        PRINT *, VALS
        END
```

Following is the display produced by Program 6-5.

```
DISPLAY OF VALS() BY EXPLICIT ELEMENT
        8       16        9       52
        3       15       27        6
      -14       25        2       10
DISPLAY OF VALS() USING NESTED DO LOOPS
        8       16        9       52
        3       15       27        6
       14       25        2       10
DISPLAY OF VALS() USING ARRAY NAME OUTPUT
8    3    14    16    15    25    9    27    2    52    6    10
```

The first display of the VALS array produced by Program 6-5 is constructed by explicitly designating each array element. The second display of array element values, which is identical to the first, is produced using a nested DO loop. Nested loops are especially useful when dealing with two dimension arrays because they allow the programmer to easily designate and cycle through each element. In Program 6-5, the variable I controls the outer loop, and the variable J, used within an implied DO loop, controls the inner loop. Each pass through the outer loop corresponds to a single row, with the inner loop supplying the appropriate column elements. After a complete column is printed, a new line is started for the next row. The effect is a display of the array in a row-by-row fashion. The final display was created by the single array output statement:

```
PRINT *, VALS
```

The array output statement is particularly convenient when a quick debugging check of array elements is needed. This same display can be produced by the nested implied DO loop statement:

```
PRINT *, ((VALS(I,J), I = 1,3), J=1,4)
```

Just as implied DO loops and array names can be used for two dimension array output, both of these techniques can be used to initialize two dimension array elements. For example, the statements:

```
READ *,VALS
```

and:

```
READ *, ((VALS(I,J), I = 1,3), J=1,4)
```

require the user to enter 12 data values, which are stored in the VALS array. In both cases the elements must be entered in the column order previously illustrated in Figure 6-5.

Once two dimension array elements have been assigned using either READ, DATA, or assignment statements, array processing can begin. Typically, DO loops are used to process two dimension arrays because, as was previously noted, they allow the programmer to easily designate and cycle through each array element. For example, the first nested DO loop illustrated in Program 6-6 is used to multiply each element in the VALS array by the scalar number 10. The second nested DO loop uses an implied inner DO loop (the same as that used in Program 6-5) to produce the final array display.

Program 6-6

```
      PROGRAM MAIN
        INTEGER I, J, VALS(3,4)
        DATA VALS/ 8,3,14,16,15,25,9,27,2,52,6,10/
*** MULTIPLY EACH ARRAY ELEMENT BY 10
        DO 10 I = 1,3
          DO 5 J = 1,4
            VALS(I,J) = 10 * VALS(I,J)
   5      CONTINUE
  10      CONTINUE
*** DISPLAY THE RESULTING ARRAY ELEMENTS
        PRINT *, 'DISPLAY OF MULTIPLIED ARRAY ELEMENTS'
        DO 15 I = 1,3
          PRINT *, (VALS(I,J), J = 1,4)
  15      CONTINUE
        END
```

Following is the output produced by Program 6-6.

```
DISPLAY OF MULTIPLIED ARRAY ELEMENTS
         80   160    90   520
         30   150   270    60
        140   250    20   100
```

Larger Dimension Arrays

Although arrays with more than two dimensions are not commonly used, FORTRAN does allow larger arrays to be specified. This is done by listing the maximum size of all indices for the array. For example, the declaration INTEGER RESPON(4,10,6) specifies a three dimension array. The first element in the array is designated as RESPON(1,1,1), and the last element as RESPON(4,10,6).

Conceptually, as illustsrated in Figure 6-6, a three dimension array can be viewed as a book of data tables. Using this visualization, the first index value can be thought of as the location of the desired row in a table, the second index value as the desired column, and the third index value, which is often called "rank", as the page number of the selected table.

Similarly, arrays having at most seven dimensions can be specified. Conceptually, a four dimension array can be represented as a shelf of books, where the fourth dimension is used to specify a desired book on the shelf, and a five dimension array can be viewed as a bookcase filled with books, where the fifth dimension refers to a selected shelf in the book case. Using the same analogy, a six dimension array can be considered as a single row of bookcases, where the sixth dimension references the desired bookcase in the row. Finally, a seven dimension array can be considered as multiple rows of bookcases, where the seventh dimension references the desired row. Alternatively, arrays of three, four, five, six, and seven dimension arrays can be viewed as mathematical *n*-tuples of order three, four, five, six, and seven, respectively.

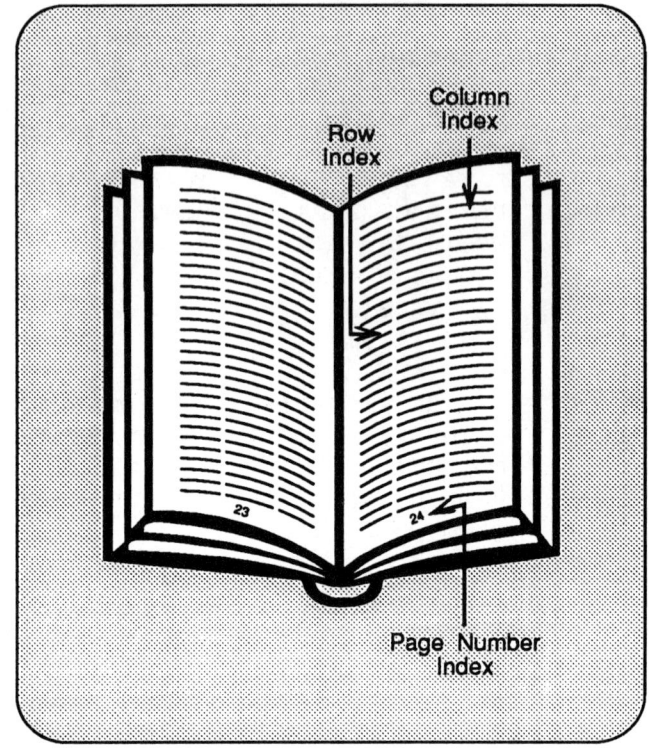

Figure 6-6   Representation of a Three Dimension Array

Exercises

1. Write appropriate declaration statements for:

   a. an array of integers with 6 rows and 10 columns named NUMS

   b. an array of integers with 2 rows and 5 columns named NUMS

   c. an array of single characters with 7 rows and 12 columns named CODES

   d. an array of single characters with 15 rows and 7 columns named CODES

   e. an array of real numbers with 10 rows and 25 columns named VALS

   f. an array of real numbers with 16 rows and 8 columnsnamed VALS

2. Determine the output produced by the following program:

```
PROGRAM MAIN
   INTEGER I, J, VALS(3,4)
   DATA VALS/ 8,3,14,16,15,25,9,27,2,52,6,10/
   DO 10 I = 1,3
     DO 5 J = 1,4
       PRINT *, VALS(I,J)
 5       CONTINUE
10       CONTINUE
   END
```

3a. Write a FORTRAN program that adds the values of all elements in the VALS array used in Exercise 2 and displays the total.

b. Modify the program written for Exercise 3a to display the total of each column separately.

Note for Exercises 4 through 7: **If you have been programming with subroutines,** write each of the following programs with a single subroutine that is called from the MAIN program unit.

4. Write a FORTRAN program that adds equivalent elements of the two dimension arrays named FIRST and SECND. Both arrays should have two rows and three columns. For example, element (1,2) of the resulting array should be the sum of FIRST(1,2) and SECND(1,2). The FIRST and SECND arrays should be initialized as follows:

```
FIRST              SECND
16  18  23         24  52  77
54  91  11         16  19  59
```

5a. Write a FORTRAN program that finds and displays the maximum value in a two dimension array of integers. The array should be specified as a four-by-five array of integers and initialized using the statement:

```
DATA NUMS/16,22,99,4,18,-258,4,101,5,98,105,6,15,2,45,33,88,72,16,3/
```

b. Modify the program written in Exercise 5a so that it also displays the maximum value's row and column subscript numbers.

6. Write a FORTRAN program to select the values in a four by five array of integers in increasing order and store the selected values in the single dimension array named SORT. Use the data statement given in Exercise 5a to initialize the two dimension array.

7a. A professor has constructed a two dimension array of real numbers having three rows and five columns. This array currently contains the test grades of the students in the professor's advanced compiler design class. Write a FORTRAN program that uses an array input statement to read 15 array values and then determine the total number of grades in the ranges less than 60, greater than or equal to 60 and less than 70, greater than or equal to 70 and less than 80, greater than or equal to 80 and less than 90, and greater than or equal to 90.

b. Entering 15 grades each time the program written for Exercise 7a is run is cumbersome. What method, therefore, is appropriate for initializing the array during the testing phase?

c. How might the program you wrote for Exercise 7a be modified to include the case of no grade being present? That is, what grade could be used to indicate an invalid grade, and how would your program have to be modified to exclude counting such a grade?

6.4 Applications

Arrays are extremely useful for plotting data on either a video screen or a standard line printer. In this section we present a simple method of constructing such plots. The first application presents the basic method and uses it to produce modest plots. The second application incorporates data scaling to ensure that the plot fits within the area of the video screen or paper, regardless of the range of data plotted.

Application 1: Curve Plotting

Two basic constraints must be considered in graphing data on either a video screen or a printer. The first constraint is that both devices automatically move in a forward direction, which means that our graphs should avoid the need to "back up" (although there are methods for reversing the cursor motion on a video screen, all of our programs will be constructed to work for both printers and screens). The second constraint is that both printer paper and video displays are restricted in the horizontal direction to displaying a maximum of either 80 or 132 characters. No such restriction exists in the vertical direction because the paper length is effectively unlimited and the video display scrolls forward. For this reason our plots will always be constructed "sideways," with the *Y* axis horizontal and the *X* axis vertical. With these two constraints in mind, consider the plot shown in Figure 6-7.

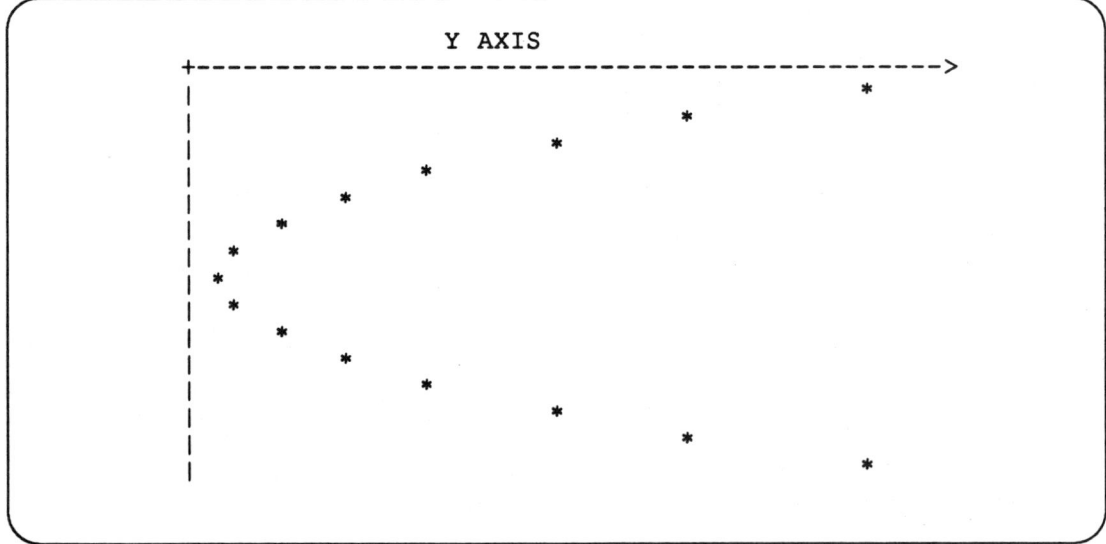

Figure 6-7 A Sample Graph

In Figure 6-7, the graph is plotted with the *Y* axis displayed across the top of the graph and the *X* axis displayed down the side. Omitting, for the moment, the two header lines:

```
                            Y AXIS
+----------------------------------------------------->
```

the actual graph of the data points consists of 15 individual lines, as follows;

```
Line  1:  |                                              *
Line  2:  |                                       *
Line  3:  |                                 *
Line  4:  |                        *
Line  5:  |                *
Line  6:  |           *
Line  7:  |      *
Line  8:  |    *
Line  9:  |     *
Line 10:  |        *
Line 11:  |            *
Line 12:  |                 *
Line 13:  |                       *
Line 14:  |                             *
Line 15:  |                                      *
```

Notice that individually each line consists of only two printed symbols, a bar (|) and an asterisk (*). The bar is always displayed in column one, and the asterisk is positioned to indicate an appropriate *Y* value. With these points in mind, it is rather easy to construct these 15 lines. To do this we will first construct an exact image of the first line to be printed in an array of characters. After the array is constructed and printed, it will be used to construct an image of the second line. After the second image is displayed, the same array is used to construct an image of the third line, and so on, until all 15 lines have been displayed. To make sure that the elements in the array can be displayed on a page with sufficient room for a right-hand margin, the array will be specified as 72 characters long (any value less than the maximum horizontal width of either the paper or video screen can be used).

As illustrated in Figure 6-8, the array, called LINE, is filled with blanks, except for the first element, which stores the bar symbol, and one other element, which stores an asterisk.

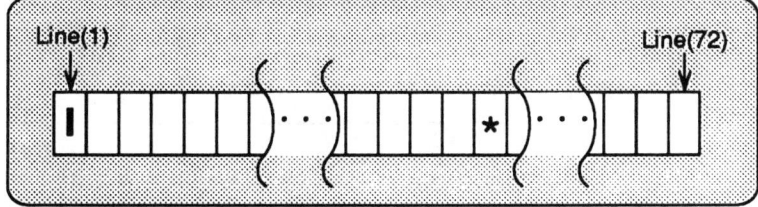

Figure 6-8   The LINE Array

Using the LINE array to store the image of each line before it is printed, our graphing approach is:

1. Store an asterisk in the desired array element
2. Print the array
3. Reset the element to a blank
4. Repeat steps 1 through 3 until the required number of lines have been displayed
   These four steps are easily implemented using a DO loop having the form:

```
DO 10 X = 1,15
   calculate a value for Y
   LINE(Y) = '*'
   PRINT *, LINE
   LINE(Y) = ' '
10    CONTINUE
```

The calculation of the Y value, which is then used as a subscript for the LINE array, depends on the graph being plotted. For the graph illustrated in Figure 6-7, the equation $Y = (X-8)^2 + 3$ was used.* Incorporating this into the DO loop yields:

```
DO 10 X = 1,15
   Y = (X-8)**2 + 3
   LINE(Y) = '*'
   PRINT *, LINE
   LINE(Y) = ' '
10    CONTINUE
```

Program 6-7 includes this code within a working program.

 Program 6-7

```
PROGRAM MAIN
   INTEGER X,Y
   CHARACTER LINE(72)
   DATA LINE/'|',71*' '/
   DO 10 X = 1,15
      Y = (X-8)**2 + 3
      LINE(Y) = '*'
      PRINT *, LINE
      LINE(Y) = ' '
10    CONTINUE
   END
```

---

* To use the Y value as a subscript for the LINE array requires that this value be an integer between the numbers 0 and 72, inclusive. The curve $Y = (X-8)^2 + 3$ was selected precisely because it yielded Y values within this range. In the next application an algorithm is presented for scaling any Y values into the required range.

Notice in Program 6-7 that after the LINE array is specified, a DATA statement initializes LINE(1) with the bar symbol and the remaining 71 elements with blanks. The DO loop then calculates a Y value, uses this value as a subscript to locate where the asterisk should be placed in the LINE array, displays the array, and restores a blank in place of the asterisk. This process is repeated fifteen times, resulting in the plot illustrated in Figure 6-9.

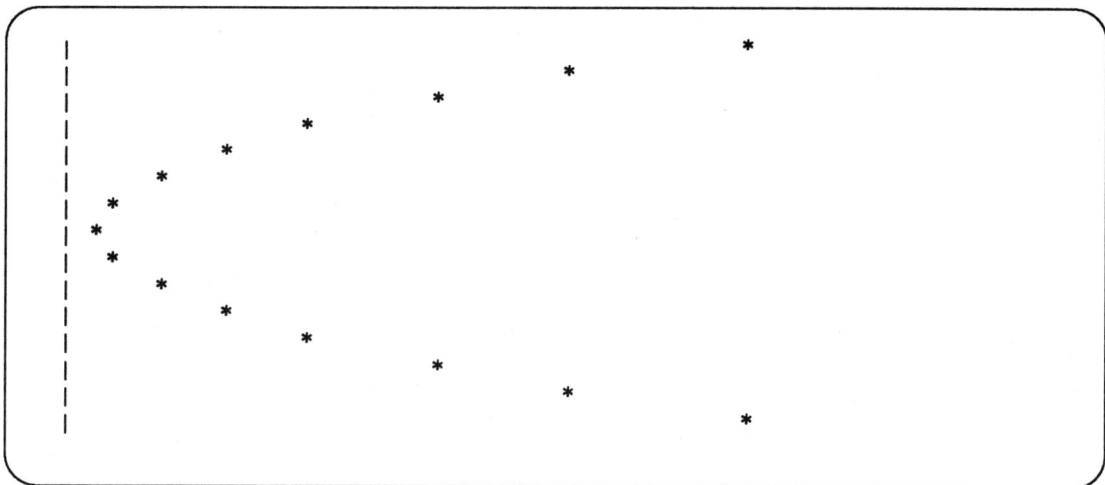

Figure 6-9   The Display Produced by Program 6-7

Two observations must be made about Program 6-7. First, a Y axis has not been explicitly included on the output. This is a minor omission that is rectified by Program 6-8.

 Program 6-8

```
PROGRAM MAIN
   INTEGER X,Y
   CHARACTER LINE(72), YAXIS(72)
   DATA LINE/'|',71*' '/
   DATA YAXIS/'+',53*'-','>',17*' '/
   PRINT *,'                    Y AXIS'
   PRINT *,YAXIS
   DO 10 X = 1,15
      Y = (X-8)**2 + 3
      LINE(Y) = '*'
      PRINT *, LINE
      LINE(Y) = ' '
10    CONTINUE
   END
```

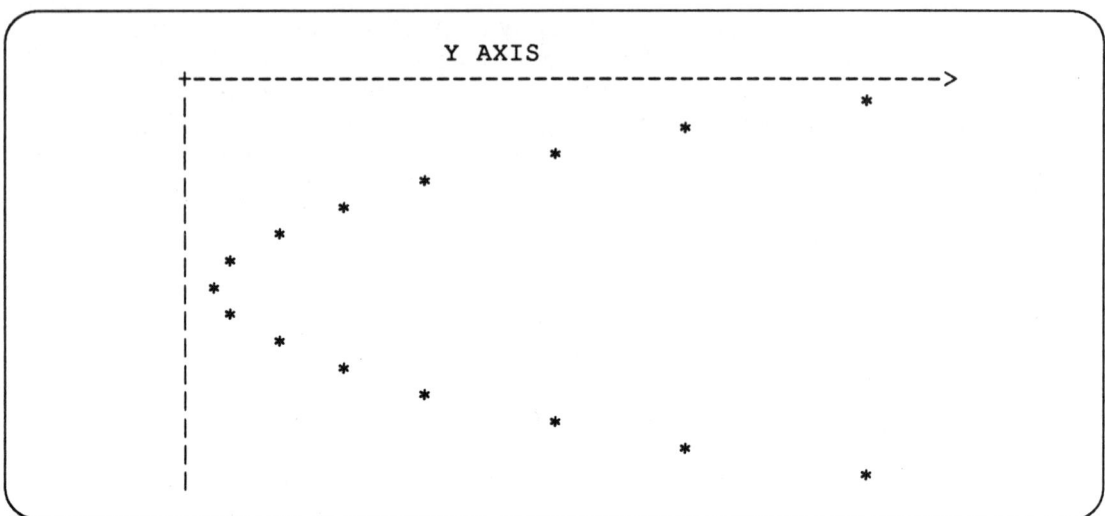

Figure 6-10   The Display Produced by Program 6-8

Notice that Program 6-8 is essentially the same as Program 6-7 with the addition of the YAXIS array specification and initialization and the two PRINT statements. The PRINT statements are placed before the DO loop to display the header lines. Program 6-8 produces the completed plot shown in Figure 6-10.

A more serious problem with both Program 6-7 and Program 6-8 is that negative Y values and Y values greater than 72 cannot be accommodated as a subscript to the LINE array. Accommodation of graphs with such values requires scaling of the Y values to fit within the LINE array's subscript range. The scaling algorithm to do this, which ensures that our plotting program works for any Y value, is presented in the next application.

Application 2: Data Scaling

A common problem encountered in plotting data is the need to scale values to fit within the width of the paper or video screen before a plotting routine can be used. Equation 1 provides the required scaling formula:

$$(EQ.\ 1)\quad Scaled\ Y\ value\ =\ \frac{Original\ Y\ value - Minimum\ Y\ value}{Maximum\ Y\ value - Minimum\ Y\ value}\ x\ (W-1)$$

where the maximum and minimum values are the respective maximum and minimum values for the complete set of data values being plotted, and W is the desired width of the paper or video display.

The term:

$$\frac{Original\ Y\ value - Minimum\ Y\ value}{Maximum\ Y\ value - Minimum\ Y\ value}$$

in equation 1 forces each original Y value to lie within the range from zero to one, with the minimum data value corresponding to zero and the maximum data value to one. Multiplying this result by the term $(W-1)$ produces values between zero and $(W-1)$, for a total width of W.

For example, the second column in Table 6-4 lists Y values of the equation $Y = X^3$ for values of X between -5 and 5, in increments of 0.5. As shown in column two, the maximum and minimum Y values are $+125$ and -125, respectively.

Table 6-4   Values of the Equation $Y = X^3$

X	Y	Scaled Y	Rounded
-5 0	-125.000	0.000	0
-4.5	-91.125	9.485	9
-4.0	-64.000	17.080	17
-3.5	-42.875	22.995	23
-3.0	-27.000	27.440	27
-2.5	-15.625	30.625	31
-2.0	-8.000	32.760	33
-1.5	-3.375	34.055	34
-1.0	-1.000	34.720	35
-0.5	-0.125	34.965	35
0.0	0.000	35.000	35
0.5	0.125	35.035	35
1.0	1.000	35.280	35
1.5	3.375	35.945	36
2.0	8.000	37.240	37
2.5	15.625	39.375	39
3.0	27.000	42.560	43
3.5	42.875	47.005	47
4.0	64.000	52.920	53
4.5	91.125	60.515	61
5.0	125.000	70.000	70

For purposes of illustration, assume that the width of the display area for plotting each Y value in column two is 72 characters wide. Also assume that a single character of this display area, for example, the bar (|), is to be used for an axis symbol. This leaves a total width, W, of 71 for the actual data display. Applying equation 1 to the data of column two with $W = 71$ and using the correct minimum and maximum values of -125 and 125, respectively, yields the values listed in column three of the table. Notice that the minimum value of -125 is converted to the value 0.000, and the maximum value of 125 is converted to the value 70.000. The last column in the table is the rounded, integerized values of the scaled numbers listed in the third column. Notice that the values in column four range from 0 to 70, for a total range of 71 possible Y values. These values can be used directly by the curve-plotting routine presented in the previous application to create a graph similar to that shown in Figure 6-11.

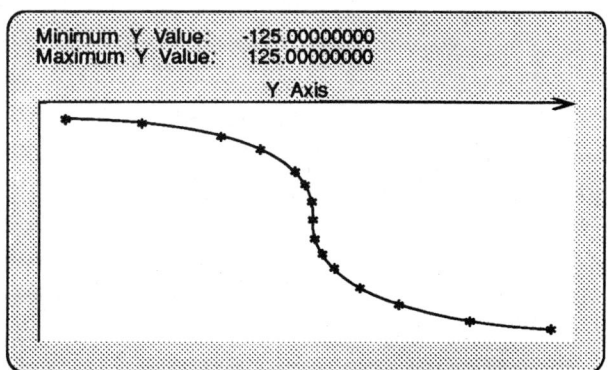

Figure 6-11   The Display Produced by Program 6-9

Program 6-9, which was used to create Figure 6-11, includes the data-scaling algorithm in the curve plotting routine used in Program 6-8.

 Program 6-9

```
PROGRAM MAIN
   INTEGER I, NPTS, NVAL(100)
   REAL X, YMIN, YMAX, WIDTH, SVAL(100)
   CHARACTER LINE(72), YAXIS(72)
   DATA YAXIS/'+',70*'-','>'/
   DATA LINE/'|',71*' '/
   DATA YMAX,YMIN /1E-5,1E5/
   X = -5.0
   XINC = 0.5
   NPTS = 21
   WIDTH = 70
*** LOAD UP THE DATA TO BE PLOTTED AND FIND THE MAX AND MIN VALUES
   DO 10 I = 1,NPTS
      SVAL(I) = X**3
      IF (SVAL(I).GT.YMAX) YMAX = SVAL(I)
      IF (SVAL(I).LT.YMIN) YMIN = SVAL(I)
      X = X + XINC
10    CONTINUE
*** SCALE ALL Y VALUES TO BE PLOTTED
   DO 15 I = 1, NPTS
      FVAL = ( (SVAL(I) - YMIN)/(YMAX - YMIN) ) * WIDTH
      NVAL(I) = INT(FVAL + .5)
15    CONTINUE
*** PRODUCE THE PLOT
   PRINT *,'MINIMUM Y VALUE: ',YMIN
   PRINT *,'MAXIMUM Y VALUE: ',YMAX
   PRINT *,' Y AXIS'
   PRINT *,YAXIS
   DO 20 I = 1,NPTS
      LINE(NVAL(I)+2) = '*'
      PRINT *, LINE
      LINE(NVAL(I)+2) = ' '
20    CONTINUE
   END
```

Additional Exercises for Chapter 6

1. Enter and run Program 6-8 on your computer system.

2. Modify Program 6-8 to plot the curve $Y = X^3 - 4X^2 + 3X + 2$ for X equal to 0, 1, 2, 3, 4, 5, and 6.

3. When the switch illustrated in Figure 6-12 is closed at time $t = 0$, the voltage, V, across the capacitor is given by the equation $V = E[1 - e^{-t/(RC)}]$, where E is the voltage of the battery, R is the circuit resistance, C is the value of the capacitance, and t is time in seconds. Assuming that $E = 60$, $R = 2500.5$, and $C = .005$, modify Program 6-8 to plot the voltage across the capacitor from $t = 1$ to $t = 30$, in increments of 1 second.

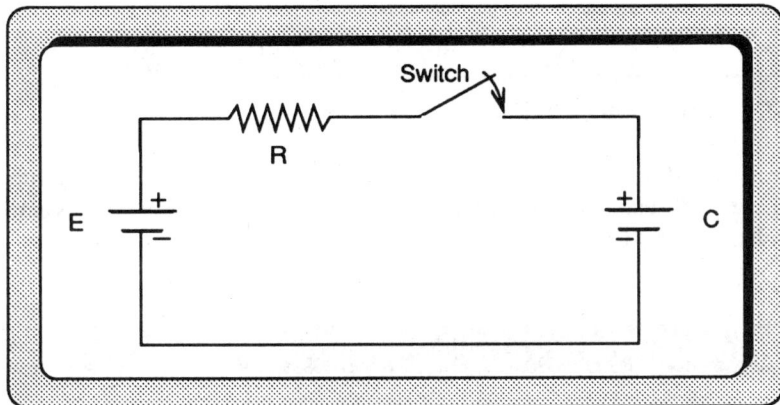

Figure 6-12   A Simple RC Circuit

4. Enter and run Program 6-9 on your computer system.

5. Modify Program 6-8 to plot the curve $Y = X^3 - 4X^2 + 3X + 10$ for X between 1 and +5, in increments of 0.25.

6. Modify Program 6-8 to plot the curve $Y = 4X^3 - X^4$ for X between -10 and $+10$, in increments of 0.5.

7. Figure 6-13 illustrates a *harmonic oscillator,* which consists of an object of mass M fastened to one end of a spring. The other end of the spring is attached to a wall, and the object is free to slide over a frictionless surface. Assuming the object is initially at rest (that is, the spring is neither stretched or compressed) and then pulled to position A at time $t = 0$, the position of the mass at any other time, t, is described by the equation $X = A \cos[(\sqrt{k/m})\, t]$, where k is the spring constant, in Newtons/meter; m is the mass, in units of kilograms; and A is the initial displacement, in units of centimeters. Assuming A is 100 centimeters, k is 50 Newtons/meter, and m is 1 kilogram, modify Program 6-9 to plot the displacement of the mass from $t = 0$ to $t = 60$ seconds, in increments of 1 second. (*Hint:* Remember to convert all angles to radian measure.)

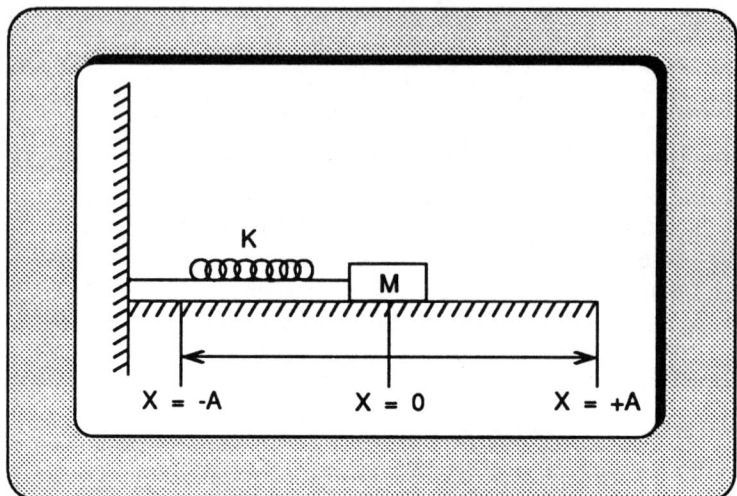

Figure 6-13   A Harmonic Oscillator

8. Modify Program 6-9 to plot the voltage across the capacitor illustrated in Figure 6-12 from $t = 0$ to $t = 30$ seconds, in increments of 1 second. For this problem, assume that $E = 100$ volts, $R = 2500.5$, and $C = .005$.

6.5   Common Programming Errors

There are seven common errors associated with using arrays.

1. The first error is forgetting to declare the array. This error results in a compiler error message equivalent to "SUBSCRIPT USED WITH UNDIMENSIONED VARI-ABLE" each time a subscripted variable is encountered on the left-hand side of an assignment statement or in a READ statement. When the subscripted variable is used on the right-hand side of an assignment statement, in a PRINT statement, or in a WRITE statement, the compiler interprets the variable as a function. In this case a message such as "UNRESOLVED EXTERNAL" or "UNDEFINED FUNC-TION" is displayed.

2. The most common programming error is to use a subscript that references a nonexistent array element—for example, declaring the array to be of size 20 and using a subscript value of 25. This error is typically not detected by most FORTRAN compilers. It will, however, result in a runtime error that results either in a program crash or in a value that has no relation to the intended element being accessed from memory. In either case, it is usually an extremely trouble-some error to locate. The only solution to this problem is to make sure, either by specific programming statements or by careful coding, that each subscript references a valid array element.

3. Related to the previous error is not using a large enough terminal value in a DO loop counter to cycle through all the array elements. This error usually occurs when an array is initially specified to be of size N and there is a DO loop within the program of the form DO 10 I = 1, N. The array size is then expanded, but the programmer forgets to change the interior DO loop parameters. Using the PARAMETER statement presented in Section 3.4 can ensure that this error will not occur. For example, the staements:

```
INTEGER N
PARAMETER (N=30)
INTEGER NUMS (N)
```

are valid. The DO loop can then be written as:

```
DO 10 I=1,N
```

4. Using a variable name to specify an array. For example, if N is an integer variable, the statements:

```
INTEGER NUMS(N)
N = 30
```

cannot be used to specify an array of size 30. Similarly, the sequence:

```
N = 30
INTEGER NUMS(N)
```

is also incorrect, because all declaration statements must precede any executable statement. The correct method of using N as an array size is to make it a named constant using the parameters statement as illustrated above in error 3.

5. Forgetting to initialize the array. Although many compilers automatically set all elements of integer and real value arrays to zero, and all elements of character arrays to blanks, it is up to the programmer to ensure that each array is correctly initialized before processing of array elements begins.

6. Using the same name for both an array and a scalar variable. Once an array name is declared, this same name cannot be used as a scalar variable.

7. Omitting the comma before setting the subscript parameters in an implied DO loop. For example, writing PRINT * (A(I) I = 1,5) instead of PRINT *, (A(I), I = 1,5). The reason for this error is that the first comma is not present in the more commonly used DO statement.

6.6 · Chapter Summary

1. A single dimension array is a data structure that can be used to store a list of values of the same data type. Such arrays are either explicitly data typed and sized using a data declaration statement or implicitly typed using a DIMENSION statement. Explicit array declarations require listing the data type of the array, its name, and the array size. For example, the declaration:

```
INTEGER NUM(100)
```

creates an array of 100 integers. Integer and real arrays can also be data typed implicitly using a DIMENSION statement. For example, the statement:

```
DIMENSION NUM(100), AREA(25)
```

creates an integer array named NUM with 100 elements and a real array named AREA consisting of 25 elements.

2. Array elements are stored in sequential locations in memory and referenced using the array name and a subscript. For example, the variable NUMS(34) refers to the 34th element in the NUMS array. Any integer-value expression can also be used as a subscript.

3. Arrays may be initialized using DATA statements. The general form of a DATA statement is:

```
DATA variable list /value list/, variable list /value list/ ...
```

Each value list must have the same number of values as there are in its associated variable list. For example, the statement:

```
DATA A,B,C,D / 22.4, 16.3, 71.2, 18.6/
```

contains one variable list and one value list, with each list having the same number of items. The first value is assigned to the first variable, the second value to the second variable, and so on, until all variables have been initialized.

4. Arrays may be referenced using implied DO loops. An implied DO loop for a single dimension array has the form:

```
(array name(I), I = initial value, terminal value, increment)
```

where the subscript I may be replaced by any other integer variable name. Implied DO loops may be used with either DATA, READ, PRINT, or WRITE statements for array input and output. Both list-directed and format-controlled versions of the input and output statements can be used with the implied DO loop. Examples of these statements are:

```
READ *, (A(I), I = 1,10)
READ 15, (VOLTS(K), K = 2,12,2)
PRINT *, (NUMS(M), M = 5,16)
PRINT 20, (NUMS(J), J = 2,12,2)
WRITE(6,*) (FACTOR(NNN), NNN = 1,15)
WRITE(6,20) (FACTOR(NNN), NNN = 1,15)
```

5. Arrays may also be referenced by name, without any subscript value, in DATA, READ, PRINT, and WRITE statements. For input and output statements, both list-directed and format-controlled versions can be used. When referenced by name in a READ statement, sufficient values must be entered for each element in the array. When referenced by name in either a PRINT or a WRITE statement, all element values are displayed.

6. FORTRAN permits the specification of arrays with a maximum of seven dimensions. For example, a two dimension array is declared by listing both a row and a column size with the data type and name of the array. Thus, the specification:

```
REAL WATTS(5,7)
```

creates a two dimension array consisting of five rows and seven columns of real values. Multidimensional arrays may also be implicitly declared using DIMENSION statements.

6.7   Enrichment Study: Sorting Methods

Most programmers encounter the need to sort a list of data items at some time in their programming careers. For example, experimental results might have to be arranged in either increasing (ascending) or decreasing (descending) order for statistical analysis, lists of names may have to be sorted in alphabetical order, or a list of dates may have to be rearranged in ascending date order.

For sorting data, two major categories of sorting techniques exist, called internal and external sorts, respectively. *Internal sorts* are used when the data list is not too large and the complete list can be stored within the computer's memory, usually in an array. *External sorts* are used for much larger data sets that are stored in large external disk or tape files and cannot be accommodated within the computer's memory as a complete unit.

In this section we present two common internal sorts, called the selection sort and the exchange sort, respectively. Although the exchange sort, also known as a "bubble sort," is the more common of the two, we will see that the selection sort is easier and frequently more efficient.

Selection Sort

In a selection sort the smallest (or largest) value is initially selected from the complete list of data and exchanged with the first element in the list. After this first selection and exchange, the next smallest (or largest) element in the revised list is selected and exchanged with the second element in the list. Since the smallest element is already in the first position in the list, this second pass need only consider the second through last elements. For a list consisting of n elements, this process is repeated $n-1$ times, with each pass through the list requiring one less comparison than the previous pass.

For example, consider the list of numbers illustrated in Figure 6-14. The first pass through the initial list results in the number 32 being selected and exchanged with the first element in the list. The second pass, made on the reordered list, results in the number 155 being selected from the second through fifth elements. This value is then exchanged with the second element in the list. The third pass selects the number 307 from the third through fifth elements in the list and exchanges this value with the third element. Finally, the fourth and last pass through the list selects the remaining minimum value and exchanges it with the fourth list element. Although

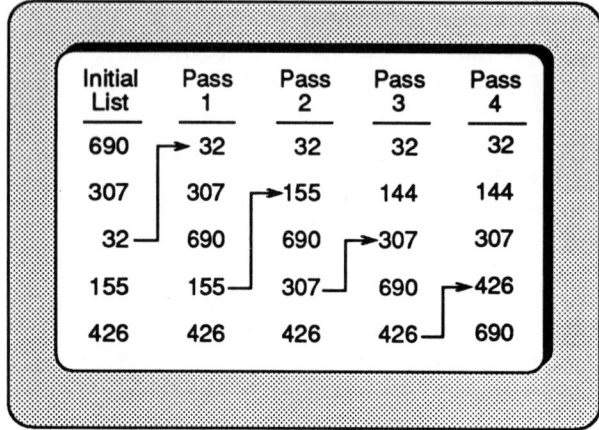

Initial List	Pass 1	Pass 2	Pass 3	Pass 4
690	32	32	32	32
307	307	155	144	144
32	690	690	307	307
155	155	307	690	426
426	426	426	426	690

Figure 6-14   A Sample Selection Sort

each pass in this example resulted in an exchange, no exchange would have been made in a pass if the smallest value were already in the correct location.

Program 6-10 implements a selection sort for a list of 10 numbers that are stored in an array named NUMS. For later comparison to an exchange sort, the number of actual moves made by the program to get the data into sorted order is counted and displayed.

Program 6-10 uses a nested DO loop to perform the selection sort. The outer DO loop causes nine passes to be made through the data, which is one less than the total number of data items in the list.

 Program 6-10

```
PROGRAM MAIN
   INTEGER I, TEMP, MOVES, MIN, MININD, NUMS(10)
   DATA NUMS/22,55,67,98,45,32,101,99,73,10/
   MOVES = 0
   DO 10 I = 1,9
     MIN = NUMS(I)
     MININD = I
     DO 5 J = I+1,10
       IF (NUMS(J).LT.MIN) THEN
         MIN = NUMS(J)
         MININD = J
       ENDIF
5    CONTINUE
*** PERFORM THE SWITCH
     IF(MIN .LT. NUMS(I)) THEN
       TEMP = NUMS(I)
       NUMS(I) = NUMS(MININD)
       NUMS(MININD) = TEMP
       MOVES = MOVES + 1
     ENDIF
10   CONTINUE
   PRINT *, 'THE SORTED LIST, IN ASCENDING ORDER, IS:'
   PRINT *, NUMS
   PRINT *
   PRINT *, MOVES, ' MOVES WERE MADE TO SORT THIS LIST'
   END
```

For each pass, the variable MIN is initially assigned the value NUMS(I), where I is the outer DO loop's counter variable. Since I begins at 1 and ends at 9, each element in the list is successively designated as the next exchange element.

The inner loop is used in Program 6-10 to cycle through the elements below the designated exchange element to select the next smallest value. Thus, this loop begins at the index value I+1 and continues through the end of the list. When a new minimum is found, its value and position in the list are stored in the variables named MIN and MININD, respectively. Upon completion of the inner loop, an exchange is made only if a value less than that in the designated exchange position was found.

Following is the output produced by Program 6-10.

```
THE SORTED LIST, IN ASCENDING ORDER, IS:
        10      22      32      45      55      67      73      98      99      101
        8 MOVES WERE MADE TO SORT THIS LIST
```

Clearly, the number of moves displayed depends on the initial order of the values in the list. An advantage of the selection sort is that the maximum number of moves that must be made is $n-1$, where n is the number of items in the list. Further, each move is a final move that results in an element residing in its final location in the sorted list.

A disadvantage of the selection sort is that $n(n-1)/2$ comparisons are always required, regardless of the initial arrangement of the data. This number of comparisons is obtained as follows: the last pass always requires one comparison, the next-to-last pass requires two comparisons, and so on, to the first pass, which requires $n-1$ comparisons. Thus, the total number of comparisons is:

$$1 + 2 + 3 + \ldots n-1 = n\,(n-1)\,/\,2$$

Exchange Sort

In an exchange sort, successive values in the list are compared, beginning with the first two elements. If the list is to be sorted in ascending (from smallest to largest) order, the smaller value of the two being compared is always placed before the larger value. For lists sorted in descending (from largest to smallest) order, the smaller of the two values being compared is always placed after the larger value.

For example, assuming that a list of values is to be sorted in ascending order, if the first element in the list is larger than the second, the two elements are interchanged. Then the second and third elements are compared. Again, if the second element is larger than the third, these two elements are interchanged. This process continues until the last two elements have been compared and exchanged, if necessary. If no exchanges were made during this initial pass through the data, the data is in the correct order and the process is finished; otherwise, a second pass is made through the data, starting from the first element and stopping at the next-to-last element. The reason for stopping at the next-to-last element on the second pass is that the first pass always results in the most positive value "sinking" to the bottom of the list.

As a specific example of this process, consider the list of numbers illustrated in Figure 6-15. The first comparison results in the interchange of the first two element values, 690 and 307. The next comparison, between elements two and three in the

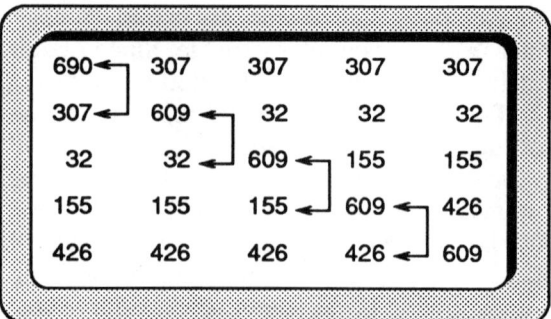

Figure 6-15   The First Pass of an Exchange Sort

revised list, results in the interchange of values between the second and third elements, 609 and 32. This comparison and possible switching of adjacent values is continued until the last two elements have been compared and possibly switched. This process completes the first pass through the data and results in the largest number moving to the bottom of the list. As the largest value sinks to its resting place at the bottom of the list, the smaller elements slowly rise, or "bubble," to the top of the list. This bubbling effect of the smaller elements gave rise to the name "bubble sort" for this sorting algorithm.

As the first pass through the list ensures that the largest value always moves to the bottom of the list, the second pass stops at the next-to-last element. This process continues with each pass stopping at one higher element than the previous pass, until either n–1 passes through the list have been completed or no exchanges are necessary in any single pass. In both cases the resulting list is in sorted order.

Program 6-11 implements an exchange sort for the same list of 10 numbers used in Program 6-10. For comparison to the earlier selection sort, the number of adjacent moves (exchanges) made by the program is also counted and displayed.

As illustrated in Program 6-11, the exchange sort requires a nested loop. The outer loop in Program 6-11 is a WHILE loop that checks if any exchanges were made in the last pass. It is the inner DO loop that does the actual comparison and exchanging of adjacent element values.

Immediately before the inner loop's DO statement is encountered, the value of the logical variable OUTORD is set to .TRUE., to indicate that the list is initially out of order (not sorted) and to force the first pass through the list. If the inner loop then detects an element is out of order, OUTORD is again set to .TRUE., which indicates that the list is still unsorted. The OUTORD variable is then used by the outer loop to determine whether another pass through the data is to be made. Thus, the sort is stopped either because OUTORD is .FALSE. after at least one pass has been completed or n–1 passes through the data have been made. In both cases, the resulting list is in sorted order.

Following is the output produced by Program 6-11.

```
THE SORTED LIST, IN ASCENDING ORDER, IS:
    10    22    32    45    55    67    73    98    99    101
    20 MOVES WERE MADE TO SORT THIS LIST
```

Program 6-11

```
      PROGRAM MAIN
        INTEGER I, MOVES, NPTS, TEMP, NUMS(10)
        LOGICAL OUTORD
        DATA NUMS/22,55,67,98,45,32,101,99,73,10/
        MOVES = 0
        NPTS = 10
        OUTORD = .TRUE.
5       IF (OUTORD .AND. NPTS .GT. 1) THEN
          OUTORD = .FALSE.
          DO 10 I = 1, NPTS - 1
            IF (NUMS(I).GT.NUMS(I+1)) THEN
              TEMP = NUMS(I+1)
              NUMS(I+1) = NUMS(I)
              NUMS(I) = TEMP
              OUTORD = .TRUE.
              MOVES = MOVES + 1
            ENDIF
10        CONTINUE
          NPTS = NPTS - 1
          GO TO 5
        ENDIF
        PRINT *, 'THE SORTED LIST, IN ASCENDING ORDER, IS:'
        PRINT *, NUMS
        PRINT *, MOVES, ' MOVES WERE MADE TO SORT THIS LIST'
        END
```

As with the selection sort, the number of moves required by an exchange sort depends on the initial order of the values in the list.

An advantage of the exchange sort is that processing is terminated whenever a sorted list is encountered. In the best case, when the data is in sorted order to begin with, an exchange sort requires no moves (the same for the selection sort) and only $n-1$ comparisons (the selection sort always requires $n(n-1)/2$ comparisons). In the worst case, when the data is in reverse sorted order, the selection sort does better. Here both sorts require $n(n-1)/2$ comparisons, but the selection sort needs only $n-1$ moves while the exchange sort needs $n(n-1)/2$ moves. The additional moves required by the exchange sort result from the intermediate exchanges between adjacent elements to "settle" each element into its final position. In this regard the selection sort is superior, because no intermediate moves are necessary. For random data, such as that used in Programs 6-10 and 6-11, the selection sort generally performs equal to or better than the exchange sort.

Modularity
Using Functions

Chapter Seven

As we have seen, each FORTRAN program must contain a MAIN program unit. In addition to this required unit, FORTRAN programs may also contain any number of additional program units, which are collectively referred to as *subprograms*. Each FORTRAN subprogram must begin with one of the keywords FUNCTION, SUBROUTINE, or BLOCK DATA. In this chapter we learn how to write FUNCTION program units, pass data to them, process the passed data, and return a result. Additionally, in this chapter's Enrichment section we present the economic motivation for constructing modular programs.

7.1 Functions

FORTRAN provides three types of functions: intrinsic, subprogram, and statement. We are already familiar with intrinsic functions, such as ABS, SQRT, EXP, and so on, which are provided as an intrinsic part of the FORTRAN language. Subprogram and statement functions perform in a manner identical to intrinsic functions except that they are user written. A subprogram function is a distinct program unit containing multiple statements while a statement function is a single FORTRAN statement, much like an assignment statement.

The purpose of all functions, whether intrinsic, subprogram, or statement, is to receive data, operate on the data, and return a single value. In using a function, we must be concerned with both the function and how it interfaces with other units of the program. In this section we review calling a function and correctly using the returned value.

All functions are called, or used, in the same manner as intrinsic functions: by giving the function's name and passing any data to it in the parentheses following the function name (see Figure 7-1). At the same time the function is called, provision must also be made to correctly use its calculated value.

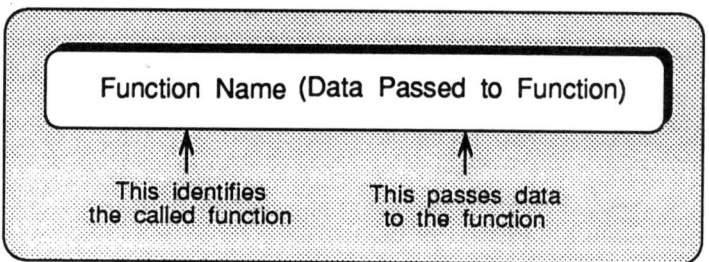

Figure 7-1   Calling and Passing Data to a Function

To clarify the process of sending data to a function and using its returned value, consider Program 7-1, which calls a function named FMAX. The program as shown is not yet complete. Once the function FMAX is written and included in Program 7-1, the completed program can be run.

Let us review calling the function FMAX. (In the next section we will write FMAX as a function subprogram that accepts the passed data and returns the maximum value of the two passed values.) The function FMAX is referred to as the *called function*, since it is called, or summoned into action, by its reference in the MAIN program unit. The program unit that does the calling, in this case, MAIN, is referred to as the *calling unit*. The terms *called* and *calling* come from standard telephone usage, where one party calls the other on a telephone. The party initiating the call is referred to as the calling party, and the party receiving the call is referred to as the called party. The same terms describe function calls.

Calling a function is rather simple. All that is required are that the name of the function be used and that any data passed to the function be enclosed within the

Program 7-1

```
PROGRAM MAIN
  REAL FIRNUM, SECNUM, THEMAX, FMAX
  PRINT *, 'ENTER A NUMBER: '
  READ *, FIRNUM
  PRINT *, 'GREAT! PLEASE ENTER A SECOND NUMBER: '
  READ *, SECNUM
*
  THEMAX = FMAX(FIRNUM,SECNUM)
  PRINT *, 'THE MAXIMUM VALUE IS ', THEMAX
*
  END
```

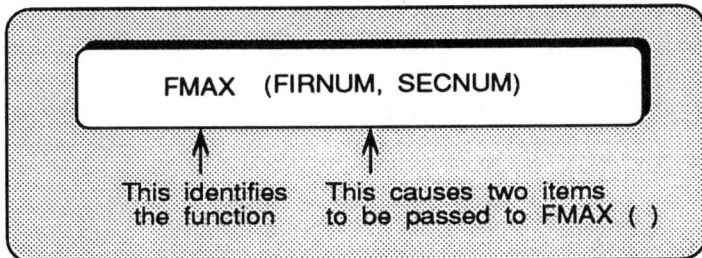

Figure 7-2   Calling and Passing Two Values to FMAX

parentheses following the function name. The items enclosed within the parentheses are called *actual arguments* of the called function (see Figure 7-2).

At the time that a function is called, provision must also be made to use the value that is provided by the function. To use the returned value, we must either provide a variable to store the value or use the value directly in an expression. Storing the returned value in a variable is accomplished using a standard assignment statement. For example, the assignment statement in Program 7-1:

```
THEMAX = FMAX(FIRNUM, SECNUM)
```

can be used to store FMAX's returned value in the variable named THEMAX. This assignment statement does two things. First, the right-hand side of the assignment statement calls FMAX; then the result returned by the FMAX function is stored in the variable THEMAX. Since the value returned by FMAX is real, the variable THEMAX must also be declared as a real variable within the calling function's variable declarations.

The second method of calling a function and using its returned value is to include the function within any valid FORTRAN expression. For example, the statement:

```
PRINT *, FMAX(FIRNUM, SECNUM)
```

can be used to directly call FMAX and display its value. Similarly, an expression such as 2.0 * FMAX(FIRNUM, SECNUM) is also valid, as long as the expression is correctly used within a complete FORTRAN statement. In both of these function calls, the variables FIRNUM and SECNUM have been used as actual arguments. More generally, any valid FORTRAN expression can be used as an actual argument.

Lastly, the calling program unit must "know" the data type of the value returned by the function. The returned value's data type is formally referred to as the function's data type. Thus, if a function returns a real value, the function's data type is REAL. Similarly, if a function returns an integer value, the function's data type is INTEGER.

One method of specifying a function's data type is to explicitly declare the function name in the same way that a variable is declared. Notice that in Program 7-1 FMAX has been declared as a REAL, which means that FMAX returns a REAL value. In the absence of an explicit declaration, the compiler will assign a data type in accordance with FORTRAN's implicit typing rules (see Section 2.2).

Although the data types of intrinsic functions are specified internally within the compiler, the intrinsic function names were selected to reflect their data types. For example, intrinsic function names beginning with one of the letters I, J, K, L, and M, such as INT, LEN, and MAX, all return integer values except that some intrinsic function names beginning in L return a logical value.

Exercises

1a. An extremely useful programming algorithm for rounding a real number to n decimal places is:

Step 1. Multiply the number by 10^n
Step 2. Add .5
Step 3. Delete the fractional part of the result
Step 4. Divide by 10^n

For example, using this algorithm to round the number 78.374625 to three decimal places yields:

Step 1. $78.374625 \times 10^3 = 78374.625$
Step 2. $78374.625 + .5 = 78375.125$
Step 3. Retain the integer part = 78375
Step 4. 78375 divided by $10^3 = 78.375$

Using this algorithm, write a program that accepts a user-entered value of money, multiplies the entered amount by an 8.675 percent interest rate, and displays the result rounded to two decimal places.

b. Enter, compile, and execute the program written for Exercise 1a.

2a. Write a FORTRAN program that returns the fractional part of any user-entered number. For example, if the number 256.879 is entered, the number .879 should be displayed. (*Hint:* Use the INT function.)

b. Enter, compile, and execute the program written for Exercise 2a.

3. Write a FORTRAN program that accepts 10 integers and determines whether each entered integer is even or odd. (*Hint:* Use the MOD function.) Enter, compile, and execute your program.

7.2   Subprogram Functions

A subprogram function is a distinct program unit in its own right, separate from a MAIN program unit. In keeping with our original definition of a function, subprogram functions are restricted to returning a single value (see Figure 7-3).

Like all program units, a subprogram function consists of two parts, a function header and a function body, as illustrated in Figure 7-4. The purpose of the function header is to identify the data type returned by the function, provide the function with a name, and specify the number and order of arguments expected by the function. The purpose of the function body is to ensure correct access to the function's arguments and then operate on the passed data and return a single value back to the calling function.

The function header is always the first line of a function and must include the type of value that will be returned by the function, the keyword FUNCTION, the name of the function, and the names of the arguments that will be used by it. For example, the following function declaration can be used for a subprogram function named FMAX that is to receive two values and return a single REAL value:

```
REAL FUNCTION FMAX(X,Y)
```

The names of the arguments in the function declaration line, in this case, X and Y, are chosen by the programmer. Since the header declaration for FMAX includes two arguments, this function expects to receive two actual arguments when it is called. Any two valid variable names could have been used instead of the argument names X and Y. The argument names in the header declaration line are referred to as either *dummy* or *formal* arguments (the two names are synonymous) and must match, in type, number, and order, the actual arguments used in calling the function. The dummy arguments are used internal to the function to refer to the data passed to the function. For example, if the calling program unit called FMAX using the statement:

```
THEMAX = FMAX(16.2, 42.3)
```

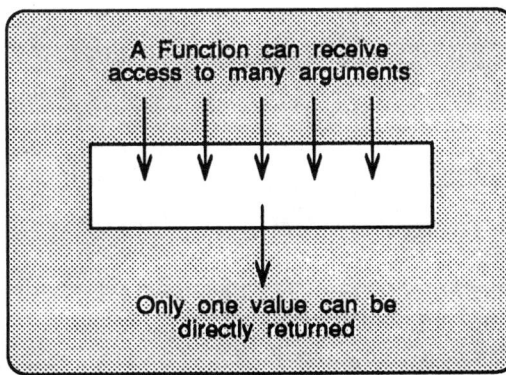

Figure 7-3   A Function Returns a Single Value

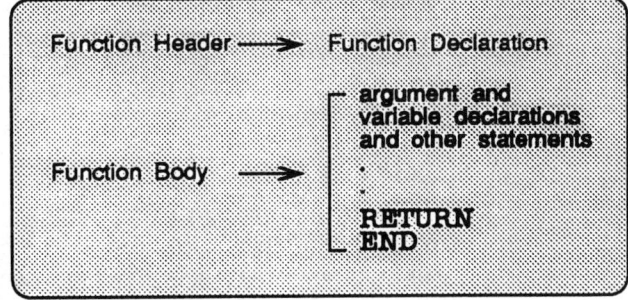

Figure 7-4   General Format of a Function Subprogram

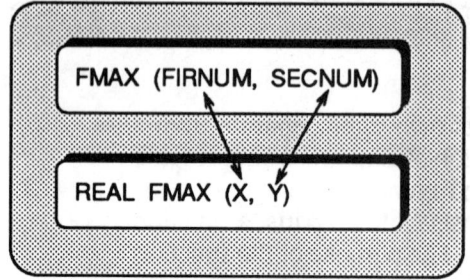

Figure 7-5   Assigning Actual Arguments to Formal Arguments

the argument X would be used to reference the number 16.2, and the argument Y to reference the number 42.3. Similarly, as illustrated in Figure 7-5, if the call from another program unit was:

```
THEMAX = FMAX(FIRNUM, SECNUM)
```

the formal argument X, within FMAX, would reference the value in FIRNUM and the formal argument Y would reference the value in SECNUM. The function itself does not know which program unit made the function call.

The two arguments of the function FMAX, X and Y, are treated like variables. As such, they must be declared and then can be used anywhere within the FMAX function. The declaration of these two arguments is given by an argument declaration statement that is placed immediately after the function declaration line and that formally begins the function's body.

Argument declarations, as the name implies, declare the data type of the arguments expected by the function. Assuming that X and Y are to reference real values, any of the following argument declaration statements can be used:

```
REAL X,Y          REAL Y,X          REAL X          REAL Y
                                    REAL Y          REAL X
```

As illustrated by these statements, the order of the argument declarations is not important. The only requirement is that each argument be specified. Notice that these argument declarations are identical to variable declarations. From a programming viewpoint, arguments can be considered as variables whose values are assigned outside the function and passed to the function when it is called.

Putting all this together, a valid function header and argument declaration for the FMAX function is:

```
REAL FUNCTION FMAX(X,Y)
  REAL X,Y
```

Although the data type of the function and the data type of its arguments happen to agree in this example, this is not required. For example, if X were an integer and Y a character of size one, the function header and argument declarations for FMAX would be:

```
REAL FMAX(X,Y)
  INTEGER X
  CHARACTER Y
```

Having constructed a function header and argument declarations for FMAX, we can now complete construction of the function's body. For purposes of illustration, let us assume that FMAX is to receive two real arguments, select the largest argument, and return this number to the calling program unit. Realizing that a function is simply a program unit, like the MAIN unit, makes the construction of FMAX's body a familiar task. A subprogram function's body requires any necessary variable declarations followed by any valid FORTRAN statements and ends with the keyword END. This is illustrated in Figure 7-4. This is essentially the same basic structure used in all the MAIN program units we have written, with two new features.

The first new feature is that the function body must contain a statement that assigns a value to the function name, which is typically accomplished using an assignment statement of the form:

$$\boxed{function \ name \ = \ expression}$$

(Although a READ statement can also be used, in practice it defeats the purpose of using the function to calculate the returned value.) In our FMAX function this statement takes the specific form:

$$\boxed{FMAX \ = \ expression}$$

This is the statement that assigns a value to FMAX, which is the value returned by the function. The expression in this statement may include the formal arguments, variables declared and assigned values within the function, or other function calls. In no case, however, may a function reference itself within its body. Thus, the statement:

```
FMAX = FMAX(A,B)
```

is invalid within the FMAX function. Functions that internally reference themselves are referred to as self-referential or recursive functions (the two terms are synonymous) and are not permitted in FORTRAN 77. (This restriction against a functions internally referencing itself does not preclude using a function as an actual argument to itself when it is called from another program unit. Thus, the statement THEMAX = FMAX(FMAX(A,B), FMAX(C,D)) is valid in any unit except the FMAX function and is equivalent to a statement such as VAL = SQRT(SQRT(A)).)

The second new feature is the inclusion of a RETURN statement. When this statement is executed, the value assigned to the function name is returned to the calling function. As with all program units, the END statement is the last statement used to close the unit. Unlike in earlier versions of FORTRAN, the END statement in a FORTRAN 77 subprogram function actually performs two tasks: it both marks the physical end of the program unit and acts as a RETURN statement. This makes an explicit RETURN statement immediately before an END statement theoretically unnecessary, and its inclusion in future programs will be omitted.[*]

---

[*] There are two counterarguments for always including a RETURN statement. First, some compilers require it. If you are using such a compiler, the RETURN statement is mandatory. For these compilers the END statement is considered a nonexecutable statement that is used only to mark the physical end of a program unit. In this role the END statement tells the compiler to stop reading any more statements and to begin the actual compilation. Here the last statement to be compiled and translated into machine language is the statement immediately preceding the END statement, which is the RETURN statement. During program execution it is the machine-language version of the RETURN that is actually executed. The second reason for including a RETURN is one of programming style. Many programmers feel that the RETURN statement clearly indicates a subprogram function's exit point. As subprogram functions can have multiple exit points, it is felt that all return points in a function, including the one at the end of the function, should clearly be marked with a RETURN statement.

Let us now put all of this together to write the complete FMAX function. Using an IF-ELSE statement to select the maximum of the two passed arguments, the complete function code is:

```
REAL FUNCTION FMAX(X,Y)
  REAL X,Y
  IF (X .GT. Y) THEN
    FMAX = X
  ELSE
    FMAX = Y
  ENDIF
  END
```

Program 7-2 includes the FMAX function within a working program.

 Program 7-2

```
PROGRAM MAIN
  REAL FIRNUM, SECNUM, THEMAX, FMAX
  PRINT *, 'ENTER A NUMBER: '
  READ *, FIRNUM
  PRINT *, 'GREAT! PLEASE ENTER A SECOND NUMBER: '
  READ *, SECNUM
  THEMAX = FMAX(FIRNUM,SECNUM)
  PRINT *, 'THE MAXIMUM VALUE IS ', THEMAX
  END
* FOLLOWING IS THE FUNCTION FMAX
  REAL FUNCTION FMAX(X,Y)
  REAL X,Y
  IF (X .GT. Y) THEN
    FMAX = X
  ELSE
    FMAX = Y
  ENDIF
  END
```

Program 7-2 can be used to select and print the maximum of any two real numbers entered by the user. Following is a sample run using Program 7-2:

```
ENTER A NUMBER:
22.0
GREAT! PLEASE ENTER A SECOND NUMBER:
78.0
THE MAXIMUM VALUE IS 78.000000
```

The placement of the FMAX function after the MAIN program unit in Program 7-2 is a matter of choice. Some programmers prefer to put all subprogram functions at the top of a program and make MAIN the last unit listed. We prefer to list the MAIN program unit first because it is the driver function that should give anyone reading the program an idea of what the complete program is about before encountering the details of each function. Either placement approach is acceptable in FORTRAN, and you will encounter both styles in your programming work. (Other programming languages such as Pascal are more restrictive in their placement of subprogram units.)

It is important to note the four items we have introduced in relation to functions in Program 7-2. The first item is the declaration of FMAX within MAIN. This alerts MAIN to the data type that FMAX will be returning. The second item to notice in MAIN is the use of an assignment statement to call FMAX and its storage of the returned value in a suitably specified variable.

The last two items of note concern the coding of the FMAX function. The first line of FMAX declares that the function will return a REAL value, and within FMAX a value of the correct type is assigned to FMAX. Thus, FMAX is internally consistent in sending a real value back to MAIN, and MAIN has been correctly alerted to receive and use the returned value.

In writing your own subprogram functions, you must always keep these four items in mind. For another example, see if you can identify these four items in Program 7-3.

 Program 7-3

```
      PROGRAM MAIN
       INTEGER COUNT
       REAL FAHREN, TEMVER
       DO 10 COUNT = 1, 4
          PRINT *, 'ENTER A FAHRENHEIT TEMPERATURE: '
          READ *, FAHREN
          PRINT *, 'THE CELSIUS EQUIVALENT IS:', TEMVER(FAHREN)
  10      CONTINUE
       END
      REAL FUNCTION TEMVER(INTEMP)
* THE FOLLOWING FUNCTION CONVERTS A FAHRENHEIT TEMPERATURE
*   INTO ITS EQUIVALENT CELSIUS VALUE
       REAL INTEMP
       TEMVER = (5.0/9.0) * (INTEMP - 32.0)
       END
```

In reviewing Program 7-3, let us first analyze the function TEMVER. The complete definition of the function begins with the function's declaration line and ends with the keyword END. The function is declared as REAL, which means the function returns a REAL value. Within TEMVER, INTEMP is specified as a REAL argument, and a real valued expression is assigned to TEMVER.

On the receiving side, MAIN has a declaration statement for TEMVER that agrees with TEMVER's function declaration. As with all declaration statements, multiple declarations of the same type may be made within the same statement. Thus, the single declaration:

```
REAL FAHREN, TEMVER
```

is used to declare both the variable FAHREN and the function TEMVER as REAL. No additional variable is specified in MAIN to store the returned value from TEMVER because the returned value is immediately used by the PRINT statement.

As subprogram functions are independent program units in their own right, formal argument names, variable names, and statement numbers within a function may be identical to those used in both the MAIN program unit and any other user-written functions or subroutines. No confusion exists because each program unit is treated as a separate entity by the compiler. In fact, since individual program units are by definition independent, they may even be stored in separate files and compiled separately from any other units. Doing this requires that all the program units be explicitly linked together before the complete program can be run. A discussion of linking separate files is contained in Appendix A.

Notes of Caution

It is important to know that when a variable is used as an actual calling argument, the called function receives direct access to the variable. This means that the function can inadvertently alter a calling program unit's variable. For example, the calling statement FMAX(FIRNUM,SECNUM) in Program 7-2 gives FMAX access to MAIN's variables FIRNUM and SECNUM, even though these variables are "known" as X and Y within FMAX. Thus, if the assignment statement X = 22.5 is contained in the function, both the value in X and the value in FIRNUM, within MAIN, are changed. The reason for this, as illustrated in Figure 7-6, is that both FIRNUM and X refer to the same storage location and are simply different names for the same variable. Similarly, both SECNUM and Y refer to the same variable stored in memory. Because of this equivalence, it is important that functions never assign values to their arguments.

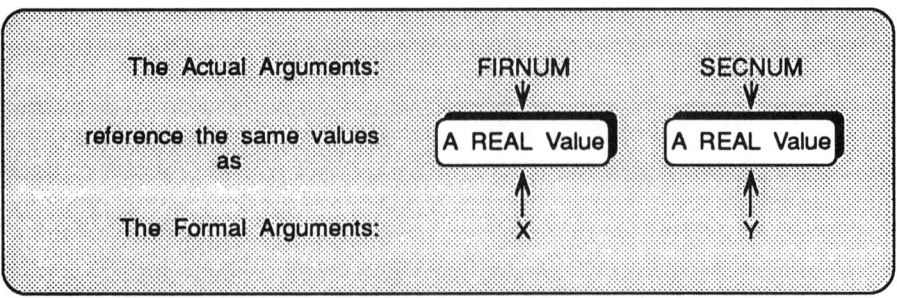

Figure 7-6   The Relationship Between Actual and Formal Arguments

If a function must use an argument in a way that will alter its value, the argument should first be assigned to a new variable declared within the function. This variable name should then be used in subsequent expressions in place of the argument name. Then, any change to the variable inside the function, even if the variable has the same name as a variable in another program unit, has no effect outside of the function.

The second point to note is that the programmer must ensure that each function actually assigns a value to the function name because it is the function name that is used for the returned value.

Finally, it is essential that the function header declare the same data type as that specified in the calling program unit. A disagreement in data types will result in either a compiler "TYPE REDEFINED" error or a logic error that is extremely troublesome to locate. If the compiler does not catch the data type mismatch error, the value actually returned by the function will have no obvious relationship to the value received by the calling program unit. The reason for this is that the storage location for the returned value is accessed as one data type by the function and as another data type by the calling unit.

Skill Builder Exercises

1. For the following function header and argument declarations, determine the number, type, and order (sequence) of the values that must be passed to the function:

   a. `INTEGER FUNCTION FTORAL(N)`
      `INTEGER N`
   b. `REAL FUNCTION PRICE(TYPE, YIELD, MATRTY)`
      `INTEGER TYPE`
      `REAL YIELD, MATRTY`
   c. `REAL FUNCTION YIELD(TYPE, PRICE, MATRTY)`
      `CHARACTER TYPE`
      `REAL PRICE, MATRTY`
   d. `CHARACTER FUNCTION FLAG(INTRST, PRICE, TIME)`
      `CHARACTER INTRST`
      `INTEGER PRICE, TIME`
   e. `INTEGER FUNCTION TOTAL(RATE, AMOUNT)`
      `REAL RATE, AMOUNT`
   f. `REAL FUNCTION ROI(A,B,C,D,E,F)`
      `INTEGER A,D,F`
      `CHARACTER B`
      `   REAL C,E`
   g. `REAL FUNCTION GETVAL(ITEM, ITER, DFLAG, DELIM)`
      `CHARACTER ITEM, DFLAG`
      `REAL ITER`
      `INTEGER DELIM`
   h. `CHARACTER FUNCTION LOCASE(C)`
      `CHARACTER C`

2. For each of the function headers listed in Exercise 1, write explicit function declarations that should be included in a program unit that calls the listed function.

3. For the following sections of code, write a variable declaration that should be included in the function for the variable ABNUM.

   a. REAL FUNCTION ITEM(A,B,C,D)

   ```
         .
         .
         .
      ITEM = ABNUM
      END
   ```

   b. REAL FUNCTION SIM(NUM)

   ```
         .
         .
         .
      SIM = ABNUM
      END
   ```

   c. CHARACTER FUNCTION KEY(LETTER)

   ```
         .
         .
         .
      KEY = ABNUM
      END
   ```

   d. INTEGER FUNCTION FACTOR(N)

   ```
         .
         .
         .
      FACTOR = ABNUM
      END
   ```

4. For each section of code listed in Exercise 3, write a function declaration, variable declaration, and assignment statement that could be used by a calling function to correctly call the above functions and store the returned value.

Programming Exercises

5. Rewrite Program 7-2 to have the function FMAX accept two integer arguments and return an integer value to MAIN. Make sure to modify MAIN in order to pass two integer values to FMAX and accept and store the integer value returned by FMAX.

6a. Rewrite the function TEMVER in Program 7-3 to accept a temperature and a character as arguments. If the character passed to the function is the letter F, the function should convert the passed temperature from Fahrenheit to Celsius. However, if the passed character is the letter C, the function should convert the passed temperature from Celsius to Fahrenheit; otherwise, the function should return the value 1 E10.

   b. Modify the MAIN function in Program 7-3 to call the function written for Exercise 6a. Your MAIN function should ask the user for the type of temperature being entered and pass the type (F or C) into TEMVER.

7a. Write a function named CHECK, with three arguments. The first argument should accept an integer number, the second argument a real number, and the third argument a character of length four. The body of the function should just display the values of the data passed to the function when it is called.

(*Note:* When tracing errors in functions, it is very helpful to have the function display the values it has been passed. Quite frequently, the error is not in what the body of the function does with the data but in the data received and stored. This type of error occurs when a different data type is passed to the function than the data type specified for the arguments.)

b. Include the function written in Exercise 7a in a working program. Make sure your function is called from the MAIN program unit. Test the function by passing various data to it.

8a. A second-degree polynomial in x is given by the expression $ax^2 + bx + c$, where a, b, and c are known numbers and a is not equal to zero. Write a function named POLY2(A,B,C,X) that computes and returns the value of a second-degree polynomial for any passed values of a, b, c, and x.

b. Include the function written in Exercise 8a in a working program. Make sure your function is called from the MAIN program unit. Test the function by passing various data to it.

9a. Write a function that produces a table of the numbers from 1 to 10, their squares, and their cubes. The function should produce the same display as that produced by Program 5-10.

b. Include the function written in Exercise 9a in a working program. Make sure your function is called from the MAIN program unit. Test the function by passing various data to it.

10a. Modify the function written for Exercise 9 to accept the starting value of the table, the number of values to be displayed, and the increment between values. Name your function SELTAB. A call to SELTAB(6,5,2) should produce a table of five lines, the first line starting with the number six and each succeeding number increasing by two.

b. Include the function written in Exercise 10a in a working program. Make sure your function is called from the MAIN program unit. Test the function by passing various data to it.

7.3 Statement Functions

Frequently the value computed by a function can be calculated using a single statement. For such a case FORTRAN provides a one-line statement function. Unlike subprogram functions, which are independent program units, a statement function is a FORTRAN statement included within its calling program unit. The general form of a statement function is:

```
function-name(argument list) = expression
```

The function name can be any valid FORTRAN symbolic name, such as the names used for variables. The argument list is list of zero or more variables, where multiple variables must be separated by commas. A variable included in the argument list is referred to as either a formal or a dummy argument (the terms are synonymous). Finally, the expression can be any valid FORTRAN expression using constants, the formal arguments of the function, and any other valid functions except the one being defined.

Examples of valid statement functions are:

```
FTOC(INTEMP) = 5.0 /9.0 * (INTEMP - 32.0)
AREA(LENGTH, WIDTH) = LENGTH * WIDTH
TESTD(A,B,C) = A**2 - 4.0 * B * C
```

The first statement function has one formal argument, the second function has two formal arguments, and the third function has three formal arguments.

As with FORTRAN's subprogram functions, statement functions cannot reference themselves. Thus, the statement function:

```
FACTOR (N) = N * FACTOR (N-1)
```

is invalid.

A statement function must be placed in its calling program unit immediately after all declaration statements and before any executable statements. In addition, the calling unit's declaration statements must declare the data type of the function and its arguments. Once this is done, the function can be used in the same manner as all of FORTRAN's intrinsic functions. Program 7-4 illustrates the use of the statement function FTOC within a MAIN program unit.

 Program 7-4

```
PROGRAM MAIN
  INTEGER COUNT
  REAL FTOC, INTEMP, FAHREN
  FTOC(INTEMP) = 5.0 /9.0 * (INTEMP - 32.0)
  DO 10 COUNT = 1, 4
    PRINT *, 'ENTER A FAHRENHEIT TEMPERATURE: '
    READ *, FAHREN
    PRINT *, 'THE CELSIUS EQUIVALENT IS:', FTOC(FAHREN)
10  CONTINUE
  END
```

The key points to note in Program 7-4 are the declaration statement for FTOC, INTEMP, and FAHREN and the statement immediately following that defines the function FTOC. Statement functions must always be placed immediately after the last declaration statement. Notice that once the function is properly defined, it is called within Program 7-4 in the same manner as both intrinsic and subprogram functions are called.

Exercises

1. Modify Program 7-4 to include a new function named CTOF that converts a Celsius temperature to its equivalent Fahrenheit value. Additionally, modify the MAIN program unit to accept a temperature and a character as arguments (recall that character input must be surrounded by apostrophes). If the entered character is an F, the function FTOC should be called and its returned value displayed; if the entered character is a C, the function CTOF should be called and its returned value displayed. Otherwise, a message informing the user that an invalid code has been entered should be displayed. Compile and execute your program and manually verify the displayed converted temperatures.

2. Write a statement function named MULT that accepts two real numbers as arguments, multiplies these two numbers, and returns the result. Include MULT in a MAIN program unit that passes various values to the function and displays the returned value. Manually verify that the displayed value is correct.

3. Write a statement function named HYPTNS that accepts the lengths of two sides of a right triangle and determines the triangle's hypotenuse. (The hypotenuse of a right triangle is equal to the square root of the sum of the squares of the other two sides.) Include HYPTNS in a MAIN program unit and verify that it works properly by passing various values to it, displaying the returned value, and checking that the displayed value is correct.

4. Write a statement function named POLY(A,B,C,X) that computes and returns the value of the polynomial $ax^2 + bx + c$ for any passed values of $a, b, c,$ and x. Include the function POLY in a working program and test the function by passing various data to it, displaying the returned value, and checking that the displayed value is correct.

5. Write a statement function named ABSDIF(X,Y) that returns the absolute value of the difference between two real numbers. For example, the function call ABSDIF(-1,-10) should return the value 9, and the call ABSDIF(-2,10) should return the value 12. Include the function ABSDIF in a MAIN program unit and test the function by passing various numbers to it, displaying the returned value, and checking that the displayed value is correct.

6a. Write a statement function named FRACPT that returns the fractional part of any real number passed to the function. For example, if the number 256.879 is passed to FRACPT, the number 0.879 should be returned. Have the function FRACPT call the intrinsic function INT. The number returned by FRACPT can then be determined as the number passed to it less its integer part.

 b. Include the function written in Exercise 6a in a working program. Make sure your function is called from MAIN and correctly returns a value to MAIN. Have MAIN use a PRINT statement to display the returned value. Test the function by passing various data to it and verifying the displayed value.

7a. Write a statement function named ROUND(XNUM) that rounds any real value to two decimal places. Rounding to two decimal places is obtained using the following steps:

Step 1: Multiply the passed number by 100
Step 2: Add 0.5 to the number obtained in step 1
Step 3: Take the integer part of the number obtained in step 2
Step 4: Divide the result of step 3 by 100

b. Include the function written in Exercise 7a in a working program. Make sure your function is called from MAIN and correctly returns a value to MAIN. Have MAIN use a PRINT statement to display the returned value. Test the function by passing various data to it and verifying the displayed value.

8a. Modify the statement function written for Exercise 6a to accept two values. The second passed value is the number of decimal places to which the first passed value should be rounded. For example, ROUND(27.6485,2) should return the value 27.65, and ROUND(27.6485,3) should return the value 27.649.

b. Include the function written in Exercise 8a in a working program. Make sure your function is called from MAIN and correctly returns a value to MAIN. Have MAIN use a PRINT statement to display the returned value. Test the function by passing various data to it and verifying the displayed value.

7.4 Applications

In this section we present two applications using functions. In the first application we create a random number generator function and incorporate it in a FORTRAN program that produces a series of 10 random numbers. In the second application the random number generator is used to simulate a coin-tossing experiment.

Application 1: Random Number Generation

There are many mathematical and engineering problems in which probability must be considered or statistical sampling techniques must be used. For example, in simulating automobile traffic flow or telephone usage patterns, statistical models are required. Additionally, applications such as simple computer games and more involved "strategy games" in business and science can only be described statistically. All of these statistical models require the generation of random numbers.

One method of generating random numbers is the power residue method. In one version of this method a suitable n-digit "seed" number, where n is an even number, is multiplied by the value $(10^{n/2} - 3)$. Using the lowest n digits of the result (the "residue") produces a new seed. Continuing this procedure produces a series of random numbers, with each new number used as the seed for the next number. If the original seed has 4 or more digits (n equal to or greater than 4) and is not divisible by either 2 or 5, this procedure yields $5 \times 10^{(n-2)}$ random numbers before a sequence of numbers repeats itself. For example, starting with a 6-digit seed ($n = 6$), for example, 654,321, a series of $5 \times 10^4 = 50,000$ random numbers can be generated. Using a power residue algorithm, we will write a statement function random number generator.

The specific power residue algorithm employed consists of the following steps:

1. Have the user enter a 6-digit integer seed that is not divisible by 2 or 5—this means the number should be an odd number not ending in 5.
2. Multiply the seed number by 997, which is $10^3 - 3$.

3. Extract the lower 6 digits of the result produced by step 2. Use this random number as the next seed.
4. Repeat steps 2 and 3 for as many random numbers as needed.

Thus, if the user entered seed number is 654,321 (step 1), the first random number generated would be calculated as follows:

2. 654,321 x 997 = 652,358,037
3. Extract the lower 6 digits of the number obtained in step 2. This is accomplished using a standard programming "trick." The trick involves:

3a. Dividing the number by $10^6 = 1,000,000$
For example, $652,358,037 / 1,000,000 = 652.358037$

3b. Taking the integer part of the result of Step 3a
For example, INT(652.358037) = 652

3c. Multiplying the previous result by 10^6
For example, $652 \times 10^6 = 652,000,000$

3d. Subtracting this result from the original number
For example, $652,358,037 - 652,000,000 = 358,037$

All of these steps can be incorporated into the single statement function:

```
RAND(X) = 997.0 * X - INT(997.0 * X/1.E6)*1.E6
```

Program 7-5 uses this random number generator function to produce a series of 10 random numbers.

 Program 7-5

```
PROGRAM MAIN
 REAL SEED, X, RAND
 RAND(X) = 997.0 * X - INT(997.0 * X/1.E6)*1.E6
 PRINT *,'ENTER AN ODD 6 DIGIT NUMBER NOT ENDING IN 5: '
 READ *, SEED
 DO 20 I = 1,10
   SEED = RAND(SEED)
   PRINT *, SEED
20     CONTINUE
 END
```

Following is a sample run using Program 7-5:

```
ENTER AN ODD 6 DIGIT NUMBER NOT ENDING IN 5:
876543
                    913344.000000
                    603968.000000
                    156096.000000
                    627712.000000
                    828864.000000
                    377408.000000
                    275776.000000
                    948672.000000
                    825984.000000
                    506048.000000
```

Conventionally, random number generators are used to produce random numbers within the range 0.0 to 1.0. To produce such numbers using Program 7-5's RAND function simply requires dividing the returned value by 10^6.

Application 2: Coin Toss Simulation

A common use of random numbers is to simulate events using a program, rather than going through the time and expense of constructing a real-life experiment. For example, statistical theory tells us that the probability of having a tossed coin turn up heads is 50 percent. Similarly, there is a 50 percent probability of having a single tossed coin turn up tails.

Using these probabilities, we would expect a single coin that is tossed 1000 times to turn up heads 500 times and tails 500 times. In practice, however, this exact result is seldom realized for a single experiment consisting of 1000 tosses. Instead of actually tossing a coin 1000 times, however, we can use a random number generator to simulate these tosses. In particular, we will use the random number function developed in the previous application.

Since the function:

```
RAND(X) = 997.0 * X - INT(997.0 * X/1.E6)*1.E6
```

returns a random number between 0 and 999,999, we divide the returned value by 1,000,000 to produce a random number between 0 and 1. Using this "normalized" random number, the algorithm to simulate 1000 coin tosses is given by the pseudocode:

Initialize the heads count to zero
Initialize the tails count to zero
Do 1000 times
  Generate a random number between 0 and 1
  If the random number is greater than .5
    consider this as a head and
    add one to the heads count
  Else
    consider this as a tail and
    add one to the tails count
  Endif
Enddo

Calculate the percentage of heads as the number of heads divided by 1000 x 100%
Calculate the percentage of tails as the number of tails divided by 1000 x 100%
Print the percentage of heads and tails obtained

   Program 7-6 codes this algorithm in FORTRAN.

 Program 7-6

```
      PROGRAM MAIN
*** A PROGRAM TO SIMULATE THE TOSSING OF A COIN 1000 TIMES
      INTEGER HEADS, TAILS, I
      REAL SEED, X, RAND, FLIP, PERHD, PERTL
      RAND(X) = 997.0 * X - INT(997.0 * X/1.E6)*1.E6
      PRINT *,'ENTER AN ODD 6 DIGIT NUMBER NOT ENDING IN 5: '
      READ *, SEED
      HEADS = 0
      TAILS = 0
*** SIMULATE 1000 TOSSES OF A COIN
      DO 10 I = 1,1000
         SEED = RAND(SEED)
         FLIP = SEED / 1.E6
         IF (FLIP .GT. 0.5) THEN
            HEADS = HEADS + 1
         ELSE
            TAILS = TAILS + 1
         ENDIF
 10      CONTINUE
*** CALCULATE THE PERCENTAGE OF HEADS
      PERHD = (HEADS / 1000.0) * 100.0
*** CALCULATE THE PERCENTAGE OF TAILS
      PERTL = (TAILS / 1000.0) * 100.0
      PRINT *, 'HEADS CAME UP ', PERHD, ' PERCENT OF THE TIME.'
      PRINT *, 'TAILS CAME UP ', PERTL, ' PERCENT OF THE TIME.'
      END
```

   Following are two sample runs using Program 7-6:

```
ENTER AN ODD 6 DIGIT NUMBER NOT ENDING IN 5:
654321
HEADS CAME UP          51.900002 PERCENT OF THE TIME.
TAILS CAME UP          48.099998 PERCENT OF THE TIME.
```

and:

```
ENTER AN ODD 6 DIGIT NUMBER NOT ENDING IN 5:
234567
HEADS CAME UP          46.800000 PERCENT OF THE TIME.
TAILS CAME UP          53.200000 PERCENT OF THE TIME.
```

Writing and executing Program 7-6 is certainly easier than tossing a coin 1000 times. It should be noted that the validity of the results produced by the program depends on how random the numbers produced by the random number function actually are.

Additional Exercises for Chapter 7

1. Modify Program 7-6 so that it requests the number of tosses from the user. (Be sure to have the program correctly determine the percentages of heads and tails obtained.)

2. (Central Limit Theorem Simulation) Modify Program 7-6 so that it automatically generates 20 simulations, with each simulation having 1000 tosses. Print out the percentage for each run and the percentages for the 20 runs combined.

3a. Write a FORTRAN program that uses a user-entered six-digit integer to produce a random integer between 1 and 100. The program should then give the user seven tries to guess the generated random number. If the user guesses the correct number, the message "HOORAY! YOU WIN!" should be displayed. After each incorrect guess, the computer should display the message "WRONG NUMBER: TRY AGAIN" and indicate the number of guesses left. After seven incorrect guesses, the computer should display the message "SORRY, YOU LOSE." (*Hint:* To generate an integer between 1 and 100 from a random number function RAND(X) that generates numbers between 0.0 and 1.0 requires the use of the expression 1 + INT(100 * RAND(X)).)

b. Modify the program written for Exercise 3a to allow the user to run the game again after a game has been completed. The program should display the message "WOULD YOU LIKE TO PLAY AGAIN: Y/N?: " and restart if the user enters either Y or y.

4. In the game of Blackjack the cards 2 through 10 are counted at their face values, regardless of suit; all picture cards (jack, queen, and king) are counted as 10; and an ace is counted as either a 1 or a 11, depending on the total count of all the cards in a player's hand. The ace is counted as 11 only if the total value of all cards in a player's hand does not exceed 21; otherwise, it is counted as a 1. Using this information, write a FORTRAN program that uses a random number generator to select three cards (a 1 initially corresponding to an ace, a 2 corresponding to a face card of 2, and so on), calculate the total value of the hand appropriately, and display the value of the three cards with a printed message.

5. Write a FORTRAN function that determines the quadrant in which a line drawn from the origin resides. The determination of the quadrant is made using the angle that the line makes with the positive X as follows:

Angle from the positive X axis	Quadrant
Between 0 and 90 degrees	1
Between 90 and 180 degrees	2
Between 180 and 270 degrees	3
Between 270 and 360 degrees	4

Note: If the angle is exactly 0, 90, 180, or 270 degrees, the corresponding line does not reside in any quadrant but lies on an axis. For such a case your function should return a 0.

6. All years that are evenly divisible by 400 or are evenly divisible by 4 and not evenly divisible by 100 are leap years. For example, since 1600 is evenly divisible by 400, the year 1600 was a leap year. Similarly, since 1988 is evenly divisible by 4 but not by 100, the year 1988 was also a leap year. Using this information, write a FORTRAN function that accepts the year as a user input and returns a 1 if the passed year is a leap year or a 0 if it is not.

7. Based on an automobile's model year and weight, the state of New Jersey determines the car's registration fee using the following schedule:

Model year	Weight	Registration fee
1970 or earlier	Less than 2700 lbs	$16.50
	2700 to 3800 lbs	25.50
	More than 3800 lbs	46.50
1971 to 1979	Less than 2700 lbs	27.00
	2700 to 3800 lbs	30.50
	More than 3800 lbs	52.50
1980 or later	Less than 3500 lbs	19.50
	3500 or more lbs	52.50

Using this information, write a FORTRAN subprogram function that accepts the year and weight of an automobile and returns its registration fee.

7.5 Common Programming Errors

The most common programming error related to functions is passing arguments to a function that is not prepared to receive them. The actual arguments passed to a function must correspond in number, data type, and order to the formal arguments declared within the function. For subprogram functions the simplest way to verify that correct values have been passed is to display all received values within a function's body before any calculations are made. Once this verification has taken place, the display is not needed.

Another common error is omitting a declaration for the called function's data type within the calling function or declaring an incorrect data type. In the absence of an explicit declaration, the received value's data type is determined by FORTRAN's implicit data typing for the called function's name. Similarly, if an incorrect data type is declared, the returned value will be converted to the declared data type. It is always a good idea during program development to display the value calculated by a function immediately after it is returned to help catch this type of error. For subprogram functions this value can also be displayed from within the function prior to its return.

A third error that can occur with subprogram functions is caused by either not assigning a value to the function's name within the function or assigning a value having an incorrect data type.

The last and most difficult error to detect occurs when the arguments passed to a subprogram functions are changed within the function. Even if a function's formal argument name differs from the variable name used as a calling argument, a change in the function's formal argument value alters the value in the corresponding calling argument. This is because both names refer to the same memory location used to store the value.

7.6 Chapter Summary

1. All functions (intrinsic, statement, and subprogram) calculate and return a single value.

2. A function is called by giving its name and passing any data to it in the parentheses following the name.

3. Function statements are defined at the beginning of a program unit, immediately following the last specification statement, and have the general form:

   ```
   function-name(argument list) = expression
   ```

   For example, the function statement:

   ```
   TAREA(BASE,HEIGHT) = 0.5 * BASE * HEIGHT
   ```

   can be used to calculate the area of a triangle.

4. The general form of a subprogram function is:

   ```
   function-type  function-name(argument list)
    argument and variable declarations
    other FORTRAN statements
    function-name = expression
    RETURN
    END
   ```

   Compilers that define the END statement as an executable statement do not require a RETURN statement before the END statement.

5. A function's type determines the data type of the value returned by the function.

6. The data type of statement and subprogram functions should be specified in the calling function and determines the type of value received by the calling program. In the absence of an explicit specification, the data type of the returned value is implicitly typed using FORTRAN's implicit typing rule. This rule types any function or variable beginning in either I, J, K, L, M, or N as an integer and all other names as reals.

7. Formal argument specifications within a function determine the data type of the values passed to the function. For subprogram functions, the formal arguments are listed within the parentheses following the function name.

8. The arguments passed to a function must agree in type, order, and number with the function's formal arguments.

7.7   Enrichment Study: Programming Costs

Any project that requires a computer incurs both hardware and software costs. The costs associated with the hardware consist of all costs relating to the physical components used in the system. These components include the computer itself, peripherals, and any other items, such as air conditioning, cabling, and associated equipment, required by the project. The software costs include all costs associated with initial program development and subsequent program maintenance. As illustrated in Figure 7-7, the major cost of most computer-based engineering projects, be they research or development, has become the software costs.

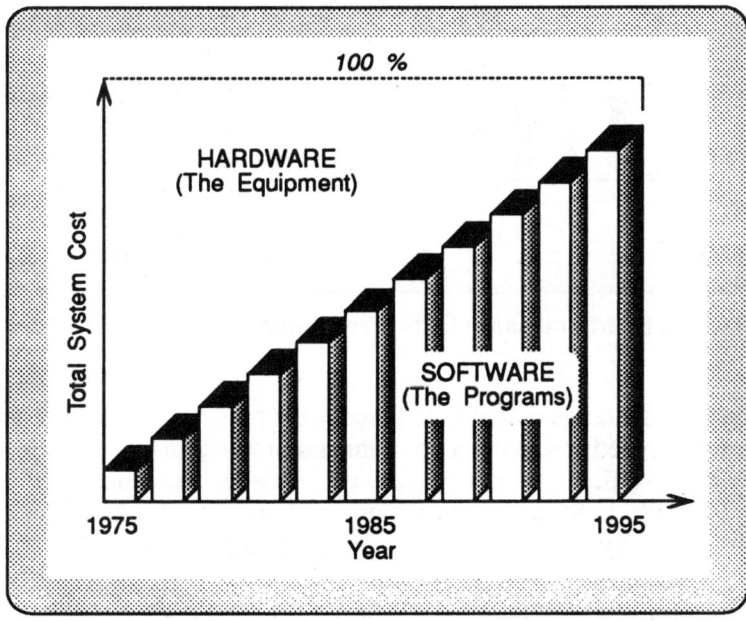

Figure 7-7   Software Is the Major Cost of Most Engineering Projects

The reason that software costs contribute so heavily to total project costs is that these costs are closely related to human productivity (are labor intensive), while hardware costs are more directly related to manufacturing technologies. For example, microchips that cost over $500 per chip 10 years ago can now be purchased for under $1 per chip.

It is far easier, however, to dramatically increase manufacturing productivity by a thousand, with the consequent decrease in hardware costs, than it is for people to double either the quantity or the quality of their thought output. So as hardware costs have plummeted, software costs have actually increased. Thus, the ratio of software costs to total system costs (hardware plus software) has increased dramatically.

Looking at just software costs (see Figure 7-8), we find that the maintenance of existing programs accounts for approximately 75 percent. Maintenance includes the correction of newly found errors and the addition of new features and modifications to existing programs.

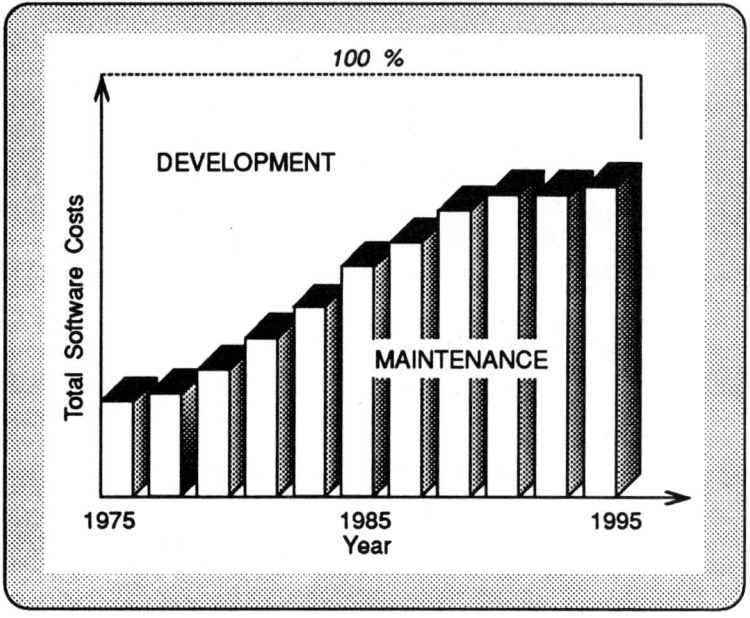

Figure 7-8   Maintenance Is the Predominant Software Cost

Students generally find it strange that maintenance is the predominant software cost because they are accustomed to solving a problem and moving on to a different one. Science and engineering fields do not operate this way. In these fields, one application or idea is typically built on a previous one and may require months or years of work. This is especially true in programming. Once a program is written, new features become evident. Advances in technology such as networking, fiber optics, genetic engineering, and graphical displays also open up new software possibilities.

How easily a program can be maintained (debugged, modified, or enhanced) is related to the ease with which the program can be read and understood, which is directly related to the modularity with which the program was constructed. Modular programs are constructed using one or more program units, each of which performs a clearly defined and specific task. If each program unit (module) is clearly structured internally and the relationships between program units are clearly specified, each unit can be tested and modified with a minimum of disturbance or undesirable interaction with the other units in the program.

Just as hardware designers frequently locate the cause of a hardware problem by using test methods designed to isolate the offending hardware subsystem, modular software permits the software engineer to similarly isolate program errors to specific software units.

Once a bug has been isolated, or a new feature needs to be added, the required changes can be confined to appropriate program units without radically affecting other program units. Only if the affected unit requires different input data or produces different outputs are its surrounding program units affected. Even in such a case the changes to the surrounding modules are clear: they must either be modified to output the data needed by the changed module or be changed to accept the new input data. Modules help the programmer determine where the changes must be made, while the internal structure of the module itself determines how easy it will be to make the change.

Although there are no hard-and-fast rules for well-written program units, specific guidelines do exist. The total number of instructions in a unit generally should not exceed 50 lines. This allows the complete program unit to fit on a standard 8 1/2-by-11-inch sheet of paper for ease of reading. Each program unit should have one entrance point and one exit point, and each control structure in the unit (such as a DO-WHILE or DO loop) should also contain a single entry and exit. This makes it easy to trace the flow of data when errors are detected. All the FORTRAN statements that alter the normal sequential program flow, including the IF and DO statements, conform to this single input–single output model.

As we have stressed throughout the text, the instructions contained within a module should use variable names that describe the data and are self-documenting. This means that they tell what is happening without a lot of extra comments. For example, the statement:

```
X = (A - B) / (C - D)
```

does not contain intelligent variable names that give an indication of what is being calculated. A more useful set of instructions, assuming that a slope is being calculated, is:

```
SLOPE = (Y2 - Y1) / (X2 - X1)
```

Here, the statement itself "tells" what the data represents, what is being calculated, and how the calculation is being performed. Always keep in mind that the goal is to produce programs that make sense to any programmer reading them, at any time. The use of mnemonic data names makes excessive comments unnecessary. The program should, however, contain a sufficient number of comments explaining what a program unit does and any other pertinent information that would be helpful to other programmers; however excessive comments are usually a sign of insufficient program design or poorly constructed coding.

Another sign of a good program is the use of indentation to alert a reader to nested statements and indicate where one statement ends and another begins. Consider version 1 of the pseudocode listed in the module "What to Wear":

if it is below 60 degrees
if it is snowing
wear your lined raincoat
else
wear a topcoat
if it is below 40 degrees
wear a sweater also
if it is below 30 degrees
wear a jacket also
else if it is raining
wear an unlined raincoat

Because the if and else statement matchings are not clearly indicated, the instructions in the module are open to multiple interpretations. For example, using this pseudocode, try to determine what to wear if the temperature is 35 degrees and it is raining. Now consider version 2 of "What to Wear":

if it is below 60 degrees
  if it is snowing
    wear your lined raincoat
  else
    wear a topcoat
  if it is below 40 degrees
    wear a sweater also
    if it is below 30 degrees
    wear a jacket also
else if it is raining
  wear an unlined raincoat

Version 2 is indented, making it clear that we are dealing with one main if-else statement. If it is below 60 degrees, the set of instructions indented underneath the first if will be executed; otherwise the condition *if it is raining* will be checked.

Subroutines Revisited

Chapter Eight

Functions, such as FORTRAN's intrinsic functions introduced in Chapter 3 and the user-created functions described in Chapter 7, are designed to calculate and return a single value. Many times, however, it is necessary to have more than a single value returned. For such applications, subroutines must be used. Although subroutines were introduced in Chapter 1 and have been used intermittently throughout the text, it is now time to understand and develop their capabilities fully.

8.1 Subroutines

As we have already seen, a subroutine is a distinct program unit in its own right, similar to a MAIN program unit. Its purpose is to receive data, operate on the data, and return as few or as many values as required. Unlike functions, the name of a subroutine is not associated with a returned value. A subroutine's name is simply a user-selected name that contains no more than six characters, the first of which must be a letter.

All subroutines are called, or used, by a CALL statement having the general form:

```
CALL subroutine name(argument list)
```

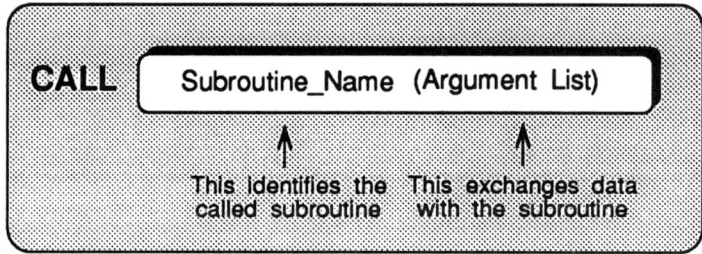

Figure 8-1   Calling a Subroutine

The keyword CALL tells the computer that a transfer into a subroutine is to take place. The subroutine name identifies the subroutine that is to be executed, and the argument list is used to exchange data with the called subroutine (see Figure 8-1).

To clarify the process of calling a subroutine and using its results, consider Program 8-1, which calls a subroutine named SWAP. The program as shown is not yet complete. Once the subroutine SWAP is written and included in Program 8-1, the completed program can be run.

 Program 8-1

```
PROGRAM MAIN
  REAL FIRNUM, SECNUM
  PRINT *, 'ENTER TWO NUMBERS: '
  READ *, FIRNUM, SECNUM
  PRINT *, 'THE VALUE IN FIRNUM IS: ',FIRNUM
  PRINT *, 'THE VALUE IN SECNUM IS: ',SECNUM
  CALL SWAP(FIRNUM, SECNUM)
  PRINT *
  PRINT *, 'THE VALUE IN FIRNUM IS NOW:', FIRNUM
  PRINT *, 'THE VALUE IN SECNUM IS NOW:', SECNUM
  END
```

The SWAP subroutine referenced in Program 8-1 is referred to as the called subroutine, since it is called or summoned into action by a CALL statement. The program unit that does the calling, in this case MAIN, is referred to as the calling unit. When SWAP is called, two items are made available to it, the variables FIRNUM and SECNUM. We now write the SWAP subroutine to accept these data items and interchange their values.

Like all program units, a subroutine consists of two parts, a subroutine header and a subroutine body, as illustrated in Figure 8-2. In addition to naming the subroutine, the subroutine header is used to exchange data between the subroutine and its calling program unit. The purpose of the subroutine body is to process the passed data and produce any values that are to be returned to the calling program unit.

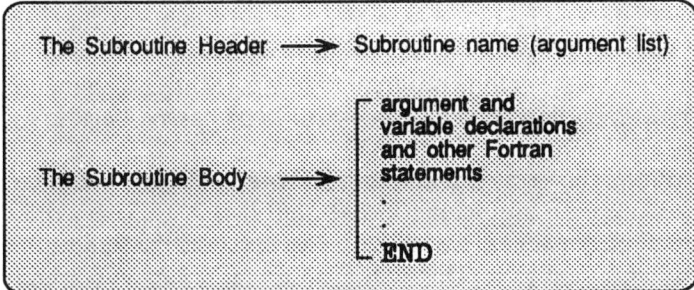

Figure 8-2   General Format of a Subroutine

The subroutine header must include the keyword SUBROUTINE, the name of the subroutine, and the names of the arguments that will be used by it. For example, the following header can be used for the SWAP subroutine:

```
SUBROUTINE SWAP (XNUM, YNUM)
```

The names of the arguments in the subroutine header line, in this case, XNUM and YNUM, are programmer selected. Any two valid symbolic names could have been used instead of the argument names XNUM and YNUM. These argument names are referred to as either *dummy* or *formal* arguments (the two terms are synonymous) and are used internally within the subroutine to refer to the actual arguments used in the CALL statement. As such, they must match, in type, number, and order, the actual arguments in the CALL statement. As pointed out earlier in Section 2.5, actual and formal argument names do not have to be the same.

Having constructed a subroutine header for SWAP, we now construct its body. As far as the SWAP subroutine is concerned, the dummy arguments XNUM and YNUM are treated like variables. They must be declared and can then be used anywhere within the SWAP subroutine. The declaration of these two arguments is given by an argument declaration statement placed immediately after the subroutine header line. Argument declarations, as the name implies, declare the data type of the arguments expected by the subroutine. Assuming that XNUM and YNUM are to reference real values, any of the following argument declaration statements can be used:

```
REAL XNUM,YNUM      REAL YNUM,XNUM      REAL XNUM       REAL YNUM
                                        REAL YNUM       REAL XNUM
```

As illustrated by these statements, the order of the argument declarations is not important. The only requirement is that each argument be declared. Notice that these argument declarations are identical to variable declarations.

Realizing that a subroutine is simply a program unit, like the MAIN unit, makes the construction of the rest of SWAP's body a familiar task, once we have defined what SWAP must do. As illustrated in Figure 8-2, a subroutine's body begins by declaring its arguments and any variables that will be used by the subroutine, followed by any valid FORTRAN executable statements, and ending with the keyword END. You should recognize this structure as the same basic structure used for constructing both MAIN and subprogram function program units.

The END statement within a subroutine performs two distinct functions, similar to those performed in the MAIN program unit. In both subroutines and MAIN program units, the END statement signals the end of the unit. The second function of an END statement in a subroutine is to cause control to be passed from the subroutine to the statement following its call within the calling program unit.* In a MAIN program unit the END terminates program execution and causes control to be passed back to the operating system.

For purposes of illustration, let us now assume that SWAP must be constructed to interchange the values within the arguments XNUM and YNUM. Before writing SWAP to perform this function, however, we will first verify that the subroutine actually receives the data items sent to it. This will ensure that we have correctly matched the type, order, and number of actual and formal arguments. The following version of SWAP does the job.

```
SUBROUTINE SWAP(XNUM,YNUM)
    REAL XNUM, YNUM
    PRINT *, ' THE VALUE IN XNUM IS: ',XNUM
    PRINT *, ' THE VALUE IN YNUM IS: ',YNUM
    END
```

Program 8-2 includes this subroutine into a working program.

---

* Some compilers require that a RETURN statement be placed before the END statement. If you are using such a compiler, a RETURN statement must be included in the subroutine immediately preceding the END statement. For such compilers the END statement is a nonexecutable statement that informs the compiler that the end of a section of code has been reached and compilation of the code can begin. In this case the END statement does not get translated into executable code and the RETURN is necessary because it becomes the last executable statement to be translated. Additionally, some programmers prefer using a RETURN statement because it clearly indicates a subroutine's exit point. As subroutines can have multiple exit points, it is felt that all return points, including the one at the end of a subroutine, should clearly be marked with a RETURN statement.

Program 8-2

```
PROGRAM MAIN
  REAL FIRNUM, SECNUM
  PRINT *, 'ENTER TWO NUMBERS: '
  READ *, FIRNUM, SECNUM
  PRINT *, 'THE VALUE IN FIRNUM IS: ',FIRNUM
  PRINT *, 'THE VALUE IN SECNUM IS: ',SECNUM
  CALL SWAP(FIRNUM, SECNUM)
  PRINT *
  PRINT *, 'THE VALUE IN FIRNUM IS NOW:', FIRNUM
  PRINT *, 'THE VALUE IN SECNUM IS NOW:', SECNUM
  END
*
  SUBROUTINE SWAP(XNUM,YNUM)
  REAL XNUM, YNUM
  PRINT *
  PRINT *, ' THE VALUE IN XNUM IS: ',XNUM
  PRINT *, ' THE VALUE IN YNUM IS: ',YNUM
  END
```

Following is a sample run using Program 8-2:

```
ENTER TWO NUMBERS:
22.5 33.0
THE VALUE IN FIRNUM IS:        22.500000
THE VALUE IN SECNUM IS:        33.000000

  THE VALUE IN XNUM IS:        22.500000
  THE VALUE IN YNUM IS:        33.000000

THE VALUE IN FIRNUM IS NOW:    22.500000
THE VALUE IN SECNUM IS NOW:    33.000000
```

In reviewing the output produced by Program 8-2, notice that the values first displayed for FIRNUM and SECNUM are generated by the two PRINT statements within MAIN immediately before the call to SWAP. The CALL statement in MAIN then invokes the SWAP subroutine, which displays the values referenced by XNUM and YNUM. These are the same values previously displayed for FIRNUM and SECNUM, because FIRNUM and SECNUM are used as the actual arguments in the call to SWAP.

After SWAP receives and displays the values referenced by its arguments, its END statement is encountered. This statement forces control to be passed back to MAIN, where the final two PRINT statements are executed. Since the values referenced by FIRNUM and SECNUM were not altered by SWAP, the values displayed immediately after the CALL statement are identical to those displayed immediately before the call was made.

In calling the SWAP subroutine, it is extremely important to note the connection between the actual arguments used in the CALL statement and the dummy arguments used in the subroutine header. *Both reference the same data items.* The significance of this is that the value in the actual (calling) argument can be altered within the subroutine using the dummy argument name (this provides the basis for returning values from a subroutine, described shortly). Thus, the dummy arguments XNUM and YNUM do not store copies of the values in FIRNUM and SECNUM but directly access the locations in memory set aside for FIRNUM and SECNUM. This type of subroutine call, where a subroutine's dummy arguments reference the same memory locations as the actual arguments of the calling unit, is formally referred to as a *call by reference* or *call by location.* This equivalence between argument names is illustrated in Figure 8-3.

Since both XNUM and FIRNUM refer to the same item, any change to the value in XNUM automatically alters the value in FIRNUM. Similarly, any change to YNUM's value automatically changes SECNUM, because both YNUM and SECNUM also refer

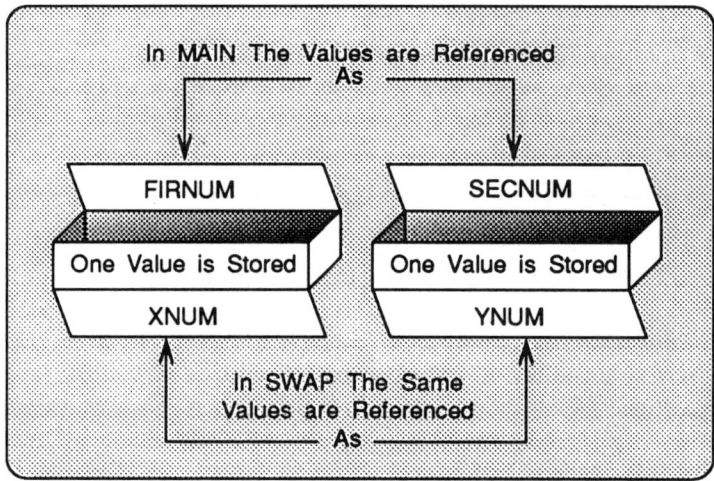

Figure 8-3   The Equivalence of Actual and Dummy Arguments

to the same data item. Since XNUM is equivalent to FIRNUM, and YNUM to SECNUM, swapping the values in XNUM and YNUM within SWAP automatically swaps the values in FIRNUM and SECNUM within the MAIN program unit. The values in XNUM and YNUM can be interchanged using the following three-step interchange algorithm (see also Figure 8-4):

1. Store XNUM's value in a temporary location
2. Change XNUM's value to YNUM's value
3. Change YNUM's value to the value stored in the temporary location used in step 1

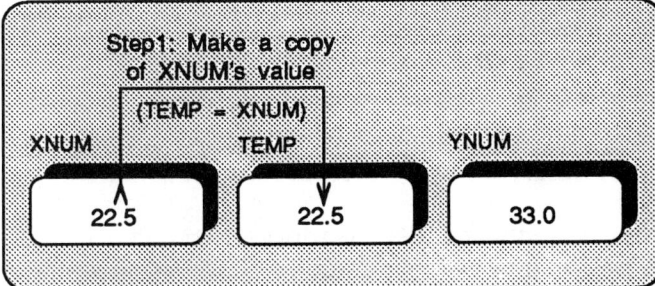

Making a Copy of XNUM's **Value**

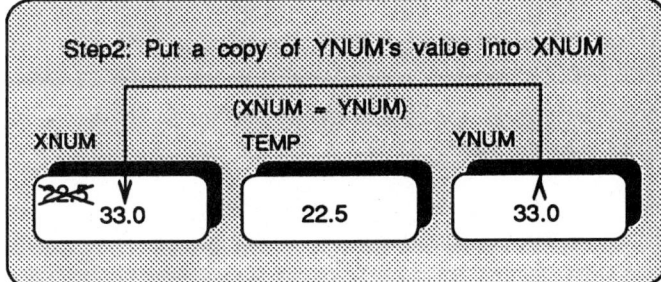

Replacing XNUM 's **Value with** YNUM's **Value**

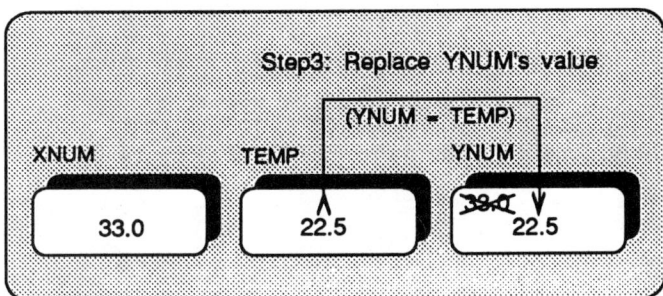

Replacing YNUM's **Value**

Figure 8-4 Interchanging the Values Stored in Two Variables

Program 8-3

```
PROGRAM MAIN
  REAL FIRNUM, SECNUM
  PRINT *, 'ENTER TWO NUMBERS: '
  READ *, FIRNUM, SECNUM
  PRINT *, 'THE VALUE IN FIRNUM IS: ',FIRNUM
  PRINT *, 'THE VALUE IN SECNUM IS: ',SECNUM
  CALL SWAP(FIRNUM, SECNUM)
  PRINT *
  PRINT *, 'THE VALUE IN FIRNUM IS NOW:', FIRNUM
  PRINT *, 'THE VALUE IN SECNUM IS NOW:', SECNUM
  END
*
SUBROUTINE SWAP(XNUM,YNUM)
  REAL XNUM, YNUM
  REAL TEMP
  TEMP = XNUM
  XNUM = YNUM
  YNUM = TEMP
  END
```

Program 8-3 contains the final form of SWAP, using this interchange algorithm. The following sample run was obtained using Program 8-3:

```
ENTER TWO NUMBERS:
22.5 33.0
THE VALUE IN FIRNUM IS:          22.500000
THE VALUE IN SECNUM IS:          33.000000
THE VALUE IN FIRNUM IS NOW:      33.000000
THE VALUE IN SECNUM IS NOW:      22.500000
```

In reviewing this output, notice that the values displayed for the variables FIRNUM and SECNUM have been swapped immediately after the call to the SWAP subroutine. This is because these two variables were used as actual arguments in the CALL statement, which gives SWAP access to them. Within SWAP these arguments are known as XNUM and YNUM, respectively. As illustrated by the final displayed values, the interchange of XNUM's and YNUM's value within SWAP is reflected in MAIN as the interchange of FIRNUM's and SECNUM's values.

The equivalence between actual calling arguments and dummy subroutine arguments illustrated by Program 8-3 provides the basis for returning any number of values from a subroutine. For example, assume that a subroutine is required to accept three values, compute their sum and product, and return these computed results to the calling routine. Naming the subroutine CALC and providing five dummy arguments (three for the input data and two for the returned values), the following subroutine can be used:

```
SUBROUTINE CALC(X,Y,Z,TOTAL,PROD)
   REAL X,Y,Z,TOTAL,PROD
   TOTAL = X + Y + Z
   PROD = X*Y*Z
   END
```

This subroutine declares five dummy arguments, named X, Y, Z, TOTAL, and PROD, all declared as real arguments. Within the subroutine, only the last two arguments are altered. The value of the fourth argument, TOTAL, is calculated as the sum of the first three arguments, and the last argument, PROD, is computed as the product of the arguments X, Y, and Z. Program 8-4 includes this subroutine in a complete program.

 Program 8-4

```
PROGRAM MAIN
   REAL FIRNUM, SECNUM, THRNUM, SUM, PRDCT
   PRINT *, 'ENTER THREE NUMBERS: '
   READ *, FIRNUM, SECNUM, THRNUM
   CALL CALC(FIRNUM, SECNUM, THRNUM, SUM, PRDCT)
   PRINT *, 'THE SUM OF THE ENTERED NUMBERS IS: ',SUM
   PRINT *, 'THE PRODUCT OF THE ENTERED NUMBERS IS: ',PRDCT
   END
*
SUBROUTINE CALC(X,Y,Z,TOTAL,PROD)
   REAL X,Y,Z,TOTAL,PROD
   TOTAL = X + Y + Z
   PROD = X*Y*Z
   END
```

Within the MAIN program unit, subroutine CALC is called using the five actual arguments FIRNUM, SECNUM, THRNUM, SUM, and PRDCT. As required, these arguments agree in number, type and order with the dummy arguments declared by subroutine CALC. Of the five actual arguments passed, only FIRNUM, SECNUM, and THRNUM have been assigned values when the call to CALC is made. The remaining two arguments have not been initialized and will be used to receive values back from CALC. Depending on the compiler used, these arguments will initially contain either zeros or "garbage" values.

Once CALC is called, it uses its first three arguments to calculate values for TOTAL and PROD and then returns control to MAIN. Because of the order of its actual calling arguments, the MAIN program unit knows the values calculated by CALC as SUM and PRDCT, which are then displayed.

Following is a sample run using Program 8-4:

```
ENTER THREE NUMBERS:
2.5 6.0 10.0
THE SUM OF THE ENTERED NUMBERS IS:          18.500000
THE PRODUCT OF THE ENTERED NUMBERS IS:      150.000000
```

Although all of the examples we have used have illustrated calling a subroutine from a MAIN program unit, this is not required in FORTRAN. A subroutine can be called by any program unit, including another subroutine, with one exception: a subroutine must never call itself, either directly or indirectly. Thus, the following subroutine is invalid because it calls itself:

```
SUBROUTINE DOIT(A,B,C)
        .
        .
        .
  CALL DOIT(X,Y,Z)
        .
        .
        .
  END
```

Similarly, the following sequence of subroutines is invalid because the first subroutine references itself indirectly through the second subroutine.

```
SUBROUTINE ONE
        .
        .
        .
  CALL TWO
        .
        .
        .
  END
SUBROUTINE TWO
        .
        .
        .
  CALL ONE
        .
        .
        .
  END
```

The actual arguments used in calling a subroutine can be variables, as illustrated in Program 8-4, single constants, or more complex expressions yielding the correct argument data type. For example, a valid call to CALC using constant and variable arguments in Program 8-4 is:

```
CALL CALC(2.0,3.0,6.2,SUM,PROD)
```

When an actual argument is either a constant value or an expression that yields a constant value, the corresponding dummy argument in the called subroutine must never be used on the left-hand side of an assignment statement. To do so would be an attempt to change the value of a constant within the calling program unit.

In addition to its dummy arguments, a subroutine may declare as many variables as needed to complete its task. These variable declarations can either be made on a line by themselves or be included within the declarations of the dummy arguments. For example, if I, J, and K are integer dummy arguments, and KOUNT and MAXVAL are integer variables within a subroutine named FINMAX, a valid subroutine heading and declaration statement are:

```
SUBROUTINE FINMAX(I,J,K)
   INTEGER I, J, K, KOUNT, MAXVAL
```

Alternatively, the variable declarations can be made on a line by themselves using the following arrangement:

```
SUBROUTINE FINMAX(I,J,K)
   INTEGER I, J, K
   INTEGER KOUNT, MAXVAL
```

Although FORTRAN permits both arguments and variables to be intermingled in any order within a declaration statement, for program clarity, arguments should always be declared prior to variables.

Variable Scope

By their very nature, FORTRAN subroutines are constructed to be independent modules. The implication of this is that variables declared in one program unit cannot be accessed by another program unit unless specific provisions are made to allow such access. As we have seen, one such access is provided through a subroutine's argument list. Seen in this light, an appropriate analogy for a subroutine is a closed box (see Figure 8-5), with slots at the top to exchange values with the calling program unit.

The analogy of a closed box is useful because it emphasizes the fact that what goes on inside the subroutine, except for the altering of an argument's value, is hidden from the view of all other program units. This includes any variables declared within the subroutine. These internally declared variables, which are available only to the subroutine itself, are said to be local to the subroutine, or *local variables*. This term refers to the *scope* of a variable, where scope is defined as the section of the program where the variable is valid or "known." Local variables are meaningful only when used in expressions

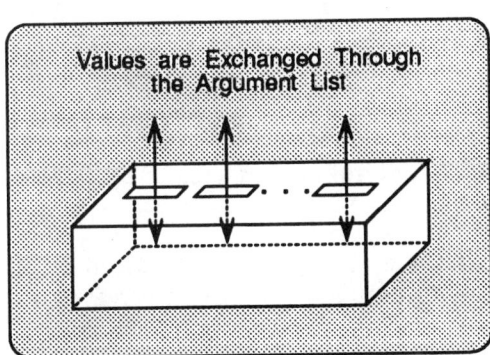

Figure 8-5   A Subroutine Can Be Considered a Closed Box

or statements inside the subroutine that declared them. This means that the same variable name can be declared and used in more than one subroutine. For each subroutine that declares the variable, a separate and distinct variable is created. For example, consider Program 8-5.

Program 8-5

```
PROGRAM MAIN
   INTEGER INUM
   INUM = 20
   PRINT *, 'THE VALUE IN INUM, WITHIN MAIN IS ', INUM
   CALL SHOW
   PRINT *, 'THE VALUE IN INUM, AGAIN FROM MAIN IS ', INUM
   END
SUBROUTINE SHOW
   INTEGER INUM
   INUM = 0
   PRINT *, ' THE VALUE IN INUM, WITHIN SHOW IS ', INUM
   END
```

Program 8-5 contains two separate local variables, both named INUM. Storage for the INUM variable used in the MAIN program unit is created by the declaration statement located in this unit. A different storage area for the INUM variable used in the subroutine named SHOW is created by the declaration statement located in the subroutine (see Figure 8-6).

Each of the variables named INUM is local to the program unit in which it is declared, and each of these variables can be used only from within the appropriate program unit. Thus, when INUM is used in the MAIN program unit, the storage area referenced by the first declaration statement is accessed;

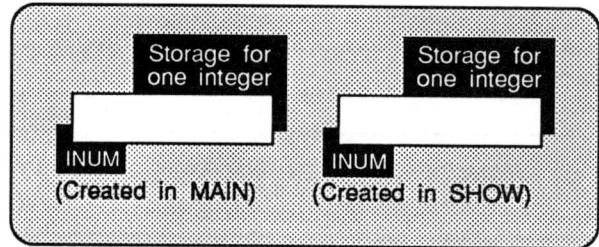

Figure 8-6   The Storage Areas Created by Program 8-5

when INUM is used in the SHOW subroutine, the storage area referenced by its declaration statement is accessed. The following output is produced when Program 8-5 is executed:

```
THE VALUE IN INUM, WITHIN MAIN IS          20
 THE VALUE IN INUM, WITHIN SHOW IS               0
THE VALUE IN INUM, AGAIN FROM MAIN IS          20
```

Since each program unit only "knows" its own local variables, the MAIN program unit can only display the value of its INUM variable, which is 20. This display is made both before and after the call to the SHOW subroutine. From within SHOW the value displayed for its INUM variable has no connection with any variable declared outside of this subroutine, regardless of the similarity in names. The value displayed for INUM within SHOW is zero because of the assignment statement INUM = 0 contained within this subroutine. The setting of this variable to zero, however, has no effect on the INUM declared in the MAIN unit. As illustrated, this variable still retains its value of 20 after the call to SHOW has been completed.

By definition, since all FORTRAN variables are declared within a program unit, all FORTRAN variables are local variables. FORTRAN does, however, provide two different means of extending the scope of a local variable from one program unit into another. One way is to use a variable as an argument in a CALL statement. For lengthy argument lists that must be shared between many subroutines, this becomes awkward and cumbersome. The second method is to use a COMMON block, which is the subject of Section 8.3.

Exercises

1. Write subroutine headers, argument declarations, and CALL statements for the following:

   a. A subroutine named TEST having a real dummy argument named EXPER. The corresponding actual argument used in calling TEST is named VALUE.

   b. A subroutine named MINUTE having an integer dummy argument named TIME. The corresponding actual argument used in calling MINUTE is named SECOND.

   c. A subroutine named KEY having a character dummy argument named CODE. The corresponding actual argument used in calling KEY is also named CODE.

   d. A subroutine named YIELD having a real dummy argument named INTRST and an integer dummy argument named N. The corresponding actual arguments used in calling YIELD are named RATE and YEARS, respectively.

   e. A subroutine named RAND having two real dummy arguments named SEED and RANDNO, respectively. The corresponding actual arguments used in calling RAND are named SEED and RVAL, respectively.

2a. Write a subroutine named FMAX that accepts two dummy integer arguments named FIRNUM and SECNUM and returns the largest of these arguments in a dummy argument named MAX.

   b. Include the FMAX subroutine written for Exercise 2a in a working program. The MAIN program unit should correctly call FMAX and display the value returned by the subroutine.

3a. Write a subroutine named CHANGE that accepts a real number and four actual integer arguments named QUART, DIMES, NICKEL, and PENNY. The subroutine should determine the number of quarters, dimes, nickels, and pennies in the number passed to it and write these values directly to the calling program unit.

   b. Include the CHANGE subroutine written for Exercise 3a in a working program. The MAIN program unit should correctly call CHANGE and display the values returned by the subroutine.

4a. The time in hours, minutes, and seconds is to be passed to a subroutine named TOTSEC. Write TOTSEC to accept these values, determine the total number of seconds in the passed data, and return the calculated value to the calling program unit.

b. Include the TOTSEC subroutine written for Exercise 4a in a working program. The MAIN program unit should correctly call TOTSEC and display the value returned by the subroutine.

5a. Write a subroutine named TIME that accepts an integer number of seconds named in the dummy argument named TOTSEC and returns the number of hours, minutes, and seconds corresponding to the total seconds in the three dummy integer arguments named HOURS, MIN, and SEC.

b. Include the TIME subroutine written for Exercise 5a in a working program. The MAIN program unit should correctly call TIME and display the three values returned by the subroutine.

6. Write a subroutine named DAYCNT that accepts a month, a day, and a year as its input arguments, calculates an integer representing the total number of days from the turn of the century corresponding to the passed date, and returns the calculated integer to the calling program unit. For this problem, assume that each year has 365 days, and each month has 30 days. Test your subroutine by verifying that the date 1/1/00 returns a day count of one.

7. Write a subroutine named LIQUID that is to be called using the statement CALL LIQUID(TOTCUP, GALONS, QUARTS, PINTS). The subroutine is to determine the number of gallons, quarts, pints, and cups in the passed value named TOTCUP and to directly alter the respective arguments in the calling subroutine. Use the relationships of 2 cups to a pint, 4 cups to a quart, and 16 cups to a gallon.

8a. A common method of sorting dates into either ascending (increasing) or descending (decreasing) order is to first convert a date having the form month/day/year into an integer number using the formula $date = year * 10000 + month * 100 + day$. For example, using this formula, the date 12/6/88 converts to the integer 881,206, and the date 2/28/90 converts to the integer 900,228. Sorting the resulting integer numbers automatically puts the dates into the correct order. Using this formula, write a subroutine named CONVRT that accepts a month, a day, and a year as individual integer arguments; converts the passed data into a single date integer; and returns the integer to the calling program unit.

b. Include the CONVRT subroutine written for Exercise 8a in a working program. The MAIN program unit should correctly call CONVRT and display the integer returned by the subroutine.

9a. Write a subroutine named DATE that accepts an integer of the form described in Exercise 8a; determines the corresponding month, day, and year; and returns these three values to the calling program unit. For example, if DATE is called using the statement:

```
CALL DATE(901116,MONTH,DAY,YEAR)
```

the number 11 should be returned in MONTH, the number 16 in DAY, and the number 90 in YEAR.

b. Include the DATE subroutine written for Exercise 9a in a working program. The MAIN program unit should correctly call DATE and display the three values returned by the subroutine.

10. The following program uses the same variable names in both the calling and called the subroutine. Determine if this causes any problem for the computer.

```
PROGRAM MAIN
   INTEGER MIN, HOUR, SEC
   PRINT *, 'ENTER TWO NUMBERS :'
   READ *, MIN, HOUR
   CALL TIME(MIN,HOUR,SEC)
   PRINT *, 'THE TOTAL NUMBER OF SECONDS IS ', SEC
   END
SUBROUTINE TIME(MIN,HOUR,SEC)
   INTEGER MIN, HOUR, SEC
   SEC = (HOUR * 60 + MIN) * 60
   END
```

11. An extremely troublesome logic error occurs when the data types of actual and formal arguments are mismatched. For example, consider the following program, which intentionally introduces this error:

```
        PROGRAM MAIN
           REAL FIRNUM, SECNUM
           INTEGER SUM
           FIRNUM = 22.2
           SECNUM = 10.3
           CALL ADDIT(FIRNUM, SECNUM, SUM)
           PRINT *, 'THE SUM OF 22.2 AND 10.3 IS ', SUM
           END
*****
        SUBROUTINE ADDIT(A,B,C)
           REAL A, B, C
           C = A + B
           END
```

In the subroutine ADDIT, the formal arguments A and B are used to access values supplied by the calling program unit, and C is used to return a value. The subroutine thus accepts two real values and correctly returns their sum. On the receiving side the sum is referenced as the integer variable SUM. Although you might think that the returned real value would be truncated and converted to an integer value, this does not happen. Run this program on your computer to determine what value is received by the MAIN program unit. Explain why you received the answer that you did.

8.2   Arrays as Arguments

An individual array element is passed to a subroutine in the same manner as any scalar variable. For a single array element this is done by including the element as a subscripted variable in a CALL statement's argument list. For example, the subroutine call:

```
CALL FMAX(TEMP(2),TEMP(6))
```

makes the individual array elements TEMP(2) and TEMP(6) available to the subroutine FMAX.

Passing a complete array to a subroutine is in many respects an easier operation than passing individual elements. For example, if TEMP is an array, the statement CALL FMAX(TEMP) makes the complete TEMP array available to the FMAX subroutine.

On the receiving side, the called subroutine must be alerted that an array is being made available. For example, assuming TEMP was declared as INTEGER TEMP(5), a suitable subroutine heading and argument declaration for the FMAX subroutine are:

```
SUBROUTINE FMAX(VALS)
  INTEGER VALS(5)
```

In this subroutine heading, the argument name VALS is local to the subroutine. However, VALS refers to the original array created outside the subroutine. This is made clear in Program 8-6.

 Program 8-6

```
PROGRAM MAIN
  INTEGER TEMP(5)
  DATA TEMP /2,18,1,27,6/
  CALL FMAX(TEMP)
  END
*
SUBROUTINE FMAX(VALS)
  INTEGER VALS(5)
  INTEGER I, MAX
  MAX = VALS(1)
  DO 10 I = 2,5
    IF (MAX .LT. VALS(I)) MAX = VALS(I)
10    CONTINUE
  PRINT *, 'THE MAXIMUM VALUE IS ', MAX
  END
```

Only one array is created in Program 8-6. In PROGRAM MAIN this array is known as TEMP, and in FMAX the array is known as VALS. As illustrated in Figure 8-7, both names refer to the same array. Thus, in Figure 8-7 VALS(3) is the same element as TEMP(3).

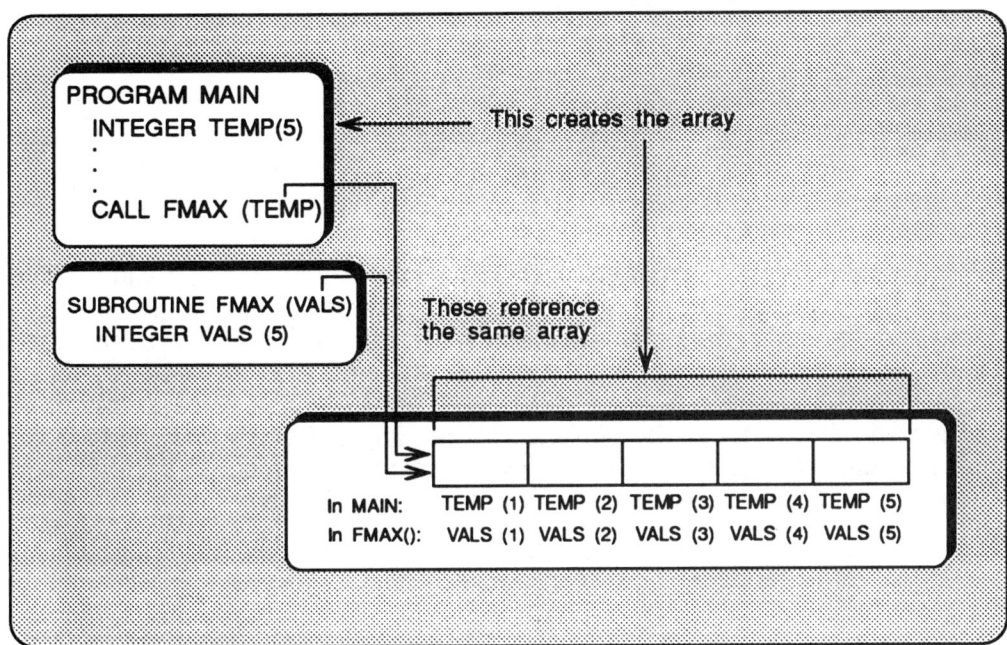

Figure 8-7   Only One Array Is Created

The argument declaration in FMAX actually contains extra information that is not required by the subroutine. All that FMAX must know is that the argument VALS references an array of integers. Since the array has been created in PROGRAM MAIN, and no additional storage space is needed in FMAX, the declaration for VALS can omit the size of the array. Thus, an alternative subroutine heading is:

```
SUBROUTINE FMAX(VALS)
    INTEGER VALS(*)
```

This form of argument declaration is referred to as an *assumed size* array declaration. Assumed size declarations make more sense when you realize that only one item is actually passed to FMAX when the subroutine is called. As you might have suspected, the item passed is the starting location of the TEMP array. This is illustrated in Figure 8-8.

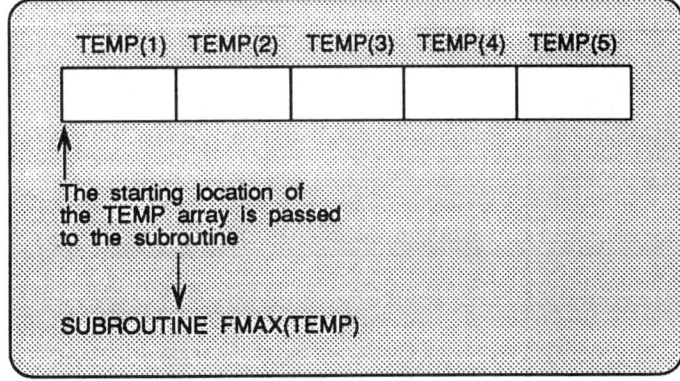

Figure 8-8   The Starting Location of the Array Is Passed

Since only one item is passed to FMAX, the number of elements in the array need not be included in the declaration for VALS. In fact, it is generally advisable to omit the size of the array in the argument declaration. For example, consider the more general form of FMAX, which can be used to find and return the maximum value of an integer array of arbitrary size.

```
SUBROUTINE FMAX(VALS,NELS,MAX)
    INTEGER VALS(*), NELS, MAX
    INTEGER I
    MAX = VALS(1)
    DO 10, I = 2, NELS
      IF (MAX .LT. VALS(I)) MAX = VALS(I)
10    CONTINUE
    END
```

The more general form of FMAX finds and returns the maximum value in any single-dimensioned integer array passed to it. The subroutine expects that an integer array and the number of elements in the array that must be inspected will be passed into it as arguments. Then, using the number of elements as the boundary for its search, the subroutine's DO loop causes each array element to be examined in sequential order to locate the maximum value. This value is passed back to the calling routine through the third dummy argument in the subroutine's argument list. Program 8-7 illustrates the use of FMAX in a complete program.

 Program 8-7

```
PROGRAM MAIN
    INTEGER TEMP(5), N, MAX
    N = 5
    DATA TEMP /2,18,1,27,6/
    CALL FMAX(TEMP, N, MAX)
    PRINT *, 'THE MAXIMUM VALUE IS ', MAX
    END
*
SUBROUTINE FMAX(VALS,NELS,MAX)
    INTEGER VALS(*), NELS, MAX
    INTEGER I
    MAX = VALS(1)
    DO 10, I = 2, NELS
      IF (MAX .LT. VALS(I)) MAX = VALS(I)
10    CONTINUE
    END
```

The output displayed when Program 8-7 is executed is:

```
THE MAXIMUM VALUE IS          27
```

It should be noted that the value of N passed into FMAX need not be the same as the number of elements in the passed array. The passed array is completely declared by the assumed size declaration:

```
INTEGER VALS(*)
```

and the value of N is used to tell FMAX how many elements of this array to examine. Thus, for example, the call:

```
CALL FMAX(TEMP,3,MAX)
```

gives FMAX complete access to TEMP but only specifies that three elements be examined within FMAX.

A third method of passing single dimension arrays to subroutines is to use *adjustable* array declarations. Here, the dimension of the array is passed as a separate argument, which is then used in the dummy argument declaration for the array size. For example, the subroutine heading:

```
SUBROUTINE FMAX(VALS,NELS)
   INTEGER NELS, VALS(NELS)
```

uses an adjustable array declaration to declare the passed array length. It is important to note that a dummy argument, such as NELS, can only be used as an array size if its data type is declared before the array argument's name. Since NELS is declared before VALS, and NELS' value is set by the calling program unit, the size of the VALS array is well defined within the subroutine. Notice, however, that this array declaration method cannot be used in a MAIN program unit using a variable to declare the array size. This is because a value cannot be assigned to the variable prior to the array's declaration.

Passing Multidimension Arrays

Passing multidimension arrays into subroutines is a process identical to passing single dimension arrays. The called subroutine receives access to the entire array. For example, assuming that the following multidimension arrays named TEST, FACTOR, and GRADES are declared as:

```
INTEGER TEST(2,3)
REAL FACTOR(3,5)
REAL GRADES(3,5,10)
```

the following subroutine calls are valid:

```
CALL FMAX(TEST)
CALL SELECT(FACTOR)
CALL AVERGE(GRADES)
```

On the receiving side, the called subroutine must be alerted to the size of the passed array. As with single dimension arrays, this may be done by declaring the exact size of the passed array. For example, suitable subroutine headings and argument declarations for the previous subroutines are:

```
SUBROUTINE FMAX(NUMS)      SUBROUTINE SELECT(VAL)      SUBROUTINE AVERGE(GDS)
   INTEGER NUMS(2,3)          REAL VAL(3,5)               REAL GDS(3,5,10)
```

In each of these subroutine headings, the argument names chosen are local to the subroutine. However, the internal local names used by the subroutine still refer to the original array created outside the subroutine. Program 8-8 illustrates passing a two dimension array into a subroutine that displays the array's values.

 Program 8-8

```
PROGRAM MAIN
  INTEGER VAL(3,4)
  DATA VAL /8,3,14,16,15,25,9,27,2,52,6,10/
  CALL DISPLY(VAL)
  END
*
SUBROUTINE DISPLY(NUMS)
  INTEGER NUMS(3,4),I, J
  DO 10 I = 1, 3
    PRINT *, (NUMS(I,J), J = 1,4)
10   CONTINUE
  END
```

Only one array is created in Program 8-8. This array is known as VAL in the MAIN program unit and as NUMS in DISPLY. Thus, VAL(1,2) refers to the same element as NUMS(1,2). The display produced by Program 8-8 is:

```
 8    16     9    52
 3    15    27     6
14    25     2    10
```

The argument declaration for NUMS in DISPLY contains extra information that is not required by the subroutine. The declaration for NUMS can use an asterisk (*) for the column dimension. Thus, an alternative subroutine heading is:

```
SUBROUTINE DISPLY(NUMS)
  INTEGER NUMS(3,*)
```

The asterisk can be used only as the last dimension (this is also true for passing larger-dimensioned arrays). Additionally, as for single-dimensioned arrays, multi-dimensioned arrays can be passed using adjustable sizing. For example, the heading:

```
SUBROUTINE DISPLY(EXPER, I, J, K)
  INTEGER I, J, K, EXPER(I, J, K)
```

uses adjustable sizing for passing the three dimension EXPER array.

Exercises

1. The following declaration was used to create the MFACTR array:

   ```
   INTEGER MFACTR(500)
   ```

   Write a subroutine header and two different argument declarations for a subroutine named SORTAR that accepts the MFACTR array as an argument named INARRY.

2. The following declaration was used to create the CODE array:

   ```
   CHARACTER CODE(256)
   ```

   Write a subroutine header and two different argument declarations for a subroutine named FINDCD that accepts the CODE array as an argument named SELCT.

3. The following declaration was used to create the WATTS array:

   ```
   REAL WATTS(140)
   ```

   Write a subroutine header and two different argument declarations for a subroutine named POWER that accepts the WATTS array as an argument named WATTS.

4a. Modify the FMAX subroutine in Program 8-7 to locate the minimum value of the passed array.

b. Include the subroutine written in Exercise 4a in a complete program and run the program on a computer.

5. Write a program that has a DATA statement in its main program unit that stores the following numbers into a array named GRADES: 65.3, 72.5, 75.0, 83.2, 86.5, 94.0, 96.0, 98.8, 100. There should be a subroutine call to SHOW that accepts the GRADES array as an argument named GRADES and then displays the numbers in the array.

6a. Write a program that has a DATA statement in PROGRAM MAIN to store the characters 'V','A','C','A','T','I','O','N',' ','I','S',' ','N','E','A','R' into an array named MESSGE.

   There should be a subroutine call to DISPLY that accepts MESSGE in an argument named STRNG and then displays the message.

b. Modify the DISPLY subroutine written in Exercise 6a to display the first eight elements of the MESSGE array.

7. Write a program that declares three single dimension arrays named VOLTS, CURRNT, and RESIST. Each array should be declared in PROGRAM MAIN and should be capable of holding 10 real numbers. The numbers that should be stored in CURRNT are 10.62, 14.89, 13.21, 16.55, 18.62, 9.47, 6.58, 18.32, 12.15, 3.98. The numbers that should be stored in RESIST are 4, 8.5, 6, 7.35, 9, 15.3, 3, 5.4, 2.9, 4.8. Your program should pass these three arrays to a subroutine called CALCV, which should calculate the elements in the VOLTS array as the product of the equivalent elements in the CURRNT and RESIST arrays (for example, VOLTS(1) = CURRNT(1) * RESIST(1)). After CALCV has put values into the VOLTS array, the values in the array should be displayed from within the MAIN program unit.

8. Write a program that includes two subroutines named AVERGE and VRANCE. The AVERGE subroutine should calculate and return the average of the values stored in an array named TEST. The TEST array should be declared in the MAIN program unit and include the values 89, 95, 72, 83, 99, 54, 86, 75, 92, 73, 79, 75, 82, 73. The VRANCE subroutine should

calculate and return the variance of the data. The variance is obtained by subtracting the average from each value in TEST, squaring the values obtained, adding them, and dividing by the number of elements in TEST. The values returned from AVERGE and VRANCE should be displayed using PRINT statements in the MAIN program unit.

9. The following declaration was used to create the FACTRS array:

```
REAL FACTRS(3,5,10)
```

Write a subroutine header and three different argument declarations for a subroutine named LOCATE that accepts the FACTRS array as an argument named XINARY.

10. Modify Program 8-8 to use adjustable array sizing for the dummy array argument NUMS in DISPLY. The row size should be declared using an argument named ROWSIZ and the column size by an argument named COLSIZ. These two arguments should also be used as final counter parameters in the subroutine's explicit and implied DO loops.

11. Write a subroutine that multiplies each element of a three-row-by-four-column integer array by an integer number. Both the array name and the number by which each element is to be multiplied are to be passed into the subroutine as arguments.

12. Write a subroutine that adds the values of all elements in a two dimension array that is passed to the subroutine. Assume that the array is an array of real numbers having four rows and five columns.

13. Write a subroutine that adds respective values of two double dimension arrays named FIRST and SECND, respectively. Both arrays have two rows and three columns. For example, element (1,2) of the resulting array should be the sum of FIRST(1,2) and SECND(1,2).

14a. Write a subroutine that finds and displays the maximum value in a two dimension array of integers. The array should be declared as a four-row-by-five-column array of integers in the MAIN program unit.

b. Modify the subroutine written in Exercise 14a so that it also displays the row and column number of the element with the maximum value.

c. Can the subroutine you wrote for Exercise 14a be generalized to handle any size two dimension array?

8.3 COMMON Blocks

As we have seen in Section 8.1, all FORTRAN variables declared within a program unit are local to that unit. In practical terms this means that, unless special provisions are made, one unit's variables cannot be accessed by another unit. One method of providing for the mutual access of variables between a subroutine and its calling unit is to use subroutine argument lists. This method is unwieldy, however, when many variables must be shared among many subroutines. A more suitable approach in this situation is to use the second method provided by FORTRAN for extending the scope of a variable beyond the borders of its originating program unit. This second method is to use a COMMON block.

A COMMON block is a block of memory locations that can be made available to any and all program units. FORTRAN provides two classes of COMMON block types: COMMON blocks that are assigned individual names, called *named* COMMON, and a single unnamed COMMON block. Once an individual variable has been assigned space in a COMMON block, any program unit that needs the variable can gain access to the block by correctly referencing the desired COMMON area.

Unnamed COMMON

Unnamed COMMON, which is also referred to as *blank* COMMON, is created with the COMMON declaration statement:

```
COMMON list of variables
```

The keyword COMMON must be present and specifies that a common block is being defined. The list of variables defines the variables that are to be included in the COMMON block. For example, the statement :

```
COMMON FACTOR, WEIGHT, MASS, DENSTY
```

places the four variables FACTOR, WEIGHT, MASS, and DENSTY into the computer's unnamed COMMON area. A program unit desiring access to this area must place this declaration statement after the data type declarations for the four variables. If the variables have not been explicitly typed, the compiler assigns data types to COMMON variables using FORTRAN's implicit typing rules.

All program units that desire access to the computer's unnamed common area must include a COMMON declaration. As with arguments, the variable names in each COMMON statement do not have to be the same, but the number, type, and order of the variables in each COMMON statement must be identical. For example, consider the following MAIN program unit and subroutine:

```
PROGRAM MAIN
   INTEGER MASS, N1, N2
   REAL FACTOR, WEIGHT, DENSTY
   COMMON FACTOR, WEIGHT, MASS, DENSTY
     .
     .
     .
   CALL SOLVE(N1,N2)
     .
     .
     .
   END
SUBROUTINE SOLVE(K,J)
   INTEGER K,J
   INTEGER MSS
   REAL SCALE, WT, DN
   COMMON SCALE, WT, MSS, DN
     .
     .
     .
   END
```

In this example the two program units communicate using both arguments and the computer's unnamed COMMON area. As illustrated in Figure 8-9, the variables FACTOR and SCALE refer to the same memory locations, the variables WEIGHT and WT refer to the same memory locations, the variables MASS and MSS refer to the same memory locations, and the variables DENSTY and DN refer to the same memory locations.

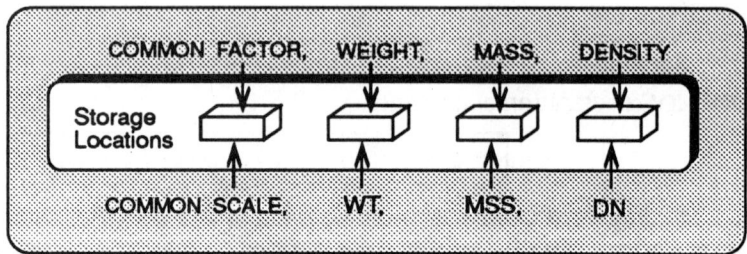

Figure 8-9   Equivalent Variable Designations

We now include an unnamed COMMON within a working program. Consider, for example, Program 8-9.

 Program 8-9

```
PROGRAM MAIN
   INTEGER FIRNUM,SECNUM
   COMMON FIRNUM
   FIRNUM = 10
   SECNUM = 20
   PRINT *, 'FROM PROGRAM MAIN: FIRNUM = ',FIRNUM
   PRINT *, 'FROM PROGRAM MAIN: SECNUM = ',SECNUM
   CALL ALTVAL
   PRINT *
   PRINT *,'FROM PROGRAM MAIN AGAIN: FIRNUM = ',FIRNUM
   PRINT *,'FROM PROGRAM MAIN AGAIN: SECNUM = ',SECNUM
   END
*
SUBROUTINE ALTVAL
   INTEGER FIRNUM, SECNUM
   COMMON FIRNUM
   SECNUM = 30
   PRINT *
   PRINT *,'FROM ALTVAL: FIRNUM = ',FIRNUM
   PRINT *,'FROM ALTVAL: SECNUM = ',SECNUM
   FIRNUM = 40
   END
```

In this program the unnamed COMMON declaration in the MAIN program unit places this unit's local variable FIRNUM into the system's unnamed COMMON area. This makes this variable available to any other program unit that also specifies the unnamed COMMON area. As the ALTVAL subroutine also specifies the unnamed COMMON block, the variable FIRNUM can be directly accessed within ALTVAL. Since ALTVAL has declared the same name for its COMMON variable, both program units reference the common variable using the name FIRNUM. Additionally, Program 8-9 contains two separate local variables, both named SECNUM. Storage for the SECNUM variable named in PROGRAM MAIN is created by the declaration statement located in PROGRAM MAIN. A different storage area for the SECNUM variable in ALTVAL is created by the declaration statement located in the ALTVAL subroutine. Figure 8-10 illustrates the three distinct storage areas reserved by Program 8-9.

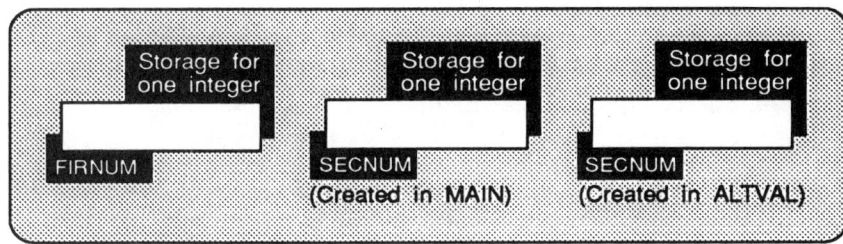

Figure 8-10   The Three Storage Areas Created by Program 8-9

Each of the variables named SECNUM is local to the program unit in which its storage is created, and each of these variables can only be used from within the appropriate subroutine. Thus, when SECNUM is used in PROGRAM MAIN, the storage area reserved by this program unit for its SECNUM variable is accessed; when SECNUM is used in ALTVAL, the storage area reserved by ALTVAL for its SECNUM variable is accessed. The following output is produced when Program 8-9 is run:

```
FROM PROGRAM MAIN: FIRNUM =            10
FROM PROGRAM MAIN: SECNUM =            20

FROM ALTVAL: FIRNUM =          10
FROM ALTVAL: SECNUM =          30

FROM PROGRAM MAIN AGAIN: FIRNUM =            40
FROM PROGRAM MAIN AGAIN: SECNUM =            20
```

Let us analyze the output produced by Program 8-9. Since FIRNUM is in unnamed COMMON declared by both the MAIN program unit and the ALTVAL subroutine, both of these units can use and change its value. Initially, both program units print the value of 10 that PROGRAM MAIN stored in FIRNUM. Before returning, ALTVAL changes the value of FIRNUM to 40, which is the value displayed when FIRNUM is next displayed from within the MAIN program unit.

Since each program unit only "knows" its own local variables, the MAIN program unit can only display the value of its SECNUM, and ALTVAL can only display the value of its SECNUM. Thus, whenever SECNUM is displayed from PROGRAM MAIN, the value 20 is output; whenever SECNUM is displayed from ALTVAL, the value

30 is output. The values of the two SECNUM variables are not confused by the computer because only one program unit can execute at a given moment.

Arrays and Unnamed COMMON

In addition to scalar variables, array names may also be included in a COMMON declaration. Doing so places the complete array in the COMMON block. For example, assume that TEST has been declared as an array of real values using the declaration:

```
REAL TEST(500)
```

If TEST is now placed into unnamed COMMON using the statement:

```
COMMON TEST
```

then all 500 elements of the TEST array are made available to any program unit that accesses the unnamed COMMON block.

An additional feature of placing arrays into COMMON areas is that integer and real valued arrays can be dimensioned at the same time they are included in a COMMON statement. For example, the statement:

```
COMMON ARR(100)
```

both dimensions ARR to be an array of 100 elements and places this array into the COMMON area. If another program unit uses the statement:

```
COMMON SEC(100)
```

both ARR and SEC refer to the same array. When dimensioned in this manner, the data type of the array is determined by FORTRAN's implicit typing rules. In this case the array is an array of real values because the initial letter of the array's name does not begin in either I, J, K, L, M, or N.

It must be emphasized that all of the variables and arrays included in an unnamed COMMON statement must match the type, order, and number of the variables and arrays in every other unnamed COMMON statement. For example, if the previous COMMON statement was incorrectly changed to COMMON ITEMP(100), the program unit using this statement would be using the values in the COMMON array as integer values, while the program unit accessing the COMMON array as ARR would think it was dealing with real values. The resulting error would be extremely difficult to find. Retaining the same scalar and array variable names in all unnamed COMMON declarations will help to prevent such an error. Additionally, when a change is made to an unnamed COMMON statement in one program unit, the change must be correctly reflected in every program unit in which the unnamed COMMON statement appears.

Named COMMON Blocks

In addition to FORTRAN's single unnamed COMMON area, multiple named COMMON areas can be established. A named COMMON area is declared using the general format:

```
COMMON /name/ list of variables
```

Examples of named COMMON declarations are:

```
COMMON /GRAPH/ X,Y,Z,FACTOR
COMMON /PARA/ WATTS, VOLTS, RESIST
COMMON /PARB/ DENSTY, MASS, WEIGHT, AREA, GRAV
```

The first COMMON declaration establishes a COMMON area named GRAPH, which include the four variables x, y, z, and FACTOR; the second declaration establishes a COMMON area named PARA containing the variables WATTS, VOLTS, and RESIST; and the last declaration creates a COMMON area named PARB containing the variables DENSTY, MASS, WEIGHT, AREA, and GRAV.

The advantage of named COMMON areas is that individual subroutines need reference only those COMMON areas containing variables they need to share. This helps isolate the shared variables between the program units that actually need them and avoids the need to list all COMMON variables in each subroutine.

An individual variable cannot be included in more than one named COMMON block. Thus, if the same variable is required by two subroutines, each sharing a different named COMMON block with the MAIN program unit, either a new COMMON block containing the desired variable must be established or the variable must be passed through each subroutine's argument list. In addition to scalar variables, arrays may also be included in any named COMMON block. When an array is assigned to named COMMON block, it follows the same rules as previously described for unnamed COMMON.

BLOCK DATA Program Units

Scalar and array variables contained within COMMON blocks, either named or unnamed, may be initialized in DATA statements. These statements must, however, be collected together within a special type of program unit, called a BLOCK DATA subprogram. This program unit has the form:

```
BLOCK DATA
   variable declarations
   COMMON declarations
   DATA statements
   END
```

An example of a BLOCK DATA subprogram that initializes the named COMMON areas called GRAPH and PARA is:

```
BLOCK DATA
   REAL X,Y,Z,WATTS,VOLTS,RESIST
   COMMON /GRAPH/ X,Y,Z
   COMMON /PARA/ WATTS, VOLTS, RESIST
   DATA X, Y, Z, WATTS, VOLTS, RESIST /3.2,4.6,5.0,5.2,7.8,9.7/
   END
```

To provide for multiple BLOCK DATA subprograms, where each subprogram is used to initialize specific COMMON areas, FORTRAN permits a BLOCK DATA subprogram to be named. An example of a named BLOCK DATA subprogram is:

```
BLOCK DATA PLOT
```

Any valid FORTRAN symbolic name may be selected for a BLOCK DATA subprogram. Although a complete FORTRAN program can contain any number of named BLOCK DATA subprograms, only one unnamed BLOCK DATA subprogram is allowed.

Exercises

1. Assuming that each of the following three COMMON statements are separately contained within their own individual program units, determine the correspondence between variables:

```
COMMON A,B,C,D,I,J,K
COMMON X,Y,Z,P,NCOUNT, MTEMP, LSHOW
COMMON SNAP, CRACLE, POP, PIP, MM, KK, II
```

2. Determine the error in the following program:

```
PROGRAM TEST
   INTEGER I, M, N
   REAL A,B,C,D,E,X,Y,Z,T(100),S(100)
   COMMON E,X,Y,IKOUNT,T,S,A
   CALL CALC
   END
SUBROUTINE CALC
   INTEGER J,K,L
   REAL F,G,H,U(100),V(100),P,Q
   COMMON F,G,H,P,U,V,Q
   .
   .
   .
   END
```

3. Rewrite Exercise 3 in Section 8.1 so that all arguments are exchanged through unnamed COMMON rather than through argument lists.

4. Rewrite Exercise 4 in Section 8.1 so that all arguments are exchanged through unnamed COMMON rather than through argument lists.

5. Rewrite Exercise 5 in Section 8.1 so that all arguments are exchanged through unnamed COMMON rather than through argument lists.

8.4 Applications

In this section two applications are presented to further illustrate the use of subroutines and the method of passing data through an argument list. In the first application a subroutine is constructed to accept a list of grades, determine the average and standard deviation of the passed data, and return these calculated quantities to the calling routine for display. In the second application a subroutine is used to insert an item's part number into an existing list that is maintained in a sorted order.

Application 1: Grade Analysis

A subroutine that accepts a list of grades as input and determines and returns both the average and standard deviation of the grades is to be developed.

Subroutine Development

Realizing that a subroutine is a small program in its own right, the top-down development procedure described in Chapter 2 can be applied to developing the required unit. Using this procedure we have:

Step 1: Determine the Desired Output

The statement of the problem indicates that two output values are required: an average and a standard deviation.

Step 2: Determine the Input Items

The input item defined in the problem statement is a list of grades. Because the size of the list is not specified in the problem statement and to make our subroutine as general as possible, the subroutine will be designed to handle any size list passed to it. This requires that the exact number of elements in the list must also be passed to the subroutine at the time of the subroutine call. From the subroutine's viewpoint this means that it must be capable of receiving two input items, an array of arbitrary size and an integer number corresponding to the number of elements in the passed array, as arguments.

Step 3a: Determine an Algorithm

The I/O specifications determined in steps 1 and 2 imply that the argument list must be capable of receiving two items consisting of an array and an integer and must return two items consisting of an average and a standard deviation. These output items are determined as follows:

Calculate the average by adding the grades and dividing by the number of grades that were added.

Determine the standard deviation by:
1. Subtracting the average from each individual grade. This results in a set of new numbers, each of which is called a deviation.

2. Square each deviation found in the previous step.

3. Add the squared deviations and divide the sum by the number of deviations.

4. *The square root of the number found in the previous step is the standard deviation.*

Step 3b: Do a Hand Calculation

To ensure that we understand the required processing, we will do a hand calculation. For this calculation we will arbitrarily assume that the average and standard deviation of the following ten grades are to be determined: 98, 82, 67, 54, 78, 83, 95, 76, 68, and 63.

The average of this data is determined as:

Average = (98 + 82 + 67 + 54 + 78 + 83 + 95 + 76 + 68 + 63)/10 = 76.4

The standard deviation is calculated by first determining the sum of the squared deviations and then taking the square root of the sum divided by 10.

$$
\begin{aligned}
\text{Sum of squared deviations} &= (98 - 76.4)^2 + (82 - 76.4)^2 \\
&\quad + (67 - 76.4)^2 + (54 - 76.4)^2 \\
&\quad + (78 - 76.4)^2 + (83 - 76.4)^2 \\
&\quad + (95 - 76.4)^2 + (76 - 76.4)^2 \\
&\quad + (68 - 76.4)^2 + (63 - 76.4)^2 \\
&= 1730.400700
\end{aligned}
$$

Standard deviation = $\sqrt{1739.4007/10}$ = $\sqrt{173.94007}$ = 13.154470

Step 3c: Select Variable Names

The selection of variable names for the input and output quantities for a subroutine corresponds to selecting argument names for the argument list. For this problem we will use the argument names ARRAY and NUMEL for the passed array and number of elements, and the names AV and ST for the calculated average and standard deviation. Internal to the subroutine we will use a variable named SUMGRD for the sum of the grades used in calculating the average and the variable named SUMDEV for the squared deviations used in calculating the standard deviation.

Step 4: Write the Subroutine

In writing the subroutine, it is convenient to initially concentrate on the header line and the appropriate declaration of arguments. The body of the subroutine can then be written to process the input arguments correctly to produce the desired results.

Calling our subroutine STATS and using the argument names selected in Step 3c, the subroutine header becomes:

```
SUBROUTINE STATS(ARRAY, NUMEL, AV, ST)
```

The order of the arguments within the argument list is entirely arbitrary. For convenience we have placed those arguments that will be used as input to the subroutine first and those arguments that will be used as output to return the average and standard deviation last. (Keep in mind, however, that from FORTRAN's standpoint each of the four arguments really provides a two-way swinging door in which values may be exchanged in any direction between the calling program unit and the subroutine.)

The declarations for the subroutine's arguments, which are placed immediately below the header, become:

```
REAL ARRAY(*), AV, ST
INTEGER NUMEL
```

Although the order within the declaration does not have to match the order of the arguments within the argument list, listing the arguments close to the order in which they appear in the argument list helps to ensure that all arguments have been declared. The remaining body of the subroutine calculates the average and standard deviation according to the algorithm described in step 3a of the development procedure. Thus, the completed subroutine becomes:

```
        SUBROUTINE STATS(ARRAY, NUMEL, AV, ST)
          REAL ARRAY(*), AV, ST, SUMGRD, SUMDEV
          INTEGER NUMEL, I
***       CALCULATE THE AVERAGE    ***
          SUMGRD = 0.0
          DO 10 I = 1, NUMEL
            SUMGRD = SUMGRD + ARRAY(I)
   10       CONTINUE
          AV = SUMGRD / NUMEL
***       CALCULATE THE STANDARD DEVIATION ***
          SUMDEV = 0
          DO 20 I = 1, NUMEL
            SUMDEV = SUMDEV + (ARRAY(I) - AV)**2
   20       CONTINUE
          ST = SQRT(SUMDEV/NUMEL)
          END
```

Notice that the calculation portion of the subroutine uses one DO loop to sum the individual grades and a second DO loop to determine the sum of the squared deviations. Because calculation of the squared deviations requires the average, the standard deviation can be calculated only after the average has been computed. Notice also that the termination value of the loop counter in both DO loops is NUMEL, which is the number of grades that is passed to the subroutine through the argument list. The use of this argument gives the subroutine its generality and allows it to be used for lists of any number of grades. For example, calling the subroutine with the statement:

```
CALL STATS(GRADES,10,AVERGE,STDDEV)
```

tells the subroutine that NUMEL is 10 and that the GRADES array consists of 10 values, while the statement:

```
CALL STATS(GRADES,1000,AVERGE,STDDEV)
```

tells STATS that NUMEL is 1000 and that the GRADES array consists of 1000 grades. In both CALL statements the actual arguments named GRADES, AVERGE, and STDDEV correspond to the dummy arguments ARRAY, AV, and ST within the STATS subroutine.

Step 5: Test the Subroutine

Testing a subroutine requires writing a MAIN program unit to call the subroutine and display the returned results. Program 8-10 uses such a MAIN unit to set up a GRADES array with the data previously used in our hand calculation and to call the STATS subroutine.

 Program 8-10

```
    PROGRAM MAIN
      REAL GRADES(10), AVERGE, STDDEV
      DATA GRADES /98, 82, 67, 54, 78, 83, 95, 76, 68, 63/
      CALL STATS(GRADES, 10, AVERGE, STDDEV)
      PRINT *, 'THE AVERAGE OF THE GRADES IS', AVERGE
      PRINT *, 'THE STANDARD DEVIATION OF THE GRADES IS', STDDEV
      END
***
      SUBROUTINE STATS(ARRAY, NUMEL, AV, ST)
      REAL ARRAY(*), AV, ST, SUMGRD, SUMDEV
      INTEGER NUMEL, I
***   CALCULATE THE AVERAGE    ***
      SUMGRD = 0.0
      DO 10 I = 1, NUMEL
        SUMGRD = SUMGRD + ARRAY(I)
   10   CONTINUE
      AV = SUMGRD / NUMEL
***   CALCULATE THE STANDARD DEVIATION ***
      SUMDEV = 0
      DO 20 I = 1, NUMEL
        SUMDEV = SUMDEV + (ARRAY(I) - AV)**2
   20   CONTINUE
      ST = SQRT(SUMDEV/NUMEL)
      END
```

A test run using Program 8-10 produces the following display:

```
THE AVERAGE OF THE GRADES IS       76.400000
THE STANDARD DEVIATION OF THE GRADES IS       13.154470
```

Since this result agrees with our previous hand calculations, and the subroutine contains no additional calculations that have not been verified, the subroutine has been completely tested.

Application 2: Insertion Update

A common problem in programming is to maintain a list in either numerical or alphabetical order. For example, telephone and mailing lists are traditionally kept in alphabetical order, while lists of part numbers are kept in numerical order.

As part of an overall maintenance program, a subroutine is to be written that correctly inserts a three-digit identification code within a list of numbers that is maintained in increasing order. Such a subroutine will be written in this application. A maximum list size of 100 values will be allowed, and a sentinel value of 9999 will be used to indicate the end of the list. Thus, for example, if the current list contains nine identification codes, the tenth position in the list will contain the sentinel value.

Subroutine Development

Using a top-down development approach, we have:

Step 1: Determine the Desired Output
The required output is an updated list of three-digit codes in which the new code has been inserted correctly into the existing list.

Step 2: Determine the Input Items
The input items for this subroutine are the existing array of identification codes and the new code that is to be inserted into the list.

Step 3a: Determine an Algorithm
To insert an identification code into the existing list requires the following processing:

Determine where in the list the new code should be placed
>   *This is done by comparing the new code to each value in*
>   *the current list until either a match is found, an*
>   *identification code larger than the new code is located,*
>   *or the end of the list is encountered*

If the new code matches an existing code.
>   *display a message that the code already exists*

Else
>   *to make room for the new element in the array, move*
>   *each element down one position. This is done by*
>   *starting from the sentinel value and moving each*
>   *item down one position until the desired position*
>   *in the list is vacated*

insert the new code in the vacated position

Step 3b: Do a Hand Calculation
For our hand calculation assume that the list of identification codes consists of the numbers illustrated in Figure 8-11a. If the number code 142 is to be inserted into this list, it must be placed in the fourth position in the list, after the number 136.

To make room for the new code, all of the codes from the fourth position to the end of the list must be moved one position over, as illustrated on Figure 8-11b. The move is always started from the end of the list and proceeds from the sentinel value back until the desired position in the list is reached. (You can convince yourself that if the copy proceeded forward from the fourth element, the number 144 would be reproduced in all subsequent locations until the sentinel value was reached.)

After the movement of the necessary elements, the new code is inserted in the correct position. This creates the updated list shown in Figure 8-11c.

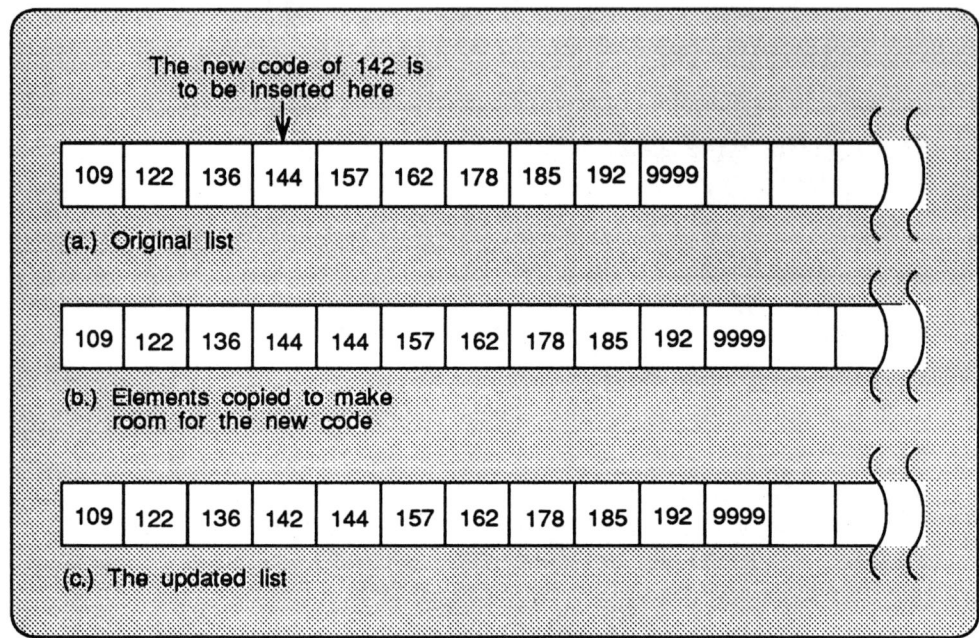

Figure 8-11   Updating an Ordered List of Identification Numbers

Step 3c: Select Variable and Argument Names

For this problem we will use the argument names IDCODE and NEWCDE for the passed array of identification numbers and the new code number to be inserted into the array. Here, the passed array is used both for receiving the original array of numbers and as the final, updated array. Internal to the subroutine we will use a variable named NEWPOS to hold the position in the list where the new code is to be inserted and the variable named TRLPOS to hold the position value of the sentinel. The variable I will be used as a running index value.

Step 4: Write the Subroutine

The subroutine named INSERT performs the required processing. After accepting the code array as the argument IDCODE and the new code as the argument NEWCDE, the INSERT subroutine performs four major tasks, corresponding to the algorithm selected in step 3a.

```
      SUBROUTINE INSERT(IDCODE, NEWCDE)
         INTEGER IDCODE(*), NEWCDE
         INTEGER I, NEWPOS, TRLPOS
         I = 1
***   FIND CORRECT POSITION TO INSERT NEW CODE
```

```
   10    IF(IDCODE(I) .LT. NEWCDE) THEN
            I = I + 1
            GO TO 10
         ENDIF
         IF (IDCODE(I) .EQ. NEWCDE) THEN
            PRINT *, 'THIS IDENTIFICATION CODE IS ALREADY IN THE LIST'
         ELSE
            NEWPOS = I
***   FIND THE END OF THE LIST
   20       IF (IDCODE(I) .NE. 9999) THEN
               I = I + 1
               GO TO 20
            ENDIF
         TRLPOS = I
***   MOVE IDCODES DOWN ONE POSITION
            DO 30 I = TRLPOS, NEWPOS, -1
               IDCODE(I+1) =IDCODE(I)
   30       CONTINUE
***   INSERT NEW CODE
            IDCODE(NEWPOS) = NEWCDE
         ENDIF
         END
```

The first task accomplished by the subroutine is determining the correct position for the new code. This is done by cycling through the list as long as each value encountered is less than the new code. Since the sentinel value of 9999 is larger than any new code, the looping will stop if the sentinel value is reached.

After the correct position is determined, the position of the sentinel value, which is the last element in the list, is found. Starting from this last position, each element in the list is copied over by one position, until the value in the required new position is reached. Finally, the new identification code is inserted in the correct position.

Step 5: Test the Subroutine

Program 8-11 incorporates the INSERT subroutine within a complete program. This allows us to test the subroutine with the same data used in our hand calculation.

A test run using Program 8-11 produces the following display:

```
ENTER THE NEW IDENTIFICATION CODE:
142
THE UPDATED LIST IS:
109    122    136    142    144    157    162    178    185    192    9999
```

Although this result agrees with our previous hand calculation, it does not constitute full testing of the program. To be sure that the program works for all cases, test runs should be made that duplicate an existing code, that place a new identification code at the beginning of the list, and that place a new identification code at the end of the list.

Program 8-11

```
PROGRAM MAIN
  INTEGER ID(100), NEWCDE, I
  DATA (ID(I), I=1,10)/109,122,136,144,157,162,178,185,192,9999/
  PRINT *, 'ENTER THE NEW IDENTIFICATION CODE: '
  READ *, NEWCDE
  CALL INSERT(ID,NEWCDE)
PRINT *, 'THE UPDATED LIST IS:'
PRINT *, (ID(I), I = 1,11)
END
***
  SUBROUTINE INSERT(IDCODE, NEWCDE)
    INTEGER IDCODE(*), NEWCDE
    INTEGER I, NEWPOS, TRLPOS
    I = 1
***   FIND CORRECT POSITION TO INSERT NEW CODE
  10    IF(IDCODE(I) .LT. NEWCDE) THEN
          I = I + 1
          GO TO 10
        ENDIF
        IF (IDCODE(I) .EQ. NEWCDE) THEN
          PRINT *, 'THIS IDENTIFICATION CODE IS ALREADY IN THE LIST'
        ELSE
          NEWPOS = I
***   FIND THE END OF THE LIST
  20      IF (IDCODE(I) .NE. 9999) THEN
            I = I + 1
            GO TO 20
          ENDIF
          TRLPOS = I
***   MOVE IDCODES DOWN ONE POSITION
          DO 30 I = TRLPOS, NEWPOS, -1
            IDCODE(I+1) =IDCODE(I)
  30      CONTINUE
***   INSERT NEW CODE
          IDCODE(NEWPOS) = NEWCDE
        ENDIF
        END
```

Additional Exercises for Chapter 8

1. Modify Program 8-10 so that the grades are entered into the GRADES array using a subroutine named ENTGRD.

2. Rewrite Program 8-10 to have the STATS subroutine additionally determine the average and standard deviation of the following list of fifteen grades: 68, 72, 78, 69, 85, 98, 95, 75, 77, 82, 84, 91, 89, 65, 74.

3. Modify Program 8-10 so that the STATS subroutine additionally determines both the highest and lowest grades in the passed array and returns these values to the MAIN program unit for display.

4. Modify Program 8-10 so that the STATS subroutine additionally returns the number of As, Bs, Cs, Ds, and Fs in the passed grade list. For this purpose assume the following scale:

Numerical grade	Letter grade
90 or above	A
Greater than or equal to 80 and less than 90	B
Greater than or equal to 70 and less than 80	C
Greater than or equal to 60 and less than 70	D
Less than 60	F

5. Modify Program 8-10 so that a subroutine named SORT is called after the call to the STATS subroutine. The SORT subroutine should sort the grades into increasing order for display by the MAIN program unit.

6a. Test Program 8-11 using an identification code of 86. The program should place this new code at the beginning of the existing list.

b. Test Program 8-11 using an identification code of 200. The program should place this new code at the end of the existing list.

7a. Determine an algorithm for deleting an entry from an ordered list of numbers.

b. Write a subroutine named DELETE, that uses the algorithm selected in Exercise 6a to delete an identification code from the list of numbers illustrated in Figure 8-11a.

8. Assume the following names are stored in an array called NAMES: BRONSON, JONES, KLEIN, MONTROSE, SMITH. Write and test a subroutine named ADNAME that accepts both the NAMES array and a new name as arguments, and inserts the new name in the correct alphabetical order in the NAMES array. For this problem assume that the maximum size of each name is 15 characters.

8.5   Common Programming Errors

The common errors associated with subroutines are:

1. Forgetting to use the word SUBROUTINE on the header line before the subroutine's name.
2. Forgetting to place an END statement as the last statement in a subroutine.
3. Using an actual argument list that disagrees in type, number, or order with the subroutine's dummy argument list. For example, assume that a subroutine named CIRCLE has the header line:
   ```
   SUBROUTINE CIRCLE(RADIUS)
   ```
   where RADIUS is declared as a real argument. Now assume that this subroutine is inadvertently called by the statement:
   ```
   CALL CIRCLE(IRAD)
   ```
   where IRAD is an integer variable. Although you might expect that CIRCLE would convert the actual integer argument into the proper type for the declared dummy argument, this is not what happens at all. What does happen is illustrated in Figure 8-12.*

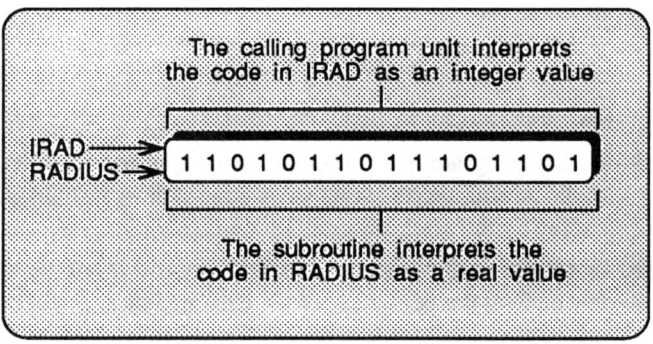

Figure 8-12   Argument Type Mismatch Error

   As illustrated in Figure 8-12, the actual argument IRAD and its equivalent dummy argument within the subroutine, RADIUS, both reference the same starting storage location in memory. Thus, the computer's internal code for the calling unit's actual integer argument is interpreted within the subroutine as the code of a real value. This creates a number within the subroutine that bears no obvious relationship to the calling unit's actual integer argument.

   The simplest way to prevent this type of error is to display all passed values within a subroutine's body before any calculations are made. Once the verification has taken place, the display is not needed. Similarly, all values passed back to the calling unit should be displayed initially to ensure that correct values have been received from the subroutine.

4. Attempting to alter the value of a passed constant. For example, assume that a subroutine named AREA has the header line:
   ```
   SUBROUTINE AREA(RADIUS)
   ```

---

* Some conpilers give a warning message for this error.

and is called using the statement:
```
CALL AREA(RAD)
```

Here, the value in RAD is referenced within the subroutine as the argument RADIUS. If the subroutine subsequently alters the value of RADIUS, the value of RAD is also changed. This is a consequence of the fact that both RAD and RADIUS reference the exact same storage location area.

Now, however, assume that the subroutine is called using the following statement:
```
CALL AREA(3.62)
```

Within AREA, and assuming that RADIUS has been declared as a real argument, the value referenced by RADIUS is 3.62. However, the value in RADIUS cannot be changed within AREA. An attempt to do so is effectively an attempt to redefine the value of the constant 3.62, which results in an error.

The errors commonly associated with COMMON blocks are:

1. Not having COMMON blocks that agree in type, number, and order. This type of error can occur in subtle ways. For example, assume that in one program unit the following two statements appear:
```
INTEGER FIRNUM
COMMON FIRNUM
```

   while in a second program unit the variable declaration is omitted and only the statement:
```
COMMON FIRNUM
```

   is used. In the absence of the explicit variable declaration, the compiler reverts to implicit data typing, which means the second COMMON block is expecting a real value, while the first block references an integer value.

   Another subtle way in which COMMON blocks lose their consistency is when a change in a COMMON statement is made within a MAIN program unit and a single subroutine but is not made in the remaining subroutines that use the same COMMON block. This error occurs because the programmer is concentrating on the interchange of information between the MAIN unit and a particular subroutine and may forget that the same interchange of data is made with other subroutines that are not being actively considered.

2. Misplacing the slashes that surround a named COMMON block's name. This usually occurs because the programmer is used to writing DATA statements where the slashes occur at the end of the statement in the form:

   ```
   DATA list of variable names /list of values/
   ```

   In named COMMON the slashes occur in the middle of the statement in the form:

   ```
   COMMON /name/ list of variables
   ```

8.6 Chapter Summary

1. The general form of a subroutine is:

   ```
   SUBROUTINE name(list of arguments)
       argument and variable declarations
       other FORTRAN statements
   END
   ```

   The arguments of a subroutine are referred to as dummy *arguments*. A dummy argument may be an array name, a variable name, a function or subroutine name, or an asterisk (see Appendix E).

2. A subroutine is called using a CALL statement having the form:

   ```
   CALL subroutine-name(list of arguments)
   ```

   The arguments in the CALL statement are referred to as *actual arguments* and may be constants, variables, or expressions using combinations of constants and variables. The data type, number, and order of the actual arguments used in the CALL statement must agree with the data type, number, and order of the corresponding dummy arguments in the subroutine's argument list.

3. Every variable used in a program unit has a *scope,* which determines where in the program the variable can be used. The scope of all variables used within a subroutine is *local.* This means that the variable only has meaning within the subroutine in which it is declared (either explicitly or implicitly). If the same variable name is used in two different subroutines, two distinct variables are created.

4. The scope of a variable can be extended from one program unit to another through either argument lists or COMMON blocks. Both of these methods make a variable in one program unit available to another program unit.

5. Arrays are passed to subroutines by using the name of the array as an argument. Within the subroutine a formal argument must be specified for the passed array name.

6. Within a subroutine an array argument must be declared explicitly and must include the size of the dummy array. The size of the dummy argument may be specified as less than or equal to the size of the actual array being passed or may have an assumed size of (*).

7. A COMMON block is a block of memory locations that can be made available to any and all program units in which they are declared.

8. In unnamed COMMON, the common area is declared using the statement:

   ```
   COMMON list of variables
   ```

   The list of variables defines the variables that are to be included in the COMMON block. All program units using this common area must include a COMMON statement having the same number, type, and order of variables in their variable lists.

9. A named COMMON area is declared using the declaration statement:

   ```
   COMMON /name/ list of variables
   ```

   An individual variable cannot appear in more than one named COMMON block.

10. COMMON blocks and DATA statements initializing variables in the COMMON blocks may be collected together within a BLOCK DATA subprogram. This program unit has the general form:

    ```
    BLOCK DATA optional name
          variable declarations
          COMMON declarations
          DATA statements
          END
    ```

    A FORTRAN program can contain any number of named BLOCK DATA subprograms, but only one unnamed BLOCK DATA subprogram is permitted.

Data Files

Chapter Nine

The data for the programs we have seen so far has either been assigned internally within the programs or entered interactively during program execution. In this chapter we learn how to store data outside of a program. This external data storage permits a program to use the data without having to recreate it each time the program is run. Additionally, it provides the basis for sharing data between programs, so that the data output by one program can be input directly to another program.

Any collection of data that is stored together under a common name on a storage medium other than the computer's main memory is called a *data file*. Typically, data files are stored on floppy diskettes, hard disks, or magnetic tapes. This chapter describes the FORTRAN statements needed to create data files, to write data to them, and to read the data from them.

9.1 Creating and Using List-Directed Data Files

A data file is physically stored by a computer using a unique file name. Typically, most computers require that the file name consist of no more than eight characters followed by an optional period and an extension of up to three characters. (This convention has been adopted by most computer systems; however, the maximum number of characters allowed for a file name is system dependent.) Using this convention, the following are all valid computer data file names:

```
MATH.DAT          DJAVG.STK          RECORDS
INFOR.DAT         EXPER1.DAT         RESULTS.MEM
```

Computer data file names should be chosen to indicate the file's information content. For data files the first eight characters typically are used to describe the data, and the three characters after the decimal point either are used to describe the application or are set equal to DAT to indicate a data file. For example, the file name EXPER1.DAT could be used for a file of data pertaining to experiment number 1. Similarly, the filename DJAVG.STK could be used for Dow Jones averages required in a stock-related program.

Within a FORTRAN program a file is always referenced using a unit number rather than the file's actual name. The unit number is a programmer-selected positive integer that corresponds to the file's computer name. The correspondence between unit number and computer file name is assigned by an OPEN statement.

An OPEN statement is an executable statement that performs two tasks. First, it physically opens a data file for use by a program. Second, opening a file equates the data file's name to the integer unit number used by the program to reference the file. The simplest form of the OPEN statement that accomplishes these tasks is:

```
OPEN(unit number, FILE = filename)
```

The keyword OPEN and the parentheses are required and identify this as an OPEN statement. As indicated, the OPEN statement requires a user-selected unit number, which is either a constant or an integer expression that evaluates to a number between 1 and 63, and the name of the data file assigned to this unit number. The file name can either be a character constant, in which case it must be enclosed in apostrophes, or a character variable. For example, the statement:

```
OPEN(1,FILE = 'EXPER1.DAT')
```

opens a file named EXPER1.DAT and assigns this to unit number one. The number 1 is a programmer-selected value for the file and represents how the file is referenced within the FORTRAN program containing the OPEN statement.

As an executable statement, an OPEN statement can be placed anywhere within a program unit after the unit's declaration statements. When the computer encounters an OPEN statement, it checks whether the file currently exists on the system. If a file having the indicated file name exists, the file is opened. If the file does not exist, a blank file having the indicated name is created.

Writing to a File

After a file is opened, data can be written to it using any WRITE statement that correctly references the file's unit number (the PRINT statement cannot be used because it implicitly references the system's standard output unit). The general form of a file WRITE statement is identical to the WRITE statement introduced in Section 2.4 and has the form:

> WRITE(*unit number*, *n*) *expression list*

For example, the statement:

    WRITE(1,*) WEIGHT, FACTOR, BALNCE

causes the values of the variables WEIGHT, FACTOR, and BALNCE to be written to a file previously opened as unit number 1. The asterisk in this WRITE statement indicates that values will be written using the system's list-directed default format. Similarly, the statement:

    WRITE(1,15) WEIGHT, FACTOR, BALNCE

causes these same three variable values to be written to file number 1 using the format specified in FORMAT statement 15.

Notice that these file WRITE statements are used in the same manner as a WRITE statement used to display values on the system's standard output device, with the replacement of the standard output unit number with the file's unit number. The file unit number directs the output to a specific file instead of to the standard display device. Program 9-1 illustrates the use of an OPEN statement and two subsequent WRITE statements for writing data to an opened file.

 Program 9-1

```
PROGRAM MAIN
    REAL WEIGHT, SLOPE, MASS
    DATA WEIGHT, SLOPE, FACTOR/165.0,7.5,2.0625/
    OPEN(1,FILE = 'TEST.DAT')
    WRITE(1,*) WEIGHT
    WRITE(1,*) SLOPE, FACTOR
    END
```

When Program 9-1 is executed, a file named TEST.DAT is created by the computer. After the file is opened, two WRITE statements are used to write two lines to the TEST.DAT file. Formally, each line in a file is referred to as a record, when a record consists of one or more data items. Thus the file produced by this program consists of the following two records:

```
165.000000
  7.500000        2.062500
```

The WRITE statements in Program 9-1 use the system's list-directed format, designated by the asterisk before the closing parentheses, to write values into the file. If an explicit user-selected format is desired, the asterisk must be replaced by either a FORMAT statement label or a format character string contained within apostrophes (see Section 9.2).

As illustrated in Program 9-1, writing to a file is essentially the same as writing to the standard output device, except for the explicit designation of the file's unit number in the WRITE statement. This means that all of the techniques you have learned for creating standard output displays apply to file writes as well. For example, Program 9-2 illustrates storing data from an array into a file opened as unit number 3.

 Program 9-2

```
PROGRAM MAIN
    INTEGER I
    REAL RESULT(5)
    DATA RESULT/16.25,17.0,15.75,18.0,19.5/
    OPEN(3,FILE = 'EXPER.DAT')
    DO 10 I = 1,5
      WRITE(3,*) I, RESULT(I)
10  CONTINUE
    CLOSE(3)
    END
```

When Program 9-2 is executed, a file named EXPER.DAT is opened by the computer (if the file does not exist, it is automatically created). After the file is opened, a DO loop is used to write five records to the file, with each record containing two items. The file produced by this program consists of the following five records:

```
1        16.250000
2        17.000000
3        15.750000
4        18.000000
5        19.500000
```

Closing a File

A CLOSE statement is included in Program 9-2. This statement is used to formally break the link established by the OPEN statement and releases the unit number, which can then be used for another file. The simplest form of this statement is:

```
CLOSE(n)
```

where n is the unit number assigned to the data file when it was opened. Since all computers have a limit on the maximum number of files that can be open at one time, closing files that are no longer needed makes good sense. In the absence of a specific CLOSE statement, as in Program 9-1, any open files existing at the end of normal program execution are automatically closed by the operating system.

When a file is closed, a special end-of-file (EOF) marker is automatically placed by the operating system as the last character in the file. The EOF character has a unique numerical code that has no equivalent representation as a printable character. This special numerical value, which is system dependent, ensures that the EOF character can never be confused with a valid character contained within the file. As we will see shortly, this EOF character can be used as a sentinel when reading data from a file.

Reading a File

Once a file has been created and written to, READ statements can be used to read data from the file. Reading data from a file is almost identical to reading data from a standard keyboard, with the addition of an explicit file unit number to indicate from where the data is coming. For example, the statement:

```
READ(3,*) A,B,C
```

causes three values to be read from file 3 using the system's list-directed format, while the statement:

```
READ(3,10) A,B,C
```

causes values to be read into the variables A, B, and C using FORMAT statement 10.

The format designated for reading data from a file requires that the programmer know how the data was originally written to the file. This is necessary for correct "stripping" of the data from the file into appropriate variables for storage. Thus, for example, if list-directed formatting was used in writing a file, list-directed format-ting would be used for reading the file. Program 9-3 illustrates this by using a list-directed READ statement to read the data in the EXPER.DAT file created by Program 9-2.

 Program 9-3

```
PROGRAM MAIN
  INTEGER I, N
  REAL VAL
  OPEN(3,FILE = 'EXPER.DAT')
  DO 10 I = 1,5
    READ(3,*) N, VAL
    PRINT *, N, VAL
10  CONTINUE
  CLOSE(3)
  END
```

Program 9-3 reads five records from the EXPER.DAT file. Each time the file is read, an integer and a real value are input to the program. The display produced by Program 9-3 is:

```
1          16.250000
2          17.000000
3          15.750000
4          18.000000
5          19.500000
```

In addition to using a DO loop to read a specific number of lines, as is done in Program 9-3, the EOF marker appended to each file can be used as sentinel value. When the EOF marker is used in this manner, the following algorithm can be used to read and display each line of the file:

While not end-of-file
  Read a line

To implement this WHILE loop, FORTRAN provides an option to the READ statement that detects when the EOF marker has been reached. This option is activated by including the phrase END = *statement number* after the format specifier in the READ statement. For example, the statement:

```
READ(3,*,END = 10) I, VAL
```

will read values for I and VAL *unless* the end of file has been reached, in which case control is transferred to statement number 10. Program 9-4 uses the END option to read the EXPER.DAT file previously read in Program 9-3.

 Program 9-4

```
     PROGRAM MAIN
      INTEGER I
      REAL VAL
      OPEN(3,FILE = 'EXPER.DAT')
5     READ(3,*,END = 10) I, VAL
        PRINT *, I, VAL
        GO TO 5
10    CONTINUE
      CLOSE(3)
      END
```

The output produced by Program 9-4 is identical to that produced by Program 9-3. The WHILE loop used in Program 9-4 to produce this output consists of the code:

```
5       READ(3,*,END = 10) I, VAL
          PRINT *, I, VAL
          GO TO 5
10      CONTINUE
```

Here the READ statement will read a value for I and VAL unless the end of file has been reached. Thus, when the READ statement is first executed, record one of the file is read and immediately displayed by the PRINT statement. The GO TO statement then transfers control back to the READ statement for another trip through the loop. When the EOF marker is detected by the READ statement, which occurs after the fifth line has been read and displayed, control is transferred to statement 10, which terminates the loop. The WHILE loop illustrated in Program 9-4 is extremely useful whenever the total number of lines in a file is either not known or subject to change.

A few general comments are in order in reference to the file-handling programs we have used. Any attempt to read a newly created blank file always results in a runtime error message. More troublesome is an attempt to write to an existing file containing data. Writing to an existing file automatically erases all existing records after the written record. This means that if a write is made to an existing file before any reads are made, all of the information in the file is effectively erased. This occurs because the first line written to a newly opened file is, by default, written at the start of the file. These constraints on reading and writing to a file are a result of the defaults assumed by the OPEN statement we have been using. In Section 9.4 these default settings are described in detail, and options for overriding them are presented.

Rewinding and Backspacing

The data files we have created have all been sequential files. The term *sequential* refers both to the placement of data in the file and to the method in which these data are subsequently accessed. In *sequential access* the data is read and written in a sequential manner. This means that data items are read and written one after another, in order, with no skipping or jumping over items. Thus, for example, to read the fifth value in a sequential access file, the previous four values must be read first.

The position in a file of the next item to be read or written is maintained by a system file pointer, which is created automatically by the computer system and set to the start of the file whenever a file is opened. Reading from a file does not alter the values in the file, but each time an item is read, the computer's internal file pointer is moved to the next item in the file. Similarly, each time a value is written to a file, the file pointer is updated.

The FORTRAN statements, BACKSPACE and REWIND can be used to alter the normal sequential access to a file. The REWIND statement resets the current position to the start of the file. REWIND requires the file's unit number as its only argument. For example, the statement:

```
REWIND(1)
```

resets file number 1 to the start of the file. A REWIND is done automatically each time a file is opened.

The BACKSPACE statement allows the programmer to move the computer's internal file pointer back one record. For example, if a file has been opened, and three records of the file have been read or written to, the file pointer is automatically incremented and points to record 4. This is the next record to be read or written. If a BACKSPACE statement is executed, the internal file pointer is decremented and points to record 3. A second BACKSPACE decrements the file pointer to record 2, and so on. Once the file pointer is set to the first record in the file, either by opening the file, by using a REWIND statement, or by using a BACKSPACE statement, a subsequent BACKSPACE statement has no effect. Program 9-5 illustrates the use of the REWIND and BACKSPACE statements.

 Program 9-5

```
PROGRAM MAIN
  INTEGER N
  REAL VAL
  OPEN(1,FILE = 'EXPER.DAT')
  DO 10 I = 1,3
    READ (1,*) N, VAL
10    CONTINUE
  READ (1,*) N, VAL
  PRINT *, N, VAL
  BACKSPACE(1)
  BACKSPACE(1)
  READ (1,*) N,VAL
  PRINT *, N, VAL
  REWIND(1)
  READ (1,*) N, VAL
  PRINT *, N, VAL
  CLOSE(1)
  END
```

Assuming the file EXPER.DAT contains the following data:

```
1          16.250000
2          17.000000
3          15.750000
4          18.000000
5          19.500000
```

The output of Program 9-5 is:

```
4          18.000000
3          15.750000
1          16.250000
```

This output is produced as follows: the DO loop in Program 9-5 causes the first three records in the file to be read. Upon completion of the DO loop the computer's internal file pointer points to the fourth record in the file. The READ statement immediately after the DO loop reads this record, which is then displayed by the next PRINT statement. The computer's internal file pointer now points to the fifth record. The first BACKSPACE statement then moves the file pointer back to the start of the fourth record, and the second BACKSPACE sets the pointer to the start of the third record. This record is then read and displayed. The REWIND statement then sets the file pointer to the start of the file. The final READ statement reads this first record, which is then displayed by the final PRINT statement.

Physical Device Files

The unit numbers we have used are called logical unit numbers. A *logical unit number* is one that references a file of logically related data that has been saved under a common name, that is, a data file. In addition to logical unit numbers, FORTRAN also supports physical unit numbers. A *physical unit number* references a hardware device such as a keyboard, screen, or printer.

As we have already seen, the physical device assigned to your program for data entry is formally called the standard input file. Usually this is a keyboard. When a program is run, this standard input device is automatically opened and assigned a unit number, usually either 1 or 5. Similarly, the output device used for display is also automatically opened and assigned a unit number, usually either 1 or 6. These unit numbers are always available for programmer use without the need for a formal OPEN statement.

In addition to the standard input and output devices, other devices can be used for input or output if the name assigned to them by the system is known. For example, on most IBM and IBM-compatible personal computers, a video screen is the standard output device. Frequently, however, an application requires that a report or graph be displayed on the printer.

Since the IBM personal computer operating system (DOS) assigns the names PRN and LPT1 to the printer, these names can be used within an OPEN statement to connect the printer to a FORTRAN program. For example, the statement OPEN(1, FILE = 'PRN') makes the printer available for direct output from the program as file number 1. Any subsequent WRITE statement of the form WRITE(1, k) will cause its display to be sent to the printer. As always, the value of k determines the format of the output: if k is an integer number between 1 and 99999, it references a user-determined FORMAT statement; if k is an asterisk (*), list-directed output is selected for the display.

Exercises

1. Using the reference manuals provided with your computer's operating system, determine:

   a. the maximum number of characters that can be used to name a file for storage by the computer system

   b. the maximum number of data files that can be open at the same time

   c. the file numbers that are reserved by the computer system and the file numbers that are available for programmer use

2. Would it be appropriate to call a saved FORTRAN program a file? Why or why not?

3. Write individual OPEN statements to link the following data file names to the corresponding unit numbers:

External name	Unit number
MATH.DAT	2
BOOK.DAT	3
RESIST.DAT	4
EXPER2.DAT	7
PRICES.DAT	8
RATES.MEM	9

4. Write CLOSE statements for each of the files opened in Exercise 3.

5a. Write a FORTRAN program that stores the following numbers into a file named RESULT.DAT: 16.25, 18.96, 22.34, 18.94, 17.42, 22.63.

   b. Write a FORTRAN program to read the data in the RESULT.DAT file created in Exercise 5a and display the data. Additionally, it should compute and display the sum and average of the data. Using a hand calculation, check the sum and average displayed by your program.

6a. Write a FORTRAN program that prompts the user to enter five numbers. As each number is entered, the program should write the number into a file named USER.DAT.

   b. Write a FORTRAN program that reads the data in the USER.DAT file created in Exercise 6a and displays each individual data item.

7a. Create a file containing the following car numbers, number of miles driven, and numbers of gallons of gas used by each car:

Car no.	Miles driven	Gallons used
54	250	19
62	525	38
71	123	6
85	1322	86
97	235	14

   b. Write a FORTRAN program that reads the data in the file created in Exercise 7a and displays the car number, miles driven, gallons used, and miles per gallon for each car. The output should additionally display the total miles driven, total gallons used, and average miles per gallon for all the cars. These totals should be displayed at the end of the output report.

8a. Create a data file containing the following part numbers, opening balances, numbers of items sold, and minimum stocks required:

Part number	Initial amount	Quantity sold	Minimum amount
310	95	47	50
145	320	162	20
514	34	20	25
212	163	150	160

b. Write a FORTRAN program to create an inventory report based on the data in the file created in Exercise 8a. The display should consist of the part number, the current balance, and the amount necessary to bring the inventory to the minimum level.

9a. Create a file containing the following data:

Identification number	Rate	Hours
10031	6.00	40
10067	5.00	48
10083	6.50	35
10095	8.00	50

b. Write a FORTRAN program that uses the information contained in the file created in Exercise 9a to produce the following pay report:

```
ID no.    Rate    Hours    Regular pay    Overtime pay    Gross pay
```

Any hours worked above 40 hours are paid at time and a half. The program should display the totals of the regular, overtime, and gross pay columns.

10a. Store the following data in a file:

```
5 96 87 78 93 21 4 92 82 85 87 6 72 69 85 75 81 73
```

b. The data is arranged in the file so that each group of numbers is preceded by the number of data items in the group. Thus, the first number in the file, 5, indicates that the next five numbers should be grouped together. The number 4 indicates that the following four numbers are a group, and the 6 indicates that the last six numbers are a group. (*Hint:* Use a nested loop. The outer loop should be executed three times.)

Write a FORTRAN program to calculate and display the average of each group of numbers in the file created in Exercise 10a.

11. Enter and execute Program 9-2 so that the EXPER.DAT file created by this program exists on your computer system. Then, using the BACKSPACE statement, write a FORTRAN program that reads and displays the contents of the EXPER.DAT file in reverse line order.

12. Rotech Systems is a distributor of high-speed memory devices for specialized computer applications. Each memory device in stock is stored by its tolerance, where lower tolerance devices are sold at a premium and used for more critical applications that require a tighter tolerance. Having just completed an annual check of inventory in stock, Rotech has found it has the following quantities of memory devices in stock:

Device number	5% tolerance	2% tolerance	1% tolerance
4016	464	612	129
4314	742	1215	375
4311	517	820	298
4364	684	105	22
4464	771	200	358

Rotech wants a report based on this data showing how many devices should be ordered to ensure that it has at least 800 of each item in stock. Your first task is to create a file containing this inventory data. Each record in the file should consist of a device number and the three inventory levels for that part number. When the file has been created, use it in a program that reads the data into a two dimension array, searches the array, and prints a report listing the amount of each item that must be ordered.

13a. Write a FORTRAN program that uses either the random number generator described in Section 7.4 or one supplied by your computer system to select 1000 random numbers having values between 1 and 100. As each number is selected, it should be written to a file called NUMBER.

b. Using the NUMBER file created in Exercise 13a, write a FORTRAN program that reads the data in the file, computes the average of the 1000 data items, and writes a new file consisting of all values that are 10 percent above or below the calculated average.

14. Instead of using an actual file name in an OPEN statement, a character variable can be used instead. For example, the statement:

```
OPEN (7, FILE = FNAME)
```

equates unit number 7 to the file name assigned to the variable FNAME. Here the variable FNAME must be declared as a character variable of sufficient length to hold a valid file name. The following code illustrates how this OPEN statement could be used in practice:

```
PROGRAM MAIN
   CHARACTER*12 FNAME
   PRINT *, 'ENTER A FILE NAME: '
   READ (*,'(A)') FNAME
   OPEN (7,FILE = FNAME)
```

The variable declaration statement in this code creates a character variable named FNAME having a length of 12 characters. This length was chosen because it is large enough to hold an actual file name consisting of 8 initial characters, a period, and 3 extension characters. The code then requests that the file name be entered by the user. The entered name is stored in the character variable FNAME, which then is used by the OPEN statement. (*Note:* The entered name does not have to be enclosed in single quotes because user-formatting is used by the READ statement. If the list-directed statement READ *, FNAME were used, the entered name would have to be enclosed in single quotes.)

a. Using this code, rewrite Program 9-2 so that the name of the data file is entered when the program is executed.

b. Modify the READ statement used in the program written for Exercise 14a so that it references a FORMAT statement rather than including the format directly within the READ statement.

c. Modify the program written for Exercise 14a so that the data file name is requested and returned using a subroutine.

In addition to the list-directed format we have been using for writing and reading file data, explicit user-designated formats may also be used. In this section we present the user-formatted READ and WRITE statements as they relate to data files.

Writing Formatted Files

The WRITE statement required to produce a user-formatted data file is identical to the WRITE statement used to produce user-formatted standard display output. As presented in Sections 2.4 and 9.1, the general form of this statement is:

```
WRITE(unit number, format specifier) expression list
```

For writing to a file, the unit number in the WRITE statement must be either an integer number designating a previously opened file or an integer expression that evaluates to a valid integer file number. The format specifier designates the specific placement of the data written to the file. Acceptable format specifiers for file writes are the same as those for writing to the standard output device. These include:

1. an asterisk, which specifies a list-directed format
2. the statement number of a FORMAT statement
3. a literal format control character constant enclosed in parentheses that are themselves contained within apostrophes

For user-selected formatting the last two options are used. For example, the statement:

```
WRITE(1,15) VALUE, SLOPE, NUMBER
```

references FORMAT statement 15, and the statement:

```
WRITE(1,'(I4,1X,I3,2X,I3)') VALUE, SLOPE, NUMBER
```

includes a literal format character constant directly within the WRITE statement. The format specifications for writing to a file are identical to the format specifications described in Section 2.4 for standard output units. It is the unit number in the WRITE statement that directs the formatted output to a disk or tape unit rather than to the standard output unit. There is one difference, however, in sending data to a disk or tape unit rather than to a display unit such as a video screen or printer: disk and tape units cannot respond to the carriage control characters required by video screens and printers. Thus, a carriage control character must not be included in a data file format specification. The creation of a user-formatted file using a formatted WRITE statement is illustrated in Program 9-6.

Program 9-6 uses the format specification 5X,I2,3X,F5.2 contained in FORMAT statement 20 for writing an integer and a real value to each record in the TEST.DAT file. This format specifies that each record written will include a blank field of five spaces (note that the first space is not taken as a carriage control character), followed by an integer placed in a field consisting of two spaces, followed by a blank field of three spaces, followed by a real value with two decimal positions to the right of its decimal point placed within a field width of five spaces. The file produced by

Program 9-6

```
PROGRAM MAIN
   INTEGER I
   REAL RESULT(5)
   DATA RESULT/26.5,18.0,44.75,33.25,52.0/
   OPEN(1,FILE='TEST.DAT')
   DO 10 I = 1,5
      WRITE(1,20) I, RESULT(I)
10    CONTINUE
20    FORMAT(5X,I2,3X,F5.2)
   END
```

Program 9-6 is illustrated in Figure 9-1. The italicized numbers in the figure indicate the column position occupied by each data item.

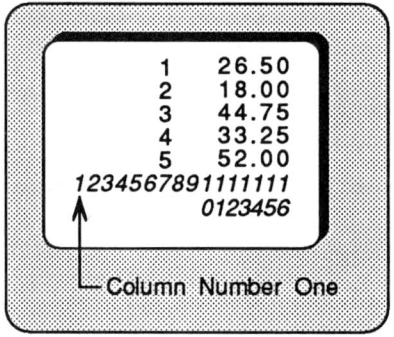

Figure 9-1 The Structure of the TEST.DAT **File**

The Complete WRITE Statement

The WRITE statement we have been using for output is an abbreviated form of the more complete WRITE statement:

```
WRITE(UNIT=u, FMT=fmt, IOSTAT=var, ERR=stl) expression list
```

where *u* and *fmt* are a unit number and a format specifier, respectively. The terms UNIT, FMT, IOSTAT and ERR are optional keywords that may be placed in any order within the parentheses; *var* is a user-specified integer variable; and *stl* is a user-specified statement label (blank spaces may be used freely within the parentheses). If the keyword UNIT is not explicitly included in the statement, the unit number must be the first item in parentheses. If the FMT keyword is omitted, the format specifier must be the second item in the list, and the keyword UNIT must also be omitted.

If the IOSTAT keyword is present, it must be followed by an equal sign and an integer variable name (scalar or array element). The value assigned to the variable depends on the output status produced by the WRITE statement. The value assigned to the integer variable is zero if the WRITE statement executed without an error or a positive value if an error was encountered (the actual positive value assigned to the variable is compiler dependent). The value assigned to the variable may be displayed using either a PRINT or a WRITE statement. For example, the sequence of statements:

```
WRITE(6, 20, IOSTAT=IVAL) A, B, C
PRINT *, 'IVAL = ', IVAL
```

will output the values of the variables A, B, and C to file number 6 using format statement 20 and assign an I/O status value to the variable IVAL. The value of IVAL is then displayed on the standard output unit using a PRINT statement.

The ERR option specifies a statement label to which control is transferred if any error condition is encountered during the WRITE. If the ERR option is omitted and an output error does occur, a runtime error will be produced.

Formatted READ Statements

Both user-formatted and list-directed input from a file require a READ statement that permits designation of the file's unit number. As previously described in Section 3.3, the most commonly used form of this statement is:

```
READ(unit, fmt) variable list
```

where *unit* is a file unit number, and *fmt* is a format specifier. The unit number, as always, designates the unit supplying the data. For data files the unit number must be either an integer number corresponding to an open file or an integer expression yielding such an integer. Just as in the WRITE statement, the *fmt* contained in the READ statement can be either:

1. an asterisk, which specifies a list-directed format
2. the statement number of a FORMAT statement
3. a literal format control character constant enclosed in parentheses that are themselves contained within apostrophes

List-directed input, as we have seen, is especially convenient for keyboard input of numerical values because it recognizes spaces and commas as data separators. User-formatted input is typically used for reading data files where the format is the same for every line in the file. For example, assume that the variables NUM1 and NUM2 have been declared as integers. Then, the statement:

```
READ(2,10) NUM1,NUM2
```

specifies that two integers are to be read from file number 2 using the format defined in FORMAT statement 10. For purposes of illustration, assume the following FORMAT statement:

```
10 FORMAT(I2,3X,I4)
```

This FORMAT statement specifies that the input record consists of two integer fields separated by three spaces. The first integer must occupy columns 1 and 2 of the record, and the second, columns 6 through 9. This format requires that the data in the file conform exactly to the fields specified. For example, consider the sequence of statements:

```
      INTEGER NUM1, NUM2
      OPEN(2,FILE='TEST.DAT')
      READ (2,10) NUM1, NUM2
   10 FORMAT(I2,3X,I4)
```

If the data stored in the TEST.DAT file is:

```
   45  6732         ←—— data in the file
   123456789        ←—— column number
```

the value 45 is assigned to the variable NUM1, and the value 732 is assigned to NUM2. If, however, the data in the file is:

```
   4   673 2        ←—— data in the file
   123456789        ←—— column number
```

the number 4 is assigned to NUM1, and the number 732 is assigned to NUM2. Note that this assumes blanks embedded in each field are effectively ignored. (Some compilers are configured to interpret blank spaces as zeros.)

The format specifications for reading integer, real, and character data and for skipping over designated input fields are the same as those used for writing these items previously described in Section 3.3.

The Complete Formatted READ Statement

The READ statement we have used for inputting data from a file is an abbreviated form of the more complete READ statement:

```
READ(UNIT=u, FMT=fmt, IOSTAT=var, ERR=st1, END=st2) variable list
```

where u and *fmt* are a unit number and a format specifier, respectively. The words UNIT, FMT, IOSTAT, ERR, and END are optional keywords that may be placed in any order within the parentheses; *var* is a user-selected integer variable (scalar or subscripted); and *st1* and *st2* are statement labels (blank spaces may be used freely within the parentheses and have no effect on the statement). If the keyword UNIT is not explicitly included in the statement, the unit number must be the first item in parentheses. If the FMT keyword is omitted, the format specifier must be the second item in the list, and the keyword UNIT must also be omitted. The IOSTAT, ERR, and END keywords provide optional error recovery from specific exceptional conditions.

If the IOSTAT keyword is present, it must be followed by an equal sign and an integer scalar or array variable. The value assigned to the variable depends on the I/O status produced by the READ statement. The value assigned to the integer variable is zero if the READ statement executed without an error, a negative value if an end of file was detected, and a positive value for any other detected error condition. The actual value assigned to the variable (not the signs, which are defined by the FORTRAN 77 standard) are compiler dependent and may be displayed using either a PRINT or a WRITE statement. Thus, the sequence of statements:

```
READ(2, 30, IOSTAT=IVAL) A, B, C
PRINT *, 'IVAL = ', IVAL
```

will input three values from file number 2 into the variables A, B, and C and will assign an I/O status value to the variable IVAL. The value of IVAL is then displayed on the standard output unit using a PRINT statement.

The ERR option specifies a statement label to which control is transferred if any error condition is encountered except an end of file, while the END option specifies a statement label for transfer of control when the end of the file is detected. The statement labels specified by the ERR and END options can be the same. If the ERR option is omitted, an input error will produce a runtime error. The specifics of the END option were presented in Section 9.1 in connection with list-directed input of data files.

Of the three options provided by the READ statement, the END option is the most useful because it permits the construction of a WHILE loop to continuously read data from a file until the end of the file is reached. The general form of this loop is:

```
n  READ(unit  number,  fmt,  END = k)  variable  list.
                         .
                         .
                         .
          any  other  statements  in  here
                         .
                         .
                         .
       GO  TO  n
k this  statement  is  executed  when  the  file  has  no  more  data
```

Notice that the GO TO statement transfers control back to the READ statement. Until the end of file has been reached, the READ statement executes as if the END option were not present. When the end of the file is encountered, the END option transfers control to statement k. Program 9-7 illustrates this loop for reading the TEST.DAT file previously produced by Program 9-6 (see Figure 9-1).

Program 9-7

```
PROGRAM MAIN
    INTEGER I
    REAL RESULT
5   FORMAT (5X, I2, 3X, F5.2)
    OPEN (1, FILE='TEST.DAT')
    PRINT *, ' EXPERIMENT'
    PRINT *, ' NUMBER       RESULT'
    PRINT *, ' ------------------------'
10  READ (1, 5, END=20) I, RESULT
      PRINT *, I, RESULT
    GO TO 10
20  END
```

The output produced by Program 9-7 is:

```
EXPERIMENT
NUMBER        RESULT
------------------------
    1         26.500000
    2         18.000000
    3         44.750000
    4         33.250000
    5         52.000000
```

Exercises

1. List the starting and ending column numbers for all input fields defined by the following statements:

   a. 10 FORMAT(I2,F6.3,I4)
   b. 20 FORMAT(F7.2,I2,A6)
   c. 30 FORMAT(5X,F5.2,7X,A25)
   d. 40 FORMAT(3(2X,I4))
   e. 60 FORMAT(6X,I2,3X,F6.2,3(3X,I2))

2. The following is a valid FORTRAN program.

```
PROGRAM MAIN
    INTEGER NUM1, NUM2 OPEN (3, 'TEST.DAT')
    READ (3,10) NUM1, NUM2
10  FORMAT (I4, I3)
    PRINT *, NUM1, NUM2
    END
```

Assume that the following data is stored in the file named TEST.DAT:

```
1 23 45
1234567
↑
Column number 1
```

Determine the output produced by the program.

3a. The following is a valid FORTRAN program:

```
PROGRAM MAIN
    INTEGER NUM1, NUM2, I
    OPEN (3, 'TEST.DAT')
    DO 20 I = 1,4
        READ(3,30) NUM1, NUM2
        PRINT *, NUM1, NUM2
20      CONTINUE
30      FORMAT(1X,F7.2,2X,F5.2)
    END
```

Determine the output produced by this program, assuming that the following data are stored in the file named TEST.DAT:

```
    6.78     23.4
    6.78     23.4
          678     345
  678            234
  123456789111111
            012345
  ↑
  Column number 1
```

b. Verify your answers for Exercise 3a by first creating the TEST.DAT file given in the problem and then running the listed program. (You may create TEST.DAT either by using an editor or by writing a FORTRAN program that reads the data from the keyboard and writes it to the file.) Using the display produced by your program, determine whether your compiler ignores blank spaces within an input field or considers them as zeros.

c. Rewrite the program listed in Exercise 3a using the END option of the READ statement to replace the DO loop with a DO-WHILE structure.

4. Determine the output produced by the following program:

```
PROGRAM MAIN
    INTEGER NUM1, NUM2
    OPEN(1,FILE='TEST.DAT')
    NUM1 = 45
    NUM2 = 67
    NUM3 = 32
    WRITE(1,5) NUM1, NUM2, NUM3
5       FORMAT(3(1X,I2))
    REWIND(1)
    READ(1,10)NUM1, NUM2
10      FORMAT(1X,I2,1X,I4)
    PRINT *, NUM1, NUM2
    END
```

5. Determine if the following program will work. Discuss what should be changed in the program, if anything.

```
PROGRAM MAIN
   CHARACTER*8, MESSGE
   INTEGER NUM1, NUM2
   OPEN(2,FILE='RESULT.DAT')
   READ(2,10) MESSGE, NUM1, NUM2
   WRITE(6,10) MESSGE, NUM1, NUM2
10    FORMAT(1X,A,2(1X,I3))
   END
```

6a. Rewrite Program 9-6 to include the format specification as a literal character constant directly within the WRITE statement.

b. Rewrite Program 9-6 using list-directed formatting for records written to the TEST.DAT file.

c. Rewrite Program 9-7 to input and display the data in the file produced by the program written for Exercise 6b.

7a. Write a FORTRAN program that writes the four real numbers 92.65, 88.72, 77.46, and 82.93 to a file named RESULT using the FORMAT statement:

```
10 FORMAT(4(1X,F5.2))
```

After writing the data to the file, your program should read the data from the file, determine the average of the four numbers read, and display the average.

b. Compile and run the program written for Exercise 7a. Additionally, verify the output produced by your program by manually calculating the average of the four input numbers.

8a. Using the FORMAT statement:

```
10 FORMAT(4(1X,F5.2))
```

write a FORTRAN program that creates a file named POINTS and writes the following numbers to the file:

```
6.3 8.2 18.25 24.32      ←——— 1st record
4.0 4.0 10.0 -5.0        ←——— 2nd record
-2.0 5.0 4.0 5.0         ←——— 3rd record
```

b. Using the data in the POINTS file created in Exercise 8a, write a FORTRAN program that reads each record and interprets the first and second numbers in each record as the coordinates of one point and the third and fourth numbers as the coordinates of a second point. Using the formulas given in Exercise 11 of Section 3.1, have your program compute and display the slope and midpoint of the two points entered. Your program should use the END option of the formatted READ statement.

c. Compile, run, and manually verify the output produced by the program written for Exercise 8b.

9a. Using the FORMAT statement:
```
10 FORMAT(4(I3,2X))
```

write a FORTRAN program that creates a file named GRADES and writes the following numbers to the file:

```
 100, 100, 100, 100
100,  0, 100,  0
86, 83, 89, 94
78, 59, 77, 85
89, 92, 81, 88
```

b. Using the data in the GRADES file created in Exercise 9a write, compile, and run a FORTRAN program that reads each record in the GRADES file, computes the average for each record, and displays the average.

10. Redo Exercise 12 of Section 9.1 using a formatted file. Your first task is to create a file containing the inventory data. Each line in the file should consist of a device number and the three inventory levels for that part number and should be written using the FORMAT statement:

```
10 FORMAT(I4,3(2X,I4))
```

After the file has been created, write, compile, and run a FORTRAN program that reads the date in the file into a two dimension array, searches the array, and prints a report listing the amount of each device that must be ordered.

9.3   Applications

Once a data file has been created, the majority of applications are concerned with updating the file's records to maintain currently accurate data.

In this section two such applications are presented. The first application uses a file as a data base for storing the 10 most recent pollen counts, which are used in the summer as allergy "irritability" measures. As a new reading is obtained, it is added to the file, and the oldest stored reading is deleted.

The second application presents an expanded file update procedure. In this application a file containing inventory data, consisting of book identification numbers and quantities in stock, is updated by information contained in a second file. This application requires that identification numbers in the two files be matched before a record is updated.

Application 1: Pollen Counts

Pollen count readings, which are taken from August through September in the northeastern region of the United States, measure the number of ragweed pollen grains in the air. Pollen counts in the range of 10 to 200 grains per cubic meter of air are typical during this time of year. Typically, pollen counts above 10 begin to affect a small percentage of hay fever sufferers, counts in the range of 30 to 40 will noticeably bother approximately 30 percent of hay fever sufferers, while counts between 40 and 50 adversely affect over 60 percent of all hay fever sufferers.

A program is to be written that updates a file containing the 10 most recent pollen counts. As a new count is obtained, it is to be added to the end of the file, and the oldest count is to be deleted from the file. (This type of data storage is formally referred to as a first-in first-out (FIFO) list, also called a *queue*. If the list is maintained in last-in first-out order, it is called a *stack*.) Additionally, the averages of the old and new files' data must be calculated and displayed. For purposes of illustration, assume that a file name POLLEN, containing the data shown in Figure 9-2, has already been created.

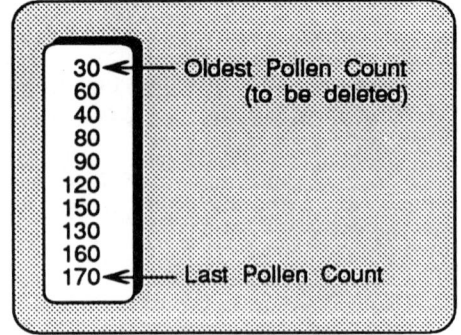

Figure 9-2   Data Currently in the POLLEN File

The pseudocode for the file update program is:

Display a message indicating what the program does
Request the name of the data file
Request a new pollen count reading
Open the data file
Do for ten data items
    Read a value into an array
    Add the value to a total
Enddo
Calculate and display the old ten-day average
Calculate and display the new ten-day average
Rewind the data file
Write the nine most recent pollen counts from the array to the file
Write the new pollen count to the file
Close the file

In reviewing this algorithm, notice that an array is used for temporarily storing the contents of the file. Thus, when the file is initially read, the first pollen count in the file is stored in the first array element, the second pollen count in the second array element, and so on, as illustrated on Figure 9-3. Once the data is "captured" in the array, the data file can be rewound and written over with the latest 10 counts. As further illustrated in Figure 9-3, the first 9 values written to the file are taken from array elements 2 through 10, respectively. Finally, the last count written to the file is the most recent value. Program 9-8 expresses this algorithm in FORTRAN.

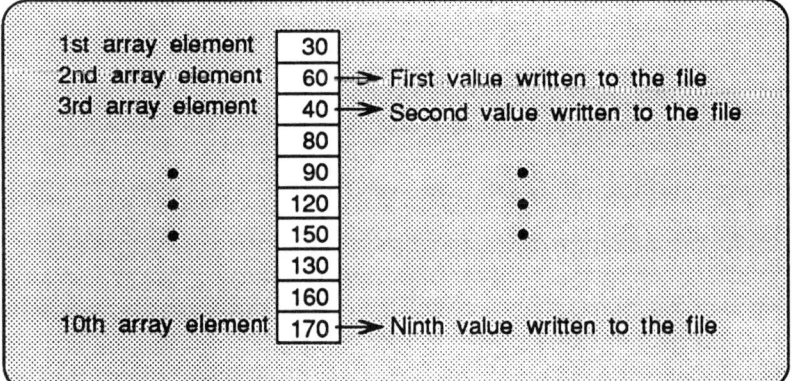

Figure 9-3   The Update Process

Program 9-8

```
      PROGRAM MAIN
        INTEGER A(10), NEWCNT, SUM, I
        CHARACTER*12 FNAME
***   GET THE DATA FILE NAME AND MOST RECENT POLLEN COUNT
        PRINT *,'          THIS PROGRAM UPDATES THE POLLEN COUNT FILE'
        PRINT *,'            AND CALCULATES TEN COUNT AVERAGES'
        PRINT *
        PRINT *, 'ENTER THE POLLEN COUNT FILE NAME (IN APOSTROPHES): '
        READ *, FNAME
        PRINT *, 'ENTER THE NEW POLLEN COUNT READING: '
        READ *, NEWCNT
***   OPEN THE FILE AND READ THE EXISTING DATA
        OPEN(1,FILE = FNAME)
        DO 5 I = 1,10
          READ(1,*) A(I)
          SUM = SUM + A(I)
    5     CONTINUE
***   COMPUTE AND DISPLAY OLD AND NEW AVERAGES
        PRINT *, '     THE OLD 10 COUNT AVERAGE IS: ', SUM/10
        SUM = SUM - A(1) + NEWCNT
        PRINT *, '     THE NEW 10 COUNT AVERAGE IS: ', SUM/10
***   WRITE UPDATED DATA TO THE FILE
        REWIND(1)
        DO 15 I = 1,9
          WRITE(1,*) A(I+1)
   15     CONTINUE
        WRITE(1,*) NEWCNT
        CLOSE(1)
        PRINT *
        PRINT *, ' AN UPDATED DATA FILE HAS BEEN WRITTEN'
        END
```

Following is a sample run using Program 9-8:

```
    THIS PROGRAM UPDATES THE POLLEN COUNT FILE
         AND CALCULATES TEN COUNT AVERAGES

ENTER THE POLLEN COUNT FILE NAME (IN APOSTROPHES):
'POLLEN'
ENTER THE NEW POLLEN COUNT READING:
200
     THE OLD 10 COUNT AVERAGE IS:          103
     THE NEW 10 COUNT AVERAGE IS:          120

AN UPDATED DATA FILE HAS BEEN WRITTEN
```

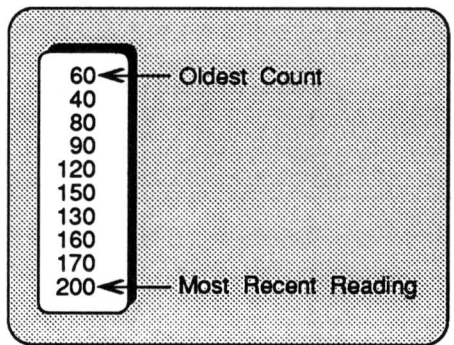

Figure 9-4   The Updated POLLEN File

The updated file created by Program 9-8 is illustrated in Figure 9-4. In reviewing the contents of this file, notice that the most current reading has been added to the end of the file and that the other counts are obtained from the original file shown in Figure 9-3, but moved up one position in the file.

Application 2: Master/Transaction File Update

A common form of file update occurs when the update data is itself contained in a file. Here, the file to be updated is referred to as a master file, and the file containing the update data is referred to as a transactions file.

As a specific example of this type of update, assume that the current master file, named OLDBK.MAS, contains the book identification numbers and quantities in stock illustrated in Table 9-1.

A transactions file, named BOOK.TRN, contains the quantities of each book bought, sold, or returned to stock each day. For purposes of illustration, assume that the BOOK.TRN file is sorted by ID number at the end of each month and contains the data illustrated in Table 9-2.

Notice in Table 9-2 that the date information is contained in apostrophes. The apostrophes are only necessary because the file will be read using a list-directed READ statement. If the file were read using a user-formatted READ statement, the apostrophes would not be required.

There are two methods of updating the master file once the transaction file has been created. The direct access method, where any record in the master file can be read, updated, and written back to the file directly, is presented in Section 9.5. For the type of files we have been using, each record in the file must be read in the order it is located in the file. Additionally, a record can only be written to the end of the file because writing a record automatically erases all records from that point to the end of the file. This constraint effectively prohibits updating a record within an existing file because an update, by definition, requires that an existing record be rewritten.

The solution to this problem is to use an update algorithm in which all records that need to be are updated at the same time, so that a completely new and updated master file is created when the update is completed. The key to creating this new updated master file is that the records in the transaction file be sorted by ID number to correspond to the order of ID numbers in the master file. Notice in Tables 9-1 and 9-2 that this is indeed the case for the data in the BOOK.TRN and OLDBK.MAS files.

Once the two files are in the same ID number order, the procedure for creating an updated master file consists of reading one master record from the existing master file and one record from the transaction file. If the ID numbers of the two records match, the transaction record's information is applied to the data in the master record, and another transaction record is read. As long as the transaction record's ID number matches the master record's ID number, the update of the master record continues. When the transaction record's ID number does not match the master record's ID number, indicating that there is no further update data to be applied to the master record, an updated record is written to the new master file. Let's see how this procedure works with the two files shown in Tables 9-1 and 9-2.

Table 9-1 Data Contained in the OLDBK.MAS File

Book ID no.	Quantity in stock
125	98
289	222
341	675
467	152
589	34
622	125

Table 9-2 Data Contained in the Transaction File Named BOOK.TRN

ID no.	Date	Sold	Returned	Bought
289	' 1/10/90'	125	34	50
341	' 1/10/90'	300	52	0
467	' 1/15/90'	50	20	200
467	' 1/20/90'	225	0	160
589	' 1/31/90'	75	10	55

The first record read from the master file has ID number 125, while the first transaction record has ID number 289. Since the ID numbers do not match, the update of this first master record is complete (in this case, there is no update information), and the existing master record is written, without modification, to the new master file. Then the next master record, which has an ID number of 289, is read. Since this ID number matches the transaction ID number, the inventory balance for book number 289 is updated, yielding a new balance of 181 books. Because the transaction file can contain multiple update records for the same ID number (notice the two records for ID number 467), the next transaction record is read and checked before writing an updated record to the new master file. Since the ID number of the next transaction record is not 289, the update of this book number is complete, and an updated master record is written to the new master file.

This algorithm continues, record by record, until the last master record has been updated. Should the end of the transaction file be encountered before the last master record is read from the existing master file, the remaining records in the existing master file are written directly to the new master file with no need to check for update information.

Since this update procedure uses two master files, a notation must be established to clearly distinguish between them. By convention, the existing master file is always referred to as the old master file, and the updated master file is called the new master file. Using these terms, the pseudocode description of the update procedure is:

Open the old master file
Open the transaction file
Open the new master file (initially blank)
Read the first old master record
Do for all records in the transaction file
  Read a transaction record
  While the transaction ID does not match the old master ID
    Write an updated master record to the new master file
    Read the next master record
  Endwhile
  If the ID numbers do match
    Calculate a new balance
Enddo
*** *To get here the last transaction record has just been read*
Write the last updated master to the new master file
While there are any remaining records in the old master file
  Read an old master record
  Write a new master record
Endwhile
Close all files

In FORTRAN, this update procedure is described by Program 9-9.

Program 9-9

```
        PROGRAM MAIN
          INTEGER IDM, IDT, BAL, SOLD, RETURN, BOUGHT
          CHARACTER*8 DATE
          OPEN(1,FILE = 'OLDBK.MAS')
          OPEN(2,FILE = 'BOOK.TRN')
          OPEN(3,FILE = 'NEWBK.MAS')
          READ(1,*) IDM, BAL
   10     READ(2,*, END = 20) IDT,DATE,SOLD,RETURN,BOUGHT
***    IF NO MATCH KEEP WRITING AND READING THE MASTER FILE
   15       IF(IDT .GT. IDM) THEN
               WRITE(3,*) IDM, BAL
               READ(1,*) IDM, BAL
               GO TO 15
            ENDIF
***    UPDATE THE MASTER AND GET ANOTHER TRANSACTION
            BAL = BAL + BOUGHT - SOLD + RETURN
            GO TO 10
***    WRITE THE LAST UPDATED MASTER
   20     WRITE(3,*) IDM, BAL
***    WRITE THE REMAINING OLD MASTER FILE TO THE NEW FILE
   25     READ(1,*,END = 30) IDM, BAL
            WRITE(3,*) IDM, BAL
            GO TO 25
   30     PRINT *, '...FILE UPDATE COMPLETE...'
          END
```

The new master file created by Program 9-9 is:

```
125        98
289       181
341       427
467       257
589        24
622       125
```

Additional File Exercises

---

1. Write a FORTRAN program to create the POLLEN file illustrated in Figure 9-2.

2. An alternate update algorithm to the one used in Program 9-8 is to use two files. The first file is the POLLEN file illustrated in Figure 9-2, and the second file is the updated file. Using two files, the update algorithm becomes:

   Open both files
     Read and add the first POLLEN record to a total
     Do for the next nine POLLEN records
       Read a pollen count
       Add the count to the total
       Write the count to the new file
     Enddo
     Request the current pollen count reading
     Write the current pollen count to the new file
     Close both files
     Calculate and display the previous ten-day average
     Calculate and display the current ten-day average

   Write a FORTRAN file update program using this algorithm.

3a. A file named POLAR.DAT contains the polar coordinates needed in a graphics program. Currently this file contains the following data:

Distance (inches)	Angle (degrees)
2	45
6	30
10	45
4	60
12	55
8	15

   Write a FORTRAN program to create this file on your computer system.

 b. Using the POLAR.DAT file created in Exercise 3a, write a FORTRAN program that accepts distance and angle data from the user and adds the data to the end of the file.

 c. Using the POLAR.DAT file created in Exercise 3a, write a FORTRAN program that reads this file and creates a second file named XYCORD.DAT. The entries in the new file should contain the rectangular coordinates corresponding to the polar coordinates in the POLAR.DAT file. Polar coordinates are converted to rectangular coordinates using the equations:

   $x = r \cos(\Theta)$
   $y = r \sin(\Theta)$

   where r is the distance coordinate, and Θ is the radian equivalent of the angle coordinate in the POLAR.DAT file.

4a. Write a FORTRAN program to create the both the OLDBK.MAS file, illustrated in Table 9-1, and the BOOK.TRN file, illustrated in Table 9-2. (*Note:* Do not include the column headings in the file.)

b. Using the files created in Exercise 4a, enter and run Program 9-9 to verify its operation.

c. Modify Program 9-9 to prompt the user for the names of the old master file, the new master file, and the transaction file. The modified program should accept these file names as input while the program is executing.

d. Using the BOOK.TRN file create in Exercise 4a, write a FORTRAN program that reads this file and displays the transaction data in it, including the heading lines shown in Table 9-2.

5a. Write a FORTRAN program to create a data file containing the following information:

```
Student        Student           Course       Course      Course
ID nunber      name              name         credits     grade
---------      -------------     ------       -------      ------
2333021        BOKOW,  R.        NS201        3            A
2333021        BOKOW,  R.        MG342        3            A
2333021        BOKOW,  R.        FA302        1            A
2574063        FALLIN,  D.       MK106        3            C
2574063        FALLIN,  D.       MA208        3            B
2574063        FALLIN,  D.       CM201        3            C
2574063        FALLIN,  D.       CP101        2            B
2663628        KINGSLEY,  M.     QA140        3            A
2663628        KINGSLEY,  M.     CM245        3            B
2663628        KINGSLEY,  M.     EQ521        3            A
2663628        KINGSLEY,  M.     MK341        3            A
2663628        KINGSLEY,  M.     CP101        2            B
```

b. Using the file created in Exercise 5a, write a FORTRAN program that creates student grade reports. The grade report for each student should contain the student's name and identification number, a list of courses taken, the credits and grade for each course, and a semester grade point average. For example, the grade report for the first student is:

```
STUDENT NAME: BOKOW,  R.
STUDENT ID NUMBER:

COURSE      COURSE      COURSE
NAME        CREDITS     GRADE
------      -------     ------
NS201       3           A
MG342       3           A
FA302       1           A

TOTAL SEMESTER COURSE CREDITS COMPLETED: 7
SEMESTER GRADE POINT AVERAGE: 4.0
```

The semester grade point average is computed in two steps. First, each course grade is assigned a numerical value ($A = 4$, $B = 3$, $C = 2$, $D = 1$, $F = 0$), and the sum of each course's grade value times the credits for each course is computed. This sum is then divided by the total number of credits taken during the semester.

6a. Write a FORTRAN program to create a data file containing the following information:

Student ID number	Student name	Course credits	Cumulative grade point average (GPA)
---------	------------	-------	-------------
2333021	BOKOW, R.	48	4.0
2574063	FALLIN, D.	12	1.8
2663628	KINGSLEY, M.	36	3.5

b. Using the file created in Exercise 6a as a master file and the file created in Exercise 5a as a transactions file, write a file update program to create an updated master file.

9.4 Formatted and Unformatted Files *

All of the files created in the previous three sections have been formatted. Specifically, the files created in Section 9.1 used implicit, list-directed formatting, while the files created in Section 9.2 used explicit, user-designated formats. Collectively, both list-directed and user-formatted files are referred to as *text* files. In addition to text files (both list-directed and user-formatted), FORTRAN permits the construction of unformatted files, which are also referred to as *binary* files.*

The primary difference between formatted and unformatted files resides in the codes used to store data in the file. In this section the specifics of formatted (text) and unformatted (binary) data storage are presented, the relative merits of each file type are described, and the mechanics of designating a file's type explicitly when the file is opened are specified. In addition to the option of selecting the file's type, other file options are also available when the file is opened. The complete set of available file options allowed by the OPEN statement is presented at the end of this section.

Formatted (Text) File Storage

Each character in the formatted files that we have been using is stored using a character code, such as the ASCII or EBCDIC codes introduced in Section 2.1. Both of these codes assign a specific code to each letter in the alphabet, to each of the digits 0 through 9, and to special symbols such as the decimal point and dollar sign. The ASCII and EBCDIC uppercase letter codes were previously listed in Table 2-1. Table 9-3 lists the correspondence between the decimal digits 0 through 9 and their ASCII and EBCDIC representations, in both binary and hexadecimal notation. Additionally, the ASCII and EBCDIC codes for a decimal point, blank space, carriage return, and line feed character are included in the table.

Using Table 9-3, we can determine how the decimal number 67432.83, for example, is stored in a data file using the ASCII code. In ASCII, this sequence of digits and decimal point requires eight character storage locations and is stored using the codes illustrated in Figure 9-5.

---

* This topic may be omitted on first reading without loss of subject continuity.

Table 9-3 Selected ASCII Codes

Character	ASCII Binary Value	ASCII Hex. Value	EBCDIC Binary Value	EBCDIC Hex. Value
0	00110000	30	11110000	F0
1	00110001	31	11110001	F1
2	00110010	32	11110010	F2
3	00110011	33	11110011	F3
4	00110100	34	11110100	F4
5	00110101	35	11110101	F5
6	00110110	36	11110110	F6
7	00110111	37	11110111	F7
8	00111000	38	11111000	F8
9	00111001	39	11111001	F9
.	00101110	2E	01001011	4B
Blank space	00100000	20	01000000	40
Carriage return	00001101	0D	00001101	0D
Line feed	00001010	0A	00001010	0A

| 36 | 37 | 34 | 33 | 32 | 2E | 38 | 33 |

Figure 9-5   The Number 67432.83 Represented in ASCII Code

The advantage of using ASCII or EBCDIC code for data files is that the file can be read and displayed by any word processing or editor program that is provided by your computer system. Such editor and word processing programs are called text editors because they are designed to process alphabetical text. The word processing program can read the ASCII or EBCDIC code in the data file and display the letter, symbol, or digit corresponding to the code. This permits a data file created in FORTRAN to be examined and changed by other than FORTRAN programs.

A formatted file is the default file type created in FORTRAN when a sequential file is opened. An option within the OPEN statement permits explicit selection of this file type or selection of the alternative unformatted form. The explicit selection of a formatted (text) file is made by adding the term FORM = 'FORMATTED' within the OPEN statement after the file name is specified. As an example employing this option, assume that the following list of experimental results is to be stored in a formatted file named EXPER.DAT.

Experiment number	Result
1	8
2	12
3	497

Program 9-10 opens a file named EXPER.DAT to store this data. Additionally, the OPEN statement uses the FORM option to explicitly create a formatted (text) file.

Program 9-10

```
PROGRAM MAIN
  INTEGER I, RESULT(3)
  DATA RESULT/8,12,497/
  OPEN(1, FILE = 'EXPER.DAT', FORM = 'FORMATTED')
  DO 10 I = 1,3
    WRITE(1,*) I, RESULT(I)
10  CONTINUE
  CLOSE(1)
  END
```

When Program 9-10 is executed, a file named EXPER.DAT is created and saved by the computer. The file is a formatted file consisting of the following three records:

```
1         8
2        12
3       497
```

The spacing between data items in the file is due to the list-directed formatting invoked by the WRITE statement. This specific formatting can, of course, be changed by having the WRITE statement reference a format control string. In either case, selecting a formatted file requires that some format for the data be designated by the user (hence the name formatted file).

The formatted file created by Program 9-10 contains 73 characters. These characters consist of the codes used to store the required digits (one code per digit or letter, which is the hallmark of a text file) plus the blank spaces before each number, a carriage return and new-line character at the end of each data line, and a special EOF marker placed as the last item in the file when it is closed.

Assuming characters are stored using the ASCII code listed in Table 9-3, the EXPER.DAT data file is stored physically as shown in Figure 9-6. For convenience, the character corresponding to each hexadecimal code is listed below the code. Although the actual code used for the EOF marker is system dependent, the hexadecimal code 00 is commonly used because this code has no equivalent character representation. The number of spaces (Hexcode 20) illustrated is also system dependent.

Unformatted (Binary) Files[*]

An alternative to text files, where each character in the file is represented by a unique code, is unformatted files. Unformatted files, also referred to as binary files, store numerical values using the computer's internal numerical code. For example, assume that the computer stores numbers internally using 16 bits in the two's complement format described in Section 1.7. Using this format, the decimal number

---

[*] This topic assumes that you are familiar with the computer storage concepts presented in Section 1.7.

```
20 20 20 20 20 20 20 20 20 20 31 20 20 20 20 20 20 20 20 20 20 38 0D 0A
                              1                                8 CR LF

20 20 20 20 20 20 20 20 20 20 32 20 20 20 20 20 20 20 20 20 31 32 0D 0A
                              2                             1  2 CR LF

20 20 20 20 20 20 20 20 20 20 33 20 20 20 20 20 20 20 20 34 39 37 0D 0A 00
                              3                          4  9  7 CR LF EOF
```

Figure 9-6 The EXPER.DAT File as Stored by the Computer

8 is represented as the binary number 0000 0000 0000 1000, the decimal number 12 as 0000 0000 0000 1100, and the decimal number 497 as 0000 0001 1111 0001.

The advantages of using this format are that no intermediary conversions are required for storing or retrieving the data (since the external storage codes match the computer's internal storage representation), no format specifications must be supplied, and the resulting file usually requires less storage space than its formatted counterpart. The disadvantages are that the file can no longer be visually inspected using a text-editing program or transferred between computers that use different internal number representations.

The specification for explicitly creating an unformatted file is made by adding the term FORM = 'UNFORMATTED' within the OPEN statement after the file name is specified. For example, the statement:

```
OPEN(1, FILE = 'EXPER.BIN', FORM = 'UNFORMATTED')
```

opens the file named EXPER.BIN as an unformatted file assigned to unit number 1. This OPEN statement is used in Program 9-11 to create a binary file of the EXPER.DAT text file previously created as a formatted file in Program 9-10.

Program 9-11

```
      PROGRAM MAIN
        INTEGER I, RESULT(3)
        DATA RESULT/8,12,497/
        OPEN(1, FILE = 'EXPER.BIN', FORM = 'UNFORMATTED')
        DO 10 I = 1,3
          WRITE(1) I, RESULT(I)
10      CONTINUE
        CLOSE(1)
        END
```

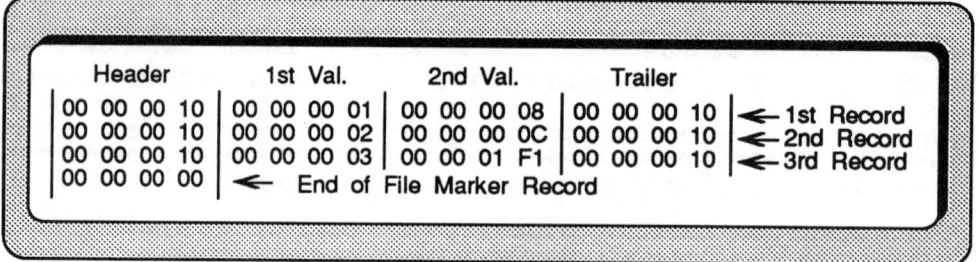

Figure 9-7   The EXPER.BIN **File as Stored by the Computer**

In reviewing Program 9-11, notice that the WRITE statement does not contain a format specification. In writing or reading an unformatted file, it is essential that no format specification be indicated, because the format has already been set by the FORM option in the OPEN statement. Other than the required omission of a format specification, the WRITE and READ statements for unformatted I/O are identical to their formatted I/O counterparts.

The unformatted file created by Program 9-11 is illustrated in Figure 9-7, which uses hexadecimal values to indicate the equivalent binary values. Although the figure separates the file's records into individual lines, with bars (|) used to distinguish individual items in each record, in actuality the file is stored as a consecutive sequence of codes.

As shown in the figure, each record in a binary file is preceded by a header value and followed by a trailer value. The values in the header and trailer are always equal and contain the number of bytes in the record (each hexadecimal value is one byte in length—review Section 1.7 for a description of a byte). For example, the first record contains 16 bytes, which is indicated by the hexadecimal value 10. Between each header and trailer value are the record's data items. As indicated in Figure 9-7, each record contains two integer values, with each integer stored using four bytes (32 bits). The hexadecimal values shown on the first line correspond to the decimal numbers 1 and 8, the values on the second line to the decimal numbers 2 and 12, and the values on the third line to the decimal numbers 3 and 497. These are the same values previously illustrated in Figure 9-6 using the ASCII code. Although the number of bytes used to store an integer is system dependent, the layout of all binary files corresponds to the form shown in Figure 9-7.

The fact that the EXPER.BIN file uses a binary storage code does not preclude us from displaying the results in a text form. For example, Program 9-12 opens the EXPER.BIN file in the unformatted mode, reads the file using an unformatted READ statement, and displays the data using a list-directed (formatted) PRINT statement. In its most general form, the unformatted READ statement is the same as the formatted READ statement described in Section 9.2, except for the required omission of the format specification.

Program 9-12

```
PROGRAM MAIN
   INTEGER I, N, VALUE
   OPEN(1, FILE = 'EXPER.BIN', FORM = 'UNFORMATTED')
   DO 10 I = 1,3
      READ(1) N, VALUE
      PRINT *,N, VALUE
10    CONTINUE
   CLOSE(1)
   END
```

The display produced by Program 9-12 is illustrated below:

```
1          8
2          12
3          497
```

The OPEN Statement Revisited

In establishing the connection between an external data file and a FORTRAN program, the OPEN statement defines the properties of the external data file being accessed. As we have seen, in the absence of explicit designations, certain default specifications, such as the form of the file (formatted or unformatted), are supplied by the compiler.

In its most general form, the OPEN statement has the general form:

```
OPEN (UNIT = u, FILE = name, STATUS = stype, FORM = file-type,
ACCESS = atype, RECL = rln, BLANK = ch, IOSTAT = var, ERR = n)
```

The words UNIT, FILE, STATUS, FORM, ACCESS, RECL, BLANK, IOSTAT, and ERR are optional keywords, called file specifiers, that may be placed in any order within the parentheses. Each of these file specifiers designates a specific file characteristic and is described below. (Blank spaces may be used freely within the parentheses and have no effect on the statement. However, if the statement extends beyond a single line, it must be properly designated as a continuation line.) Except for the UNIT specification, all other file specifiers are optional and may be omitted from the OPEN statement. If the keyword UNIT is not included explicitly in an OPEN statement, the unit number must be the first item listed in parentheses.

File Specifiers

The unit specifier, UNIT = u, designates the unit number assigned to the file. The u in this specifier may be either an integer expression that evaluates to a nonnegative value or an asterisk, which designates a default system-specified unit. If the term UNIT = is omitted, the unit number must be the first item in parentheses.

The name specifier, FILE = *name*, designates the name of the file being opened, which can be any character expression. If this file specifier is not included in the OPEN statement, a default system-specified file is selected. If a character constant is used for the name, it must be enclosed in apostrophes. For example, the specifier FILE = 'TEST.DAT' identifies the file TEST.DAT as the file to be opened.

The STATUS file specifier, STATUS = *stype*, designates the status of the file. The character expression *stype* must evaluate to one of the values NEW, OLD, SCRATCH, or UNKNOWN. A status of NEW causes a new file to be created. If an existing file has the same name as the file being opened, an error will be reported when the OPEN statement is executed. Files opened as OLD already exist on the system. Files opened as UNKNOWN will be created if they do not exist or opened as OLD files if they do exist. UNKNOWN is the default status selected in the absence of an explicit status designation. A SCRATCH status indicates that the file is temporary and will be deleted upon closing the file or program termination.

The FORM specifier, FORM = *file-type*, designates whether the file is formatted (text) or unformatted (binary). The character expression *file-type* must evaluate to one of the constants FORMATTED or UNFORMATTED, respectively. If this file specifier is omitted, the file is assumed to be FORMATTED if it is a sequential access file or UNFORMATTED if it is a direct access file.

The ACCESS file specifier, ACCESS = *atype*, designates whether the records in a file are accessed in a sequential or a direct manner (see Section 9.5 for a complete discussion of file access methods). The character expression *atype* must evaluate to one of the constants SEQUENTIAL or DIRECT. Files created as SEQUENTIAL must subsequently be opened with this access type and files created as DIRECT also must subsequently be opened using DIRECT access. If the access specification is omitted, the file is opened as SEQUENTIAL by default. If the access specification ACCESS = 'DIRECT' is used, the record length specifier, RECL = *rln*, must be used.

The RECL file specifier, RECL = *rln*, designates the record length of a direct access file. The integer expression *rln* must evaluate to a positive value. This specifier must be present when the ACCESS = 'DIRECT' specifier is used and must be omitted for sequential access files. For formatted direct access files the record length is the number of characters allowed in a record, for unformatted direct access files the record length is typically the number of words allowed in a record. For existing direct access files the record length must always be specified as the same value used when the file was created.

The BLANK file specifier, BLANK = *ch*, determines the interpretation of blank spaces in numeric input fields. The character expression *ch* must evaluate to one of the constants NULL or ZERO, respectively. When BLANK = 'NULL,' is specified blank spaces embedded within an input number are ignored. When BLANK = 'ZERO' is specified, embedded blank spaces in a numeric input field are interpreted as zeros. In both cases a completely blank field is assigned the value zero. If the BLANK file specifier is omitted, a NULL default is used. (As noted previously, some compilers are configured to assume a ZERO default.) The BN and BZ format specifiers (see Appendix B) can always be used to override the BLANK file specifier.

The IOSTAT file specifier, IOSTAT = *var*, designates an integer variable that will be assigned an I/O status code. The value assigned to the variable depends on the I/O status produced by the OPEN statement. It is zero if the OPEN statement executed without an error, and it is assigned a computer-dependent positive value for any other detected error condition. The value assigned to the IOSTAT variable may be displayed using either a PRINT or a WRITE statement.

The ERR file specifier, ERR = n, designates a statement label to which control is transferred if any error condition is encountered when the OPEN statement is executed.

Exercises

1. Write individual OPEN statements that explicitly open files having the following characteristics:

   a. A formatted sequential file named TEST.DAT that is to be assigned to unit number 3.

   b. A file named DESCRI that is a new, direct access file with individual record lengths of 80. The file is to be assigned to unit number 4.

   c. A file named NAMES that is an old, sequential, formatted file that is to be assigned to unit number 1. The I/O status of the file is to be assigned to the variable IOS, and the OPEN statement should transfer control to statement label 850 if an error in opening the file is detected.

   d. An existing formatted sequential file named TYPES that is to be assigned to unit number 4. The I/O status of the file is to be assigned to the variable ISTAT, and the OPEN statement should transfer control to statement label 835 if an error in opening the file is detected.

   e. An existing unformatted sequential file named TYPES that is to be assigned to unit number 4. The I/O status of the file is to be assigned to the variable ISTAT, and the OPEN statement should transfer control to statement label 860 if an error in opening the file is detected.

   f. An existing formatted direct access file with record length 80 named TYPES that is to be assigned to unit number 7. The I/O status of the file is to be assigned to the variable MST, and the OPEN statement should transfer control to statement label 870 if an error in opening the file is detected. Explicitly designate that blank spaces within all numeric fields in the file are to be interpreted as zeros.

   g. Redo Exercise 1f but explicitly designate that blank spaces within all numeric fields in the file are to be ignored.

2. Redo Exercise 1 but omit all explicit file specifiers from the OPEN statement when the desired specifiers are correctly selected by FORTRAN's default values.

3. Write, compile, and run a FORTRAN program that writes the four real numbers 92.65, 88.72, 77.46, and 82.93 to an unformatted sequential file named RESULT. After writing the data to the file, your program should read the data from the file, determine the average of the four numbers read, and display the average. Verify the output produced by your program by manually calculating the average of the four input numbers.

4a. Write, compile, and execute a FORTRAN program that creates an unformatted sequential file named POINTS and writes the following numbers to the file:

```
6.3   8.2   18.25   24.32      ⟵——— 1st record
4.0   4.0   10.0    -5.0       ⟵——— 2nd record
-2.0  5.0   4.0     5.0        ⟵——— 3rd record
```

b. Using the data in the POINTS file created in Exercise 4a write, compile, and run a FORTRAN program that reads each record and interprets the first and second numbers in each record as the coordinates of one point and the third and fourth numbers as the coordinates of a second point. Using the formulas given in Exercise 11 of Section 3.1, have your program compute and display the slope and midpoint of the two points entered. Your program should use the END option of the formatted READ statement.

5a. Write, compile, and run a FORTRAN program that creates an unformatted sequential file named GRADES and writes the following numbers to the file:

```
100, 100, 100, 100
100, 0, 100, 0
86, 83, 89, 94
78, 59, 77, 85
89, 92, 81, 88
```

b. Using the data in the GRADES file created in Exercise 5a, write, compile, and run a FORTRAN program that reads each record in the GRADES file, computes the average for each record, and displays the average.

6. Redo Exercise 12 in Section 9.1 using an unformatted sequential file.

9.5   Direct Access Files *

The manner in which records in a file are written and retrieved is called *file access*. All of the files created so far have used *sequential access*, which means that each record in the file is accessed sequentially, one after another. Thus, for example, the fourth record in a sequentially accessed file cannot be read without first reading the first three records in the file, the last record in the file cannot be read without first reading all of the previous records, and no record can be replaced without erasing all subsequent records. Because records within a sequential file cannot be replaced, updating a sequential access file requires using a file update procedure in which a completely new file is created for each update (see, for example, Application 2 in Section 9.3). For those applications in which every record in a file must be updated, such as updating a monthly payroll file, sequential access conforms to the way the file must be updated and is not a restriction.*

---

* This topic may be omitted on first reading without loss of subject continuity.

In some applications direct access to each record in the file, where an individual record in the middle of the file can be retrieved, modified, and rewritten without reading or writing to any other record, is preferable. *Direct access* files, also referred to as *random access* files, provide this capability. In this section we will see how to create and use direct access files. Since the access method (sequential or direct) refers to how data in the file is accessed and not to the codes used in storing the data, both sequential and direct access files may be created in both formatted (text) and unformatted (binary) forms.

Unless a file is explicitly specified as a direct access file, it will be opened in sequential access mode. The specification of a direct access file is made by including both the ACCESS = 'DIRECT' and the RECL = *rln* file specifiers in the file's OPEN statement. For example, the statement:

```
OPEN(1, FILE='BK.DAT', FORM='FORMATTED', ACCESS='DIRECT', RECL=20)
```

opens the formatted file named BK.DAT as a direct access file, where each record in the file has a maximum length of 20 characters. If the FORM specifier were omitted, the file would be opened by default as an unformatted file (this is in keeping with the FORM defaults described in the previous section: a direct access file defaults to an unformatted form, and a sequential file to a formatted form). The record length specified for direct access formatted files corresponds to the maximum number of characters that can be stored in a record. Each time a direct access file is opened, the same record length must be specified as when the file was initially created. It is the record length that tells the computer how many characters must be retrieved and written each time a record is accessed.

Once a direct access file has been opened, either as a formatted or an unformatted file, reading and writing to the file are identical to their sequential access file counterparts, with one exception: both the READ and the WRITE statements used must include a REC = *record number* specifier to indicate which record is to be accessed. For example, the statement:

```
WRITE (1, 15, REC = 5) IDNO, QUANTY, PRICE
```

writes the values of IDNO, QUANTY, and PRICE to the fifth record in file number 1 using the format specified in FORMAT statement 15. Similarly, the statement:

```
WRITE (3, *, REC = 226) A, B, C
```

writes the values of A, B, and C to the 226th record of file number 3 using the compiler's list-directed format. For unformatted direct access files the format specification in both READ and WRITE statements, as for unformatted sequential access files, must be omitted.

In general, the record number in both READ and WRITE statements can be any integer expression that evaluates to a positive number. Since records in a direct access file are accessed by record number, applications that use direct access files must contain either an identification number or an account code, to be used either directly or indirectly as a record number, as part of each record. For example, assume that a direct access formatted file that contains the data shown in Table 9-4 is to be created.

Creating a direct access file of the data in Table 9-4, either as a formatted or an unformatted file, requires that five records be written. Each record in the file is used to store a product identification number, the quantity of the product in stock, and the product's selling price. The product identification number has been selected as a four-digit number so that subtracting 1000 from the number yields the correct record number. Thus, the data for product identification number 1001 would be stored in record number 1, the data for product identification number 1002 would be stored in record number 2, and so on. (Converting an identification code to a record number is formally called *hashing*.)

Table 9-4 Product Information to Be Stored in a Direct Access File

Product number	Quantity in stock	Selling price
1001	476	28.00
1002	348	32.50
1003	517	51.00
1004	284	23.75
1005	165	35.25

Program 9-13 creates the required file.

Program 9-13   Creation of a Formatted Direct Access File

```
PROGRAM CREATE
    INTEGER RECNO, IDNO, QUANTY
    REAL PRICE
    OPEN(1, FILE = 'PRDCT.DAT', FORM = 'FORMATTED',
   +     ACCESS = 'DIRECT', RECL = 20)
    DO 20 I = 1, 5
      PRINT *, 'ENTER THE IDENTIFICATION NUMBER: '
      READ *, IDNO
      RECNO = IDNO - 1000
      PRINT *, 'ENTER THE QUANTITY IN STOCK: '
      READ *, QUANTY
      PRINT *, 'ENTER THE SELLING PRICE: '
      READ *, PRICE
      WRITE (1,15,REC = RECNO) IDNO,QUANTY,PRICE
15    FORMAT(I5,3X,I3,3X,F6.2)
20  CONTINUE
    CLOSE(1)
    END
```

```
1001    476    28.00
1002    348    32.50
1003    517    51.00
1004    284    23.75
1005    165    35.25
1234567891111111112
           01234567890
↑
└─Column Number One
```

Figure 9-8   The Formatted File Produced by Program 9-13

The OPEN statement in Program 9-13 opens the PRDCT.DAT file as a formatted direct access file that will be known as unit number 1 within the program. The record length of 20 in the OPEN statement was obtained by adding the field width specifiers in FORMAT statement 15, since it is this format that is used to write each individual record to the file. (*Note:* A larger record length can be specified, but a smaller record length will result in a runtime "direct record overflow" error.) When Program 9-13 is executed, and assuming that the data in Table 9-4 is entered correctly, the file illustrated in Figure 9-8 will be created (since it is a formatted file, it can be listed using any word processing or text editor program).

Program 9-14 illustrates the use of a formatted READ statement to read the data in the direct access file created by Program 9-12. In reviewing this program, notice that the file specifiers used in the OPEN statement are identical to those used when the file was created. Also notice that the READ statement includes a REC = *record number* specifier and uses the same format specification for reading each record in

Program 9-14   Reading and Listing a Direct Access File

```
       PROGRAM MAIN
       INTEGER RECNO, IDNO, QUANTY
       REAL PRICE
       OPEN(1, FILE = 'PRDCT.DAT', FORM = 'FORMATTED',
    +        ACCESS = 'DIRECT', RECL = 20)
 5     FORMAT(1X,'                   QUANTITY')
10     FORMAT(1X,'STOCK NO.      IN STOCK      PRICE')
15     FORMAT(1X,'---------      --------      -------')
20     FORMAT(I5,3X,I3,3X,F6.2)
25     FORMAT(2X,I5,10X,I3,7X,'$',F6.2)
       PRINT 5
       PRINT 10
       PRINT 15
       RECNO = 1
30     READ(1, 20, REC = RECNO, END = 35) IDNO, QUANTY, PRICE
          PRINT 25, IDNO, QUANTY, PRICE
          RECNO = RECNO + 1
       GOTO 30
35     CLOSE(1)
       END
```

the file as was used when the file was written. The program begins at record number 1 and continuously reads each record in increasing record number order until the end of the file is detected, at which point control is transferred to statement label 35.

The output produced by Program 9-14 is as follows:

```
                 QUANTITY
STOCK NO.        IN STOCK      PRICE
---------        --------     -------
    1001            476       $ 28.00
    1002            348       $ 32.50
    1003            517       $ 51.00
    1004            284       $ 23.75
    1005            165       $ 35.25
```

Notice that although direct access is used in Program 9-14, the data in the PRDCT.DAT file is read in a sequential order, starting from record number 1. The real advantage to direct access files is that records in the file can be read and written in any order. To illustrate this, consider Program 9-15, which requests a user to enter any identification number. If the record corresponding to the desired identification number is located, the user is requested to enter a new quantity in stock number, and the updated data is written to the existing record; otherwise, the user is informed that no record exists for the entered stock number.

In reviewing Program 9-15, notice that the OPEN statement contains the same file specifiers as used in Program 9-13 when the PRDCT.DAT file was created. Also notice the use of the ERR specifier in the READ statement to direct the program to display an error message when the appropriate record is not found.

◻ Program 9-15   Updating a Formatted Direct Access File

```
      PROGRAM MAIN
        INTEGER RECNO, STKNO, IDNO, QUANTY, CURRNT
        REAL PRICE
   5    FORMAT(I5)
  10    FORMAT(I3)
  15    FORMAT(I5,3X,I3,3X,F6.2)
*
        OPEN(1, FILE = 'PRDCT.DAT', FORM = 'FORMATTED',
   +        ACCESS = 'DIRECT', RECL = 20)
        PRINT *, 'ENTER AN IDENTIFICATION NUMBER OR 999 TO STOP: '
*
        READ *, STKNO
  20    IF (STKNO .NE. 999) THEN
          RECNO = STKNO - 1000
          READ(1, 15, REC=RECNO, ERR=25) IDNO, QUANTY, PRICE
***     RECORD HAS BEEN FOUND - ENTER UPDATED QUANTITY
          PRINT *, 'ENTER THE CURRENT QUANTITY IN STOCK: '
          READ *, CURRNT
***     WRITE THE UPDATED RECORD
          WRITE(1,15, REC=RECNO) IDNO,CURRNT,PRICE
  25      IF (STKNO.NE.IDNO) THEN
            PRINT *, 'THERE IS NO RECORD FOR THIS STOCK NUMBER'
            PRINT *, 'PLEASE RECHECK THE NUMBER'
          ENDIF
          PRINT *, 'ENTER ANOTHER STOCK NUMBER OR 999 TO STOP: '
          READ *, STKNO
          GO TO 20
        ENDIF
        CLOSE(1)
        END
```

Additional Exercises for Chapter 9

1a. Enter, compile, and execute Program 9-13 on your computer.

  b. Modify the record length in the OPEN statement in Program 9-13 to be 10. Run the program and determine the effect produced by this change.

  c. What effect do you think will be made if the record length in the OPEN statement in Program 9-13 is changed to 200?

2. Modify Program 9-13 so that an unformatted file is created. (*Hint:* Typically, an unformatted file requires less space per record than does a formatted file. More generally, the record length for an unformatted file is the number of words needed to store a record in the binary format used by your computer. If the record length is not large enough, a runtime error will occur when the record is being written because of the insufficient storage allocation.)

3. Modify Program 9-14 to read and list the contents of the unformatted direct access file produced in Exercise 2.

4. Modify Program 9-15 to update the unformatted direct access file created in Exercise 2.

5. Modify Program 9-15 so that both the quantity and the price in each record can be modified. Additionally, have your program check that an identification number between 1001 and 9999 has been entered; if a valid identification number is not currently in the file, have your program create a record for the new item.

6. Redo Exercise 12 in Section 9.1 using a formatted direct access file. To do this, you will have to assign product codes that can be translated into record numbers.

9.6   Common Programming Errors

Five programming errors are common when using files. The most obvious of these is incorrect use of the OPEN statement. This statement must include at minimum a unit number and the FILE = '*filename*' specifier.

A second error is omitting the unit number when using a file READ or WRITE statement. Programmers used to writing these statements for standard input and output devices, where a specific file designator is not required, sometimes forget to include a unit number when accessing data files.

A third error is attempting to use the PRINT statement and replacing the list-directed asterisk with a unit number. The PRINT statement can only access the standard output device. If a unit number is used in this statement, the compiler will consider it to be a FORMAT statement label.

A fourth error occurs when a formatted READ or WRITE is attempted on an unformatted (binary) file. This frequently occurs because the programmer is accustomed to writing formatted I/O statements (list directed or user formatted) to standard I/O units.

A fith error occurs when the record number specification is omitted from READ or WRITE statements used with direct access files.

9.7 Chapter Summary

1. A data file is any collection of data stored together on an external storage medium under a common name. Formally, each line of data stored on the file is called a *record*.
2. The manner in which records are written to and read from a file is called the file's access method.
   a. In a *sequential access file* each record must be accessed in a sequential manner. This means that the second record in the file cannot be read until the first record has been read, the third record cannot be read until the first and second records have been read, and so on, until the last record is read. Similarly, a record cannot be written until all previous records have been written and a record cannot be replaced without destroying all following records.

   b. In a *direct access file* any record can be read, written, or replaced without affecting any other record in the file. A disadvantage of direct access files is that the record length must be specified. Additionally, each record in a direct access file must contain a value that can be translated into a record number needed for record access.
3. In addition to the access method selected for a file, a file can be either a formatted or an unformatted file.
   a. A *formatted file* is one in which each data item in the file is formatted, using either explicit user-designated formats or the compiler's list-directed format. A formatted file is also referred to as a text file.

   b. An *unformatted file* is one is which each data item in the file is stored using the computer's internal binary code. An unformatted file is also referred to as a binary file.
4. An OPEN statement is required to connect a file name to a program unit number. The most basic form of the OPEN statement is:

   ```
   OPEN(unit number, FILE = 'filename')
   ```

   This form of the OPEN statement, by default, designates the file as both sequential and formatted. If the file does not exist, the OPEN statement creates a file having the indicated name.
   a. Including the specifier FORM = 'UNFORMATTED' in the parentheses opens the file as a binary file.

   b. Including the specifier ACCESS = 'DIRECT' in the parentheses opens the file as a direct access file. If the file is opened for direct access, the record length specifier RECL = *rln* must also be used, where *rln* is the length of an individual record.

5. A file must always be opened using the specifiers with which the file was originally created.

6. Data is written to a file using a WRITE statement.
   a. The basic form of this statement for writing to a sequential formatted file is:

   ```
   WRITE(unit number, format specifier) expression list
   ```

   b. The basic form of this statement for writing to a sequential unformatted file is:

   ```
   WRITE(unit number) expression list
   ```

   c. The basic form of this statement for writing to a direct access formatted file is:

   ```
   WRITE(unit number, format specifier, REC = recno)
   expression list
   ```

   d. The basic form of this statement for writing to a direct access unformatted file is:

   ```
   WRITE(unit number, REC = recno) expression list
   ```

   The unit number in all WRITE statements must be either an integer number designating a previously opened file or an integer expression that evaluates to a valid integer file number. The format specifier can be either an asterisk, which specifies a list-directed format, the statement number of a FORMAT statement, or a literal format control character constant surrounded by parentheses and enclosed in apostrophes. For direct access files *recno* can be any integer expression yielding a positive record number.

7. Data is read from an existing file using a READ statement.
   a. The most basic form of this statement for reading from a sequential formatted file is:

   ```
   READ(unit number, format specifier) variable list
   ```

   b. The most basic form of this statement for reading from a sequential unformatted file is:

   ```
   READ(unit number) variable list
   ```

   c. The most basic form of this statement for reading from a direct access formatted file is:

   ```
   READ(unit number, format specifier, REC = recno)
   variable list
   ```

d. The most basic form of this statement for reading from a direct access unformatted file is:

```
READ(unit number, REC = recno) variable list
```

The unit number in all READ statements must be either an integer number designating a previously opened file or an integer expression that evaluates to a valid integer file number. The format specifier can be either an asterisk, which specifies a list-directed format, the statement number of a FORMAT statement, or a literal format control character constant surrounded by parentheses and enclosed in apostrophes. The format used for reading data from a formatted file must be identical to the format used when data was written to the file. For direct access files *recno* can be any integer expression yielding a positive record number.

8. In addition to files opened explicitly within a program, the standard input and output files are automatically opened when a FORTRAN program is executed. The standard input file corresponds to the physical device used for data entry, and the standard output file is the physical device used for data display. Each of these files is assigned a unit number by the system. On many systems an asterisk can be used in place of a unit number to designate the standard I/O device. This asterisk is distinct from the asterisk used to select list-directed formatting.

9. The current position in a sequential file can be altered using the REWIND and BACKSPACE statements. The REWIND statement sets the current position of an internal file pointer to the start of the file. The BACKSPACE statement moves the pointer back one record in the file.

10. Files are formally closed using a CLOSE statement. The most common format of this statement is:

```
CLOSE (unit number)
```

All files are automatically closed when the program they are opened in finishes executing.

9.8 Enrichment Study: Writing Control Codes

In addition to responding to the codes for letters, digits, and special punctuation symbols, which are collectively referred to as printable characters, physical device files such as printers and CRT screens can also respond to a small set of control codes. Because control codes have no equivalent character that can be displayed, they are also referred to as nonprintable characters.

Four of these codes that are extremely useful in applications are the page eject, bell, line feed, and carriage return control codes. When a page eject control code is sent to a printer, a page of paper is ejected, and printing begins on the next sheet of paper. If care is taken to align the printer to the top of a new page when printing is started, the page eject control character can be used as an equivalent "top-of-page" command. The bell code is used to sound the bell or speaker contained within every display terminal, the line feed code is used to advance the output display by one line, and the carriage return code moves the display cursor or print head to column 1 on the current line.

Sending control codes to an output device is done in a similar manner to sending a printable character to a file. Instead of sending an actual character to the output device, the numerical value of the control code is used. For computers that use the ASCII code, this amounts to substituting the equivalent ASCII numerical value for the appropriate letter. Referring to Table 2.1 in Section 2.1, we see that the ASCII code for an A, for example, is the decimal number 65. This numerical value can be converted to a character by using FORTRAN's intrinsic CHAR function. Thus, the statement PRINT *, CHAR(65), for example, causes an A to be output to the standard output unit. This statement produces the same display as the statement PRINT *, 'A'.

The importance of using the CHAR function and the numerical code for the letter is only realized when a control code rather than a character code must be transmitted. Since no equivalent character exists for control codes, the numerical value for the code must be used within the CHAR function. For all computers that use the ASCII code, the bell, line feed, and carriage return codes correspond to the decimal numbers 7, 10, and 13, respectively. For most printers the decimal page eject code is a decimal 12. For example, using this code and assuming the printer is the standard output device, the statement:

```
PRINT *, CHAR(12)
```

causes the printer to eject the current page. Similarly, if the CRT is the standard output device, the code:

```
        PRINT *, CHAR(7), CHAR(7), CHAR(7)
        DO 10 I = 1,25
          PRINT *, CHAR(10)
10      CONTINUE
```

causes the bell to be "beeped" three times and the screen to be cleared. The clearing of the screen is accomplished by sending 25 consecutive line feeds to it. Program 9-16 illustrates how this code could be included in a working program, using individual subroutines to sound the bell and clear the screen. In each subroutine the appropriate codes have been equated to more meaningful character variable names.

Program 9-16 will also work if the printer is the standard output device, except that 66 line feeds are required to eject a standard page. For printers, however, it is easier to send the single page eject code. If the printer is not the standard output device, it must first be opened before the eject code is transmitted.

Program 9-16

```
PROGRAM MAIN
   CALL BELL3
   CALL CLEAR
   END
*
   SUBROUTINE BELL3
   CHARACTER BELL
   BELL = CHAR(7)
   PRINT *, BELL, BELL, BELL
   END
*
   SUBROUTINE CLEAR
   CHARACTER LINEFD
   LINEFD = CHAR(10)
   DO 10 I = 1,25
      PRINT *, LINEFD
10 CONTINUE
   END
```

For IBM personal computers the printer has the file name PRN. Program 9-17 illustrates using this name to open a printer connected to an IBM or IBM-compatible personal computer and then to send a page eject code to it.

 Program 9-17

```
PROGRAM MAIN
   CHARACTER EJECT
   EJECT = CHAR(12)
   OPEN (1, FILE = 'PRN')
   WRITE (1,*) EJECT
   END
```

Additional Data Types

Chapter Ten

In addition to the four data types we have discussed so far (integer, real, character, and logical), FORTRAN provides two other data types. In this chapter these two additional data types, double precision and complex, are presented. Additional processing techniques are also presented for working with character variables, and the implementation of data structures using parallel arrays is described.

10.1   Double Precision Data

As we discussed in Chapter 1, most FORTRAN compilers provide approximately six significant digits of accuracy. However, there are times when that is not enough—for example, when calculating the angle of intercept of a rocket with a planet 10^9 (1 billion) miles away. An error in the sixth digit in such a calculation could result in the rocket's missing its target by over 1000 miles ($10^{-6} * 10^9$).

In order to gain additional significant digits, FORTRAN provides double precision constants and variables. A double precision constant must be written in scientific notation (see Section 2.1) using a "D" to indicate the exponent. Examples of valid double precision constants are:

```
  4.645D+2
 -5.322728D+08
  3.45678D-02
 -6.466789039D-03
  1.2345678D5          (same as 1.2345678D+5)
 -2.9876D2             (same as -2.9876D+2)
```

As illustrated by these examples, the plus sign (+) may be omitted immediately following the D when the exponent is positive. In all cases, an exponent must be present as an integer number. The value preceding the D, which is called the *mantissa,* may be either an integer or a real number (some compilers require the mantissa to be real). The number of digits in the mantissa actually stored by the computer is the amount of significant digits retained for the double precision value (see Appendix D for a description of real and double precision number storage).

Examples of invalid double precision constants are:

```
45.3       (missing exponent)
D+4        (missing mantissa)
3.4D-.5    (exponent must be an integer value)
```

Although a double precision constant need not necessarily store twice as many significant digits as are used for real values (often called *single precision* constants), typically they do. Thus, if your compiler retains 6 significant digits for a real number, it typically will retain at least 12 digits for a double precision constant. Even if you specify more digits, only the first 12 (or however many are stored by your compiler) will be retained. Second, execution of arithmetic with double precision values is considerably slower than that with single precision numbers because the extra length of each double precision value must be carried through each computation. Third, since each double precision value typically uses twice the memory space of a single precision constant, the total memory space needed by the program is increased. For these reasons, double precision data should be used only when the additional accuracy they provide is necessary.

Computations using double precision values follow the same rules as computation with reals and integers, with one addition: when an operation is being performed on a double precision number and another number, the other number is first converted to double precision length, and then the arithmetic is executed. For example, the mixed-mode computation 6 * 2.7D4 + 3.0D–1D0**2 / 3.0 proceeds as follows:

```
= 6 * 2.7D4 + .090000000000 / 3.        (exponentiation performed)
= 162000.000000 + .09000000000000 / .03 (multiplication  performed)
= 162000.000000 + .03000000000000       (division performed)
= 162000.030000                         (addition performed)
```

Notice that in each case the operand with the highest precision determines the precision to which the other operand is converted. Assuming that the length of a double precision value is 12 digits, each intermediate value in the previous calculation results in a 12-digit number. If the same computation were done using real values capable of holding only 6 significant digits, the value of the final result would be 1.62000E5, and the last 2 digits, 03, corresponding to the seventh and eighth significant digits, would be lost. Similarly, for example, the real computation 2.0/7.0 results in the value 0.285714, while the double precision computation 2.D0/7.D0 results in the value 0.285714285714 (again, the exact number of retained digits is compiler dependent).

The general form of a declaration statement for double precision variables is:

> DOUBLE PRECISION *variable list*

Thus, the declaration:

```
DOUBLE PRECISION LENGTH, DSTNCE, TOTSAL
```

declares the three variables LENGTH, DSTNCE, and TOTSAL as double precision variables. Assignment statements using double precision variables follow the same pattern as assignment statements using real or integer variables, except that double precision values should be used on the right side of the equal sign. Assuming LENGTH and MEASMT have been declared as double precision variables, the following assignments can be made:

```
LENGTH = 3.75D+05
MEASMT = 4.1567D-10
```

If a real value is assigned to a double precision variable, the real value is padded with zeros to the appropriate length. Conversely, if a double precision value is assigned to a real variable, the double precision value is truncated to the allowed number of significant digits. Similarly, an integer assigned to a double precision variable is first converted to a double precision value, and a double precision value assigned to an integer variable is truncated to an integer.

Intrinsic functions are also available in double precision form (see Appendix F for a complete list of intrinsic functions). All double precision functions begin with the letter D, and most require double precision arguments. For example, DSQRT(DX) returns the double precision square root of its double precision argument DX, and DLOG(DX) returns the double precision natural logarithm of its double precision argument DX.

For formatted READ statements using double precision variables, the F format descriptor must be used. The following program segment, in which a double precision value is read from the standard input unit, illustrates this:

```
      DOUBLE PRECISION A, B
      READ 3, A, B
   3  FORMAT (F13.6, 3X, F12.8)
```

For the following input:

```
123456.789098    765.43212345
123456789111111111222222222
          0123456789012345678
```

↑
Column number 1

the value assigned to A is 123456.789098, and the value assigned to B is 765.43212345.

Output of double precision variables can be performed in the same manner as output of real variables and can be made in either exponential or fixed-point form. For display in exponential form, however, double precision values must use a D format specifier rather than the E specifier used for real values. Thus, to display the double precision variables A and B in exponential format on the standard output device, the following statements are valid:

```
      PRINT 4, A, B
   4  FORMAT (' ', D18.10, 4X, D15.7)
```

Assuming A and B have the values assigned by the previous READ statements, the output resulting from the PRINT statement is:

```
  0.1234567891D+06        0.7654321D+03
123456789111111111222222222233333333
          0123456789012345678901234567
```

↑
Column number 1

Here, the value of A is printed in a field of width 18; 10 digits are printed after the decimal, and the D+06 indicates the placement of the decimal in the value of the number. This is followed by 4 blanks (from the 4X). Then B is printed in a field of width 15, with 7 digits after the decimal, and with D+03 indicating that the decimal is placed between the 5 and the 4. When using the D$w.d$ format specification, as with the E descriptor, the width w must be at least 7 more than the number of decimal places d in order to allow room for a sign, a leading zero, decimal point, and power of 10. If the width of the field is too small, the field is filled with asterisks. If the field width is too large, the number is right justified in the field.

A double precision variable may also be formatted using an F format specifier; in this case, the output is displayed in decimal rather than exponential notation. For example, A and B (above) can be displayed with the following statements:

```
      PRINT 5, A, B
   5  FORMAT ( ' ', 2F8.1)
```

The output resulting from these statements is:

```
123456.8    765.4
1234567891111111
         0123456
```

↑
Column number 1

Double precision expressions may also be used as subroutine and function arguments, as long as each argument is suitably declared in both the MAIN program and the subprogram. A function will return a double precision value if the name of the function is declared to be double precision. This may be done either in the function header or in a type declaration statement within the body of the function. For example, the following function returns the hypotenuse of a right triangle whose other two sides are declared as double precision arguments:

```
DOUBLE PRECISION FUNCTION HYP (X, Y)
   DOUBLE PRECISION X, Y
   HYP = DSQRT ( X ** 2 + Y ** 2 )
   END
```

Skill Builder Exercises

1. Write each of the following double precision constants in standard decimal notation. Assume the computer retains 12 significant digits.

   a. 0.372D 04   d. −7.53852D+04

   b. 0.4512D−03   e. −0.437D+01

   c. 4.2375D 06   f. −0.242D−05

2. Write each of the following decimal values in double precision scientific notation.

   a. −37654390000.

   b. .00004562000000

   c. 234563.5300

   d. −.002356000000

3. Write each of the following constants in double precision form.

   a. 5/8

   b. 1/6

   c. 0.75

   d. 0.37

4. Assume that the double precision variable DB has been assigned the value 375.26359, and the statement PRINT 10, DB is executed. Show the output that is produced by each of the following format statements.

   a. 10 FORMAT (' ', D16.8)
   b. 10 FORMAT (' ', D10.9)

c. 10 FORMAT (' ', D12.5)
d. 10 FORMAT (' ', D8.2)

Programming Exercises

5. Consider the following two equations:

X = 3.14159 - .98888 + .98888 - .14159
Y = X^2 - X - 6.

Algebraically, of course, these equations yield $X = 3$ and $Y = 0$. Write a program to calculate the values of X and Y when these variables are declared as single precision, and then display the calculated values. Then change X and Y to double precision variables and rerun the program.

6. Redo Exercise 4 of Section 3.1 using double precision variables and compare the result to that obtained with a calculator.

7. Redo Exercise 5 of Section 3.1 using double precision variables and the double precision square root function. Compare your results to those obtained using single precision variables.

8. Redo Exercise 16 of Section 3.1 with A, B, and C declared as double precision variables.

10.2   Complex Data

A complex number is represented in FORTRAN as an ordered pair of either real or integer numbers that are separated by a comma and enclosed in parentheses. (Some compilers require both components of a complex number to be real values.) Examples of valid complex constants are:

```
(7,5)
(2.5,6.7)
(-.2, 14)
(0, 6)
(3.6, 0)
```

Examples of invalid complex constants are:

```
-3, 5           (missing parentheses)
(4.,)           (missing second component)
(, 7.)          (missing first component)
```

Computation involving complex numbers follows the standard mathematical definitions. For example, $(8,10) + (3,4)$ equals $(11,14)$, and $(8,10) - (3,4)$ equals $(5,6)$. Computation between a complex number and a real or integer value results in the real or integer being converted to a complex number with an imaginary part of 0; complex arithmetic is then performed. For example, $5 + (2,-3) = (5,0) + (2,-3) = (7,-3)$. Computation between a complex number and a double precision number is not allowed.

The general form of a declaration statement used to declare complex variables is:

```
COMPLEX variable list
```

Thus, the declaration:

```
COMPLEX ROOT1, ROOT2
```

declares that the variables ROOT1 and ROOT2 are complex variables. Complex constants may be assigned to complex variables using assignment statements, as in the assignment statement ROOT1 = (3,–2). If, however, both components of the complex number are not constants, the intrinsic CMPLX function must be used. The following example illustrates this:

```
COMPLEX COM2
REAL X, Y
   .
   .
   .
X = 4.3
Y = 5.2
COM2 = CMPLX (X, Y)
```

Once a variable has been declared as complex, it may be read using either a list-directed or a user-formatted READ statement. Similarly, complex values may be displayed using list-directed or user-formatted PRINT and WRITE statements. The following illustrates the input and output of two complex numbers using list-directed I/O:

```
COMPLEX C, D
READ *, C, D
PRINT *, C, D
```

To input the complex numbers (3.0,–4.0) and (7.0,6.0) the input line should be:

```
(3., -4.)   (7., 6.)
```

When the values of C and D are displayed, they will appear in a similar form, with each number enclosed in parentheses, as follows:

```
(3.00000, -4.00000)   (7.00000, 6.00000)
```

User-formatted input and output of a single complex number require the use of two format descriptors, one for each component of the complex number. Consider the following section of code:

```
    COMPLEX E, F
    READ 3, E, F
3   FORMAT (F5.1, F5.1, F4.1, F4.1)
    PRINT 4, E, F
4   FORMAT (' ', 'E:', 2F6.1, 2X, 'F:', 2F6.1)
```

The input format specifies that both components of the first complex number are to be input as real values using an F5.1 format. Similarly, both components of the second complex number are to be input using an F4.1 format. Thus, if the input is:

```
3.5   4.2   2.1 -3.8
123456789111111111
          012345678
```

↑

Column number 1

the variables E and F are assigned the values (3.5,4.2) and (2.1,–3.8), respectively. The output produced by this section of code is:

```
E:    3.5    4.2  F:    2.1  -3.8
123456789111111111122222222223
          012345678901234567890
```

↑

Column number 1

Intrinsic functions that operate on complex numbers are included in Appendix F. Descriptions of the more commonly used complex functions follow:

The intrinsic function REAL(C) returns the real portion of the complex number C, while the function AIMAG(C) returns the imaginary portion of C. The intrinsic function CABS(C) returns the magnitude, or absolute value, of C, which is defined to be the sum of its two components, and CMPLX(X, Y), as we have already seen, converts two scalar arguments into a complex number.

Exercises

1. Write each of the following FORTRAN complex constants in the algebraic form $a + bi$, where i is the imaginary number equal to the square root of –1.

   a. (4.8, 0)   c. (0, –8)

   b. (3, –7)   d. (–2, 5)

2. Assume that the complex variables CA and CB are assigned the values (3,2) and (4,–5), respectively. For these assignments determine the value of the following expressions.

   a. $CA + CB$ e. $CA ** 2$

   b. $CB - CA$ f. REAL (CA)

   c. $CA * CB$ g. AIMAG (CB)

   d. CB / CA

3. Assume that C is a complex number with a value of (7,–6), and x is a real variable assigned the value –6. For these values determine the value of each of the following.

   a. $C + X$ c. $C * X$

   b. $C - X$ d. C / X

4. Assume that CD is a complex number with a value of (–2.5, 3.4) and that the statement PRINT 15, CD is executed. Show the output that would be produced by each of the following FORMAT statements.

a. 15   FORMAT (' ', 2F6.1)
b. 15   FORMAT (' ', F5.2, 2X, F5.2)
c. 15   FORMAT (' ', '(', F5.1, ',', F5.1, ')')

Programming Exercises

5. Write a program to compute the value of each of the expressions listed in Exercise 3.

6. If n is an integer greater than zero, the equation $x^n = 1$ has n complex solutions that may be obtained by substituting $k = 0, 1, 2, \ldots n-1$ in the formula:

$r_{k+1} = (\cos(2k/n), \sin(2k/n))$

For example, $x^4 = 1$ has 4 roots, which may be found by letting $k = 0, 1, 2$, and 3 in the above formula, as follows:

$r_1 = (\cos(2 * 0 / 4), \sin(2 * 0 / 4))$
$r_2 = (\cos(2 * 1 / 4), \sin(2 * 1 / 4))$
$r_3 = (\cos(2 * 2 / 4), \sin(2 * 2 / 4))$
$r_4 = (\cos(2 * 3 / 4), \sin(2 * 3 / 4))$

Using this information, write a FORTRAN program to find and display the three roots of $x^3 = 1$. Use complex numbers for all three roots.

10.3   String and Substring Processing

In Chapter 2 we saw that a string is another name for a character constant or character variable consisting of one or more characters. In this section we present techniques for processing strings.

The only specific string operator provided in FORTRAN is the concatenation operator, denoted as //. This operator is used to join two strings into a single string, as illustrated by the following code:

```
CHARACTER*3 CHAR1, CHAR2, CHAR3*6, CHAR4*7
CHAR1 = 'HOT'
CHAR2 = 'DOG'
CHAR3 = CHAR1 // CHAR2
```

Here the variable CHAR3 is assigned the string 'HOTDOG'. To insert a blank space between the words HOT and DOG, the following statement should be used:

```
CHAR4 = CHAR1 // ' ' // CHAR2
```

In addition to being concatenated, strings may be compared for equality or inequality. Recall that each character in a string is stored in binary according to either the ASCII or the EBCDIC code. Although the codes are different, they have some characteristics in common. In each of them, a blank precedes (is less than) all letters and numbers; the letters of the alphabet are stored in order from A to Z; and the digits are stored in order from 0 to 9. (It is important to note that in ASCII the letters come before, or are less than, the digits, whereas in EBCDIC the letters follow, or are greater than, the digits.)

When two strings are compared, if their lengths are unequal the shorter string is padded on the right with enough blanks to make the lengths the same. Then the characters are compared, a pair at a time (both first characters, then both second characters, and so on). If no differences are found, the strings are equal; if a difference is found, the string with the first lower character is considered the smaller string. Thus:

'ABC' is less than 'ABCD', since 'ABC' is padded to 'ABC ', and a blank is less than a D
'SMITH' is greater than 'JONES', because S is greater than J
'123' is greater than '1227', since '123' is padded to '123 ', and 3 is greater than 2
'123' is less than '1237', since '123' is first padded with a trailing blank space, and the blank space is less than 7
'FORTRAN' and 'FORTRAN ' are equal, because the shorter string is first padded with two blank spaces to make its length the same as that of the longer string

Using FORTRAN's relational operators, it is possible to put character data in alphabetical order using a sort in much the same way that we would sort numerical data. Program 10-1 uses an exchange sort to put a list of names in alphabetical order (the exchange sort was presented in Section 6.7).

Program 10-1: Sorting Character Data

```
PROGRAM NAMSRT
    CHARACTER*10 NAMES(25), TEMP
    INTEGER I, J, N
    OPEN(UNIT = 20, FILE = 'DATA', STATUS = 'OLD')
    DO 10 I = 1, 25
      READ(20, 15, END = 99) NAMES(I)
15    FORMAT(A10)
      N = I
10    CONTINUE
99    DO 20 I = 1, N-1
        DO 30 J = 1, N - I
          IF ( NAMES (J) .GT. NAMES (J+1) ) THEN
            TEMP = NAMES(J)
            NAMES(J) = NAMES(J+1)
            NAMES(J+1) = TEMP
          ENDIF
30      CONTINUE
20    CONTINUE
    PRINT 25, (NAMES(I), I = 1, N)
25    FORMAT (' ', A10)
    END
```

In reviewing Program 10-1, notice that each line in the file being read must begin in the same column. For example, if the file consisted of the three lines:

```
JONES
 ZEBEDIAH
  ADAMS
```

the string 'ZEBEDIAH' would be the first name displayed by the program, the string ' ADAMS' would be the next, and the string 'JONES' would be last. This is because blanks have a lower value in both ASCII and EBCDIC codes than do any letters.

Substrings

A *substring* of a character string is a subsection of contiguous characters. For example, all possible substrings of the string 'COMPUTE' are:

```
'C'   'CO'   'COM'   'COMP'   'COMPU'   'COMPUT'   'COMPUTE'
'O'   'OM'   'OMP'   'OMPU'   'OMPUT'   'OMPUTE'
'M'   'MP'   'MPU'   'MPUT'   'MPUTE'
'P'   'PU'   'PUT'   'PUTE'
'U'   'UT'   'UTE'
'T'   'TE'
'E'
```

It is possible to extract a substring from a character constant, character variable, or character array element using the (:) operator. The general form of this operator is:

$$exp1(exp2:exp3)$$

where *exp1* is either a string variable, a string constant, an array element name, or a string expression using the concatenation operator, *exp2* is an integer expression that specifies the leftmost character position of the substring, and *exp3* is an integer expression that specifies the rightmost character of the substring. For example, TEXT(3:8) specifies a substring containing the characters in positions three through eight of the string TEXT. If TEXT contains the string 'A STITCH IN TIME', then TEXT(3:8) equals 'STITCH'.

An error occurs if the value of *exp2* is less than one, the value of *exp2* is greater than the value of *exp3,* or the value of *exp3* is greater than the length of the original string. Additionally, if the value of *esp2* is omitted, a value of 1 is assumed; if the value of *exp3* is omitted, a value equal to the length of the original string is assumed. For example, assuming that DEMO, DEMO1, DEMO2, and DEMO3 are all string variables of length 10 and that DEMO has been assigned the value 'ABCDEFGHIJ', the assignments:

```
DEMO1 = DEMO (3:5)
DEMO2 = DEMO ( :6)
DEMO3 = DEMO (3: )
```

store the third through fifth characters of DEMO to the string DEMO1, the first through sixth characters of DEMO to DEMO2, and the third through last characters of DEMO to DEMO3. In each case the substring is stored left justified and is padded on the right with blanks, if necessary. As with strings, substrings may be concatenated using the concatenation operator.

In-Memory String Conversions

As we have seen in the previous chapter, both READ and WRITE statements can be used to read and write data from external data files. In addition, these statements can be used to read and write data directly from or to a character string. Character strings used in this manner are referred to as *internal files* because the READ and WRITE statements transfer data from one internal location to another. For example, consider the following statements:

```
INTEGER I
REAL VAL1, VAL2
CHARACTER TEXT*15
TEXT = '22.35 17.258 53'
READ(TEXT,*) VAL1, VAL2, I
```

In this section of code, the READ statement receives its input directly from the internal variable TEXT, just as it would from the keyboard or an external data file. Thus, the value 22.35 is stored in the real variable VAL1, the value 17.258 is stored in the real variable VAL2, and the value 53 is stored in the integer variable I. Since the input from the string effectively involves converting from either the ASCII or EBCDIC code used to store the string into the data type of the receiving variables, this type of input is also referred to as in-memory string conversion.

An extremely useful application of in-memory conversion is in "stripping off" of undesirable characters in a data file. For example, assume that a record in a data file contains a price containing a dollar sign and followed by a description, such as:

```
$32.50  Right-front light assembly
```

If each record in the file is first read into a character variable named LINE, the price and description in the record can be obtained using the statements:

```
    READ(LINE, 10) PRICE, DESCRP
10  FORMAT(1X,F5.2,A)
```

In a similar manner, writing to an internal file allows us to "assemble" a string from one or more variables before a complete line is written to either a data file or the standard output device. For example, assuming that TEXT is a character variable of length 14, AMOUNT is an integer variable, and PRICE is a real variable, the statements:

```
   WRITE(TEXT,3) AMOUNT, PRICE
3  FORMAT(I3,3X,'$',F7.2)
```

would place the values in AMOUNT and PRICE into the TEXT string as the first three and last seven characters, respectively.

Skill Builder Exercises

1. Indicate whether the following are true or false.

    a. `'ABC' .GT. 'AC'`

    b. `'FIFTY' .LT. 'FIVE'`

    c. `'48' .GT. '476'`

    d. `48 .GT. 476`

    e. `'TODAY' .EQ. 'FRIDAY'`

2. For the following FORTRAN statements:

```
CHARACTER*30 ONE, TWO, THREE
ONE = 'THIS IS THE FIRST SENTENCE'
TWO = 'EIGHTH ONE NOT HERE'
THREE = 'HERE''S THE THIRD'
```

    a. Determine the result of the following substring extractions.

        (1) `ONE(12:17)`

        (2) `TWO(8:9)`

        (3) `THREE(4:7)`

    b. Determine the result of the following concatenations.

        (1) `ONE(13:15)//TWO(10:11)//ONE(13:14)//TWO(3:5)//THREE(2:3)`

        (2) `ONE(2:4)//TWO(7:8)//THREE(15:15)//' '//THREE(:3)//'S'`

        (3) `ONE(26:)//TWO(:2)//THREE(10:10)`

Programming Exercises

3. Write a program to read in a name having the form *first name last name* and display it the form *last name, first name*. (*Hint:* After reading the name, check for blank spaces. The first blank indicates the end of the first name, and the second blank indicates the end of the last name. You will want to store the desired output in a second character string, along with the comma and blank, before printing it; use concatenation to do this.)

4. Write a program that reads in a list of names from a file named NAME.DAT, sorts the names in reverse alphabetical order (use any sort other than the bubble sort to do this), and outputs the names in sorted order.

5. A mail order catalog codes its catalog numbers with five digits followed by a letter. The digits indicate the item number, and the letter indicates what additional information is needed, according to the following codes:

```
S       size only
C       color only
B       both size and color
N       no additional information needed
```

Write a program to read in a catalog number, look at the letter in the sixth position, and print a statement of what additional information is needed.

6. Modify the program written in Exercise 5 to accommodate a catalog number consisting of five digits and one letter in any order.

10.4   Data Structures as Parallel Arrays

A data structure is a data type consisting of several elements, not all of which need to be the same data type (recall that an array is a data structure in which all elements are of the same data type). A single data structure consists of a number of individual items, called *fields*. For example, consider Figure 10-1, which illustrates a single structure consisting of a book title, a cat-alog number, and a price field. The *form* of this structure consists of the three field names, the data types that can be stored in each field, and the arrangement of the fields. The *contents* of each field refers to the actual data stored in the field.

The real usefulness of structures is realized when the same structure form is used for lists of data. In this situation the

Book Title	Catalog Number	Price
PC Tools	CB3027	$28.50

Figure 10-1   A Book Inventory Record

contents of each structure would contain the data for a particular member of a larger group. For example, Figure 10-2 illustrates a list of insurance company structures, where each structure contains the data for a single individual. Notice that the form of each structure is the same and consists of a series of fields to hold the name, street address, city and state, zip code, age, premium amount, and renewal date. Clearly, some of these fields must be character, but some (for example, premium amount) must be numeric.

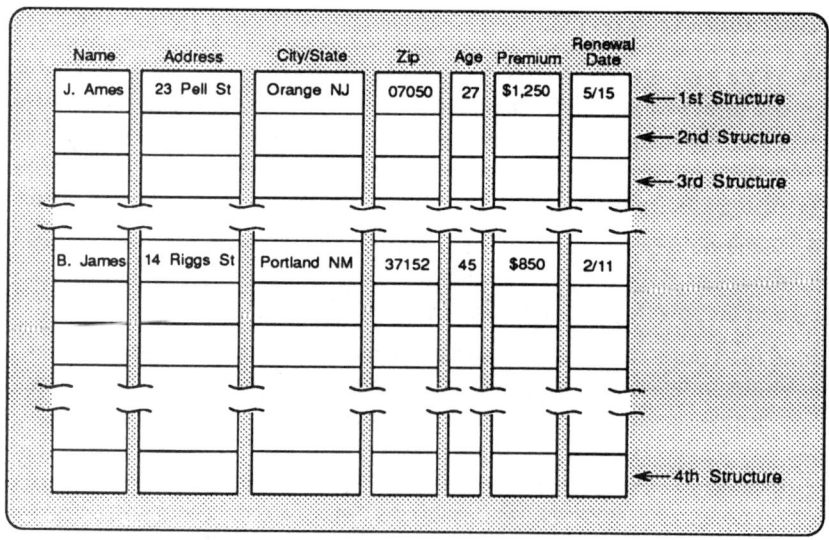

Figure 10-2   A List of Structures

If an array could hold several types of data, a list of structures could be easily implemented using a two dimension array. Instead, such structures are implemented in FORTRAN 77 using a series of parallel linear arrays.* Each linear array holds a single field; in the example above, we could use a character array for the name, another character array for the street address, and so on, using an integer array for the age and a real array for the premium amount. As shown in Figure 10-3, each individual's data would be stored in the same position in all arrays.

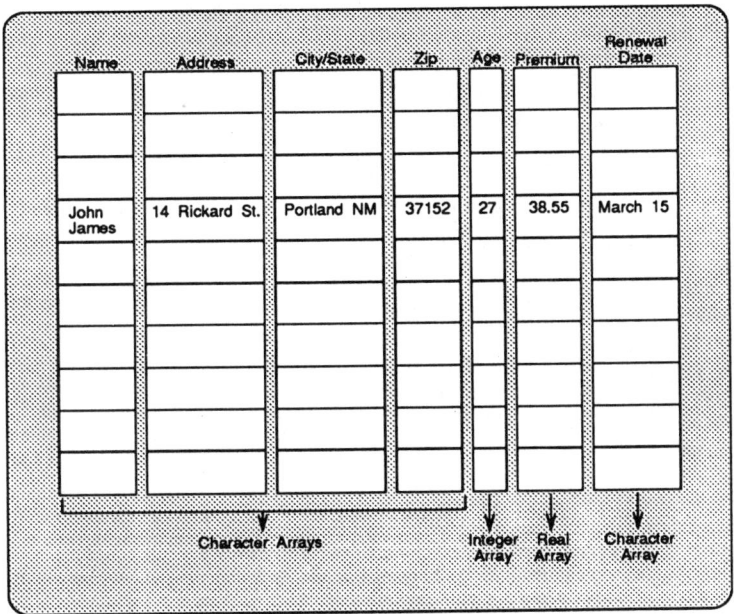

Figure 10-3   A List of Structures Implemented with Parallel Arrays

Program 10-2 illustrates the use of parallel arrays for storing and processing data input from a data file containing a maximum of fifty records. Each record in the data file consists of a student name and three test grades. The program inputs all of the records into a set of parallel arrays and then determines and displays the letter grade for each student based on the average of three tests. For each student, the name, three exam grades, the numerical average, and the letter grade are stored using six parallel linear arrays. The data for the first four arrays (name, first test grade, second test grade, and third test grade) are input from the external data file; the data for the fifth and sixth arrays (numerical average and letter grade) are calculated by the program. Figure 10-4a, b, and c provide the appropriate flowcharts for this program.

---

* In the proposed new FORTRAN standard, sturctures can be implemented directly as a derived data type (see Section 12.5).

Program 10-2

```
PROGRAM STRUCT
  CHARACTER*10 NAME(50), GRADE*1(50)
  REAL AVG(50)
  INTEGER EX1(50), EX2(50), EX3(50), I, N
  OPEN(UNIT = 22, FILE = 'GRADES', STATUS = 'OLD')
  DO 10 I = 1, 50
    READ(22,15,END = 99) NAME(I), EX1(I), EX2(I), EX3(I)
    N = I
10    CONTINUE
99    CALL AVERAGE (EX1, EX2, EX3, AVG, N)
  CALL LETGRD (AVG, GRADE, N)
  DO 20 J = 1, N
    PRINT 25, NAME(J),EX1(J),EX2(J),EX3(J),AVG(J),GRADE(J)
20    CONTINUE
15    FORMAT (A, 3I5)
25    FORMAT(' ',A, 3X, 3I5, 2X, F6.2, 2X, A )
  END
***
  SUBROUTINE AVERAGE (EX1, EX2, EX3, AVG, N)
  INTEGER EX1(50), EX2(50), EX3(50), N, I
  REAL AVG(50)
  DO 10 I = 1, N
    AVG(I) = (EX1(I) + EX2(I) + EX3(I)) / 3.
10    CONTINUE
  END
***
  SUBROUTINE LETGRD (AVG, GRADE, N)
  CHARACTER GRADE(50)
  REAL AVG(50)
  INTEGER I, N
  DO 10 I = 1, N
    IF ( AVG(I) .GE. 90) THEN
      GRADE(I) = 'A'
    ELSE IF ( AVG (I) .GE. 80) THEN
      GRADE(I) = 'B'
    ELSE IF ( AVG (I) .GE. 70) THEN
      GRADE(I) = 'C'
    ELSE IF ( AVG (I) .GE. 60) THEN
      GRADE(I) = 'D'
    ELSE
      GRADE(I) = 'F'
    ENDIF
10    CONTINUE
  END
```

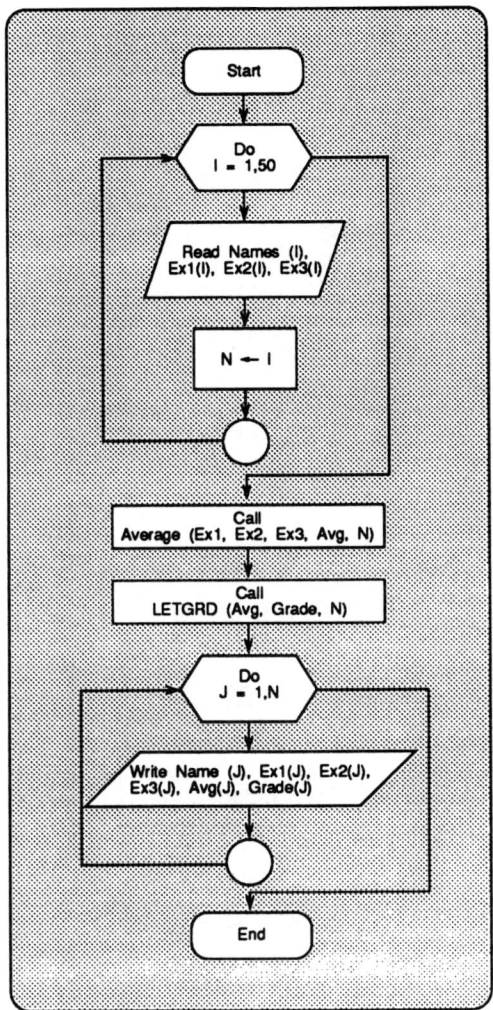

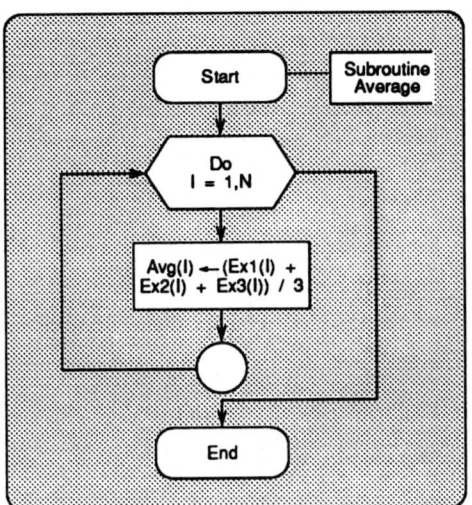

Figure 10-4b   continued

**Figure 10-4a   Flowcharts for
Program 10-2**

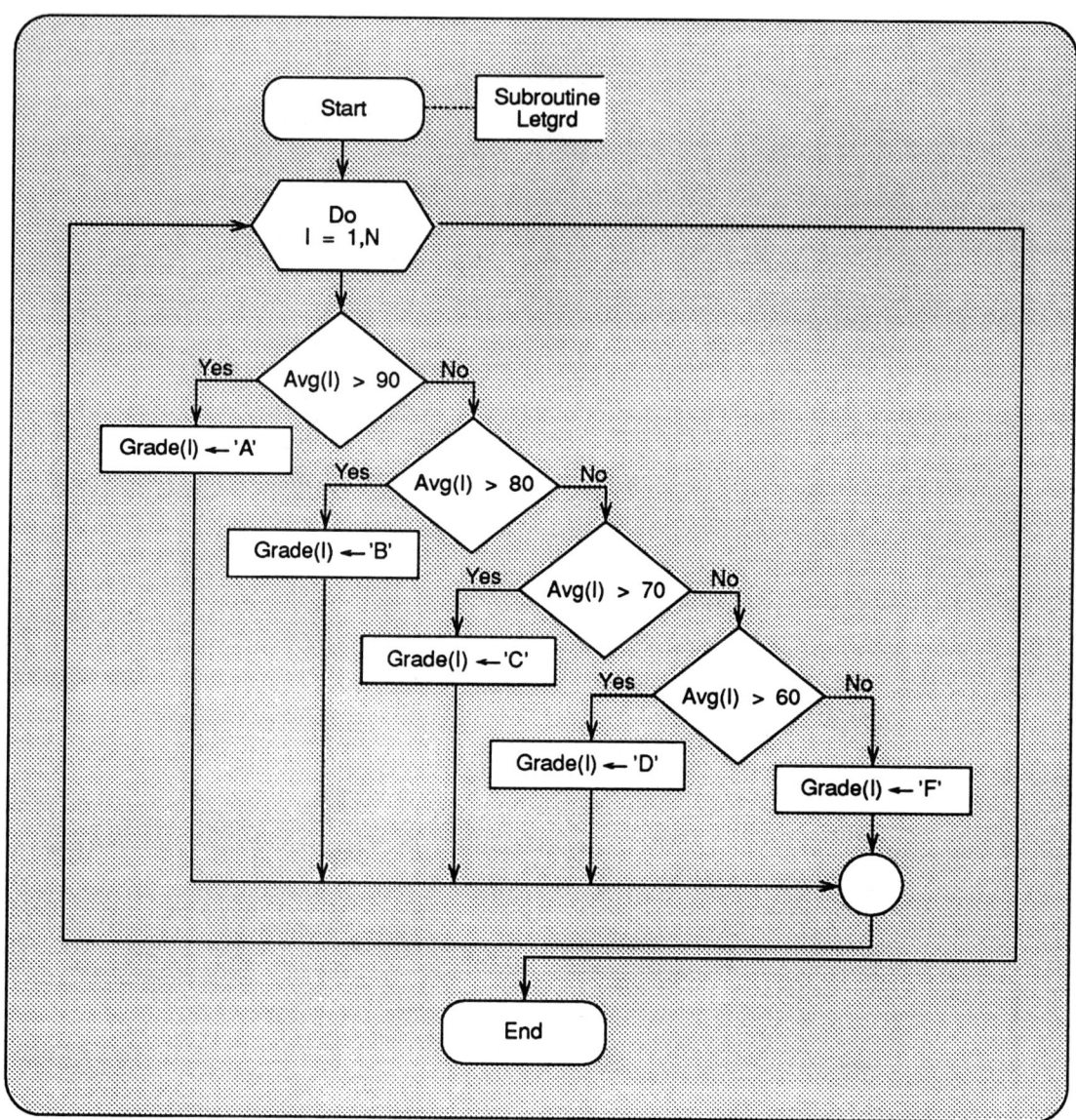

Figure 10-4c   continued

Skill Builder Exercises

1. List the fields found on your driver's license.

2. French Creek Marina stores 500 boats for the winter. Records must be maintained on each boat, detailing the owner's name, the length of the boat, the boat license number, the boat slip number, and the warehouse in which the boat is stored. Determine suitable array names and data types that would be required to store this data.

3. Shown is part of a data file that contains student records. Each record consists of the student's name, student's birthday, the number of credits for which the student is registered this semester, and the student's year in school (FR, freshman; SO, sophomore; JR, junior; SR, senior; GR, graduate student). For this data determine a pair of READ-FOR-MAT statements that could be used to input this data from the data file.

```
JONES,  JOHN      011457 15      FR
SMITH,  SUSAN     102270 12      SO
COOKE,  PAUL      042837  6      GR
MICRO,  MARVIN    121867 18      SR
1234567891111111111222222222233333
          01234567890123456789012 34
↑
Column number 1
```

Programming Exercises

4. Write a program to read in the data given in Exercise 3; add more data so you have a total of at least 20 records representing at least 4 students from each year (FR, SO, JR, and so on). Have your program compute the average number of credits taken and then display the data for all the freshmen, followed by that for all the sophomores, and so on. Additionally, compute the average number of credits for each year, and print that information.

5. The chart below shows the information kept on file by the New Hope Computerized Dating Service. The numbers indicate the number of phone calls each participant received monthly through NHCDS. Write a program to read in the data; then compute the total number of phone calls per month and the total number of phone calls per participant.

NAME	JA	FE	MA	AP	MA	JN	JL	AU	SE	OC	NO	DE
SMOTHERS	3	4	5	2	1	7	8	5	4	3	2	4
JANKE	1	4	2	3	5	6	7	8	3	2	5	6
LIGIN	3	1	2	3	5	3	0	8	6	3	1	2
MELLOW	4	3	1	6	3	0	4	2	8	4	3	1
BILLS	2	4	1	6	4	3	2	7	5	4	2	3
HENRY	1	2	1	0	2	1	3	0	3	4	3	1

6. French Creek Marina (see Exercise 2) needs its bills computed from the data given below. Each record gives the boat owner's name, the boat length, the month the boat went into storage, and the month the boat came out of storage. Storage charges are $1.50 per foot of boat length per month. For example, storage costs for a 20-foot boat that is stored from September until May (9 months) would be $270 (20 x 1.5 x 9). Write a program to read the given data, compute storage costs for each boat, and display the given data as well as each boat's storage costs.

```
KING         22    SEPT    MAY
KING         31    AUG     MAY
KING         18    SEPT    JUNE
ROGERS       18    OCT     JUNE
ROGERS       24    AUG     MAY
SMITHSON     22    AUG     JUNE
SMITHSON     45    SEPT    MAY
CARDWELL     34    AUG     APR
CAUGHEY      42    SEPT    APR
CAUGHEY      18    AUG     MAY
JONES        21    OCT     APR
JONES        45    SEPT    MAY
JONES        15    SEPT    APR
MARTIN       28    OCT     MAY
```

7. Modify the program written for Exercise 6 to calculate and display the total charges for each boat owner.

10.5   Applications

In this section we present two applications of the topics covered in this chapter. First look at a program for analyzing text using the substring (:) operator. Then examine a program that uses parallel linear arrays to simulate data structures.

Application 1: Word Analysis

When writing an article, an author often finds it desirable to have a count of the number of words in the article. The computer can aid in this task. Since each word in a sentence is followed by a blank space, it would seem that we could determine the number of words in a line of text by counting the number of blanks it contains. However, we should look at an example to be sure that this method works. The sentence "this is a sentence" has three blank spaces and four words; so far, the number of words is not equal to the number of blanks. However, if we were to store that sentence (or string) in a character variable called LINE, of length 80, then LINE would look like Figure 10-5. Notice that each word is followed by at least one blank, and the end of the sentence is now followed by more than one blank space. So if the program counted blank spaces, the number of blanks would give us the number of words, as long as we only counted the series of blanks after the last word as a single

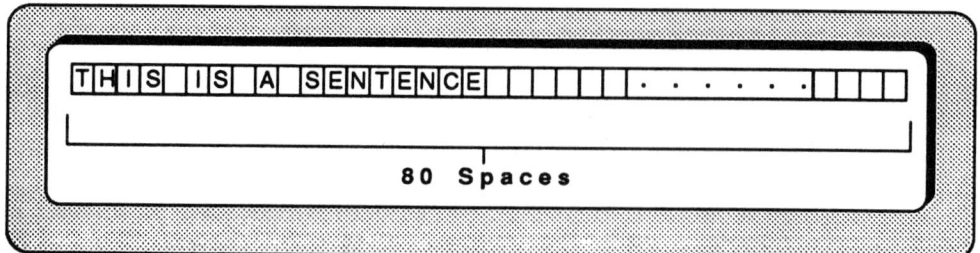

Figure 10-5   A Sample Line of Words

blank. Our program could check for a blank space using the substring (:) operator to step across the line. Remember that LINE(I:I) looks at the character in the *I*th position, so a DO loop that allowed *I* to run from 1 to the end of the string would look at each character in turn. Using a comparison such as:

```
IF (LINE (I:I) .EQ. ' ')
```

we would be able to locate each blank space in the sentence. Note, again, that if we just counted the blanks in the line, we would think there were more words than there are, because once the sentence is read in, the rest of LINE is padded on the right with blanks. So how do we know when we have reached the end of the series of words? Look at Figure 10-5 again and see that the last word in the sentence is followed by at least two blanks. So two blanks in a row will tell us that the end of the sentence has been reached. When we reach the end of the sentence (as indicated by two blank spaces in a row), the number of blanks (counting the double at the end as a single blank) gives us the number of words. The flowchart for determining the number of words in a single line of text is illustrated in Figure 10-6.

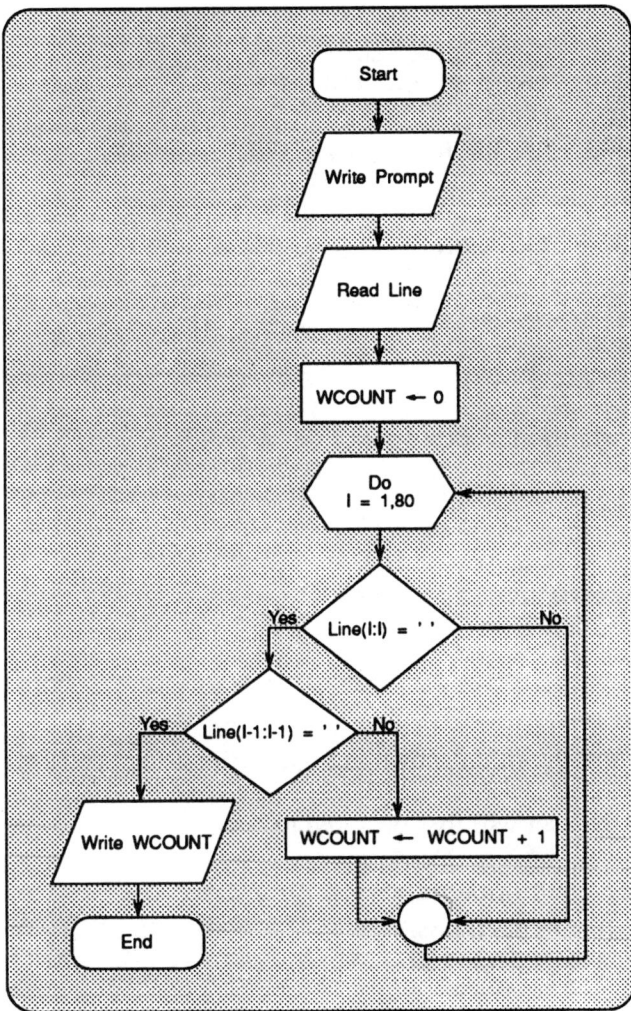

Figure 10-6   Flowchart for Counting the Words in a Single Line of Text

Program 10-3

```
      PROGRAM WORDCT
         CHARACTER*80 LINE
         INTEGER WCOUNT, I
***   READ THE LINE INTO MEMORY
         PRINT*, 'ENTER THE LINE TO BE CHECKED'
         PRINT*, 'DO NOT USE MORE THAN 78 CHARACTERS'
         READ (5,2) LINE
***   SEARCH THE LINE FOR BLANKS; AT EACH BLANK, COUNT A WORD
         WCOUNT = 0
         DO 10 I = 1, 80
           IF ( LINE (I:I) .EQ. ' ') THEN
***   CHECK FOR END OF LINE
              IF ( LINE(I-1:I-1) .EQ. ' ') THEN
                 WRITE (6,3) WCOUNT
                 STOP
              ENDIF
***   IF NOT THE END OF LINE, WE HAVE FOUND END OF A WORD
              WCOUNT = WCOUNT + 1
           ENDIF
10         CONTINUE
2          FORMAT (A)
3          FORMAT (' ', 'NUMBER OF WORDS IS', I5)
           END
```

Program 10-3 implements the algorithm shown in Figure 10-6 using FORTRAN code.

When this program is run, the user will first be asked to:

```
ENTER THE LINE TO BE CHECKED
DO NOT USE MORE THAN 78 CHARACTERS
```

The user might now respond with the following:

```
THIS IS A SENTENCE WHOSE WORD COUNT I WANT CHECKED
```

The computer will then respond with the following:

```
NUMBER OF WORDS IS    10
```

The exercises at the end of this section will offer you the opportunity to modify this program by entering a series of lines and counting sentences as well as words.

Application 2: Weight Loss Club

The following data represent individuals at the U-Watch-Ur-Weight Club. The first column contains the initials of the dieter, the second column gives the dieter's initial weight, and the third column gives the dieter's final weight.

```
KLK        132    115
FPD        225    210
DMC        176    154
RJK        165    151
CAJ        182    176
```

We want to write a program to find the weight loss for each individual and the average weight loss for all of the individuals together. To do this, we will read the data into three parallel arrays, one each for the dieter's initials, initial weight, and final weight, respectively. A fourth array will be used to store the weight loss for each individual. The pseudocode for our program is:

Open the data file and input each record into the first
  three parallel arrays of a four-array data structure
DO for each individual
  compute a weight loss and store this value in a fourth array
  add the weight loss to a total
Enddo
Calculate the average weight loss
Display the values in the data structure

Program 10-4 is the FORTRAN implementation of this pseudocode. As written, Program 10-4 stores the data from the data file into three parallel arrays, which are named INIT, INITWT, and TERMWT. The program then uses a DO loop to step through the initial and final weight arrays. Each final weight is subtracted from the initial weight, and the result (the weight loss) is stored in the WTLOSS array. The computation of the sum of weight losses is made within the same loop by adding the individual losses into the SUM variable. Finally, the average weight loss is determined by dividing the sum of the weight lost by the number of dieters, and the input data and calculated data are displayed together.

When Program 10-4 is run with the given data as input, the following output is produced:

```
KLK   132   115    17
FPD   225   210    15
DMC   176   154    22
RJK   165   151    14
CAJ   182   176     6
THE AVERAGE WEIGHT LOSS IS   14.8
```

The first column contains the initials, the second and third columns contain the initial and final weights, respectively, and the fourth column contains the weight loss. The last output line displays the average weight loss.

Program 10-4

```
      PROGRAM DIET
       CHARACTER*3 INIT(50)
       INTEGER INITWT(50), TERMWT(50), WTLOSS(50), SUM, I, N
       REAL AVG
*
*   READ THE DATA
*
       OPEN (UNIT = 7, FILE = 'WEIGHT')
       DO 5 I = 1, 50
          READ (7, 15, END = 99) INIT(I), INITWT(I), TERMWT(I)
    5  CONTINUE
*
*   COMPUTE INDIVIDUAL AND TOTAL WEIGHT LOSS
   99     N = I - 1
          SUM = 0
          DO 10 I = 1, N
             WTLOSS(I) = INITWT(I) - TERMWT(I)
             SUM = SUM + WTLOSS(I)
   10     CONTINUE
*
*    COMPUTE AVERAGE LOSS
*
          AVG = SUM / FLOAT(N)
*
* DISPLAY THE INPUT AND COMPUTED DATA TOGETHER *
          DO 30 I = 1, N
             WRITE(6,25) INIT(I), INITWT(I), TERMWT(I), WTLOSS(I)
   30     CONTINUE
          WRITE(6,35) AVG
   15     FORMAT ( A, 2X, I3, 2X, I3 )
   25     FORMAT(' ', A, 3( 2X, I3 ) )
   35     FORMAT(' ', 'THE AVERAGE WEIGHT LOSS IS ', F5.1)
          END
```

Additional Exercises for Chapter 10

1. Modify Program 10-3 to accept five lines of input. Have the program count the number of sentences as well as the number of words; assume all the sentences end with periods. Then have the program compute the average number of words per sentence. Test the program on this exercise.

2. Modify the program you wrote in Exercise 1 so that a sentence may end with a period, a question mark, or an exclamation point.

3. Modify Program 10-3 so that it counts the number of letters in each word of a sentence. Have the program then compute the average word length of the sentence.

4. Write a program to read the following city names and temperatures from either the keyboard or a data file into two parallel single-dimensioned arrays.

```
Boston      45      Minneapolis     22
Fresno      66      San Diego       74
New York    51      San Francisco   69
Mobile      73      Houston         70
Madison     -2      Cortland        27
Miami       88      Nashville       65
Chicago     57      Portland        61
Trenton     30      Seattle         54
```

   Display the contents of the arrays, with column headings. Calculate and display the average temperature, the minimum temperature, and the maximum temperature.

5. Modify the program written for Exercise 4 to determine the number of balmy days (temperature over 70 degrees Fahrenheit), the number of moderate days (temperature between 50 and 70 degrees Fahrenheit), the number of chilly days (temperature between 25 and 49 degrees Fahrenheit), and the number of cold days (temperature below 25 degrees Fahrenheit). Display this information in a second table, with appropriate headings.

6. Modify the program written for Exercise 4 to display a single table showing the temperatures in decreasing order. Include the names of the cities in the table.

7. Modify the program written for Exercise 4 to display a table that lists the cities in alphabetical order. Include the temperatures in the table.

8. Write a FORTRAN program to read the following student names and grades from either the keyboard or a data file.

```
Adams       94      Turner          66
Baker       88      Lundberg        42
Morris     100      Jeffers         87
Parker      73      Weston          89
Stine       75      Rogers          96
Godley      54      Feissner        99
```

   Have your program display the data in a table with column headings. Also have your program determine and print the average grade, the maximum and minimum grades, and the range (maximum minus minimum).

9. Modify the program written for Exercise 8 to have it determine the distribution of grades, that is, the number of As (90 or above), Bs (80 to 89), Cs (70 to 79), Ds (60 to 69), and Fs (below 60). Display the distribution using appropriate descriptions.

10. Modify the program written for Exercise 8 to produce a table listing the grades in increasing numerical order. Include the students' names in the table.

11. Modify the program written for Exercise 8 to produce a table listing the students' names in alphabetical order. Include the grades in the table.

10.6   Common Programming Errors

The errors commonly associated with the material presented in this chapter are:

1. Forgetting to explicitly declare double precision variables and functions that return a double precision value. If a double precision variable is not explicitly declared, it will be implicitly typed according to its first letter.

2. Using single precision intrinsic functions with double precision arguments or double precision intrinsic functions with single precision arguments.

3. Inadvertently assigning a double precision value to either a real or an integer variable. In such a case the extra precision is lost because the double precision value is either converted to a single precision real value or truncated to an integer value.

4. Forgetting to explicitly declare complex variables and functions that return complex values. If a complex variable is not explicitly declared, it will be implicitly typed according to its first letter.

5. Inadvertently assigning a complex variable or value to a real variable. This results in the loss of the imaginary part of the complex number.

6. Forgetting to explicitly declare all character variables. If a character variable is not explicitly declared, it will be implicitly typed according to its first letter.

7. Confusing a character string of numbers with the number itself. The string '2345' consists of four symbols and is a separate entity from the number 2345. The string '2345' cannot be combined with a numeric variable, nor can it be compared with a numeric.

8. Using the substring operator STRING(I:J) incorrectly. I and J must be no less than 1 and no greater than the length of STRING. In addition, I must be less than or equal to J.

9. Attempting to use the concatenation operator (//) with noncharacter data. Only character variables and values may be concatenated.

10.7   Chapter Summary

1. In order to achieve greater precision than that provided by real values, FORTRAN provides the double precision data type. A double precision variable must be explicitly declared as DOUBLE PRECISION.

2. A double precision constant must be written in scientific notation using a "D" to indicate the exponent.

3. Intrinsic functions exist for double precision data. Most begin with D, and most require that the argument(s) be double precision.

4. A user-written function that is intended to return a double precision value must be declared double precision in both the calling program and the function itself.

5. A complex number is represented in FORTRAN as an ordered pair of either real or integer numbers that are separated by a comma and enclosed in parentheses. The first number in parentheses is the real part of the number and the second number is the imaginary part. Complex arithmetic in FORTRAN follows the same rules as does complex arithmetic in mathematics.

6. Complex variables must be explicitly declared as COMPLEX.

7. If a complex value is written with a list-directed PRINT or WRITE statement, it is written in ordered pair form. If it is written with a formatted PRINT or WRITE statement, two format descriptors must be given, one for the real part and one for the imaginary part.

8. A function that is intended to return a complex value must be declared complex in both the calling program and the function itself. Additionally, intrinsic functions exist for complex data. Most begin with C, and most require that their argument(s) be complex.

9. Concatenation of strings is accomplished using the concatenation operator (//).

10. A substring is a group of contiguous letters that form part of a string. The substring operator (:) is used to extract a substring from a larger string variable.

11. A single data structure is a collection of fields that need not be of the same data type. A list of structures is implemented in FORTRAN 77 using parallel linear arrays. The proposed new FORTRAN standard has a provision for directly implementing structures.

Numerical Techniques and Applications

Chapter Eleven

In this chapter we present and apply several programming techniques to solve a variety of commonly encountered numerical applications. The solving of simultaneous equations is presented first. This is followed by root finding and numerical integration techniques.

11.1   Solving Simultaneous Linear Equations

A linear equation in two unknowns, x and y, is an equation of the form:

$$ax + by = k \qquad (1)$$

where a, b, and k are known numbers, and a and b are not both zero. For example, the equation $3x + 2y = 10$ is linear because it has the form of equation 1, with $a = 3$, $b = 2$, and $k = 10$. Although we have defined a linear equations for two unknowns, the definition may be extended to include any number of unknowns. For example, the equation $x + 3y + 2z = 5$ is a linear equation in the three unknowns x, y, and z. What makes the equation linear is that each unknown quantity is raised only to the first power and is multiplied by a known number.

Two Linear Equations with Two Unknowns

A simultaneous set of two linear equations in two unknowns are two linear equations having the general form:

$$a_1x + b_1y = k_1$$
$$a_2x + b_2y = k_2$$

where x and y are the unknowns. For example, the equations:

$$2.3x + 4y = 21.75$$
$$3x + 1.5y = 13.5$$

are a simultaneous set of two linear equations in two unknowns. Here the constants a_1, b_1, k_1, a_2, b_2, and k_2 are the numbers 2.3, 4, 21.75, 3, 1.5, and 13.5, respectively, and the unknowns are the values of x and y that satisfy both equations.

The solution to two simultaneous linear equations in two unknowns, if one exists, can easily be solved for using Cramer's rule, which requires the use of determinants. A determinant is a square array of elements enclosed in straight lines, such as:

$$\begin{vmatrix} 3 & 6 \\ 2 & 5 \end{vmatrix}$$

that has the same number of rows as it has columns and can be evaluated to yield a result. The number of rows or columns in a determinant determines its order. For example, the determinant:

$$\begin{vmatrix} 6 & 9 \\ 0 & -2 \end{vmatrix}$$

is a second-order determinant, because it has two rows and two columns. The general form of a second-order determinant is:

$$\begin{vmatrix} a_1 & b_1 \\ a_2 & b_2 \end{vmatrix}$$

where a_1 and b_1 refer to the first and second elements in the first row, respectively, and a_2 and b_2 refer to the first and second elements of the second row, respectively.

The value of this determinant is then calculated as $a_1 * b_2 - a_2 * b_1$. Thus, the value of the determinant:

$$\begin{vmatrix} 3 & 6 \\ 2 & 5 \end{vmatrix}$$

is $(3 * 5) - (2 * 6) = 3$, and:

$$\begin{vmatrix} 6 & 9 \\ 0 & -2 \end{vmatrix}$$

is $(6 * (-2)) - (0 * 9) = -12$.

Let us now relate the evaluation of determinants to solving sets of two linear equations. Cramer's rule states that the solution of the set of linear equations:

$$a_1x + b_1y = k_1$$
$$a_2x + b_2y = k_2$$

is:

$$x = \frac{\begin{vmatrix} k_1 & b_1 \\ k_2 & b_2 \end{vmatrix}}{\begin{vmatrix} a_1 & b_1 \\ a_2 & b_2 \end{vmatrix}}$$

and:

$$y = \frac{\begin{vmatrix} a_1 & k_1 \\ a_2 & k_2 \end{vmatrix}}{\begin{vmatrix} a_1 & b_1 \\ a_2 & b_2 \end{vmatrix}}$$

As an example using these formulas, consider the set of linear equations:

$$2x + 3y = 130$$
$$10x + 5y = 330$$

Using Cramer's rule, we obtain the solution for this set of equations as:

$$x = \frac{\begin{vmatrix} 130 & 3 \\ 330 & 5 \end{vmatrix}}{\begin{vmatrix} 2 & 3 \\ 10 & 5 \end{vmatrix}} = \frac{(130 * 5) - (330 * 3)}{(2 * 5) - (10 * 3)} = \frac{650 - 990}{10 - 30} = \frac{-340}{-20} = 17$$

$$y = \frac{\begin{vmatrix} 2 & 130 \\ 10 & 330 \end{vmatrix}}{\begin{vmatrix} 2 & 3 \\ 10 & 5 \end{vmatrix}} = \frac{(2 * 330) - (10 * 130)}{(2 * 5) - (10 * 3)} = \frac{660 - 1300}{10 - 30} = \frac{-640}{-20} = 32$$

Notice that the same determinant is used as the denominator in solving for both unknowns. When this denominator determinant is equal to zero, no unique solution can be found that solves the equations. Also notice that the numerator used in solving for x is the same as the denominator, with the first column replaced by the coefficients on the right side of the equations (k_1 and k_2). Likewise, the numerator in the solution for y replaces the second column of the denominator determinant with the coefficients k_1 and k_2. This pattern lends itself to ease of programming and also carries over to the solution of a larger number of equations.

 Program 11-1

```
PROGRAM MAIN
   REAL A1, B1, K1, A2, B2, K2, X, Y, DET2, VALDET
   PRINT *,'ENTER A1, B1, K1, A2, B2, K2: '
   READ *, A1, B1, K1, A2, B2, K2
   VALDET = DET2 (A1, B1, A2, B2)
   IF (ABS (VALDET) .GE. 0.001) THEN
      X  = DET2 (K1, B1, K2, B2) / VALDET
      Y  = DET2 (A1, K1, A2, K2 ) / VALDET
      PRINT *, 'THE SOLUTION IS:'
      PRINT *, '     X = ', X
      PRINT *, '     Y = ', Y
   ELSE
      PRINT *, 'A UNIQUE SOLUTION DOES NOT EXIST'
   ENDIF
   END
*
* SUBPROGRAM FUNCTION TO EVALUATE 2X2 DETERMINANT   | A  B |
*                                                   | C  D |
   REAL FUNCTION DET2 (A, B, C, D)
      REAL A, B, C, D
*
      DET2 = A * D - B * C
*
      END
```

Program 11-1 allows us to enter the numerical coefficients for two linear equations and solve for the two unknowns, x and y, when a unique solution exists. The values of all three determinants required to solve the set of two linear equations are evaluated using a single subprogram function.

Following is the output produced by Program 11-1 when it is used to solve the set of equations:

$$2x + 3y = 130$$
$$10x + 5y = 330$$

```
ENTER A1, B1, K1, A2, B2, K2:
2 3 130 10 5 330
THE SOLUTION IS:
      X =        17.000000
      Y =        32.000000
```

Application: Battery Charger

As an example of solving two equations with two unknowns consider the electrical equivalent circuit of an automobile battery charger, shown in Figure 11-1. The circuit models the car's electrical system after the car has been started. The purpose of the generator (or alternator) is to supply power to (that is, recharge) the battery. A real voltage source, such as a generator or battery, can be modeled by an ideal source in series with a resistor representing the internal resistance of that source. The components shown in the circuit diagram are:

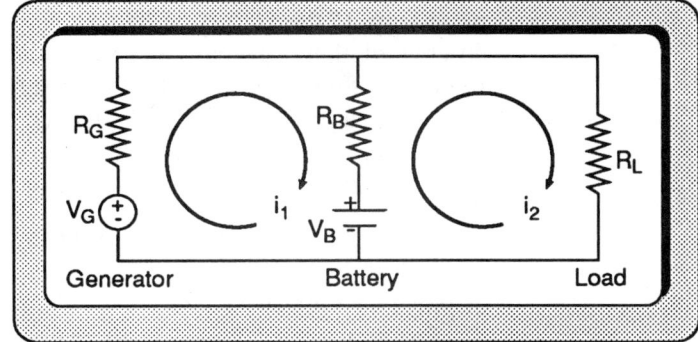

Figure 11-1   Automobile Battery-Charging Circuit

V_G : ideal generator voltage
R_G : generator internal resistance
V_B : ideal battery voltage (for example, 12 volts)
R_B : battery internal resistance
R_L : load resistance (that is, equivalent resistance of all devices drawing energy, such as headlights and radio)

If the component values are known, we can set up two linear equations in terms of the two loop currents, i_1 and i_2. By solving for the two unknowns, we can determine the voltage, current, or power for any source or resistor. By applying circuit laws to the two loops, we obtain the following equations:

$$-V_G + R_G\, i_1 + R_B\, (i_1 - i_2) + V_B = 0$$
$$-V_B + R_B\, (i_2 - i_1) + R_L\, i_2 = 0$$

These equations result from the fact that the sum of all voltages around a closed circuit path (that is, a loop) is zero, and that the voltage across a resistor (in volts) is equal to its current (in amperes, or amps for short) multiplied by the resistance value (in ohms). We notice that the current through the generator is i_1 flowing upward, and the load current is i_2 flowing downward. The battery has both loop currents circulating through it in opposite directions, so that its current can be specified as $i_1 - i_2$ flowing downward, or equivalently, $i_2 - i_1$ flowing upward.

The equations can be easily rearranged so that they are in the standard form shown previously. This results in:

$$(R_G + R_B)\, i_1 \quad - R_B\, i_2 = V_G - V_B$$
$$-R_B\, i_1 + (R_B + R_L)\, i_2 = V_B$$

In terms of previous notation we see that:

$$a_1 = R_G + R_B$$
$$b_1 = a_2 = -R_B$$
$$b_2 = R_2 + R_L$$
$$k_1 = V_G - V_B$$
$$k_2 = V_B$$

Suppose we want to determine whether the battery is charging or discharging its energy. If the battery is being charged by the generator, its net current flows downward; that is the case if current i_1 is larger than i_2. Otherwise, if i_2 is larger than i_1, current flows upward, and the battery is discharging. Once i_1 and i_2 have been solved for, a program segment such as:

```
IF (I1 .GT. I2) THEN
   PRINT *, 'BATTERY CHARGING'
ELSE
   PRINT *, 'BATTERY DISCHARGING'
ENDIF
```

displays the battery's status.

Program 11-2 allows us to read in the voltage source and resistor values, calculates the two loop currents, and determines whether the battery is charging or discharging.

The results of two sample runs are shown below, using realistic values for voltages and resistances:

```
ENTER VG AND VB IN VOLTS:
12.5, 12
ENTER RG, RB, AND RL IN OHMS:
0.15, 0.1, 1

GENERATOR CURRENT = 6.603773 AMPS
LOAD CURRENT = 11.50944 AMPS
BATTERY DISCHARGING
```

and:

```
ENTER VG AND VB IN VOLTS:
15, 12
ENTER RG, RB, AND RL IN OHMS:
0.15, 0.1, 1

GENERATOR CURRENT = 16.981130 AMPS
LOAD CURRENT = 12.452829 AMPS
BATTERY CHARGING
```

Further analysis of this problem shows that for a 12-volt car battery and the given resistor values, a generator voltage of at least 13.8 volts is required to keep the battery charging. The generator voltage must be higher than the battery voltage to overcome the loss in the internal source resistances.

Program 11-2

```
PROGRAM MAIN
   REAL VG, VB, RG, RB, RL, I1, I2
   REAL A1, B1, A2, B2, K1, K2, VALDET, DET2
   PRINT *, 'ENTER VG AND VB IN VOLTS: '
   READ *, VG, VB
   PRINT *, 'ENTER RG, RB, AND RL IN OHMS: '
   READ *, RG, RB, RL
   A1 = RG + RB
   B1 = - RB
   A2 = - RB
   B2 = RB + RL
   K1  = VG - VB
   K2  = VB
   VALDET  = DET2 (A1, B1, A2, B2)
   I1  = DET2 (K1, B1, K2, B2) / VALDET
   I2  = DET2 (A1, K1, A2, K2) / VALDET
   PRINT *
   PRINT *, 'GENERATOR CURRENT = ', I1, ' AMPS'
   PRINT *, 'LOAD CURRENT = ', I2, ' AMPS'
   IF (I1 .GT. I2) THEN
      PRINT *, 'BATTERY CHARGING'
   ELSE
      PRINT *, 'BATTERY DISCHARGING'
   ENDIF
   END
*
* SUBPROGRAM FUNCTION TO EVALUATE 2X2 DETERMINANT  | A  B |
*                                                  | C  D |
   REAL FUNCTION DET2 (A, B, C, D)
      REAL A, B, C, D
*
   DET2 = A * D - B * C
*
   END
```

Three Linear Equations with Three Unknowns

Cramer's rule also applies to the solution of three linear equations in three unknowns, having the general form:

$$a_1x + b_1y + c_1z = k_1$$
$$a_2x + b_2y + c_2z = k_2$$
$$a_3x + b_3y + c_3z = k_3$$

As for the case of two linear equations in two unknowns, each unknown in a set of three linear equations in three unknowns can be evaluated as a ratio of two determinants. In this case, however, each determinant is of the third order. Specifically, for the equations above, the solution is:

$$x = \det_x / \det_3$$
$$y = \det_y / \det_3$$
$$z = \det_z / \det_3$$

where:

$$\det_x = \begin{vmatrix} k_1 & b_1 & c_1 \\ k_2 & b_2 & c_2 \\ k_3 & b_3 & c_3 \end{vmatrix}$$

$$\det_y = \begin{vmatrix} a_1 & k_1 & c_1 \\ a_2 & k_2 & c_2 \\ a_3 & k_3 & c_3 \end{vmatrix}$$

$$\det_z = \begin{vmatrix} a_1 & b_1 & k_1 \\ a_2 & b_2 & k_2 \\ a_3 & b_3 & k_3 \end{vmatrix}$$

$$\det_3 = \begin{vmatrix} a_1 & b_1 & c_1 \\ a_2 & b_2 & c_2 \\ a_3 & b_3 & c_3 \end{vmatrix}$$

As we saw in the two-equation case, the numerator determinant corresponding to each unknown is evaluated by replacing the entries of the appropriate column of the denominator determinant ($\det_3$) by the coefficients on the right side of the equations (k_1, k_2, and k_3). As in the two-equation case, when the denominator determinant is zero, no unique solution exists.

The actual evaluation of a third-order determinant can be made by multiplying each element of any arbitrarily chosen row or column by the remaining second-order determinant after removing the row and column corresponding to the element. The selected row or column is called the pivot row or pivot column, respectively, and the resulting evaluation proceeds by alternating additions and subtractions. For example, arbitrarily selecting the first column as a pivot column, the three-by-three determinant:

$$\begin{vmatrix} a & b & c \\ d & e & f \\ g & h & i \end{vmatrix}$$

can be evaluated as:

$$a * \begin{vmatrix} e & f \\ h & i \end{vmatrix} - d \begin{vmatrix} b & c \\ h & i \end{vmatrix} + g * \begin{vmatrix} b & c \\ e & f \end{vmatrix}$$

Program 11-3 uses this evaluation method to compute the determinants required to solve three linear equations in three unknowns. This permits the program to make use of the subprogram function DET2() previously developed for Program 11-1.

Program 11-3

```
PROGRAM MAIN
  REAL A1,B1,C1,A2,B2,C2,A3,B3,C3,K1,K2,K3
  REAL X, Y, Z, VALDET, DET3
  PRINT *, 'ENTER A1,B1,C1,A2,B2,C2,A3,B3,C3: '
  READ *, A1,B1,C1,A2,B2,C2,A3,B3,C3
  PRINT *, 'ENTER K1, K2, K3: '
  READ *, K1, K2, K3
  VALDET = DET3 (A1,B1,C1,A2,B2,C2,A3,B3,C3)
  IF (ABS (VALDET) .GE. 0.001) THEN
    X  = DET3 (K1,B1,C1,K2,B2,C2,K3,B3,C3) / VALDET
    Y  = DET3 (A1,K1,C1,A2,K2,C2,A3,K3,C3) / VALDET
    Z  = DET3 (A1,B1,K1,A2,B2,K2,A3,B3,K3) / VALDET
    PRINT *, 'THE SOLUTION IS:'
    PRINT *, '   X = ', X
    PRINT *, '   Y = ', Y
    PRINT *, '   Z = ', Z
  ELSE
    PRINT *, 'A UNIQUE SOLUTION DOES NOT EXIST'
  ENDIF
  END
*
* SUBPROGRAM FUNCTION TO EVALUATE 3X3 DETERMINANT    | A  B  C |
*                                                    | D  E  F |
*                                                    | G  H  I |
      REAL FUNCTION DET3 (A, B, C, D, E, F, G, H, I)
        REAL A, B, C, D, E, F, G, H, I, DET2
*
        DET3 = A*DET2(E,F,H,I)-D*DET2(B,C,H,I)+G*DET2(B,C,E,F)
*
      END
*
* SUBPROGRAM FUNCTION TO EVALUATE 2X2 DETERMINANT    | A  B |
*                                                    | C  D |
      REAL FUNCTION DET2 (A, B, C, D)
        REAL A, B, C, D
*
        DET2 = A * D - B * C
*
      END
```

Following is a sample run of Program 11-3 used to solve the system of linear equations:

$$x + y + z = 32.5$$
$$10x + 5y + 4z = 240$$
$$1.5x + 0y + 10z = 49$$

```
ENTER A1,B1,C1,A2,B2,C2,A3,B3,C3:
1 1 1 10 5 4 1.5 0 10
ENTER K1, K2, K3:
32.5 240 49
THE SOLUTION IS:
   X =          16.000000
   Y =          14.000000
   Z =           2.500000
```

Exercises

1. Compile and run Program 11-1 on a computer. Enter the data necessary to solve the linear equations:

$$3x + 4y = 5$$
$$3x + 5y = 4$$

2a. Notice that the two equations below cannot be solved.

$$x + 2y = 5$$
$$3x + 6y = 8$$

In contrast, the equations:

$$x + 2y = 5$$
$$3x + 6y = 15$$

result in many solutions. Can you see what the problem is?

b. Compile and run Program 11-1 for the equations in Exercise 2a.

3. Modify Program 11-1 to read the coefficients in from a data file COEFF.DAT rather than from the keyboard. Create the data file on a computer with the coefficients from Exercise 1. Then compile and run the modified program and verify the results of Exercise 1.

4. Modify Program 11-1 to evaluate the second-order determinant using a subroutine rather than a subprogram function. Compile and run the modified program, and again verify the result of Exercise 1.

5. Compile and run Program 11-2 on a computer, for a 12-volt battery charger with the following resistor values in ohms:

$$R_G = 0.2 \qquad R_B = 0.2 \qquad R_L = 1.0$$

Noting that 12 must be entered for V_B, enter a higher value of volts for V_G. Rerun the program, varying only the generator voltage. By trial and error, find the minimum V_G required (to one decimal place) to cause the battery to charge rather than discharge.

6a. Modify Program 11-2 to allow you to enter values for V_B, R_G, R_B, and R_L from the keyboard. The currents i_1 and i_2 are to be calculated for all values of V_G ranging from

12.5 to 15.0 volts, in steps of 0.1 volt. Rather than displaying a message as to whether the battery is charging or discharging, print the results in a table with the headings shown below.

VG	I1	I2
(volts)	(amps)	(amps)
-------	------	------

b. Compile and run the modified program on a computer. Enter the values:

$$V_B = 12 \qquad R_G = 0.15 \qquad R_B = 0.1 \qquad R_L = 1$$

c. Repeat Exercise 6b for the values used in Exercise 5.

7. Compile and run Program 11-3 on a computer. Enter the data necessary to solve the linear equations:

$$2x + y - 2z = 8$$
$$x - 5y + 3z = 6$$
$$3x - 3y - 2z = 10$$

8. Modify Program 11-3 to read the coefficients in from a data file COEFF.DAT rather than from the keyboard. Create the data file on a computer with the coefficients from Exercise 7, then compile and run the modified program and verify the results of Exercise 7.

9. A common numerical problem is to find the equation of a straight line that best fits a set of N data points, denoted as (x_1, y_1), (x_2, y_2), (x_3, y_3), ... (x_N, y_N). The equation of a straight line is given by $y = mx + b$, where m is the slope of the line, and b is called the y intercept. One technique for determining the values of m and b is called a linear least-squares fit. For such a fit, the unknowns m and b are related by the set of two simultaneous linear equations:

$$Nb + \left(\sum_{i=1}^{N} x_i \right) m = \sum_{i=1}^{N} y_i$$

$$\left(\sum_{i=1}^{N} x_i \right) b + \left(\sum_{i=1}^{N} x_i^2 \right) m = \sum_{i=1}^{N} x_i y_i$$

a. Using Program 11-1 as a starting point, write a FORTRAN program that accepts the given x and y values as inputs, determines the coefficients of the two equations, and then solves for the values of m and b. (*Hint:* Accept the number of data points as the first input and store the actual data points in two arrays named X and Y, respectively. A DO loop will be useful in calculating the summations. Test your program using the data points (1,0.5), (2,1.5), (3,1), and (4,2).

b. Using the program developed for Exercise 9a, determine the equation of the straight line that best fits the following data points: (1,3), (2,1), (3,2), (4,1), (6,2), and (8,5).

10. Experimental results on an unknown resistor produced the following table of voltages and currents.

Voltage (volts)	Current (amps)
1	0.018
2	0.043
3	0.056
4	0.085
5	0.092
6	0.100
7	0.102

The equation relating voltage, V; current, I; and resistance, R, is given by Ohm's law, which states that $V = R * I$. Use the program developed in Exercise 9a to assist you in finding the "best" guess at the resistance value, R.

11. Fitting a quadratic curve to a set of N data points, denoted as (x_1,y_1), (x_2,y_2), (x_3,y_3), ... (x_N,y_N), requires determining the values of a, b, and c for the equation $y = a + bx + cx^2$ that fit the data in some best manner. One technique for determining the values of a, b, and c is called the quadratic least-squares fit. For such a fit, the unknowns a, b, and c are related by the set of equations:

$$Na + b \sum_{i=1}^{N} x_i + c \sum_{i=1}^{N} x_i^2 = \sum_{i=1}^{N} y_i$$

$$a \sum_{i=1}^{N} x_i + b \sum_{i=1}^{N} x_i^2 + c \sum_{i=1}^{N} x_i^3 = \sum_{i=1}^{N} x_i y_i$$

$$a \sum_{i=1}^{N} x_i^2 + b \sum_{i=1}^{N} x_i^3 + c \sum_{i=1}^{N} x_i^4 = \sum_{i=1}^{N} x_i^2 y_i$$

Using Program 11-3 as a starting point, write a FORTRAN program that accepts the given x and y values as inputs, determines the coefficients of the three equations, and then solves for the values of a, b, and c. (*Hint:* Accept the number of data points as the first input and store the actual data points in two arrays named X and Y, respectively.) Test your program using the data points $(1,3)$, $(2,1)$, $(3,2)$, and $(4,1)$.

12a. The official United States population for each census taken since the year 1900 is listed below. The population figures are in millions of people and are rounded off to one fractional digit.

Year	U.S. population
1900	76.2
1910	92.2
1920	106.0
1930	123.2
1940	132.2
1950	151.3
1960	179.3
1970	203.3
1980	226.5

Using the program developed for Exercise 11, determine the equation of the least-squares quadratic curve for this data.

b. Using the equation determined in Exercise 12a, determine an estimate for the population of the United States in the year 2000.

11.2   Root Finding

Although the solution to sets of linear equations can be obtained using methods such as Cramer's rule, presented in Section 11.1, and individual quadratic equations, such as:

$$x^2 + 2x - 35 = 0$$

can be solved for x with the aid of the quadratic formula (see Section 4.4), no such computationally simple solutions exist for equations such as:

$$x^4 + 5x^3 + 12x^2 - 7x + 21 = 0$$

and:

$$\sin(5x) - 3x^2 + e^{4.8x} = 12$$

Although both of these equations have only a single unknown quantity, they are extremely difficult to solve because they both are nonlinear equations. By solve, of course, we mean finding values for x that when substituted into the equation yield a value for the equation's left side equal to that on its right side. More formally, such a value of x is called a root of the equation. Not unexpectedly, then, the methods of solving these equations are referred to as root-finding methods.

All root-finding methods require that the equation whose roots are being sought be written as the equation of a curve. In general, this involves the following two steps:

Step 1: Rewrite the equation to have all of the unknowns and constants on one side of the equation and a zero on the other side. For example, the equation $x^2 + 2x = 35$ can be rearranged in this form by subtracting 35 from both sides of the equation to yield $x^2 + 2x - 35 = 0$.

Step 2: Set the side of the equation with the unknowns equal to another variable, such as y. For example, setting $y = x^2 + 2x - 35$ converts the original equation into the equation of a curve. For each value of x in this equation, a value of y can be computed.

Once the given equation has been transformed into the equation of a curve, the root-finding problem reduces to locating values of x for which y is zero. Three such methods are now presented.

All of the methods presented, as indeed do all root-finding methods, rely on guessing at a value of x, finding the corresponding value of y, and then modifying the value of x until a y value of zero is reached. The difference in methods is based on the procedure used to modify each guess until a root is located.

Fixed-Increment Iterations

In the fixed-increment root-finding method, each value of x is obtained from the previous value by adding or subtracting a fixed amount. To understand how this procedure works, consider Program 11-4, which tabulates values of the curve $y = x^2 + 2x - 35$ for integer values of x ranging from -10 to $+10$ (see Section 5.4 to review this use of a DO loop).

Program 11-4

```
PROGRAM MAIN
  INTEGER X, Y
  PRINT *,'          X VALUE       Y VALUE'
  PRINT *,'          -------       -------'
  DO 20 X = -10, 10
    Y = X ** 2 + 2 * X - 35
    PRINT *, X, Y
20    CONTINUE
  END
```

The output produced by Program 11-4 is:

X VALUE	Y VALUE
-10	45
-9	28
-8	13
-7	0
-6	-11
-5	-20
-4	-27
-3	-32
-2	-35
-1	-36
0	-35
1	-32
2	-27
3	-20
4	-11
5	0
6	13
7	28
8	45
9	64
10	85

The roots of the curve correspond to those values of x for which the calculated values of y are zero, in this case, $x = -7$ and $x = 5$. Figure 11-2 is a plot of the curve using the tabulated values. The roots are the values of x corresponding to the points where the curve intersects the x axis, namely, at $x = -7$ and $x = 5$.

Now let us modify Program 11-4 to display the two roots without listing the entire table. We do this by eliminating the printing of the headings in Program 11-4 and replacing the PRINT statement inside the DO loop with a conditional PRINT of x only if y is zero. Program 11-5 accomplishes this.

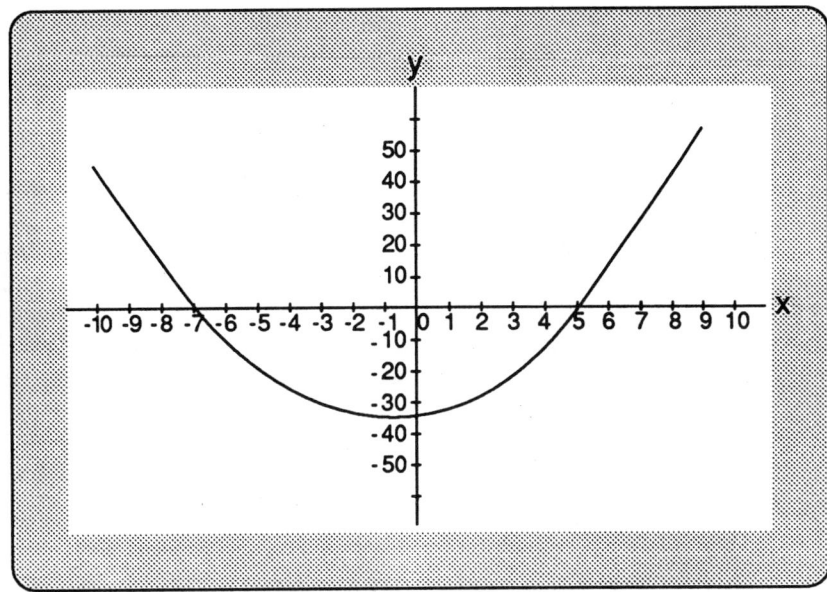

Figure 11-2   The Graph of the Curve $y = x^2 + 2x - 35$

Program 11-5

```
PROGRAM MAIN
   INTEGER X, Y
   DO 20 X = -10, 10
      Y = X ** 2 + 2 * X - 35
      IF ( Y .EQ. 0 ) PRINT *, 'A ROOT IS AT X = ', X
20    CONTINUE
   END
```

The output produced by this program is the following:

```
A ROOT IS AT X =          -7
A ROOT IS AT X =           5
```

Of course it should be apparent that Program 11-5 found the solutions to the equation for us because the roots happen to be integers. Noninteger roots cannot be located by this routine because X is declared as an integer, so that only integer values are entered into the equation. To consider the more general case of noninteger roots, we consider the equation:

$$x^2 + 2.1x - 16.96 = 0$$

From the quadratic formula, the roots of this equation are $x = -5.3$ and $x = 3.2$. However, let us assume that we do not know where the roots are, as would be the case for a higher-order equation or one with trigonometric or exponential functions. For this more general noninteger case, the variables X and Y in the program need to be declared as REAL variables. The step size in the DO loop, which defaults to one in Program 11-5, needs to be decreased to enable the finding of noninteger root locations. Also, we need to decide how close to zero the function needs to be to qualify a value as a root (recall from Section 4.5 that, because of round-off errors exact equality to zero is not always possible for real values). In Program 11-6 the step size used in the loop (called INCR) and the allowable deviation from zero, referred to as the allowable error, are read from the keyboard. The value of Y is calculated within the loop, and the root value is printed out only if the absolute value of Y does not exceed the allowable error.

Program 11-6

```
PROGRAM MAIN
   REAL X, Y, INCR, ERROR
   PRINT *, 'ENTER STEP SIZE: '
   READ *, INCR
   PRINT *, 'ENTER THE ALLOWABLE ERROR: '
   READ *, ERROR
   DO 20 X = -10.0, 10.0, INCR
     Y = X ** 2 + 2.1 * X - 16.96
     IF (ABS(Y) .LE. ERROR) PRINT *, 'A ROOT IS AT X = ', X
20   CONTINUE
   END
```

The results of three sample runs using Program 11-6 are:

```
ENTER STEP SIZE:
0.01
ENTER THE ALLOWABLE ERROR:
0.1
A ROOT IS AT X =        -5.309893
A ROOT IS AT X =        -5.299892
A ROOT IS AT X =        -5.289892
A ROOT IS AT X =         3.190131
A ROOT IS AT X =         3.200131
A ROOT IS AT X =         3.210131
```

and:

```
ENTER STEP SIZE:
0.01
ENTER THE ALLOWABLE ERROR:
0.01
```

```
A ROOT IS AT X =          -5.299892
A ROOT IS AT X =           3.200131
```

and:

```
ENTER STEP SIZE:
0.01
ENTER MINIMUM FUNCTION ERROR:
0.001
A ROOT IS AT X =          -5.299892
```

The results illustrate the care that needs to be taken in choosing both the step size and the allowable error. The step size determines the total number of iterations that are made, while the allowable error determines the range of y values that are close enough to zero to qualify a given x value as a root. As shown in the first run, too large an allowable error may qualify too many roots, while too small a value, as shown in the last run, may cause valid roots to be missed. In this latter case the root location at 3.2, is not found because of round-off error.

Although the second run correctly locates the two roots of the equation using a step size of 0.01 and an allowable error of the same value, this relationship between step size and allowable error cannot be generalized. However, the problem of selecting too large or small a value for the allowable function error can be eliminated by using a different approach.

Referring to Figure 11-2, notice that the crossing of the x axis by the curve causes the sign of y to change. The table of values printed by Program 11-4 also shows the sign changes. As x is increased from −10, the values of y are positive, and they then change to negative as the root x = −7 is passed. The values of y remain negative until the second root, x = 5, is reached, whereupon y is again positive for larger values of x. All curves exhibit sign changes in y when a root is encountered, with one exception. The exception is the occurrence of a curve that is tangent to the x axis at some point, whereupon the sign of y will not change even though a root exists (this is referred to as a repeated root).

Taking advantage of the sign change feature allows us to have our program calculate two successive values of y within the loop, corresponding to a value of x and to x plus a chosen increment. If the two values of y differ in sign, then a root is identified. The root, however, is between the two values of x used. Rather than simply use one of the x values, we obtain a more accurate computation of the root using interpolation. In Figure 11-3 a small portion of a curve is shown for both a positive slope and negative slope case; x_1 and x_2 represent two successive values of x between which a root exists. The actual root location, x_r, is approximated by drawing a straight line between the points (x_1, y_1) and (x_2, y_2). Where this interpolation line crosses the x axis determines x_r. From the triangles drawn in Figure 11-3 the slopes of the lines can be equated, resulting in the equation:

$$\frac{y_1}{x_r - x_1} = \frac{-y_2}{x_2 - x_r}$$

for the negatively sloped case (the equation is the same for the positively sloped case because the minus sign is simply transposed from y_2 to y_1).

By solving the equation above for x_r, the approximate root value is:

$$x_r = \frac{x_2\,y_1 - x_1\,y_2}{y_1 - y_2} = x_1 + \frac{y_1}{y_1 - y_2}\,(x_2 - x_1)$$

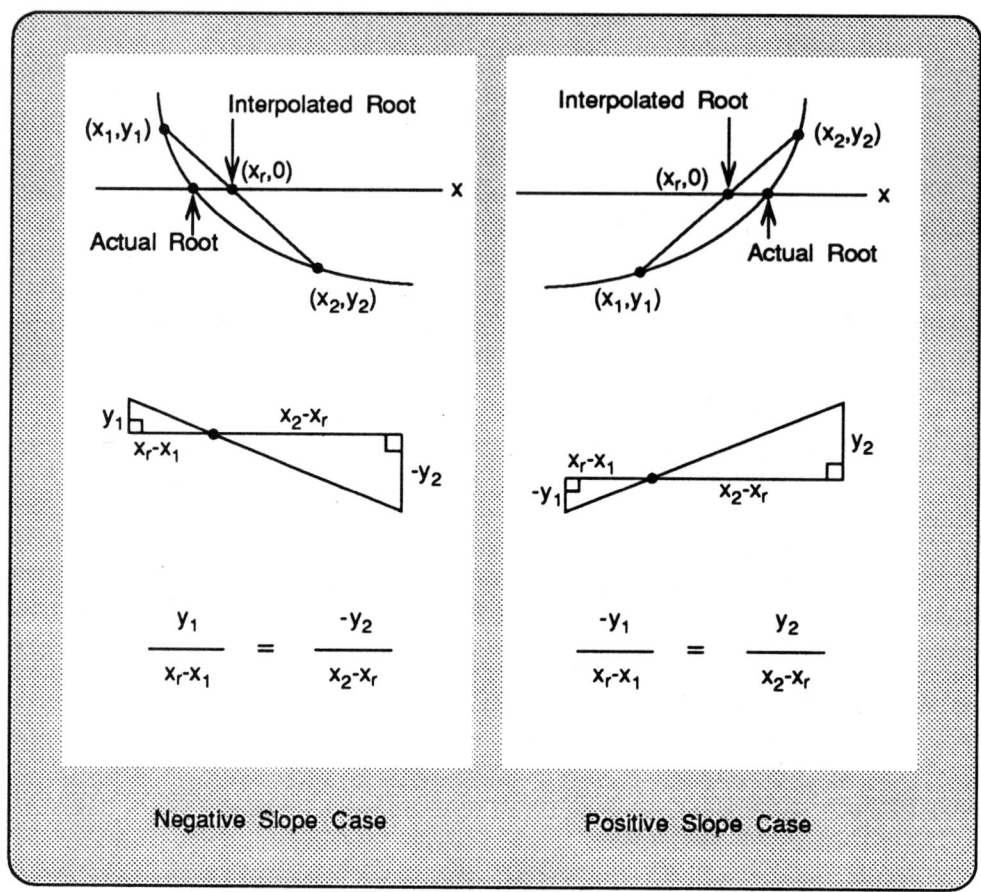

Figure 11-3 Approximating a Root by Interpolation

Program 11-7 incorporates this interpolation formula to locate the roots of the curve $y = x^2 + 2.1x - 16.96$.

Following are four sample runs of Program 11-7 using different step sizes:

```
ENTER STEP SIZE:
1
 A ROOT IS AT X =        -5.276404
 A ROOT IS AT X =         3.182417

ENTER STEP SIZE:
0.5
 A ROOT IS AT X =        -5.292857
 A ROOT IS AT X =         3.193023
```

```
ENTER STEP SIZE:
0.1
  A ROOT IS AT X =       -5.300000
  A ROOT IS AT X =        3.200000

ENTER STEP SIZE:
0.01
  A ROOT IS AT X =       -5.300000
  A ROOT IS AT X =        3.200000
```

 Program 11-7

```
PROGRAM MAIN
   REAL INCR, X, X1, X2, Y1, Y2, XROOT, YRATIO, F
   F(X) = X ** 2 + 2.1 * X - 16.96
   PRINT *, 'ENTER STEP SIZE: '
   READ *, INCR
   DO 20 X = -10.0, 10.0 - INCR, INCR
      X1 = X
      X2 = X + INCR
      Y1 = F (X1)
      Y2 = F (X2)
      IF (Y1 * Y2 .LT. 0) THEN
         YRATIO = Y1 / (Y1 - Y2)
         XROOT = X1 + YRATIO * ( X2 - X1 )
         PRINT *, ' A ROOT IS AT X = ', XROOT
      ENDIF
20    CONTINUE
   END
```

The three important points to observe from Program 11-7 are:

1. The calculation of y values for the curve is relegated to a function statement. This statement can easily be changed for different curves.

2. Although two values of x (X1 and X2) and two values of y (Y1 and Y2) need to be calculated inside the loop, care is taken not to change the loop's index value, X. The maximum index value is set to 10-INCR to ensure that X2 does not exceed 10.

3. Since the two values Y1 and Y2 must be of different sign for a root to exist, simply multiplying them and examining the sign of the result provides a convenient test. If both values are positive or if both are negative, the product is a positive number, and the statements within the IF block are ignored.

We see from the results that by testing for a sign change and interpolating to find the root, the accuracy is quite good, and the danger of missing a root has been diminished. Even incrementing X by 1 each time results in roots that are less than 1 percent in error from their true value. For step sizes of 0.1 and lower, the roots rounded to 6 fractional digits are identical to the expected values of –5.3 and 3.2. Clearly, however, a root will be missed if the range of X values used in the DO loop does not include the root.

The Bisection Method

All fixed-increment root-finding algorithms require the computer to iterate through a fixed number of x values, calculate corresponding y values, and identify the roots in some manner. When the step size is small, this can be extremely time-consuming, especially when the general vicinity of the roots is not known. In such cases it may be necessary to search over a wide range of x values to avoid missing a root. For reasons of computational efficiency, various techniques have been developed to permit the search to proceed much more rapidly than is possible when simply incrementing x by a fixed step size. One such method is the bisection method.

The rationale for the bisection method can be better understood by first considering a game called High-Low. In High-Low an integer is selected between 1 and 99, and a player is required to find the number with as few guesses as possible. The game is often played against a calculator or computer, in which case the player must guess a randomly selected integer. Upon each guess, the player is told whether the choice is too high or too low. When the correct number is chosen, the game is over, and the number of guesses is tallied.

If we approach this game as a fixed-step iteration problem, we would begin by selecting 1 as our first guess. If that is incorrect, we will be told that our guess is too low. We would then begin incrementing our guess by 1 each time, proceeding to guess the numbers 2, 3, 4, and so on, until we locate the right number. Clearly, the number of tries is going to equal the selected number. If a low number was selected we are in luck, but in the worst case it could take 99 guesses.

There is, however, a better approach to the game. Rather than selecting 1 as our first guess, let us select a number at the middle of the range, namely, 50. Now, if we are told that the guess is too low, we have instantly eliminated all integers below 50 as well as 50 itself. Conversely, a response of too high removes from further consideration the numbers in the range 50 to 99. In either case the range has been cut approximately in half. Our next guess repeats this strategy: if the new range is 1 to 49, we choose 25, and if the new range is 51 to 99, we choose 75. In either case we again eliminate half of the remaining numbers (assuming that we have not been so fortunate as to hit the number already). You can see that this process will locate the correct number quite rapidly. An illustrative example is shown below:

```
Number selected by opponent:   59

Range      Guess        Message
-----      -----        -------
 1-99       50       Too low
51-99       75       Too high
51-74       63       Too high
51-62       57       Too low
58-62       60       Too high
58-59       58       Too low
   59       59       Correct
```

Notice that the correct number was identified in seven guesses, without any "lucky" guesses; that is, the number was not identified until it was the only possible one left. It is always the case that the maximum number of guesses required by halving each range is seven, regardless of the number originally selected (recall that the fixed-step iteration method might require 99 guesses).

Let us now apply the underlying strategy of High-Low to root finding. To do this, consider a curve that is known to have a single root, denoted as x_r, between the values $x = a$ and $x = b$, as illustrated in Figure 11-4(a). Although the illustrated curve has a positive slope, the technique works equally well with a curve having a negative slope. Regardless of the curve's slope, the value of the curve at $x = a$ differs in sign from the value at $x = b$.

Using the bisection method, we initially calculate y values corresponding to the left and right bounds on the x axis, namely $x = a$ and $x = b$. Then we select the midpoint of these two x values and replace one of the x values by this midpoint in such a manner that the root lies in the remaining range. For this procedure the midpoint of the values $x = a$ and $x = b$ is calculated as:

$mid = (a+b) / 2.0$

If the calculated midpoint lies to the left of the root, as is the case in Figure 11-4(a), the left half of the curve segment (between $x = a$ and $x = mid$) can be discarded; otherwise, the right half between $x = mid$ and $x = b$ can be removed from further consideration. In either case the root is within the reduced interval. Figure 11-4(b) shows the removal of the left half of the curve segment, with the value of a replaced by the previously calculated value of mid. The second calculation of mid, using this new value of a, results in a value larger than the root. In this case the right half of the remaining segment is discarded, and the value of b is replaced by the newly calculated mid. Figure 11-4(c) shows the original segment reduced to one-fourth of its size. A third calculation of mid is seen to be smaller than the root, so that the next step would be to replace a by mid.

We see that each step of this procedure reduces the interval between $x = a$ and $x = b$ by a factor of two, or in other words bisects the interval. Now we can see the analogy of this procedure with the High-Low game. The initial values a and b correspond to the initial range of integers in the High-Low game, which was 1 to 99 in our illustration. The calculation of mid corresponds to the "guessing" of a number at the middle of the range. If mid is larger than the root, the "guess" was too high, and the upper half of the range is eliminated; alternatively, a low "guess" of mid, which is less than the root, removes the lower half of the interval from further consideration.

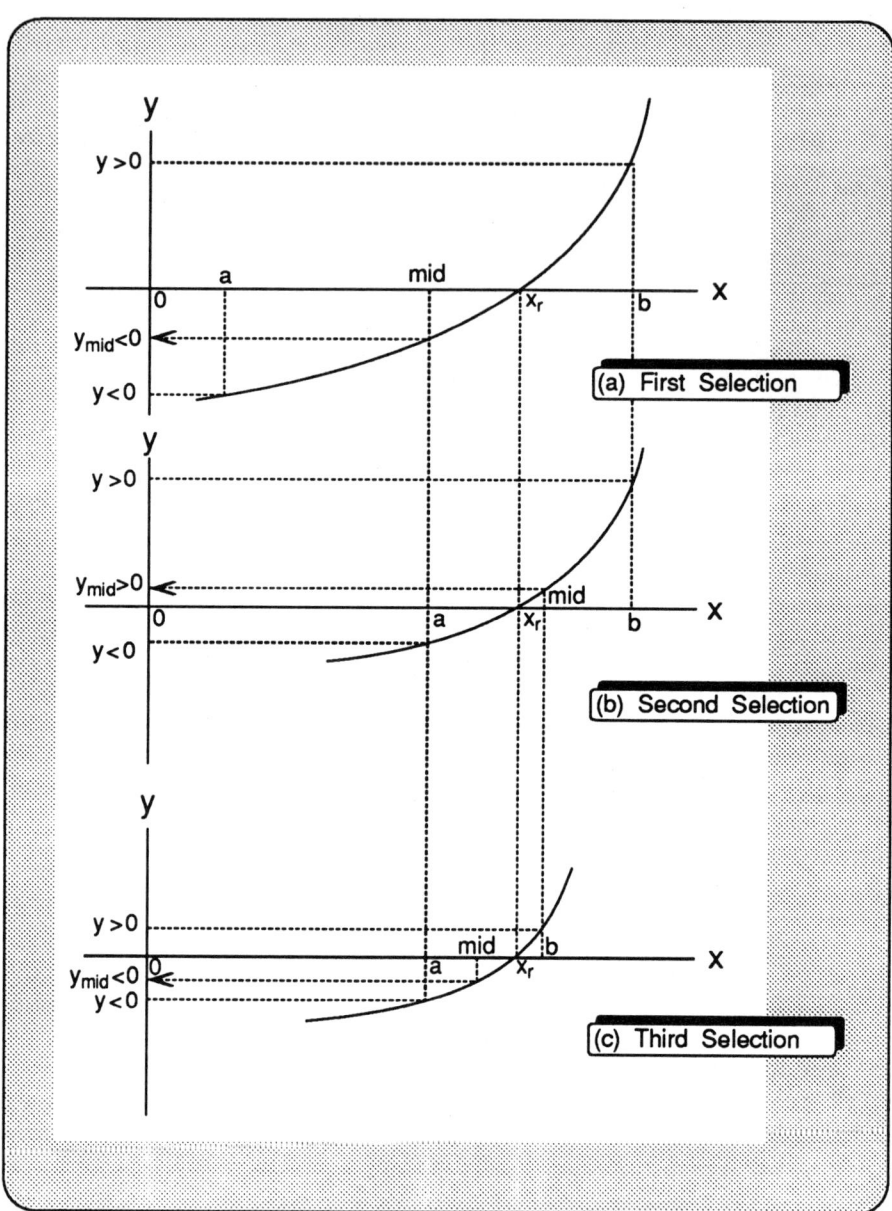

Figure 11-4   Illustration of the Bisection Technique

Since the High-Low game involves only integers, an exact answer will always be obtained after a relatively small number of guesses. Because the roots of equations are generally real numbers subject to round-off error, finding an exact answer, regardless of the root-finding method, is generally not possible. We must, therefore, agree beforehand on an allowable error in the computation of the root. We can also provide further control on the computation time by limiting the number of iterations. If we specify too small an error and too few iterations, we run the risk of not finding the root. If that happens, however, we can then adjust one (or both) of these criteria and rerun the program. With this as background, the pseudocode for the bisection algorithm is as follows:

enter an allowable error for the root
  and the maximum number of iterations
initialize left and right bounds of x
repeat until acceptable root found or maximum iterations reached
    calculate midpoint of current interval
    if function value at left bound and at midpoint differ in sign then
      set new right bound to midpoint value
      display root value and number of iterations
      stop
    else
      set new left bound to midpoint value
display message indicating no root found

Program 11-8 implements this pseudocode for the curve $y = x^2 + 2.1x - 16.96$.

Notice that Program 11-8 uses a loop with a fixed number of iterations that contains an IF statement to terminate the program if a root is found. The actual termination is caused by the STOP statement, which is executed after the root value and number of iterations are printed. (Recall that an END statement, which also stops execution, cannot be used because only one END statement is permitted in the MAIN program. Using END in place of STOP would result in a compiler error, since it is not the last statement of the program.) Also notice that the value of the root is computed by averaging the last values of A and B, which yields a more accurate approximation to the root than either A or B alone.

A disadvantage of the bisection procedure is that two roots within an interval can cause problems because no sign change in y values will occur (can you see why?). The solution to this problem is to select an interval that encloses only one root and then to rerun the program for the additional roots. The sample runs shown below for Program 11-8 illustrate how both roots of the curve $y = x^2 + 2.1x - 16.96$ are found by modifying the range of the search interval.

```
ENTER MAXIMUM ROOT ERROR:
0.0001
ENTER MAXIMUM NUMBER OF ITERATIONS:
30
ENTER LEFT AND RIGHT BOUNDS OF X   (A, B):
-100, 100
A ROOT IS AT X =       -5.300021
ROOT FOUND AFTER           22 ITERATIONS

ENTER MAXIMUM ROOT ERROR:
0.0001
ENTER MAXIMUM NUMBER OF ITERATIONS:
30
ENTER LEFT AND RIGHT BOUNDS OF X   (A, B):
0, 100
A ROOT IS AT X =        3.200006
ROOT FOUND AFTER           20 ITERATIONS
```

Program 11-8

```
PROGRAM MAIN
  INTEGER I, N
  REAL A, B, X, XERROR, MID, XROOT, F
  F(X) = X ** 2 + 2.1 * X - 16.96
  PRINT *, 'ENTER MAXIMUM ROOT ERROR: '
  READ *, XERROR
  PRINT *, 'ENTER MAXIMUM NUMBER OF ITERATIONS: '
  READ *, N
  PRINT *, 'ENTER LEFT AND RIGHT BOUNDS OF X  (A, B): '
  READ *, A, B
  DO 20 I = 1, N
   MID = (A + B) / 2
   IF (F(A) * F(MID) .LT. 0) THEN
     B = MID
     IF (B - A .LE. XERROR) THEN
       XROOT = (A+B) / 2
       PRINT *, 'A ROOT IS AT X = ',XROOT
       PRINT *, 'ROOT FOUND AFTER ',I, ' ITERATIONS'
       STOP
     ENDIF
   ELSE
     A = MID
   ENDIF
20    CONTINUE
  PRINT *, 'NO ROOT FOUND AFTER ',N,' ITERATIONS'
  END
```

In the first run the initial interval includes both roots and the program correctly locates the root at $x = -5.3$ but misses the positive root. The next run locates the positive root at $x = 3.2$ because the search interval includes this root while excluding the negative root.

The Secant Method

The secant method is a variation on the bisection technique just described. Rather than selecting the midpoint of an interval at each step to estimate the root value, the intersection of a secant line with the x axis is used as the next estimate. A *secant line* is a straight line that connects two points on the curve, as illustrated on Figure 11-5.

Figure 11-5 also shows the process of estimating the root location through the use of successive secant lines. The initial interval of the curve is defined by the values x_1 and x_2; notice that these points correspond to points a and b respectively, for the bisection method. In Figure 11-5(a) the first secant line drawn crosses the x

axis at x_3; for the curve shown it is to the left of the actual root, but only because of the bending of the curve.

A second secant line, shown in Figure 11-5(b) connects the points of the curve corresponding to x_2 and x_3; the intersection of this secant line with the x axis is then x_4. Again, the last two values of x, namely x_3 and x_4, define the points on the curve corresponding to the next secant line. As shown in Figure 11-5(c), the third secant line intersects the x axis at x_5. The process would then continue, using x_4 and x_5 to define the next curve segment.

Notice that the point x_5 in this illustration falls outside of the interval between x_3 and x_4. This is one difference between the secant method and the bisection method, where each point chosen is halfway between the two previous points. The fact, that a point may fall outside the interval defined by the previous two points does not imply that the secant method is diverging. In fact for most cases it converges more rapidly than does the bisection method, which means that the intersections of the secant lines with the x axis are

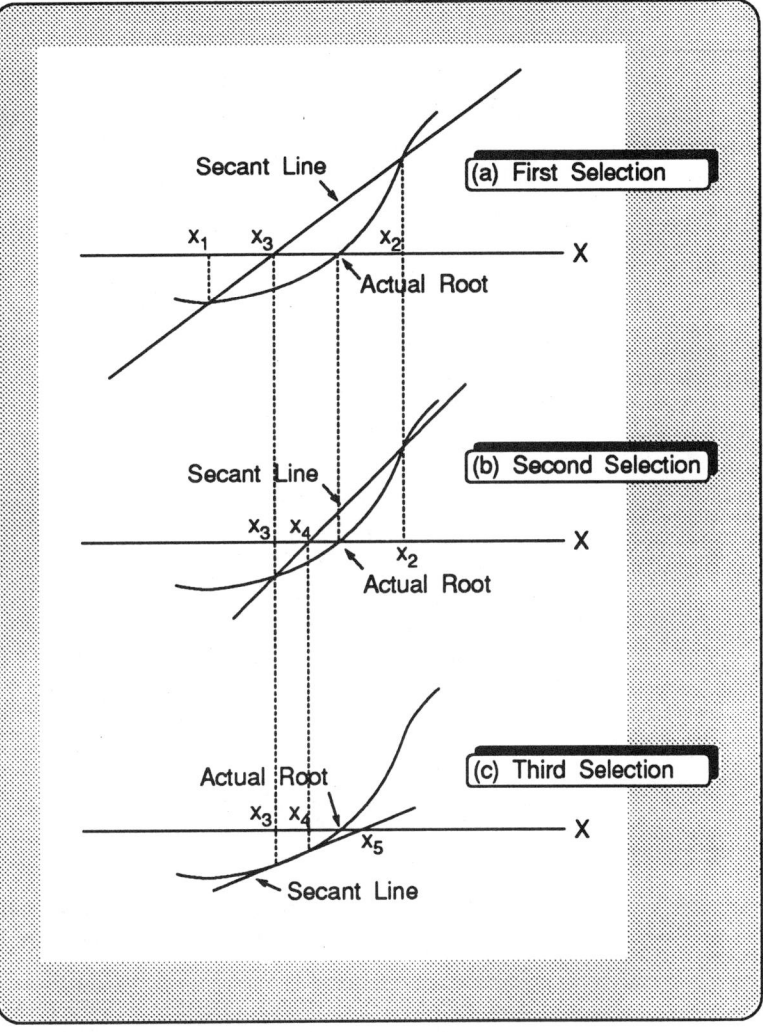

Figure 11-5   Illustration of Root Finding Using Secant Method

more rapidly approaching the actual root location. However, as with the bisection method, there are potential problems when multiple roots are involved.

A program to implement the secant method is no more complex than Program 11-9, which implements the bisection method. The secant method requires repeated calculation of the intersection of the line with the x axis in place of the simpler calculation of the midpoint when bisection is used. However, the bisection method includes for each step a test of whether the function value at the midpoint has the same sign as the value at one of the endpoints; the IF-ELSE structure within the DO loop of Program 11-9 implements this test. The test is necessary to determine whether the left or right end of the previous interval is used as a bound for the next interval. Since the secant method always uses the two most recent values of x to define the next interval, regardless of the value of the function at any point, the test is unnecessary.

We can terminate the secant method's root search when the function's value for the most recent value of x is arbitrarily close to zero. As with the bisection method, we can terminate the program before finding a root when a desired maximum number of iterations have been completed.

The pseudocode for the secant method is:

enter acceptable error for root and maximum iterations
initialize left and right bounds of x
repeat until acceptable root found or maximum iterations reached
　　calculate location of secant line intersection with
　　x *axis for current bounds*
　　use secant intersection value to update bound locations
display root value and number of iterations, or message
indicating no root found

Recall the calculation of the secant line's intersection with the x axis shown in Figure 11-3 and implemented in Program 11-7. Notice that the result of the single calculation of x_r from x_1 and x_2 in Figure 11-3 can be applied to the repeated calculation of $x_3, x_4, x_5, \ldots$ illustrated in Figure 11-5. We are now finding x_{i+2} from x_i and x_{i+1}, starting with $i = 1$, where the first two values x_1 and x_2 are the initial bounds to be entered into our program.

The relationship:

$$x_r = x_1 + \frac{y_1}{y_1 - y_2} (x_2 - x_1)$$

previously shown, now becomes:

$$x_{i+2} = x_i + \frac{y_i}{y_i - y_{i+1}} (x_{i+1} - x_i) \qquad\qquad (i = 1, 2, 3, \ldots)$$

where x_{i+2} is the location of the intersection of the current secant line with the x axis, x_{i+1} and x_i are the previously calculated secant line intersections, and y_{i+1} and y_i are the function values corresponding to x_{i+1} and x_i, respectively.

Program 11-9 implements the secant method for the same quadratic function used previously, namely $x^2 + 2.1x - 16.96$.

It is convenient to use single-dimension arrays in this program to repeatedly calculate the values of x and y. Arrays X and Y have 102 memory locations assigned to them as a result of their declaration statement. This allows us to perform as many as 100 iterations, noting that the first two array elements are reserved for the values entered into X(1) and X(2) and calculated for Y(1) and Y(2). Notice that it is necessary to use a variable name other than X in the function statement to avoid a conflict with the array named X. A function subprogram or subroutine to calculate F would not be subject to this restriction, since the same variable name can be used in different program units.

Another feature to notice is the formatted PRINT statement inside the DO loop. Its purpose is to simply display for us the result of each calculation of the secant line intersection with the x axis. It is a useful aid in debugging such a program and offers some insight into the degree of convergence of this method; it can, of course, be eliminated from the program.

Program 11-9

```
PROGRAM MAIN
 INTEGER I, N
 REAL YERROR, XX, XROOT, YRATIO, F
 REAL X(102), Y(102)
 F(XX) = XX ** 2 + 2.1 * XX - 16.96
 PRINT *, 'ENTER MAXIMUM FUNCTION ERROR: '
 READ *, YERROR
 PRINT *, 'ENTER MAXIMUM NUMBER OF ITERATIONS (<=100): '
 READ *, N
 PRINT *,'ENTER LEFT AND RIGHT BOUNDS OF X  (X(1),X(2)): '
 READ *, X(1), X(2)
 DO 20 I = 1, N
   Y(I) = F (X(I))
   Y(I+1) = F (X(I+1))
   YRATIO = Y (I) / (Y(I) - Y(I+1))
   X(I+2) = X(I) + YRATIO * (X(I+1) - X(I))
   PRINT 30, I+2, X(I+2)
30         FORMAT (' ', 'X (', I3, ') = ', F12.6)
   Y(I+2) = F (X(I+2))
   IF (ABS(Y(I+2)) .LE. YERROR) THEN
      XROOT =X(I+2)
      PRINT *, 'A ROOT IS AT X = ',XROOT
      PRINT *, 'ROOT FOUND AFTER ',I, ' ITERATIONS'
      STOP
   ENDIF
20         CONTINUE
 PRINT *, 'NO ROOT FOUND AFTER ',N,' ITERATIONS'
 END
```

Several sample runs of Program 11-9 are shown below along with comments on the results. For each run the acceptable function error is entered as 0.0001, and a 30-iteration limit is specified.

```
ENTER MAXIMUM FUNCTION ERROR:
0.0001
ENTER MAXIMUM NUMBER OF ITERATIONS (<=100 ):
30
ENTER LEFT AND RIGHT BOUNDS OF X  (X(1),X(2)):
-100, 100
X (  3) = -4753.829000
X (  4) =   102.191200
X (  5) =   104.479600
X (  6) =    51.223000
X (  7) =    34.021730
```

```
X (  8) =    20.146090
X (  9) =    12.482530
X ( 10) =     7.729481
X ( 11) =     5.084414
X ( 12) =     3.772313
X ( 13) =     3.298430
X ( 14) =     3.206143
X ( 15) =     3.200070
X ( 16) =     3.200000
A ROOT IS AT X =        3.200000
ROOT FOUND AFTER          14 ITERATIONS
```

When the same values were entered for the bisection program, the smaller root $x = -5.3$ was found after 22 iterations. Here the larger rather than the smaller root was found, but with fewer iterations. Notice that the large range specified results in the first calculation of X(3) being far removed from the root. This is not surprising in view of the fact that the parabolic function evaluates to about 10,000 for $x = -100$ and for $x = 100$.

```
ENTER MAXIMUM FUNCTION ERROR:
0.0001
ENTER MAXIMUM NUMBER OF ITERATIONS (<=100 ):
30
ENTER LEFT AND RIGHT BOUNDS OF X   (X(1),X(2)):
100, -100
X (  3) = -4753.829000
X (  4) =   -97.985660
X (  5) =   -96.051970
X (  6) =   -49.123580
X (  7) =   -33.097030
X (  8) =   -20.504140
X (  9) =   -13.506220
X ( 10) =    -9.209970
X ( 11) =    -6.856354
X ( 12) =    -5.735712
X ( 13) =    -5.364632
X ( 14) =    -5.303129
X ( 15) =    -5.300024
X ( 16) =    -5.300000
A ROOT IS AT X =       -5.300000
ROOT FOUND AFTER          14 ITERATIONS
```

For this run we "fool" the program by reversing the bound numbers entered; despite the prompt message, the right bound is entered before the left bound, and the program has no provision for rejecting the entry. Notice that the first calculation is the same as that for the previous run; a secant line is drawn between the same two points, regardless of which one we choose as X(1). The next calculation, that of X(4), and subsequent ones differ from those from the first run (can you see why?). The result is that the negative root rather than the positive root has been found in the same number of iterations.

```
ENTER MAXIMUM FUNCTION ERROR:
0.0001
ENTER MAXIMUM NUMBER OF ITERATIONS (<=100 ):
30
```

```
ENTER LEFT AND RIGHT BOUNDS OF X   (X(1),X(2)):
-100, 0
X (   3) =       -.173241
X (   4) =       8.802341
X (   5) =       1.438618
X (   6) =       2.400397
X (   7) =       3.437145
X (   8) =       3.176111
X (   9) =       3.199350
X ( 10) =        3.200002
A ROOT IS AT X =          3.200002
ROOT FOUND AFTER          8 ITERATIONS
```

This result illustrates a problem with the secant method when more than one root exists. Only the negative root is enclosed within the initial bound (–100 to 0), yet the positive root is the one found. The problem, as we saw for the curve shown in Figure 11-5 is that the last two secant line intersections with the *x* axis do not always stay between the root we are searching for. As a result, the process can converge to another root, as is the case for this run.

```
ENTER MAXIMUM FUNCTION ERROR:
0.0001
ENTER MAXIMUM NUMBER OF ITERATIONS (<=100 ):
30
ENTER LEFT AND RIGHT BOUNDS OF X   (X(1),X(2)):
-10, 0
X (   3) =        -2.146835
X (   4) =      -362.119600
X (   5) =        -2.193387
X (   6) =        -2.239640
X (   7) =        -9.375102
X (   8) =        -3.989268
X (   9) =        -4.825817
X ( 10) =        -5.392557
X ( 11) =        -5.294594
X ( 12) =        -5.299942
X ( 13) =        -5.300000
A ROOT IS AT X =          -5.300000
ROOT FOUND AFTER          11 ITERATIONS
```

For this run we chose the left interval as –10 rather than –100, and the negative root was found. However, the convergence was not as rapid as we might have expected, since an apparently small slope for the second secant line constructed resulted in a large negative value for X(4). This again illustrates that this method is rather sensitive to the nature of the curve.

```
ENTER MAXIMUM FUNCTION ERROR:
0.0001
ENTER MAXIMUM NUMBER OF ITERATIONS (<=100 ):
30
ENTER LEFT AND RIGHT BOUNDS OF X   (X(1),X(2)):
-6, -4
X (   3) =        -5.184810
X (   4) =        -5.321136
X (   5) =        -5.299710
X (   6) =        -5.299999
```

```
A ROOT IS AT X =          -5.299999
ROOT FOUND AFTER              4 ITERATIONS
```

For this run it is assumed that we had some knowledge that the negative root was in the vicinity of $x = -5$. By choosing the initial interval to be very narrow in comparison to those used in the previous runs, we converged on the enclosed root quite rapidly.

From the results of these runs, we can conclude that the secant method does indeed converge more rapidly than does the bisection method in most cases, and certainly far more rapidly than the fixed-count iteration method presented at the beginning of this section. However, where more than one root exists, it is not always apparent how to locate all the roots with a very small number of runs. You may want to try other functions with this method to gain more insight into the problem.

Exercises

1a. Modify Program 11-4 to calculate and display a table of integer values of the function:

$$y = x^4 + 4x^3 - 7x^2 - 22x + 24$$

in the interval from $x = -10$ to $x = 10$. Compile and run the program on a computer. Can you determine the roots of this function from your display?

b. Modify Program 11-5 to calculate and display the roots of this function. Compile and run the program.

2. Modify Program 11-6 using the function from Exercise 1. Run the program four times using a step size of 0.01 for each run and allowable errors of 0.1, 0.01, 0.003, and 0.001, respectively.

3. Modify Program 11-7 using the function from Exercise 1. Run the program five times using step sizes of 1, 0.5, 0.499, 0.1, and 0.01, respectively. Explain your results.

4. Consider the function $y = \cos(x)$ in the interval from $x = 0$ to $x = 20$.

   a. Sketch the curve for the function by hand and determine from it the number of roots in this interval and their location.

   b. Modify Program 11-6 using this function and run the program. By trial and error set a step size and an allowable error that will display each root in the interval only once.

5. Modify Program 11-7 using the function from Exercise 4. Run the program four times using step sizes of 1, 0.5, 0.1, and 0.01, respectively. Explain your results.

6. Modify Program 11-8 using the function from Exercise 1. Run the program several times, entering 0.001 for the allowable error and 30 for the maximum number of iterations. For the various runs select left and right bounds to enable you to find all the roots in the interval from $x = -10$ to $x = 10$.

7. Repeat Exercise 6 using the function $y = \cos(x)$ in the interval from $x = 0$ to $x = 20$.

8. Modify Program 11-9 using the function from Exercise 1. Run the program several times, entering 0.001 for the maximum function error and 30 for the maximum number of iterations. For the various runs, select left and right bounds to enable you to find all the roots in the interval from $x = -10$ to $x = 10$. Compare the number of iterations required for the secant method and for the bisection method. Did the presence of multiple roots cause any problems in using the secant method?

9. Repeat Exercise 8 using the function $y = \cos(x)$ in the interval from $x = 0$ to $x = 20$.

10. The equation:

$$2e^{-x} - 1 = 0$$

has a root between $x = 0$ and $x = 1$.

a. Modify and run Program 11-8 to locate the root using the bisection method, using the interval from 0 to 1 and an allowable error of 0.001, and have your program display the number of iterations made. Then modify Program 11-9 to locate the root using the secant method, using the same allowable error. Compare the number of iterations required by both programs.

b. Repeat Exercise 10a using an interval from 0 to 5 and determine the number of iterations required to locate the root using both the bisection and secant methods.

c. Repeat Exercise 10a using an interval from 0 to 10 and determine the number of iterations required to locate the root using both the bisection and secant methods. Note that convergence may be a problem with the secant method.

11.3   Numerical Integration

Integration is a calculus technique that can be used to find the area under a portion of a curve. Frequently, in engineering and statistical problems, the calculated areas correspond to physical quantities. For example, the area under a normal bell-shaped curve in statistical applications is used in calculating probabilities, and the area under a band of frequencies in engineering applications is used to calculate power consumption. As in the root-finding methods discussed in the previous section, there are approximation methods that can be easily programmed on a computer for determining these areas when exact solutions do not exist.

Rectangular Approximations

To illustrate the rectangular approximation method, consider Figure 11-6. As illustrated in this figure, an arbitrary function $y = f(x)$ is shown within an interval bounded by $x = a$ and $x = b$. The area under the curve refers to the area between the curve and the horizontal x axis, bounded by the vertical lines drawn at a and b. An approximation to the true area under the curve can be obtained by dividing the area into N rectangles of equal widths, denoted as w in the figure, and adding the area of each rectangle. The integer N is arbitrary, but larger values chosen for N generally result in more accurate approximations. The width of each subinterval is the total interval width divided by the number of subintervals. Therefore, we have:

$$w = \frac{b - a}{N}$$

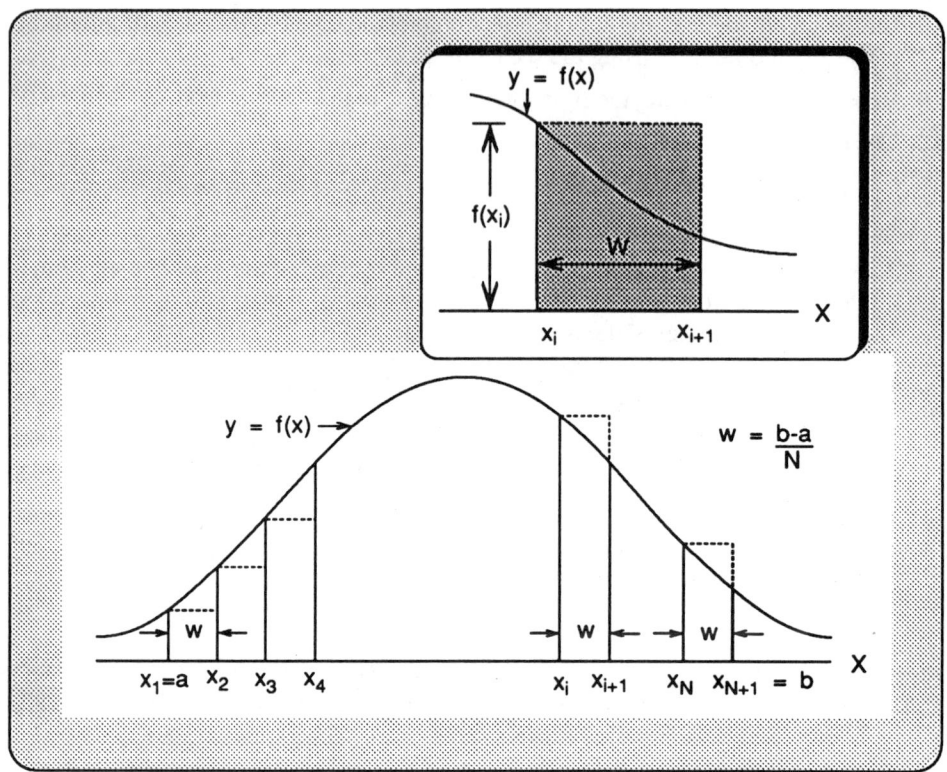

Figure 11-6   Rectangular Approximation to Area Under a Curve

The start of each subinterval is designated by $x_1, x_2, x_3, \ldots x_N$. Using a variable index, i, the start of subinterval i is at x_i where $i = 1, 2, 3, \ldots N$.

The start of the first subinterval, x_1, corresponds to a, and the end of the Nth subinterval, which we can call x_{N+1}, is equal to b. Also, since the subintervals are of equal width:

$$x_{i+1} = x_i + w \qquad \text{for } i = 1, 2, 3, \ldots N$$

The total area under the curve between a and b is clearly the sum of the areas under the N subintervals. As the name of the rectangular approximation technique implies, it simply approximates the area under each subinterval by that of a rectangle. As seen in the enlarged drawing of the ith subinterval in Figure 11-6, the value of y at the start of the interval determines the height of the rectangle. Since the area of a rectangle is simply width multiplied by height, and the width is w, the area of the ith subinterval can be expressed as:

$$A_i = w * f(x_i)$$

This corresponds to the shaded area shown in Figure 11-6. The total area is then:

$$\text{Area} = A_1 + A_2 + A_3 + \ldots + A_N$$

$$= \sum_{i=1}^{N} A_i$$

$$= w \sum_{i=1}^{N} f(x_i)$$

where:

$$w = \frac{b-a}{N}$$

$$x_1 = a$$

$$x_{i+1} = x_i + w$$

for all i from 1 to N. This result then approximates the area under the curve between limits $x = a$ and $x = b$.

This technique can be programmed with the aid of a looping procedure that calculates each subinterval area and then updates the value of x. The pseudocode for this procedure is given by:

enter the left and right bounds (a and b) and the number of subintervals (N)
calculate width (w)
initialize x
set total area to zero
do for all rectangles
  calculate the y value corresponding to x
  calculate the area of the recangle
  add the rectangular area to the total area
  update value of x
enddo
display total area

To illustrate this approximation method, we will choose a curve for which the exact area is known, so that we may compare the calculated approximation to the actual area. Figure 11-7 shows a circle centered at the origin of the x–y coordinate system. Consider the area under the portion of the circle in the upper right quadrant, shown by the shaded region in Figure 11-7. From symmetry, the shaded area is one-fourth of the total area of the circle, which we know to be π multiplied by the radius squared (where π = 3.141593, accurate to six decimal places). Therefore, the exact area of the shaded area is:

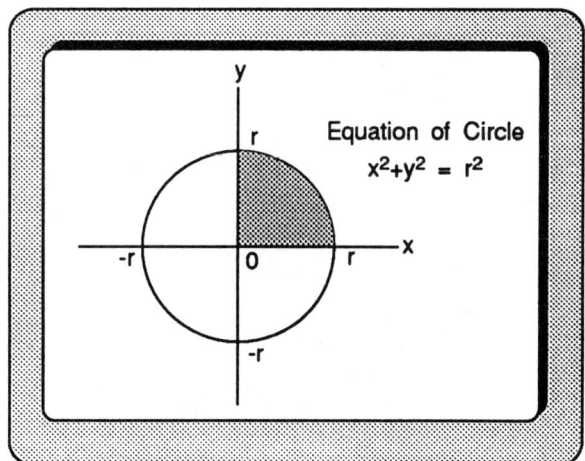

Figure 11-7 Area Under a Circle

$$\text{Area} = \pi * r^2 / 4$$

For a circle of radius equal to 2, the area is then π, or 3.141593.

The equation of a circle centered at the origin is given by:

$$x^2 + y^2 = r^2$$

For a circle with a radius of 2, this becomes:

$$x^2 + y^2 = 4$$

Solving for y, in terms of x, we obtain:

$$y = \sqrt{4 - x^2}$$

To limit ourselves to the upper right quadrant requires that x be bounded by 0 and 2 and the positive (rather than negative) square root be taken for y. The requirement on the sign of the root is no problem, because FORTRAN's square root function (SQRT) always returns the positive root.

Program 11-10 calculates and displays the area of this circle using rectangular approximation.

Program 11-10

```
PROGRAM MAIN
   REAL X, A, B, WIDTH, AREA, F
   INTEGER I, N
   F (X) = SQRT ( ABS (4 - X ** 2))
   PRINT *, 'ENTER LEFT AND RIGHT BOUNDS OF X   (A, B): '
   READ *, A, B
   PRINT *, 'ENTER NUMBER OF SUBINTERVALS   (N): '
   READ *, N
   WIDTH = (B - A) / N
   X = A
   AREA = 0
   DO 20 I = 1, N
      AREA = AREA + WIDTH * F (X)
      X = X + WIDTH
20    CONTINUE
   PRINT *, 'APPROXIMATE TOTAL AREA USING RECTANGULAR'
   PRINT *, '  METHOD = ', AREA
   END
```

Notice that although we used subscripted x values in the discussion of the method, the difference between x_{i+1} and x_i is a constant for all i. It is therefore unnecessary to use arrays in the program to store many values of x at once. After each value is used in calculating the area of the subinterval, it is updated by the statement X = X + WIDTH. This calculation in effect replaces each x_i by the next value, x_{i+1}. Notice also the index I in the program simply functions as a counter, allowing the areas of the N subintervals to be summed. The equation of the circle is specified by the function statement placed after the declaration statement. The absolute value intrinsic function (ABS) was inserted to prevent taking the square root of a negative number, a condition that would cause an error.

The sample runs for Program 11-10 are shown below, varying only the number of subintervals, N.

```
ENTER LEFT AND RIGHT BOUNDS OF X   (A, B):
0 2
ENTER NUMBER OF SUBINTERVALS   (N):
2
APPROXIMATE TOTAL AREA USING RECTANGULAR
 METHOD =        3.732051

ENTER LEFT AND RIGHT BOUNDS OF X   (A, B):
0 2
ENTER NUMBER OF SUBINTERVALS   (N):
10
APPROXIMATE TOTAL AREA USING RECTANGULAR
 METHOD =        3.304518

ENTER LEFT AND RIGHT BOUNDS OF X   (A, B):
0 2
ENTER NUMBER OF SUBINTERVALS   (N):
50
APPROXIMATE TOTAL AREA USING RECTANGULAR
 METHOD =        3.178269

ENTER LEFT AND RIGHT BOUNDS OF X   (A, B):
0 2
ENTER NUMBER OF SUBINTERVALS   (N):
1000
APPROXIMATE TOTAL AREA USING RECTANGULAR
 METHOD =        3.143558
```

As expected, the accuracy improves as N gets larger. For example, if only two subintervals are used the approximated area is about 20 percent greater than the exact area ($\pi = 3.141593$, accurate to six decimal places); however, if 50 subintervals are used, the error is about 1 percent. Obviously, the improved accuracy is gained at the expense of a longer running time for the program.

Modified Rectangular Approximations

A modified form of the rectangular method, called the *midpoint* method, is illustrated in Figure 11-8. The only difference from the standard rectangular method is that the value of y at the midpoint of the subinterval rather than at the start of the subinterval is used as the height of the rectangle.

From Figure 11-8 it is seen that the midpoint of the ith rectangle, m_i, is calculated as:

$$m_i = \frac{x_i + x_{i+1}}{2} = \frac{x_i + (x_i + w)}{2} = x_i + \frac{w}{2}$$

where w is the width of each rectangle. The height of the ith rectangle is the y value for $x = m_i$, which is:

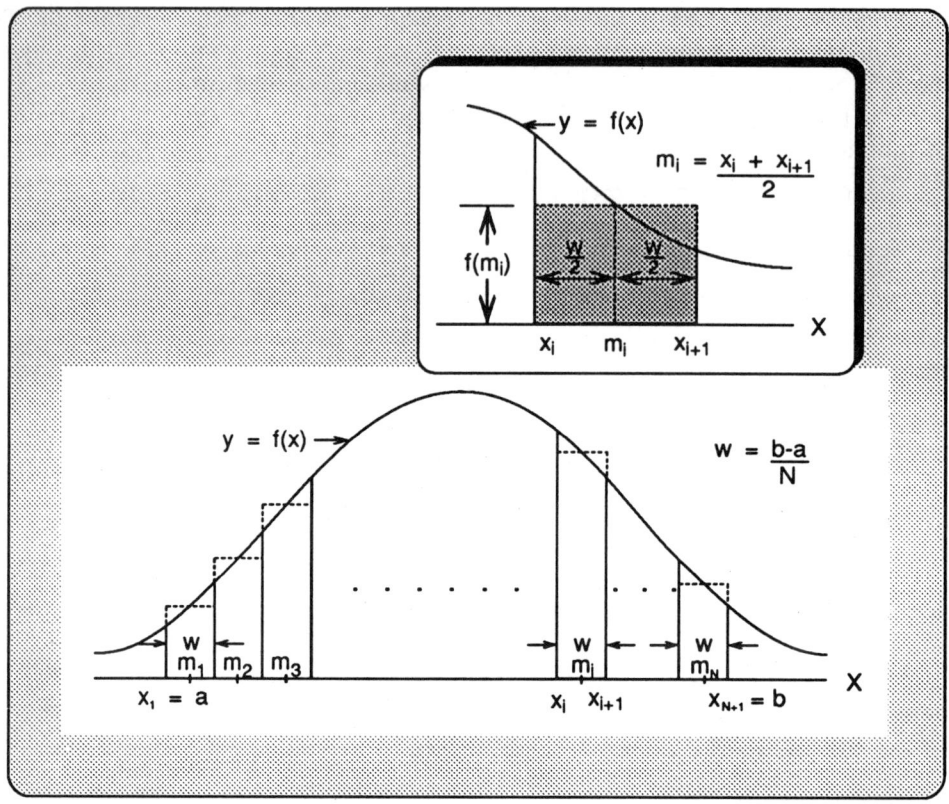

Figure 11-8   Modified Approximation to Area Under a Curve

$$f(m_i) = f(x_i + \frac{w}{2})$$

and the area of the ith rectangle is then:

$$A_i = w * f(x_i + \frac{w}{2})$$

Finally, the total area under the curve is approximated by:

$$Area = w \sum_{i=1}^{N} f(x_i + \frac{w}{2})$$

where the width, w, of each rectangle is calculated as $(b - a) / N$.

From a programming perspective, this approximation formula for the total area can be programmed using a DO loop that calculates each rectangular area, adds the calculated area to a sum, and then updates the value of x. The pseudocode for this procedure is:

enter the left and right bounds (a and b and the number of subintervals (N).
calculate width (w)
initialize x
set total area to zero
do for all rectangles
  calculate the x midpoint and its corresponding y value
  calculate the area of the rectangle
  add the rectangular area to the total area
  update the value of x
enddo
display total area

Program 11-11 calculates and displays the area of this circle using the midpoint approximation method. The only difference between Programs 11-10 and 11-11 is the assignment statement for AREA within the DO loop. In this statement the function call F(X) in Program 11-10 is replaced by F (X + WIDTH/2) in Program 11-11.

Program 11-11

```
PROGRAM MAIN
   REAL X, A, B, WIDTH, AREA, F
   INTEGER I, N
   F(X) = SQRT ( ABS(4 - X ** 2) )
   PRINT *, 'ENTER LEFT AND RIGHT BOUNDS OF X  (A, B): '
   READ *, A, B
   PRINT *, 'ENTER NUMBER OF RECTANGLES (N): '
   READ *, N
   WIDTH = (B - A) / N
   X = A
   AREA = 0
   DO 20 I = 1, N
     AREA = AREA + WIDTH * F (X + WIDTH/2)
     X = X + WIDTH
20       CONTINUE
   PRINT *, 'APPROXIMATE TOTAL AREA USING THE'
   PRINT *, ' MODIFIED RECTANGULAR METHOD = ',AREA
   END
```

Notice that after each midpoint value is used to calculate a corresponding *y* value, and the area of each rectangle is computed, this area is immediately added into the total area. Notice also that the index I in the program only acts as a counter, allowing the areas of the *N* rectangles to be summed. The equation of the circle is specified by the function statement placed after the declaration statement.

Four sample runs using Program 11-11 follow, showing the areas calculated when 2, 10, 50, and 1000 rectangles are used.

```
ENTER LEFT AND RIGHT BOUNDS OF X   (A, B): 0, 2
ENTER NUMBER OF RECTANGLES   (N): 2
APPROXIMATE TOTAL AREA USING THE
  MODIFIED RECTANGULAR METHOD =           3.259367

ENTER LEFT AND RIGHT BOUNDS OF X   (A, B): 0, 2
ENTER NUMBER OF RECTANGLES   (N): 10
APPROXIMATE TOTAL AREA USING THE
  MODIFIED RECTANGULAR METHOD =           3.152411

ENTER LEFT AND RIGHT BOUNDS OF X   (A, B): 0, 2
ENTER NUMBER OF RECTANGLES   (N): 50
APPROXIMATE TOTAL AREA USING THE
  MODIFIED RECTANGULAR METHOD =           3.142566

ENTER LEFT AND RIGHT BOUNDS OF X   (A, B): 0, 2
ENTER NUMBER OF RECTANGLES   (N): 1000
APPROXIMATE TOTAL AREA USING THE
  MODIFIED RECTANGULAR METHOD =           3.141631
```

As expected, the accuracy improves as the number of approximating rectangles, N, is increased. When using only two rectangles, the approximation differs by less than 5 percent from the exact area (3.141593). This compares to a 20 percent difference using the standard rectangular method. For $N = 50$, the error is less than 0.01 percent of its true value, which compares to an error of 1 percent using the same number of subintervals with the standard rectangular method. Referring again to Figures 11-6 and 11-8, it seems reasonable to expect that using the midpoint for the height of each rectangle method would give a more accurate result than using the endpoint, as in the standard rectangular method. If the curve does not exhibit unusual bending within a subinterval, the use of the midpoint to define the height of the rectangle will give a better approximation to the subinterval area than if the left endpoint of the subinterval (or the right endpoint, for that matter) were used.

Trapezoidal Approximation

In Figure 11-9, which illustrates the trapezoidal approximation method, the interval is divided into subintervals in the same manner as for the rectangular methods. However, the curve is now approximated by connecting a straight line between the points on the curve corresponding to the start and end of the subinterval. As shown by the enlarged drawing of the ith subinterval, the approximate area (the shaded portion) is that of a trapezoid made up of a rectangle plus a triangle. Since the area of a triangle is one-half of the product of width and height, the area of the ith subinterval shown in Figure 11-9 is then:

$$A_i = \text{area of rectangle} + \text{area of triangle}$$
$$= w f(x_{i+1}) + 0.5w \left[f(x_i) - f(x_{i+1}) \right]$$
$$= 0.5w \left[f(x_i) + f(x_{i+1}) \right]$$

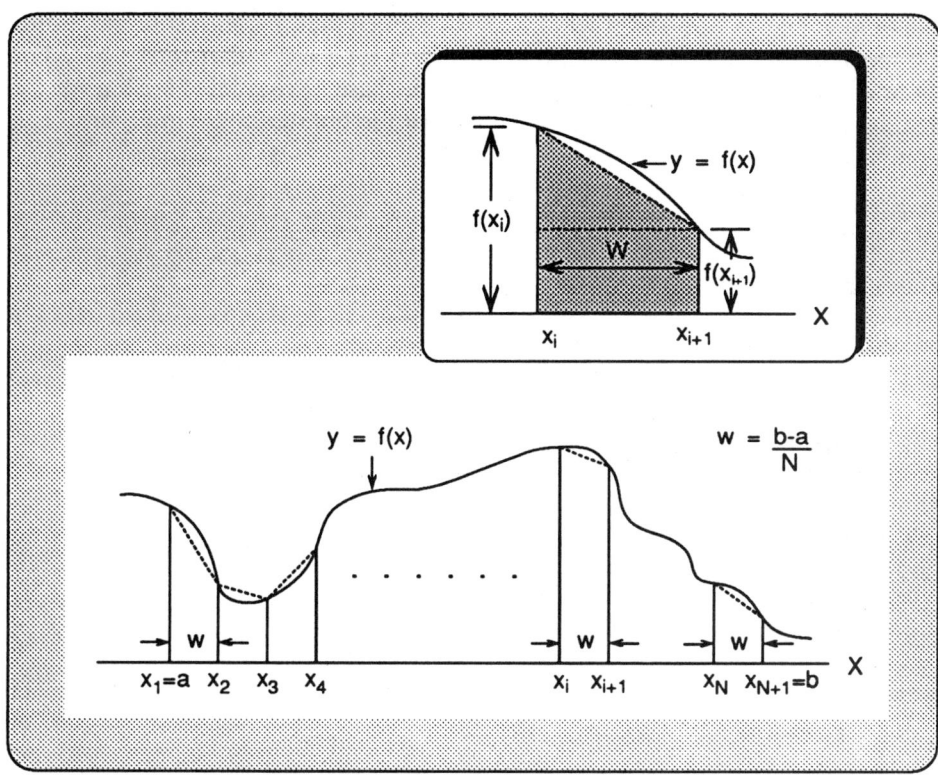

Figure 11-9   Trapezoidal Approximation to Area Under a Curve

The total area is then:

$$
\begin{aligned}
\text{Area} &= A_1 + A_2 + A_3 + \ldots + A_N \\
&= 0.5w\,[f(x_1) + f(x_2)] \\
&\quad + 0.5w\,[f(x_2) + f(x_3)] \\
&\quad + 0.5w\,[f(x_3) + f(x_4)] \\
&\quad + \ldots \\
&\quad + 0.5w\,[f(x_N) + f(x_{N+1})] \\
&= 0.5w\,[f(x_1) + f(x_{N+1})] \\
&\quad + w\,[f(x_2) + f(x_3) + f(x_4) + \ldots + f(x_N)]
\end{aligned}
$$

Since x_1 and x_{N+1} are the interval endpoints a and b, respectively, we can write the total area as:

$$
\text{Area} = 0.5\,w\,[f(a) + f(b)] + w\sum_{i=2}^{N} f(x_i)
$$

where $w = \dfrac{b-a}{N}$ and $x_{i+1} = x_{i+1} + w$.

The computation of the total area can now be done in a manner similar to that used for the rectangular methods. After entering a, b, and N the area can be initialized to:

$$
0.5w\,[f(a) + f(b)]
$$

and the term $wf(x_i)$ can be added within a loop. Notice that in contrast to the results for the rectangular methods, the summation starts for $i = 2$ rather than $i = 1$. The initial loop index value is therefore 2 for this case. Program 11-12 uses the trapezoidal approximation to compute the area of the quarter circle in Figure 11-7, with radius $r = 2$.

Program 11-12

```
PROGRAM MAIN
  REAL X, A, B, WIDTH, AREA, F
  INTEGER I, N
  F(X) = SQRT ( ABS (4 - X ** 2) )
  PRINT *, 'ENTER LEFT AND RIGHT BOUNDS OF X  (A, B): '
  READ *, A, B
  PRINT *, 'ENTER NUMBER OF SUBINTERVALS  (N): '
  READ *, N
  WIDTH = (B - A) / N
  X = A + WIDTH
  AREA = 0.5 * WIDTH * ( F(A) + F(B) )
  DO 20 I = 2, N
    AREA = AREA + WIDTH * F(X)
    X = X + WIDTH
20      CONTINUE
  PRINT *, 'APPROXIMATE TOTAL AREA USING TRAPEZOIDAL'
  PRINT *, ' METHOD = ', AREA
  END
```

As with the rectangular methods, the four sample runs for the trapezoidal method shown below display the approximate area for 2, 10, 50, and 1000 subintervals, respectively.

```
ENTER LEFT AND RIGHT BOUNDS OF X  (A, B):
0 2
ENTER NUMBER OF SUBINTERVALS  (N):
2
APPROXIMATE TOTAL AREA USING TRAPEZOIDAL
 METHOD =        2.732051

ENTER LEFT AND RIGHT BOUNDS OF X  (A, B):
0 2
ENTER NUMBER OF SUBINTERVALS  (N):
10
APPROXIMATE TOTAL AREA USING TRAPEZOIDAL
 METHOD =        3.104518
```

```
ENTER LEFT AND RIGHT BOUNDS OF X  (A, B):
0 2
ENTER NUMBER OF SUBINTERVALS  (N):
50
APPROXIMATE TOTAL AREA USING TRAPEZOIDAL
 METHOD =       3.138269

ENTER LEFT AND RIGHT BOUNDS OF X  (A, B):
0 2
ENTER NUMBER OF SUBINTERVALS  (N):
1000
APPROXIMATE TOTAL AREA USING TRAPEZOIDAL
 METHOD =       3.141557
```

The results for this example show that the trapezoidal method is considerably more accurate than the standard rectangular method but not quite as accurate as the modified rectangular (midpoint) method. Although we cannot generalize our conclusions for all curves, the use of the two endpoints of each subinterval should in most cases enable a better approximation of the area than will the use of only one endpoint. This justifies the trapezoidal approach as compared to the standard rectangular method. The midpoint method, unlike the standard method, is actually using the two endpoint values of x in calculating the subinterval's midpoint. We would therefore expect comparable accuracy between the midpoint and the trapezoidal methods. The results for the area of the quarter circle support that conclusion.

Simpson's Method

In addition to obtaining a more accurate estimate of the area under a curve by increasing the number of approximating subintervals, it is frequently possible to increase the accuracy by using a better approximation for the area of each subinterval. Simpson's method effectively achieves this result by fitting a parabolic curve to the endpoints of two successive intervals, as illustrated in Figure 11-10.

Notice that the two subintervals shown in Figure 11-10 share a common endpoint at x_{i+1}, providing three points to which the parabolic curve is being fit. Since two subintervals are being fitted at a time, the total number of subintervals,

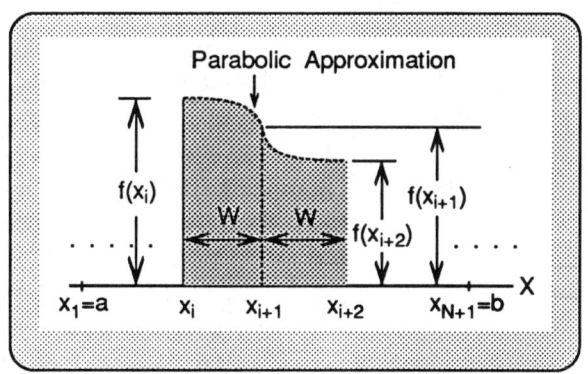

Figure 11-10   Parabolic Approximation to the Area Under a Curve

N, must be an even integer when Simpson's method is used.

The shaded area shown in Figure 11-10 is the approximation to the actual area under curve between the two intervals bounded by $x = x_i$ and $x = x_{i+2}$. The area under a parabolic curve cannot be determined simply as the height times the width, as it can be for a rectangle. With the aid of calculus, however, it can be shown that the shaded area is equal to:

$$A_i + A_{i+1} = \frac{w}{3} * [\, f(x_i) + 4\, f(x_{i+1}) + f(x_{i+2})\,]$$

where A_i is the area of the interval starting at x_i, and A_{i+1} the area of the adjacent next interval, starting at x_{i+1}. Notice that if the curve encompassed within two adjacent intervals is flat (zero slope), then $f(x_i) = f(x_{i+1}) = f(x_{i+2})$, and the shaded area becomes two equal-sized rectangles, each of width w and height equal to $f(x_i)$. In this case the previous expression reduces to:

$$A_i + A_{i+1} = \frac{w}{3} * [f(x_i) + 4f(x_i) + f(x_i)]$$

$$= \frac{w}{3} * [6f(x_i)] = 2wf(x_i)$$

as expected.

The total area under the curve, between the limits $x = a$ and $x = b$, is again a summation of areas A_i for all i from 1 to N. However, since the expression above includes two adjacent intervals, the sum is taken for $i = 1, 3, 5,$ and all other odd values of i up to and including $N-1$. That is:

$$Area = \sum_{i=1}^{N-1} (A_i + A_{i+1})$$

(odd i only)

$$= \frac{w}{3} * \sum_{i=1}^{N-1} [f(x_i) + 4f(x_{i+1}) + f(x_{i+2})]$$

(odd i only)

We will find it more convenient to evaluate this expression in its present form using a DO loop than to expand out the expression. As in Program 11-10, a routine to implement Simpson's method must input the values of a and b and the number of intervals (N) and calculate the width (WIDTH). The calculation of the total area is then completed using the following statements:

```
          X = A
          AREA = 0
          DO 20 I = 1, N-1, 2
             TEMP = F(X) + 4 * F(X + WIDTH) + F(X+2*WIDTH)
             AREA = AREA + WIDTH * TEMP / 3
             X = X + 2 * WIDTH
20        CONTINUE
```

Starting with the leftmost interval, X is initialized to A, and AREA to 0. Within the loop, the index advances by two each time, and X is incremented by twice the width, to account for the handling of two intervals at a time. Additionally, a temporary variable (TEMP) is introduced to avoid an overly lengthy statement line for the calculation of AREA.

Program 11-13 includes these statements in applying Simpson's method to approximate the area of the quarter circle with radius $r = 2$.

Program 11-13

```
PROGRAM MAIN
   REAL X, A, B, TEMP, WIDTH, AREA, F
   INTEGER  I, N
   F(X) = SQRT ( ABS(4 - X ** 2) )
   PRINT *, 'ENTER LEFT AND RIGHT BOUNDS OF X  (A, B): '
   READ *, A, B
   PRINT *, 'ENTER EVEN NUMBER OF INTERVALS  (N): '
   READ *, N
   WIDTH = (B - A) / N
   X = A
   AREA = 0
   DO 20 I = 1, N-1, 2
      TEMP = F(X) + 4 * F(X + WIDTH) + F(X + 2 * WIDTH)
      AREA = AREA + WIDTH * TEMP / 3
      X = X + 2 * WIDTH
20    CONTINUE
   PRINT *, 'APPROXIMATE TOTAL AREA USING SIMPSON METHOD'
   PRINT *, ' = ', AREA
   END
```

The sample runs below show the results for 2, 10, 50, and 1000 intervals.

```
ENTER LEFT AND RIGHT BOUNDS OF X  (A, B): 0 2
ENTER EVEN NUMBER OF INTERVALS  (N): 2
APPROXIMATE TOTAL AREA USING SIMPSON METHOD
 =         2.976068

ENTER LEFT AND RIGHT BOUNDS OF X  (A, B): 0 2
ENTER EVEN NUMBER OF INTERVALS  (N): 10
APPROXIMATE TOTAL AREA USING SIMPSON METHOD
 =         3.127031

ENTER LEFT AND RIGHT BOUNDS OF X  (A, B): 0 2
ENTER EVEN NUMBER OF INTERVALS  (N): 50
APPROXIMATE TOTAL AREA USING SIMPSON METHOD
 =         3.140298

ENTER LEFT AND RIGHT BOUNDS OF X  (A, B): 0 2
ENTER EVEN NUMBER OF INTERVALS  (N): 1000
APPROXIMATE TOTAL AREA USING SIMPSON METHOD
 =         3.141579
```

Table 11-1 summarizes the results for each of the four numerical integration methods used to approximate the area of the quarter circle with radius r = 2.

Table 11-1.   Comparison of Area Approximations for F(X) = $\sqrt{4-X^2}$ Over the Interval X = 0 to X = 1.

N	Standard rectangular method	Midpoint rectangular method	Trapezoidal method	Simpson's method
2	3.372051	3.259367	2.732051	2.976068
10	3.304518	3.152411	3.104518	3.127031
50	3.178269	3.142466	3.138269	3.140298
1000	3.143558	3.141603	3.141557	3.141579

(Exact area = 3.141593)

To further compare the two methods listed in Table 1-1, consider the half-cycle sine wave shown in Figure 11-11. The exact area under the curve from $x = 0$ to $x = \pi$ ($\pi = 3.141593$, accurate to six decimal places) can be shown using calculus to be 2.0. To approximate this value using numerical integration, Programs 11-10 through 11-13 were modified by replacing the function statement in each case by:

```
F(X)  =  SIN (X)
```

The bounds 0 and 3.141593 were entered when the programs were running. The tabulated results for the sine wave are listed in Table 11-2.

Table 11-2.   Comnparison of Area Approximation for F(X) = SIN(X) Over the Interval X = 0 to X = π

N	Standard rectangular method	Midpoint rectangular method	Trapezoidal method	Simpson's method
2	1.570796	2.221442	1.570796	2.094395
10	1.983524	2.008249	1.983523	2.000109
50	1.999342	2.000329	1.999342	2.000000
1000	1.999998	2.000001	1.999998	2.000000

(Exact area = 2.000000)

Using Tables 11-1 and 11-2, we can compare the four methods for the two examples, still far too few from which to draw any general conclusions, however. For the quarter circle the standard rectangular method has the poorest accuracy, and the trapezoidal method the next poorest. Both methods have the same accuracy for the half-cycle sine wave, which is coincidental and arises from the special properties of the symmetrical sine wave. For the quarter circle, the modified rectangular and Simpson's methods converge to the correct result equally fast as N increases.

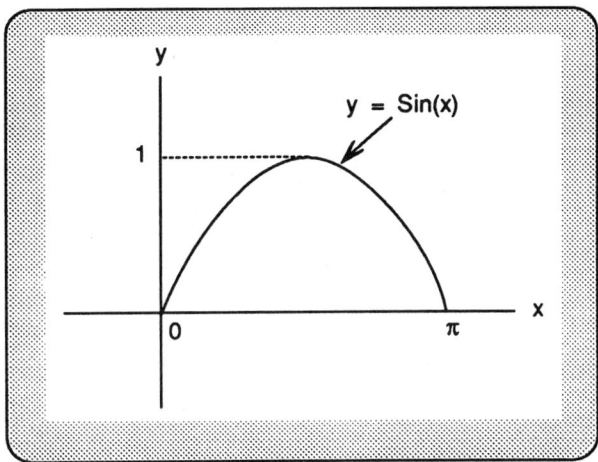

Figure 11-11   Half-Cycle of a Sine Wave

Application: Finding Average and RMS Values

The techniques for finding the area under a curve can also be used to find the average, or root-mean-squared (RMS), value of a waveform described by a function $y = f(x)$. This subject is of importance in electrical instrumentation, in which many voltage- and current-measuring instruments are calibrated to the average or RMS value of a periodic signal (such as a sine wave).

Refer again to Figure 11-6 illustrating the rectangular approximation to the area under a general curve $y = f(x)$. The average value of the function can be approximated by selecting a reasonably large number of equally spaced points on the curve, adding their y values, and dividing by the total number of points selected. Notice that this procedure is analogous to finding the average quiz grade for a class by adding the individual quiz grades and dividing by the size of the class. The average value corresponding to N points on the curve corresponding to $x_1, x_2, x_3, \ldots x_N$ is then:

$$Average = \frac{f(x_1) + f(x_2) + f(x_3) + \ldots + f(x_N)}{N}$$

$$= \frac{1}{N} \sum_{i=1}^{N} f(x_i)$$

where the x values are separated by the fixed interval width:

$$w = \frac{b-a}{N}$$

as before. Notice that the expression above can be written as:

$$Average = \frac{1}{Nw} \, w \sum_{i=1}^{N} f(x_i)$$

$$= \frac{1}{b-a} \, w \, \sum_{i=1}^{N} f(x_i)$$

$$= \frac{\textit{Approximate area under curve}}{\textit{Total interval width}}$$

This should satisfy our intuitive notion that the average height of a curve is the area divided by the base or total width.

The RMS value of a set of function values is also an average or "mean." As the name suggests, the root-mean-squared value is the square root of the average of the individual squared values. For our notation, the RMS value can be written as:

$$RMS = \sqrt{\frac{f^2(x_1) + f^2(x_2) + f^2(x_3) + \ldots + f^2(x_N)}{N}}$$

Program 11-14 is a modification of the rectangular approximation technique shown in Program 11-10. The calculation of AREA has been replaced in the loop by the calculation of the sum of the values of the function (SUM) and the sum of the squared values of the function (SUMSQR). After N iterations we exit from the loop and calculate the average by dividing SUM by N and the RMS value by dividing SUMSQR by N and taking the square root of the result. A sine wave is used for illustration.

 Program 11-14

```
PROGRAM MAIN
   REAL X, A, B, WIDTH, SUM, SUMSQR, AVERGE, RMS, F
   INTEGER I, N
   F(X) = SIN (X)
   PRINT *, 'ENTER LEFT AND RIGHT BOUNDS OF X  (A, B): '
   READ *, A, B
   PRINT *, 'ENTER NUMBER OF SUBINTERVALS  (N): '
   READ *, N
   WIDTH = (B - A) / N
   X = A
   SUM = 0
   SUMSQR = 0
   DO 20 I = 1, N
     SUM = SUM + F (X)
     SUMSQR = SUMSQR + F(X) ** 2
     X = X + WIDTH
20    CONTINUE
   AVERGE = SUM / N
   RMS = SQRT (SUMSQR / N)
   PRINT *, 'APPROXIMATE AVERAGE VALUE =', AVERGE
   PRINT *, 'APPROXIMATE RMS VALUE    =', RMS
   END
```

Sample runs for Program 11-14 are shown below.

```
ENTER LEFT AND RIGHT BOUNDS OF X   (A, B):
0, 3.141593
ENTER NUMBER OF SUBINTERVALS   (N):
10
APPROXIMATE AVERAGE VALUE =      0.631375
APPROXIMATE RMS VALUE      =      0.707107

ENTER LEFT AND RIGHT BOUNDS OF X   (A, B):
0, 3.141593
ENTER NUMBER OF SUBINTERVALS   (N):
50
APPROXIMATE AVERAGE VALUE =      0.636410
APPROXIMATE RMS VALUE      =      0.707107

ENTER LEFT AND RIGHT BOUNDS OF X   (A, B):
0, 6.283186
ENTER NUMBER OF SUBINTERVALS   (N):
50
APPROXIMATE AVERAGE VALUE =     -4.523840E-08
APPROXIMATE RMS VALUE      =      0.707107
```

The first two runs approximate the average and RMS values for the half-cycle sine wave shown in Figure 11-13, from $x = 0$ to $x = \pi$ (where $\pi = 3.141593$). Recall that the exact area under this curve is 2.0, and since the total interval width is π, the actual average value is:

Average $= 2 / \pi = 2 / 3.141593 = 0.636620$

The RMS value can be derived with the aid of calculus and is found to be:

RMS $= 1 / \sqrt{2}$ 0.707107

Notice that the computed average is closer to the exact value for larger N, as expected. The RMS value, interestingly, is nearly exact for the smaller as well as the larger value of N. As a result of the special properties of the sine function, you will obtain nearly the exact RMS value for any N (try it out for yourself!).

The final sample run shown is for a full cycle of the sine wave, from $x = 0$ to $x = 2 * \pi$. The sine wave in the interval from π to $2 * \pi$ has the same shape as in Figure 11-11 but flipped over to the negative direction. The sum of positive and negative values then cancel one another, resulting in an average value of zero. However, the negative values when squared become positive values and the resulting RMS value is the same as for the half-cycle case (do you see why?). The results of the last run support these conclusions.

Exercises

1a. Modify Program 11-10 to approximate the area under the curve:

$$y = x^3 + 2x^2 + 3x + 1$$

in the interval from $x = 0$ to $x = 1$. Run the program four times for $N = 2, 10, 50$, and 1000, respectively. The exact area is:

$$AREA = 41/12 = 3.416666$$

b. Repeat Exercise 1a using the modified rectangular method (Program 11-11).

2a. Repeat Exercise 1a using the trapezoidal method (Program 11- 12).

b. Repeat Exercise 1a using Simpson's method (Program 11-13).

c. Compare the results of Exercises 1 and 2.

3. Modify Program 11-11 to calculate and display a table of values of area for the quarter circle used in the text examples, for $N = 1, 2, 3, \ldots 10$. Also tabulate for each area the percent error between the approximate area and the exact area of $\pi = 3.141593$. Notice that the input of N from the keyboard needs to be replaced by a second loop in the program in which N is an index varying from 1 to 10. The original loop in the program should be nested inside this second loop. The output should be displayed using the heading below.

```
N     APPROXIMATE AREA      PERCENT ERROR
---   ----------------      -------------
```

4. The centroid is an important concept in engineering mechanics, as it represents the location of the center of gravity of a body of uniform density and thickness. For a curve described by the equation $y = f(x)$, it can be shown that the centroid is located at a point (x_c, y_c) where:

$$x_c = \frac{\text{Area under function } x f(x)}{\text{Area under function } f(x)}$$

$$y_c = \frac{\text{Area under function } f^2(x) / 2}{\text{Area under function } f(x)}$$

Notice that finding the centroid location requires the computation of the areas under three different functions, each related to $f(x)$.

a. Modify Program 11-11 to calculate and display the approximate centroid location for the function:

$$y = x^2$$

in the interval from $x = 0$ to $x = 1$.

b. Compile the program from Exercise 4a and run it for $N = 5, 10$, and 50. Comment on the relative accuracies of x_c and y_c. The exact centroid location is:

$$x_c = 0.75, \quad y_c = 0.3$$

5. Repeat Exercise 4 for the function:

$$y = x^4$$

in the interval from $x = 0$ to $x = 1$. The exact centroid location, accurate to six decimal places, is $x_c = 5/6 = 0.833333$, and $y_c = 5/18 = 0.277777$.

6a. Modify Program 11-14 to calculate and display the average and RMS values of the function $y = \sin(2x)$ in the interval $x = 0$ to $x = \pi = 3.141593$. Run the program for $N = 10$ and again for $N = 50$. Compare the results with those obtained from the sample runs shown of Program 11-14 for the function $y = \sin(x)$ in the same interval.

b. Repeat Exercise 6a for the function $y = e^{-x} \sin(x)$.

7. An unusual method of approximating the area under a curve can be made using a Monte Carlo simulation algorithm. To understand this algorithm, consider Figure 11-12, in which a rectangle of base (a,b) is superimposed on the curve $y = f(x)$ such that the height of the rectangle, H, is larger than any y value on the curve.

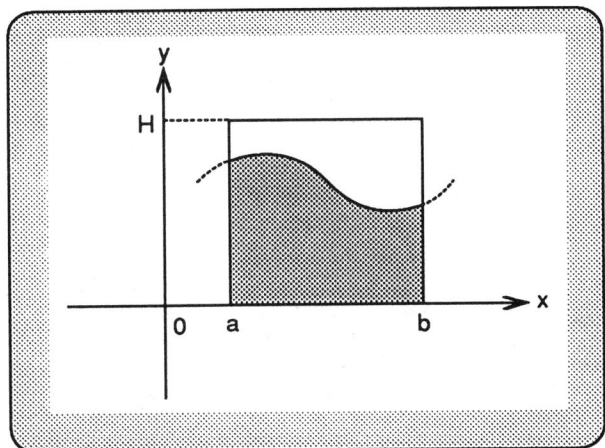

Now consider throwing N darts at Figure 11-12 and calculating the total number of darts, M that land in the shaded region. Probability theory states that for a large number of darts, the ratio of the M darts that land in the shaded area to the total number of N darts thrown is the same as the ratio of the shaded area to the total area. That is:

Figure 11-12

$$\frac{M}{N} = \frac{\text{Shaded area}}{\text{Rectangular area}}$$

Solving this formula for the shaded area under the curve yields:

$$\text{Shaded area} = (M/N) * \text{Rectangular area}$$

Using this information, write a FORTRAN program to approximate the area under the curve:

$$y = \sqrt{4 - x^2}$$

from $x = 0$ to $x = 1$. Generate random values of x and y between 0 and 1 using the random number generation algorithm presented in Section 7.5. If the resultant point (x,y) lies below the curve, the generated point is considered as landing in the shaded region; otherwise, it is considered as landing outside of the shaded region. Run your program using 2, 10, 50, and 1000 random points, respectively, and compare the results obtained with those presented in Table 11-1.

11.4   Common Programming Errors

The common errors associated with the techniques presented in this section include the following:

1. Although a real-valued loop index is often used for convenience in root-finding techniques, as it is in Programs 11-6 and 11-7, this practice can lead to problems in determining the exact number of iterations performed. Specifically, due to round-off errors, the real variable index may cause the loop to terminate one step earlier than expected. For example, the loop:

```
      REAL X
      DO 20 X = 0.1, 10.0, 0.1
               .
               .
               .
  20      CONTINUE
```

may exit after X = 9.9 rather than X = 10.0 as intended. The reason is that after the last increment of the index, its value may round off to 9.999999, or possibly to 10.000001. In the latter case the loop is exited because the index value exceeds the upper limit of 10.0. This problem can be avoided, when necessary, by using an integer variable as a loop index. For example, using an integer loop counter, the following routine can be used to replace the previous loop.

```
      REAL X
      INTEGER I
      X = 0.1
      DO 20 I = 1, 100
               .
               .
               .
         X = X + 0.1
  20      CONTINUE
```

The cost of this solution is the additional complexity of the resultant code.

2. Unless numerical iteration algorithms are carefully programmed, their execution times can be excessive. Both root-finding and numerical integration programs containing only single loops may exhibit a noticeable delay in completion when the number of iterations is larger than 50. For such programs it is frequently possible to decrease the runtime by performing a calculation outside the loop rather than inside. For example, consider the following segment of code from Program 11-11.

```
      X = A
      AREA = 0
      DO 20 I = 1, N
         AREA = AREA + WIDTH * F (X + WIDTH/2)
         X = X + WIDTH
  20      CONTINUE
```

Recall that in this program X represents the start of each interval with the midpoint at X + WIDTH/2. Within the loop the function F is repeatedly evaluated at the interval midpoint, requiring WIDTH/2 to be repeatedly added to X. By initializing X to the midpoint of the first interval, however, we can move this calculation outside the loop. Similarly, the returned value of F is multiplied by WIDTH within the existing loop before being added to the previously stored value of AREA. Since WIDTH has a constant value, this multiplication can be done after the loop is exited. The previous segment of code can, therefore, be replaced by:

```
      X = A + WIDTH/2
      AREA = 0
      DO 20 I = 1, N
        AREA = AREA + F(X)
        X = X + WIDTH
   20 CONTINUE
      AREA = WIDTH * AREA
```

Since the updating of AREA inside the loop now involves fewer calculations, the program will run faster. For the sake of readability, you may want to use a name other than AREA inside the loop, since the value returned when the loop is exited is not the actual area until it is multiplied by the subinterval width.

11.5 Chapter Summary

1. The solution of linear equations with two or three unknowns can be easily programmed. One such method uses *Cramer's rule* and is conveniently programmed using a subroutine function for the calculation of the required determinants. This algorithm is not efficient, however, for larger numbers of equations and unknowns.

2. There are several programming techniques for finding the real roots of an equation $y = f(x)$. In *fixed-increment* techniques the value of x is incremented by a constant step size over a range of values that includes the roots of interest. The value of y is calculated for each x, and a root is assumed to exist wherever the absolute value of y is arbitrarily small. Alternatively, the roots can be located where the function changes sign for two successive values of x. Although fixed-increment methods are easy to program, particularly with the aid of DO loops, such programs generally require a relatively long time to run.

3. The *bisection method* for root finding locates roots more rapidly than do fixed-increment methods. When a bisection algorithm is used, the interval of x is repeatedly bisected. For each bisection the half-interval that maintains the sign change at the endpoints is retained, and the other half interval is discarded from further consideration. The process continues until the interval is arbitrarily small. The presence of multiple roots can cause problems with this method.

4. The *secant method* for root finding is usually more efficient than the bisection method. Rather than bisecting the interval, a secant line is drawn from the points on the function's curve corresponding to the endpoints of the interval. The intersection of the secant line with the x axis is then used as one of the endpoints of the next interval. The process terminates when the absolute value of y is arbitrarily small. Like the bisection method, the secant method may have difficulties handling multiple roots.

5. Numerical integration is a technique for approximating the area under an interval of a curve described by a function $y = f(x)$. The most commonly used techniques divide the interval into N subintervals, where N is an arbitrary number, and adds the subinterval areas in sequence. Within each subinterval the curve can be approximated by a constant value, in which case the total area is a sum of rectangular areas. Alternatively, a straight line can be connected between the endpoints of the subinterval, leading to the addition of trapezoidal areas. *Simpson's method* involves approximating the function in two successive subintervals using a parabolic curve. All of the approximation techniques can be applied to finding the average and root-mean-square (RMS) values of functions.

The Proposed New FORTRAN Standard

Chapter Twelve

FORTRAN is one of the most versatile, powerful, and easy to use computer languages available for numeric applications, as it has been since its introduction over thirty years ago as the first high-level language. Since that time, however, many changes have occurred in both computer hardware and software design. For example, thirty years ago, when only 4000 memory locations might be available for a program, computer memory was considered a very scarce resource. Since current computers generally provide over half a million memory locations for a programmer to use, some early FORTRAN innovations such as the EQUIVALENCE statement, which allowed programmers to share computer memory between variables, have become unnecessary. Similarly, in the software arena, various capabilities more recently pioneered by such languages as Pascal and C are not yet available in FORTRAN. In recognition that programming environments do change, the American Standards Association, which later became the American National Standards Institute (ANSI), developed the first official standard for FORTRAN in 1966. This standard, which was developed over four years and used earlier versions of FORTRAN as its basis, was officially designated FORTRAN 66.

In 1978 a second standard was established, which was officially designated as FORTRAN 77. Unlike the earlier standard, which brought together the then existing versions of FORTRAN under a common standard, FORTRAN 77 included new features. Most of these features were concerned with supplying structured capabilities (such as the block IF statement) that were not available in FORTRAN 66 and with standardizing file-handling capabilities needed for the direct access disk storage that was rapidly displacing older sequential magnetic tape file devices.

Immediately after the FORTRAN 77 standard was released in April 1978, the ANSI American Standards Committee for Information Processing Systems, X3, initiated the process for establishing the next FORTRAN standard. This process included the establishment of the X3J3 technical committee, which was charged with developing a draft revision of the FORTRAN standard. Each draft revision developed by the X3J3 technical committee is first submitted to the X3 committee for preliminary acceptance. If accepted, the draft is published and submitted for public review and comment over a four-month period. After the public review period, every comment on the draft must be responded to and results either in an amendment to the draft by the X3J3 committee or rejection of the comment with supporting rationale. As this book is being written, the draft revision is in its second public review phase, which commenced on July 27, 1989, and ended on November 24, 1989. After the public review phase, the X3 committee determines whether to recommend to ANSI that the proposed standard be officially adopted.

The remaining sections of this chapter describe the new features of the proposed new standard as they are described in the second public review draft. (A copy of this draft, formally referred to as X3J3/S8—Version 112, dated June 1989, may be obtained from Global Engineering Documents, 2805 McGraw Avenue, Irvine, California 92714.) It is important to note that all existing features of FORTRAN 77 are supported in the new standard, which means that any program written under the FORTRAN 77 standard will compile under the new standard.

12.1   New Names and Additional Features

The central philosophy of the X3J3 committee in developing a new FORTRAN standard has been to "modernize Fortran so that it may continue its long history as a scientific and engineering program language" (p. 1, Foreword to draft X3J3/S8—Version 112). Additionally, the X3J3 committee has recommended that except for the official designation of FORTRAN 66 and FORTRAN 77, the name of the language be spelled as Fortran. We adhere to this recommendation in the remainder of this chapter.

The official name of the new Fortran standard (when approved), however, has not been established. Although names such as Fortran 88 and Fortran Extended have been suggested, the final standard's name will not, most likely, be decided until some time in early 1990, when the status of the draft revision is more certain. Regardless of the final name, the public review draft of the proposed new standard appears to have faithfully adhered to X3J3's stated philosophy to maintain Fortran as a modern language, geared to the numerical computing community. The major proposed additions to the language, as described in the most recent draft revision, include:

1. *Enhanced array operations*. FORTRAN 77's arithmetic, logical, and character operations and intrinsic functions have been extended to operate on complete arrays. A new intrinsic function, for example, has been specified to sum the elements of an array.

2. *Additional numerical capabilities*. The new standard has specifications for setting the numeric precision of data items and inquiry into the characteristics of numeric representation.

3. *Parameterized character data type*. This feature facilitates the inclusion of additional character sets, such as Chinese or Japanese characters, within the language. It also facilitates the inclusion of mathematical, chemical, and musical character sets.

4. *A new program unit type*. This feature permits a new program unit, called a module, to be accessed by as many or as few other program units as necessary. In its broadest applications this feature permits a singly defined global data area to be accessed by all program units in the same file without the need for further specification. As such, this feature is a generalization and replacement for the block data program unit.

5. *Support for direct implementation of structures*. This feature permits the construction of data structures that can contain elements having differing data types. As such, this feature removes the necessity of constructing parallel arrays of different data types, as described in Section 10.4, to simulate structures.

6. *Inclusion of pointers*. This feature permits the construction of a new type of variable whose content is the memory address of another variable. Since the address effectively "points to" where another variable is located, the name *pointer* is commonly used to describe this new type of variable. Pointer variables are extremely helpful in constructing data lists where each element in the list, unlike in an array, need not be stored consecutively.

7. *A mechanism for language evolution*. A mechanism is included in the new standard for deleting features from a previous standard. This involves defining certain features as obsolete. An obsolete feature becomes a candidate for removal from the next standard.

8. *Addition of new control statements*. The proposed standard includes a DO WHILE and a CASE statement. The DO WHILE is a repetition statement that can be used to construct WHILE loops (see Section 5.1) without using the block IF, GO TO, and ENDIF statements required for such loops in FORTRAN 77. The CASE statement is a multilevel selection statement that can be used to replace IF-ELSEIF structures.

In more general terms, these eight proposed new features are the most significant of many other features added to the new Fortran standard. These other proposed features include a new free-form source code more adaptable to keyboard input; increased length of variable names from 6 to 31 characters; an enhanced declaration statement; recursive capabilities; dynamically allocated arrays that can be expanded or contracted during program execution; the addition of binary, octal, and hexadecimal specification of integer constants; the addition of bit manipulation intrinsic functions; new edit descriptors that permit the formatted input and output of binary, octal, and hexadecimal constants; and the extension of READ and WRITE statements to read and write individual characters in a complete input and output record.

Following are descriptions of the new symbolic name capability, the expanded declaration statement, and the new free-form source code. Descriptions of pointers, structures, and the additional DO WHILE and CASE control structures are presented in the remaining sections of this chapter.

Symbolic Names

In the proposed standard, the length of symbolic names has been increased from 6 to 31 characters, the first of which must be a letter. Additionally, the underscore character, _, has been included in the proposed new character set. Thus, under the proposed new standard the following are all valid symbolic names:

```
A1
NAME_LENGTH
EXPERIMENT
S_P_R_E_A_D__OUT
FINAL_
```

Variable Declarations

In the proposed standard a variable may have an attribute as well as a data type. To include the attribute, the general form of variable declaration statements has been expanded to:

```
data type, attribute_1, attribute_2, . . .   :: list of variables
```

where the comma before each attribute and the :: symbol are only required if an attribute is included. For example, since the declaration:

```
REAL SUM
```

has no attributes, the comma after the data type is omitted, and the :: symbol does not have to be included. This symbol can be used, however, resulting in the equivalent declaration:

```
REAL :: SUM
```

Similarly, the declaration:

```
INTEGER, POINTER :: A, B
```

declares two variables, A and B, to have the attribute POINTER and data type INTEGER (the meaning of the POINTER attribute is described in Section 12.4). Notice that multiple variables can be declared using the new declaration statement, as in

FORTRAN 77. Thus, in the new standard, the following two declarations can both be used and mean the same thing:

```
INTEGER NUM1, NUM2, NUM3
INTEGER :: NUM1, NUM2, NUM3
```

Another addition is the way in which character variables are specified. Under the proposed standard the length of a character variable can be specified by including the term (LEN = *n*) after the CHARACTER type designation. Thus, the declarations:

```
CHARACTER*20 NAME
CHARACTER(LEN = 20) NAME
CHARACTER*20 :: NAME
CHARACTER(LEN = 20) :: NAME
```

are all equivalent.

Free-Form Source Code

As described in the proposed standard, "In free source form, each source line may contain from zero to 132 characters and there are no restrictions on where a statement may appear within a line." Although the free-form source code exists in addition to the fixed-form FORTRAN 77 source code the forms may not be intermixed in the same program.

In free-form source entry blanks may be inserted freely within a line, except within designated keywords, such as PRINT, READ, and WRITE. Additionally, blanks must be used to separate names, constants, and labels from adjacent names, constants, and labels. For example, in the statements:

```
INTEGER NUM
READ 10
50 DO I=1,3
```

the blanks are required after the words INTEGER, READ, and DO and after label 50.

The start of a comment in the free-form source code is signified by an exclamation point. For example, the declaration statement:

```
INTEGER NUM  !THIS DECLARES AN INTEGER VARIABLE:
```

contains the comment THIS DECLARES AN INTEGER VARIABLE. In all cases the comment extends to the end of the source line. If the first nonblank character on the line is an exclamation point, the line is called a comment line. A line containing all blanks is also considered a comment line and does not require the ! symbol.

The ampersand character, &, is used to indicate that the current statement is continued on the next line that is not a comment line. Thus, in free-form source entry, the continuation mark is placed on the line being continued rather than on the continuation line, as in the fixed-form source code required in FORTRAN 77. In no case can a statement have more than 39 continuation lines, and comment lines cannot be continued.

Finally, multiple statements may appear on the same line when separated by a semicolon (;). Thus, the line:

```
INTEGER NUM; REAL TOTAL; CHARACTER(LEN = 10) :: CODE
```

contains the three individual statements:

```
INTEGER NUM
REAL TOTAL
CHARACTER(LEN = 10) :: CODE
```

and the single line:

```
NUM = 5; TOTAL = 0.0
```

contains the two statements:

```
NUM = 5
TOTAL = 0.0
```

12.2 The CASE Construct

The IF-ELSEIF structure (see Section 4.3) is used in programming applications where one set of instructions must be selected from many possible alternatives. The CASE construct provides an alternative to the IF-ELSEIF structure. The common form of a Fortran CASE construct is:

```
SELECT CASE (expression)
  CASE (value_1)
    statement1
    statement2
        .
        .
        .

  CASE (value_2)
    statementm
    statementn
        .
        .
        .

  CASE (value_n)
    statementw
    statementx
        .
        .
        .

  CASE DEFAULT
    statementaa
    statementbb
END SELECT              ! END OF CASE CONSTRUCT
```

The CASE construct uses three new Fortran statements, a single SELECT CASE statement, one or more CASE statements, and a required END SELECT statement. Let us see how these statements are used. The SELECT CASE statement, which has the general form:

> SELECT CASE (*expression*)

identifies the start of the CASE construct. The expression in parentheses in this statement is evaluated, and the result of the expression is compared to various alternative values contained within each CASE statement.

Internal to the CASE construct, the CASE statement, which has the form:

> CASE (value)

is used to identify individual values that are compared to the value of the SELECT CASE expression. The expression's value is compared to each of these CASE values, in the order that these values are listed, until a match is found. When a match occurs, execution begins with the statement immediately following the matching CASE and ends when either the next CASE or an END SELECT statement is encountered. The CASE construct is then exited, and program execution continues with the statement following the END SELECT statement, which formally "closes off" the CASE construct. Thus, as illustrated in Figure 12-1, the value of the expression determines where in the CASE construct execution actually begins.

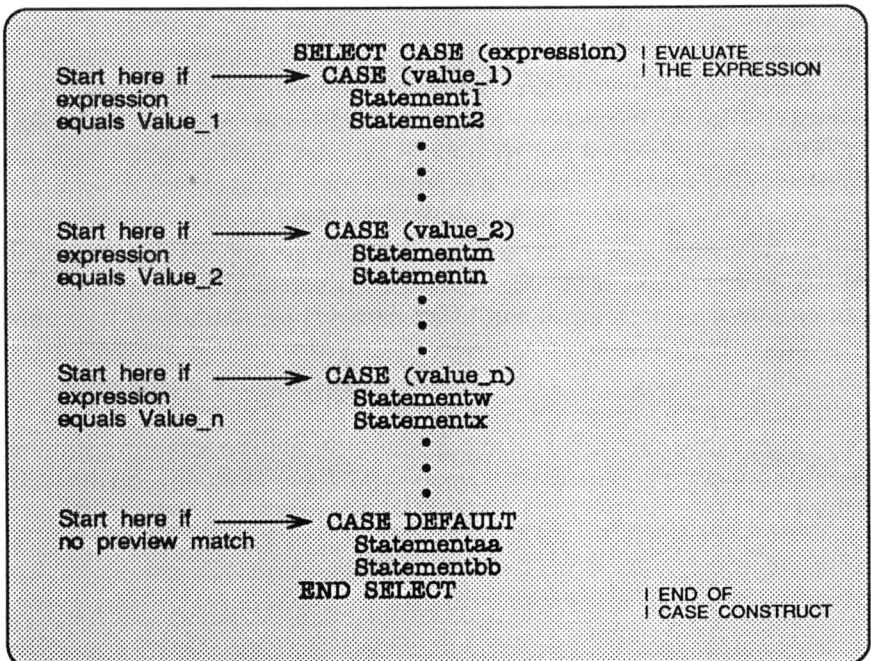

Figure 12-1   The Expression Determines an Entry Point

Any number of CASE labels may be contained within a CASE construct, in any order; the only requirement is that the values in each CASE statement must be of the same type as the expression in the CASE SELECT statement. If the value of the expression does not match any of the case values, however, no statement within the CASE construct is executed unless a CASE DEFAULT statement is encountered. The word DEFAULT is an optional "value" for the CASE statement that produces the same effect as the last ELSE in an IF-ELSEIF structure. If the value of the SELECT CASE expression does not match any of the CASE values, and the CASE DEFAULT statement is present, execution begins with the statement following the word DEFAULT.

Once an entry point has been located by the CASE construct, all further case evaluations are ignored, and execution continues until either a CASE or an END SELECT statement is encountered.

When writing a CASE construct, multiple CASE values may be included in the same CASE statement, and the DEFAULT case is optional. For example, consider the following CASE construct:

```
SELECT CASE (NUMBER)
  CASE (1)
    PRINT *, 'HAVE A GOOD MORNING'
  CASE (2)
    PRINT *, 'HAVE A HAPPY DAY'
  CASE (3, 5)
    PRINT *, 'HAVE A NICE EVENING'
  CASE (4, 6:10)
    PRINT *, 'HAVE A GOOD NIGHT'
END SELECT
```

If the value stored in the variable NUMBER is 1, the message HAVE A GOOD MORNING is displayed. Similarly, if the value of NUMBER is 2, the second message is displayed. The third CASE statement checks for a NUMBER equal to either 3 or 5, in which case the message HAVE A NICE EVENING is displayed. Finally, the last case checks for a value of 4 or any value between 6 and 10, inclusive, which is indicated by the colon (:) between the numbers 6 and 10. When a colon is included between two values, as it is in the last CASE statement, a match occurs if the expression's value is greater than or equal to the lower value and less than or equal to the upper value. Since this sample CASE construct does not include a DEFAULT case, no message is printed if the value of NUMBER is not one of the listed case values. Although it is good programming practice to list case values in increasing order, this is not required by the CASE construct. A CASE construct may have any number of case values, in any order; only the values being tested for need be listed.

Program 12-1 uses a CASE construct to select the arithmetic operation (addition, multiplication, or division) to be performed on two numbers depending on the value of the variable OPSELECT.

Program 12-1

```
PROGRAM MAIN
  INTEGER OPSELECT
  REAL FNUM, SNUM, FINAL
  PRINT *, 'PLEASE TYPE IN TWO NUMBERS'
  READ *, FNUM, SNUM
  PRINT *, 'ENTER A SELECT CODE:
  PRINT *,'         1 FOR ADDITION'
  PRINT *,'         2 FOR MULTIPLICATION'
  PRINT *,'         3 FOR DIVISION: '
  READ *, OPSELECT

  SELECT CASE (OPSELECT)
    CASE (1)
      FINAL = FNUM + SNUM
      PRINT *, 'THE SUM OF THE NUMBERS ENTERED IS', FINAL
    CASE (2)
      FINAL = FNUM * SNUM
      PRINT *, 'THE PRODUCT OF THE NUMBERS ENTERED IS', FINAL
    CASE (3)
      FINAL = FNUM / SNUM
      PRINT *, 'THE FIRST NUMBER DIVIDED BY THE SECOND IS', FINAL
  END SELECT         ! END OF CASE CONSTRUCT
  END                ! END OF PROGRAM UNIT
```

The following display clearly identifies the cases that would be selected in two hypothetical runs of Program 12-1.

```
PLEASE TYPE IN TWO NUMBERS:
12 3
ENTER A SELECT CODE:
        1 FOR ADDITION
        2 FOR MULTIPLICATION
        3 FOR DIVISION:
2
THE PRODUCT OF THE NUMBERS ENTERED IS 36.000000
```

and:

```
PLEASE TYPE IN TWO NUMBERS:
12 3
ENTER A SELECT CODE:
        1 FOR ADDITION
        2 FOR MULTIPLICATION
        3 FOR DIVISION:
3
THE FIRST NUMBER DIVIDED BY THE SECOND IS 4.000000
```

In addition to being used to select a case based on an integer expression, the CASE construct can be used for logical, character, and real valued expressions. For example, assuming that CHOICE is a character variable, the following CASE construct is valid:

```
SELECT CASE (CHOICE)
  CASE ('a', 'e', 'i', 'o', 'u')
    PRINT *, 'THE CHARACTER IN CHOICE IS A VOWEL'
  CASE DEFAULT
    PRINT *, 'THE CHARACTER IN CHOICE IS NOT A VOWEL'
END SELECT
```

Range of Values

As we saw in the first CASE construct example, the values being selected may be included in a range by using a colon to separate the end points of the selected range. Thus, a case value of $-1:10$ indicates all values between -1 and 10, inclusive, and a case value of $2.2:3.6$ indicates all values between 2.2 and 3.6, inclusive. Additionally, case values may take the form *low:* or *:high,* as in the examples 10:, -3.2:, :-2, and :25. When a colon follows a value, as in 10:, and no upper value is listed after the colon, a match occurs if the expression in the SELECT CASE statement is greater than or equal to the value indicated. Similarly, when a colon precedes a value, as in :25, and no lower value is listed before the colon, a match occurs if the expression in the SELECT CASE statement is less than or equal to the value indicated. For example, consider the CASE construct:

```
SELECT CASE (REALNUM)
  CASE (:-1.0)
    WEIGHT = -1
  CASE (1.0:)
    WEIGHT = 1
  CASE DEFAULT
    WEIGHT = 0
END SELECT
```

The first case tested in this CASE construct is whether the value of REALNUM is less than or equal to -1.0, in which case the variable WEIGHT is assigned the value -1. The next case tested is whether the value of REALNUM is greater than or equal to 1.0, in which case WEIGHT is assigned the value 1. Finally, if none of these two cases is selected, WEIGHT is assigned a value of 0 by the DEFAULT CASE.

Exercises

1. Rewrite the following IF-ELSEIF structure using a CASE construct:

```
IF (LETTER_GRADE .EQ. 'A')
  PRINT *, 'THE NUMERICAL GRADE IS BETWEEN 90 AND 100'
ELSEIF (LETTER_GRADE .EQ. 'B')
  PRINT *, 'THE NUMERICAL GRADE IS BETWEEN 80 AND 89.9'
ELSEIF (LETTER_GRADE .EQ. 'C')
  PRINT *, 'THE NUMERICAL GRADE IS BETWEEN 70 AND 79.7'
ELSEIF (LETTER_GRADE .EQ. 'D'
  PRINT *, 'HOW ARE YOU GOING TO EXPLAIN THIS ONE'
ELSE
```

```
      PRINT *, 'OF COURSE I HAD NOTHING TO DO WITH MY GRADE.'
      PRINT *, ' THE PROFESSOR WAS REALLY OFF THE WALL.'
   ENDIF
```

2. Rewrite the following IF-ELSEIF structure using a CASE construct:

```
IF (FACTOR .EQ. 1)
   CALL IN_DATA
   CALL CHECK
ELSEIF (FACTOR .EQ. 2)
   CALL DATES
   CALL LEAP_YR
ELSEIF (FACTOR .EQ. 3)
   CALL YIELD
   CALL RESULTS
ELSEIF (FACTOR .EQ. 4 .OR. FACTOR .EQ. 5 .OR. FACTOR .EQ. 6)
   CALL VOLTS
   CALL ROI
   CALL FILES
   CALL SAVE
ENDIF
```

3. Modify Program 12-1 to use a character variable for the select code.

12.3   The DO WHILE Construct

The DO WHILE structure introduced in Section 5.1 required a block IF, GO TO, and ENDIF statement for its construction. In the proposed new Fortran standard the DO WHILE structure, referred to as a DO WHILE construct, can be created using a DO WHILE statement. The general form of the new DO WHILE construct is:

```
DO WHILE (relational expression)
   statement_1
   statement_2

        .
        .
        .

   statement_n
ENDDO
```

The DO WHILE construct introduces two new Fortran statements, the DO WHILE statement and the ENDDO statement. The general form of the DO WHILE statement, which begins a DO WHILE construct, is:

```
DO WHILE (relational expression)
```

Within the context of a DO WHILE construct, the DO WHILE statement performs as follows. The relational expression contained within the parentheses is evaluated, and, if the expression is true, the statements between the DO WHILE and ENDDO statements are executed repeatedly as long as the expression remains true. This naturally means that somewhere in the DO WHILE construct there must be a statement that alters the value of the tested expression. As we will see, this is indeed the case. Thus, the process used by the computer in evaluating a DO WHILE construct is to:

1. test the expression
2. If the expression is true
   a. execute the statements between the DO WHILE and ENDDO statements
   b. go back to step 1

   else

   exit the DO WHILE construct and continue execution with the statement following the ENDDO statement

Notice that this is essentially the same sequence of operation listed for the DO WHILE structure introduced in Section 5.1. The transfer of control back to the start of a DO WHILE statement by step 2b forces the DO WHILE statement to recheck its expression and results in a program loop. This looping process was previously illustrated in Figure 5-1, which is reproduced as Figure 12-2.

As an example of a DO WHILE loop, consider the following set of instructions:

```
COUNT = 1
DO WHILE (COUNT .LE. 10)
   PRINT *, COUNT
   COUNT = COUNT + 1
ENDDO
```

The first assignment statement sets COUNT equal to one. The DO WHILE construct is then entered, and the expression in the DO WHILE statement is evaluated for the first time. Since the value of COUNT is less than or equal to 10, the expression is true, and the statements between the DO WHILE and the ENDDO statement are executed. The first statement within the construct causes the PRINT statement to display the value of COUNT. The next statement adds one to the value currently stored in COUNT, making this value equal to two. The ENDDO statement then causes the program to loop back to retest the condition. Since COUNT is still less than or equal to 10, the statements within the construct are again executed. This process continues until the value of COUNT reaches 11. Program 12-2 illustrates these statements in an actual program.

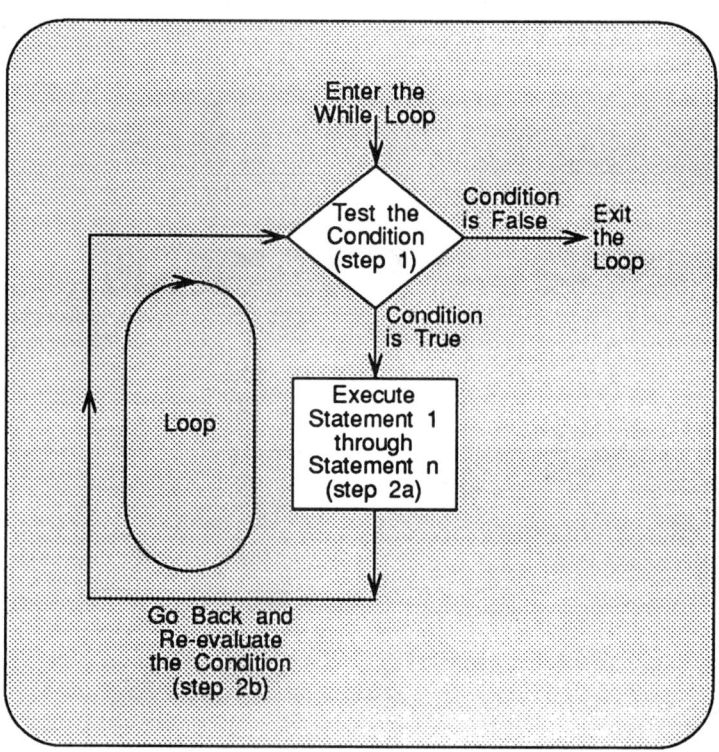

Figure 12-2   Operation of a DO WHILE Loop

Program 12-2

```
PROGRAM MAIN
  INTEGER COUNT
  COUNT = 1
  DO WHILE (COUNT .LE. 10)
    PRINT *, COUNT
    COUNT = COUNT + 1
  END DO
  END
```

The output that would be produced by Program 12-2 is:

```
1
2
3
4
5
6
7
8
9
10
```

There is nothing special about the variable COUNT used in Program 12-2, and any valid integer or real variable could have been used in its place. Additionally, the statement COUNT = COUNT + 1 can be replaced with any statement that changes the value of COUNT in a way that ultimately ensures exit from the loop. A statement such as COUNT = COUNT + 2, for example, would cause every second integer to be displayed. It is the programmer's responsibility, however, to ensure that COUNT is changed in a way that ultimately leads to a normal exit from the loop. For example, if we replace the statement COUNT = COUNT + 1 with the statement COUNT = COUNT − 1, the value of COUNT will never reach 11, and an infinite loop is created.

Consider now the task of printing a table of numbers from one to 10 with their squares and cubes. This can be done with the simple DO WHILE structure illustrated in Program 12-3.

Program 12-3

```
PROGRAM MAIN
  INTEGER NUM
  PRINT *, '          NUMBER      SQUARE      CUBE'
  PRINT *, '          ------      ------      ----'

  NUM = 1
  DO WHILE (NUM .LT. 11)
    PRINT *, NUM, NUM**2, NUM**3
    NUM = NUM + 1
  ENDDO
END
```

The output that would be produced by Program 12-3 is:

NUMBER	SQUARE	CUBE
1	1	1
2	4	8
3	9	27
4	16	64
5	25	125
6	36	216
7	49	343
8	64	512
9	81	729
10	100	1000

Note that the condition used in Program 12-3 is NUM .LT. 11. For the integer variable NUM, this condition can be replaced by the equivalent condition NUM .LE. 10. Which to use is entirely up to the programmer.

Although we have illustrated using the DO WHILE statement to construct loops that are executed a fixed count number of times, this is not required by the DO WHILE statement. For example, consider Program 12-4, where the DO WHILE statement is used to generate a program loop that terminates when a sentinel value is entered. In this program data is continuously requested and accepted until a number larger than 100 is entered. Entry of a number higher than 100 alerts the program to exit the DO WHILE loop and to display the sum of the numbers entered.

Program 12-4

```
PROGRAM MAIN
  REAL GRADE, TOTAL
  TOTAL = 0.0
  PRINT *, 'TO STOP ENTERING GRADES, TYPE IN ANY NUMBER'
  PRINT *, ' GREATER THAN 100.'
  DO WHILE (GRADE .LE. 100)
    PRINT *, 'ENTER A GRADE: '
    READ *, GRADE
    TOTAL = TOTAL + GRADE
  ENDDO
  PRINT *, 'THE TOTAL OF THE GRADES IS ', TOTAL - GRADE
END
```

As long as grades less than or equal to 100 are entered, the program continues to request and accept additional data. When a number greater than 100 is entered, the program adds this number to the TOTAL and exits the WHILE loop. Outside of the loop and within the PRINT statement, the value of the sentinel that was added to TOTAL is subtracted and the sum of the legitimate grades that were entered is displayed. Here is how a sample run using Program 12-4 would look:

```
TO STOP ENTERING GRADES, TYPE IN ANY NUMBER
 GREATER THAN 100.
ENTER A GRADE:
84
ENTER A GRADE:
75
ENTER A GRADE:
93
ENTER A GRADE:
88
ENTER A GRADE:
101
THE TOTAL OF THE GRADES IS      340.000000
```

Notice that Program 12-4 differs from previous examples in that termination of the loop is controlled by an externally supplied value rather than by a fixed count condition. The loop in Program 12-4 will continue indefinitely until the sentinel value is encountered. DO WHILE statements are well suited to handle sentinel values because the statement evaluates a relational expression.

The EXIT and CYCLE Statements

Two useful statements in connection with Fortran's DO statements are the proposed EXIT and CYCLE statements. The general form of the EXIT statement is:

```
EXIT
```

An EXIT statement, as its name implies, forces an immediate EXIT from any DO loop within which it is contained. For example, execution of the following DO WHILE loop is immediately terminated if a number greater than 76 is entered.

```
DO WHILE (COUNT .LE. 10)
   PRINT *, 'ENTER A NUMBER: '
   READ *, NUM
   IF (NUM .GT. 76) THEN
     PRINT *, 'YOU LOSE!'
     EXIT            ! EXIT OUT OF THE LOOP
   ELSE
   PRINT *, 'KEEP ON TRUCKIN!'
   ENDIF
ENDDO
! EXIT FORCES CONTROL TO HERE
```

The EXIT statement violates pure structured programming principles because it provides a second, nonstandard exit from a loop. Nevertheless, the EXIT statement is extremely useful and valuable for exiting loops when an unusual condition is detected.

The general format of a CYCLE statement, which also can be used only in conjunction with DO loops, is:

```
CYCLE
```

When CYCLE is encountered in a loop, the next iteration of the loop is immediately begun. For DO WHILE loops this means that execution is automatically transferred to the top of the loop, and reevaluation of the tested expression is initiated, in the same manner as if the ENDDO statement had been encountered.

As a general rule the CYCLE statement is less useful than the EXIT statement, but it is convenient for skipping over data that should not be processed while remaining in a loop. For example, invalid grades are simply ignored in the following section of code, and only valid grades are added into the total:

```
DO WHILE (COUNT .LT. 30)
  PRINT *, 'ENTER A GRADE: '
  READ *, GRADE
  IF(GRADE .LT. 0 .OR. GRADE .GT. 100) CYCLE
  TOTAL = TOTAL + GRADE
ENDDO
```

Exercises

1. Rewrite Program 12-2 to print the numbers from –10 to –1 in increments of one.

2. Rewrite Program 12-2 to print the numbers 2 to 10 in increments of two. The output of your program should be:

```
2
4
6
8
10
```

3. For the following program determine the total number of items displayed. Also determine the first and last numbers printed.

```
PROGRAM MAIN
  INTEGER NUM = 0
  DO WHILE (NUM .LE. 20)
    NUM = NUM + 1
    PRINT *, NUM
  ENDDO
  END
```

12.4   Pointers and Targets

As illustrated in Figure 12-3, every variable has two major items associated with it: the value stored in the variable and the address of the variable. Programmers are usually concerned only with the value assigned to a variable (its contents) and give little attention to where the value is stored (its address).

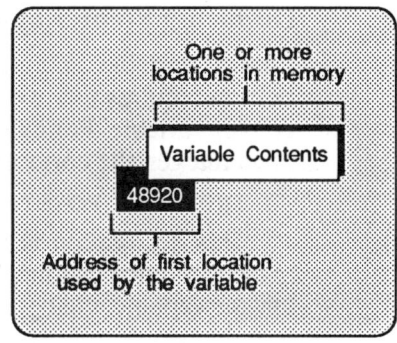

In the proposed Fortran standard, it is possible to store the address of one variable into another suitably declared variable. For example, the statement:

```
NUMADR => NUM
```

stores the address corresponding to the variable NUM in the variable NUMADR. Notice that we have introduced a new assignment symbol, =>, which is composed of the two individual symbols, = and >. In the proposed standard, this new assignment symbol means "store the address of the variable to the right of the symbol in the variable to the left of the symbol." Thus, the statements:

Figure 12-3   A Typical Variable

```
D => M

TABPTR => LIST

CHRPTR => CH
```

store the addresses of the variables M, LIST, and CH in the variables D, TABPTR, and CHRPTR, respectively, as illustrated in Figure 12-4.

The variables NUMADR, D, TABPTR, and CHRPTR are all called pointer variables, or pointers. *Pointers* are simply variables that are used to store the addresses of other variables. In programming, another way of saying that one variable contains the address of a second variable is

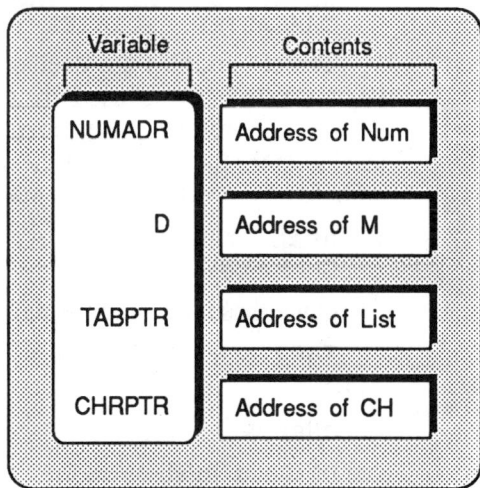

Figure 12-4   Storing Addresses

to say that the first variable "points to" where the second variable is located in memory. The variable containing the address is called the pointer variable, or pointer, and the variable whose address is being stored is called the target variable, or target. Thus, for the previous assignment NUMADR => NUM, it is correct to say that the pointer NUMADR "points to" the target NUM, typically shortened to saying NUMADR points to NUM. Similarly, since the address of the variable M was stored in the pointer variable D by the statement D => M, we can say that D points to M. Here D is the pointer and M the target. This interpretation, of course, is reinforced by the notation =>, which can be read "points to."

As we shall see in Section 12.6, when we construct a linked list, the ability to store one variable's address into another variable would provide Fortran programmers with an extremely powerful programming tool. First, however, we must see how to declare pointer and target variables.

Declaring Pointer and Target Variables

Like all variables, pointers and targets must be declared before they can be used. Fortran requires that we specify the type of variable pointed to when we declare a pointer variable. For example, if the address in the pointer NUMADR is the address of an integer, the correct declaration for the pointer is:

```
INTEGER, POINTER :: NUMADR
```

This declaration is read as "the variable named NUMADR is a pointer to an integer." Notice that the declaration specifies three things: the name of the variable, that the variable will be used as a pointer, and that the variable pointed to by NUMADR is an integer. Similarly, if the pointer TABPTR will be used as a pointer to (contain the address of) a real valued variable, and CHRPTR will be used as a pointer to (contain the address of) a character variable, the required declarations for these pointers are:

```
REAL, POINTER :: TABPTR
CHARACTER, POINTER :: CHRPTR
```

Target variables are declared in a similar manner as pointers except that the keyword TARGET is used instead of the keyword POINTER (both TARGET and POINTER are referred to as *attributes* in the new standard). Thus, if TABPTR will be used to store the address of the variable LIST, and CHRPTR will be used to store the address of the variable CH, suitable declarations for these two target variables are:

```
REAL, TARGET :: LIST
CHARACTER, TARGET :: CH
```

Once these declarations have been made, the address assignments:

```
TABPTR => LIST
```

and:

```
CHRPTR => CH
```

can be made. In all cases the data type of the pointer must match the data type of the target, or an error will occur. Thus, the data type of the pointer TABPTR must be the same as the data type of the target LIST (they are both REAL variables), and the data type of the pointer CHRPTR must be the same as that of its target, CH (both are character variables of length one).

Using Pointers

Once a pointer has been assigned a target, which means that the address of the target variable has been stored in the pointer, the pointer name may be used in place of the target to access the target's value. For example, consider Program 12-5:

 Program 12-5

```
PROGRAM SHOWPT
  INTEGER, POINTER :: A
  INTEGER, TARGET :: B
  INTEGER C
  A => B !STORE B'S ADDRESS INTO A
  B = 22
  PRINT *, A
  PRINT *, B
  A = 15
  PRINT *, A
  PRINT *, B
  C = A
  PRINT *, C
  END
```

The output that would be produced by Program 12-5 is:

```
22
22
15
15
15
```

Let us see how this output is obtained. As previously described, an assignment such as A = > B in Program 12-5 causes B's address to be stored in the pointer variable named A. Henceforth, until A is assigned to another target, referencing the variable A automatically forces the computer to use the address in A to locate the desired target. Thus, the statement PRINT *, A causes the computer to use the address in A to locate its target, which in this case is the variable B. It is the contents of the target that is displayed. Thus, the output of the statement PRINT *, A is the value 22, which is the same output produced by the statement PRINT *, B. In the first case the computer "knows" to use the address of A correctly because A has been declared as a pointer. Similarly, the assignment A = 15 is interpreted by the computer to mean "store a 15 in the location pointed to by A," which again is the variable B. Thus, the second set of two consecutive PRINT statements in Program 12-5 both display the value 15. Finally, the variable C is assigned the value pointed to by A. Thus, the value displayed by the last PRINT statement is also 15.

Now we can see why pointer declarations must include the type of value being pointed to. Although it certainly would have been simpler if the pointer A used in Program 12-5 could have been declared as POINTER A, such a declaration conveys no information as to the type of variable that ultimately must be accessed. This additional information is essential when the pointer is used in statements such as PRINT *, A and C = A. Here the address stored in A only provides the starting location of the ultimate target and does not tell the computer whether an integer, character, or real valued datum must be accessed. Since these differing data types typically are stored using differing amounts of storage (see both Sections 1.7 and Appendix D for a description of data storage concepts), the computer must know not only that A is a pointer but also the type of data A ultimately references.

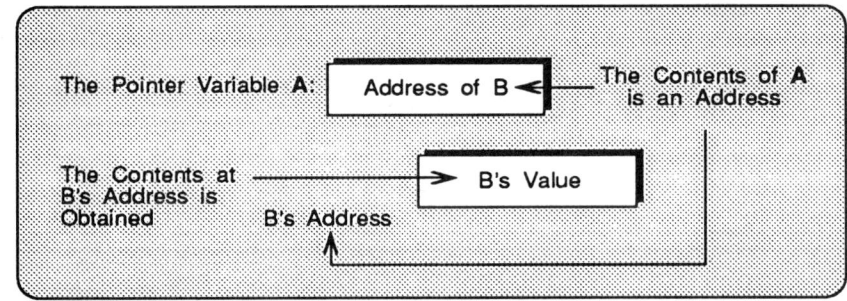

Figure 12-5   Using a Pointer Variable

When using a pointer variable, as illustrated in Figure 12-5, the value that is finally accessed is always found by first going to the pointer variable for an address. The address contained in the pointer is then used to get the desired contents. Certainly, this is a rather indirect way of getting to the final value, and the term *indirect addressing* is used to describe this procedure.

Since using a pointer requires the computer to do a double lookup (first the address is retrieved; then the address is used to retrieve the actual data), it is a worthwhile to ask why you would want to store an address in the first place. The answer must be deferred until we get to a real application, such as presented in Section 12.6, where the use of pointers becomes invaluable. However, given what we know about variables, the idea of storing an address in a variable should not seem overly strange.

12.5   Structures

In Chapter 10 we saw how structures can be represented in FORTRAN 77 using parallel arrays. In the new proposed Fortran standard, structures may be defined directly. We first briefly review the concept of a structure and then show how structures may be implemented under the proposed new Fortran standard.

In the broadest sense, structure refers to the way individual elements of a group are arranged or organized. For example, a corporation's structure refers to the organization of the people and departments in the company, and a government's structure refers to its form or arrangement. In programming, a structure refers to the way individual data items are arranged to form a cohesive and related unit. For example, consider the data items typically used in preparing mailing labels, as illustrated in Figure 12-6.

Each of the data items listed in the figure is an entity by itself. Taken together,

```
Name:
Street Address:
City:
State:
Zip Code:
```

Figure 12-6   Typical Mailing List Components

all the data items form a single unit, representing a natural organization of the data for a mailing label. This larger grouping of related individual items is commonly called a structure.

Although there could be thousands of names and addresses in a complete mailing list, the form of each mailing label, or structure, is identical. In dealing with structures, it is important to distinguish between the form of the structure and the data content of the structure.

The *form* of a structure consists of the symbolic names, data types, and arrangement of individual data items in the structure. The *contents* of a structure refers to the actual data stored in the symbolic names. Figure 12-7 shows acceptable contents for the structure illustrated in Figure 12-6.

```
Rochelle Bokow
333 14th Street
New York
NY
10033
```

Figure 12-7   The Contents of a Structure

Using structures requires three steps. The first step requires that we specify the form of the structure. Once a structure form has been specified, variables may be declared to have this form. Specific values can then be assigned to the individual structure elements.

The first step, specifying the form of the structure, requires listing the data types, data names, and arrangement of data items. For example, the declaration:

```
TYPE DATE
   INTEGER MONTH
   INTEGER DAY
   INTEGER YEAR
END TYPE DATE
```

defines the form of a structure. More precisely, a new data type called DATE is created. This new data type consists of three data items, which are called *members of the structure*. In this case the structure members consist of three integers, called MONTH, DAY, and YEAR, respectively. Since a structure is derived using other data types for its members, Fortran formally refers to a structure as a derived data type.

Once a structure form has been specified, variable names may be declared for this new data type. For example, the declaration:

```
TYPE(DATE) :: BIRTH
```

declares BIRTH to be a variable of the form DATE. As with all Fortran data types, multiple variables may be declared in the same declaration statement. Thus, the declaration:

```
TYPE(DATE) :: BIRTH, CURRENT
```

declares both BIRTH and CURRENT to be of type DATE.

Once a variable has been declared as a structure type, assigning actual data values to the individual structure members is called *populating the structure* and is a relatively straightforward procedure. Each member of a structure is accessed by giving both the structure's variable name and the individual member name, separated by a percent sign, %. Thus, BIRTH % MONTH refers to the first member of the BIRTH structure, BIRTH % DAY refers to the second member, and BIRTH % YEAR refers to the third member. Program 12-6 illustrates assigning values to the individual members of the BIRTH structure and displaying the contents of these members.

Program 12-6   Specifying and Populating a Structure

```
      PROGRAM MAIN
        ! SPECIFY A STRUCTURE TYPE NAMED DATE
        TYPE DATE
           INTEGER MONTH
           INTEGER DAY
           INTEGER YEAR
        END TYPE DATE
        ! DECLARE A VARIABLE TO BE OF THE SPECIFIED TYPE
        TYPE(DATE) :: BIRTH
        ! ASSIGN VALUES TO MEMBERS OF THE BIRTH STRUCTURE
        BIRTH % MONTH = 12
        BIRTH % DAY = 28
        BIRTH % YEAR = 52
        ! DISPLAY THE MEMBER VALUES
        PRINT 10, BIRTH % MONTH, BIRTH % DAY, BIRTH % YEAR
10      FORMAT(1X,'MY BIRTH DATE IS: ',I2,'/',I2,'/',I2)
        END
```

The output that would be produced by Program 12-6 is:

```
MY BIRTH DATE IS 12/28/52
```

The individual members of a structure are not restricted to being integer data types, as illustrated in Program 12-6. Any valid Fortran data type can be used. For example, consider an employee record consisting of the following data items:

```
Name:
Identification number:
Regular pay rate:
Overtime pay rate:
```

A suitable structure specification for these data items is:

```
TYPE PAYREC
   CHAR (LEN = 20) :: NAME
   INTEGER IDNUM
   REAL REG_RATE
   REAL OT_RATE
END TYPE PAYREC
```

Once the form, or template, for PAYREC is specified, a specific structure having the PAYREC form may be declared. For example, the declaration:

```
TYPE(PAYREC) :: EMPLOYEE
```

creates a structure named EMPLOYEE of the PAYREC type. Assignment statements such as:

```
EMPLOYEE % NAME = 'HARRY ROLLBY'
EMPLOYEE % IDNUM = 73562
```

are then valid.

Notice that a single structure is simply a convenient method for combining and storing related items under a common name. Although a single structure is useful in clearly identifying the relationship among its members, the individual members could be defined as separate variables. The real advantage to using structures is only realized when the same structure form is used in a list many times over. Creating lists with the same structure form is discussed shortly.

Before leaving single structures, it is worth noting that the individual members of a structure can be any valid Fortran data type, including arrays, structures, and pointers. Accessing an element of a member array requires giving the structure's name, followed by a percent symbol, followed by the array designation. For example, assuming the integer array VAL is a member of an EXPERIMENT structure, EXPERIMENT % VAL(5) refers to the fifth value in the VAL array.

Including a structure within a structure follows the rules for including any data type in a structure. For example, assume that a structure is to consist of a name and a date of birth, where a DATE structure has been declared as:

```
TYPE DATE
   INTEGER MONTH
   INTEGER DATE
   INTEGER YEAR
END TYPE DATE
```

A suitable specification of a structure that includes a name and a date structure is:

```
TYPE INDIVIDUAL
   CHARACTER (LEN = 20)  :: NAME
   TYPE(DATE)  :: BIRTH
END TYPE INDIVIDUAL
```

Notice that in specifying both the DATE and INDIVIDUAL structures, the symbolic names DATE and INDIVIDUAL are structure types, while the variable BIRTH is a specific structure having the form of a DATE structure. Before individual structure can be used, specific variables must also be declared for this type. Thus, for example, the declaration:

```
TYPE(INDIVIDUAL)  :: PERSON
```

declares PERSON to be a variable of type INDIVIDUAL. Here PERSON is the name of a specific structure. Individual members in the PERSON structure are accessed by preceding the desired member with the structure name followed by a percent symbol. For example, PERSON % BIRTH % MONTH refers to the MONTH variable in the BIRTH structure contained in the PERSON structure.

Arrays of Structures

The real power of structures is realized when the same structure is used for lists of data. For example, assume that the data shown in Table 12-1 must be processed.

Clearly, the employee numbers can be stored together in an array of integers, the names in an array of characters, and the pay rates in an array of real values. In organizing the data in this fashion, each column in Table 12-1 is considered as a separate list, which is stored in its own array. Using arrays in this manner, as previously described in Section 10.4, the correspondence between items for each individual employee is maintained by storing an employee's data in the same position in each array.

Table 12-1   A List of Employee Data

Employee number	Employee name	Employee pay rate
12479	ADAMS, C.	5.72
13623	BRENER, D.	7.54
14145	DUNSON, P.	6.56
15987	FRANKLIN, S.	8.43
16203	JAMASON, T.	5.72
16417	KLINE, H.	9.64
17634	OPPER, G.	7.29
18321	SMITH, S.	8.67
19435	VOELMER, L.	5.50
19567	WILSON, R.	7.35

The separation of the complete list into three individual arrays is unfortunate, since all of the items relating to a single employee constitute a natural organization of data into structures, as illustrated in Figure 12-8.

	Employee Number	Employee Name	Employee Pay Rate
1st structure →	12479	ADAMS, C.	5.72
2nd structure →	13623	BRENNER, D.	7.54
3rd structure →	14145	DUNSON, P.	6.56
4th structure →	15987	FRANKLIN, S.	8.43
5th structure →	16203	JAMASON, T.	5.72
6th structure →	16417	KLINE, H.	9.64
7th structure →	17634	OPPER, G.	7.29
8th structure →	18321	SMITH, S.	8.67
9th structure →	19435	VOELMER, L.	5.50
10th structure →	19567	WILSON, R.	7.35

Figure 12-8   A List of Structures

Using a structure, the integrity of the data organization as a whole can be maintained and reflected by the program. Under this approach, the list in Figure 12-8 can be processed as a single array of 10 structures.

Declaring an array of structures is the same as declaring an array of any other variable type. For example, if the structure type PAYREC is specified as:

```
TYPE PAYREC
   INT IDNUM
   CHARACTER (LEN = 20)  :: NAME
   REAL RATE
END TYPE PAYREC
```

then an array of 10 such structures can be declared as:

```
TYPE(PAYREC)  ::  EMPLOYEE(10)
```

This declaration statement constructs an array of 10 elements, each of which is a structure of the type PAYREC. Notice that the declaration of an array of 10 structures has the same form as the declaration of any other array. For example, creating an array of 10 integers named EMPLOYEE requires the declaration:

```
INTEGER EMPLOYEE(10)
```

In this declaration the data type is integer, while in the former declaration for EMPLOYEE the data type is a structure of the form PAYREC.

Once an array of structures is declared, a particular data item is referenced by giving the position of the desired structure in the array followed by a percent symbol and the appropriate structure member. For example, the variable EMPLOYEE(1) % RATE references the RATE member of the first structure in the EMPLOYEE array. Including structures as elements of an array permits a list of structures to be processed using standard array programming techniques. For example, the first five employee structures in the EMPLOYEE array can be displayed using the DO loop:

```
      DO 10 I = 1, 5
         PRINT *, EMPLOYEE(I)  %  IDNUM
         PRINT *, EMPLOYEE(I)  %  NAME
         PRINT *, EMPLOYEE(I)  %  RATE
10    CONTINUE
```

Finally, extremely useful programs can be constructed when a pointer is included as a member of a structure. The inclusion of a pointer within a structure permits the construction of linked lists, the topic of the next section.

Exercises

1. Specify a structure type named TEMP for each of the following:

   a. A mailing list consisting of the items previously illustrated in Figure 12-6.

   b. A student record consisting of a student identification number, number of credits completed, and cumulative grade point average.

   c. A student record consisting of a student's name, date of birth, number of credits completed, and cumulative grade point average.

   d. A stock record consisting of the stock's name, price, and date of purchase.

e. An inventory record consisting of an integer part number, part description, number of parts in inventory, and integer reorder number.

2. Declare arrays of 100 structures for each of the structures specified in Exercise 1.

3. Using the specification:

```
TYPE MONTHS
  CHARACTER (LEN = 10) :: NAME
  INTEGER DAYS
END TYPE MON_DAYS
```

declare an array of 12 structures of type MON-DAYS. Name the array CONVERT. Individual structure elements in the array should be named MONTH_DAYS.

4a. Specify a single structure type suitable for an employee record of the type illustrated below:

```
Number   Name       Rate   Hours
------   -------     ----   -----
23462    BLATT       8.62    40
46793    ERNST       8.83    38
56985    JOHNSON     6.22    45
77834    JONES       9.89    40
78867    SMITHSON    8.43    35
99002    WALTON      9.75    42
```

b. Declare an array of sufficient size to hold all of the data listed in Exercise 4a.

5a. Specify a single structure type suitable for a car record of the following type:

```
Car number   Miles driven   Gallons used
----------   ------------   -------------
25           1450            62
36           3240           136
44           1792            76
52           2360           105
68           2124            67
```

b. Declare an array of sufficient size to hold all of the data listed in Exercise 5a.

12.6 Linked Lists

A classic data-handling problem is making additions or deletions to lists that are maintained in a specific order. This is best illustrated by considering the alphabetical list of names shown in Figure 12-9. We desire to add new names to this list in the proper alphabetical sequence and to delete existing names in such a way that the storage for deleted names is eliminated.

```
ADAMS,   JOHN
EVANS,   MARTHA
KINGSLEY, LEN
NORTAN,  WILLIAM
ZEBART,  HELEN
```

Figure 12-9 A List of Names in Alphabetical Order

Although the insertion or deletion of ordered names can be accomplished using an array of names, such arrays are not efficient representations for adding and deleting names because arrays are fixed and prespecified in size. Deleting a name from an array creates an empty slot that requires either special marking or shifting up of all elements below the deleted name to close the empty slot. Similarly, adding a name to an array requires that all elements below the addition be shifted down to make room for the new entry, or the new element could be added to the bottom of the existing array and the array then resorted to restore the proper name order. Thus, either adding or deleting names to such a list generally requires restructuring and rewriting the list—a cumbersome, time-consuming, and inefficient practice.

A linked list provides a convenient method for maintaining a constantly changing list without the need to continually reorder and restructure the complete list. A linked list is simply a set of structures in which each structure contains at least one member whose value is the address of the next logically ordered structure in the list. Rather than requiring each structure to be physically stored in the proper order, each new structure is physically added either to the end of the existing list or wherever the computer has free space in its storage area. The structures are "linked" together by including the address of the next structure in the structure immediately preceding it. From a programming standpoint, the current structure being processed contains the address of the next structure, no matter where the next structure is actually stored.

The concept of a linked list is illustrated in Figure 12-10. Although the actual data for the KINGSLEY structure illustrated in the figure may be physically stored anywhere in the computer, the additional member included at the end of the EVANS structure maintains the proper alphabetical order. This member provides the starting address of the location where the KINGSLEY structure is stored. As you might expect, this member is a pointer.

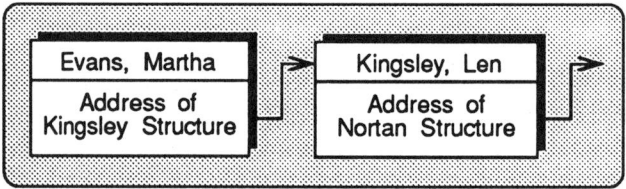

Figure 12-10   Linking Structures with Pointers

To see the usefulness of the pointer in the EVANS structure, let us add the name JUNE HAGAR into the alphabetical list in Figure 12-9. The data for JUNE HAGAR is stored in a data structure using the same form as that used for the existing structures. To ensure that the name HAGAR is correctly inserted into the list after EVANS, the address in the EVANS structure must be altered to point to the HAGAR structure, and the address in the HAGAR structure must be set to point to the KINGSLEY structure. This is illustrated in Figure 12-11.

Notice that the pointer in each structure simply points to the location of the next ordered structure, even if that structure is not physically located in order. Removal of a structure from the ordered list is the reverse process of adding a structure. The actual structure is logically removed from the list by simply changing the address

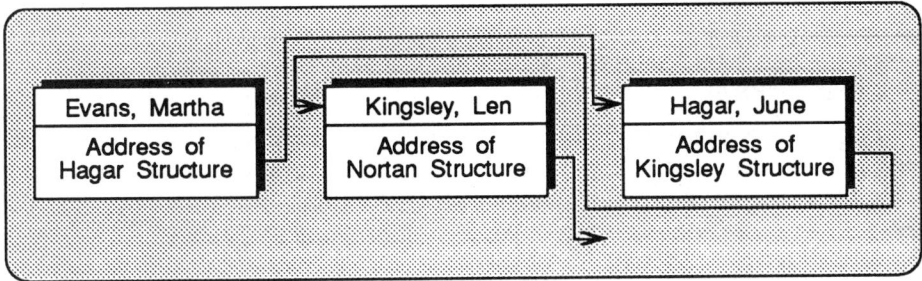

Figure 12-11   Adjusting Addresses to Point to Appropriate Structures

in the structure preceding it to point to the structure immediately following the deleted structure.

Each structure in a linked list has the same format; however, it is clear that the last structure cannot have a valid pointer value that points to another structure, since there is none. Fortran provides a special pointer value that can be used as a sentinel or flag to indicate when the last record has been processed. This value is placed into a pointer using the NULLIFY statement. This statement has the general form:

```
NULLIFY(list of pointers)
```

For example, if VALPTR and TEMP_ADDR are pointers, the statement NULLIFY(VALPTR, TEMP_ADDR) would set the addresses in these pointers to a system dependent value indicating that the pointers are not associated with any target variables. Formally, the NULLIFY statement is said to dissociate a pointer.

In addition to dissociating the last pointer, an extra pointer must also be provided for storing the address of the first structure in the list. Figure 12-12 illustrates the

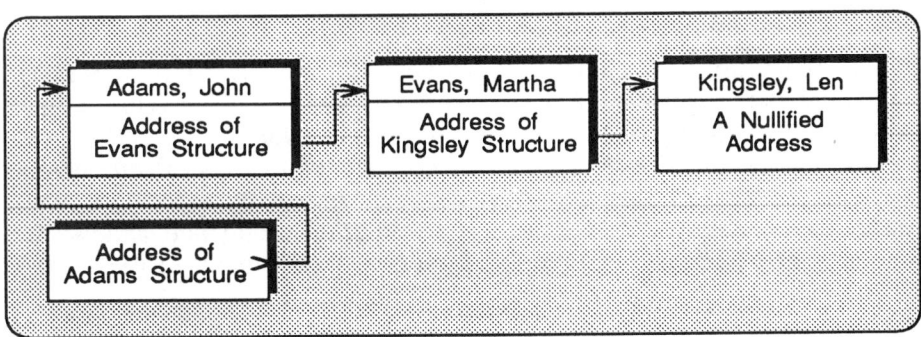

Figure 12-12   A Complete Linked list

complete set of pointers and structures for a linked list consisting of three names.

The inclusion of a pointer in a structure should not seem surprising. As we discovered in the previous section, a structure can contain any Fortran data type. For example, the structure declaration:

```
TYPE TEST
  INTEGER :: ID_NUM
  REAL, POINTER :: PT_PAY
END TYPE TEST
```

specifies a structure type named TEST consisting of two members. The first member is an integer variable named ID_NUM, and the second variable is a pointer named PT_PAY, which is a pointer to an integer value. Program 12-7 illustrates that the pointer member of a structure is used like any other pointer variable.

 Program 12-7

```
PROGRAM MAIN
  TYPE TEST
    INTEGER :: ID_NUM
    REAL, POINTER :: PT_PAY
  END TYPE TEST
  TYPE(TEST) :: EMPLOYEE
  REAL, TARGET :: PAY

  PAY = 456.20
  EMPLOYEE % ID_NUM = 12345
  EMPLOYEE % PT_PAY => PAY
  PRINT 10, EMPLOYEE % ID_NUM, EMPLOYEE % PT_PAY
10  FORMAT(1X,'EMPLOYEE NUMBER ',I5,' WAS PAID $',F6.2)
  END
```

The output that would be produced by Program 12-7 is:

```
EMPLOYEE NUMBER 12345 WAS PAID $456.20
```

Figure 12-13 illustrates the relationship between the members of the EMPLOYEE structure defined in Program 12-7 and the variable named PAY. The value assigned to EMPLOYEE % ID_NUM is the number 12345, and the value assigned to PAY is 456.20. The address of the PAY variable is then assigned to the structure member EMPLOYEE % PT_PAY by the pointer assignment statement EMPLOYEE % PT_PAY => PAY. Since this member has been defined as a pointer to a real value, and PAY was declared as a target variable, having EMPLOYEE % PT_PAY point to PAY (that is, placing the address of the real variable PAY in the variable EMPLOYEE % PT_PAY) is a valid pointer assignment. The use of the pointer variable in the PRINT statement automatically forces the computer to use the pointer correctly to obtain the address of the target variable. It is the contents of

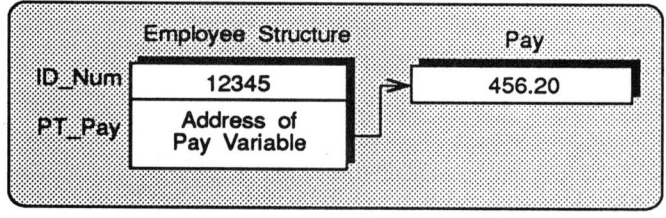

Figure 12-13   Storing an Address in a Structure Member

this target variable that is ultimately accessed and displayed.

Although the pointer defined in Program 12-7 has been used in a rather trivial fashion, the program illustrates the concept of including a pointer in a structure. This concept can be easily extended to create the linked list of structures illustrated in Figure 12-12. The following declaration creates a form for such a structure:

```
TYPE TELE_TYP
   CHARACTER (LEN = 30) :: NAME
   TYPE(TELE_TYP), POINTER :: NEXT_NAME
END TYPE TELE_TYP
```

The TELE_TYP form consists of two members. The first member is a character variable suitable for storing a name with a maximum of 30 letters. The second member is a pointer suitable for storing the address of a structure of the TELE_TYP type.

Program 12-8 illustrates the use of the TELE_TYP structure by specifically declaring three structures having this form. The three structures are named T1, T2, and T3, respectively. The name members of each of these structures are assigned the names JOHN ADAMS, MARTHA EVANS, and LEN KINGSLEY, respectively, and the correct structure addresses are assigned using pointer assignments.

Program 12-8

```
PROGRAM MAIN
   TYPE TELE_TYP
      CHARACTER (LEN = 30) :: NAME
      TYPE(TELE_TYP), POINTER :: NEXT_NAME
   END TYPE TELE_TYP
   TYPE(TELE_TYP), TARGET :: T1, T2, T3
   TYPE(TELE_TYP), POINTER :: FIRST
   ! POPULATE THE NAME MEMBERS
   T1 % NAME = 'ADAMS, JOHN'
   T2 % NAME = 'EVANS, MARTHA'
   T3 % NAME = 'KINGSLEY, LEN'
   ! ASSOCIATE THE POINTERS
   FIRST => T1                  ! STORE T1'S ADDRESS IN FIRST
   T1 % NEXT_NAME => T2   ! STORE T2'S ADDRESS
   T2 % NEXT_NAME => T3   ! STORE T3'S ADDRESS
   NULLIFY(T3 % NEXT_NAME)
   ! USE THE POINTERS TO LOCATE THE NAMES
   PRINT *, FIRST % NAME
   PRINT *, T1 % NEXT_NAME % NAME
   PRINT *, T2 % NEXT_NAME % NAME
   END
```

The output that would be produced by Program 12-8 is:

```
ADAMS, JOHN
EVANS, MARTHA
KINGSLEY, LEN
```

The assignment of member names for each of the structures declared in Program 12-8 is straightforward. The second member of each structure is a pointer. To create a linked list, each structure pointer must be assigned the address of the next structure in the list. Additionally, a pointer variable is provided for storing the first structure in the list. In Program 12-8 this initial pointer is named FIRST. As illustrated in Figure 12-14, the pointer member of each structure contains the address of the next structure in the list.

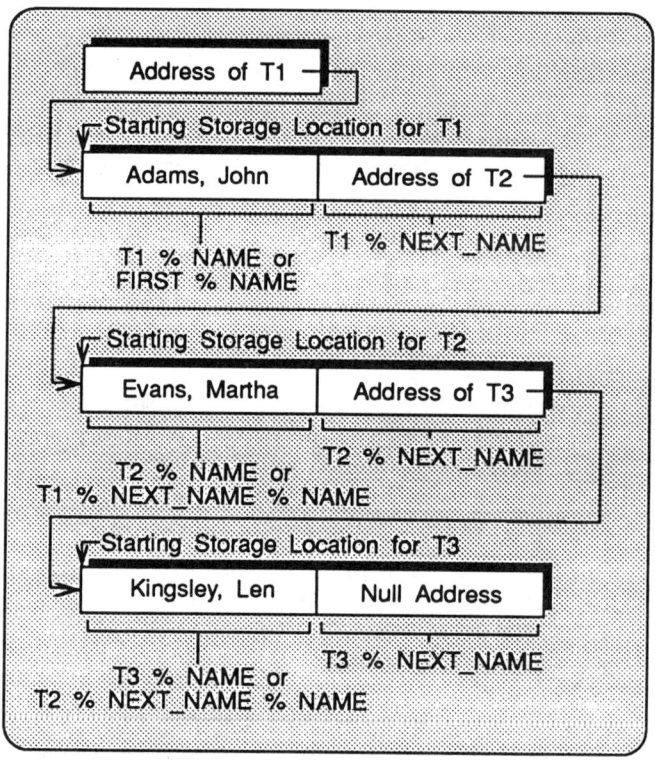

Figure 12-14   The Relationship Between Structures in Program 12-8

The three pointer assignment statements in Program 12-8 perform the correct assignments. To link the structures as shown in Figure 12-14, the expression FIRST => T1 stores the address of the first structure in the pointer variable named FIRST. The statement T1 % NEXT_NAME => T2 stores the starting address of the T2 structure into the pointer member of the T1 structure, and the statement T2 % NEXT_NAME => T3 stores the starting address of the T3 structure into the pointer member of the T2 structure. Finally, the pointer member of the T3 structure is nullified because it is the last element in the list.

Once a value has been assigned to each structure's name member and correct pointer assignments have been made, the addresses in the pointers are used to access each structure's name member. For example, the expression T1 % NEXT_NAME % NAME refers to the NAME member of the structure whose address is in the NEXT_NAME member of the T1 structure. Since T1 % NEXT_NAME contains the address of the T2 structure, the proper name is accessed.

An alternative method for cycling through each structure in a linked list is to continually update a single pointer that is dedicated for pointing to the next structure to be processed, as illustrated in Program 12-9. As each subsequent structure is accessed, it can either be examined to select a specific value or used to print out a complete list. Program 12-9 illustrates the use of a DO WHILE loop that uses the address in a single pointer to cycle through the list and successively display the name stored in each structure.

  Program 12-9

```
PROGRAM MAIN
   TYPE TELE_TYP
      CHARACTER (LEN = 30) :: NAME
      TYPE(TELE_TYP), POINTER :: NEXT_NAME
   END TYPE TELE_TYP
   TYPE(TELE_TYP), TARGET :: T1, T2, T3
   TYPE(TELE_TYP), POINTER :: CURRENT
   ! POPULATE THE NAME MEMBERS
   T1 % NAME = 'ADAMS, JOHN'
   T2 % NAME = 'EVANS, MARTHA'
   T3 % NAME = 'KINGSLEY, LEN'
   ! ASSOCIATE THE POINTERS
   CURRENT => T1             ! STORE T1'S ADDRESS
   T1 % NEXT_NAME => T2    ! STORE T2'S ADDRESS
   T2 % NEXT_NAME => T3    ! STORE T3'S ADDRESS
   NULLIFY(T3 % NEXT_NAME)
   ! USE THE CURRENT POINTER TO "WALK THROUGH" THE LIST
   DO WHILE (ASSOCIATED(CURRENT) .EQ. .TRUE.)
      PRINT *, CURRENT % NAME
      CURRENT => CURRENT % NEXT_NAME
   ENDDO
   END
```

Except for the DO WHILE loop in Program 12-9, which introduces a new Fortran intrinsic function, the declaration of structures and assignment of pointers are the same as in Program 12-8. Let us, then, examine the DO WHILE construct used in Program 12-9.

The relational expression ASSOCIATED(CURRENT) .EQ. .TRUE. compares the result returned by the proposed intrinsic function named ASSOCIATED with the logical .TRUE. value. The ASSOCIATED function is called with a pointer variable and determines whether or not the address in the pointer is associated with a target. If the pointer is associated with a target, the ASSOCIATED function returns a .TRUE. value; otherwise, a .FALSE. value is returned.

Notice that when the DO WHILE statement in Program 12-8 is first encountered, the address in the pointer CURRENT is the address of the T1 structure. Thus, CURRENT is associated, and the ASSOCIATED function returns a .TRUE. value. Within the DO WHILE loop the name member of the structure pointed to by CURRENT is displayed by the statement PRINT *, CURRENT % NAME. Then the address in CURRENT is set to the target pointed to by the address in CURRENT % NEXT_NAME, which is the T2 structure. The end of the loop is then encountered, and the relational expression is reevaluated by the DO WHILE statement.

For this second reevaluation the address in CURRENT is associated with the T2 structure, so the loop is again traversed. This pass through the loop causes the name member of T2 to be displayed and the address in the T2 structure to be copied into CURRENT. On the third pass through the loop the name member of the T3 structure is displayed, and the address in the pointer member of the T3 structure is copied into CURRENT. This last address, however, is not associated because it was previously nullified. When the last address is passed to the ASSOCIATED function, a .FALSE. value is returned. This makes the relational expression .FALSE., and the DO WHILE loop is exited.

We can make one simple modification to the expression evaluated by the DO WHILE statement. Since the ASSOCIATED function returns either a .TRUE. or a .FALSE. value, the statement:

```
DO WHILE (ASSOCIATED(CURRENT) .EQ. TRUE)
```

can be replaced by the equivalent statement:

```
DO WHILE (ASSOCIATED(CURRENT))
```

When the address in CURRENT is associated with a target, both expressions being evaluated have a .TRUE. value, and when the address in CURRENT is not associated, both expressions have a .FALSE. value.

A disadvantage of Programs 12-8 and 12-9 is that exactly three structures are declared in both programs by name, and storage for them is reserved at compile time. Should a fourth structure be required, the additional structure would have to be declared and the program recompiled. The proposed Fortran provides for dynamically allocating and releasing storage for structures as it is required at runtime. Only when a new structure is to be added to the list, and while the program is running, is storage for the new structure created. Similarly, when a structure is no longer needed and can be deleted from the list, the storage for the deleted structure can be relinquished and returned to the computer.

12.7 Chapter Summary

1. The public review phase of the proposed new Fortran standard ended on November 24, 1989. The proposed standard could become the official standard some time in 1990.

2. All features of FORTRAN 77 are included in the proposed new standard. Additionally, several new features may be added. The major additions would include:

    a. Enhanced array operations in which FORTRAN 77's arithmetic, logic, character operators, and intrinsic functions have been extended to operate on complete arrays.

    b. Additional numeric capabilities that permit the explicit setting of a data item's numeric precision at the bit level.

    c. Enhancement of the character set making it possible to include foreign language, mathematical, chemical, and other specialized character sets.

    d. A new MODULE program unit that expands the capabilities of the BLOCK DATA program unit.

    e. Support for the direct implementation of structures (see item 11 below).

    f. Inclusion of pointers (see item 8 below).

    g. A mechanism for removing features from future standards. This mechanism involves designating certain features as obsolete, making them candidates for removal from the next standard.

    h. Addition of several new control statements, including a CASE and a DO WHILE statement (see items 4 and 5 below, respectively).

3. Other new features in the proposed standard include a new free-form source code more adaptable to keyboard input; increased length of symbolic names to 31 characters; inclusion of the underscore symbol in the character set; an enhanced declaration statement; recursive capabilities; dynamically allocated arrays; the addition of binary, octal, and hexadecimal integer constants; the addition of bit manipulation intrinsic functions; new edit descriptors for the formatted input and output of binary, octal, and hexadecimal values; and the extension of the READ and WRITE statements for partial record I/O as character streams.

4. The CASE construct is a multipath decision structure equivalent to an IF-ELSEIF construct. For the CASE construct the value of an expression is compared to a number of constants. Program execution is transferred to the first matching case. The general form of the CASE construct is:

```
SELECT CASE (expression) !START OF CASE CONSTRUCT
  CASE (value_1)
    statement1
    statement2

         .
         .
         .

  CASE (value_2)
    statementm
    statementn

         .
         .
         .

  CASE (value_n)
    statementw
    statementx

         .
         .
         .

  CASE DEFAULT
    statementaa
    statementbb
END SELECT                    ! END OF CASE  CONSTRUCT
```

CASES within the CASE construct may appear in any order, and the DEFAULT case is optional. The DEFAULT case, if present, is executed only if none of the other cases is matched.

5. The DO WHILE statement is a repetition statement having the general form:

```
DO WHILE (relational expression)
```

This statement must always be used with an ENDDO statement to form DO WHILE loops having the form:

```
DO WHILE (relational expression)
   statement_1
   statement_2
         .
         .
         .
       statement_n
ENDDO
```

The DO WHILE statement evaluates the relational expression before any other statement in the loop. This requires that any variables in the relational expression have values assigned before the DO WHILE statement is encountered. If the relational expression is true, the statements within the loop are executed, and the expression is reevaluated; otherwise, control is transferred to the first executable statement following the ENDDO statement. Within a DO WHILE loop there must be either a statement that alters the tested expression's value or an EXIT statement.

6. An EXIT statement forces immediate exit from the loop within which it is contained.

7. A CYCLE statement forces immediate transfer to the top of the DO loop in which the CYCLE statement is contained. For DO WHILE loops this means that control is transferred to the DO WHILE statement, and the tested expression is reevaluated.

8. A pointer is a variable that is used to store the address of another variable. Variables that will be used as pointers must include the keyword POINTER as an attribute within the variable's declaration statement. For example, the declaration:

```
INTEGER, POINTER :: NAME_ADDR
```

declares that NAME_ADDR is a variable that will be used as a pointer.

9. A target is a variable whose address can be stored in a pointer. Variables that will be used as targets must include the keyword TARGET as an attribute within the variable's declaration statement. For example, the declaration:

```
INTEGER, TARGET :: NAME
```

declares that NAME is an integer variable whose address may be stored in a pointer.

10. The data types of a pointer and its target must agree. A pointer is assigned to a target using the pointer assignment operator =>. Thus, if NAME and NAME_ADDR have been declared as the same data types, where NAME has the TARGET attribute and NAME_ADDR has the POINTER attribute, the pointer assignment:

```
NAME_ADDR => NAME
```

stores the address of NAME into NAME_ADDR. NAME_ADDR is then said to "point to" NAME.

11. A structure allows individual variables to be grouped under a common variable name. Each variable in a structure is referenced by its structure name, followed by a percent symbol, %, followed by its individual variable name.

12. Individual members of a structure can be any valid Fortran data type, including structures, arrays, and pointers. When a pointer is included as a structure member, a linked list can be created. Such a list uses the pointer in one structure to "point to" (contain the address of) the next logical structure in the list.

Appendix A

Program Entry,
Compilation, and Execution

In this appendix we examine the general steps that must be taken for a FORTRAN program to be entered into a computer, compiled, and executed.

As illustrated in Figure A-1, a computer can be thought of as a self-contained world that is entered by a special set of steps called a log-in procedure. For some computers such as IBM, Apple, and other desk-top computers, the log-in procedure is usually as simple as turning on the computer's power switch. Larger multiuser systems such as DEC VAX and Prime computers typically require a log-in procedure consisting of turning on a terminal and supplying an account number and password.

Once you have successfully logged in to your computer system, you are automatically under the control of a computer program called the operating system (unless the computer is programmed to switch you into a specific application program). The *operating system* is the program that effectively runs the computer. It is used to gain access to the services provided by the computer, including the programs needed for entering, compiling, and executing a FORTRAN program.

Communicating with the operating system is always accomplished using a specific set of commands that are recognized by the operating system. Although each computer system (IBM, Apple, DEC, Prime, and so on) has its own set of operating system commands, all operating systems provide commands that allow you to log in to the system, exit from the system, create your own programs, and quickly list, delete, copy, or rename your programs.

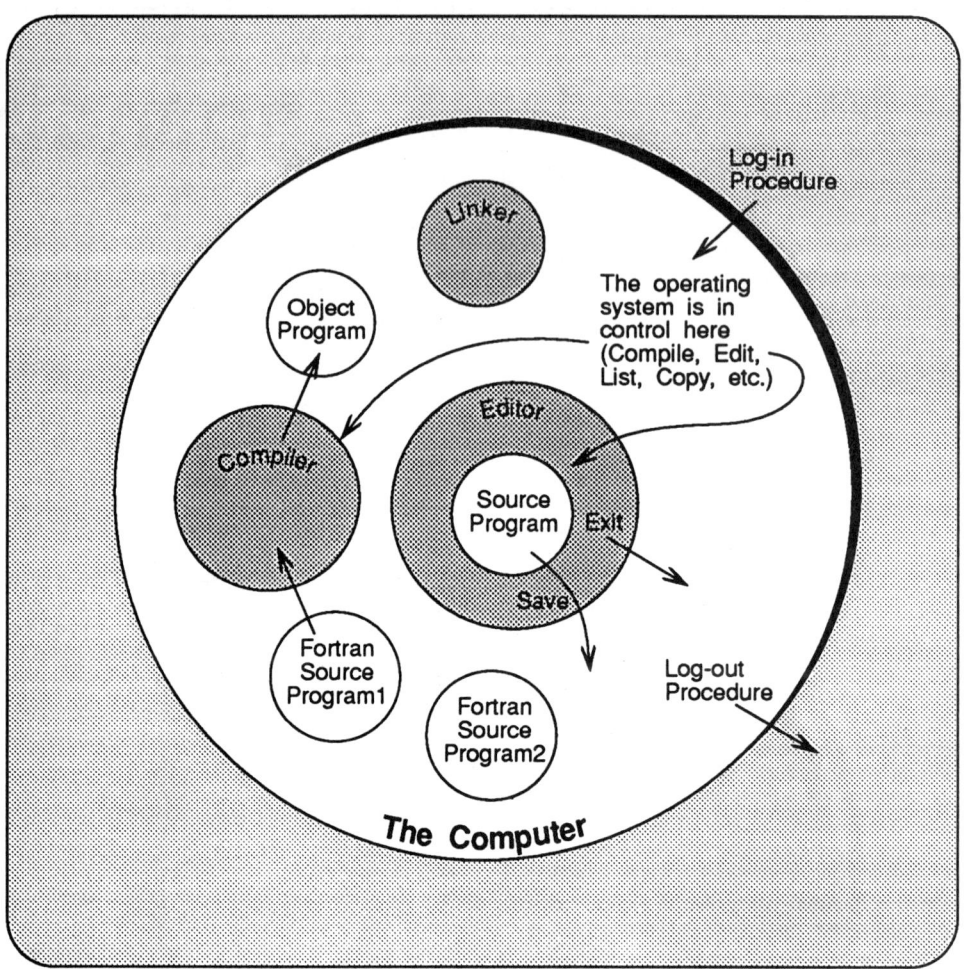

Figure A-1   Viewing a Computer as a Self-Contained World

The specific operating system commands and any additional steps used for exiting from a computer, such as turning off the power, are collectively referred to as the log-out procedure. Make sure you know the log-out procedure for your computer at the time you log-in to ensure that you can effectively "escape" when you are ready to leave the system. The operating system command for listing programs typically has a name such as LIST, TYPE, or PRINT; the command for deleting a program typically has a name such as DELETE, DEL, ERASE, UNSAVE, or REMOVE; the command for copying a program typically has a name such as COPY, COP, or CP; and the operating system command for renaming a program typically has a name such as RENAME, REN, or RN. Use Table A-1 to list the specific operating system command names used by your system to perform these tasks.

Table A-1   Operating System Commands (Fill in for Your System)

Task	Command(s)	Example
Log-in procedure		
Log-out procedure		
List a program		
Copy a program		
Delete a program		
Rename a program		

The commands to list, copy, delete, or rename a FORTRAN program are all concerned with manipulating existing programs. Let us now turn our attention to creating, compiling, and executing a new FORTRAN program. The procedures for doing these tasks are illustrated in Figure A-2. As shown in this figure, the procedure for creating an executable FORTRAN program consists of three distinct operations: editing, compiling, and linking.

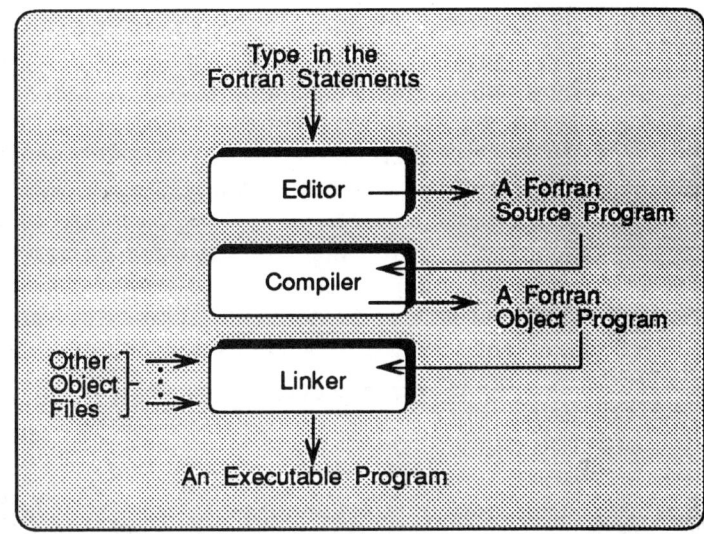

Figure A-2   Creating an Executable FORTRAN Program

A.1   Editing

Both the creation of a new FORTRAN program and the modification of an existing FORTRAN program require the use of an editor program. The function of such a program is to allow a user to type statements at a keyboard and to save the typed statements together under a common name, called a *source program file*.

As illustrated in Figure A-1, an editor program is contained within the environment controlled by the operating system. Like all services provided by the operating system, this means that the editor program can only be accessed using an operating system command.

Once the editor program has been requested, the operating system relinquishes control to the editor program. Again, as illustrated in Figure A-1, this means that you temporarily leave the world controlled by the operating system and its commands and enter the world controlled by the editor. The editor, like the operating system, has its own set of services and commands. The services provided by the editor include entering FORTRAN statements, modifying and deleting existing statements in a program, listing a program, naming a program, saving a program, and exiting from the editor back into the operating system with or without saving the program.

When using an editor, you must carefully distinguish between entering a FORTRAN statement and entering an editor command. Some editors make this distinction by using special keys to alert the editor that what is being typed is a command to the editor rather than the line of a program (for example, in BASIC the line number automatically informs the editor that the entered line is a statement, and the absence of a line number informs the editor that the entered line is an editor command). Other editors contain two modes: a text mode for entering and modifying program statements and a command mode for entering editor commands. For the latter type of editor there is always a means of switching from text to command mode and back from command to text mode. In both cases the commands recognized by the editor depend on the editor being used. After filling in the operating system command needed to enter the editor, use Table A-2 to list the specific editor command names or procedures provided by your editor.

```
Operating system command
to enter the editor:_____
```

A.2   Compiling and Linking

The translation of a FORTRAN source program into a form that can be executed by the computer is accomplished using a program called a compiler. The compiler, like the editor, is accessed using an operating system command. Each operating system uses a different command for calling the compiler into action and giving the compiler the name of the source file to be translated. Determine and then list the command used by your computer for performing this operation.

```
Operating system command
to compile a program:_____
```

The output produced by the compiler is called an object program. An *object program* is simply a translated version of the source program that can be executed by the computer system with one more processing step. Let us see why this is so.

Most FORTRAN programs contain statements that use preprogrammed routines, called intrinsic functions, for finding such quantities as square roots, logarithms, trigonometric values, absolute values, and other commonly encountered mathematical calculations. Additionally, a large FORTRAN program may be stored in two

Table A-2.   Editor Commands (Fill in)

Task	Command(s)	Example
Save the program and exit from the editor		
Save the program without exiting from the editor		
Exit from the editor without saving the program		
Switch to text mode (if applicable)		
Switch to command mode (if applicable)		
List the complete program from within the editor		
List a set of lines from within the editor		
List a single line from within the editor		
Delete the complete program from within the editor		
Delete a set of lines from within the editor		
Delete a single line from within the editor		
Name a program from within the editor		

separate program files. In such a case, if the program is correctly divided into multiple sections using the modular programming techniques discussed in the text, each section can be compiled separately. However, both sections must ultimately be combined to form a single program before the program can be executed. In both of these cases it is the task of the linker to combine all of the intrinsic functions and individual object files into a single program ready for execution. This final program is called an executable program.

As with the compiler, the linker program is accessed using a single operating system command. For ease of operation, however, all operating systems provide a single command that both compiles a FORTRAN program and links it correctly with any required other object programs using one command. Determine and then list the command used by your computer for performing this operation.

```
Operating system command
to compile and link a program:_____
```

Finally, once the FORTRAN source program has been compiled and linked, it must be run. Determine and then list the command used by your computer for this operation.

```
Operating system command to
execute a compiled and linked program:_____
```

Appendix B

FORMAT Specifications

A format is used with formatted PRINT, WRITE, and READ statements and provides information that directs the conversion between internal data representations (see Section 1.7 and Appendix D) and external data representations in a file. A format specifier is designated by:

1. an asterisk, which invokes an implicit compiler-defined format
2. the statement number of a FORMAT statement, which contains explicit user-defined format descriptors
3. a literal format control character constant that is enclosed in parentheses and surrounded by apostrophes

Formally, method 1 is referred to as list-directed I/O, and methods 2 and 3 are referred to as user-formatted I/O, usually shortened to the term formatted I/O. The edit descriptors that can be used with user-formatted I/O are listed in Table B-1.

Edit descriptors are interpreted from left to right in a format specification, and input and output records are edited from left to right. If there are insufficient edit descriptors in a format specification for an input or output list, format control is transferred to the first open parentheses in the specification.

Table B-1   Edit Descriptors

Descriptor	Description
rIw	Edits integer data
rFw.d	Edits both real and double precision data in decimal format
rEw.d	Edits real data in exponential format
rDw.d	Edits double precision data in exponential format
rGw.d	Edits both real and double precision data in exponential format
rLw	Edits logical data
rAw	Edits character data
'a..a'	Specifies a character constant
Tc	Tabs to position c
TLn	Tabs backward n positions
TRn	Tabs forward n positions
nX	Skips over n positions (same as TRn)
/	Causes the current record to be written or the next record to be read
SS	Suppresses printing of plus sign
BN	Ignores blank spaces in a field
BZ	Considers blank spaces in a field to be zeros
kP	Multiplies each number by 10^{-k} on input and 10^{k} on output. The scale factor must precede an E, F, D, or G descriptor.

Notes: r is an optional unsigned nonzero positive integer used as repeat count.

w is an unsigned nonzero positive integer that specifies the data field width.

d is an unsigned positive integer that specifies the number of places to the right of the decimal point.

a is any character.

c is an unsigned positive nonzero integer.

n is an unsigned positive nonzero integer.

k is an unsigned positive nonzero integer.

Appendix C

Operator Precedence Table

Table C-1 presents the symbols, precedence, descriptions, and associativity of FORTRAN's operators. Operators toward the top of the table have a higher precedence than those toward the bottom. Operators within each category have the same precedence and associativity.

Arithmetical operations that are undefined mathematically are also undefined in FORTRAN 77. Thus, it is illegal to divide by zero, raise a zero-valued operand to a zeroth or negative power, or raise a negative operand to a real or double precision power.

Table C-1   Summary of FORTRAN **Operators**

Operator	Description	Associativity
( )	Parentheses	Inner to outer
**	Exponentiation	Right to left
*	Multiplication	Left to right
/	Division	Left to right
+	Addition	Left to right
–	Subtraction	Left to right
//	Concatenation	Left to right
.GT.	Relational	Left to right
.GE.	Relational	Left to right
.LT.	Relational	Left to right
.LE.	Relational	Left to right
.EQ.	Relational	Left to right
.NE.	Relational	Left to right
.NOT.	Logical negation	Left to right
.AND.	Logical conjunction	Left to right
.OR.	Logical inclusion	Left to right
.EQV.	Logical equivalence	Left to right
.NEQV.	Logical nonequivalence	Left to right

Appendix D

Floating Point Number Storage[*]

The two's-complement binary code used to store integer values was presented in Section 1.7. In this appendix we present the binary storage format typically used to store single precision and double precision numbers. Single precision values are called real values in FORTRAN, and both single and double precision numbers are collectively referred to as floating point values.[*]

Like their decimal number counterparts that use a decimal point to separate the integer and fractional parts of a number, floating point numbers are represented in a conventional binary format using a binary point for the same purpose. For example, consider the binary number 1011.11. The digits to the left of the binary point (1011) represent the integer part of the number, and the digits to the right of the binary point (11) represent the fractional part.

A code similar to that for decimal exponential notation is used to store a floating point binary number. To obtain this code, the conventional binary number format is separated into a mantissa and an exponent. The following examples illustrate floating point numbers expressed in this exponential notation.

Conventional binary notation	Binary exponential notation
1010.0	1.01 exp 011
-10001.0	-1.0001 exp 100
0.001101	1.101 exp -011
-0.000101	-1.01 exp -100

---

[*] Reprinted by permission of AT&T from "32-Bit Microprocessors–A Primer Plus" (pages 489–493) by G. Bronson and H. Silver, Copyright 1988, AT&T.

In binary scientific notation, the term *exp* stands for exponent. The binary number in front of the exp term is the mantissa, and the binary number following the exp term is the exponent value. Except for the number 0, the mantissa always has a single leading 1 followed immediately by a binary point. The exponent represents a power of 2 and indicates the number of places the binary point should be moved in the mantissa to obtain the conventional binary notation. If the exponent is positive, the binary point is moved to the right. If the exponent is negative, the binary point is moved to the left. For example, the exponent 011 in the number:

```
1.01 exp 011
```

means to move the binary point three places to the right, so that the number becomes 1010. The –011 exponent in the number:

```
1.101 exp -011
```

means to move the binary point three places to the left, so that the number becomes:

```
.001101.
```

In storing floating point numbers, the sign, mantissa, and exponent are stored individually within separate fields. The number of bits used for each field determines the precision of the number. Single precision (32-bit), double precision (64-bit), and extended precision (80-bit) real data formats are defined by the Institute of Electrical and Electronics Engineers (IEEE) Standard 754-1985 to have the characteristics given in Table D-1. The format for a single precision real number is illustrated in Figure D-1.

Table D-1   IEEE **Standard 754-1985 Floating Point Specification**

Data format	Sign bits	Mantissa bits	Exponent bits
Single Precision	1	23	8
Double Precision	1	52	11
Extended Precision	1	64	15

The sign bit shown in Figure D-1 refers to the sign of the mantissa. A sign bit of 1 represents a negative number, and a 0 sign bit represents a positive value. Since all mantissas except for the number 0 have a leading 1 followed by their binary points, these two items are never stored explicitly. The binary point implicitly resides immediately to the left of mantissa bit 22, and a leading 1 is always assumed. The binary number 0 is specified by setting all mantissa and exponent bits to 0. For this case only, the implied leading mantissa bit is also 0.

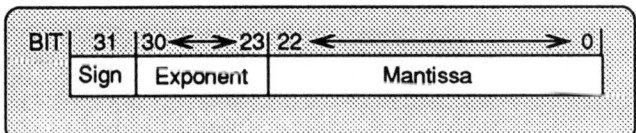

Figure D-1   **Single Precision Real Number Storage Format**

The exponent field contains an exponent that is biased by 127. For example, an exponent of 5 would be stored using the binary equivalent of the number 132 (127 + 5). Using eight exponent bits, this is coded as 100000100. The addition of 127 to each exponent allows negative exponents to be coded within the exponent field without the need for an explicit sign bit. For example, the exponent –011, which correspond to –3, would be stored using the binary equivalent of +124 (127 – 3).

Figure D-2 illustrates the encoding and storage of the decimal number 59.75 as a 64-bit single precision binary number. The sign, exponent, and the mantissa are determined as follows: The conventional binary equivalent of –59.75 is –111011.11. Expressed in binary exponential notation, this becomes –1.1101111 exp 101. The

SIGN	EXPONENT	MANTISSA
1	10000100	11011110000000000000000

Figure D-2   The Encoding and Storage of a Decimal Number

minus sign is signified by setting the sign bit to 1. The mantissa's leading 1 and binary point are omitted, and the 23-bit mantissa field is encoded as 11011110000000000000000. The exponent field encoding is obtained by adding the exponent value of 101 to 1111111, which is the binary equivalent of the 127_{10} bias value.

$$
\begin{array}{rcl}
1\ 1\ 1\ 1\ 1\ 1\ 1 & = & 127_{10} \\
+\ 1\ 0\ 1 & = & +\ 5_{10} \\
\hline
1\ 0\ 0\ 0\ 0\ 1\ 0\ 0 & = & 132_{10}
\end{array}
$$

Appendix E

Additional Capabilities

E.1   Additional Subprogram Statements
E.2   Additional Specification Statements
E.3   Additional Selection Statements
E.4   Summary of Additional Statements

The major premise of this text is that FORTRAN programs should be constructed in a modular fashion using structured blocks of code having single-entry and single-exit points. The reason for this, as emphasized throughout the text, is that programs so constructed are more easily written, tested, debugged, modified, and maintained than programs that do not conform to this structure. Simply put, fewer program errors are introduced when programs are designed using a structured, modular approach, and those errors that are coded into such programs can be more easily detected and corrected than those in nonstructured programs.

Except for the first three statements presented in this appendix (the SAVE, EXTERNAL, and INTRINSIC statements), the remaining statements are nonstructured statements that permit programs written in earlier versions of FORTRAN to be compiled using FORTRAN 77 and later compilers. In general, these statements should not be used in a modular FORTRAN program because they violate the principles of structured, modular programming. As such, their use invites numerous program errors and debugging problems that are best avoided by not using these statements.

E.1   Additional Subprogram Statements

This section presents additional FORTRAN statements applicable to subroutine and function subprograms. These include the SAVE, EXTERNAL, INTRINSIC, and alternate subroutine ENTRY and RETURN statements. The first three of these statements provide features that are sometimes required in a particular program application. The last two features, alternate subroutine entry and return, are presented for completeness only. As these two features violate the single-entry, single-exit characteristic of structured program units, their use should be avoided.

The SAVE Statement

When a subroutine returns control to its calling unit, the FORTRAN 77 standard allows the storage for its local variables to be released to the computer's operating system. For example, consider Program E-1, where subroutine TEST is called four times.

Program E-1

```
PROGRAM MAIN
   INTEGER COUNT
   DO 10 COUNT = 1,4
   CALL TEST
10    CONTINUE
   END
SUBROUTINE TEST
   INTEGER NUM
   NUM = 0
   PRINT *, 'THE VALUE OF NUM IS ', NUM
   NUM = NUM + 1
   END
```

The output produced by Program E-1 is:

```
THE VALUE OF NUM IS          0
THE VALUE OF NUM IS          0
THE VALUE OF NUM IS          0
THE VALUE OF NUM IS          0
```

Each time TEST is called, the local variable NUM is created and initialized to zero. When the subroutine returns control to MAIN, the variable NUM is destroyed along with any value stored in it. Thus, the effect of incrementing NUM in TEST is lost.

The initialization used in TEST is called a runtime initialization because the initialization occurs each time the subroutine containing this statement is run. There are cases, however, where we would like a subroutine to retain values between subroutine calls. This usually can be accomplished using the DATA statement introduced in Section 6.2. The DATA statement initializes its variables only once, when the program is first compiled. Thereafter, the value is not reset to zero each time the subroutine is called. To see how this works, consider Program E-2.

Program E-2

```
PROGRAM MAIN
   INTEGER COUNT
   DO 10 COUNT = 1,4
   CALL TEST
10    CONTINUE
   END
  SUBROUTINE TEST
   INTEGER NUM
   DATA NUM /0/
   PRINT *, 'THE VALUE OF NUM IS: ', NUM
   NUM = NUM + 1
   END
```

The output produced by Program E-2 is:

```
THE VALUE OF NUM IS:          0
THE VALUE OF NUM IS:          1
THE VALUE OF NUM IS:          2
THE VALUE OF NUM IS:          3
```

As illustrated by the output of Program E-2, the variable NUM is set to zero only once. The subroutine TEST then increments this variable just before relinquishing control to MAIN, and the value that NUM has when TEST is reentered is retained and displayed when the subroutine is next called.

Although the FORTRAN 77 standard ensures that the DATA statement performs a compile-time initialization, it does not require that a subroutine's local variables, such as NUM, retain their values between subroutine calls. This is the purpose of the SAVE statement. This statement has the form:

```
SAVE list of variables
```

and ensures that the variables listed will retain their values between subroutine calls. This means that the last value stored in the variable when the subroutine is finished executing is available to the subroutine the next time it is called.

SAVE variables should always be initialized using a DATA statement (using an assignment initialization defeats the purpose of a SAVE variable by resetting its value each time the subroutine is called). Including a SAVE statement in Program E-2a results in the following program:

Program E-2a

```
PROGRAM MAIN
   INTEGER COUNT
   DO 10 COUNT = 1,4
   CALL TEST
10    CONTINUE
   END
SUBROUTINE TEST
   INTEGER NUM
   SAVE NUM
   DATA NUM /0/
   PRINT *, 'THE VALUE OF NUM IS: ', NUM
   NUM = NUM + 1
   END
```

The EXTERNAL Statement

In certain situations a programmer may want to either rewrite one of FORTRAN's intrinsic functions, use an intrinsic function name for a user-written subprogram, or use a user-written subprogram as an actual argument in a CALL statement. In these situations, an EXTERNAL statement must be used. The general form of this statement is:

```
EXTERNAL list of subprogram names
```

For example, the statement:

```
EXTERNAL DSQRT, SIN
```

specifies that when these names are encountered within a program, they do not refer to the intrinsic functions having these names but will be supplied as user-written subprograms (functions or subroutines). This permits the programmer to write versions of these functions that might execute faster or provide more options than those supplied with the intrinsic functions of the same names. For example, Program E-3 uses the EXTERNAL statement to tell the compiler that the name SIN refers to a user-written subprogram rather than to an intrinsic function.

Program E-3

```
      PROGRAM MAIN
***       THIS PROGRAM COMPUTES THE SINE OF THE NUMBERS 0.1 TO 1.0,
***       IN INCREMENTS OF 0.1, USING A USER-WRITTEN SIN FUNCTION
      EXTERNAL SIN
      REAL XNUM, SIN
      INTEGER I
      PRINT *, ' NUMBER      SIN'
      PRINT *, '  ------      ------'
      DO 10 I = 1, 10
        XNUM = I * 0.1
        PRINT 20, XNUM, SIN(XNUM)
   10   CONTINUE
   20   FORMAT(4X,F3.1,5X,F8.6)
      END
******
      REAL FUNCTION SIN(VAL)
*         THIS FUNCTION COMPUTES THE SINE OF A NUMBER USING 15 TERMS
*         OF A TAYLOR SERIES. THE FIRST APPROXIMATION IS THE VALUE OF
*         THE PASSED ARGUMENT AND THE NEXT 14 TERMS ARE CALCULATED
*         USING A DO LOOP.
      REAL VAL, FCTORL
      INTEGER I
      SIN = VAL
      DO 10 I = 1, 14
        SIN = SIN + (-1)**I * VAL**(2*I+1) / FCTORL(2*I+1)
   10   CONTINUE
      END
******
      REAL FUNCTION FCTORL(NUM)
*       THIS FUNCTION COMPUTES THE FACTORIAL OF A NUMBER
      INTEGER NUM, I
      FCTORL = 1
      DO 10 I = 2, NUM
        FCTORL = I * FCTORL
   10   CONTINUE
      END
```

The SIN function used in Program E-3 uses a Taylor series to approximate the sine of the passed argument (see Section 3.5 for a description of this approximation method). The output produced by this program is:

```
NUMBER          SIN

-------         -------
    .1          .099833
    .2          .198669
    .3          .295520
    .4          .389418
    .5          .479426
    .6          .564642
    .7          .644218
    .8          .717356
    .9          .783327
   1.0          .841471
```

The interested reader should compare this output to that produced when FORTRAN's intrinsic SIN function is used instead of the user-written version contained within Program E-3.

The INTRINSIC Statement

The intrinsic functions provided by FORTRAN consist of both generic and specific names. For example, the generic name of the square root function is SQRT. Three specific function names exist for this generic square root function: SQRT, DSQRT, and CSQRT. These three specific functions are used for calculating the square roots of integer, real, and complex numbers, respectively.

A useful feature of FORTRAN is that the generic function name can be used in place of all specific function names, and the compiler will select the appropriate version based on the arguments used. For example, using the complex number (25,4) in the statement:

```
PRINT *, SQRT((25,4))
```

automatically invokes the complex version of the square root function and produces the display:

```
(5.015874,3.987341E-01)
```

In this case the compiler "knows" which specific square root function to use because of the argument's data type.

A function's generic name can always be used in place of a specific name. However, when a specific name different from the generic name is used as an argument, the specific name must be declared using an INTRINSIC statement. For example, consider Program E-4:

Program E-4

```
PROGRAM MAIN
  INTRINSIC CSQRT
  PRINT *, SQRT(SQRT((25,4)))
  PRINT *, SQRT(CSQRT((25,4)))
  END
```

In Program E-4, the specific function name CSQRT is used as an argument to another function. As such, this specific function name must be specified using an INTRINSIC statement. The output produced by this program is:

```
(2.241380,8.894835E-02)
(2.241380,8.894835E-02)
```

The results displayed by both PRINT statements are identical because the first statement automatically uses the complex version of the SQRT function due to the data types of the arguments used in the statement. As the second PRINT statement contains the CSQRT function as an argument, this function must be specified using an INTRINSIC statement. The general form of this statement is:

```
INTRINSIC funcname-1, funcname-2, . . . funcname-n
```

where *funcname* is the name of an intrinsic function that will be used as an actual argument.

The ENTRY Statement

The ENTRY statement permits entry into a subprogram other than at the entry point defined by the header line. The general form of this statement is:

```
ENTRY name (list of arguments)
```

An ENTRY statement may be placed at any point within a subprogram, and a subprogram may contain multiple ENTRY statements. The list of arguments in the ENTRY statement perform the same function as but are independent of the arguments in a subprogram's header line. This means that an ENTRY statement's arguments do not have to agree in either type, number, or order with the argument list defined in the subprogram header. For example, consider the ENTRY statements contained in the following subroutine:

```
SUBROUTINE FLOW(A,B,D)
        .
        .
        .
ENTRY FLOW1(X,Y)
        .
        .
        .
ENTRY FLOW2(A,X,Z)
        .
        .
        .
END
```

To enter this subroutine at either the program header or alternative entry points designated by the ENTRY statements, a CALL statement must be used. If the CALL statement references the header name, as in the statement:

```
CALL FLOW(FIRST,SECOND,THIRD)
```

the subroutine is entered at the header line, and the actual arguments FIRST, SECOND, and THIRD are equated to the dummy arguments A, B, and C, respectively. As ENTRY statements are nonexecutable, the subsequent two ENTRY statements have no effect on the subroutine's execution. If the CALL statement reference the name listed in the first ENTRY statement, as in the statement:

```
CALL FLOW1(POINT1,POINT2)
```

the subroutine is entered at the entry point designated as FLOW1, and the actual arguments POINT1 and POINT2 are equated to the dummy arguments X and Y, respectively. In this case, subroutine execution begins with the first executable statement following the FLOW1 entry point. Any subsequent ENTRY statements encountered have no effect on the subroutine's execution. Finally, if the CALL statement references the name listed in the second ENTRY statement, subroutine execution begins with the first executable statement following the FLOW2 entry point, and the actual arguments in the CALL statement are equated to the dummy arguments A, X, and Z.

Alternate Subprogram Return

The RETURN statement is used to return program control to the calling program unit. A subprogram can contain multiple RETURN statements. When a RETURN is encountered, control is normally transferred to the first executable statement following the CALL statement that transferred control to the subroutine. If a subprogram contains no RETURN statement, the END statement will return control to the calling program.

In addition to providing this normal return from a subprogram, a RETURN statement can be used to return control to alternative points in the calling program as follows.

The CALL statement used to call a subprogram having alternative return points must contain one or more statement labels in its actual argument list. The statement label must be preceded by an asterisk. For example, the statement:

```
CALL TRY(FIRST, SECOND, *10, *22, *55)
```

contains five actual arguments, including the three statement labels 10, 22, and 55. To accept statement labels as arguments requires that the called subprogram use asterisks as dummy arguments. Thus, a suitable header line for the TRY subroutine is:

```
SUBROUTINE TRY(A, B, *, *, *)
```

This header indicates that the last three dummy arguments will be used to receive statement labels from the calling program unit. The general form of the RETURN statement needed to access the statement labels passed to a subprogram is:

```
RETURN integer expression
```

The value of the integer expression is used to return control to the first, second, third, and so on statement labels designated in the argument list used to call the subprogram. For example, the statement:

```
RETURN 1
```

causes control to be transferred to the first statement label in the actual argument list, and the statement:

```
RETURN 3
```

causes control to be transferred to the third statement label in the actual argument list. A runtime error occurs if the integer expression evaluates to either a nonpositive integer or an integer having no corresponding statement label.

E.2   Additional Specification Statements

The additional specification statements provided by FORTRAN 77 are the EQUIVALENCE and IMPLICIT statements. The capabilities provided by these statements follow.

The EQUIVALENCE Statement

An EQUIVALENCE statement reserves the same area in memory for two or more variables, each of which must be of the same data type. The general form of this statement is:

```
EQUIVALENCE (name-1, name-2, name-3, . . . name-n)
```

For example, the statement:

```
EQUIVALENCE (OHMS, RESIST, VALUE)
```

permits the variable names OHMS, RESIST, and VALUE to be used interchangeably, because all three names refer to the same storage area. Similarly, the statement:

```
EQUIVALENCE (SLOPE, A(5))
```

permits both SLOPE and A(5) to be used interchangeably. The same variable cannot, however, be used in two equivalence statements. Thus, the sequence of statements:

```
EQUIVALENCE (A, B, C)
EQUIVALENCE (A, VAL)
```

is invalid because the variable A has been used twice.

Once two or more variables have been equivalenced, a change to one of the variables included in the EQUIVALENCE statement automatically changes the value referenced by all other variables in the statement (notice that this is the same relationship between an actual and a dummy argument in a subroutine call). For example, assuming that SLOPE and A(5) have been equivalenced, the sequence of statements:

```
A(5) = 20.2
SLOPE = 45.6
PRINT *, 'THE VALUE OF A(5) IS ', A(5)
```

produces the display:

```
THE VALUE OF A(5) IS        45.600000
```

The first statement, A(5) = 20.2, causes the value 20.2 to be assigned to the storage area reserved for this variable. Since both A(5) and SLOPE refer to the same storage area, the next statement, SLOPE = 45.6, causes the value stored in this area to be replaced by the value 45.6. Finally, the PRINT statement causes the value stored in the area referenced by A(5) to be displayed. As the last value assigned to this area is the value 45.6, this value is displayed.

In the early days of FORTRAN, when computer storage was the most costly component of a computer system, the EQUIVALENCE statement provided a means of sharing this expensive resource. This was especially useful when two or more large arrays could use the same storage locations but were accessed by different names. Thus, for example, one array might use the storage area at the start of a program; a second array could use the same storage area later on, when the first array was no longer needed. Inevitably, however, multiple use of the same storage area results in messy debugging problems when the values associated with one usage inadvertently affect the values assumed by the second usage. In the current computer environment, where software costs far exceed hardware costs (see Section 7.7), the potential debugging problems associated with the EQUIVALENCE statement dictate that it should be avoided.

The IMPLICIT Statement

As described in Chapter 2, the data type of FORTRAN variables can be either explicitly or implicitly declared. In the absence of an explicit declaration, all variables beginning in one of the letters I, J, K, L, M, and N are created as integer variables, and all other variables are created as real variables. This implied data typing can be changed using the IMPLICIT statement. For example, the statement:

```
IMPLICIT DOUBLE PRECISION (A-H,O-P)
```

specifies that all scalar and subscripted variables beginning in the letters A through H and O through P that are not explicitly declared will be created as double precision variables rather than as reals. Similarly, the statement:

```
IMPLICIT INTEGER (A-Z)
```

specifies that all scalar and subscripted variables in a program that are not otherwise explicitly declared will be created as integers. Finally, multiple implicit declarations can be incorporated within the same IMPLICIT statement. For example, the statement:

```
IMPLICIT CHARACTER*8 (C), LOGICAL (L), DOUBLE PRECISION (M-Z)
```

specifies that in the absence of an explicit declaration, all variables beginning in a C will be created as character variables of length eight, all variables beginning in an L will be created as logical variables, and all variables beginning in the letters M through Z will be created as double precision variables.

E.3   Additional Selection Statements

The additional selection statements provided in FORTRAN 77 permit upward compatibility with older versions of the language (such as FORTRAN IV and FORTRAN 66) and permit programs written in these earlier versions to be compiled using a FORTRAN 77 compiler. All of these statements provide multipath selection that are more effectively structured using FORTRAN 77's block IF, ELSEIF, and ELSE statements.

The Arithmetic IF Statement

The arithmetic IF statement is a three-way selection statement, that has the general form:

```
IF (arithmetic expression) n1, n2, n3
```

The *arithmetic expression* in this statement may be any valid arithmetic expression, and n_1, n_2, and n_3 are statement labels of executable statements (the same label may be repeated in this IF statement). The arithmetic expression in the statement is evaluated first, and if its value is negative, control is transferred to statement label n_1; if the expression's value is zero, control is transferred to statement label n_2; and if the expression's value is positive, control is transferred to statement label n_3. For example, the statement:

```
IF (POWER - 15.8) 10, 20, 30
```

transfers control to statement label 10 if the expression POWER − 15.8 is negative, to statement label 20 if the expression evaluates to zero, and to statement label 30 if the expression is positive. A complete structure using this specific arithmetic IF statement would typically appear as follows:

```
      IF (POWER - 15.8) 10, 20, 30
10    statements to be executed if the
      expression is negative
      GO TO 40
20    statements to be executed if the
      expression is zero
      GO TO 40
30    statements to be executed if the
```

```
                 expression is positive
     40      CONTINUE
```

Using a block IF statement combined with an ELSEIF and ELSE statement, this can be rewritten as:

```
IF (POWER .LT. 15.8) THEN
    statements to be executed if this
    condition is true
ELSEIF (POWER .EQ. 0.0) THEN
    statements to be executed if this
    condition is true
ELSE
    statements to be executed if the
    previous two conditions are false
ENDIF
```

Besides being easier to read, the block IF version permits the test for exact zero equality to be modified, which avoids the numerical round-off problem described in Section 4.5.

The Computed GO TO Statement

The computed GO TO statement is a multipath selection statement that has the general form:

```
GO TO (n₁, n₂, n₃, . . . n) integer expression
```

where the ns are statement labels of executable statements, which may be the same, and the integer expression is any valid FORTRAN integer expression. The integer expression is evaluated first. If its value is 1, control is transferred to statement label n_1; if its value is 2, control is transferred to statement label n_2; if it value is 3, control is transferred to statement label n_3, and so on. For example, assuming ICODE is an integer variable, the statement:

```
GO TO (5, 10, 15, 20) ICODE
```

transfers control to statement label 5, 10, 15, or 20, depending on an ICODE value of 1, 2, 3, or 4, respectively. If ICODE has a value less than 1 or greater than 4, control is transferred to the next executable statement following the computed GO TO statement. A complete structure using this computed GO TO statement would typically appear as follows:

```
             GO TO (5, 10, 15, 20) ICODE
     5           statements to be executed if
                 ICODE is 1
                 GO TO 40
     10          statements to be executed if
                 ICODE is 2
                 GO TO 40
     15          statements to be executed if
                 ICODE is 3
                 GO TO 40
     20          statements to be executed if
                 ICODE is 4
     40      CONTINUE
```

Using a block IF statement combined with an ELSEIF statement, this can be rewritten as:

```
IF (ICODE .EQ. 1) THEN
    statements to be executed if this
    condition is true
ELSEIF (ICODE .EQ. 2) THEN
    statements to be executed if this
    condition is true
ELSEIF (ICODE .EQ. 3) THEN
    statements to be executed if this
    condition is true
ELSEIF (ICODE .EQ. 4) THEN
    statements to be executed if this
    condition is true
ENDIF
```

Besides being easier to read, the block IF version permits a more varied set of conditions, including a default case, to be incorporated into the selection structure.

The ASSIGN and Assigned GO TO Statements

The last selection statement provided in FORTRAN is composed of two parts: an ASSIGN statement and an assigned GO TO statement. The general form of the ASSIGN statement is:

```
ASSIGN integer constant TO integer variable
```

and the general form of the assigned GO TO statement is:

```
GO TO integer variable (n₁, n₂, n₃, . . . n)
```

where the integer variable in both statements is the same name, and the ns are distinct statement labels of executable statements. The integer variable in the assigned GO TO statement must contain a number equal to one of the statement labels in parentheses. This value can only be assigned to the integer variable using the ASSIGN statement. If the integer variable contains a value not equal to one of the ns, a runtime error will occur.

The assigned GO TO was used to select a set of statements to be executed based on the value assigned to the integer variable. For example, consider the sequence of instructions:

```
IF (DSCRIM .LT. 0.0) THEN
  ASSIGN 5 TO IFLAG
ELSEIF (DSCRIM .EQ. 0.0) THEN
  ASSIGN 10 TO IFLAG
ELSE
  ASSIGN 15 TO IFLAG
ENDIF
GO TO IFLAG (5, 10 15)
```

In this sequence of statements, the block IF statement is used to assign a value to the integer variable IFLAG, which must be one of the statement label values contained within the assigned GO TO statement. Based on the value assigned, control is transferred to either statement label 5, 10, or 15. As with the previous two IF statements presented in this section, the assigned GO TO statement can be replaced with a block IF statement.

E.4 Summary of Additional Statements

This chapter presents additional program statements provided in FORTRAN 77. Except for the SAVE, EXTERNAL, and INTRINSIC statements, the statements described in this chapter have been retained in FORTRAN 77 to permit programs written in older versions of FORTRAN to be compiled using a FORTRAN 77 compiler. A summary of the statements presented follows:

1. The SAVE statement has the form:

```
SAVE list of variables
```

and ensures that the variables listed will retain their values between subroutine calls. This means that the last value stored in the variable when the subroutine is finished executing is available to the subroutine the next time it is called.

2. The EXTERNAL statement is used to alert the compiler that an intrinsic FORTRAN function name will be used to reference a user-supplied subprogram or that a user-written subprogram is to be used as an actual argument. The general form of this statement is:

```
EXTERNAL list of subprogram names
```

3. When a specific intrinsic function name different from the generic name is used as an actual argument, the specific name must be declared using an INTRINSIC statement. The general form of this statement is:

```
INTRINSIC funcname-1, funcname-2, ... funcname-n
```

where *funcname* is the name of an intrinsic function that will be used as an actual argument.

4. The ENTRY statement permits entry into a subprogram other than at the entry point defined by the header line. The general form of this statement is:

```
ENTRY name (list of arguments)
```

An ENTRY statement may be placed at any point within a subprogram, and a subprogram may contain multiple ENTRY statements.

5. In addition to providing normal return from a subprogram, a RETURN statement can be used to return control to alternative points in the calling program. The general form of the RETURN statement needed to access statement labels passed to a subprogram is:

> RETURN *integer expression*

The value of the integer expression is used to return control to the first, second, third, and so on statement labels designated in the argument list used to call the subprogram.

6. An EQUIVALENCE statement reserves the same area in memory for two or more variables, each of which must be of the same data type. The general form of this statement is:

> EQUIVALENCE (name-1, name-2, name-3, ... name-n)

7. In the absence of an explicit declaration, all variables beginning in one of the letters I, J, K, L, M, and N are created as integer variables, and all other variables are created as real variables. This implied data typing can be changed using the IMPLICIT statement. This statement has the general form:

> IMPLICIT *data type (default letters)*

8. The arithmetic IF statement is a three-way selection statement. The general form of this statement is:

> IF (*arithmetic expression*) n_1, n_2, n_3

where *arithmetic expression* is any valid arithmetic expression, and n_1, n_2, and n_3 are statement labels of executable statements. The same statement label may be repeated within this IF statement.

9. The computed GO TO statement is a multipath selection statement. The general form of this statement is:

> GO TO (n_1, n_2, n_3, . . . n) *integer expression*

where the *n*s are statement labels of executable statements, which may be the same, and the integer expression is any valid FORTRAN integer expression.

10. The last selection statement provided in FORTRAN is composed of two parts: an ASSIGN statement and an assigned GO TO statement. The general form of the ASSIGN statement is:

> ASSIGN *integer constant* TO *integer variable*

and the general form of the assigned GO TO statement is:

$$\text{GO TO } integer\ variable\ (n_1,\ n_2,\ n_3,\ .\ .\ .\ n)$$

where the integer variable in both statements is the same name, and the ns are distinct statement labels of executable statements. The integer variable in the assigned GO TO statement must contain a number equal to one of the statement labels in parentheses. This value can only be assigned to the integer variable using the ASSIGN statement. If the integer variable contains a value not equal to one of the ns, a runtime error will occur.

Appendix F

Intrinsic Function Reference

FORTRAN 77's intrinsic functions may be referenced by a specific or generic name. When referenced by specific name, the function requires specific argument data types and returns a value of the specified type. Generally, this returned value agrees with the data type of the arguments. When referenced by generic name, the function returns a value based on the arguments used with the function.

All arguments of an intrinsic function, for both specific and generic forms, must be of the same data type. If arguments of differing data types are used, they will all be converted to the data type of the first argument. Additionally, all angle arguments must be in radians. Table F-1 provides a listing of FORTRAN's intrinsic fucntions by generic and specific name.

Table F-1   FORTRAN 77 Intrinsic Functions

Generic Name	Specific Name	Number of Arguments	Argument Type	Result Type	Description
ABS	IABS	1	Integer	Integer	Absolute value
	ABS		Real	Real	
	DABS		Double	Double	
	CABS		Complex	Complex	
ACOS	ACOS	1	Real	Real	Arcosine
	DACOS		Double	Double	
ANINT	ANINT	1	Real	Real	Nearest whole number
	DNINT		Double	Double	
ASIN	ASIN	1	Real	Real	Arcsine
	DASIN		Double	Double	
ATAN	ATAN	1	Real	Real	Arctangent
	DATAN		Double	Double	

Generic Name	Specific Name	Number of Arguments	Argument Type	Result Type	Description
ATAN2	ATAN2	2	Real	Real	Arctangent of (arg1/arg2)
	DATAN2		Double	Double	
CHAR	CHAR	1	Integer	Character	Convert to character
CMPLX	—	1 or 2	Integer	Complex	Convert to complex
	—		Real	Complex	
	—		Double	Complex	
CONJG	CONJG	1	Complex	Complex	Complex conjugate
COS	COS	1	Real	Real	Cosine
	DCOS		Double	Double	
	CCOS		Complex	Complex	
COSH	COSH	1	Real	Real	Hyperbolic cosine
	DCOSH		Double	Double	
DBLE	DFLOAT	1	Integer	Double	Conversion to double (real part only)
	DBLE		Real	Double	
	DBLE		Complex	Double	
DIM	IDIM	2	Integer	Integer	Positive difference (arg1 − arg2)
	DIM		Real	Real	
	DDIM		Double	Double	
EXP	EXP	1	Real	Real	Exponential (e**arg)
	DEXP		Double	Double	
	CEXP		Complex	Complex	
ICHAR	ICHAR	1	Character	Integer	Conversion to integer
IMAG	AIMAG	1	Complex	Real	Extract imaginary part
INDEX	INDEX	2	Character	Integer	Return starting position of arg2 within arg1
INT	INT	1	Integer	Integer	Conversion to integer
	INT		Real	Integer	
	INT		Complex	Integer	
	IFIX		Real	Integer	
	IDINT		Double	Integer	
LEN	LEN	1	Character	Integer	Length of string
LGE	LGE	2	Character	Logical	True if arg1 > = arg2; else False
LGT	LGT	2	Character	Logical	True if arg1 > arg2; else False
LLE	LLE	2	Character	Logical	True if arg1 < = arg2; else False
LLT	LLT	2	Character	Logical	True if arg1 < arg2; else False
LOG	ALOG	1	Real	Real	Natural logarithm (base e)
	DLOG		Double	Double	
	CLOG		Complex	Complex	
LOG10	ALOG10	1	Real	Real	Common logarithm (base 10)
	DLOG10		Double	Double	
MAX	MAX0	> = 2	Integer	Integer	Largest value of all arguments
	AMAX0		Integer	Reeal	
	AMAX1		Real	Real	
	DMAX1		Double	Double	
	MAX1		Real	Integer	

Generic Name	Specific Name	Number of Arguments	Argument Type	Result Type	Description
MIN	MIN0	>= 2	Integer	Integer	Smallest value of all arguments
	AMIN0		Integer	Real	
	AMIN1		Real	Real	
	DMIN1		Double	Double	
	MIN1		Real	Integer	
MOD	MOD	2	Integer	Integer	Remainder of $arg_1 - (int(arg_1/arg_2)*arg_2)$
	AMOD		Real	Real	
	DMOD		Double	Double	
REAL	REAL	1	Integer	Real	Convert to real (real part only); same as REAL
	REAL		Real	Real	
	REAL		Complex	Real	
	FLOAT		Integer	Real	
	SNGL		Double	Real	
SIGN	ISIGN	2	Integer	Integer	Transfer of sign (sign of arg_1 = sign of arg_2)
	SIGN		Real	Real	
	DSIGN		Double	Double	
SIN	SIN	1	Real	Real	Sine
	DSIN		Double	Double	
	CSIN		Complex	Complex	
SINH	SINH	1	Real	Real	Hyperbolic sine
	DSINH		Double	Double	
SQRT	SQRT	1	Real	Real	Square root ($arg**0.5$)
	DSQRT		Double	Double	
	CSQRT		Complex	Complex	
TAN	TAN	1	Real	Real	Tangent
	DTAN		Double	Double	
TANH	TANH	1	Real	Real	Hyperbolic tangent
	DTANH		Double	Double	

Solutions

Section 1.1

2. One possible solution:
   a. Make sure the car is parked, the engine is off, and the
      key is out of the ignition switch
      Go to the trunk
      Put the correct key into the trunk
      Open the trunk
      Remove the spare tire and the jack
      Put the jack under the car ... and so on

   b. Go to a phone
      Remove the handset from the phone
      Wait for the dial tone
      Take out the correct change for the call
      Put the correct change into the phone
      Dial the number

3. Step 1: Pour the contents of the first cup into the third cup
   Step 2: Rinse out the first cup
   Step 3: Pour the contents of the second cup into the first cup
   Step 4: Rinse out the second cup
   Step 5: Pour the contents of the third cup into the second cup

5. Step 1: Compare the first number with the second number and
           use the smallest of these numbers for the next step
   Step 2: Compare the smallest number found in step 1 with the
           third number. The smallest of these two numbers is
           the smallest of all three numbers.

7a. Step 1: Compare the first name in the list with the name
            JONES. If the names match, stop the search; else go
            to step 2.
    Step 2: Compare the next name in the list with the name
            JONES. If the names match, stop the search; else
            repeat this step.

Section 1.2

1. POWER - valid and mnemonic
   DENSITY - invalid, more than six characters
   M123$ - invalid, contains the special symbol $
   1234 - invalid, does not begin with a letter
   ABCD - valid and not mnemonic
   TOTAL - valid and mnemonic
   TANGENT - invalid, too many letters
   ABSVAL - valid and mnemonic
   MARRIED - invalid, too many letters
   B34A - valid and not mnemonic
   34AB - invalid, does not start with a letter
   TAXES$ - invalid, contains the special symbol $
   A2-B3 - invalid, contains the special symbol -
   NEWBAL - valid and mnemonic
   MIN-VAL - invalid, contains the special symbol -
   SINE - valid and mnemonic
   $SINE - invalid, contains the special symbol $
   COSINE - valid and mnemonic
   INVOICES - invalid, more than six characters
   NETPAY - valid and mnemonic
   BALANCE - invalid, more than six characters
   SOLD - valid and mnemonic
   AVERAGE - invalid, more than six characters

3. PROGRAM MAIN
       ITEMS
       SALETX
       BALNCE
       STOP
       END

5a. For a case insensitive compiler:
    AVERAG and averag are equivalent
    MODE, Mode, and moDE are equivalent
    BESSEL and besseL are equivalent
    Total and total are equivalent
    TeMp and TEMP are equivalent

 b. In a case sensitive compiler, none of the names are
equivalent.

 c. AVERAG, MODE, BESSEL, and TEMP

9. Determine the courses needed for graduate school
   Take the right courses
   Maintain an appropriate grade average
   Prepare for the graduate record exam (GRE)
   Contact engineering graduate schools for admission
     interview requirements
   Establish contacts for letters of recommendation

11. Select and reserve a camp site
    Prepare a list of items to take along
    Purchase needed supplies
    Reserve a camper at a rental agency (optional)
    Arrange for someone to feed plants and watch house
    Make arrangements for pet care, if needed
    Check and service automobile

Exercise 1.3

1. ```
   123456789 Column Number
           PROGRAM MAIN
           CALL GROPAY
           CALL TAXES
           CALL NETPAY
           CALL DISPLAY
           STOP
           END
   ```

3. ```
   123456789 Column Number
   * THIS PROGRAM DISPLAYS A FOUR LINE POEM
           PROGRAM MAIN
           CALL POEM
           STOP
           END
           SUBROUTINE POEM
   * THE NUMBERS 10, 20, 30, AND 40 IN THE NEXT FOUR STATEMENTS
   * ARE STATEMENT LABELS THAT BELONGS IN THE LABEL FIELD
       10    PRINT *, 'COMPUTERS, COMPUTERS EVERYWHERE'
       20    PRINT *, '   AS FAR AS I CAN SEE'
       30    PRINT *, 'I REALLY, REALLY LIKE THOSE THINGS'
       40    PRINT *, '   OH JOY, OH JOY FOR ME'
           STOP
           END
   ```

5. ```
   123456789 Column Number
           PROGRAM MAIN
           CALL TEST
               STOP
           END
           SUBROUTINE TEST
   * THE NUMBERS 100 AND 200 IN THE NEXT TWO STATEMENTS ARE
   * LABELS THAT BELONG IN THE LABEL FIELD
       100    FORMAT(1X,A,2X,A)
       200    FORMAT(1X,I5,2X,F5.3)
   * THE FOLLOWING TWO STATEMENTS ARE CALLED DECLARATION STATEMENTS
           REAL VALUE
           INTEGER COUNT
           PRINT 100, 'VALUE', 'SIN'
           PRINT 100, '-----', '---'
           DO 10 COUNT = 1, 20
   * FOR APPEARANCE ONLY, BEGIN THE NEXT TWO STATEMENTS IN COLUMN 11
             VALUE = 0.1 * I
             PRINT 200, VALUE, SIN(VALUE)
   * THE 10 IN THE NEXT STATEMENT IS A STATEMENT NUMBER
       10    CONTINUE
           STOP
           END
   ```

7. PROGRAM is spelled incorrectly
   ```

9. The statement number 100 should be placed within columns 1 through 5

11. The statement should begin in column 7 or beyond

13. 123456789 Column Number
```
    C THE NEXT LINE IS AN INITIAL LINE OF A STATEMENT
            PRINT 100, 'THE AVERAGE IS',
    C AND THE NEXT LINE IS A CONTINUATION LINE
          1 AVERAGE
```

Section 1.4

```
1. PROGRAM MAIN
      CALL DISPLY
      END
   SUBROUTINE DISPLY
      PRINT *, 'JOHN JONES'
      PRINT *, '212 SOMEPLACE STREET'
      PRINT *, 'NONESUCH, NJ, 07078'
      END
```

3. Six PRINT or WRITE statement should be used, one for each line.

Chapter Two - Data and Operations

Section 2.1

```
1 a. REAL
  b. INTEGER
  c. REAL
  d. INTEGER
  e. REAL
  f. CHARACTER
```

3. 1.26E2 6.5623E2 3.42695E3 4.8931E3 3.21E-1 1.23E-2 6.789E-3

5a.
```
-----------------------------------------------------------------
| 01001101 | 01000001 | 01010010 | 01010100 | 01001000 | 01000001 |
-----------------------------------------------------------------
```

b.
```
-----------------------------------------------------------------
| 11010100 | 11000001 | 11011001 | 11100011 | 11001000 | 11000001 |
-----------------------------------------------------------------
```

```
7a. 2 * 3 + 4 * 5
 b. (6 + 18) / 2
 c. 4.5 / (12.2 - 3.1)
 d. 4.6 * (3.0 + 14.9)
 e. (12.1 + 18.9) * (15.3 - 3.8)
```

```
9.
a. 27   b. 8.0   c. 1.0   d. 220.0   e. 22.5   f. 19.67
g. 6.0  h. 2.0
```

11. Since all of the operands are integers, the result of each
intermediate operation is an integer.
a. 5   b. 10   c. 24   d. 0 (due to truncation)
e. 3   f. -50   g. -2   h. 10   i. 53
15. A program might alert the computer to the amount of storage
needed for the various values in the program by specifying the
numbers of each type of value that will be used by the program.

Section 2.2

1. PROD-A is invalid because of the special symbol -
   C1234 is valid
   ABCD is valid
   -C3 is invalid because of the special symbol -
   12345 is invalis because it does not begin in a letter
   NEWBAL is valid
   WATTS is valid
   $TOTAL is invalid because of the special symbol $
   NEW$AL is invalid because of the special symbol $
   A1B2C3D4 is invalid because it contains more than six characters
   9AB6 is invalid because it does not begin with a letter
   SUM.OF is invalid because it contains a period
   AVERAGE is invalid because it contains more than six characters
   GRADE1 is valid
   FINGRAD is invalid because it contains more than six characters

3a. INTEGER COUNT
 b. REAL GRADE
 c. CHARACTER KEYCH

5a. INTEGER FIRNUM, SECNUM
 b. REAL PRICE, YIELD, COUPON
 c. CHARACTER CH, LET1*3, LET2*3, LET3*7, LET4*9

7. A name and a value

9a. RATE is stored starting at memory location 159
    CH1 is stored starting at memory location 163
    CH2 is stored starting at memory location 164
    CH3 is stored starting at memory location 165
    CH4 is stored starting at memory location 166
    NUM is stored starting at memory location 167
    COUNT is stored starting at memory location 168

11. MILES is stored in byte locations 159 through 162
    COUNT is stored in byte locations 163 and 164
    NUM is stored in byte locations 165 and 166
    KEY is stored in byte location 167
    KEY2*3 is stored in byte locations 168, 169, and 170
    KEY is stored in byte location 171

Section 2.3

1. CIRCUM = 2 * 3.1416 * RADIUS

3. CELSUS = 5.0 / 9.0 * (FAHREN - 32.0)

5. ETIME = TOTDIS / AVSPED

7. HEIGHT = V**2 * SIN (THETA) **2 / (2.0 * 32.2)

9. FORCE = K * Q1 * Q2 / R**2

11. THE FIRST INTEGER DISPLAYED IS 4
    THE SECOND INTEGER DISPLAYED IS 4

13. THE SUM IS   0.000000
    THE SUM IS 26.270000
    THE FINAL TOTAL IS 28.238000

15. LENGTH is not initialized before it is used in the last statement

17. The last statement should be AREA = LENGTH * WIDTH

19. THE VALUE OF TOTAL IS INITIALLY SET TO 247
        TOTAL IS NOW 247
        TOTAL IS NOW 247
        TOTAL IS NOW 247
        THE FINAL VALUE IN TOTAL IS 247

25.   PROGRAM MAIN
```
         REAL MINRAD, MAXRAD, CIRCUM
         MINRAD = 2.5
         MAXRAD = 6.4
         CIRCUM = 3.1416 * (2 * (MINRAD**2 + MAXRAD**2))**(0.5)
         PRINT *, 'THE CIRCUMFERENCE IS ', CIRCUM
         END
```

27.   PROGRAM MAIN
```
         REAL X1, X2, Y1, Y2, SLOPE
         X1 = 3.0
         Y1 = 7.0
         X2 = 8.0
         Y2 = 12.0
         SLOPE = (Y2 - Y1) / (X2 - X1)
         PRINT *, 'THE SLOPE OF THE LINE IS ', SLOPE
         END
```

Section 2.4

1a.
```
   7
123456789 ←Column number
```

b.
```
      7
123456789 ←Column number
```

c.
```
****
123456789 ←Column number
```

d.
```
7.92
123456789 ←Column number
```

e.
```
5.76
123456789 ←Column number
```

f.
```
82.63
123456789 ←Column number
```

g.
```
*****
123456789 ←Column number
```

h.
```
*****
123456789 ←Column number
```

```
i. THE NUMBER IS   26.27
   THE NUMBER IS  682.30
   THE NUMBER IS    1.97
   12345678911111111122 ←Column number
           012345678901
j. 26.27
   682.30
     1.97
   ------
   710.54
   123456789 ←Column number

k.     26.27
       682.30
         1.97
       ------
       710.54
   123456789 ←Column number

l.         34.16
           10.00
           ------
           44.17
   1234567891111 ←Column number
            0123
```

3. Same display as for Exercise 1

```
7.      PROGRAM MAIN
        REAL RES1, RES2, RES3, TOTRES
        RES1 = 1000.0
        RES2 = 1000.0
        RES3 = 1000.0
        TOTRES = 1.0 / (1.0/RES1 +1.0/RES2 + 1.0/RES3)
        PRINT 10, TOTRES
   10   FORMAT (' ','THE COMBINED RESISTANCE IS ',F7.2, ' OHMS')
        END

9.      PROGRAM MAIN
        REAL WEIGHT, LENGTH, XLEN,BEND
        WEIGHT = 500.0
        LENGTH = 25.0
        XLEN = 10.0
        BEND = XLEN * WEIGHT * (LENGTH - XLEN) / LENGTH
        PRINT 10, BEND
   10   FORMAT(1X,'THE MAXIMUM BENDING MOMENT IS ',F9.4)
        END
```

Section 2.5

1a. One output: the dollar amount
 b. Five Inputs: halfdollars, quarters, dimes, nickels, pennies
 c. Dollar amount = 0.50 * halfs + 0.25 * quarters + 0.10 * dimes
                  + 0.05 * nickels + 0.01 * pennies

3a. One output : the amount of Ergies
 b. Four inputs: pi, mu, e, and fergies

5a. One output: distance
 b. Three inputs: s, d, and t
7a. Four outputs: weekly gross and net pay for two people
 b. Four inputs: two hourly rates, income tax rate, medical rate

9a. One output: the value of y
 b. Four inputs: , r, x, and pi

Section 2.6

5a.

```
        PROGRAM CONVRT
          REAL CELSUS, FAHREN
          FAHREN = 98.6
          CELSUS = 5.0/9.0 * (FAHREN - 32.0)
          PRINT *, 'FOR A FAHRENHEIT TEMPERATURE OF ', FAHREN, ' DEGREES'
          PRINT *, 'THE CELSIUS TEMPERATURE IS ', CELSUS, ' DEGREES'
          END
```

7a.

```
        PROGRAM ELAPSE
          REAL ETIME, DIST, AVSPED
          DIST = 183.67
          AVSPED = 58.0
          ETIME = DIST /AVSPED
          PRINT *, 'THE TIME FOR THE TRIP WAS ', ETIME, ' HOURS'
          END
```

9a.

```
        PROGRAM COOL
          REAL TFIN, TINIT, ATEMP, K, TIME
          TINIT = 150.0
          ATEMP = 60.0
          K = 0.0367
          TIME = 20.0
          TFIN = (TINIT - ATEMP) * 2.71828 ** (-K*TIME) + ATEMP
          PRINT *, 'THE FINAL TEMPERATURE IS ', TFIN
          END
```

11a.

```
        PROGRAM MONEY
          REAL FINAMT, BEGAMT, RATE, M, N
          RATE = 0.06
          M = 4.0
          N = 10.0
          BEGAMT = 5000.00
          FINAMT = BEGAMT * (1.0 + RATE/M)** (M * N)
          PRINT 10, FINAMT
   10     FORMAT(1X,'THE FINAL AMOUNT OF MONEY IS $',F7.2)
          END
```

13a.

```
        PROGRAM VALUE
          REAL  PVALUE, FAMT, RATE, YEARS
          FAMT = 8000.00
          RATE = 0.08
          YEARS = 9.0
          PVALUE = FAMT / (1.0 + RATE)**YEARS
          PRINT 10, PVALUE
   10     FORMAT (1X,'THE PRESENT VALUE IS $',F7.2)
          END
```

Section 2.9

```
1a. SUBROUTINE TEST(EXPER)
        REAL EXPER

    CALL TEST(VALUE)

 b. SUBROUTINE MINUTE(ITIME)
        INTEGER ITIME

    CALL MINUTE(LSECND)

 c. SUBROUTINE KEY(CODE)
        CHARACTER CODE

    CALL KEY(CODE)

 d. SUBROUTINE YIELD(RATE,N)
        REAL RATE
        INTEGER N

    CALL YIELD(COUPON,IYEARS)

 e. SUBROUTINE RAND(SEED,RANDNO)
        REAL SEED, RANDNO

    CALL RAND(SEED,RVAL)
```

```
3b.
        PROGRAM TEST
          CALL TOTAMT(26,80,100,216)
          END
        SUBROUTINE TOTAMT(IQUART, IDIMES, NICKEL, IPENNY)
          INTEGER IQUART, IDIMES, NICKEL, IPENNY
          REAL DOLLAR
          DOLLAR = (25*IQUART + 10*IDIMES + 5*NICKEL + IPENNY)/100.0
          PRINT *, 'THE AMOUNT OF MONEY IN THE BANK IS $ ', DOLLAR
          END
```

Chapter Three - Completing the Basics

Section 3.1

```
1a.  SQRT(6.37)
 b.  SQRT(X-Y)
 c.  SIN(30 * 3.1416/180.0)
 d.  SIN(60 * 3.1416/180.0)
 e.  INT(19.37)
 f.  ABS( A**2 - B**2)
 g.  MOD(7,2)
 h.  EXP(3)

3a.  B = SIN(X) - COS(X)
 b.  B = SIN(X)**2 - COS(X)**2
 c.  AREA = (C * B * SIN(A))/2
 d.  C = SQRT(A**2 + B**2)
 e.  P = SQRT( ABS(M - N) )
```

```
   f.   SUM = A*(R**N - 1) / (R - 1)
   g.   X = AMAX1(P,Q,R,S,T)
   h.   Y = AMIN1(P,Q,R,S,T)
```

5.
```
        PROGRAM DISTNS
          REAL DIST, X1, Y1, X2, Y2
          X1 = 7.0
          Y1 = 12.0
          X2 = 3.0
          Y2 = 9.0
          DIST = SQRT( (X1 - X2)**2 + (Y1 - Y2)**2 )
          PRINT *, 'THE DISTANCE IS ', DIST
          END
```

7.
```
        PROGRAM MAXHT
          REAL HEIGHT, VELCTY, THETA
          VELCTY = 15.0
*** MAKE SURE TO CONVERT DEGREES TO RADIANS
          THETA = 60.0 * 3.1416/180.0
          HEIGHT = (0.5 * VELCTY**2 * (SIN(THETA))**2)/9.80
          PRINT *, 'THE MAXIMUM HEIGHT REACHED IS ', HEIGHT, ' METERS'
          END
```

9.
```
        PROGRAM XYCORD
          REAL X, Y, R, THETA
          R = 10.0
          THETA = 30 * 3.1416/180.0
          X = R * COS(THETA)
          Y = R * SIN(THETA)
          PRINT *, 'THE X COORDINATE IS ', X
          PRINT *, 'THE Y COORDINATE IS ', Y
          END
```

11.
```
        PROGRAM REMAIN
          REAL RMAT, OMAT, N
          OMAT = 100.0
          N = 1000.0
          RMAT = OMAT * EXP(-0.00012 * N)
          PRINT *, 'THE REMAINING MATERIAL IS ', RMAT, ' GRAMS'
          END
```

13.
```
        PROGRAM AMPLFY
          REAL POUT, PIN, AMP
          POUT = 50.0
          PIN = 1.0
          AMP = 10 * LOG10(POUT/PIN)
          PRINT *, ' THE AMPLIFICATION IS ', AMP, ' DECIBELS'
          END
```

Section 3.2

```
1.a. READ *, NUMBER   or   READ(5,*) NUMBER
  b. READ *, GRADE     or   READ(5,*) GRADE
  c. READ *, KEYVAL    or   READ(5,*) KEYVAL
  d. READ *, MONTH, YEAR, SCORE   or   READ(5,*) MONTH, YEAR, SCORE
  e. READ *, CH, NUM1, NUM2   or   READ(5,*) CH, NUM1, NUM2
  f. READ *, CAPTAL, RATE, AMOUNT   or   READ(5,*) CAPTAL, RATE, AMOUNT
```

g. READ *, LETTR1, LETTR2, KEY, NUM1, NUM2, NUM3
   or READ(5,*) LETTR1, LETTR2, KEY, NUM1, NUM2, NUM3
h. READ *, OHMS1, OHMS2, OHMS3, VOLTS1, VOLTS2, VOLTS3
   or READ(5,*) OHMS1, OHMS2, OHMS3, VOLTS1, VOLTS2, VOLTS3

3. Assuming 5 is the standard unit output number, the correct forms
are
   a. READ(5,*) NUM1, NUM2, VAL2
   b. READ(5,*) NUM1, NUM2
   c. READ(5,*) NUM1, I4
   d. READ(5,*) TEMP, AMBINT
   e. READ(5,*) VAL1, VAL2
   f. READ(5,*) NUM1, TEMP

5.
```
        PROGRAM CIRCAR
          REAL RADIUS, AREA
          PRINT *,'ENTER THE RADIUS OF A CIRCLE'
          READ *, RADIUS
          AREA = 3.1416 * RADIUS**2
          PRINT *, 'RADIUS = ', RADIUS, ' AREA = ', AREA
          END
```

7.
```
        PROGRAM AVERAG
          REAL AVRGE, NUM1, NUM2, NUM3, NUM4
          PRINT * ,'ENTER A NUMBER:'
          READ *, NUM1
          PRINT *, 'ENTER A SECOND NUMBER:'
          READ *, NUM 2
          PRINT *, 'ENTER A THIRD NUMBER:'
          READ *, NUM3
          PRINT *, 'ENTER A FOURTH NUMBER:'
          READ *, NUM4
          AVRGE = (NUM1 + NUM2 + NUM3 + NUM4)/4.0
          PRINT *, 'THE AVERAGE IS ', AVRGE
          END
```

9.
```
        PROGRAM BACTER
          REAL BTERIA, TIME
          PRINT *, 'ENTER THE REFRIGERATION TIME:'
          READ *, TIME
          BTERIA = 300000.0 * EXP(-0.032*TIME)
          PRINT *, 'THE NUMBER OF REMAINING BACTERIA IS: ', BTERIA
          END
```

11.
```
        PROGRAM MAIN
          REAL NUMBER, FRTHRT
          PRINT *, 'ENTER A NUMBER:'
          READ *, NUMBER
          FRTHRT = SQRT(SQRT(NUMBER))
          PRINT *, 'THE FOURTH ROOT IS ', FRTHRT
          END
```

Section 3.3

1a. REAL WATTS
 b. REAL TEMP
 c. INTEGER COUNT

```
    d. INTEGER NUM1, NUM2
       REAL VALUE
       CHARACTER CH1*6
    e. INTEGER COUNT
       REAL VOLTS, OHMS
    f. REAL AVERGE
       INTEGER IFLAG
       CHARACTER*6 KEY, CODE
```

3a. The first field starts at column 1 and ends at column 4
    The second field starts at column 5 and ends at column 9
    The third field starts at column 10 and ends at column 14

 b. The first field starts at column 1 and ends at column 5
    The second field starts at column 6 and ends at column 11
    The third field starts at column 12 and ends at column 19

 c. The first field fills column 1 only
    The second field starts at column 2 and ends at column 6
    The third field starts at column 7 and ends at column 8
    The fourth field starts at column 9 and ends at column 28

 d. The first field fills column 1 only
    The second field starts at column 2 and ends at column 6
    The third field fills column 7 only
    The fourth field starts at column 8 and ends at column 12

 e. First field: Column 1
    Second field: Columns 2, 3, and 4
    Third field: Columns 5 and 6
    Fourth field: Columns 7, 8, and 9
    Fifth field: Columns 10 and 11
    Sixth field: Columns 12, 13, 14, 15, and 16
    Seventh field: Column 17
    Eighth field: Columns 18, 19, and 20
    Ninth field: Column 21
    Tenth field: Columns 22, 23, and 24

5. The program will work. However, it is advisable to display a
prompt for the user that explains what input is requested and the
format that should be used. It is also generally advisable to use
separate FORMAT statements for both input and output statements, so
that a change can be made in one of the formats without effecting
the other. Note also that the first 1X in the format is used
differently on input than it is on output (recall the carriage
control character on output).

7a.
```
        PROGRAM MAIN
         REAL NUM1, NUM2
         PRINT *, 'ENTER TWO NUMBERS:'
*** THE FOLLOWING TWO PRINT STATEMENTS ARE TO HELP
***  THE USER CORRECTLY ALIGN THE INPUT
         PRINT *, '123456789111111'
         PRINT *, '         012345'
         READ(5,10) NUM1, NUM2
10       FORMAT(1X,F7.2,2X,F5.2)
         PRINT *, NUM1, NUM2
         END
```

9a.
```
        PROGRAM MAIN
        REAL X1, X2, XMID, Y1, Y2, YMID
        PRINT *, 'ENTER FOUR COORDINATES'
*** THE FOLLOWING PRINT STATEMENT IS TO HELP
***    THE USER CORRECTLY ALIGN THE INPUT
        PRINT *,' X1X.XX Y1Y.YY X2X.XX Y2Y.YY'
        READ 10, X1, Y1, X2, Y2
  10    FORMAT(4(1X,F6.2))
        XMID = (X1 + X2) / 2.0
        YMID = (Y1 + Y2) / 2.0
        PRINT *, 'X MIDPOINT = ', XMID
        PRINT *, 'Y MIDPOINT = ',YMID
        END
```

Section 3.4

1.
```
        PROGRAM MAIN
        REAL TIME, HEIGHT, GRAV
        PARAMETER (GRAV = 32.2)
        HEIGHT = 800
        TIME = SQRT(2.0 * HEIGHT / GRAV)
        PRINT *, 'IT WILL TAKE ', TIME, ' SECONDS'
        PRINT *, ' TO FALL ', HEIGHT, ' FEET.'
        sEND
```

3.
```
        PROGRAM MAIN
        REAL RADIUS, CIRCUM, AREA, PI
        PARAMETER (PI = 3.1416)
        PRINT *, 'ENTER A RADIUS'
        READ *, RADIUS
        CIRCUM = 2.0 * PI * RADIUS
        AREA = PI * RADIUS**2
        PRINT *, 'THE CIRCUMFERENCE IS ', CIRCUM
        PRINT *, 'THE AREA IS ', AREA
        END
```

Section 3.5

3. The mistake in this program is that the output statements for the headings are made before the input prompts. This has the effect of "sandwiching" the input between the desired output, as shown by the following sample run.

```
        SINE         APPROXIMATION    DIFFERENCE
     ------------    -------------    ------------
ENTER AN ANGLE (IN DEGREES)
30
     5.000011E-01    5.236000E-01     2.359891E-02
     5.000011E-01    4.996752E-01     3.258522E-04
     5.000011E-01    5.000032E-01     2.098380E-06
```

5.

```
        PROGRAM BELL
          REAL X, MU, R, Y, PI
          PARAMETER (PI = 3.1416)
          PRINT *, 'ENTER A VALUE FOR MU:'
          READ *, MU
          PRINT *, 'ENTER A VALUE FOR X:'
          READ *, X
          PRINT *, 'ENTER A VALUE FOR R:'
          READ *, R
          Y = EXP(-(0.5*(X-MU)/R)**2) / (R* SQRT(2.0*PI))
          PRINT *, 'THE VALUE OF Y IS ', Y
          END
```

7.

```
        PROGRAM CYLVOL
          REAL VOL, PI, RADIUS, DIST
          PARAMETER (PI = 3.1416)
          PRINT *, 'ENTER THE RADIUS OF THE TANK:'
          READ *, RADIUS
          PRINT *, 'ENTER THE DISTANCE MEASUREMENT:'
          READ *, DIST
          VOL = PI * RADIUS**2 * (200.0 - DIST)
          PRINT *, 'THE VOLUME OF OIL IN THE TANK IS ', VOL
          END
```

Chapter Four - Selection

Section 4.1

1a. True　　b. True　　c. True　　d. True　　e. 10
　f. False　g. False　h. True　　i. False

3a. False　b. False　c. True

Section 4.2

1a. IF (ANGLE .EQ. 90) THEN
```
        PRINT *, 'THE ANGLE IS A RIGHT ANGLE'
    ELSE
        PRINT *, 'THE ANGLE IS NOT A RIGHT ANGLE'
    ENDIF
```

　b. IF (TEMP .GT. 100) THEN
```
        PRINT *, 'ABOVE THE BOILING POINT OF WATER'
    ELSE
        PRINT *, 'BELOW THE BOILING POINT OF WATER'
    ENDIF
```

c. IF (NUM .GE. 0.0) THEN
```
        POSSUM = POSSUM + NUM
    ELSE
        NEGSUM = NEGSUM + NUM
    ENDIF
```

```
d.  IF (VOLTGE .LT. 0.5) THEN
       FLAG = 0
    ELSE
       FLAG = 1
    ENDIF

e.  IF (ABS(VOLTS1-VOLTS2) .LT. 0.001) THEN
       APPROX = 0.0
    ELSE
       APPROX = (VOLTS1 - VOLTS2)/ 2.0
    ENDIF

f.  IF (FREQ .GT. 60) PRINT *, 'FREQUENCY IS TOO HIGH'

g.  IF (ABS(TEMP1-TEMP2) .GT. 2.3) ERROR = (TEMP1-TEMP2)*FACTOR

h.  IF (X .GT. Y .AND. X .LT. 20) READ *, P

i.  IF (DIST .GT. 20 .AND. DIST .LT. 35) READ *, TIME
```

3.
```
          PROGRAM  MAIN
            REAL INCOME, TAXES
            PRINT *,'PLEASE TYPE IN THE TAXABLE INCOME'
            READ *,INCOME
            IF (INCOME .LE. 20000.00) THEN
               TAXES = .02 * INCOME
            ELSE
               TAXES = .025 * (INCOME - 20000.00) + 400.00
            ENDIF
            PRINT 10, TAXES
     10     FORMAT(1X,'THE TAXES ARE $',F7.2)
            END
```

5.
```
        PROGRAM MAIN
          REAL NYRS
          PRINT *, 'ENTER THE NUMBER OF YEARS'
          READ *, NYRS
          CALL RATE(NYRS)
          END
*
        SUBROUTINE RATE(NYRS)
          REAL NYRS, INTRST
          IF (NYRS .GT. 2.0) THEN
             INTRST = 8.5
          ELSE
             INTRST = 7.0
          ENDIF
          PRINT 10, INTRST
     10   FORMAT (1X,'THE INTEREST RATE IS ',F3.1,' PERCENT')
          END
```

7.
```
      PROGRAM MAIN
        REAL HOURS
        PRINT *, 'ENTER THE NUMBER OF HOURS WORKED'
        READ *, HOURS
        CALL PAY(HOURS)
        END
*
      SUBROUTINE PAY(HOURS)
        REAL HOURS, SALRY
        IF (HOURS .GT. 40.0) THEN
          SALRY = 320.00 + 12.00 * (HOURS - 40.0)
        ELSE
          SALRY = 8.00 * HOURS
        ENDIF
        PRINT 10, SALRY
10      FORMAT(1X,'THE SALARY IS $ ',F7.2)
        END
```

9.
```
      PROGRAM MAIN
        CHARACTER STATUS
        PRINT *, 'ENTER THE STATUS CODE (IN APOSTROPHES):'
        READ *, STATUS
        CALL DISPLY(STATUS)
        END
*
      SUBROUTINE DISPLY(STATUS)
        CHARACTER STATUS
        IF (STATUS .EQ. 'S') THEN
          PRINT *, 'THE SENIOR SALESPERSON''S SALARY IS $400.00'
        ELSE
          PRINT *, 'THE JUNIOR SALESPERSON''S SALARY IS $275.00'
        ENDIF
        END
```

11.
```
      PROGRAM MAIN
        CHARACTER CH
        PRINT *, 'TYPE IN ANY CHARACTER ENCLOSED IN APOSTROPHES:'
        READ *, CH
        CALL CTYPE(CH)
        END
*
      SUBROUTINE CTYPE(CH)
        CHARACTER CH
        IF (CH .GE. 'a' .AND. CH .LE. 'z') THEN
          PRINT *, 'THE CHARACTER ENTERED IS A LOWERCASE LETTER'
        ELSE
          PRINT *, 'THE CHARACTER ENTERED IN NOT A LOWERCASE LETTER'
        ENDIF
        END
```

Section 4.3

1.

```
      PROGRAM MAIN
        CHARACTER MRCODE
        PRINt *,'ENTER A MARITAL CODE (IN APOSTROPHES): '
        READ *, MRCODE
*
        IF (MRCODE .EQ. 'M' .OR. MRCODE .EQ. 'm') THEN
          PRINT *,'INDIVIDUAL IS MARRIED.'
        ELSEIF (MRCODE .EQ. 'S' .OR. MRCODE .EQ. 's') THEN
          PRINT *,'INDIVIDUAL IS SINGLE.'
        ELSEIF (MRCODE .EQ. 'D' .OR. MRCODE .EQ. 'd') THEN
          PRINT *,'INDIVIDUAL IS DIVORCED.'
        ELSEIF (MRCODE .EQ. 'W' .OR. MRCODE .EQ. 'w') THEN
          PRINT *,'INDIVIDUAL IS WIDOWED.'
        ELSE
          PRINT *,'AN INVALID CODE WAS ENTERED.'
        ENDIF
*
        END
```

3.

```
      PROGRAM MAIN
        REAL ANGLE
        PRINT *, 'ENTER AN ANGLE:'
        READ *, ANGLE
        CALL ATYPE(ANGLE)
        END
*
      SUBROUTINE ATYPE(ANGLE)
        REAL ANGLE
        IF (ANGLE .LT. 90.0) THEN
          PRINT *, 'THE ANGLE IS ACUTE'
        ELSEIF (ANGLE .GT. 90.0) THEN
          PRINT *, 'THE ANGLE IS OBTUSE'
        ELSE
          PRINT *, 'THE ANGLE IS A RIGHT ANGLE'
        ENDIF
        END
```

5.

```
      PROGRAM MAIN
        REAL GRADE
        PRINT *, 'ENTER THE STUDENT''S NUMERICAL GRADE'
        READ *, GRADE
        CALL LETTER(GRADE)
        END
*
      SUBROUTINE LETTER(GRADE)
        REAL GRADE
        CHARACTER LGRADE
        IF (GRADE .GE. 90.0) THEN
          LGRADE = 'A'
        ELSEIF (GRADE .GE. 80.0) THEN
          LGRADE = 'B'
        ELSEIF (GRADE .GE. 70.0) THEN
          LGRADE = 'C'
        ELSEIF (GRADE .GE. 60.0) THEN
          LGRADE = 'D'
        ELSE
          LGRADE = 'F'
        ENDIF
```

```
             PRINT *, 'THE LETTER GRADE FOR THIS STUDENT IS ', LGRADE
             END
```

7.

```
         PROGRAM MAIN
           REAL TEMP
           CHARACTER TYPE
           PRINT *,'ENTER A TEMPERATURE AND ITS TYPE (''F'' OR ''C''):'
           READ *, TEMP, TYPE
           CALL CONVER(TEMP,TYPE)
           END
*
         SUBROUTINE CONVER(TEMP, TYPE)
           REAL TEMP, CELSUS, FAHREN
           CHARACTER TYPE
           IF (TYPE .EQ. 'F') THEN
              CELSUS = (5.0/9.0) * (TEMP - 32.0)
              PRINT *, 'THE EQUIVALENT CELSIUS TEMPERATURE IS ', CELSUS
           ELSEIF (TYPE .EQ. 'C') THEN
              FAHREN = (9.0/5.0) * TEMP + 32.0
              PRINT *, 'THE EQUIVALENT FAHRENHEIT TEMPERATURE IS ', FAHREN
           ELSE
              PRINT *, 'AN INVALID TEMPERATURE CODE WAS ENTERED'
           ENDIF
           END
```

9a. The program will run.
b. The program determines whether the monthly sales is less than or greater than 10000. If monthly sales is less than 10000.00 then it determines the correct income. If monthly sales are greater than or equal to 10000.00, regardless of how much greater, the income is calculated as 200.00 + .03 * MSALES.
c. The correct income is calculated for sales less than $10,000 and for sales between $10,000 and $20,000.

Section 4.4

1a.

```
         PROGRAM MAIN
           REAL NUM1, NUM2
           INTEGER CODE
           PRINT *, 'ENTER TWO NUMBERS'
           READ *, NUM1, NUM2
           PRINT *, 'ENTER A CALCULATION CODE AS FOLLOWS:'
           PRINT *, '    1 FOR ADDITION'
           PRINT *, '    2 FOR MULTIPLICATION'
           PRINT *, '    3 FOR DIVISION'
           READ *, CODE
           CALL CALC(NUM1, NUM2, CODE)
           END
*
         SUBROUTINE CALC(NUM1, NUM2, CODE)
           REAL NUM1, NUM2, RESULT
           INTEGER CODE
           IF (CODE .EQ. 1) THEN
              RESULT = NUM1 + NUM2
              PRINT *, 'THE SUM OF THE ENTERED NUMBERS IS ', RESULT
           ELSEIF (CODE .EQ. 2) THEN
              RESULT = NUM1 * NUM2
              PRINT *, 'THE PRODUCT OF THE ENTERED NUMBERS IS ', RESULT
           ELSEIF (CODE .EQ. 3) THEN
              RESULT = NUM1/NUM2
```

```
          PRINT *, 'THE FIRST NUMBER DIVIDED BY THE SECOND IS ', RESULT
        ELSE
          PRINT *, 'AN INCORRECT CALCULATION CODE WAS ENTERED'
        ENDIF
        END
```

3a.

```
      PROGRAM MAIN
       REAL ANGLE
       PRINT *, 'ENTER AN ANGLE BETWEEN O AND 360'
       READ *, ANGLE
       CALL QUAD(ANGLE)
       END
*
      SUBROUTINE QUAD(ANGLE)
       REAL ANGLE
       IF (ANGLE .GT. 0.0 .AND. ANGLE .LT. 90.0) THEN
         PRINT *, ' THE ANGLE IS IN QUADRANT 1 '
       ELSEIF (ANGLE .GT. 90.0 .AND. ANGLE .LT .180.0) THEN
         PRINT *, ' THE ANGLE IS IN QUADRANT 2'
       ELSEIF (ANGLE .GT. 180.0 .AND. ANGLE .LT. 270.0) THEN
         PRINT *, ' THE ANGLE IS IN QUADRANT 3'
       ELSEIF (ANGLE .GT. 270.0 .AND. ANGLE .LT. 360.0) THEN
         PRINT *, ' THE ANGLE IS IN QUADRANT 4'
       ELSEIF (ANGLE .EQ. 0.0 .OR. ANGLE .EQ. 180.0 .OR.
     +         ANGLE .EQ. 360.0) THEN
         PRINT *, ' THE ANGLE IS ON THE X AXIS'
       ELSEIF (ANGLE .EQ. 90.0 .OR. ANGLE .EQ. 270.0) THEN
         PRINT *, ' THE ANGLE IS ON THE Y AXIS'
       ELSE
         PRINT *, ' THE ANGLE ENTERED IS NOT BETWEEN 0 AND 360'
          PRINT *, '  DEGREES'
       ENDIF
       END
```

5.

```
      PROGRAM MAIN
       INTEGER YEAR
       REAL WEIGHT
       PRINT *, 'ENTER THE CAR''S YEAR AND WEIGHT: '
       READ *, YEAR, WEIGHT
       CALL FECLSS(YEAR,WEIGHT)
       END
*
      SUBROUTINE FECLSS(YEAR, WEIGHT)
       INTEGER YEAR, WTCLSS
       REAL WEIGHT
       IF (YEAR .LE. 1970) THEN
         IF (WEIGHT .LT. 2700.0) THEN
           FEE = 16.50
           WTCLSS = 1
         ELSEIF (WEIGHT .LE. 3800.0) THEN
           FEE = 25.50
           WTCLSS = 2
         ELSE
           FEE = 46.50
           WTCLSS = 3
         ENDIF
       ELSEIF (YEAR .LE. 1979) THEN
         IF (WEIGHT .LT. 2700.0) THEN
           FEE = 27.00
           WTCLSS = 4
         ELSEIF (WEIGHT .LE. 3800.0) THEN
```

```
                  FEE = 30.50
                  WTCLSS = 5
                ELSE
                  FEE = 52.50
                  WTCLSS = 6
                ENDIF
              ELSE
                IF (WEIGHT .LT. 3500.0) THEN
                  FEE = 19.50
                  WTCLSS = 7
                ELSE
                  FEE = 52.50
                  WTCLSS = 8
                ENDIF
              ENDIF
              PRINT 10, WTCLSS
              PRINT 20, FEE
10            FORMAT(1X,'THE WEIGHT CLASS IS ',I1)
20            FORMAT(1X,'THE REGISTRATION FEE IS $ ',F5.2)
              END
```

Chapter 5 - Repetition

Section 5.1

1.
```
        PROGRAM MAIN
          INTEGER COUNT
          COUNT = 2
5       IF (COUNT .LE. 10) THEN
            PRINT *, COUNT
            COUNT = COUNT + 2
            GO TO 5
          ENDIF
          END
```

3a. Twenty-one numbers are printed. The first number printed is 1 and the last number printed is 21.

5.
```
        PROGRAM MAIN
          CALL CONVER
          END
*
        SUBROUTINE CONVER
          INTEGER FEET
          REAL METER
          PRINT *, 'FEET    METERS'
          PRINT *, '----    ------'
          FEET = 3
10      IF(FEET .LE. 30) THEN
            METER = FEET / 3.28
            PRINT 20, FEET, METER
            FEET = FEET + 3
            GO TO 10
          ENDIF
20        FORMAT(1X,I3,4X,F5.2)
          END
```

7.

```
      PROGRAM MAIN
       CALL TRAVEL
       END
*
      SUBROUTINE TRAVEL
       REAL HOURS, DIST
       HOURS = 0.5
       PRINT *, 'HOURS   DISTANCE'
       PRINT *, '-----   --------'
  10   IF (HOURS .LE. 4.0) THEN
          DIST = 55.0 * HOURS
          PRINT 20, HOURS, DIST
          HOURS = HOURS + 0.5
          GO TO 10
       ENDIF
  20   FORMAT(1X,F4.1,5X,F6.2)
       END
```

9.

```
      PROGRAM MAIN
       CALL EULER
       END
*
      SUBROUTINE EULER
       REAL E, DENOM, OLDVAL, NEWVAL
       DENOM = 1
       NUM = 1
       OLDVAL = 1
       NEWVAL = 2
  10   IF (ABS(OLDVAL - NEWVAL) .GE. 10E-7) THEN
          NUM = NUM + 1
          DENOM = DENOM*NUM
          OLDVAL = NEWVAL
          NEWVAL = NEWVAL + 1.0/DENOM
          GO TO 10
       ENDIF
       PRINT *, 'THE APPROXIMATE VALUE OF E IS ', NEWVAL
       END
```

Section 5.2

1. The only modification required is to change the 4 to an 8 in the block IF statement.

3. The program yields the correct result. The recomputation of a new average for each number, however, is unnecessary, as it is only the last average that has any meaning. Thus, the average should only be computed once, after the final total has been computed.

5.

```
      PROGRAM MAIN
       INTEGER COUNT, TOTNUM
       REAL NUM, TOTAL, AVERGE
*
       PRINT *, 'THIS PROGRAM WILL ASK YOU TO ENTER SOME NUMBERS.'
       PRINT *, 'PLEASE TYPE IN THE TOTAL NUMBER OF DATA VALUES'
       PRINT *, ' TO BE AVERAGED'
       READ *, TOTNUM
```

```
        COUNT = 1
        TOTAL = 0
10      IF (COUNT .LE. TOTNUM) THEN
           PRINT *, 'ENTER A NUMBER: '
           READ *,  NUM
           TOTAL = TOTAL + NUM
           COUNT = COUNT + 1
           GO TO 10
        ENDIF
        COUNT = COUNT - 1
        AVERGE = TOTAL / COUNT
        PRINT *, 'THE AVERAGE OF THE NUMBERS IS ', AVERGE
        END
```

7a.

```
        PROGRAM MAIN
         REAL NUM, MAX
         INTEGER COUNT
         PRINT *, 'THIS PROGRAM WILL ASK YOU TO ENTER 10 NUMBERS'
         MAX = -1E20
         COUNT = 1
10       IF (COUNT .LE. 10) THEN
            PRINT *, 'ENTER NUMBER ', COUNT
            READ *, NUM
            IF (NUM .GT. MAX) MAX = NUM
            COUNT = COUNT + 1
            GO TO 10
         ENDIF
         PRINT *, 'THE MAXIMUM VALUE ENTERED WAS ', MAX
         END
```

9a.

```
        PROGRAM MAIN
         INTEGER COUNT
         REAL STARTM, NEWMIL, GALONS, MPG
         PRINT *, 'ENTER THE STARTING MILEAGE'
         READ *, STARTM
         PRINT *, 'THIS PROGRAM WILL NOW ASK YOU TO ENTER 8 MILEAGE'
         PRINT *, ' AND 8 GALLON VALUES'
         COUNT = 1
10       IF (COUNT .LE. 8) THEN
            PRINT *, 'ENTER A NEW MILEAGE FIGURE AND GALLONS USED'
            READ *, NEWMIL, GALONS
            MILES = NEWMIL - STARTM
            MPG = MILES / GALONS
            PRINT *, 'THE MILES/GALLON IS ', MPG
            STARTM = NEWMIL
            COUNT = COUNT + 1
            GO TO 10
         ENDIF
         END
```

11a.
```
        PROGRAM MAIN
        REAL FAHREN, VAL, SVAL, EVAL, INC
        PRINT *, 'PLEASE ENTER THE STARTING AND ENDING VALUES'
        READ *, SVAL, EVAL
        IF (SVAL .GT. EVAL) THEN
           PRINT *, 'THE STARTING VALUE MUST BE GREATER THAN'
           PRINT *, 'THE ENDING VALUE'
           STOP
        ENDIF
        PRINT *, 'PLEASE ENTER THE INCREMENT'
        READ *, INC
        IF (INC .LT. 0) THEN
           PRINT *, 'THE INCREMENT MUST BE POSITIVE'
           STOP
        ENDIF
        PRINT *, 'CELSIUS        FAHRENHEIT'
        PRINT *, '-------        ----------'
        VAL = SVAL
10      IF (VAL .LE. EVAL) THEN
           FAHREN = (9.0/5.0) * VAL + 32.0
           PRINT 20, VAL, FAHREN
           VAL = VAL + INC
           GO TO 10
        ENDIF
20      FORMAT(1X,F7.2,5X,F7.2)
        END
```

Section 5.3

1 For each of these DO statements, the statement label 10 may be
replaced by any integer from 1 to 99999.

a. DO 10 I = 1, 20   or   DO 10 I = 1, 20, 1
b. DO 10 ICOUNT = 1, 20 , 2
c. DO 10 J = 1, 100, 5
d. DO 10 ICOUNT = 20, 1, -1
e. DO 10 ICOUNT = 20, 1, -2
f. DO 10 COUNT = 1.0, 16.2, 0.2
g. DO 10 XCNT = 20.0, 10.0, -0.5

3a. 55
 b. 1024
 c. 75
 d. -5
 e. 40320
 f. .031250

5. The following output is produced by the program:
```
        20
        16
        12
         8
         4
         0
```

7.
```
      PROGRAM MAIN
       INTEGER NUM
       PRINT *, '         NUMBER      SQUARE      CUBE'
       PRINT *, '         ------      ------      ----'
       DO 30 NUM = 10,1,-1
          PRINT*, NUM, NUM**2, NUM**3
  30     CONTINUE
         END
```

9.
```
      PROGRAM MAIN
       CALL EXPAND
       END
      SUBROUTINE EXPAND
       REAL COEFEX, INLEN, INTEMP, TEMP, INCLEN
       COEFEX = 11.7E-6
       INLEN = 7365.0
       INTEMP = 0.0
       PRINT *,' TEMPERATURE          EXPANSION'
       PRINT *,'(DEG. CELSIUS)        (METERS)'
       PRINT *,'--------------        ---------'
       DO 10 TEMP = 0.0, 40.0, 5.0
          INCLEN = COEFEX * INLEN * (TEMP -INTEMP)
          PRINT 20, TEMP, INCLEN
  10     CONTINUE
  20     FORMAT(5X,F4.1,14X,F7.4)
         END
```

11a.
```
      PROGRAM MAIN
       CALL ARIVAL
       END
*
      SUBROUTINE ARIVAL
       INTEGER X
       REAL AVARVL, PROBX
       PRINT *,'CUSTOMERS          PROBABILITY'
       PRINT *,'---------          -----------'
       AVARVL = 3.0
       DENOM = 1
       DO 10 X = 0, 20
          PROBX = AVARVL**(X) * EXP(-AVARVL) / DENOM
          PRINT 20, X, PROBX
          DENOM = DENOM * (X+1)
  10     CONTINUE
  20     FORMAT(1X,I5,12X,F8.6)
         END
```

Section 5.4

1.
```
      PROGRAM MAIN
* THIS PROGRAM DISPLAYS A TABLE OF NUMBERS, THEIR SQUARE AND CUBE
* ROOTS. THE STARTING NUMBER, FINAL NUMBER, AND INCREMENT BETWEEN
* NUMBERS IS DECIDED BY THE USER
         REAL NUM, IFINAL, IBEGIN, INC
         PRINT *, 'ENTER THE STARTING NUMBER FOR THE TABLE'
         READ *, IBEGIN
         PRINT *, 'ENTER THE FINAL NUMBER'
         READ *, IFINAL
         PRINT *, 'ENTER THE INCREMENT'
         READ *, INC
```

```
          IF (IBEGIN .LT. IFINAL .AND. INC .LT. 0.0) THEN
             PRINT *, 'INCREMENT MUST BE POSITIVE FOR THIS'
             PRINT *, 'COMBINATION OF INITIAL AND FINAL VALUES'
          ELSEIF (IBEGIN .GT. IFINAL .AND. INC .GT. 0.0) THEN
             PRINT *, 'INCREMENT MUST BE NEGATIVE FOR THIS'
             PRINT *, 'COMBINATION OF INITIAL AND FINAL VALUES'
          ELSE
             PRINT *, ' NUMBER            SQUARE                CUBE'
             PRINT *, ' ------            ------                ----'
             DO 30, NUM = IBEGIN, IFINAL, INC
                PRINT 40, NUM, NUM**2, NUM**3
   30        CONTINUE
          ENDIF
   40     FORMAT(1X,F7.2,2X,F14.2,2X,F21.2)
          END
```

3a.
```
          PROGRAM MAIN
          INTEGER YEARS
          REAL AMOUNT, RATE
          PRINT *, 'PLEASE ENTER THE INITIAL AMOUNT DEPOSITED'
          READ *, AMOUNT
          PRINT *, 'YEAR          AMOUNT'
          PRINT *, '----          ---------'
          RATE = 0.08
          DO 10 YEARS = 1, 10
             AMOUNT = AMOUNT*(1.0 + RATE)
             PRINT 20, YEARS, AMOUNT
   10     CONTINUE
   20     FORMAT(1X,I3,7X,'$',F8.2)
          END
```

5.
```
          PROGRAM MAIN
          INTEGER I
          REAL GALONS, LITERS
          PRINT *, 'THIS PROGRAM WILL ASK YOU TO ENTER 10 VALUES'
          PRINT *, 'WHERE EACH VALUE REPRESENTS A GALLON AMOUNT'
          PRINT *
          DO 50 I = 1, 10
             PRINT *, 'ENTER GALLON AMOUNT ', I
             READ *, GALONS
             LITERS = 3.785 * GALONS
             PRINT 100, LITERS
   50     CONTINUE
  100     FORMAT(1X,'THE EQUIVALENT LITER AMOUNT IS ',F8.3,/)
          END
```

7.
```
          PROGRAM MAIN
* THIS PROGRAM COMPUTES THE POSITIVE AND NEGATIVE SUMS OF A SET
* OF USER ENTERED NUMBERS
          INTEGER I, NUMS
          REAL USENUM, POSTOT, NEGTOT
          POSTOT = 0
          NEGTOT = 0
          PRINT *, 'ENTER HOW MANY NUMBERS ARE TO BE ADDED:'
          READ *, NUMS
          DO 10 I = 1, NUMS
             PRINT *, 'ENTER A NUMBER (POSITIVE OR NEGATIVE): '
             READ *, USENUM
             IF (USENUM .GT. O) THEN
                POSTOT = POSTOT + USENUM
```

```
         ELSE
            NEGTOT = NEGTOT + USENUM
         ENDIF
10       CONTINUE
         PRINT *,' THE POSITIVE TOTAL IS ', POSTOT
         PRINT *,' THE NEGATIVE TOTAL IS ', NEGTOT
         END
```

9a.
```
         PROGRAM MAIN
         REAL VAL, MAX
         PRINT *, 'THIS PROGRAM WILL ASK YOU TO ENTER FIVE NUMBERS'
         PRINT *
         MAX = -1E9
         DO 10 I = 1, 5
            PRINT *, 'ENTER NUMBER ', I
            READ *, VAL
            IF (VAL .GT. MAX) MAX = VAL
10       CONTINUE
         PRINT *, 'THE MAXIMUM NUMBER ENTERED IS ', VAL
         END
```

11.
```
         PROGRAM MAIN
         INTEGER MONTH
         REAL POP, TIME, INC
         PRINT *, 'DATE         EST. POPULATION'
         PRINT *, '-----        ----------------'
         INC = 1.0/12.0
         MONTH = 0
         DO 200 TIME = 5.0, 6, INC
            POP = 4.88 * ( 1.0 + EXP(0.02*TIME) )
            MONTH = MONTH + 1
            PRINT 300, MONTH, POP
200      CONTINUE
300      FORMAT(1X,I2,'/90',10X,F7.3)
         END
```

Section 5.5

1.
```
         PROGRAM MAIN
         INTEGER EXPER, RESULT
         REAL VALUE, TOTAL, AVERGE
         DO 200 EXPER = 1, 4
            PRINT *
            PRINT *, 'ENTER THE RESULTS OF EXPERIMENT NUMBER ', EXPER
            PRINT *, 'AS THEY ARE CALLED FOR.'
            TOTAL = 0.0
            DO 100 RESULT = 1, 6
               PRINT *, '  ENTER RESULT NUMBER ', RESULT
               READ *, VALUE
               TOTAL = TOTAL + VALUE
100         CONTINUE
            AVERGE = TOTAL / 6.0
            PRINT *, 'THE AVERAGE FOR EXPERIMENT NUMBER ', EXPER
            PRINT *, ' IS ', AVERGE
200      CONTINUE
         END
```

3a.
```
      PROGRAM MAIN
       INTEGER BOWLER, GAME
       REAL SCORE, TOTAL, AVERGE
       DO 200 BOWLER = 1, 5
         PRINT *
         PRINT *, 'ENTER THE SCORES FOR BOWLER NUMBER ', BOWLER
         PRINT *, 'AS THEY ARE CALLED FOR.'
         TOTAL = 0.0
         DO 100 GAME = 1, 3
           PRINT *, '  ENTER SCORE FOR GAME NUMBER ', GAME
           READ *, SCORE
           TOTAL = TOTAL + SCORE
 100     CONTINUE
         AVERGE = TOTAL / 3.0
         PRINT *, 'THE AVERAGE FOR BOWLER NUMBER ', BOWLER
         PRINT *, ' IS ', AVERGE
 200   CONTINUE
       END
```

5.
```
      PROGRAM MAIN
       CALL FUNCTN
       END
*
      SUBROUTINE FUNCTN
       REAL X, Y, Z
       PRINT *, 'X VALUE   Z VALUE    Y VALUE'
       PRINT *, '-------   -------    -------'
       DO 100 X = 1.0, 5.0, 1.0
         DO 50 Z = 2.0, 10.0, 2.0
           IF (ABS(X-Z) .LE. 0.00001) THEN
             PRINT 200, X, Y
           ELSE
             Y = X * Z / (X - Z)
             PRINT 210, X, Z, Y
           ENDIF
 50      CONTINUE
 100   CONTINUE
 200   FORMAT(1X,F5.2,6X,F5.2,3X,'FUNCTION UNDEFINED')
 210   FORMAT(1X,F5.2,6X,F5.2,3X,F8.3)
       END
```

Section 5.6

1b.
```
      PROGRAM MAIN
       CALL GRDVAL
       END
*
      SUBROUTINE GRDVAL
       REAL GRADE
 100     PRINT *, 'ENTER A GRADE'
         READ *, GRADE
         IF (GRADE .LT. 0.0 .OR. GRADE .GT. 100.0) THEN
           PRINT *, 'AN INVALID GRADE HAS BEEN ENTERED'
           PRINT *, 'PLEASE REENTER THE GRADE'
           GO TO 100
         ENDIF
       END
```

3a.
```
       PROGRAM MAIN
         INTEGER NUM
         PRINT *, 'PLEASE ENTER ANY INTEGER NUMBER'
         READ *, NUM
         CALL REVERS(NUM)
         END
*
       SUBROUTINE REVERS(NUM)
         INTEGER NUM, NEWNUM
         NEWNUM = 0
  100      DIGIT = MOD(NUM,10)
           NUM = NUM / 10
           NEWNUM = NEWNUM * 10 + DIGIT
         IF (NUM .NE. O) GO TO 100
         PRINT *, 'THE NUMBER, IN REVERSE DIGIT ORDER, IS ', NEWNUM
         END
```

Chapter Six - Arrays

Section 6.1

1a. REAL VOLTS(100)
 b. REAL TEMPS(50)
 c. CHARACTER CODE(30)
 d. INTEGER YEARS(100)
 e. REAL VELOCY(32)
 f. REAL DISTNC(100)
 g. INTEGER CODE(6)

3a. READ *, GRADES(1), GRADES(3), GRADES(7)
 b. READ *, VOLTS(1), VOLTS(3), VOLTS(7)
 c. READ *, AMPS(1), AMPS(3), AMPS(7)
 d. READ * DIST(1), DIST(3), DIST(7)
 e. READ *, VELOC(1), VELOC(3), VELOC(7)
 f. READ *, TIME(1), TIME(3), TIME(7)

5a. A(1)
    A(3)
    A(5)

b. B(3)
   B(6)
   B(9)

c. A(1) A(2) A(3) A(4) A(5)

d. B(3) B(6) B(9) B(12)

e. C(2) C(4) C(6) C(8) C(10)

7a.
```
       PROGRAM ARRAY
         INTEGER I
         REAL VOLTS(9)
         DO 100 I = 1,9
           PRINT *, 'ENTER ARRAY ELEMENT NO. ', I
           READ *, VOLTS(I)
```

```
100      CONTINUE
         DO 200 I = 1,9
           PRINT *, VOLTS(I)
200      CONTINUE
         END
```

  b.
```
         PROGRAM ARRAY
          INTEGER I
          REAL VOLTS(9)
          DO 100 I = 1,9
            PRINT *, 'ENTER ARRAY ELEMENT NO. ', I
            READ *, VOLTS(I)
100       CONTINUE
          PRINT 10, (VOLTS(I), I = 1,3)
          PRINT 10, (VOLTS(I), I = 4,6)
          PRINT 10, (VOLTS(I), I = 7,9)
  10      FORMAT(3(2X,F5.2))
          END
```

9.
```
         PROGRAM FNDMAX
          INTEGER I
          REAL FMAX(10), THEMAX
          THEMAX = 0.0
          DO 100, I = 1,10
            PRINT *, 'ENTER ARRAY ELEMENT NO. ', I
            READ *, FMAX(I)
            IF (FMAX(I) .GT. THEMAX) THEMAX = FMAX(I)
100       CONTINUE
          PRINT *, 'THE MAXIMUM VALUE ENTERED IS ', THEMAX
          END
```

11.
```
         PROGRAM CVOLTS
          INTEGER I
          REAL VOLTS(10), CURRNT(10), RESIST(10)
          DO 10 I = 1, 10
            PRINT *, 'ENTER CURRENT AND RESISTANCE NUMBER ', I
            READ *, CURRNT(I), RESIST(I)
            VOLTS(I) = CURRNT(I) * RESIST(I)
  10      CONTINUE
          PRINT *, '          VOLTAGE        CURRENT        RESISTANCE'
          PRINT *, '          -------        -------        ----------'
          DO 20, I = 1, 10
            PRINT *, VOLTS(I), CURRNT(I), RESIST(I)
  20      CONTINUE
          END
```

Section 6.2

```
1a.   INTEGER GRADES(10
      DATA GRADES /89,75,82,93,78,95,81,88,77,82/

 b.   REAL AMOUNT(5)
      DATA AMOUNT /10.62,13.98,18.45,12.68,14.76/

 c.   REAL RATES(100)
      DATA (RATES(I), I = 1,6) /6.29, 6.95, 7.25, 7.35, 7.42/

 d.   REAL TEMPS(64)
      DATA (TEMPS(I), I = 1,4) /78.2, 69.6, 68.5, 83.9/

 e.   CHARACTER CODES(15)
      DATA (CODES(I), I = 1,7) / 'G', 'K', 'M', 'Q', 'R', 'W', 'X' /
```

3.
```
      PROGRAM MAXMIN
       INTEGER I
       REAL SLOPES(9), MAXSLP, MINSLP
       DATA SLOPES / 17.24,25.63,5.94,33.92,3.71,32.84,35.93
      +             ,18.24,6.92/
       MAXSLP = SLOPES(1)
       MINSLP = SLOPES(1)
       DO 10 I = 2, 9
         IF (SLOPES(I) .GT. MAXSLP) MAXSLP = SLOPES(I)
         IF (SLOPES(I) .LT. MINSLP) MINSLP = SLOPES(I)
 10    CONTINUE
       PRINT *, 'THE MAXIMUM SLOPE IS ', MAXSLP
       PRINT *, 'THE MINIMUM SLOPE IS ', MINSLP
       END
```

5b.
```
      PROGRAM DISPLY
       INTEGER I
       CHARACTER*26 MESSGE(4)
       DATA MESSGE /' INPUT THE FOLLOWING DATA ',
      +            '--------------------------',
      +            'ENTER THE DATE:           ',
      +            'ENTER THE ACCOUNT NUMBER: '/
       DO 10, I = 1,4
         PRINT *, MESSGE(I)
 10    CONTINUE
       END
```

Section 6.3

```
1a. INTEGER NUMS(6,10)
 b. INTEGER NUMS(2,5)
 c. CHARACTER CODES(7,12)
 d. CHARACTER CODES(15,7)
 e. REAL VALS(10,25)
 f. REAL VALS(16,8)
```

3a.

```
PROGRAM MAIN
 INTEGER I, J, VALS(3,4), TOTAL
 DATA VALS, TOTAL / 8,3,14,16,15,25,9,27,2,52,6,10,0/
 DO 10 I = 1,3
   DO 5 J = 1,4
     TOTAL = TOTAL + VALS(I,J)
 5   CONTINUE
10 CONTINUE
 PRINT *, 'THE TOTAL OF ALL ELEMENTS IS ', TOTAL
 END
```

5a.

```
PROGRAM FNDMAX
 INTEGER I, J, NUMS(4,5), FMAX
 DATA NUMS/16,22,99,4,18,-258,4,101,5,98,105,6,15,2,
+          45,33,88,72,16,3/
 FMAX = NUMS(1,1)
 DO 10 I = 1,4
   DO 10 J = 1,5
     IF( NUMS(I,J) .GT. FMAX ) FMAX = NUMS(I,J)
10   CONTINUE
 PRINT *, 'THE MAXIMUM VALUE IS ', FMAX
 END
```

7a.

```
PROGRAM TGRADE
 INTEGER I, J, GLSS60, G6070, G7080, G8090, G90100
 REAL GRADE(3,5)
 DATA GLSS60, G6070, G7080, G8090, G90100 /5*0/
 PRINT *, 'ENTER ALL FIFTEEN GRADES ON ONE LINE'
 READ *, GRADE
 DO 10 I = 1,3
   DO 10 J=1,5
     IF (GRADE(I,J) .LT. 60) THEN
       GLSS60 = GLSS60 + 1
     ELSE IF (GRADE(I,J) .LT. 70) THEN
       G6070 = G6070 + 1
     ELSE IF (GRADE(I,J) .LT. 80) THEN
       G7080 = G7080 + 1
     ELSE IF (GRADE(I,J) .LT. 90) THEN
       G8090 = G8090 + 1
     ELSE
       G90100 = G90100 + 1
     ENDIF
10   CONTINUE
 PRINT *, GLSS60, ' GRADES LESS THAN 60'
 PRINT *, G6070, ' GRADES BETWEEN 60 AND 70'
 PRINT *, G7080, ' GRADES BETWEEN 70 AND 80'
 PRINT *, G8090, ' GRADES BETWEEN 80 AND 90'
 PRINT *, G90100, ' GRADES GREATER THAN 90'
 END
```

Section 6.4

3.

```
PROGRAM MAIN
 INTEGER X,Y
 CHARACTER LINE(72), YAXIS(72)
 DATA LINE/'|',71*' '/
 DATA YAXIS/'+',53*'-','',17*' '/
```

```
        PRINT *,'                         Y AXIS'
        PRINT *,YAXIS
        DO 10 X = 1,30
          Y =  60 * (1.0 - EXP(-X/(2500.5*0.005)))
          LINE(Y) = '*'
          PRINT *, LINE
          LINE(Y) = ' '
   10   CONTINUE
        END
```

5.

```
        PROGRAM MAIN
        REAL X
        INTEGER Y
        CHARACTER LINE(72), YAXIS(72)
        DATA LINE/'|',71*' '/
        DATA YAXIS/'+',53*'-','',17*' '/
        PRINT *,'                   Y AXIS'
        PRINT *,YAXIS
        DO 10 X = 1.0, 5.0, 0.25
          Y =  INT(X**3 - 4.0 * X**2 + 3.0 * X + 10.0)
          LINE(Y) = '*'
          PRINT *, LINE
          LINE(Y) = ' '
   10   CONTINUE
        END
```

7.

```
        PROGRAM MAIN
        INTEGER  I, NPTS, NVAL(100)
        REAL X, YMIN, YMAX, WIDTH, SVAL(100)
        CHARACTER LINE(72), YAXIS(72)
        DATA YAXIS/'+',70*'-',''/
        DATA LINE/'|',71*' '/
        DATA YMAX,YMIN /1E-5,1E5/
        X = 0.0
        XINC = 1.0
        NPTS = 61
        WIDTH = 70
*** LOAD UP THE DATA TO BE PLOTTED AND FIND THE MAX AND MIN VALUES
        DO 10 I = 1,NPTS
          SVAL(I) = 100 * COS( 3.1416/180.0 * X * SQRT(50.0) )
          IF (SVAL(I).GT.YMAX) YMAX = SVAL(I)
          IF (SVAL(I).LT.YMIN) YMIN = SVAL(I)
          X = X + XINC
   10   CONTINUE
*** SCALE ALL Y VALUES TO BE PLOTTED
        DO 15 I = 1, NPTS
          FVAL = ( (SVAL(I) - YMIN)/(YMAX - YMIN) ) * WIDTH
          NVAL(I) = INT(FVAL + .5)
   15   CONTINUE
*** PRODUCE THE PLOT
        PRINT *,'MINIMUM Y VALUE: ',YMIN
        PRINT *,'MAXIMUM Y VALUE: ',YMAX
        PRINT *,'                              Y AXIS'
        PRINT *,YAXIS
        DO 20 I = 1,NPTS
          LINE(NVAL(I)+2) = '*'
          PRINT *, LINE
          LINE(NVAL(I)+2) = ' '
   20   CONTINUE
        END
```

Chapter Seven - Modularity Using Functions

Section 7.1

1a.
```
PROGRAM MAIN
  REAL AMOUNT, RATE, INTRST, RNDINT
  RATE = .08765
  PRINT *, 'ENTER THE DOLLAR AMOUNT'
  READ *, AMOUNT
  INTRST = RATE * AMOUNT
  RNDINT = INT(INTRST * 100.0 + 0.5)/100.0
  PRINT *, 'THE INTEREST BEFORE ROUNDING IS', INTRST
  PRINT *, 'THE INTEREST AFTER ROUNDING IS', RNDINT
  END
```

3a.
```
PROGRAM TEST
  INTEGER NUMBER, I
  DO 5 I = 1, 10
    PRINT *, 'ENTER AN INTEGER NUMBER'
    READ *, NUMBER
    IF (MOD(NUMBER,2) .EQ. 0) THEN
      PRINT *, 'THE ENTERED NUMBER IS EVEN'
    ELSE
      PRINT *, 'THE ENTERED NUMBER IS ODD'
    ENDIF
5   CONTINUE
  END
```

Section 7.2

1a. The function expects one integer argument to be passed to it.
 b. The function must be passed three arguments in the order:
    one integer argument and two real arguments.
 c. The function must be passed three arguments in the order:
    one character argument and two real arguments.
 d. The function must be passed three arguments in the order:
    one character argument and two integer arguments.
 e. The function must be passed two real arguments.
 f. The function must be passed six arguments in the order:
    three integers, one character, and two real arguments.
 g. The function must be passed four arguments in the order:
    two character arguments, one real argument, one integer
    argument.
 h. The function must be passed one character argument.

3a. REAL ABNUM
 b. REAL ABNUM
 c. CHARACTER ABNUM
 d. INTEGER ABNUM

5.
```
PROGRAM MAIN
  INTEGER FIRNUM, SECNUM, THEMAX, FMAX
  PRINT *, 'ENTER AN INTEGER NUMBER: '
  READ *,  FIRNUM
  PRINT *, 'GREAT! PLEASE ENTER A SECOND INTEGER NUMBER: '
  READ *,  SECNUM
  THEMAX = FMAX(FIRNUM,SECNUM)
```
(Coninued on next page)

```
        PRINT *, 'THE MAXIMUM VALUE IS ', THEMAX
        END
* FOLLOWING IS THE FUNCTION FMAX
        INTEGER FUNCTION FMAX(X,Y)
         INTEGER X,Y
         IF (X .GT. Y) THEN
           FMAX = X
         ELSE
           FMAX = Y
         ENDIF
         RETURN
         END
```

7.
```
        PROGRAM TEST
         INTEGER CHECK, TEMP
         TEMP = CHECK(20,33.5,'AWAY')
         END
        INTEGER FUNCTION CHECK(INUM,RNUM,CH)
        INTEGER INUM
        REAL RNUM
        CHARACTER CH*4
        PRINT *, 'THE ARGUMENT VALUES RECEIVED ARE:'
        PRINT *, INUM, RNUM, CH
        END
```

9.
```
        PROGRAM TEST
         INTEGER TABLE, TEMP
         TEMP = TABLE()
         END
        INTEGER FUNCTION TABLE()
         INTEGER I
         PRINT *,'         NUMBER      SQUARE       CUBE'
         PRINT *,'         ------      ------       ----'
         DO 5 I = 1, 10
           PRINT *, I, I**2, I**3
     5    CONTINUE
         END
```

Section 7.3

1.
```
        PROGRAM MAIN
         INTEGER COUNT
         REAL FTOC, CTOF, INTEMP, TEMP
         CHARACTER TYPE
         FTOC(INTEMP) = 5.0 /9.0 * (INTEMP - 32.0)
         CTOF(INTEMP) = 9.0 / 5.0 * INTEMP + 32.0
         DO 10 COUNT = 1, 4
           PRINT *, 'ENTER A TEMPERATURE: '
           READ *, TEMP
           PRINT *, 'ENTER AN ''F'' IF THIS IS A FAHRENHEIT TEMP'
           PRINT *, ' OR AN ''C'' IF THIS IS A CELSIUS TEMPERATURE'
           READ *, TYPE
           IF(TYPE .EQ. 'F') THEN
             PRINT *, 'THE CELSIUS EQUIVALENT IS: ', FTOC(TEMP)
           ELSEIF (TYPE .EQ. 'C') THEN
             PRINT *, 'THE FAHRENHEIT EQUIVALENT IS: ', CTOF(TEMP)
           ELSE
             PRINT *, 'INCORRECT TEMPERATURE TYPE - PLEASE REDO'
           ENDIF
```

```
     10    CONTINUE
           END
```

3.
```
           PROGRAM TEST
             REAL SIDE1, SIDE2, SIDE3, HYPTNS
             HYPTNS(SIDE1,SIDE2) = SQRT(SIDE1**2 + SIDE2**2)
             PRINT *, 'ENTER THE VALUE OF TWO SIDES OF A TRIANGLE'
             READ *, SIDE1, SIDE2
             SIDE3 = HYPTNS(SIDE1,SIDE2)
             PRINT *, 'THE HYPOTENUSE IS ', SIDE3
           END
```

5.
```
           PROGRAM TEST
             REAL ABSDIF, NUM1, NUM2, A,B, TEMP
             ABSDIF(A,B) = ABS(A-B)
             PRINT *, 'ENTER ANY TWO NUMBERS'
             READ *, NUM1, NUM2
             TEMP = ABSDIF(NUM1,NUM2)
             PRINT *, 'THE ABSOLUTE DIFFERENCE OF THE NUMBERS IS', TEMP
           END
```

7.
```
           PROGRAM TEST
             REAL ROUND, XNUM, NUM
             ROUND(XNUM) = INT(XNUM * 100.0 + 0.5) / 100.0
             PRINT *, 'ENTER ANY REAL VALUED NUMBER'
             READ *, NUM
             NUM = ROUND(NUM)
             PRINT *, ' THE NUMBER, ROUNDED TO TWO DECIMAL PLACES IS', NUM
           END
```

Section 7.4

1.
```
           PROGRAM MAIN
***        PROGRAM TO SIMULATE THE TOSSING OF A COIN
             REAL SEED, X, RAND, FLIP, HEADS, TAILS, PERHD, PERTL
             INTEGER NUMS
             RAND(X) = 997.0 * X - INT(997.0 * X/1.E6) * 1.E6
             PRINT *, 'ENTER THE NUMBER OF COIN FLIPS TO BE MADE'
             READ *, NUMS
             PRINT *,'ENTER AN ODD 6 DIGIT NUMBER NOT ENDING IN 5: '
             READ *, SEED
             HEADS = 0.0
             TAILS = 0.0
***  SIMULATE 1000 TOSSES OF A COIN
             DO 10 I = 1,NUMS
               SEED = RAND(SEED)
               FLIP = SEED / 1.E6
               IF (FLIP .GT. 0.5) THEN
                 HEADS = HEADS + 1
               ELSE
                 TAILS = TAILS + 1
               ENDIF
     10      CONTINUE
***  CALCULATE THE PERCENTAGE OF HEADS
             PERHD = (HEADS / NUMS) * 100.0
***  CALCULATE THE PERCENTAGE OF TAILS
             PERTL = (TAILS / NUMS) * 100.0
             PRINT *, 'HEADS CAME UP ', PERHD, ' PERCENT OF THE TIME.'
```

```
                   PRINT *, 'TAILS CAME UP ', PERTL, ' PERCENT OF THE TIME.'
                   END

3a.
                PROGRAM MAIN
***         GUESSING GAME
                REAL SEED
                INTEGER NUM, GUESS
                RAND(X) = 997.0 * X - INT(997.0 * X/1.E6) * 1.E6
                   PRINT *,'ENTER AN ODD 6 DIGIT NUMBER NOT ENDING IN 5: '
                READ *, SEED
*** GENERATE A RANDOM NUMBER BETWEEN 0 AND 1
                   SEED = RAND(SEED)/1.E6
*** SCALE THE NUMBER TO RESIDE BETWEEN 1 AND 100
                   NUM = 1 + INT(SEED*100)
                PRINT *, 'I HAVE A NUMBER IN MIND - YOU HAVE'
                PRINT *, 'SEVEN TRIES TO GUESS THE NUMBER'
                DO 10 I = 1, 7
                   PRINT *, 'YOU NOW HAVE', 8-I, ' GUESSES'
                   PRINT *, 'ENTER GUESS NUMBER ', I
                   READ *, GUESS
                   IF (GUESS .EQ. NUM) THEN
                      PRINT *, 'HOORAY! YOU WIN'
                      STOP
                   ELSEIF (GUESS .LT. NUM) THEN
                      PRINT *, 'YOUR GUESS IS TOO LOW'
                   ELSE
                      PRINT *, 'YOUR GUESS IS TOO HIGH'
                   ENDIF
10              CONTINUE
                PRINT *
                PRINT *,'SORRY - YOU LOSE'
                PRINT *,'THE CORRECT NUMBER WAS ',NUM
                PRINT *,'BETTER LUCK NEXT TIME!'
                END


5.
                PROGRAM TEST
                REAL ANGLE
                INTEGER TEMP, QUAD
                PRINT *, 'ENTER AN ANGLE BETWEEN 0 AND 360'
                READ *, ANGLE
                TEMP = QUAD(ANGLE)
                IF (TEMP .LE. 4) THEN
                   PRINT *, ' THE ANGLE IS IN QUADRANT ', TEMP
                ELSEIF (TEMP .EQ. 5) THEN
                   PRINT *, 'THE ANGLE IS ON THE X AXIS'
                ELSEIF (TEMP .EQ. 6) THEN
                   PRINT *, 'THE ANGLE IS ON THE Y AXIS'
                ELSE
                   PRINT *, ' AN INCORRECT ANGLE WAS ENTERED'
                ENDIF
                END
                INTEGER FUNCTION QUAD(ANGLE)
*** THIS FUNCTION RETURNS THE QUADRANT OF THE PASSED ANGLE
*** QUAD = 1 FOR ANGLES BETWEEN 0 AND 90
*** QUAD = 2 FOR ANGLES BETWEEN 90 AND 180
*** QUAD = 3 FOR ANGLES BETWEEN 180 AND 270
*** QUAD = 4 FOR ANGLES BETWEEN 270 AND 360
*** QUAD = 5 IF THE ANGLE IS ON THE X AXIS
*** QUAD = 6 IF THE ANGLE IS ON THE Y AXIS
*** QUAD = 7 FOR AN ANGLE OUTSIDE OF THE LIMITS 0 TO 360
                REAL ANGLE
```

(Coninued on next page)

```
        IF (ANGLE .GT. 0.0 .AND. ANGLE .LT. 90.0) THEN
          QUAD = 1
        ELSEIF (ANGLE .GT. 90.0 .AND. ANGLE .LT .180.0) THEN
          QUAD = 2
        ELSEIF (ANGLE .GT. 180.0 .AND. ANGLE .LT. 270.0) THEN
          QUAD = 3
        ELSEIF (ANGLE .GT. 270.0 .AND. ANGLE .LT. 360.0) THEN
          QUAD = 4
        ELSEIF (ANGLE .EQ. 0.0 .OR. ANGLE .EQ. 180.0 .OR.
      +         ANGLE .EQ. 360.0) THEN
          QUAD = 5
        ELSEIF (ANGLE .EQ. 90.0 .OR. ANGLE .EQ. 270.0) THEN
          QUAD = 6
        ELSE
          QUAD = 7
        ENDIF
        END
```

7.

```
        PROGRAM TEST
        INTEGER YEAR
        REAL WEIGHT, TEMP, FEE
        PRINT *, 'ENTER THE CAR''S YEAR AND WEIGHT (IN LBS.): '
        READ *, YEAR, WEIGHT
        TEMP = FEE(YEAR,WEIGHT)
        PRINT 10, TEMP
10      FORMAT(1X,'THE REGISTRATION FEE IS $ ',F5.2)
        END
*
        REAL FUNCTION FEE(YEAR, WEIGHT)
        INTEGER YEAR
        REAL WEIGHT, AMT(8)
        DATA AMT /16.50,25.50,46.50,27.00,30.50,52.50,19.50,52.50/
        IF (YEAR .LE. 1970) THEN
          IF (WEIGHT .LT. 2700.0) THEN
            FEE = AMT(1)
          ELSEIF (WEIGHT .LE. 3800.0) THEN
            FEE = AMT(2)
          ELSE
            FEE = AMT(3)
          ENDIF
        ELSEIF (YEAR .LE. 1979) THEN
          IF (WEIGHT .LT. 2700.0) THEN
            FEE = AMT(4)
          ELSEIF (WEIGHT .LE. 3800.0) THEN
            FEE = AMT(5)
          ELSE
            FEE = AMT(6)
          ENDIF
        ELSE
          IF (WEIGHT .LT. 3500.0) THEN
            FEE = AMT(7)
          ELSE
            FEE = AMT(8)
          ENDIF
        ENDIF
        END
```

Chapter Eight - Subroutines Revisited

Section 8.1

1a. ```
     SUBROUTINE TEST(EXPER)   CALL TEST(VALUE)
       REAL EXPER
     ```

  b.  ```
      SUBROUTINE MINUTE(TIME)        CALL MINUTE(SECOND)
        INTEGER TIME
      ```

  c. ```
      SUBROUTINE KEY(CODE)   CALL KEY(CODE)
        CHARACTER CODE
      ```

  d.  ```
      SUBROUTINE YIELD(INTRST,N)     CALL YIELD(RATE,YEARS)
        REAL INTRST
        INTEGER N
      ```

  e. ```
      SUBROUTINE RAND(SEED,RANDNO)   CALL RAND(SEED,RVAL)
        REAL SEED, RANDNO
      ```

3b.
```
PROGRAM TEST
  INTEGER AMOUNT, QUART, DIMES, NICKEL, PENNY
  CALL CHANGE(93, QUART, DIMES, NICKEL, PENNY)
  PRINT *, QUART, DIMES, NICKEL, PENNY
  END
SUBROUTINE CHANGE(AMOUNT, QUART, DIMES, NICKEL, PENNY)
  INTEGER AMOUNT, TEMP, QUART, DIMES, NICKEL, PENNY
  QUART = INT(AMOUNT/25)
  TEMP = AMOUNT - QUART * 25
  DIMES = INT(TEMP/10)
  TEMP = TEMP - DIMES * 10
  NICKEL = INT(TEMP/5)
  PENNY = TEMP - NICKEL * 5
  END
```

5b.
```
PROGRAM TEST
  INTEGER HOURS, MIN, SEC
  CALL TIME(72345, HOURS, MIN, SEC)
  PRINT *, HOURS, MIN, SEC
  END
SUBROUTINE TIME(TOTSEC, HOURS, MIN, SEC)
  INTEGER TOTSEC, HOURS, MIN, SEC, TEMP
  HOURS = INT(TOTSEC/3600)
  TEMP = TOTSEC - HOURS * 3600
  MIN = INT(TEMP/60)
  SEC = TEMP - MIN * 60
  END
```

7b.
```
PROGRAM TEST
  INTEGER TOTCUP, GALONS, QUARTS, PINTS, CUPS
  TOTCUP =   261
  CALL LIQUID(TOTCUP, GALONS, QUARTS, PINTS, CUPS)
  PRINT *, GALONS, QUARTS, PINTS, CUPS
  END
SUBROUTINE LIQUID(TOTCUP, GALONS, QUARTS, PINTS, CUPS)
  INTEGER TOTCUP, GALONS, QUARTS, PINTS, CUPS, TEMP
  GALONS = INT(TOTCUP/16)
```
```

```
       TEMP = TOTCUP - GALONS * 16
       QUARTS = INT(TEMP/4)
       TEMP = TEMP - QUARTS * 4
       PINTS = INT(TEMP/2)
       CUPS = TEMP - PINTS * 2
       END
```

9b.

```
       PROGRAM TEST
        INTEGER MONTH, DAY, YEAR
        CALL DATE(901116, MONTH, DAY, YEAR)
        PRINT 10, MONTH, DAY, YEAR
   10   FORMAT(1X,I2,'/',I2,'/',I2)
        END
       SUBROUTINE DATE(DAYS, MONTH, DAY, YEAR)
        INTEGER DAYS, MONTH, DAY, YEAR, REMDAY
        YEAR = INT(DAYS/10000)
        REMDAY = DAYS - YEAR * 10000
        MONTH = INT(REMDAY/100)
        DAY = REMDAY - MONTH*100
        END
```

Section 8.2

1. ```
   SUBROUTINE SORTAR(INARRY)          or     SUBROUTINE SORTAR(INARRY)
       INTEGER INARRY(500)                       INTEGER INARRY(*)
   ```

3. ```
   SUBROUTINE POWER(WATTS)            or     SUBROUTINE POWER(WATTS)
       REAL WATTS(140)                           REAL WATTS(*)
   ```

5.

```
       PROGRAM MAIN
        REAL GRADES(9)
        DATA GRADES /65.3,72.5,75.0,83.2,86.5,94.0,96.0,98.9,100.0/
        CALL SHOW(GRADES)
        END
       SUBROUTINE SHOW(GRADES)
        REAL GRADES(*)
        INTEGER I, NUMEL
        NUMEL = 9
        PRINT *, 'THE GRADES IN THE ARRAY ARE:'
        PRINT *,  (GRADES(I), I = 1, NUMEL)
        END
```

7.

```
       PROGRAM MAIN
        INTEGER I
        REAL CURRNT(10), RESIST(10), VOLTS(10)
        DATA CURRNT / 10.62, 14.89, 13.21, 16.55, 18.62, 9.47,
      +               6.58, 18.32, 12.15, 3.98 /
        DATA RESIST / 4.0, 8.5, 6.0, 7.35, 9.0, 15.3, 3.0,
      +               5.4, 2.9, 4.8 /
        CALL CALCV(CURRNT, RESIST, VOLTS)
        PRINT *,'THE VALUES IN THE ARRAY VOLTS ARE:'
        PRINT *, (VOLTS(I), I = 1, 10)
        END
       SUBROUTINE CALCV(CURRNT, RESIST, VOLTS)
        REAL CURRNT(*), RESIST(*), VOLTS(*)
        INTEGER I
        DO 10 I = 1, 10
          VOLTS(I) = CURRNT(I) * RESIST(I)
   10   CONTINUE
        END
```

```
9.    SUBROUTINE LOCATE(XINARY)
        REAL XINARY(3,5,10)

      SUBROUTINE LOCATE(XINARY)
        REAL XINARY(3,5,*)

      SUBROUTINE LOCATE(XINARY,I,J,K)
        INTEGER I,J,K
        REAL XINARY(I,J,K)

11.
      PROGRAM TEST
        INTEGER ARR(3,4), NUM
        DATA ARR /1,2,3,4,5,6,7,8,9,10,11,12/
        NUM = 2
        CALL MSCALE(ARR,NUM)
        PRINT *, ((ARR(I,J), I = 1,3), J = 1,4)
        END
      SUBROUTINE MSCALE(ARR,NUM)
        INTEGER ARR(3,4), NUM, I, J
        DO 10 I = 1,3
          DO 10 J = 1,4
            ARR(I,J) = NUM*ARR(I,J)
 10     CONTINUE
        END
```

Section 8.3

1. The following variables refer to the same memory locations:
   A, X, AND SNAP
   B, Y, and CRACLE
   C, Z, and POP
   D, P, and PIP
   I, NCOUNT, and MM
   J, MTEMP, and KK
   K, LSHOW, and II

3.
```
      PROGRAM TEST
        INTEGER AMOUNT, QUART, DIMES, NICKEL, PENNY, TOTPEN
        COMMON TOTPEN, QUART, DIMES, NICKEL, PENNY
        TOTPEN = 93
        CALL CHANGE
        PRINT *, QUART, DIMES, NICKEL, PENNY
        END
      SUBROUTINE CHANGE
        INTEGER AMOUNT, TEMP, QUART, DIMES, NICKEL, PENNY
        COMMON AMOUNT, QUART, DIMES, NICKEL, PENNY
        QUART = INT(AMOUNT/25)
        TEMP = AMOUNT - QUART * 25
        DIMES = INT(TEMP/10)
        TEMP = TEMP - DIMES * 10
        NICKEL = INT(TEMP/5)
        PENNY = TEMP - NICKEL * 5
        END
```

5.
```
      PROGRAM TEST
        INTEGER HOURS, MIN, SEC, TOTSEC
        COMMON TOTSEC, HOURS, MIN, SEC
        TOTSEC = 72345
        CALL TIME
```

```
            PRINT *, HOURS, MIN, SEC
            END
          SUBROUTINE TIME
            INTEGER TOTSEC, HOURS, MIN, SEC, TEMP
            COMMON TOTSEC, HOURS, MIN, SEC
            HOURS = INT(TOTSEC/3600)
            TEMP = TOTSEC - HOURS * 3600
            MIN  = INT(TEMP/60)
            SEC = TEMP - MIN * 60
            END
```

Section 8.4

1.

```
          PROGRAM MAIN
            INTEGER I
            REAL GRADES(10), AVERGE, STDDEV
            CALL ENTGRD(GRADES)
            CALL STATS(GRADES, 10, AVERGE, STDDEV)
            PRINT *, 'THE AVERAGE OF THE GRADES IS', AVERGE
            PRINT *, 'THE STANDARD DEVIATION OF THE GRADES IS', STDDEV
            END
*
          SUBROUTINE ENTGRD(GRADES)
            REAL GRADES(*)
            INTEGER I
            PRINT *, 'ENTER THE GRADES AS THEY ARE CALLED FOR'
            DO 10 I = 1,10
             PRINT *, 'ENTER GRADE ', I
             READ *, GRADES(I)
  10        CONTINUE
            END
*
          SUBROUTINE STATS(ARRAY, NUMEL, AV, ST)
            REAL ARRAY(*), AV, ST, SUMGRD, SUMDEV
            INTEGER NUMEL, I
***       CALCULATE THE AVERAGE      ***
            SUMGRD = 0
            DO 10 I = 1, NUMEL
              SUMGRD = SUMGRD + ARRAY(I)
  10        CONTINUE
            AV = SUMGRD / NUMEL
***       CALCULATE THE STANDARD DEVIATION       ***
            SUMDEV = 0
            DO 20 I = 1, NUMEL
              SUMDEV = SUMDEV + (ARRAY(I) - AV)**2
  20        CONTINUE
            ST = SQRT(SUMDEV/NUMEL)
            END
```

3.

```
          PROGRAM MAIN
            INTEGER I
            REAL GRADES(10), AVERGE, STDDEV, HIGH, LOW
            DATA GRADES /98, 82, 67, 54, 78, 83, 95, 76, 68, 63/
            CALL STATS(GRADES, 10, AVERGE, STDDEV, HIGH, LOW)
            PRINT *, 'THE AVERAGE OF THE GRADES IS', AVERGE
            PRINT *, 'THE STANDARD DEVIATION OF THE GRADES IS', STDDEV
            PRINT *, 'THE HIGHEST GRADE IS ', HIGH
            PRINT *, 'THE LOWEST GRADE IS', LOW
            END
```

```
*
         SUBROUTINE STATS(ARRAY, NUMEL, AV, ST, HIGH, LOW)
           REAL ARRAY(*), AV, ST, SUMGRD, SUMDEV, HIGH, LOW
           INTEGER NUMEL, I
***      CALCULATE THE AVERAGE      ***
           SUMGRD = 0
           HIGH = ARRAY(1)
           LOW = ARRAY(1)
           DO 10 I = 1, NUMEL
             SUMGRD = SUMGRD + ARRAY(I)
             IF (ARRAY(I) .GT. HIGH) HIGH = ARRAY(I)
             IF (ARRAY(I) .LT. LOW)  LOW = ARRAY(I)
     10    CONTINUE
           AV = SUMGRD / NUMEL
***      CALCULATE THE STANDARD DEVIATION      ***
           SUMDEV = 0
           DO 20 I = 1, NUMEL
             SUMDEV = SUMDEV + (ARRAY(I) - AV)**2
     20    CONTINUE
           ST = SQRT(SUMDEV/NUMEL)
           END
```

5.

```
         PROGRAM MAIN
          ·INTEGER I
           REAL GRADES(10), AVERGE, STDDEV
           DATA GRADES /98, 82, 67, 54, 78, 83, 95, 76, 68, 63/
           CALL STATS(GRADES, 10, AVERGE, STDDEV)
           CALL SORT(GRADES)
           PRINT *, 'THE AVERAGE OF THE GRADES IS', AVERGE
           PRINT *, 'THE STANDARD DEVIATION OF THE GRADES IS', STDDEV
           PRINT *, 'THE GRADES, IN SORTED ORDER, ARE:'
           PRINT *, (GRADES(I), I = 1, 10)
           END
*
         SUBROUTINE STATS(ARRAY, NUMEL, AV, ST)
           REAL ARRAY(*), AV, ST, SUMGRD, SUMDEV
           INTEGER NUMEL, I
***      CALCULATE THE AVERAGE      ***
           SUMGRD = 0
           DO 10 I = 1, NUMEL
             SUMGRD = SUMGRD + ARRAY(I)
     10    CONTINUE
           AV = SUMGRD / NUMEL
***      CALCULATE THE STANDARD DEVIATION      ***
           SUMDEV = 0
           DO 20 I = 1, NUMEL
             SUMDEV = SUMDEV + (ARRAY(I) - AV)**2
     20    CONTINUE
           ST = SQRT(SUMDEV/NUMEL)
           END
*
         SUBROUTINE SORT(GRADES)
          REAL GRADES(10)
          INTEGER I
          NTERM = 10
          DO 10 I = 1, 9
            NTERM = NTERM - 1
            DO 5 J = 1, NTERM
              IF (GRADES(J) .GT. GRADES(J+1)) THEN
                TEMP = GRADES(J+1)
                GRADES(J+1) = GRADES(J)
```

```
            GRADES(J) = TEMP
          ENDIF
5         CONTINUE
10        CONTINUE
          END
```

Chapter Ten - Additional Data Types

Section 10.1

1. a. 3720   b. 0.0004512   c. 4237500   d. -75387.2

    e. -4.37   f. -0.00000242

3. a. 0.5D 01/0.8D 01   b. 1.0D 01/6.0D 01

    c. 0.75D 01   d. 0.37D 0

Section 10.2

1. a. 4.8   b. 3 - 7i   c. - 8i   d. -2 + 5i

3. a. 1 - 6i   b. 13 - 6i   c. -42 + 36i   d. -(7/6) + i

Section 10.3

1. a. false   b. true   c. true   d. false   e. false

Section 10.4

1. Answers will vary but may include the following:

```
    CHARACTER*15 NAME(1000), STRADR(1000), CITY*10(1000)
    CHARACTER*2 STATE(1000), ZIP*5(1000, LICNUM*25(1000)
    INTEGER CLASS(1000)
    REAL FEE(1000)
```

3.  ```
    CHARACTER*15 NAME(1200), BDATE*6(1200), YEAR*2(1200)
    INTEGER CREDIT(1200)
    ```

Chapter Eleven - Numerical Techniques and Applications

Section 11.1

1. The solution is x = 3 , y = -1

3. The modified program is:

```
    PROGRAM MAIN
      REAL A1, B1, K1, A2, B2, K2, X, Y, DET2, VALDET
      OPEN (UNIT = 10, FILE = 'COEFF.DAT', STATUS = 'OLD')
      READ (10,*) A1, B1, K1, A2, B2, K2
      D2 = DET2 (A11, A12, A21, A22)
      VALDET = DET2 (a1, b1, a2,
```
(Coninued on next page)
```

```
      X   = DET2 (K1 , B1, K2 , B2) / VALDET
      Y   = DET2 (A1, K1 , A2, K2 ) / VALDET
      PRINT *, 'THE SOLUTION IS  X = ',X, ' Y = ',Y
      CLOSE (10)
      END
*
* SUBPROGRAM FUNCTION TO EVALUATE 2X2 DETERMINANT   |  A  B  |
*                                                   |  C  D  |
      REAL FUNCTION DET2 (A, B, C, D)
      REAL A, B, C, D
      DET2 = A * D - B * C
      RETURN
      END
```

The file COEFF.DAT created prior to running the program is:

3, 4, 5, 3, 5, 4

5. The minimum V_G required to charge the battery is approximately 14.4 volts.

7. The solution is $x = 5.2$, $y = 0.8$, $z = 1$.

9a. The optimum straight line fit is $y = 0.25 + 0.4x$

11. The optimum parabolic fit is

$$y = 4.25 - 1.75\ x + 0.25\ x^2$$

Section 11.2

The results of some of the root finding exercises are dependent on the roundoff errors generated. Therefore different results may occur when the programs are run on your own computer.

1a. In Program 11-4 replace the assignment statement for Y by

$$Y = X ** 4 + 4 * X ** 3 - 7 * X ** 2 - 22 * X + 24$$

The roots are at $x = -4$, $x = -3$, $x = 1$, and $x = 2$.

b. In Program 11-5 replace the assignment statement for Y as done in Exercise 1a. The four roots are displayed.

3. In Program 11-7 replace the function statement by

$$F(X) = X ** 4 + 4 * X ** 3 - 7 * X ** 2 - 22 * X + 24$$

For a step size of 1 and 0.5 no roots are displayed, since the roots are integers and either x_1 or x_2 fall very close to the roots. Roundoff errors may result in the values of y_1 and y_2 having the same sign, in which case the root is not displayed. All four roots are displayed for the step sizes of 0.499, 0.1, and 0.01. A step size of 0.499 will ensure that all values of x_1 and x_2 do not fall very close to the roots. For smaller step sizes accumulated roundoff error makes it unlikely that values of x_1 and x_2 are very close to the roots.

5. In Program 11-7 replace the function statement by

$$F(X) = COS (X)$$

The six roots

x = 1.57, 4.71, 7.85, 11.00, 14.14, and 17.28

are displayed for each of the four step sizes.

7. In Program 11-8 replace the function statement by

$$F(X) = COS (X)$$

The six roots are located by selecting the left and right bounds of X shown below. The number of iterations required is also shown.

Left and right bounds of X	Root	Number of iterations
0 to 3	1.571	12
3 to 6	4.712	18
6 to 9	7.854	13
9 to 12	10.995	12
12 to 16	14.137	12
16 to 20	17.279	13

9. In Program 11-9 replace the function statement by

$$F(XX) = COS (XX)$$

When the same bounds of X used in Exercise 7 are entered, the following results are obtained.

Left and right bounds of X	Root	Number of iterations
0 to 3	1.571	3
3 to 6	4.712	3
6 to 9	7.853	3
9 to 12	10.996	4
12 to 16	14.137	3
16 to 20	20.420	5

The first five roots are located much more rapidly than for the bisection method. However, the last run located a root outside the interval (at x = 13 * pi / 2). If the last run is repeated, with 16 and 18 entered as the left and right bounds of X, the root at X = 17.279 is then located after 3 iterations.

Section 11.3

1a. In Program 11-10 replace the function statement by

$$F(X) = X ** 3 + 2 * X ** 2 + 3 * X + 1$$

The results of the four runs are shown below.

N	AREA
2	2.0625
10	3.1225
50	3.3569
1000	3.4136

b. In Program 11-11 replace the function statement as done in Exercise 1a. The results of the four runs are shown below.

N	AREA
2	3.3438
10	3.4138
50	3.4165
1000	3.4166

3. The modified program is:

```
      PROGRAM MAIN
      REAL X, A, B, WIDTH, AREA, F
      INTEGER I, N
      F(X) = SQRT (ABS (4 - X ** 2))
      PRINT *, 'ENTER LEFT AND RIGHT BOUNDS OF X  (A, B): '
      READ *, A, B
      PRINT *, '          N   APPROXIMATE AREA    PERCENT ERROR'
      PRINT *, '          ---  ----------------    --------------'
      DO 10 N = 1, 10
        WIDTH = (B - A) / N
        X = A
        AREA = 0
        DO 20 I = 1, N
          AREA = AREA + WIDTH * F (X + WIDTH/2)
          X = X + WIDTH
20      CONTINUE
        ERROR = (AREA - 3.14159) / AREA * 100
        PRINT *, N, AREA, ERROR
10    CONTINUE
      END
```

The following table is displayed when the program is run.

```
ENTER LEFT AND RIGHT BOUNDS OF X  (A, B): 0, 2
```

N	APPROXIMATE AREA	PERCENT ERROR
1	3.464102	9.310103
2	3.259367	3.613503
3	3.206413	2.021650
4	3.183929	1.329782
5	3.171988	0.958323
6	3.164767	0.732334
7	3.160012	0.582969
8	3.156687	0.478244
9	3.154254	0.401485
10	3.152411	0.343257

5. In the program for Exercise 4a, change the function statement to

$$F(X) = X ** 4$$

The results of the three runs are shown below.

N	x_c	y_c
5	0.8194	0.2545
10	0.8299	0.2718
50	0.8332	0.2775

The value of x_c converges more rapidly than does the value of y_c. This results from the fact that the calculation of x_c requires approximating the area under a fifth order polynomial, while the calculation of y_c involves an eighth order polynomial. The higher order polynomial presents a steeper curve which results in a poorer approximation of area by the modified rectangular method. Nevertheless the error in y_c is only about 2 % for N = 10 and less than 0.1 % for N = 50.

Index

I-2

TANH function F-3
TARGET statement 502
Telephone switching 97
Testing phase 88, 159
Text files 384
Three dimensioned arrays 267
TLn format specifier 82
Tn format specifier 82
Top-down development 88, 91
Transaction file 379
Trapezoidal approximation 470-473
TRn format specifier 82, 138
TRUE 44
Two's complement numbers 37
Two-dimensional array 263

U

Unconditional GO TO statement 205

Unformatted file 386, 399
UNFORMATTED specifier 387
Unit number 22, 121, 363
UNIT specifier 390
Unnamed COMMON 335
Upper index bound 25
User-formatted
  READ statement 133, 369
  PRINT statement 72
  WRITE statement 73, 367
User-written function 288

V

Variable 52
Variable parameters 232
Variable scope 323
Vertical spacing 73

W

White space 23
Width of format specification 76, 77, 80
Words 38
WRITE statement
  list-directed 22, 357, 367-369, 400
  user-formatted 73, 357, 367-369, 400

X

X format specification 79, 138
X3J3 Committee 486

Y, Z

Zero of a function 447